DRAMA
for Students

DRAMA
for Students

**Presenting Analysis, Context and Criticism on
Commonly Studied Dramas**

Volume 1

David Galens, Lynn Spampinato, Editors

*Barbara Dubb, Farmington/Farmington Hills School District,
Michigan, Advisor*

*Marie Slotnic, English Department Chair,
Center Line High School, Center Line, Michigan, Advisor*

GALE

DETROIT • NEW YORK • TORONTO • LONDON

STAFF

David Galens and Lynn M. Spampinato, *Editors*

Thomas Allbaugh, Craig Bentley, Terry Browne, Christopher Busiel, Stephen Coy, L. M. Domina, John Fiero, Carol L. Hamilton, Erika Kreger, Jennifer Lewin, Sheri Metzger, Daniel Moran, Terry Nienhuis, Bonnie Russell, Arnold Schmidt, William Wiles, Joanne Woolway, *Contributing Writers*

Elizabeth Cranston, Kathleen J. Edgar, Joshua Kondek, Marie Lazzari, Tom Ligotti, Marie Napierkowski, Scot Peacock, Mary Ruby, Diane Telgen, Patti Tippett, Kathleen Wilson, Pam Zuber, *Contributing Editors*

Pamela Wilwerth Aue, *Managing Editor*

Jeffery Chapman, *Programmer/Analyst*

Victoria B. Cariappa, *Research Team Manager*
Michele P. LaMeau, Andy Guy Malonis, Barb McNeil, Gary Oudersluys, Maureen Richards, *Research Specialists*
Julia C. Daniel, Tamara C. Nott, Tracie A. Richardson, Cheryl L. Warnock, *Research Associates*

Susan M. Trosky, *Permissions Manager*
Kimberly F. Smilay, *Permissions Specialist*
Sarah Chesney, *Permissions Associate*
Steve Cusack, Kelly A. Quin, *Permissions Assistants*

Mary Beth Trimper, *Production Director*
Evi Seoud, *Assistant Production Manager*
Shanna Heilveil, *Production Assistant*

Randy Bassett, *Image Database Supervisor*
Mikal Ansari, Robert Duncan, *Imaging Specialists*
Pamela A. Reed, *Photography Coordinator*

Cynthia Baldwin, *Product Design Manager*
Cover design: Michelle DiMercurio, *Art Director*
Page design: Pamela A. E. Galbreath, *Senior Art Director*

∞™ This book is printed on acid-free paper that meets the minimum requirements of American National Standard for Information Sciences—Permanence Paper for Printed Library Materials, ANSI Z39.48-1984.
ISBN 0-7876-1683-4
ISSN applied for and pending
Printed in the United States of America
10 9 8 7 6 5 4 3 2 1

Table of Contents

The Study of Drama

We study drama in order to learn what meaning others have made of life, to comprehend what it takes to produce a work of art, and to glean some understanding of ourselves. Drama produces in a separate, aesthetic world, a moment of being for the audience to experience, while maintaining the detachment of a reflective observer.

Drama is a representational art, a visible and audible narrative presenting virtual, fictional characters within a virtual, fictional universe. Dramatic realizations may pretend to approximate reality or else stubbornly defy, distort, and deform reality into an artistic statement. From this separate universe that is obviously not ''real life'' we expect a valid reflection upon reality, yet drama never is mistaken for reality—the methods of theater are integral to its form and meaning. Theater is art, and art's appeal lies in its ability both to approximate life and to depart from it. By presenting its distorted version of life to our consciousness, art gives us a new perspective and appreciation of reality. Although, to some extent, all aesthetic experiences perform this service, theater does it most effectively by creating a separate, cohesive universe that freely acknowledges its status as an art form.

And what is the purpose of the aesthetic universe of drama? The potential answers to such a question are nearly as many and varied as there are plays written, performed, and enjoyed. Dramatic texts can be problems posed, answers asserted, or moments portrayed. Dramas (tragedies as well as comedies) may serve strictly ''to ease the anguish of a torturing hour'' (as stated in William Shakespeare's *A Midsummer Night's Dream*)—to divert and entertain—or aspire to move the viewer to action with social issues. Whether to entertain or to instruct, affirm or influence, pacify or shock, dramatic art wraps us in the spell of its imaginary world for the length of the work and then dispenses us back to the real world, entertained, purged, as Aristotle said, of pity and fear, and edified—or at least weary enough to sleep peacefully.

It is commonly thought that theater, being an art of performance, must be experienced—that is, seen—in order to be appreciated fully. However, to view a production of a dramatic text is to be limited to a single interpretation of that text—all other interpretations are for the moment closed off, inaccessible. In the process of producing a play, the director, stage designer, and performers interpret and transform the script into a work of art that always departs in some measure from the author's original conception. Novelist and critic Umberto Eco, in his *The Role of the Reader: Explorations in the Semiotics of Texts,* explained, ''In short, we can say that every performance offers us a complete and satisfying version of the work, but at the same time makes it incomplete for us, because it cannot simultaneously give all the other artistic solutions which the work may admit.''

Thus Laurence Olivier's coldly formal and neurotic film presentation of Shakespeare's *Hamlet* (in which he played the title character as well as directed) shows marked differences from subsequent adaptations. While Olivier's Hamlet is clearly entangled in a Freudian relationship with his mother, Gertrude, he would be incapable of shushing her with the impassioned kiss that Mel Gibson's mercurial Hamlet (in director Franco Zeffirelli's 1990 film) does. Although each of the performances rings true to Shakespeare's text, each is also a mutually exclusive work of art. Also important to consider are the time periods in which each of these films were produced: Olivier made his film in 1948, a time in which overt references to sexuality (especially incest) were frowned upon. Gibson and Zeffirelli made their film in a culture more relaxed and comfortable with these issues. Just as actors and directors can influence the presentation of drama, so too can the time period of the production affect what the audience will see.

A play script is an open text from which an infinity of specific realizations may be derived. Dramatic scripts that are more open to interpretive creativity (such as those of Ntozake Shange and Tomson Highway) actually require the creative improvisation of the production troupe in order to complete the text. Even the most prescriptive scripts (those of Neil Simon, Lillian Hellman, and Robert Bolt, for example), can never fully control the actualization of live performance, and circumstantial events, including the attitude and receptivity of the audience, make every performance a unique event. Thus, while it is important to view a production of a dramatic piece, if one wants to understand a drama fully it is equally important to read the original dramatic text.

The reader of a dramatic text or script is not limited by either the specific interpretation of a given production or by the unstoppable action of a moving spectacle. The reader of a dramatic text may discover the nuances of the play's language, structure, and events at their own pace. Yet studied alone, the author's blueprint for artistic production does not tell the whole story of a play's life and significance. One also needs to assess the play's critical reviews to discover how it resonated to cultural themes at the time of its debut and how the shifting tides of cultural interest have revised its interpretation and impact on audiences. And to do this, one needs to know a little about the culture of the times which produced the play as well as the author who penned it.

Drama for Students supplies this material in a useful compendium for the student of dramatic theater. Covering a range of dramatic works that span from the fifth century B.C. to the 1990s, this book focuses on significant theatrical works whose themes and form transcend the uncertainty of dramatic fads. These are plays that have proven to be both memorable and teachable. *Drama for Students* seeks to enhance appreciation of these dramatic texts by providing scholarly materials written with the secondary and college/university student in mind. It provides for each play a concise summary of the plot and characters as well as a detailed explanation of its themes and techniques. In addition, background material on the historical context of the play, its critical reception, and the author's life help the student to understand the work's position in the chronicle of dramatic history. For each play entry a new work of scholarly criticism is also included, as well as segments of other significant critical works for handy reference. A thorough bibliography provides a starting point for further research.

These inaugural two volumes offer comprehensive educational resources for students of drama. *Drama for Students* is a vital book for dramatic interpretation and a valuable addition to any reference library.

Source: Eco, Umberto, *The Role of the Reader: Explorations in the Semiotics of Texts,* Indiana University Press, 1979.

Carole L. Hamilton
Author and Instructor of English
Cary Academy
Cary, North Carolina

Introduction

Purpose of Drama for Students

The purpose of *Drama for Students* (*DfS*) is to provide readers with a guide to understanding, enjoying, and studying dramas by giving them easy access to information about the work. Part of Gale's "For Students" literature line, *DfS* is specifically designed to meet the curricular needs of high school and undergraduate college students and their teachers, as well as the interests of general readers and researchers considering specific plays. While each volume contains entries on "classic" dramas frequently studied in classrooms, there are also entries containing hard-to-find information on contemporary plays, including works by multicultural, international, and women playwrights.

The information covered in each entry includes an introduction to the play and the work's author; a plot summary, to help readers unravel and understand the events in a drama; descriptions of important characters, including explanation of a given character's role in the drama as well as discussion about that character's relationship to other characters in the play; analysis of important themes in the drama; and an explanation of important literary techniques and movements as they are demonstrated in the play.

In addition to this material, which helps the readers analyze the play itself, students are also provided with important information on the literary and historical background informing each work.

This includes a historical context essay, a box comparing the time or place the drama was written to modern Western culture, a critical overview essay, and excerpts from critical essays on the play. A unique feature of *DfS* is a specially commissioned overview essay on each drama by an academic expert, targeted toward the student reader.

To further aid the student in studying and enjoying each play, information on media adaptations is provided, as well as reading suggestions for works of fiction and nonfiction on similar themes and topics. Classroom aids include ideas for research papers and lists of critical sources that provide additional material on each drama.

Selection Criteria

The titles for each volume of *DfS* were selected by surveying numerous sources on teaching literature and analyzing course curricula for various school districts. Some of the sources surveyed included: literature anthologies; *Reading Lists for College-Bound Students: The Books Most Recommended by America's Top Colleges;* textbooks on teaching dramas; a College Board survey of plays commonly studied in high schools; a National Council of Teachers of English (NCTE) survey of plays commonly studied in high schools; St. James Press's *International Dictionary of Theatre;* and Arthur Applebee's 1993 study *Literature in the Secondary School: Studies of Curriculum and Instruction in the United States.*

Input was also solicited from our expert advisory board (both experienced educators specializing in English), as well as educators from various areas. From these discussions, it was determined that each volume should have a mix of "classic" dramas (those works commonly taught in literature classes) and contemporary dramas for which information is often hard to find. Because of the interest in expanding the canon of literature, an emphasis was also placed on including works by international, multicultural, and women playwrights. Our advisory board members—current high school teachers—helped pare down the list for each volume. If a work was not selected for the present volume, it was often noted as a possibility for a future volume. As always, the editor welcomes suggestions for titles to be included in future volumes.

How Each Entry Is Organized

Each entry, or chapter, in *DfS* focuses on one play. Each entry heading lists the full name of the play, the author's name, and the date of the play's first production or publication. The following elements are contained in each entry:

- **Introduction:** a brief overview of the drama which provides information about its first appearance, its literary standing, any controversies surrounding the work, and major conflicts or themes within the work.

- **Author Biography:** this section includes basic facts about the author's life, and focuses on events and times in the author's life that inspired the drama in question.

- **Plot Summary:** a description of the major events in the play, with interpretation of how these events help articulate the play's themes. Subheads demarcate the plays' various acts or scenes.

- **Characters:** an alphabetical listing of major characters in the play. Each character name is followed by a brief to an extensive description of the character's role in the plays, as well as discussion of the character's actions, relationships, and possible motivation.

Characters are listed alphabetically by last name. If a character is unnamed—for instance, the Stage Manager in *Our Town*—the character is listed as "The Stage Manager" and alphabetized as "Stage Manager." If a character's first name is the only one given, the name will appear alphabetically by the name.

Variant names are also included for each character. Thus, the nickname "Babe" would head the listing for a character in *Crimes of the Heart,* but below that listing would be her less-mentioned married name "Rebecca Botrelle."

- **Themes:** a thorough overview of how the major topics, themes, and issues are addressed within the play. Each theme discussed appears in a separate subhead, and is easily accessed through the boldface entries in the Subject/Theme Index.

- **Style:** this section addresses important style elements of the drama, such as setting, point of view, and narration; important literary devices used, such as imagery, foreshadowing, symbolism; and, if applicable, genres to which the work might have belonged, such as Gothicism or Romanticism. Literary terms are explained within the entry, but can also be found in the Glossary.

- **Historical and Cultural Context:** This section outlines the social, political, and cultural climate *in which the author lived and the play was created.* This section may include descriptions of related historical events, pertinent aspects of daily life in the culture, and the artistic and literary sensibilities of the time in which the work was written. If the play is a historical work, information regarding the time in which the play is set is also included. Each section is broken down with helpful subheads.

- **Critical Overview:** this section provides background on the critical reputation of the play, including bannings or any other public controversies surrounding the work. For older plays, this section includes a history of how the drama was first received and how perceptions of it may have changed over the years; for more recent plays, direct quotes from early reviews may also be included.

- **For Further Study:** an alphabetical list of other critical sources which may prove useful for the student. Includes full bibliographical information and a brief annotation.

- **Sources:** an alphabetical list of critical material quoted in the entry, with full bibliographical information.

- **Criticism:** an essay commissioned by *DfS* which specifically deals with the play and is written specifically for the student audience, as well as excerpts from previously published criticism on the work.

In addition, each entry contains the following highlighted sections, set separate from the main text:

- **Media Adaptations:** a list of important film and television adaptations of the play, including source information. The list may also include such variations on the work as audio recordings, musical adaptations, and other stage interpretations.

- **Compare and Contrast Box:** an "at-a-glance" comparison of the cultural and historical differences between the author's time and culture and late twentieth-century Western culture. This box includes pertinent parallels between the major scientific, political, and cultural movements of the time or place the drama was written, the time or place the play was set (if a historical work), and modern Western culture. Works written after the mid-1970s may not have this box.

- **What Do I Read Next?:** a list of works that might complement the featured play or serve as a contrast to it. This includes works by the same author and others, works of fiction and nonfiction, and works from various genres, cultures, and eras.

- **Study Questions:** a list of potential study questions or research topics dealing with the play. This section includes questions related to other disciplines the student may be studying, such as American history, world history, science, math, government, business, geography, economics, psychology, etc.

Other Features

DfS includes "The Study of Drama," a foreword by Carole Hamilton, an educator and author who specializes in dramatic works. This essay examines the basis for drama in societies and what drives people to study such work. Hamilton also discusses how *Drama for Students* can help teachers show students how to enrich their own reading/viewing experiences.

A Cumulative Author/Title Index lists the authors and titles covered in each volume of the *DfS* series.

A Cumulative Nationality/Ethnicity Index breaks down the authors and titles covered in each volume of the *DfS* series by nationality and ethnicity.

A Subject/Theme Index, specific to each volume, provides easy reference for users who may be studying a particular subject or theme rather than a single work. Significant subjects from events to broad themes are included, and the entries pointing to the specific theme discussions in each entry are indicated in **boldface**.

Each entry has several illustrations, including photos of the author, stills from stage productions, and stills from film adaptations.

Citing **Drama for Students**

When writing papers, students who quote directly from any volume of *Drama for Students* may use the following general forms. These examples are based on MLA style; teachers may request that students adhere to a different style, so the following examples may be adapted as needed.

When citing text from *DfS* that is not attributed to a particular author (i.e., the Themes, Style, Historical Context sections, etc.), the following format should be used in the bibliography section:

> "Our Town," *Drama for Students.* Ed. David Galens and Lynn Spampinato. Vol. 1. Detroit: Gale, 1997. 8–9.

When quoting the specially commissioned essay from *DfS* (usually the first piece under the "Criticism" subhead), the following format should be used:

> Fiero, John. Essay on "Twilight: Los Angeles, 1992." *Drama for Students.* Ed. David Galens and Lynn Spampinato. Vol. 1. Detroit: Gale, 1997. 8–9.

When quoting a journal or newspaper essay that is reprinted in a volume of *DfS,* the following form may be used:

> Rich, Frank. "Theatre: A Mamet Play, 'Glengarry Glen Ross'." *New York Theatre Critics' Review* Vol. 45, No. 4 (March 5, 1984), 5–7; excerpted and reprinted in *Drama for Students,* Vol. 1, ed. David Galens and Lynn Spampinato (Detroit: Gale, 1997), pp. 61–64.

When quoting material reprinted from a book that appears in a volume of *DfS,* the following form may be used:

> Kerr, Walter. "The Miracle Worker," in *The Theatre in Spite of Itself* (Simon & Schuster, 1963, 255–57; excerpted and reprinted in *Drama for Students,* Vol. 1, ed. Dave Galens and Lynn Spampinato (Detroit: Gale, 1997), pp. 59–61.

We Welcome Your Suggestions

The editor of *Drama for Students* welcomes your comments and ideas. Readers who wish to suggest dramas to appear in future volumes, or who have other suggestions, are cordially invited to contact the editor. You may contact the editor via E-mail at: **david_galens@gale.com.** Or write to the editor at:

David Galens, *Drama for Students*
Gale Research
835 Penobscot Bldg.
645 Griswold St.
Detroit, MI 48226-4094

Literary Chronology

c. 496 B.C.: Sophocles born in Colonus, Greece, c. 496 B.C.

c. 480 B.C.: Euripides born in Athens, Greece, c. 480 B.C.

442 B.C.: *Antigone* is written as the last work in Sophocles's "Theban Trilogy."

431 B.C.: *Medea* debuts at the Great Dionysia, a festival in Athens, 431 B.C.

430 B.C.: *Oedipus the King,* the second play in Sophocles's Theban Trilogy, is produced at the Great Dionysia of 430 B.C.

c. 406 B.C.: Euripides dies an expatriot in Macedonia, c. 406 B.C.

c. 406 B.C.: Sophocles dies in Athens, Greece, c. 406 B.C.

1564: Christopher Marlowe is born in Canterbury, England, in February of 1564.

1593: Marlowe is killed by a dining companion during a tavern fight, May 30, 1593, in Deptford, England; there is considerable speculation as to whether the murder was a random act or an assassination.

1594: An early version of Marlowe's *Dr. Faustus* is posthumously produced by a theatrical troupe known as the Earl of Nottingham's Men.

1728: The son of a minister, Oliver Goldsmith is born November 10, 1728, in Ballymahon, Ireland.

1773: Goldsmith's *She Stoops to Conquer* debuts in England in 1773.

1774: Goldsmith dies on April 4, 1774, in London, England; he is buried in Temple Church in London, with a monument erected to him in Westminster Abbey.

1828: Henrik Ibsen born March 20, 1828, to Knud and Marichen (Altenburg) Ibsen, in Skien, Norway.

1856: George Bernard Shaw is born on July 26, 1856, to George Carr and Lucinda Elizabeth (Gurly) Shaw, in Dublin, Ireland.

1860: Anton Chekhov is born on January 16, 1860, to Pavel Yegorovitch and Yevgeniya Yakovlevna (Morozov) Chekhov in Taganrog, Russia.

1868: Edmond Rostand is born on April 1, 1868, in Marseilles, France, to Eugene Rostand and his wife.

1879: *A Doll's House* published on December 4, 1879 and first performed in Copenhagen, Denmark, on December 21, 1879.

1888: Eugene O'Neill is born on October 16, 1888, to James and Mary Ellen (Quinlan) O'Neill, in New York City.

1889: George S. Kaufman is born November 16, 1889, to Joseph S. and Nettie Schamberg (Myers) Kaufman, in Pittsburgh, Pennsylvania.

1890: Agatha Christie is born on September 15, 1890, to Frederick Alvah and Clarissa Miller, in Torquay, Devon, England.

1895: Oscar Hammerstein is born on July 12, 1895, to William and Alica Vivian (Nimmo) Hammerstein, in New York City.

1897: Thornton Wilder is born on April 17, 1897, to Amos Parker and Isabella Thornton (Niven) Wilder, in Madison, Wisconsin.

1897: Rostand's *Cyrano de Bergerac* is first produced at the Porte Saint-Martin Theater in Paris, France, on December 28, 1897.

1900: *The Cherry Orchard,* under its original Russian title of *Vishnyovy Sad: Komediya v chetyryokh deystriyakh,* is first produced in Moscow, Russia, at the Moscow Art Theater on January 17, 1900.

1902: Richard Rodgers is born on June 28, 1902, to William Abraham and Mamie (Levy) Rodgers, in New York City.

1904: Chekhov dies of tuberculosis July 2, 1904, in Badenweiler, Germany; he is buried in Moscow, Russia.

1904: Moss Hart is born on October 24, 1904, to Barnett and Lillian (Solomon) Hart in New York City.

1906: Ibsen dies from complications resulting from a series of strokes on May 23, 1906, in Oslo, Norway.

1906: Samuel Beckett is born on April 13, 1906, to William Frank and Mary Jones (Roe) Beckett, in Foxrock, Dublin, Ireland.

1906: Lillian Hellman is born on June 20, 1906, to Max Bernard and Julia (Newhouse) Hellman, in New Orleans, Louisiana.

1911: Tennessee Williams is born on March 26, 1911, to Cornelius Coffin and Edwina (Dakin) Williams, in Columbus, Mississippi.

1914: William Gibson is born on November 13, 1914, to George Irving and Florence (Dore) Gibson, in New York City.

1914: *Pygmalion* is first produced in London, England, at His Majesty's Theatre, April 11, 1914.

1915: Arthur Miller is born on October 17, 1915, to Isidore and Augusta (Barnett) Miller, in New York City.

1915: Jerome Lawrence is born on July 14, 1915, to Samuel and Sarah (Rogen) Lawrence, in Cleveland, Ohio.

1918: Rostand dies on December 2 (one source says December 22), 1918, in Paris, France.

1918: Robert E. Lee is born on October 15, 1918, to Claire Melvin and Elvira (Taft) Lee, in Elyria, Ohio.

1920: Alice Childress is born on October 12, 1920, in Charleston, South Carolina.

1924: Robert Bolt is born on August 15, 1924, to Ralph and Leah (Binnion) Bolt, in Sale, Manchester, England.

1925: Gore Vidal is born on October 3, 1925, to Eugene Luther and Nina (Gore) Vidal, at the U.S. Military Academy, West Point, New York.

1927: Neil Simon is born on July 4, 1927, to Irving and Mamie Simon, in Bronx, New York.

1928: Edward Albee is born on March 12, 1928, probably in Virginia; adopted by Reed A. and Frances (Cotter) Albee.

1930: Lorraine Hansberry is born on May 19, 1930, to Carl Augustus and Nannie (Perry) Hansberry, in Chicago, Illinois.

1936: Eugene O'Neill awarded the Nobel Prize in literature; he is only the second American to receive this honor.

1936: *You Can't Take it with You* is first produced on Broadway at the Booth Theatre, December 14, 1936.

1936: Hart and Kaufman are awarded the Pulitzer for their comedy.

1937: Tom Stoppard is born on July 3, 1937, to Eugene Straussler and Martha Stoppard, in Zlin, Czechoslovakia.

1938: *Our Town* is first produced in Princeton, New Jersey, on January 22, 1938; produced in New York City at the Henry Miller Theatre, February 4, 1938.

1939: Wilder's play receives the Pulitzer Prize despite initially mixed reviews of the drama.

1939: *The Little Foxes* is first produced in New York City at the National Theatre on February 15, 1939.

1944: *The Glass Menagerie* is first produced in Chicago, Illinois, in 1944; the play is produced on Broadway the following year.

1947: Williams's play is first published in 1947; the play has productions staged in both Boston and New York.

1947: Marsha Norman born on September 21, 1947, to Billie Lee and Bertha Mae (Conley) Williams, in Louisville, Kentucky.

1947: David Mamet born on November 30, 1947, to Bernard Morris and Lenore June (Silver) Mamet, in Chicago, Illinois.

1948: Williams's play is awarded the Pulitzer for drama in addition to winning the New York Drama Critics Circle Award.

1948: Ntozake Shange born on October 18, 1948, to Paul T. and Eloise Williams, in Trenton, New Jersey.

1949: *Death of a Salesman* first produced on Broadway at the Morosco Theatre, February 10, 1949.

1949: Miller's play receives the prestigious Pulitzer as well as the New York Drama Critics Circle Award for best play of the year.

1950: Shaw dies November 2, 1950, in Ayot Saint Lawrence, Hertfordshire, England.

1950: Anna Deveare Smith is born on September 18, 1950, to Deveare Young and Anna (Young) Smith, in Baltimore, Maryland.

1951: Rodgers and Hammerstein's *The King and I* makes its debut on Broadway in 1951.

1951: Tomson Highway born on December 6, 1951 (some sources say 1952), in Northwest Manitoba, Canada.

1952: Beginning its record-breaking run, *The Mousetrap* is first produced on the West End of England, at the Ambassadors' Theatre, November 25, 1952; produced Off-Broadway at the Maidman Playhouse in 1960.

1952: Beth Henley born on May 8, 1952, to Charles Boyce and Elizabeth Josephine (Becker) Henley, in Jackson, Mississippi.

1953: *Waiting for Godot* is first produced in Paris, France, at Theatre de Babylone, January 5, 1953.

1953: O'Neill dies of pneumonia on November 27, 1953, in Boston, Massachusetts; he is buried December 2, 1953, in Forest Hills Cemetery, Boston.

1954: *A Man for All Seasons* is first broadcast as a radio play by the British Broadcasting Corporation (BBC) in 1954; a televised adaptation airs on BBC-TV in 1957; a full-length play is produced in London in 1960 and in New York the following year.

1955: *Inherit the Wind* is first produced on Broadway at the National Theatre (now the Nederlander Theatre, also formerly the Billy Rose Theatre), April 21, 1955.

1955: *A Visit to a Small Planet* is produced as a radio play; an expanded edition has its first Broadway production at the Booth Theater on February 7, 1957; the play is adapted by Edmund Beloin and Henry Garson as a film starring Jerry Lewis in 1960.

1956: Following O'Neill's instructions that the play not be produced until after his death, *Long Day's Journey into Night* is first produced in Stockholm, Sweden, at the Kungliga Dramatiska Teatern, February 10, 1956; the play is produced on Broadway at the Helen Hayes Theatre, November 7, 1956.

1956: Following a posthumous production in Sweden, the first published edition of O'Neill's play receives the Pulitzer.

1957: *The Miracle Worker* debuts as a television play produced by the Columbia Broadcasting System (CBS) for the anthology series *Playhouse 90* in 1957; the play is rewritten for the stage and produced on Broadway at the Playhouse Theatre, October 19, 1959; it is adapted for film and produced by United Artists in 1962; the play comes full circle with another television adaptation by the National Broadcasting Company (NBC) in 1979.

1959: Hansberry becomes the first black female playwright to have her work produced on Broadway when *A Raisin in the Sun* debuts in 1959. She later becomes the first black playwright to win the New York Drama Critics Circle Award; she is also the youngest playwright to receive this honor.

1959: *Zoo Story* is produced for the first time in Berlin, Germany, on September 28, 1959, at the Schiller Theatre Werkstatt; the play debuted off-

Broadway at the Provincetown Playhouse on January 14, 1960.

1960: Hammerstein dies on August 23, 1960, in Doylestown, Pennsylvania.

1961: Hart dies on December 20, 1961, in Palm Springs, California.

1961: Kaufman dies following a heart attack, June 2, 1961, in New York City.

1965: Hansberry dies of cancer on January 12, 1965, in New York City. She is buried in Beth El Cemetery.

1965: *The Odd Couple* debuts on Broadway in March of 1965.

1966: Childress's *Wedding Band* receives its first production in 1966; due to concerns about the play's interracial themes, a production is not mounted on Broadway until 1972.

1966: *Rosencrantz and Guildenstern Are Dead* is first produced as an amateur production in Edinburgh, Scotland, in 1966; it has subsequent productions in London and New York in 1967.

1975: Shange's *for colored girls ...* is first produced in New York City at Studio Rivbea, July 7, 1975; it is later produced Off-Broadway at the Anspacher Public Theatre in 1976; it is produced on Broadway at the Booth Theatre, September 15, 1976.

1975: Wilder dies of a heart attack, December 7, 1975, in Hamden, Connecticut.

1976: Christie dies January 12, 1976, in Wallingford, England.

1979: Rodgers dies on December 30, 1979, in Manhattan, New York.

1979: *Crimes of the Heart* is first produced in Louisville, Kentucky, at the Actors' Theatre of Louisville, February 18, 1979; produced on Broadway at the John Golden Theatre, November 4, 1981.

1981: Henley is awarded the Pulitzer Prize in drama for her first play.

1982: Norman's *'night, Mother* is first produced at the American Repertory Theatre, Cambridge,

Massachusetts, in 1982; it is later produced on Broadway at the Golden Theatre in 1983.

1983: *Glengarry, Glen Ross* is first presented at the Cottlesloe Theatre of the Royal National Theatre, in London, England, on September 21, 1983; the play's American premier takes place at the Goodman Theatre in Chicago, Illinois, on February 6, 1984; with one cast change, the production then transfers to Broadway's Golden Theatre on March 5, 1984.

1983: Norman wins the Pulitzer for drama just two years after her southern colleague Beth Henley.

1983: Williams chokes to death on February 24, 1983, in his suite at Hotel Elysee in New York City; he is buried in St. Louis, Missouri.

1984: Mamet's play about business and greed, *Glengarry Glen Ross,* is awarded the Pulitzer for drama.

1984: Hellman dies of cardiac arrest on June 30, 1984, in Martha's Vineyard, Massachusetts.

1986: *The Rez Sisters* is first produced at the National Canadian Centre in Toronto, Ontario, in 1986.

1986: Highway's play wins both the Dora Mavor Award and is runner-up for the Floyd F. Chalmers Award for outstanding Canadian play of 1986.

1989: Beckett dies of respiratory failure, December 22, 1989, in Paris, France.

1993: Following the Los Angeles riots that inspired the work, *Twilight: Los Angeles, 1992* begins its premier run on May 23, 1993, in Los Angeles, California, at the Center Theatre Group/Mark Taper Forum.

1993: Smith's play garners several major awards, including an Obie Award, Drama Desk Award, Outer Critics Circle Award.

1994: Childress dies of cancer, August 14, 1994, in Queens, New York.

1995: Bolt dies on February 20, 1995, in Hampshire, England.

Acknowledgments

The editors wish to thank the copyright holders of the excerpted criticism included in this volume and the permissions managers of many book and magazine publishing companies for assisting us in securing reproduction rights. We are also grateful to the staffs of the Detroit Public Library, the Library of Congress, the University of Detroit Mercy Library, Wayne State University Purdy/Kresge Library Complex, and the University of Michigan Libraries for making their resources available to us. Following is a list of the copyright holders who have granted us permission to reproduce material in this volume of **DFS**. Every effort has been made to trace copyright, but if omissions have been made, please let us know.

COPYRIGHTED EXCERPTS IN DFS, VOLUME 1, WERE REPRODUCED FROM THE FOLLOWING PERIODICALS:

Ball State University Forum, v. 14, Summer, 1973. Copyright © 1973 Ball State University. Reprinted by permission of the publisher.—*Comparative Literature Studies,* v. 3, 1966. Reproduced by permission of The Pennsylvania State University Press.—*Educational Theatre Journal,* v. 16, March, 1964. Copyright © 1964, renewed 1992. Reproduced by permission of The John Hopkins University Press.—*Poet Lore,* v. 11, Winter, 1989. Copyright © 1989 by Helen Dwight Reid Educational Foundation. Reprinted with permission of the Helen Dwight Reid Educational Foundation, published by Heldref Publications, 1319 18th Street, NW, Wash-

ington, DC 20036-1802.—*The Explicator,* v. 52, Fall, 1993. Copyright © 1993 by Helen Dwight Reid Educational Foundation. Reprinted with permission of the Helen Dwight Reid Educational Foundation, published by Heldref Publications, 1319 18th Street, NW, Washington, DC 20036-1802.—*The New York Times,* April 7, 1996. Copyright © 1996 by The New York Times Company. Reproduced by permission./ February 16, 1939. Copyright © 1939, renewed 1967 by the New York Times Company. Reproduced by permission.—*The Saturday Review,* v. 28, April 14, 1945. Copyright © 1945 Saturday Review Magazine. Reprinted by permission of Saturday Review Publications, Ltd. Reproduced by permission.—*The Southern Literary Journal,* v. XXVIII, Spring, 1996. Copyright © 1996 by the Department of English, University of North Carolina at Chapel Hill. Reproduced by permission.

COPYRIGHTED EXCERPTS IN DFS, VOLUME 1, WERE REPRODUCED FROM THE FOLLOWING BOOKS:

Atkinson, Brooks. From *Onstage: Selected Theater Reviews from The New York Times, 1920-1970.* Edited by Bernard Beckerman and Howard Siegman. Arno Press, 1973. Copyright © 1973 by the New York Times Company. Reproduced by permission of The New York Times Company.—Brown, John Mason. From *Two on the Aisle: Ten Years of the American Theatre in Performance.*

W. W. Norton & Co., 1938. Reproduced by permission of the author.—Conacher, D. J. From *Euripidean Drama: Myth, Theme, and Structure.* University of Toronto Press, 1967. Copyright © 1967 by University of Toronto Press. Reprinted by permission of the publisher.—Corbin, John. From *Onstage: Selected Theater Reviews from The New York Times, 1920-1970.* Edited by Bernard Beckerman and Howard Siegman. Arno Press, 1973. Copyright © 1973 by the New York Times Company. Reproduced by permission of The New York Times Company.—Eliot, George. From *Essays of George Eliot.* Edited by Thomas Pinney. Routledge and Kegan Paul, 1963. Reproduced by permission.—Kronenberger, Louis. From an introduction to *She Stoops to Conquer; or, The Mistakes of a Night.* By Oliver Goldsmith. Heritage Press, 1964. Reproduced by permission of the author.—Nichols, Lewis. From *Onstage: Selected Theater Reviews from The New York Times, 1920-1970.* Edited by Bernard Beckerman and Howard Siegman. Arno Press, 1973. Copyright © 1973 by the New York Times Company. Reproduced by permission of The New York Times Company.—Pritchett, V. S. From *Chekhov: A Spirit Set Free.* Hodder and Stoughton, 1988. Copyright © by V. S. Pritchett 1988. All rights reserved. Reproduced by permission.

PHOTOGRAPHS AND ILLUSTRATIONS APPEARING IN *DFS*, VOLUME 1, WERE RECEIVED FROM THE FOLLOWING SOURCES:

Sophocles, photograph. Corbis-Bettmann. Reproduced by permission.—From a production still for *Antigone* by Sophocles. Donald Cooper, London. Reproduced by permission.—Chekhov, Anton, photograph. Library of Congress.—*The Cherry Orchard* production still. Donald Cooper, London. Reproduced by permission.—Rostand, Edmond, photograph. Archive Photos. Reproduced by permission.—Production still for *Cyrano de Bergerac,* by Edmond Rostand. Archive Photos. Reproduced by permission.—Miller, Arthur, photograph. Archive Photos. Reproduced by permission.—Production still for *Death of A Salesman* by Arthur Miller. Donald Cooper, London. Reproduced by permission.—Production still for *Death of A Salesman* by Arthur Miller. AP/Wide World Photos. Reproduced by permission.—Marlowe, Christopher, photograph. Corbis-Bettman. Reproduced by permission.—Production still for *Doctor Faustus* by Christopher Marlowe. Donald Cooper, London. Reproduced by permission.—Ibsen, Henrik, photograph. AP/Wide World Photos. Reproduced by permission.—Movie still from *A Doll's House,* by Henrik Ibsen. Archive Photos. Reproduced by permission.—Williams, Tennessee, photograph. AP/Wide World Photos. Reproduced by permission.—Production still for *The Glass Menagerie* by Tennessee Williams. The Raymond Mander & Joe Mitchenson Theatre Collection. Reproduced by permission.—Production still for *The Glass Menagerie* by Tennessee Williams. Archive Photos. Reproduced by permission.—Hammerstein, Oscar II, photograph. International Portrait Gallery/ Library of Congress.—Movie still for *The King and I* by Richard Rodgers and Oscar Hammerstein. AP/Wide World Photos. Reproduced by permission.—Rodgers, Richard, photograph. Archive Photos, Inc. Reproduced by permission.—Production still for *The King and I* by Richard Rodgers and Oscar Hammerstein. AP/Wide World Photos. Reproduced by permission.—Hellman, Lillian, photograph. AP/Wide World Photos. Reproduced by permission.—Production still for *The Little Foxes* by Lillian Hellman. The Raymond Mander & Joe Mitchenson Theatre Collection. Reproduced by permission.—Euripides, photograph. Archive Photos, Inc. Reproduced by permission.—Production still for *Medea* by Euripides. Hulton Deutsch Collection Limited. Reproduced by permission of Tony Stone Images.—Sophocles, photograph. Archive Photos, Inc. Reproduced by permission.—Production still for *Oedipus Rex* by Sophocles. Corbis-Bettmann. Reproduced by permission.—Wilder, Thornton, photograph by Carl Van Vechten. The Library of Congress.—Photograph for *Our Town* by Thornton Wilder. AP/Wide World Photos. Reproduced by permission.—Shaw, George Bernard, photograph. The Library of Congress. Reproduced by permission.—Production still for *Pygmalion* by George Bernard Shaw. The Raymond Mander & Joe Mitchenson Theatre Collection. Reproduced by permission.—Goldsmith, Oliver, photograph. Archive Photos. Reproduced by permission.—Production still for *She Stoops to Conquer* by Oliver Goldsmith. Billy Rose Theatre Collection. Reproduced by permission.—Williams, Tennessee, photograph. Archive Photos. Reproduced by permission.—Production still for *A Streetcar Named Desire* by Tennessee Williams. Archive Photos. Reproduced by permission.—Production still for *A Streetcar Named Desire* by Tennessee Williams. Archive Photos. Reproduced by permission.—

Kaufman, George and Moss Hart, photograph. AP/ Wide World Photos. Reproduced by permission.— Production still for *You Can't Take It with You* by Moss Hart and George Kaufman. Donald Cooper, London. Reproduced by permission.

Antigone

SOPHOCLES

c. 442 B.C.

Greek playwright Sophocles wrote the last play in the Theban Trilogy, *Antigone,* around 442 B.C. The Theban Trilogy consists of *Oedipus Rex (Oedipus the King), Oedipus at Colonus,* and *Antigone,* but the play considered the last of the three was, ironically, written first. Only seven of Sophocles's one hundred-twenty-three tragedies have survived to the modern era—with the trilogy surviving the ages intact. These three plays are perhaps the most famous of the seven, with *Antigone* performed most often.

Antigone tells the story of the title character, daughter of Oedipus (the former king of Thebes, who unknowingly killed his father and married his mother, and who renounced his kingdom upon discovering his actions), and her fight to bury her brother Polyneices against the edict of her uncle, Creon, the new king of Thebes. It is a story that pits the law of the gods—''unwritten law''—against the laws of humankind, family ties against civic duty, and man against woman.

Many playwrights in Ancient Greece used mythological stories to comment on social and political concerns of their time. This is what Sophocles may have intended when he wrote *Antigone.* Based on the legends of Oedipus, Sophocles may have been trying to send a message to the Athenian general, Pericles, about the dangers of authoritarian rule.

Sophocles

He was also a priest of the healing god Amynos and kept the sacred snake representing the god Aeschulapius while his temple was being built. He was a very well-rounded citizen, not only leading an active political and religious life but also writing one hundred and twenty-three tragedies, of which only seven remain intact for modern readers.

Sophocles was married to a woman named Nicostrata, with whom he had a son, Iophon; he also had a son (out of wedlock) with Theoris of Sicyon named Ariston. He studied music under Lamprus and tragedy under Aeschylus before writing his own tragedies. His was a wealthy family and powerful in political and religious affairs. Of his seven plays to survive, *Oedipus Rex (Oedipus the King)* (c. 430 B.C.), *Oedipus at Colonus* (c. 404 B.C.), and *Antigone* (c. 442 B.C.), comprise the "Theban Trilogy," three plays which deal with King Oedipus's tragic fall from power and the ruin of his children. Sophocles also wrote *Ajax* (c. 450 B.C.), *Trachiniae (The Women of Trachis)* (440 B.C.), and *Electra* and *Philoctetes* (both c. 409 B.C.). The titles of ninety other Sophoclean dramas survive, including *Triptolemos,* which was honored at the dramatic competition the Great Dionysia c. 468 B.C., when Sophocles defeated his onetime mentor Aeschylus.

In *Antigone,* the title character asserts that the laws of Zeus and "unwritten law" justify her burial of her brother, Polyneices. The popular general Pericles himself addressed the issue of unwritten law. To many scholars the play was Sophocles's message to Pericles on the dangers of authoritarian rule, and the playwright's assertion of the general's need to remain conscious of his duty to the citizens of Athens. It was the duty of playwrights in Athens to address social and political issues, and this play not only addresses authoritarian rule, but also familial duty and the status of women in society. When Antigone stands up to Creon she not only defies the edict, but also the traditional behavior of Greek women of the time.

These tragedies were written to be performed at the Great Dionysia (a festival in honor of the god Dionysus, the god of fertility, theater, and wine) in Athens. Attending these plays was considered a civic duty, and even criminals were let out of jail to attend. *Antigone* won Sophocles first prize at the festival and was an enormous success. It is still performed today, and has been adapted by French playwright Jean Anouilh, who set the play during World War II.

During the Golden Age of Athens, Sophocles was one of the city's most prolific and beloved playwrights. *Antigone* is still performed all over the world, and though it may seem different in theme and structure to modern works, it continues to move audiences just at it did when it was first produced. Many scholars have remarked on Sophocles's ability to create dramatic, complex, and unique characters and situations, all of which have withstood the passage of time.

AUTHOR BIOGRAPHY

Sophocles lived from c.496 to c.406 B.C., during the Golden Age of Athens (480-404 B.C.), the Greek city-state of which he was a citizen. He was an active citizen, participating in the city's infant democracy. He was involved in the war against the Samians and during the war became friends with Athens's popular general, Pericles. He founded the Thiasos of Muses (a society for the advancement of music and literature), and was an ambassador to many foreign countries throughout his lifetime.

PLOT SUMMARY

Scene I

Antigone opens shortly before dawn outside of the palace at Thebes, where Antigone meets her sister Ismene. Together they grieve over the losses their family has suffered. First, their father, Oedipus, had unknowingly murdered his own father, ascended the throne, and married his mother. When Oedipus discovered this, he put out his eyes and wandered as an exile from Thebes until his death. Then their brothers Polyneices and Eteocles had killed each other in a battle between Thebes and the city of Argos. Now, because Polyneices fought against Thebes, Creon, the new king of Thebes, has ordered that his corpse remain unburied, thus condemning his spirit to roam the earth for one hundred years.

Grieved, Antigone calls on Ismene to join her in carrying out their duty to their brother in spite of the edict. Antigone appeals to her sister's familial duty. Ismene, on the other hand, argues that, as women, they should not question the decisions of men—especially an edict from the king. Each fails to persuade the other and the sisters exit as the chorus of elders approaches.

Scene II

Because Thebes has stood victorious in the battle against Argos, the chorus calls for a celebration. Then, as they begin to wonder why they have been summoned to the palace, Creon, newly crowned as king over the city-state, comes from the palace. He asks the elders to show him the same loyalty they had previously awarded Oedipus. He restates his edict that Polyneices shall not be buried, vowing that no foe of the city shall be his friend. The chorus seems uncertain about administering Creon's edict and ask that younger men perform the task. One of the young men guarding the body of Polyneices comes forward.

The sentry guard tells Creon that someone has sprinkled dust on the body of Polyneices—an attempt at burial that violates Creon's decree. An elder suggests that the act is the work of a god. Creon disagrees and warns the old man against such foolish proclamations. It is base, he argues, to defy the state, not the glorious act of a god. The king suspects that money has provoked someone to at-

MEDIA ADAPTATIONS

- *Antigone* was adapted for a film directed by Dinos Katsourides. Starring Irene Papas and Manos Katrakis, the production is in Greek with English subtitles, released by Ivy Film, 1962; available through Ingram International Films.

- *Antigone* was re-adapted for the stage in 1987; available through Films for the Humanities & Sciences.

- *Antigone: Rites for the Dead* is a dance interpretation of Sophocles's tragedy. A filmed version was directed by Amy Greenfield, with music by Glen Branca, Paul Lemos, Eliot Sharp, Diamanda Galas, and David Van Tiegham, 1991.

tempt Polyneices's burial. Creon tells the sentry that he will be held responsible for the crime until the guard finds the actual perpetrator. He sends the sentry back to his post, commanding that he find the lawbreaker.

Scene III

The chorus praises the wonder that is man and the cunning by which he can capture all of nature, or, conversely, escape nature's snares, all, that is, except death. Then the guard returns bringing Antigone as his captive. The guard reports that just after they had removed the dust from Polyneices, Antigone was caught trying to bury her brother a second time. When questioned by Creon, Antigone admits to both attempts at burial. Creon condemns her; Antigone asserts that she has done a noble deed by honoring her family and following the "unwritten law."

Creon suspects that, due to her odd behavior earlier, Ismene may be an accomplice in her sister's crimes. When she comes forth, the chorus of elders recognizes that Ismene is innocent; her tears are not of guilt but sorrow for her sister. Yet Creon demands her confession, and she gives it. Upon hear-

TOPICS FOR FURTHER STUDY

- Research the ways in which arguments over such topics as abortion (both pro-choice and anti-abortion movements) or anti-government militia groups such as the Montana Freemen and the Republic of Texas concern conflicts over the rights of individuals and the role the state should play in determining ethical decisions. How much should the state be involved in determining or restricting the rights of the individual? How much should the rights of individuals be asserted over the good of the state and community?

- Research the differences between the concept of the nuclear family, consisting of two parents and their children, and the extended families of other cultures, in which grandparents and other relatives play important roles in the lives of family members.

- In the breakdown of what is perceived to be a traditional American family—particularly families without father figures–many young people living in urban areas find nurture and support by joining gangs. Research the ways, both positive and negative, in which young people find family values by being loyal to a gang. Based on this research, what alternatives to gangs can be suggested for youths seeking some kind of familial relationship?

- Research how organized crime "families" are structured and show the ways in which this structure is in conflict with political structures in America and the world.

- Explore the family unit during the 19th century western expansion of the American frontier. How did the early explorers and settlers organize themselves? What type of family unit was most common, nuclear or extended?

---

ing this, Antigone states that she acted alone, absolving her sister of guilt. Ismene pleads for Antigone's life, reminding the king that not only is his prisoner family (Antigone is Creon's niece), she is also betrothed to his son, Haemon. Despite this, Creon will not reverse his judgment.

Scene IV

As Antigone and Ismene are led away, Haemon appears. He appeals to his father's ego, asking that he let Antigone go free to show the people that he is a kind and forgiving ruler. Though Creon briefly considers his son's advice, when Haemon notes that citizens are concerned for Antigone's welfare, the king sees that the argument is only made to free Antigone. He rejects his son's proposal, stating that he will not have his laws questioned by a woman, nor will he accede to the desires of his son. He vows to execute Antigone in Haemon's presence, but his son leaves, vowing that his father will never see him again. Creon decides to bury Antigone alive with

enough food and water so that the city itself is not held to blame for her death.

Scene V

Antigone is led to a cavern where she will be sealed inside of a tomb. The chorus of elders mourn for her, speaking of comparisons to Persephone, who also died young and without a husband. The chorus also seems to mock Antigone, however.

Scene VI

After Antigone has been led away, Teiresias, a blind seer, is brought before Creon. The prophet warns Creon that he is responsible for a sickness that has descended on Thebes. Polyneices's unburied body has polluted the city and the gods will hear no more prayers. The body is also polluting the cities close to Thebes, causing ill will toward Creon's city-state. Creon accuses the old man of trickery, stating that some enemy must have paid the seer to come and upset him. Teiresias accuses Creon of tyranny and selfishness, warning the king that he will lose his son and great grief will befall his house.

After Teiresias exits, Creon becomes fearful. He decides to heed the advice of the elders, allow Polyneices to be buried, and set Antigone free. When he exits the elders pray to Bacchus for the safe-keeping of the city.

Scene VII

A messenger enters and reports that Haemon has taken his own life. Eurydice, Creon's wife, comes from the palace to receive this information. She learns how Creon and his men first gave Polyneices an honorable burial, and how, when they came to Antigone's crypt, they found that she had hanged herself. Haemon, in grief, tried to stab his father and, failing this, impaled himself. Eurydice bears this news in silence, returning to the palace.

Scene VIII

Creon returns to the palace bearing the body of his son. He is grief-stricken over the results of his own stubbornness. He then learns that Eurydice has also taken her own life. Creon begins to rave, calling himself a rash, foolish man whose life has been overwhelmed by death.

CHARACTERS

Antigone

Antigone, the daughter of Jocasta (sister of Creon) and daughter/half-sister of Oedipus (Jocasta's son/husband, King of Thebes), is a strong-willed young woman who decides to bury her brother Polyneices against the edict of her uncle Creon, the new king. Following what she calls "unwritten law," Antigone buries her brother and performs the rituals of the dead. Creon, upon discovering her guilt, sentences her to die by being buried alive. When Creon goes to free Antigone from her early grave on the advice of Teiresias, he finds she's already hung herself, and his son, Haemon, her fiance, commits suicide to join her in death. Antigone is a representative of allegiance to family and tradition. By defying Creon's edict, she is showing her faith and sense of duty to her family. She personifies the belief that family and human relations should be placed above politics.

Antigone is committed to her ideals. When her sister Ismene refuses to help her bury their brother, she ends their relationship, and, when caught, she refuses to let Ismene share the punishment. When Creon tells her that she dishonors her dead brother Eteocles, she replies that he is dishonoring the gods by refusing to obey the unwritten laws of Zeus. Though she laments her fate, she later faces it defiantly. Antigone also represents contradictions, first defying her role as a woman, which is to remain silent and follow Creon's edict, and then lamenting that she will never be Haemon's bride. Yet her complex emotions and strength of conviction makes her unique as a Greek woman and have rendered her a compelling heroine for centuries.

Chorus

The Chorus is another convention of Greek drama. They, in *Antigone,* act as older Theban nobles who comment on the actions of the characters in the play and underline moral points. They also fill in the background of the civil war that pitted brothers Eteocles and Polyneices against each other.

One of the choral passages in the play is called the "Ode to Man," which glorifies humankind's accomplishments but warns against ignoring the gods. The Chorus, however, supports Creon's decisions until it becomes evident that his rule has resulted in tragedy. Creon reminds the Chorus that they too signed Antigone's death warrant by supporting his policies.

Chorus Leader

See Koryphaios

Creon

Creon is Antigone's uncle, brother of her mother, Jocasta. He was proclaimed regent (or ruler) after Oedipus's tragic fall from power. He has raised his sister's children as his own following her descent into madness. He was to rule Thebes until Eteocles and Polyneices could rule together as adults. After their deaths he was proclaimed king in his own right.

Holding on to power and suppressing rebellion of any kind are Creon's main objectives when he orders Polyneices to remain unburied. When notified by a sentry that someone has defied his order, he holds the sentry responsible until the culprit is caught. Creon is unbending and will not listen to the advice of his elders (the Chorus) or Teiresias, the prophet. He is an autocrat, an absolute ruler.

Creon's refusal to obey what Antigone calls the "unwritten laws" regarding honoring the dead leads to his downfall. As the body of Polyneices "pollutes" the altars of Thebes and its neighboring kingdoms, Creon refuses to listen to advice and further angers the gods by sentencing Antigone to be buried alive as punishment for her betrayal of his edict. Even the pleas of his own son Haemon, Antigone's fiance, go unheard as he disowns his son for being less of a man for defending his love. Teiresias, the respected prophet, is branded a liar by Creon for predicting that this unbending stance will bring death to those he loves. Despite evidence that Teiresias has been right in the past, and is an honest man, Creon refuses to yield. It is only at the urging of the chorus leader that he relents but by then it is too late. Both Antigone and Haemon are dead by suicide, and their deaths are followed closely by the suicide of Creon's wife Eurydice. Creon's refusal to listen and to compromise lead to the loss of everything he loves, including power. He becomes a grief-stricken, broken man.

Eurydice

Eurydice is Creon's wife and Haemon's mother. She appears late in the play, when she senses something is wrong with her family, and is then informed of the deaths of Antigone and Haemon by a messenger. She takes refuge inside the palace, and, as the messenger tells Creon: "She stabbed herself at the altar, then her eyes went dark . . . then with her dying breath she called down torments on your head—you killed her sons."

Haemon

Haemon is the son of Creon and Eurydice and is engaged to be married to Antigone. He tries desperately to persuade his father to see reason by allowing Polyneices's burial and the release of Antigone, but Creon refuses and accuses his son of being a "slave" to Antigone. Disowned by his father, Haemon breaks into Antigone's tomb and, upon finding her dead, kills himself in front of his father. Haemon responds to Antigone's moral courage by sacrificing himself for her; his love and admiration for Antigone are so great that he cannot bear to live without her.

Ismene

Antigone's sister Ismene loves her sister and brothers, but she refuses to help Antigone bury Polyneices. She reminds her sister that according to their role as women, it is not for them to decide what is right or wrong. When Antigone is caught, Ismene is willing to share the punishment, but Antigone denies her sister's involvement. Ismene is devastated by the loss of her siblings, but because of her belief in her lack of status, she feels powerless to act on their behalf. Ismene acts as a foil for Antigone; while she demonstrates a woman living according to the traditional rules governing the behavior and status of Athenian women, Antigone represents a pioneering woman who governs herself according to a sense of personal empowerment and self-reliance.

Koryphaios

The Koryphaios is the chorus leader, who functions as an advisor to Creon. He expresses concern for Antigone, tries to support Haemon, and advises Creon to listen to Teiresias. He does, however, agree with both Creon and Antigone on some points, and support wavers between the two characters throughout the play.

Leader

See Koryphaios

Messenger

The messenger brings the news of the deaths of Antigone and Haemon to Eurydice and the news of Eurydice's death to Creon. Greek tragedy demanded that the violence take place offstage; so a messenger served to inform the audience, and the other characters, of the action that has taken place offstage. The messenger in *Antigone* asserts to Eurydice that "Truth is always best," sparing her—and any other character to whom he brings news—no details and providing the simple truth. Pointing to the Haemon's body, and hinting at the death of the queen, the messenger tells Creon: "The grief that lies at hand you've brought yourself—the rest, in the house, you'll see it all too soon."

Sentry Guard

The sentry informs Creon at the beginning of the play that someone has buried and performed death rituals for Polyneices; he is held accountable for the crime until he goes back to the scene and catches Antigone in the act. The sentry then proudly brings Antigone to Creon, glad to have cleared himself of any wrongdoing. He claims to be concerned solely with his own welfare, though expresses regret at having implicated such a young woman.

Teiresias

A respected prophet, the blind Teiresias was well known to ancient Greek audiences from the Theban legends. He is led by his boy assistant to Creon's palace to tell the king that he must reverse his edicts, bury Polyneices, and free Antigone. Using a ritual sacrifice, Teiresias determines that the "state is sick" and its altars "polluted" because Polyneices's body has been left to be eaten by animals. The live burial of Antigone only adds to the anger of the gods.

Creon accuses the prophet of lying for money, calling him a "prophetic profiteer." Teiresias counters by predicting the deaths of Haemon and Eurydice. He also predicts that the other nearby kingdoms will attack because of the pollution of their altars. Greek audiences of Sophocles's time would have readily accepted and believed Teiresias and his predictions. Oracles, fortune telling, and ritual sacrifices and offerings to the gods were part of everyday life in Greece at the time. His predictions serve to heighten the tension in the play and to set up the events for catharsis, the purging of fear and pity brought about by the events in the play.

THEMES

Thematic Overview

Antigone was written over two thousand years ago, in a land that is still considered the birthplace of democracy. Sophocles was a part of this democratic movement, but custom, tradition, and the rules of the gods also played an important role in Greek life. This is reflected in the themes present in the play: choices and their consequences; custom and tradition; gods and religion; and betrayal. These issues make *Antigone* constant in terms of its relevance to audiences of all times, as these issues represent some of the fundamental challenges faced by humankind.

Choices and Consequences

Just as in life, choices in *Antigone* have their consequences. From the outset, Antigone's decision to bury Polyneices seals her fate. Her refusal to obey Creon's edict to leave her brother's body to be consumed by wild animals leads to her capture and to her death. Similarly, Ismene's refusal to help Antigone ends her relationship with her sister. When Antigone is caught, Ismene is refused the honor of sharing her fate and instead is forced to live on alone, tortured by a loss of family and the knowledge that she may have made a cowardly choice.

Creon's unyielding government and his choice to ignore both the advice of Teiresias and the pleas of Haemon result in the loss of both his son and wife—as well as bad relationships with neighboring cities. His refusal to bend to the will of the gods effectively ruins his life. All choices in the play—Antigone's, Ismene's, and Creon's—are made freely, but the consequences are predicted by the prophet Teiresias and, therefore, are considered to be governed by fate. In Greek culture in the fifth century B.C., much emphasis was placed on fate; oracles (prophets) were commonly consulted and prophecies were made. Though the characters make choices of their own free will, the consequences of these choices are viewed as being controlled by fate, that is, determined by the gods.

Sophocles may have wanted to show that choices made for apparently logical reasons—Antigone's burial of her brother according to "unwritten law," Creon's need to keep order after a civil war, and Ismene's following of the traditional role of women—can have terrible unforeseen consequences. Though all three characters make the choice that seems right to him or her, the results are disastrous. Antigone dies, Creon loses his family and power over the state, and Ismene is doomed to live the rest of her life alone, knowing that she did not try to help her family.

Custom and Tradition

The Ancient Greeks were polytheists, which means that they believed in many gods, and each god represented a specific aspect of life. Zeus, however, was the king of the gods, and he ruled over all. Antigone invokes the name of Zeus several times in the play as she defends her burial of Polyneices. Greek custom and tradition dictated that the women in the immediate family of the deceased should carry out the burial rituals, which meant that Antigone and Ismene were responsible for the burial of both of their brothers. When Creon orders Polyneices left unburied, Antigone felt she was acting according to the "unwritten laws" of Zeus by burying him. To her, all dead should have the honor of burial, no matter what they did in life, and she felt she was justified in fulfilling this custom and obeying the law of Zeus.

Teiresias warns Creon that ignoring Zeus's "unwritten law" would bring tragedy to his house. By ignoring the prophet, Creon disregards both the gods and the long tradition of prophets and oracles in Greece. This disrespect for custom and tradition, and his arrogance in presuming that he is "absolutely right" leads to his fall from power. Most scholars agree that Sophocles wrote *Antigone* as a warning against absolute rule and authoritarianism. Greece had just become a democracy after a long period of dictatorial rule, and this play, as well as others of its time, was meant to caution all of Athens against allowing that type of government to regain power.

God and Religion

Creon's edict that Polyneices should go unburied invites disaster on Thebes. Teiresias tells Creon that "the gods reject our prayers and our sacrifices," and pleads with Creon to listen, warning the king that the furies—agents of the god of death—are angered and will seek retribution. Teiresias further tells Creon: "You have dishonored a living soul with exile in the tomb,/hurling a member of this world below./You are detaining here, moreover,/a dead body, unsanctified, and so unholy,/a subject of the nethergods." In other words, Creon has infuriated the gods by imposing his own set of laws instead of following the laws that they have set down for humankind to follow.

Betrayal

The conflict between Creon and Antigone becomes a sort of family versus state conflict that results from the betrayal each group perceives in the actions of the other. When Polyneices married into the royal family of Argos, Creon felt betrayed that one of his own should seek power in another state (and later fight against Thebes in a war), and Creon views Antigone's burial of her brother as another act of betrayal. Antigone is betrayed both by Ismene's refusal to help her bury their brother, and by Creon's actions when he learns what she has done. Finally, Eurydice expresses betrayal by Creon, who failed to save their son Haemon from suicide and failed to take action to prevent the death of their older son in the civil war that began the tragic course of events depicted in the play. In his introduction to his translation of *Antigone*, Richard Emil Braun asserted: "Betrayal of faith and disregard of family bonds are the themes of Creon's reign. Permeated with hate, life lacks cohesiveness; the polar opposite of life, the anti-world of Hades, must then contain love." Creon puts the governing of Thebes before the needs of his family, precisely the opposite of Antigone's choice to put her duty to her family before her duties to the state; both choices lead to

death, which is portrayed as the only solution to the dilemma.

STYLE

Ancient Greek playwrights in Athens wrote plays for the Great Dionysia festival that was held every Spring. It was a civic duty to attend these plays, as they dealt with moral and social issues important to the community. Sophocles based *Antigone* on the Theban myths of the legendary rulers of Thebes, using what was, even in his time, an old story to comment on such issues as the absolute rule of kings and the status of women in society.

Tragedy

Antigone is a traditional Greek tragedy. A tragedy is defined as a drama about a noble, courageous hero or heroine of excellent character who because of some tragic character flaw brings ruin upon himself or herself. Tragedy treats its subjects in a dignified and serious manner, using poetic language to help evoke pity and fear and bring about catharsis, a purging of these emotions. In the case of *Antigone* we have two characters at the center of the conflict—Antigone and Creon—who are both tragic figures. Antigone defies a royal edict to bury her brother and pays with her life, while Creon ignores the gods and loses his wife and son to suicide. Both characters evoke pity, and each meets a tragic end.

Catharsis

Catharsis is the release or purging of emotions of fear and/or pity, brought on by art, usually tragedy. It is an act that brings spiritual renewal. One of the conventions of Greek drama was to have all violence occur offstage and then conveyed verbally to the audience. This occurs in *Antigone*, as the messenger relates the story of the deaths of Antigone and Haemon to Eurydice. The words of the messenger in *Antigone* are designed to provoke catharsis in the audience without directly exposing them to the violence of the events. With *Antigone*, Sophocles hoped to illustrate to audiences the emotional price of his characters' actions, inspiring in his viewers new perspectives and a sense of caution regarding similar actions.

Chorus

Another convention in Greek drama is the chorus. Strictly defined, a chorus is a group of actors who comment on and interpret the action taking place on stage. The Greek word *choros* means "dance," and sometimes the chorus actually functioned as a character in the play, or portrayed a group of citizens very similar to the audience. In *Antigone,* Koryphaios, the chorus leader, is a character in the play; the rest of the chorus are Theban elders who alternately express loyalty to Antigone and Creon. The chorus's indecision underscores the complex nature of the issues in the play.

Dramatic License

Many scholars have expressed opinions similar to that of Braun, who argued in his introduction to his translation of *Antigone:* "Until new evidence appears, one must presume that Sophocles invented many events in the story of his *Antigone:* (1) the form of Creon's decree; (2) the quarrels between Antigone and Ismene; (3) the double burial of Polyneices by Antigone and the final creation-burial by Creon; (4) the love of Antigone and Haemon; (5) the entombment of Antigone; (6) Teiresias's intervention and Creon's change of mind; and (7) the suicides of Antigone, Haemon, and Eurydice." These events are not present in other accounts of the Theban myths, only in Sophocles's version of the story. The playwright's use of "dramatic license," or embellishment, serves to heighten the tension in the story, increase the complexity of the plot, and intensify the catharsis at the end of the play. Scholars disagree on the exact reasons for these additions, but most agree that the changes make the story more intense and immediate. Since few plays from *Antigone*'s era have survived, it can only be speculated that these events were fabricated and added to the story; however, no other known accounts of the Theban myths include this information.

HISTORICAL CONTEXT

Fifth Century Greece and Its Influence

The fifth century B.C. in Greece was a time of great advancement in philosophy, art, and government. Great writers such as Aristotle, Aeschylus, and Sophocles wrote plays, philosophy, and political tracts that would influence the world for thousands of years to come. Democracy was being established, and the "Hippocratic Oath," written by Hippocrates the Great in 429 B.C., was being taken by the first doctors; this oath is the same oath taken by contemporary doctors. The Golden Age of Athens (480-404 B.C.) was in full swing during Sophocles's lifetime, and it was during this period in history that many ideals of the modern Western world first appeared.

Bronze Age of Greece

Antigone takes place in Bronze Age Thebes, sometime during the 1200s B.C. Sophocles uses the legends of the family of Oedipus (Antigone's father) in order to explore social and political issues of his time. Attending the theater was a civic and religious duty in Sophocles's time. By setting his play in a time period 800 years before his own, he could explore social and political issues without offending those currently in power. He uses the authoritarian rule of Creon and the strong-willed Antigone to warn against the dangers of dictatorship and to highlight the status of women in Greek society.

Civil and Moral Unrest

In 429 B.C. a great plague killed almost two-thirds of the population of Athens, causing civil and moral unrest and testing the bounds of democracy. Warfare was also common at this time in Greek society, as the city-states of Greece competed with each other for trade, commerce, and artistic superiority. This unrest is reflected in the events portrayed in *Antigone,* beginning with the civil war that pits Antigone's brothers against each other and ending with the deaths of Antigone, Haemon, and Eurydice.

Democracy and Government

Sophocles was not only a respected writer, but also a member of the government in Athens. Democracy was practiced differently in Ancient Greece than it is in the modern United States. Full citizenship, which included the right to vote, was only given to free men; women and slaves were not considered full citizens and so lacked the same rights as men. They were forced to follow a different code of conduct. Despite such inequities and restrictions, the foundations laid in the fifth century B.C. provided a framework for the founders of the United States—and other world democracies—when they sought to establish a free democratic government.

Playwrights and Drama

The writers of the fifth century B.C. established the traditions of both tragedy and comedy. The first three plays at the Great Dionysia festival were tragedies, followed by the satyr play, which poked fun at the characters and situations of the earlier tragedies; ''satyr'' served as the forerunner to the modern dramatic convention of satire, which uses humor to criticize or mock. The satyr plays were then followed by a comedy by another playwright, as the competition for comedic plays was separate from the competition for tragedies.

There were strict rules for tragedy in the Great Dionysia, and the plays were viewed as valued cultural commodities. To qualify—let alone win—dramatic works had to subscribe to a strict format that had been used for many years. To preserve this cultural jewel, a great deal of importance was placed on the passing of knowledge; it was as much a role of the playwright to teach as it was to compose. Aeschylus, a great writer of tragedy, was one of the teachers entrusted to teach younger writers the methodology of tragedy. Sophocles was one of his students (who would later defeat his instructor at the Great Dionysia), and he, in turn, also shared his knowledge with younger writers. Modern plays are evaluated according to the standards set forth by plays written in Ancient Greece, and contemporary playwrights look to writers such as Sophocles and Aeschylus for instruction and inspiration.

The Sophists

Athens in the fifth century B.C. saw the rise of a revolutionary group of teachers and philosophers called the Sophists. This group broke with tradition and focused more on the study of the actions of humankind than on the standard legends of gods and goddesses. Sophocles was one of these individual teachers, who, although differing in their views as well as their standards, agreed that the main subject of their teaching should be human actions. These middle-class teachers instructed the sons of the wealthy about politics and the practice of democracy with the full support of Pericles and other leaders.

CRITICAL OVERVIEW

In the fifth century B.C., Athens was one of the great city-states of Greece. *Antigone* takes place in Thebes during the Bronze Age (1200s B.C.), 800 years before the birth of Sophocles. The story Sophocles tells is based on the oral history, or genealogy, of the ancient rulers of Thebes. By removing the action of his play to the mythic past and using heroic characters, Sophocles was able to touch on the profound and significant issues of his day from a safe distance. Athens in Sophocles's time was one of the world's first experiments in democracy. *Antigone* represents the conflict between traditional government, which advocated following the laws of the state and the absolute rule of its leader, and democracy, according to which citizens obeyed a set of laws that they themselves had helped to institute. One school of critical thought argues that the figure of Creon, who abuses his power, may have been a veiled warning to Pericles and the Athenian people about the dangers of dictatorship. In the play, Creon stubbornly insists that Antigone suffer an awful fate for her actions. His refusal to listen to any line of reasoning served to remind the Athenian audience of the terrors that tyranny could bring. Other critics, however, insist that Creon behaves as he does precisely because of the democratic ideal. As Arlene W. Saxonhouse noted in her *Fear of Diversity: The Birth of Political Science in Ancient Greek Thought:* "Creon, the political leader, categorizes and simplifies; one female equals another. . . . In a perverse way, Creon's refusal to distinguish, to particularize, to see differences, may make him more the democrat than the tyrant.'' This difference of opinion serves to underscore how complex the play is. Whether one perceives Creon as tyrant or democrat, he meets a tragic end. Sophocles respects the gods, but tends to explore human characters rather than supernatural ones. Scholar Jacqueline de Romilly stated in an essay in her *A Short History of Greek Literature:* ''The relation between men and gods . . . is a major theme in Sophocles. But it is nothing like the relation between men and gods as described by Aeschylus. In the first place, the gods are more distant. In the surviving plays, they almost never appear onstage. . . . Likewise, their influence on human emotions is less immediate; and the principles by which they act are harder to discern.'' Unlike previous writers who used the gods as characters in their plays, Sophocles tends to focus on the human characters' actions and choices. When the gods do make their presence known in Sophocles, it is usually through oracles. It is Teiresias who makes the gods' wishes known in *Antigone;* through the prophet's examination of a ritual sacrifice, the god's displeasure with Creon is revealed. Creon's unwill-

COMPARE
&
CONTRAST

- **1200s B.C.:** The states in Greece are run by dictators who are members of the royal family. Power is transferred from father to son, and never to daughters. The citizens have no say in affairs of state.

  400s B.C.: Democracy is taking hold in Greece. Athens, for example, is run by ten generals elected by the free male population. The citizens have a say in what actions their government takes.

  Today: Democracies flourish on all continents of the world. The most famous of these democracies, the United States, was founded on the Athenian experiments with democracy in the 400s B.C. Following the end of the Cold War (a state of nonmilitary aggression between democratic and Communist countries), many more countries are in the process of establishing democratic governments.

- **1200s B.C.:** Greek society was "polytheistic," meaning that the Greeks worshipped many gods. Zeus was the king of the gods, with many other gods such as Hades, the god of death, and Aphrodite, the goddess of love, who gathered with Zeus on Mount Olympus (the heavens). The Greeks believed that one must make offerings to the gods to appease them and that ritual sacrifice could influence the gods' feelings and actions regarding certain issues (such as harvests or wars).

  400s B.C.: Greek society was still polytheistic but as long as the city's gods were not neglected, worship was open to any god. Worship of the gods was still important but it became more of a civic and social duty. In art, emphasis was less on the actions of the gods and more on human actions.

  Today: Most Western societies are monotheistic, meaning that they worship only one god. Religion has become marginalized in many societies and ritual sacrifices and offerings have become taboo in most Christian sects. There is a resurgence in interest in earth-based and pagan (non-Christian) religions, but the Greek gods have disappeared into myths and legends, only resurrected in films, books, and television shows.

- **1200s B.C.:** Bronze was used to fashion weapons of war and household tools. The coming of the Bronze Age meant a great leap forward in civilization by allowing people to invent new tools and weapons to make their lives easier and more productive.

  400s B.C.: The Golden Age of Athens (480-404 B.C.) saw the rise of great tragedies and comedies in the theater, finely crafted sculptures, and advancements in democratic ideals. This age was crucial to the development of democratic ideals and the foundations of modern drama as we know them today.

  Today: The advancements in science and technology made in the latter part of the twentieth century, such as space flight, the personal computer, and alternative sources of power, will almost certainly have a very real effect on generations of humans to come.

- **1200s B.C.:** Doctors in the modern sense did not exist in Bronze Age Greece. Oracles and prophets would try to interpret the gods' will and action would be taken accordingly.

  400s B.C.: Hippocrates the Great wrote the Hippocratic Oath in 429 B.C. The oath sets out ethical standards for the medical profession and includes the passage: "I will use treatment to help the sick according to my ability and judgment, but I will never use it to injure or wrong them."

  Today: The Hippocratic Oath is still taken by doctors upon graduation from medical school, but in recent years its forbiddance of abortion has been left out by some schools.

ingness to accept what Teiresias tells him leads to his downfall. De Romilly further remarked that Sophocles "respects the gods; and in his plays only the arrogant who are about to be struck down dare to doubt the veracity of oracles. Instead of revolt or doubt we find an overwhelming sense of the distance between gods and men. Among men, everything passes, everything changes. . . . The sphere of the gods, by contrast, is the sphere of the absolute, which nothing disturbs." Creon is struck down because he refuses to acknowledge the "unwritten law" of the gods which is absolute and binding: that the dead should be respected and that those who defend this law are morally right. His further refusal to acknowledge his mistake when Teiresias gives him advice seals his fate and moves the gods to revenge.

Sophocles's characters are complex in terms of their emotions yet simplistic in terms of their moral code of conduct. De Romilly maintained that Sophocles's "characters have different mentalities because each embodies a different moral ideal, to which he or she adheres. Each knows the basis for his actions and defends his principles, making them his cause; each stands in contrast to those among whom he lives as on philosophy of life stands in contrast to others." Similarly, Richard C. Beacham, in *The International Dictionary of Theatre, Volume 1: Plays,* declared: "*Antigone* is in one sense a play of conflicting moral principles in which both sides can marshal strong arguments in their support. Creon insists on the necessity of civil order and the primacy of the rule of law; Antigone claims allegiance to a higher law, that of religious and familial duty, which must, she insists, outweigh the demands of the state. Tragedy is inherent . . . in the irreconcilable conflict between two moral imperatives each of which may be thought of as 'right.'" In other words, both characters make strong arguments but neither is able to compromise. The intensity of the tragedy in the play comes from the fact that both characters can be perceived as behaving in an appropriate manner according to the laws each is following. The audience is able to appreciate both points of view, and because both Creon and Antigone are destroyed, the play's emotional power over the audience is increased.

Antigone won first place in the Great Dionysia festival in Athens when it was first produced c. 442 B.C. The play has been celebrated since that first performance and praised by such writers as: John Keats, William Butler Yeats, George Eliot, Friedrich Nietzsche, Martin Heidegger, and Jean

Cocteau. Noted literary scholar George Steiner, in his *Antigones,* explained: "Between 1790 and 1905, it was widely held by European poets, philosophers, [and] scholars that Sophocles' *Antigone* was not only the finest of Greek tragedies, but a work of art nearer to perfection than any other produced by the human spirit." The play is also extremely popular during times of war—most recently World War II—because of its clash between individual conscience and governmental law. French playwright Jean Anouilh adapted *Antigone* in 1946, and put the characters in a modern setting. According to Colin Radford in his essay in *The International Dictionary of Theatre,* "Anouilh has been much criticized for degrading the legend, for cheapening the significance of his subject, for turning the heroine into a stubborn willful adolescent." Though Anouilh was faulted for his interpretation of the ancient tragedy, his play is considered a masterful work of drama by many critics.

CRITICISM

Thomas Allbaugh
Allbaugh holds a Ph.D. in rhetoric and composition. His essay discusses the issue of family versus community that pervades Sophocles's play.

Literary criticism of a dramatic work can help readers in several ways. It can clarify difficult passages in the play itself. It can assist readers in identifying assumptions that they bring to their viewing or reading of a play. And it can point out important issues raised in the play that warrant more thought and/or discussion. When the play in question is Sophocles's *Antigone,* criticism can be especially helpful concerning the preconceived notions a reader may have concerning the work. The play is an ancient tragedy and, as such, contemporary readers often have difficulty relating to the story and characters. A first time reader of *Antigone* may have assumptions regarding ancient classics that conflict with their own values and beliefs, assumptions that can color their reading of the play.

This is true concerning a number of issues in the play. For example, is Antigone a noble, heroic victim or a fanatical, willfully stubborn character who causes the deaths of two other innocent people? Wallace Grey noted in *Homer to Joyce* that Antigo-

WHAT DO I READ NEXT?

- *Oedipus Rex,* Sophocles's play written c. 430 B.C., years after *Antigone,* concerns the downfall of Oedipus, Antigone's father. As king of Thebes, Oedipus must remove the plague from the city of Thebes by solving the murder of Laius, who was king before Oedipus. In doing so he discovers that he has murdered his own father, married his own mother, and himself brought the plague on the city.

- French playwright Jean Anouilh's *Antigone* presents a modern version of Sophocles's play, one in which the chorus is represented by a single commentator. The play was applauded by both French resistance fighters and German Nazis during World War II.

- *Alcestis,* Euripides's play first produced in 438 B.C. presents a contrast to *Antigone* in terms of both substance and style. When considered next to Sophocles and his apparent devotion to religious ideas and to the gods, Euripides seems to be a realist. In this play, Alcestis, wife of Admetus, agrees to die for him and for his family. This action serves as a contrast to Antigone's claim that she would not die for a husband or for children.

- Kurt Vonnegut's 1976 novel *Slapstick* presents a futuristic view of a longing for relationship and for kinship, and one character's political program to make sure that every American citizen has an extended family.

- *The Godfather,* Mario Puzo's 1969 novel about an organized crime syndicate, describes a family structure that is set in opposition to mainstream American political and ethical life and is organized around ideas of kinship and blood ties.

---

ne is "the first heroine of Western drama." At the same time, he also called Antigone's stubbornness a "wrong," which, when combined with the wrong of Creon, does not make a right. In Grey's words, Antigone is a "lone individual, isolated from the gods and from other people . . . the representative Sophoclean hero or heroine." Another issue, in addition to the character of Antigone, concerns the dramatic conflict between Antigone and Creon. Critics themselves have been divided about how to understand it. Some read this conflict as one in which the rights of the individual are set in opposition to the rule of the state.

As Terence Des Pres suggests in the book *Praises and Dispraises,* reading the central conflict of *Antigone* as individual vs. the state does underscore the political elements of the drama. It sees Antigone's determination to bury her brother as a private affair of the heart. This deeply individual concern, as Des Pres reads it, is set against Creon's motivations, which are political. Noting that critics do not "ignore its political spirit," Des Pres cites

twentieth century retellings of *Antigone* by Jean Anouilh, Bertolt Brecht, and Athol Fugard as works that focus on this issue.

Yet reading the conflict as individual vs. the state has caused confusion over a key passage just before Antigone is led away to be buried alive. In this scene she makes a statement which many critics have felt is a contradiction to her character (if it is to be perceived as Des Pres describes it). It makes her appear less noble than she is in the opening scene and raises questions about her motives for burying her brother. In this difficult passage, Antigone claims that she would not make the same sacrifice for a husband or children that she is making for her brother and her father. "Never," she cries, "had I been a mother of children or if a husband had been moldering in death, would I have taken this task upon me in the city's despite." This passage has bothered readers since the seventeenth century, causing many to speculate that Antigone's motives are greater than mere familial loyalty. It has been considered a late addition to the play, though Aris-

A scene from an updated interpretation of Antigone, *produced in London*

totle, a contemporary of Sophocles's, attests to its genuineness.

In contrast to the view of the conflict as individual vs. the state, Robin Fox presented an argument which would appear to resolve the contradiction raised by Antigone's statement above. Fox wrote in *Anthropology and Literature,* that the conflict in *Antigone* is one in which Antigone's duties are not to individuality, selfhood, or to private affairs of the heart, but to her father's family, and to kinship rites of burial. It is this duty which is in conflict with the state edict. It is her duty to her father's family to which she is appealing in the questionable statement above, a blood tie which would be more important to her than her ties to a husband. In this persuasive argument, Fox accounts for an issue deeply important to citizens of ancient Athens, one in which the demands of kinship conflict with democratic rule of the city-state in the fifth century B.C.

Similar arguments about kinship and blood ties have been made to account for Antigone's statement by Sheila Murnaghan (in the *American Journal of Philology*) and Charles Segal. Segal noted in *Greek Tragedy* that the conflict in this play is between "fundamentally different concepts of life," between "Antigone's fierce personal loyalties"

and Creon's "politicization of burial." He writes that it is "through blood alone [that] Antigone makes the basis of her . . . loyalty," or "friendship." In contrast, the basis for Creon's friendships is found through obedience to the state (as he stated to the elders in Scene II, no foe of Thebes is a friend of his). Like Fox, Segal argued that Antigone's real concern with burying her brother demonstrates a valuing of kinship and blood ties, not individuality.

These ancient values of kinship and state would have been captured for Sophocles's first audiences in the Greek words *oikos,* meaning house, and *polis,* a word for city. The concept indicated in *oikos* concerns everyone related by blood and servanthood to a father's house. Connected to this is the issue that one must care for one's own blood ties, and an important part of that duty, especially for women, includes burial rites. At the same time that these allegiances to family are important and can be seen in the play, so is Creon's appeal to the welfare of the city-state. After all, the city itself has just come through a war in which one of its own—Antigone's brother Polyneices—has led the enemy. The need for obedience to a ruler's edict, to restore order and right governing, is understandable. These oppositions of these two powerful duties are the engine for the play's compelling and complex dramatic conflict.

The central opposition in the play between Antigone and Creon, and, respectively, between a duty to one's house and a duty to the city-state, is directly echoed in many images in the play. Examples include the image Creon uses of a ship to represent the state, which he believes must sail well for citizens to find the value of friendships. ''If any makes a friend of more account than his fatherland, that man has no place in my regard . . . nor would I ever deem the country's foe a friend to myself . . . our country is a ship that bears us safe, and that only while she prospers in our voyage can we make true friends.'' Creon is shown here connecting the idea of friendship, of having ''parcel of [another's] thoughts,'' as the chorus puts it, with the good of the state. In a revealing statement when he interrogates Antigone and Ismene, he vows never to allow Antigone, though she is his blood relative, to worship at the shrine of Zeus in his house. This shows him placing loyalty to the state over loyalty to blood members of his house.

That Antigone's concern is with her father's house and not with some individual, private concern is exemplified in her challenge to Ismene to fulfill her duties as a noble daughter of noble lineage. Underscoring her sense of kinship, Antigone refers to Ismene in the first scene as ''dear sister,'' as kin, when she appeals to her for help in burying their brother. After Ismene opposes this decision, Antigone calls her a foe. Similarly, after she has been condemned, Antigone states that she hopes by her actions to be welcomed to a home among the dead members of her family. In addition to these statements, a sympathetic image of the home is made in connection with Antigone by the guard who brings her captive to Creon. The guard claims first to have heard her cry bitterly like a bird, ''as when within the empty nest it sees the bed stripped of its nestlings.'' Interestingly, he also calls her a friend, suggesting that he would, if Creon were not enforcing his will as state, act more sympathetically toward her. Though Antigone is increasingly isolated, she is not asserting individuality but the importance of performing her duties to her father's house.

Many persuasive appeals are made in *Antigone* on the basis of kinship or the state. The deeply dramatic scenes of argument in the play make strong cases for both kinship and to patriotic allegiance. They form the basis on which one will find friends. Ismene's appeal to Creon for mercy to Antigone is made on the grounds of his son's love and betrothal to her. Creon has already rejected her as blood kin, and he also rejects this appeal, saying

> MANY PERSUASIVE APPEALS ARE MADE IN *ANTIGONE* ON THE BASIS OF KINSHIP OR THE STATE"

that he will not have an evil wife for his son. She is evil, at least in Creon's eyes, because she has violated an edict of the state. Haemon, after appealing to his father on the basis of the good of the state to spare Antigone, finally rejects his own father, leaving him to ''such friends as can endure you.''

On the basis of Creon's intractable adherence to his edict, the sisters' relationship is strained, kindred connections between Creon and Antigone and Ismene are rejected, and, finally, Creon's estrangement from his son. Sophocles's position in *Antigone* is complex and situated within these deeply conflicted scenes, which show a group of elders, presented as the chorus of the play, who are unable to act or offer counsel until well after the dramatic action has moved toward tragedy. They are caught in Creon's tyrannical rule, swayed between the opposing arguments of the principle characters in the drama, unable to decide finally how they should act. The dramatic movement toward discord, in which the concept of *oikos* seems rejected in favor of the *polis,* is shown as deeply wrong when Teiresias announces that the city itself has been polluted by Creon's own edict. Finally, this word reveals that both house and state have been ruined by tyranny. The end result is the downfall of Creon's own house.

As Fox suggested, citizens of early democracy in Athens encountered conflict over the issues of kinship and state rule. These issues raised in *Antigone* are issues with which modern audiences may have trouble identifying. We value the rights of the individual far more than the rights of families. Except in certain areas of the Mediterranean, blood ties are often considered weak social bonds. In the late twentieth century, we rarely use the word ''kin,'' unless we are referring to those we consider our ''kindred spirits.''

Yet Antigone's loyalty to her dead brother, her care for him, is inspiring. In Sophocles's play, the functioning of the state oversteps into areas of the demands that kinship makes, and this boundary jumping raises significant questions. How far shall the state go in determining the laws that previously concerned the family? Conversely, how far shall one's family take precedence over the laws of the state and the people? These questions are not easily answered—even in modern society—and demonstrate why Sophocles's play remains topical and important. While not providing a universal outcome of such a situation, *Antigone* offers one possible—and tragic—result of the personal and the political converging and conflicting. In this sense, the play has significant relevance to modern society and offers both an entertaining drama and valuable lesson to the contemporary reader of the play.

Source: Thomas Allbaugh, in an essay for *Drama for Students,* Gale, 1997.

George Eliot

In the following excerpt from an article that originally appeared in The Leader *on March 29, 1856, Eliot interprets* Antigone *as the conflict between "the strength of man's intellect, or moral sense, or affection" and "the rules which society has sanctioned."*

Eliot was an English novelist, essayist, poet, editor, short story writer, and translator. She is regarded as one of the greatest English novelists of the nineteenth century, and is best known for her novels The Mill on the Floss *(1860) and* Middlemarch: A Study of Provincial Life *(1871–72).*

The *Antigone* has every quality of a fine tragedy, and fine tragedies can never become mere mummies for [critics] to dispute about: they must appeal to perennial human nature, and even the ingenious dulness of translators cannot exhaust them of their passion and their poetry.

E'en in their ashes live their wonted fires.

[Matthew Arnold] said that the dramatic motive of the *Antigone* was foreign to modern sympathies, but it is only superficially so. It is true we no longer believe that a brother, if left unburied, is condemned to wander a hundred years without repose on the banks of the Styx; we no longer believe that to neglect funeral rites is to violate the claims of the infernal deities. But these beliefs are the accidents and not the substance of the poet's conception. The turning point of the tragedy is not, as it is stated to be in the argument prefixed to [an 1855 school] edition, "reverence for the dead and the importance of the sacred rites of burial," but the *conflict* between these and obedience to the State. Here lies the dramatic collision: the impulse of

sisterly piety which allies itself with reverence for the Gods, clashes with the duties of citizenship; two principles, both having their validity, are at war with each. (pp. 262–63)

It is a very superficial criticism which interprets the character of Creon as that of a hypocritical tyrant, and regards Antigone as a blameless victim. Coarse contrasts like this are not the materials handled by great dramatists. The exquisite art of Sophocles is shown in the touches by which he makes us feel that Creon, as well as Antigone, is contending for what he believes to be the right, while both are also conscious that, in following out one principle, they are laying themselves open to just blame for transgressing another; and it is this consciousness which secretly heightens the exasperation of Creon and the defiant hardness of Antigone. The best critics have agreed. . .in recognising this balance of principles, this antagonism between valid claims; they generally regard it, however, as dependent entirely on the Greek point of view, as springing simply from the polytheistic conception according to which the requirements of the Gods often clashed with the duties of man to man.

But, is it the fact that this antagonism of valid principles is peculiar to polytheism? Is it not rather that the struggle between Antigone and Creon represents that struggle between elemental tendencies and established laws by which the outer life of man is gradually and painfully being brought into harmony with his inward needs? Until this harmony is perfected, we shall never be able to attain a great right without also doing a wrong. Reformers, Martyrs, revolutionists, are never fighting against evil only; they are also placing themselves in opposition to a good—to a valid principle which cannot be infringed without harm. Resist the payment of ship-money; you bring on civil war; preach against false doctrines, you disturb feeble minds and send them adrift on a sea of doubt; make a new road, and you annihilate vested interests; cultivate a new region of the earth, and you exterminate a race of men. Wherever the strength of a man's intellect, or moral sense, or affection brings him into opposition with the rules which society has sanctioned, *there* is renewed the conflict between Antigone and Creon; such a man must not only dare to be right, he must also dare to be wrong—to shake faith, to wound friendship, perhaps, to hem in his own powers. Like Antigone, he may fall a victim to the struggle, and yet he can never earn the name of a blameless martyr any more than the society—the Creon he has defied, can be branded as a hypocritical tyrant.

Perhaps the best moral we can draw is that to which the Chorus points—that our protest for the right should be seasoned with moderation and reverence, and that lofty words. . .are not becoming to mortals. (pp. 264–65)

Source: George Eliot, ''The *Antigone* and Its Moral'' (1856), in her *Essays of George Eliot,* edited by Thomas Pinney, Routledge and Kegan Paul, 1963, pp. 261–65.

Walter H. Johns

In the following excerpt, Johns outlines Sophocles's distinctive use of violence and strong emotion in Antigone.

The stern violence of the actors in the drama is to be seen throughout: Antigone knows that if she gives Polyneices burial, she will be stoned to death. When Creon warns the members of the Chorus not to aid those who disobey his commands, the leader intimates that death would be the punishment and Creon agrees. When Antigone is revealed as the culprit, Creon regards her action as direct defiance of his commands . . . charges her with that tragic fault. . . .

When Haemon comes to plead with his father, the Chorus announce his approach with a comment on his mood of bitterness and grief. Their final word contains a foreboding note on the tragic excess of this grief. In the scene which follows, Sophocles gives one of many striking examples of his irony in the speech in which Creon bids his son reject Antigone and send her off ''to find a marriage in Hades.'' This foreshadows Haemon's own doom, later described by the messenger, in which he is said to have ''found his marriage in the halls of Hades,'' i.e. with the dead Antigone. The dramatist, as usual, draws a moral from his doom—that the greatest evil which can befall mankind is . . . (want of judgment) —a Delphic utterance which as so often in Sophocles, can be applied in two ways, to Creon as well as to Haemon.

In the long dialogue with his father, Haemon gives a veiled warning that Antigone's death may involve someone else. But Creon's [want of judgement], another tragic flaw in his nature, makes him miss the hint. The most specific threat of all, however, is found in Haemon's parting words—the last line he speaks in the whole play:

> IT IS A VERY SUPERFICIAL CRITICISM WHICH INTERPRETS THE CHARACTER OF CREON AS THAT OF A HYPOCRITICAL TYRANT, AND REGARDS ANTIGONE AS A BLAMELESS VICTIM"

. . . thou shalt in no wise gaze upon this face of mine again, *seeing it in thine eyes.*

As he departs the Chorus say:

My lord, the young man has gone, swift in his wrath: the spirit of one so young, when it is pained, is fierce. . . .

As the drama moves on to its conclusion the promises and reports of violence continue. Teiresias foretells the death of Creon's son. The messenger reports the death of Haemon by his own hand and once more brings in a reference to Haemon's *wrath* at his father for the death of his beloved Antigone.

We now come to the passage containing the disputed phrase. The messenger describes the scene in vivid detail. Creon had sent his followers to explore the cell and they had found Antigone hanging by the neck and Haemon embracing her dead body ''bewailing the loss of his bride who is with the dead, and his father's deeds and his own ill-fated love.'' Then Haemon hears his father's voice and realizes that the cause of all his grief is close at hand. The effect on the young man is described by Sophocles in brief and vivid phrases. He is mad with rage; in fact his eyes are described as those of a wild beast. In a fit of blazing anger he momentarily blinds his father by spitting in his face, then tries to kill him. But his own furious anger and his father's hurried flight foil his attempt and, instead of pursuing his father, he carries out his prime intention of suicide, turning his sword against himself and dying with his arms about the body of Antigone. Thus Sophocles has Haemon fulfil the vow he had made that his father's eyes should never gaze on him again alive, and at the same time express his supreme contempt and hatred for his sire in a manner more familiar among Mediterranean races than among those of north-western Europe. The poet's

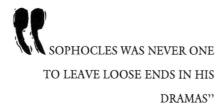

SOPHOCLES WAS NEVER ONE TO LEAVE LOOSE ENDS IN HIS DRAMAS"

phrase expressing his utter silence here strengthens the action instead of, as Bayfield suggests, serving as an anticlimax. And so to Haemon we must ascribe an act of fury and scorn, to Sophocles a carefully chosen expression which links two crucial episodes in the play: Haemon's last words as he leaves his father (and the stage) and his last acts before his own suicide.

To many this explanation may seem fanciful in the extreme if not wholly offensive, but two major points must be borne in mind. The first is that Sophocles was the most careful of the ancient dramatists to knit his plots into a close fabric of lines in which tragic irony occurs again and again, and lines spoken early in a play are recalled in later scenes to form the climax of the drama. The significant lines are seldom idly spoken. So it is here. Haemon's parting vow to his father prompts his own vicious action in the last moment of his life. Sophocles was never one to leave loose ends in his dramas.

The other point to be borne in mind is one which seems to have escaped Professor Johnson's notice. He says: "For him to spit in his father's face would . . . simply arouse disgust in the spectators." [*The Classical Journal* 41 (1945–46) 371–374]. But it must not be overlooked that this did not take place on the stage; it was simply reported by the messenger. It was placed in its context to add to the pity and horror of the final meeting between father and son just before the latter's death. It is an act of violence like the attempt of Haemon on his father's life and his own suicide or the subsequent suicide of Eurydice. Such things Sophocles carefully bars from his stage.

Again Johnson speaks of Sophocles as "an artist and as a dramatist whose effects are regularly brought about by subtle and delicate touches." But he did not hesitate to show on the stage the dead bodies of Haemon and Eurydice in the *Antigone,* the

slaughtered animals in the *Ajax,* the dead body of Clytemnestra in the *Electra,* and Oedipus with blood dripping from his ravished eyes in the *Oedipus Tyrannus.* Surely these are no subtle and delicate touches. The violence which he presents off stage and depicts only in the description of a messenger is too familiar to demand recounting here. Haemon's action is in perfect harmony with many similar instances elsewhere. . . .

Source: Walter H. Johns, "Dramatic Effect in Sophocles' *Antigone,*" *The Classical Journal,* Vol. 43, No. 2, November, 1947, pp. 99–100.

FURTHER READING

Des Pres, Terence. "Creon's Decree" in *Praises and Dispraises,* Viking (New York), 1988, pp. 3-16.
   Des Pres discusses Antigone's isolation in the play in terms that are political. He alludes to recent retellings of the story by Jean Anouilh and Bertolt Brecht.

Fox, Robin. "The Virgin and the Godfather: Kinship versus the State in Greek Tragedy and After" in *Anthropology and Literature,* edited by Paul Benson, University of Illinois Press (Urbana, IL), 1993, pp. 107-50.
   Fox presents an argument based on anthropology that Antigone's conflict has to do with kinship ties, not with contemporary notions of individuality.

Grey, Wallace. "Antigone" in *Homer to Joyce,* Macmillan (New York), 1985, pp. 59-67.
   In this short article, Grey challenges traditional readings of *Antigone,* in particular those which stress the conflicts of individual vs. the state, religion vs. the state, natural law vs. the state, and man vs. woman.

Murnaghan, Sheila. "Sophocles, *Antigone* 904-920 and the Institution of Marriage" in *American Journal of Philology,* Vol. 107, no. 2, pp. 192-207.
   Murnaghan discusses the controversial passage in which Antigone claims that what she does for her father's house she would not do for a husband's. Murnaghan suggests that Antigone's claim has to do with her blood ties to her father's house rather than exemplifying an act of self.

Segal, Charles. "*Antigone:* Death and Love, Hades and Dionysus" in *Greek Tragedy,* edited by Erich Segal, Harper & Row, 1983, pp.167-76.
   Segal provides a reading of the mythic allusions to Persephone which the chorus uses in reference to Antigone's death at a young age. The critic also

presents a reading of the play which shows the heroine confronting a politicization of burial.

SOURCES

Beacham, Richard C. "*Antigone* by Sophocles," in *The International Dictionary of Theatre, Vol. 1: Plays,* edited by Mark Hawkins-Dady, St. James Press, 1992, pp. 21-3.

Braun, Richard Emil, translator. Introduction to *Antigone,* by Sophocles, Oxford University Press, 1973, pp. 5, 12.

de Romilly, Jacqueline. "Drama in the Second Half of the Fifth Century: Sophocles, Euripides, and Aristophanes," in her *A Short History of Greek Literature,* translated by Lillian Doherty, University of Chicago Press, 1985, pp. 66-89.

Radford, Colin. "*Antigone* by Jean Anouilh," in *The International Dictionary of Theatre, Vol. 1: Plays,* edited by Mark Hawkins-Dady, St. James Press, 1992, pp. 23-4.

Saxonhouse, Arlene W. *Fear of Diversity: The Birth of Political Science in Ancient Greek Thought,* University of Chicago Press, 1992.

Steiner, George. *Antigones,* Oxford University Press, 1984.

The Cherry Orchard

ANTON CHEKHOV

1904

Anton Chekhov wrote *The Cherry Orchard* during the last year of his life. Though Chekhov intended the play to be a comedy, when it was first produced by the Moscow Art Theater on January 17, 1904, producer Konstantin Stanislavsky insisted it should be played as a tragedy. Chekhov fought against this portrayal, but to this day, most productions emphasize the tragic elements of the piece.

The Cherry Orchard is a play about the passing of an era. Some critics have said that it is a play about nothing more than a wealthy family that loses its beloved cherry orchard and estate to a man of the rising middle class. The action is quiet in this tragicomedy. Chekhov's family had lost its home to repossession in 1876, and this may have been an inspiration for the story. He also had inspiration for some of the characters while staying at the estate owned by Stanislavsky's mother in 1902.

The Cherry Orchard portrays the social climate of Russia at the beginning of the 20th century, when the aristocrats and land-owning gentry were losing their wealth and revealed themselves to be incapable of coping with their change in status. Many Socialist Soviet critics in Russia after the Revolution of 1917 tried to interpret this as an indictment of Russian society at the turn of the century; however, it is unlikely that Chekhov meant this play as an attack on the society of which he was so much a part. Though intended as a comedy, the tragedy of the situation in which Mrs. Ranevsky and her family

find themselves is derived primarily from their inability to adapt to their new social and personal responsibilities. No longer able to live on the labor provided by the serfs (slaves) who worked the land, many wealthy landowners, like Mrs. Ranevsky in *The Cherry Orchard,* lost their fortunes and their estates.

AUTHOR BIOGRAPHY

Anton Chekhov was born in Taganrog, Russia, on January 16, 1860. His grandfather had been a serf who had been able to earn enough to buy his freedom and purchase a small home. In 1876, however, Chekhov's father, a grocer, was forced to move the family to Moscow because of their many debts and the repossession of their home. Chekhov remained behind to finish his studies. His years in school at Taganrog were plagued by poverty, and he often agreed to complete other students' school work for payment in order to support himself.

In 1880 Chekhov moved to Moscow and entered medical school at the University of Moscow. He graduated with an M.D. in 1884. Chekhov had written hundreds of short stories by the time of his graduation, but he did not consider writing as a career until he moved to St. Petersburg in 1885 and became friends with A. S. Suvorin, editor of the journal *Novoe Vremja.* By 1888 Chekhov was practicing medicine only during epidemics, focusing instead on his writing.

Though his one-act plays *The Boor* and *The Marriage Proposal* were successful, his first full-length plays *Ivanov* and *The Wood Demon* were great disappointments. He did not write another full-length play until *The Seagull* in 1896. Though *The Seagull* failed in its first production due to its intense psychological realism (very unlike the fashion of the time), the Moscow Art Theater's production in 1898, which was staged under the supervision of noted producer and actor Konstantin Stanislavsky, was a great success.

This success was followed by *Uncle Vanya* in 1899, *The Three Sisters* in 1901, and ultimately *The Cherry Orchard* in 1904. Chekhov and Stanislavsky argued whether *The Cherry Orchard* was a comedy, as Chekhov maintained, or a tragedy, as Stanislavsky claimed. The play was finally produced as interpreted by Stanislavsky, and Chekhov was at first absent from the premiere on January 17, 1904, even

Anton Chekhov

though his wife Olga Knipper (whom he married in 1901) was an actress in the Moscow Art Theater and a part of the production. He was finally persuaded to attend the premiere just after the second act.

Suffering from tuberculosis during the last years of his life, Chekhov spent much time abroad in European health resorts and was often separated from his wife and family. A few months after attending the premiere of his final play, he died in a Black Forest spa in July, 1904.

PLOT SUMMARY

Act One

The Cherry Orchard opens in the nursery of Lyuba Andreyevna Ranevsky's estate. Although it is only about 2:00 A.M., it is close to daybreak, for it is May, when northern Russian days are long and the sun rises very early. Lopakhin, a businessman, and Dunyasha, a maid, anticipate the arrival of Mrs. Ranevsky, who is returning home from a self-imposed, five-year exile with her daughter, Anya, and her governess, Charlotte Ivanovna. Lopakhin speaks of his peasant background and his admiration for Mrs. Ranevsky; then the pair are briefly joined by the bumbling clerk, Yepikhodov, nick-named ''Twenty-two Calamities.''

After arriving, the travelers enter, preceded by Firs, a manservant. They are soon joined by Varya, Lyuba's adopted daughter, Leonid Gayev, Lyuba's brother, Simeonov-Pishchik, a neighboring land-owner, and Lopakhin and Dunyasha.

The reunion is very tearful. Mrs. Ranevsky sweeps about the room, overcome with joy. The family members all display great emotion, weeping uncontrollably, not just over each other, but over the cherry orchard and house, even the nursery and its furniture.

Lyuba is a generous but impractical sentimen-talist. She tears up two telegrams from France without reading them, because, as she says, ''I've finished with Paris.'' Yet she daydreams of her happy youth, and imagines, at one point, that she sees her mother wandering through the cherry or-chard. Gayev, as sentimental as his sister, has a screw or two loose; he carries on a perpetual game of mental billiards and weeps fondly over the nurs-ery's bookcase. Pishchik, also eccentric, seems less senile than mad. When Mrs. Ranevsky starts to take some medicine, he grabs her pills and swallows the lot on impulse. Firs, the old family retainer, is simply feeble. He constantly trails off his mental path into inarticulate muttering.

As the dialogue's comic shuffle continues, un-pleasant truths intrude. Mrs. Ranevsky is broke, and in her absence, Varya has not made interest pay-ments on the mortgage. The estate is to go on the auction block in August. Lopakhin proposes a prac-tical solution. He advises Lyuba to divide the estate into lots and lease them out for vacation cottages, even though that will mean sacrificing the house and orchard. Gayev, who considers Lopakhin an upstart peasant, is incensed and dismissive, calling the businessman's proposal ''utter nonsense.'' He, Lyuba, and Firs simply extol the virtues of the orchard, as impractical as it has become.

Pishchik, too, is facing the loss of his estate through his failure to pay mortgage interest. He tries to get a loan from Mrs. Ranevsky. Rebuffed, he consoles himself with the idea that ''something's bound to turn up.'' The arrival of the ''eternal student'' Peter Trofimov, who has been expelled from a university for his radical politics, prompts a new round of weeping. The forgetful Pishchik re-peats his request. Mrs. Ranevsky tells Gayev to lend him the money, but Gayev refuses.

After Mrs. Ranevsky goes off, Gayev, Varya, and Anya discuss possible solutions to her financial woes. Gayev doubts that their great-aunt, the Count-ess, will help because Lyuba had offended her relative by marrying beneath herself, but he buoys his nieces' hopes by promising to borrow money on his own while encouraging Lyuba to ask Lopakhin for help. Then, completely exhausted, all the char-acters save Peter Trofimov leave the room and go to bed.

Act Two

The scene shifts to outside a chapel near the orchard. Sunset approaches. Charlotte, Yasha (who is Firs's ambitious grandson), and Dunyasha sit on a bench. Nearby, Yepikhodov plays a guitar. After Charlotte ponders her heritage, Yepikhodov stops playing to remark on fate and his uncertainty about shooting himself. When Charlotte and the clerk leave, Dunyasha confesses her love for Yasha, but she is overcome by the smoke of his cigar and also leaves the scene.

Mrs. Ranevsky, Gayev, and Lopakhin enter. Lyuba, distraught by her admitted extravagant life-style, drops her purse, scattering gold coins on the ground. Yasha picks them up while she voices regrets about wasting money on lunch. Lopakhin again presses her to agree to his plan, but she finds his proposal ''vulgar,'' making him momentarily furious. She speaks of the death of her son and her affair with the scoundrel who left her destitute, then tries to convince Lopakhin to marry Varya.

Firs enters with Gayev's overcoat. He is fol-lowed by Trofimov, Anya, and Varya. Talking with Lopakhin, Peter voices his disgust for the Russian intelligentsia, while Lopakhin, the selfmade man, speaks of his great success at making money.

As the sun sets and the air grows still, they hear the melancholic sound of a breaking string. For a moment, they try to identify its source, but they are interrupted by a drifter asking for a handout. Lyuba, foolishly generous, gives him one of her gold coins.

After the rest leave for dinner, Anya and Peter talk. He identifies the orchard with the old, decadent Russia, and tells Anya that she must abandon it to find true happiness. Then, as they are called by Varya, the pair exit towards the river to be alone.

Act Three

It is night, the day of the auction, during a party at Mrs. Ranevsky's estate. Couples enter the drawing room from the ballroom, where a band plays and guests dance. They await the return of Gayev, who, with money borrowed from the Countess, had gone to town to try to save the estate.

A forced gaiety keeps the mood superficially buoyant. Pishchik's complaints about his debts are blunted by Charlotte's clever ventriloquism and magic tricks, but Mrs. Ranevsky's apprehension surfaces in her confession that she intends to return to the wretch of a man who had fleeced and deserted her. Later, Mrs. Ranevsky and Peter get into an argument over the heart versus the head. Trofimov claims that he is beyond love for Anya. Lyuba ridicules him for being a pseudo-intellectual. Angry, Peter storms from the room, promptly falling down a flight of stairs.

A spreading rumor of the estate's sale momentarily upsets Mrs. Ranevsky, but she is soon dancing with Pishchik, who once more presses her for a loan. Thereafter, Yepikhodov, scorned by Dunyasha, gets into an argument with Varya, who attempts to beat him with a billiard cue but accidentally hits the arriving Lopakhin instead. However, the blow does nothing to dampen his spirits, for it is he who has bought the estate. Lopakhin gives a long, self-congratulatory and triumphant speech, leaving Mrs. Ranevsky in tears with only Anya to console her.

Act Four

It is now October, and the setting is again the nursery. The room is bare except for some odd furniture. In the distance, an axe is heard; a woodsman has begun felling the cherry trees in the orchard.

The family members, getting ready to depart, have deposited their luggage near the front door. Lopakhin encourages everybody to share some champagne, but his enthusiasm only earns him bitter remarks from Trofimov. Anya enters, questioning whether the ailing Firs has been taken to the hospital. No one seems quite sure. Dunyasha then professes her love for the disdainful Yasha, who plans to return to Paris with Mrs. Ranevsky. Dunyasha will ultimately marry Yepikhodov instead.

Mrs. Ranevsky enters with Gayev, Anya, and Charlotte. She gives a tearful goodbye to the house, sadly reconciled to her fate. Gayev is more optimistic. He has secured a job in a bank. Pishchik, too, has had some luck; he has managed to escape ruin through leasing some clay-rich property. Concerned about Varya, Mrs. Ranevsky pushes Lopakhin to propose to her step-daughter. The businessman seems willing enough, but when left alone with Varya, neither is able to broach the subject.

Near the end, after the others depart for the train station, Lyuba and Gayev embrace in a tearful farewell. They, too, leave, and for a moment the stage is bare; then Firs enters, forgotten and left behind. Dejected over his fate, he plops down on a sofa and lies motionless. The doleful sound of the breaking string is heard again, then, at the final curtain, only silence save the echoing axe.

CHARACTERS

Anya
See Anya Ranevsky

Charlotte
See Charlotte Ivanovna

Dunyasha (doon-YA-sha)
Dunyasha is the maid in the Ranevsky household who dreams of being an aristocratic lady. She parodies the ladies of the household, and compares herself to them. She must give up her dreams of marrying Yasha (Mrs. Ranevsky's manservant) when he returns to Paris with Mrs. Ranevsky. She agrees to marry Yepikhodov instead.

Firs (feers)
Firs is the Ranevsky family's faithful servant who, because of his loyalty to the family, chose to stay after the serfs were freed. Sickly and somewhat senile, he marks the play's most poignant moment when he is locked inside the estate and forgotten. He laments: "Life has slipped away as if I haven't lived."

Gayev
See Leonid (lay-oh-NEED) Gayev

MEDIA
ADAPTATIONS

- *The Cherry Orchard, Part I: Chekhov, Innovator of Modern Drama,* an educational film includes select scenes and a discussion by Norris Houghton, 1968; available from Britannica Films.

- *The Cherry Orchard, Part II: Comedy or Tragedy?* from the same series as the above; scenes with discussion by Houghton; focus on technique of dramatizing interior action and concept of subtext, 1967; available from Britannica Films.

- *Chekhov and the Moscow Art Theatre,* using the Stanislavsky method, director Yuri Zavadsky stages select scenes from *The Cherry Orchard;* available from IASTA.

- *The Cherry Orchard,* on three audio cassettes, translated by Leonid Kipnis, actors include Jessica Tandy and Hume Cronyn; Caedmon/Harper Audio.

- *Anton Chekhov: A Writer's Life,* a brief biographical study of the dramatist, 1974; available from Films for the Humanities and Sciences.

- *Chekhov,* Henry Troyat's biography of Chekhov on twelve audio cassettes, read by Wolfram Kandinsky, 1989; available from Books on Tape.

- *Chekhov: Humanity's Advocate,* an audio cassette in the Classics of Russian Literature Series; Ernest Simmons discusses Chekhov's work and artistic principles, 1968; available from Audio-Forum.

- *The Seagull,* another Chekhov classic adapted to film by Sidney Lumet, starring James Mason, Vanessa Redgrave, Simone Signoret, David Warner, Harry Andrews, Eileen Herlie, Denholm Elliot, 1968; available on video from Warner Brothers.

- *The Seagull,* Russian film version with English subtitles, directed by Yuri Karasik, 1971; available from Facets Multimedia, Inc.

- *Three Sisters,* yet another Chekhov classic adapted for film by Laurence Olivier and John Sichel, starring Olivier, Joan Plowright, Alan Bates, Jeanne Watts, Louise Purnell, Derek Jacobi, 1970; available from American Film Theater.

- *Three Sisters,* video taped version of the Actors Studio production of the play, directed by Paul Bogart, starring Kim Stanley, Geraldine Page, Shelly Winters, Kevin McCarthy, and Sandy Dennis, 1966.

- *Vanya on 42nd Street,* imaginative filming of a rehearsal of David Mamet's stage adaptation of Chekhov's *Uncle Vanya,* directed by Louis Malle, with Andre Gregory as the director of the play in rehearsal and Wallace Shawn as Uncle Vanya, 1994; available from Columbia Tristar Home Video.

Leonid (lay-oh-NEED) Gayev (GUY-ev)

Gayev is Mrs. Ranevsky's brother. He is an irresponsible, unkempt man who prefers to play or pretend to play billiards than to find a solution to his family's problems. He is addicted to fruit candies, and talks a great deal—faults pointed out by his family several times in the play. Dreaming up several schemes to save the orchard, Guyev acts on none of them; instead he calls out billiard shots and

believes someone will come forward to rescue the family. Like his sister, he imagines the cherry orchard as it was in his childhood, unable to accept that it will soon be sold.

Hiker

The Hiker is a sickly homeless man who begs Mrs. Ranevsky for money. That she is in financial ruin herself and gives the hiker a gold piece emphasizes Mrs. Ranevsky's generosity and her disregard for her own predicament.

Charlotte Ivanovna (ee-VAN-ov-na)

The governess to both Anya and Varya, Charlotte is a very thin woman whose magic tricks and uncertain parentage add comic elements to the play.

little cucumber

See Dunyasha

Lopakhin

See Yermolay (yer-mo-LYE) Lopakhin

Peter Trofimov (trow-FEE-mov)

Trofimov is a shabbily dressed "eternal student." He was a tutor for Mrs. Ranevsky's son, and the sight of him when she first returns to the cherry orchard brings back terrible memories of her son's death. She remarks that Trofimov has aged badly, which is a veiled reference to his time spent as an inmate in a labor camp for those found guilty of participating in subversive political activities. Trofimov's actions sometimes do not match his words. Remarking that he and Anya are "above love," he is criticized by Mrs. Ranevsky for his outspoken behavior. She ridicules his declaration, and as he storms out he falls down a flight of stairs. Chekhov tries to keep Trofimov from being too serious by injecting humor into both the dialogue and his actions. Though he can be outspoken and critical, he is tender and supportive of Anya. He is constantly emphasizing the value of work as the salvation of Russia, and convinces Anya that the whole of Russia is her orchard. Soviet critics after the Russian Revolution of 1917 latched onto the character of Trofimov as a literary hero who exemplifies the ideals of Socialism, often citing his speech describing the trees in the orchard as souls.

Pishchik

See Boris Simeonov-Pishchik

Post Office Clerk

The post office clerk appears as a guest at the ball.

Anya Ranevsky

Mrs. Ranevsky's daughter, Anya, dresses all in white to signify her purity and innocence. Although she loves her home and the orchard that surrounds it, she realizes that all of Russia is her orchard. She looks to the future as an adventure. At seventeen, she is eager to go on with her life and to share it with Peter Trofimov, the eternal student. Anya is the opposite of her sister Varya, and is a youthful, sweet, energetic, young woman looking forward to the future. She attempts to get her aunt, the Countess, to help her family pay off the debt on the orchard, but is ready to face the future without wealth.

Lyuba Andreyevna Ranevsky

See Mrs. Ranevsky

Mrs. Ranevsky (ra-NEV-sky)

Mrs. Ranevsky is an aristocratic woman incapable of adapting to the changing social climate in Russia. When faced with the loss of her beloved orchard and estate, she is incapable of acting to save it. She is a kind and generous woman who is irresponsible when it comes to money and adult life. Though she knows that the orchard is up for auction in August, she continues to go out to lunch, throws a lavish party, and gives a gold piece to a homeless man. Her neighbor, Boris Simeonov-Pishchik, continues to borrow money from her, despite her desperate financial situation.

Having fled to Paris from Russia five years before to try to forget the deaths of her little boy and her husband, Mrs. Ranevsky has only succeeded in trading her problems at home for a new set of difficulties. She takes a villain for her lover, and is swindled out of most of her money and then is left by him for another woman. Once back in Russia, she receives telegrams from him begging her to return because he is ill. When the orchard and estate are lost to Lopakhin, she returns to her lover in Paris because she feels the need to take care of him.

Rather than living in the present, Mrs. Ranevsky pictures the orchard as it was in her childhood, with her mother walking through its aisles. She is crushed by the sale, but then freed from the worries associated with running such a large estate. Mrs. Ranevsky puts a face on the many wealthy landowners who lost their wealth and power in turn of the century Russia.

Varya Ranevsky

Varya Ranevsky is the adopted daughter of Mrs. Ranevsky. At twenty-four years of age, this daughter of a serf is allied with neither the aristocracy or the servants, but is in a world somewhere in between the two. She wears only black and is very dedicated to her work and to religion. She runs the cherry orchard to the best of her ability while her mother is gone, but is seen as a miser by the servants.

Varya is in love with Yermolay Lopakhin, a wealthy merchant who is more concerned with business than with her. She is heartbroken by his passivity, and by her family's inability to save their home. She openly criticizes her mother's generosity and irresponsibility when it comes to money, yet she has no solution to the problem.

Dreaming of entering a convent, by the end of the play Varya has taken a job as a housekeeper at a nearby estate. She is a severe woman who feels ill-at-ease without a task to attend to. She is unable to fight for what she wants—Lopakhin—and instead passively accepts her fate.

Boris Simeonov-Pishchik (seem-YOH-nov-PEE-shik)

Simeonov-Pishchik is a landowner who is constantly in debt and asking to borrow money. He expects fate to solve his financial problems, and eventually allows the English to mine his estate in order to pay off his debts. Though he pays Mrs. Ranevsky the money he owes her in the end, it is too late to save the orchard. He does not consider her financial situation when he borrows the money from her, and she is too generous to deny his request.

Stationmaster

The Stationmaster is a fun-loving guest at the ball who dances with the ladies.

Trofimov

See Peter Trofimov

Twenty-two Calamities

See Simon Yepikhodov

Varya

See Varya Ranevsky

Yasha

Yasha is Firs's grandson, but is eager to become more than a manservant. Referred to as a scoundrel by Varya, he plays with Dunyasha's emotions, and schemes to go back to Paris with Mrs. Ranevsky. He also ignores his mother every time she comes to see him, and leaves her waiting outside. He is a self-centered man who cares nothing for anyone but himself.

Yepikhodov

See Simon Yepikhodov

Simon Yepikhodov (yep-i-KHO-dov)

Yepikhodov is a financial clerk whose ineffectual management leads to the auction of the estate. Nicknamed Twenty-two Calamities, he is constantly plagued by problems (including squeaking boots) and crises. He is in love with the maid Dunyasha, who is in love with Mrs. Ranevsky's manservant Yasha. This love triangle provides some of the comic moments in *The Cherry Orchard*.

Yermolay (yer-mo-LYE) Lopakhin (lo-PA-chin)

Lopakhin is a wealthy businessman whose grandfather was once a serf on the Ranevsky estate. Though sometimes seen as a calculating opportunist, he loves the Ranevsky family and tries to persuade Mrs. Ranevsky (who helped him as a child) to cut down the orchard to clear land for building country vacation cottages for the rising middle class. He grows increasingly impatient with her as she refuses to see the solution he suggests and does nothing to save the estate. Lopakhin eventually buys the estate at the auction, and in a vulgar display during the ball, he rejoices in owning the estate his family was once forced to serve. Much is made of the fact that Varya loves Lopakhin and that the two should marry, but he is too consumed with making money to propose to her. Lopakhin represents the triumph of vulgarity and ignorance of the middle class over the traditions of nobility and elegance of Czarist Russia.

THEMES

The Cherry Orchard is about an aristocratic family that is unable to prevent its beloved estate from being auctioned off. More symbolically, it is about the growth of the middle class in Russia and the fall of the aristocracy. The once-wealthy family's estate and beloved orchard is purchased by a man who once served as a serf on the estate. Though Chekhov

TOPICS FOR FURTHER STUDY

- Investigate the Russian class structure that evolved after the emancipation of the serfs in 1861, during the reign of Tsar Alexander II, relating it to the gallery of characters in *The Cherry Orchard*.

- Research the rise of the Moscow Art Theatre, its relationship to Anton Chekhov, and the influence of its great co-director, Konstantin Stanislavsky, on the "method" school of acting that was taught by Sanford Meisner and Lee Strasberg in America and popularized by such actors as Robert De Niro, Jane Fonda, and Dennis Hopper.

- Investigate the treatment of tuberculosis in Russia and Europe at the turn of the nineteenth century and relate your findings to Chekhov's life and role as physician.

- Investigate the influence of Chekhov on modern American drama and such specific playwrights as David Mamet, Maria Irene Fornes, Spalding Gray, John Guare, Wendy Wasserstein, Neil Simon, and Lillian Hellman.

- Research daily life on the provincial estate of late nineteenth-century Russia and relate your findings to *The Cherry Orchard* and other works by Chekhov.

- Research penal conditions in Chekhov's Russia and the playwright's efforts to encourage reform in his nonfiction expose, *Sakhalin Island* (1893-94).

---

intended the play as a comedy, most productions emphasize the tragedy of the events. Mrs. Ranevsky and her family are unable to find a way to succeed within the new social order of Russia, while Lopakhin profits from the business opportunity and gains personal satisfaction in displacing those who once ruled over him.

Apathy and Passivity

For Mrs. Ranevsky, her daughters, and her brother Leonid Gayev, apathy and passivity have become a way of life, as Mrs. Ranevsky's line "if only this heavy load could be lifted from my heart; if only I could forget my past!" reveals. Mrs. Ranevsky has given up trying to change her circumstances and is resigned to taking her life as it comes. She goes out to expensive lunches, buys a gift for Anya, lends her neighbor Pishchik money, and gives a gold piece to the homeless hiker in Act Two. Mrs. Ranevsky refuses to accept that she can change her circumstances by changing her behavior. She becomes passive and allows the auction to take place. Gayev, Anya, and Varya also become passive in the situation, and continue to believe that everything

will work out. This apathy–combined with a fear of living below the standards to which they've become accustomed—is what keeps the family from saving its orchard.

The family ignores Lopakhin's suggestion of breaking up the orchard into smaller plots for country cottages. Mrs. Ranevsky considers the suggestion vulgar, declaring that the orchard is famous for being the largest and most beautiful in Russia. She and her brother do almost nothing to avert the auction and remaining passive and hoping for a solution or a savior, such as their relative the Countess, seals their fate.

A good example of this passivity is this statement from Gayev: "I've been thinking, racking my brains; I've got all sorts of remedies, lots of them, which, of course, means I haven't got one." This lack of ability to adapt to the changing social conditions in Russia at the turn of the century was very common, as many wealthy landowners lost their estates to debt. Gayev would rather mime billiard shots than find a real solution to the financial situation in which his family finds itself.

Varya also remains passive, though she tries to save money where she can by feeding the servants only dried peas. It upsets her to stand by as her mother and uncle do nothing, but she is powerless to act without their support. Varya wishes to enter a convent but does not; she is even incapable of acting on her own behalf in this instance. Similarly, Varya's passivity when it comes to her love for Yermolay Lopakhin (and his passivity toward it as well) leads to their inability to commit to one another in marriage. Both repeatedly say they have no objections to marriage, but neither proposes it, because Varya is held by social constraints and Lopakhin by his obsession with business. Mrs. Ranevsky tells Lopakhin to propose to Varya, but he fails to comply, even while he tells Mrs. Ranevsky: ''I'm ready even now. . . . Let's settle it at once and get it over. I don't feel I'll ever propose to her without you here.'' When brought together, Varya and Lopakhin remain inactive, exchanging only small talk. Lopakhin is called away and the moment is lost. Their inability to act destroys any hope of marriage.

Appearances and Reality

Mrs. Ranevsky and her family appear to be a wealthy family living on their estate. They continue to live just as they have for generations, keeping servants, throwing parties, and lending money to neighbors—even though they are nearly destitute. Their need to keep up appearances threatens their very existence. Gayev speaks of getting a job in a bank only when it becomes obvious that his financial situation is dire—this would have been unheard of in earlier times. He speaks badly of his sister, because she has been an ''immoral woman'' while living in Paris and asserts that her impropriety is what led their aunt, the Countess, to refuse to help them. This emphasis on appearance is important to the aristocracy, but in the changing social climate in which the play takes place, these things become less and less important. Gayev maintains the appearance to his family that he has the auction of the orchard under control, but in reality he has almost no control over the situation.

Choices and Consequences

For all characters in Chekhov's *The Cherry Orchard*, choices have their consequences. Free will is a powerful thing, and the Ranevsky family chooses to remain passive and allow the auction to happen with little interference. It is only Lopakhin, who chooses to buy the orchard when his advice goes unheeded, who eventually benefits from the sale. Similarly, Pishchik takes the opportunity to allow mining on his estate and benefits from this choice by making enough money to pay off his debtors. Chekhov places much of the blame for the sale of the orchard on those characters who are unable to make choices and act to save themselves.

Class Conflict

The class conflicts in this play are illustrated best through the servants. Yasha is Firs's grandson, yet their wants and needs are far different. Yasha wishes to move up in the world, and this means taking the opportunity to return to Paris with Mrs. Ranevsky. Firs, on the other hand, wishes to return to the days before the liberation of the serfs. This difference is underscored by generational differences as well. Firs is more comfortable with the old social order, while Yasha yearns for a new one.

Dunyasha, Mrs. Ranevsky's maid, wishes to be a lady and to marry a wealthy man. She is free to dream, unlike her predecessors, who were locked in servitude. There is a new hope among the servant class that they could make money like Lopakhin, or save enough to buy a small home. Peter Trofimov comments on the sociological changes in Russia when he says to Anya ''all your ancestors owned serfs. They owned living beings. Can't you see human beings looking at you from every cherry tree in your orchard, from every leaf and every tree trunk? To own living souls—that's what has changed you all so much. . . . That's why your mother, you yourself, and your uncle no longer realize that you are living on borrowed capital, at other people's expense, at the expense of those whom you don't admit farther than your entrance hall.'' This passage underscores and explains much of the class conflicts in the play. The aristocracy refuse to treat men like Lopakhin or Trofimov as social equals, despite their (the aristocracy's) fall from power.

Lopakhin and Varya are in the middle of this class conflict. Lopakhin was born the child of serfs on the Ranevsky estate, and Varya's father was a serf. Lopakhin is a wealthy man who is in a better financial situation than the Ranevskys, yet they will never accept him as a social equal. They consider him a vulgar man who has no appreciation for tradition or beauty (he suggested building ''vulgar'' cottages on the pristine orchard). Varya was adopted by Mrs. Ranevsky, so she too is caught in the middle of the struggle by virtue of not being entirely a part of the aristocracy nor of the servant class.

STYLE

Comedy vs. Tragedy

Anton Chekhov wrote his last play, *The Cherry Orchard,* as a comedy about a wealthy family that loses its beloved home and orchard to a man who was born a serf on their estate. A comedy is one of the two kinds of drama (the other is tragedy), one that is meant to amuse and typically ends happily. Chekhov referred to *The Cherry Orchard* as a farce, which is a type of comedy characterized by broad humor, outlandish incidents, and often vulgar subject matter. When Konstantin Stanislavsky decided to produce the play at the Moscow Art Theater in 1904, however, he stated in a letter to Chekhov, as quoted in *Stages of Drama: Classical to Contemporary Theater:* ''It is not a comedy, not a farce, as you wrote—it is a tragedy no matter if you do indicate a way out into a better world in the last act . . . when I read it for the second time . . . I wept like a woman, I tried to control myself, but I could not. I can hear you say: 'But please, this is a farce. . .' No, for the ordinary person this is a tragedy.'' This difference of opinion between Chekhov and Stanislavsky would lead to a great rift between the two friends. Like that first production, most contemporary productions of *The Cherry Orchard* still emphasize the play's tragic elements, rather than choosing to present Chekhov's vision of the play as a farce.

A tragedy, strictly defined, is a drama in prose or poetry about a noble, courageous hero of excellent character who, because of a tragic flaw, brings disaster upon himself. Tragedy treats its subjects in a dignified and serious manner, using poetic language to help evoke pity and fear and bring about catharsis, a spiritual awakening or renewal. *The Cherry Orchard* does not fit into the conventional definition of tragedy, but the inability of the main characters to act to save themselves or solve their own problems serves to evoke empathy in the reader/viewer. The play provokes a feeling that the circumstances depicted are tragic, despite the humorous passages.

Comic Moments

There are many comic situations in the play. Leonid Gayev's constant calling out of imaginary

FOR THE ORDINARY PERSON THIS IS A TRAGEDY''

billiard shots, and his chatter create some wonderful comic moments: his salute to the one-hundred-year-old bookcase (''Dear highly esteemed bookcase, I salute you''), and his addiction to hard candy are a few examples. Simon Yepikhodov, also known as Twenty-two Calamities, is a character included purely for comic effect. His boots squeak, and, as he states: ''Everyday, sir, I'm overtaken by some calamity. Not that I mind. I'm used to it. I just smile.'' Yepikhodov's love triangle with Dunyasha and Yasha lends comic value as well.

The elderly servant Firs's doddering ways and muttering–and the misunderstandings that result from his frailties—are also presented with comic intent. However, language is used to make Peter Trofimov comic in a much different way; his passion often gives way to comical rants. After he is chastised by Mrs. Ranevsky for his declaration that he is ''above love'' with Anya, he storms out and falls down a flight of stairs. This is played for comic effect in Chekhov's stage directions, but could easily be portrayed in a serious manner. Yasha's exchange with Dunyasha in the orchard is another comic moment. Calling Dunyasha his ''little cucumber,'' Yasha flirts with her and makes her love him, while fully intending to leave her. Again, the complexity of the characters that Chekhov has created leave room for interpretation by actors and directors.

Boris Simeonov-Pishchik is both tragic and comic at the same time. He is constantly seeking a loan from Mrs. Ranevsky to pay off his debts, though her financial situation is no better than his. Most of his pleas are comic, yet the entire situation is a dreadful one. Chekhov's idea of finding the humor in tragic circumstances is an important part of his individuality as a playwright. Pishchik's comments about his family pedigree lead to his admission that he has fallen on hard times: ''My father, may he rest in peace, liked his little joke, and speaking about our family pedigree, he used to say that the ancient Simeonov-Pishchiks came from the horse that Caligula had made a senator. But you see, the trouble is that I have no money. A hungry dog believes only in meat. I'm just the same. All I can think of is money.'' Although one can certainly find humor in Pishchik's statement, anyone who has ever worried about his or her finances can sympathize with his preoccupation with money. In numerous situations, Chekhov manages to walk a fine line between comedy and pathos, one that could fall to either side depending upon interpretation. This is a contradiction present in the play, and it illustrates why some consider it a farce and others regard it as a tragedy.

Point of View and Empathy

The point of view in this play is third-person, allowing the audience to see the events in the story from outside any particular character but without any insights into their inner thoughts or motivations. The audience often experiences empathy for these characters. Empathy is a shared sense of experience, including emotional and physical feelings, with someone or something other than oneself. When, at the end of the play, the axes begin the job of chopping the orchard down; the reader/viewer feels Mrs. Ranevsky's pain. Upon learning of her young son's death, which is followed shortly by her husband's (events that take place prior to the play's first act), the audience understands her need to run away to Paris. Similarly, when Lopakhin fails to propose to Varya, the audience can appreciate the heartbreak she experiences.

HISTORICAL CONTEXT

Politics

In 1904, the year *The Cherry Orchard* was first produced, Russia was in a state of upheaval. The Japanese declared war on Russia on February 10, 1904, following Russia's failure to withdraw from Manchuria and its continuing penetration of Korea. The Japanese defeated Russia at the Yalu River on May 1, 1904; by October of that year the Japanese had forced Russia to pull back its forces. This war was the beginning of tensions in Asia and the establishment of Japan as a military force.

On the home front, Russia's minister of the interior, Vyacheslav Plehve, exercised complete control over the public. He forbid any political assemblies, required written police permission for small social gatherings, and forbid students to walk together in the streets of St. Petersburg, Russia's capital. On Easter Sunday of 1904, 45 Jews were killed, 600 houses were destroyed in Kishenev in Bessarabia on orders from Plehve, and the police were instructed to ignore rioting in the streets. These events culminated with Plehve's assassination on July 28, 1904. This kind of civil unrest marked the beginning of a time of great conflict and transformation in Russia that ended with the Communist Revolution in 1917.

These tensions both in and outside Russia made life difficult for Russian citizens. The middle class began to assume an elevated position in society as many nobles lost their wealth and large, lavish estates. As the Ranevsky family discovers, Russia is changing and the climate is no longer hospitable to those who do not act in their own interests. Trofimov's character alludes to the strict control of the public when he speaks of the ''things he's seen'' that have caused him to age prematurely. When the serfs were freed, the landowners were forced to pay for labor, and as conditions in Russia worsened due to war and the totalitarian regime, revolution becomes imminent.

Transportation and Industry

The Trans-Siberian Railroad's link from Moscow to Vladivostok opened in 1904. This is the longest line of track in the world, spanning 3,200 miles between the two cities. In the United States, the first New York City subway line of importance opened on October 27, with the Interborough Rapid Transit, known as the IRT, running from the Brooklyn Bridge to 145th Street with stops in between. This system would grow to become the world's largest rapid transit system, covering more than 842 miles. These transportation systems are important because, as society became more urbanized around the world, it changed. Large plots of land, such as the cherry orchard in Chekhov's play, were broken up into smaller plots for building and industry. The railroads allowed people of all economic backgrounds to travel and allowed goods to be shipped long distances using much less manpower.

Science and Technology

Marie Curie discovered radium and polonium in uranium ore in 1904; these two new radioactive elements helped to fuel the nuclear age in the decades to come. Also in 1904, German physicists Julius Elster and Hans Friedrich Geitel invented the first practical photoelectric cell, which led to the invention of radio. The first wireless radio distress

COMPARE & CONTRAST

- **1904:** A Zemstvo congress meets in St. Petersburg, Russia, and demands that civil liberties are accorded to citizens and that an assembly of representatives of the people is convened.

  Today: Russia still grapples with basic civil liberties and rights after the fall of the Soviet Empire. A coup is attempted by right-wing activists, but democratically-elected President Boris Yeltsin retains his power.

- **1904:** The Trans-Siberian Railroad opens, linking Moscow to Vladivostok. The railroad's 3,200 miles of track makes it the longest line in the world.

  Today: Citizens of Vladivostok take to the streets to protest the government's failure to deliver on financial reforms. The expansive distance between Moscow and Vladivostok, though linked by communications and public transportation, makes it difficult for the central government to control the city.

- **1904:** French physicist Marie Curie discovers polonium and radium—two new radioactive elements. This discovery leads to the advent of nuclear power, nuclear weapons, and space flight.

  Today: Despite financial difficulties, the Russian space program continues to advance. The space station Mir, powered by nuclear means, continues to orbit the Earth manned by astronauts from both Russia and the United States.

- **1904:** The National Tuberculosis Association in the United States is established to fight the disease, which is also known as consumption. In Russia the disease claims the life of playwright Anton Chekhov.

  Today: Tuberculosis is on the rise again in the United States, and around the world due to HIV (Human Immunodeficiency Virus) and AIDS (Acquired Immune Deficiency Syndrome). Thought to be virtually wiped during the 1970s, tuberculosis has gained a foothold through weakened immune systems that result from viruses like HIV. However, many treatments are now available to combat tuberculosis, and the illness does not carry with it a death sentence, as it did during Chekhov's time.

---

signal was sent the same year. Clearly, the time in which Chekhov wrote *The Cherry Orchard*—during 1903 and 1904—was a time of much change and scientific advancement. The simple way of life on the orchard was being phased out of existence; a different mindset was required for the dawning age of science and industry. The Ranevsky family is unable to adapt to this new, quickly evolving world in which discoveries are made almost weekly and change is imminent.

Literature and Drama

1904 saw the first publication of such works as Lincoln Steffens's expose of urban squalor *The Shame of the Cities, The Late Mattia Pascal,* by Italian novelist Luigi Pirandello, Henry James's *The Golden Bowl,* and *Reginald,* by English writer Saki, also known as H. H. Munro. Plays which, like *The Cherry Orchard,* were first produced in 1904 include: *Riders to the Sea* by John Millington Synge, Frank Wedekind's *Pandora's Box,* George Bernard Shaw's *Candida* and *How He Lied to Her Husband,* and *Peter Pan, or The Boy Who Would Not Grow Up,* by James M. Barrie. Chekhov's style was substantially different from his contemporaries'; his self-proclaimed "farce," *The Cherry Orchard,* portrays psychology and human behavior far more realistically than many of his fellow playwrights. Unlike the other plays of its time, *The Cherry Orchard* focuses upon an historical era and examines the whole of society rather than just characters.

CRITICAL OVERVIEW

Anton Chekhov intended *The Cherry Orchard* as a farce, yet when Konstantin Stanislavsky's Moscow Art Theater decided to produce the play, it was presented as a tragedy, according to Stanislavsky's view of the play. Chekhov was so frustrated by the failure of Stanislavsky and other commentators to share his vision of the play as a farce that he burned all copies of the manuscript except for one that remained in Moscow. Chekhov was suffering in the last stages of tuberculosis, yet still managed to make the trip to Moscow to attend rehearsals almost daily. Despite his conflicts with Stanislavsky about how the play should be interpreted, he kept a close watch on the production by attending the rehearsals.

In his *The Breaking String: The Plays of Anton Chekhov,* Maurice Valency asserted:

> It is strangely ironical that Chekhov never saw his play produced as a comedy, as he intended, nor has anyone, apparently, ever ventured to produce it in this manner. *The Cherry Orchard* has many comic passages, some of them so broad as to approximate farce but, generally speaking, directors have been unable to fathom the author's comedic intention. The reason is not far to seek. The play, on the whole, is not funny. The characters have their comic side, but the situation is sad. No rationalization has ever succeeded in giving it a comic bias.

Chekhov combined elements of both kinds of drama—comedy and tragedy—in *The Cherry Orchard,* but he used those elements to underscore each other. Some critics have maintained that it is precisely because *The Cherry Orchard* cannot be viewed as a comedy or even as a tragedy in the strictest sense that it is such a successful drama; the combination of both comic and tragic components, these critics maintain, generates the realism in and the emotional impact of *The Cherry Orchard.* The heartbreak that is felt as the characters lose what they want most is diminished by the sense that these characters have not lost their sense of humor; in addition, presenting both negative and positive emotions makes the characters, and their situations, much more accessible to the audience. Francis Fergusson, in an essay included in *Chekhov: A Collection of Critical Essays,* argued: "If Chekhov drastically reduced the dramatic art, he did so in full consciousness, and in obedience both to artistic scruples and to a stricter sense of reality. He reduced the dramatic art to its ancient root, from which new growths are possible"; Chekhov was very deliberate in the crafting of the play. Though most modern productions focus on the tragic in the play, there is

no escaping the humor present in it. Chekhov honed this ability to capture the "real lives" of people and "real situations"—noting that in life there is always a mixture of the tragic and comic—and recreated it for the stage. In *The Cherry Orchard,* his last play, he combined the farcical elements of his earlier works—like *The Marriage Proposal*—with the anguish and misery found in his tragedy, *The Seagull,* and created a new type of drama.

When the play premiered on January 17, 1904, Chekhov sought to avoid it. It was only after a messenger was dispatched to report the audience had erupted in thunderous applause after the second act that he was persuaded to attend. To his horror, the play was stopped between the third and fourth acts as those present saluted the author on his twenty-five years as a writer. Weak from tuberculosis, Chekhov suffered through the evening watching what he viewed as his farce presented as what he called "a piece of sniveling sentimentality," as quoted in *Stages of Drama: Classical to Contemporary Theater.* Stanislavsky would eventually modify his view of the play in the thirty years after the initial production, but he would never see the play in the manner Chekhov had intended.

The Cherry Orchard is still performed and taught today because the characters remain very real to audiences; they personify aspects of comedy and tragedy that are present in the everyday lives of viewers. The complexities of the situations that occur in the play mirror the complexities in life. Real life may not be as balanced as is life in the play, but Chekhov manages to make the play feel like reality. The actions, or failures to act, have consequences, and not all stories have a happy ending. Hope still exists, but it is the hope that the characters can create for themselves a future that is better than the present, rather than the hope that fate will bring that better future to the characters.

Soviet critics after the 1917 Communist Revolution seized upon the character of Peter Trofimov as a hero. He is a young political radical, whose ideas and political beliefs have caused his expulsion from school. He looks forward to a more equal society, and the views he espouses in the play—especially his speech to Anya in which he likens the trees in the orchard to human souls—made him a favorite of Communist critics and scholars. Many Western scholars, however, do not view Trofimov as a hero, largely because although he makes speeches he rarely acts, and even though he presents himself as being concerned with the fate of all humanity he cannot understand those around him. Furthermore, these critics argue, Trofimov refuses Anya's love and affection and opts instead to "fall in love" with his theories about humanity. Despite such criticisms, scholars do agree that Trofimov is ardent in his beliefs and fully intends to work for better things in the future, and these personal characteristics are those which Chekhov intended to celebrate in *The Cherry Orchard.* Following the collapse of the Soviet Union (and Communist governments), Russian critics tend to emphasize the psychological significance of Trofimov rather than his political convictions.

Most scholars do agree that Chekhov's last play is his triumph, and that its strengths lie in its combination of both tragic and comic elements. By creating this balance between the two genres he creates a world where every little action and decision (or lack thereof) has its consequences, and the action in the play is very real. These characters seem to live on after the final curtain. Despite the fact that this psychological realism caused the failure of the first production of *The Seagull,* the audience was ready by 1904 to embrace the reality of the characters and to both empathize with and understand their actions. *The Cherry Orchard* is an excellent example of how one literary work can generate a variety of interpretations. Though the play was intended as a farce by Chekhov, it generally is produced more in accordance with Stanislavsky's view that it is a tragedy. It is important to note that this play is still produced and studied all over the world, because although Chekhov did not want the play to be translated due to his belief that people outside of Russia would not understand the issues it raises, *The Cherry Orchard* has proven successful largely because its themes are universal in scope.

CRITICISM

John Fiero

Fiero is an accomplished actor as well as a noted collegiate educator. In this essay he discusses Chekhov's skill as a writer of comedy and The Cherry Orchard's *status as a misperceived comedy masterpiece.*

Henri Bergson, the French philosopher, theorized in the essay collection *Comedy,* that laughter springs from our perception of "something mechanical encrusted upon the living." The comic figure,

Bergson maintained, is rigid or inflexible in circumstances that demand a resiliency of the mind or body. Moreover, laughter increases through a character's repeated failures to alter a rigid behavior, for it is repetition that transforms mere rigidity into the semblance of something mechanical, like a jack-in-a-box.

If Bergson's ideas have any validity, there is no writer who possessed a greater sense of the comic than Anton Chekhov. Nor is that sense more fully revealed than in his last play, *The Cherry Orchard,* generally considered his greatest work.

From the outset, Chekhov designed the play as comedy. In a letter to his wife, Olga, quoted in *Chekhov in Performance: A Commentary on the Major Plays,* he said that it was to "be funny, very funny, at least in conception." Furthermore, as his later correspondence indicates, he was convinced he had done what he intended. Writing to Lilina, wife to the Moscow Art Theater's great director, Konstantin Stanislavsky, he claimed that, "in places," *The Cherry Orchard* was "even a farce."

Stanislavsky and his co-director, Nemirovich-Danchenko, as they had with other Chekhov plays, chose to interpret the play as much more serious stuff than farce. On stage, they weighed it down as a serious drama, advertising it as such, much to Chekhov's annoyance. The playwright had never felt that either man had fully understood his plays, and he often bristled at their interpretations—yet he could hardly argue with the acclaim their theater won him.

Chekhov's adherence to realism, his objectivity, made it difficult for his contemporaries to see his characters in the kaleidoscopic light in which he cast them. In *The Cherry Orchard,* as in all his comedies, he created characters who confront serious, often insoluble problems. From one perspective, they do elicit sympathy, even pity, no matter how passive or inept they may also seem. If their suffering is the main element the audience perceives, the comic impulse is suppressed, for, as Bergson noted, laughter is really only possible when there is an "absence of feeling."

Farce, most particularly, depends on a hardening of the heart, an emotional distance that allows uninhibited laughter, often at the expense of a character's misfortune or suffering. Some great comic writers, including William Shakespeare, have used various methods to prevent an audience from feeling too much empathy—comic asides, for ex-

WHAT DO I READ NEXT?

- *The Bear* (1888) and *The Marriage Proposal* (1889), the best of Chekhov's early one-act farces or "curtain raisers," tap the purely comic and make an interesting contrast to his more complex and subtle comedies like *The Cherry Orchard.*

- *Miss Julie* (1888), an early naturalistic drama by August Strindberg, investigates the tragic consequences of breaking class barriers in the sexual liaison of Miss Julie and her father's valet, Jean.

- *The Three Sisters,* Chekhov's immediate predecessor to *The Cherry Orchard,* was first performed at the Moscow Art Theatre in 1901. Another play of minimal action, it introduces characters who, like those in the later play, suffer from an inertia of the will.

- *Heartbreak House* (1916), George Bernard Shaw's iconoclastic comedy, shares Chekhov's thematic interest in the breakdown of social norms based on class distinctions. Hesione Hushabye's country house, the play's setting, is a place where artificial conventions and traditions are exposed to Shaw's sardonic wit.

- *The Autumn Garden* (1951), by Lillian Hellman, reflects Chekhov's influence in its technique, structure and theme. Three generations of the Ellis family and their friends gather in the Ellis house to suffer through a shared ennui, atrophy of the will, and sense of loss.

- *The Good Doctor* (1974) is Neil Simon's dramatic tribute to Chekhov, consisting of a collection of dramatized stories adapted from the Russian writer's fictional sketches.

---

ample, or mistaken identities arising from the use of disguise. Chekhov, ever true to the limits of realism, uses no such devices. As a result, as J. L. Styan suggested in *Chekhov in Performance,* he risked misinterpretation: "Farce, which prohibits compassion for human weakness, and tragedy, which demands it, are close kin. The truth is that *The Cherry Orchard* is a play that treads the tightrope between them, and results in the ultimate form of the special dramatic balance we know as Chekhovian comedy."

The Cherry Orchard, depicting the passing world of twilight Russia (before the country's casualty-ridden involvement in both World Wars and its Communist Revolution), certainly has a tragic backdrop. Sometimes, when it cannot be repressed, an anxious awareness of that passing wells up in the characters, but it does not change them. Only Lopakhin really adapts, because to find his place in the new world, he must help destroy the old. He is not mercenary or callous, however, just practical. Although he has only a commercial interest in Mrs. Ranevsky's property, he is genuinely respectful

towards her, partly from habitual reverence that typified the Russian peasant class from which he springs. Initially, he even tries to help her, but her inability to take action finally forces him to buy her land himself. In doing so, he severs the last invisible strings of class deference, ties that bind another character, the old manservant, Firs, until death. The play confirms Lopakhin's resourcefulness, his adaptability. He is, primarily, a flexible character, and is not, therefore, comical, except, perhaps, in his stillborn efforts at wooing Varya.

The central symbol of the old Russia is the cherry orchard. In his way, Peter Trofimov, the perennial student, perceives it as such, but he sees nothing of worth in the ways of the past. The orchard only reminds him of human misery. He speaks of the ghosts of the serfs to Anya:

> Can't you see human beings looking at you from every cherry tree in your orchard, from every leaf and every tree trunk? Don't you hear their voices?

His solution is not to cut the orchard down, but rather to run from it, into "ineffable visions of the future.'' He is a utopian dreamer, as impractical and inflexible as Mrs. Ranevsky and her brother; and, therefore, unlike Lopakhin, he is more than slightly ridiculous.

The cherry orchard is not simply an emblem of a Russia that has passed. As Styan suggested, ''it represents an inextricable tangle of sentiments, which together comprise a way of life and an attitude to life.'' Its white cherry blossoms remind Mrs. Ranevsky and her brother, Gayev, of their youthful purity and innocence. To them, the orchard is a thing of great and enduring beauty, and they find Lopakhin's proposal to replace it with vacation cottages ''vulgar.'' For Firs, the orchard is ''an inviolable aesthetic symbol of the traditional order.'' Anya, on the other hand, drawn by her heart to Trofimov, accepts the student's dream of a future happiness, despite Trofimov's inconvenient belief that they must transcend love and practice celibacy to prepare for it.

On a more mundane level, the orchard is simply a white elephant. No one harvests its fruit, and, in fact, no one even enters it, except the anonymous, unseen woodsman who starts felling its trees in the last act. And while the orchard may be glimpsed through the windows of the house, it is the house itself that is the play's true setting, ''the centre and heart of the play,'' as J. B. Priestley claimed in his text *Anton Chekhov.*

Three of *The Cherry Orchard*'s four acts take place inside the house, and two of them, the first and the last, occur in the same room—the nursery. It is the setting for both the arrival and departure of Mrs. Ranevsky and her entourage. The room at first vibrates with life, brimming with the excitement of the reunited family members, who animate the room with their memories and maudlin but joyous greetings to the furniture. In contrast, at the end, it is stripped of all its furnishings, all signs of life, except some odds and ends; the flotsam of the past, now abandoned, like Firs, who seems indistinguishable from the discarded sofa on which he lies immobilized at the final curtain. Staged, the room has a more immediate impact than the orchard, for it is actually present, unlike the cherry orchard, which remains indirectly experienced through words alone. The orchard's presence is most keenly felt in the last act, in the sound of the axe that has begun its destruction.

The most poignant and haunting presence in the play is not even identified with a locale. It comes in the sound of the breaking string, heard first in the

> **❝** CHEKHOV'S ADHERENCE TO REALISM, HIS OBJECTIVITY, MADE IT DIFFICULT FOR HIS CONTEMPORARIES TO SEE HIS CHARACTERS IN THE KALEIDOSCOPIC LIGHT IN WHICH HE CAST THEM"

second act, and then at the end of the play. Maurice Valency argued in *The Breaking String: The Plays of Anton Chekhov,* that the broken string is ''the golden string that connected man with his father on earth and his father in heaven, the age-old bond that tied the present to the past.'' In general terms, it represents the passing of a way of life, but it relates, too, to the play's specific actions, especially Lopakhin's purchase of Mrs. Ranevsky's estate. The act gives him an overwhelming sense of emancipation, expressed in his triumphant monologue at the close of Act Three:

> ''I've bought the estate where my father and grandfather were slaves, where they weren't even allowed in the kitchen. I must be dreaming. I must be imagining it all. It can't be true.''

Most of the other characters suffer some anxious and painful moments in their ritual passage into the changing but uncertain world that the play foreshadows. Some, like Yepikhodov and Charlotte, experience an identity crisis, while others, like Gayev and Firs, seem sadly disoriented and confused. Yet, as Francis Fergusson claimed in *The Idea of a Theater: A Study of Ten Plays,* while *The Cherry Orchard* is ''a theater poem of the suffering of change,'' it is free ''from the mechanical order of the thesis or intrigue'' play. The tragic implications of the change drift through the comedy like the ghost of Mrs. Ranevsky's mother in the orchard, but they are not shaped into a single catastrophe and momentous reversal of fortune. The tragic elements are simply too diffuse and, like the breaking string, too distant to be distinct or fully understood.

They are also muted and even subverted by the foreground elements that provide a comic counterpoint to the tragic backdrop. Much of the play's action remains routine and mundane, even trivial.

A scene from London's Theatre Royal Haymarket 1983 production

Behind a facade of politeness, there is a quiet tension between those who fear change and those who welcome it, but when tension surfaces as anger or open aggression, Chekhov releases the pressure through some sort of comic safety valve. For example, in the third act, Trofimov, stung by Mrs. Ranevsky's attack on his perceptions of man/woman relationships and his childish whining, exits with theatrical indignation, only to fall down some off-stage stairs to a chorus of laughter. So, too, in the second act, when the frustrated Lopakhin calls Mrs. Ranevsky ''a silly old woman'' because she will not agree to his plans for the estate, Gayev defuses the situation with his billiard game prattle and non-sequitur confession to a fruit candy addiction.

Most of the play's characters are idiosyncratic, and some, like Gayev and Pishchik, are wonderfully eccentric. Most, said Priestley, if ''coldly considered,'' are also at least slightly contemptible: ''Madame Ranevsky is a foolish woman only too anxious to return to a worthless young lover; Gayev is an amiable ass who talks too much; Anya is a goose and her Trofimov a solemn windbag; Lopakhin, the practical self-made man, is confused and unhappy; Epihodov a clumsy idiot; Dunyasha a foolish girl; Yasha an insufferable jumped-up lad; and Firs far gone in senility.'' However, Chekhov never leaves

any one of them exposed to such a naked light for very long; he is too congenial for that, too, as Priestley stated, ''tender and compassionate.''

Each character also seems to have a comic foil or nemesis, Firs and Kasha, for example, or Charlotte and Yepikhodov. All also ride some sort of mental hobby horse that sporadically sends them off the track of conversation onto private, incongruous pathways, i.e., amusing non-sequiturs. Most, at the point of self-awareness, behave exactly like a jack-in-the-box, never able to suppress their foolish impulse. For example, in Act Two, Mrs. Ranevsky, berates herself for her careless waste of money, then immediately drops her purse on the ground and a moment later bestows one of her last gold coins on a panhandler. Meanwhile, Yepikhodov, ever mindful of his role as an unfortunate clod, stumbles into furniture as if to prove he was not miscast for the part.

It is possible to probe such characters to reveal some darker or more sinister personality traits. Beverly Hahn, for one, argued in *Chekhov: A Study of the Major Stories and Plays* that the weaknesses of Mrs. Ranevsky and Gayev, their lack of will, ''amounts to a complex sense of guilt and self-degradation which is both personal and yet obscurely the product of their situation of privilege.'' The Moscow Art Theatre audience of 1904 came from and returned to the world depicted in Chekhov's plays, and they experienced such inner guilt first hand—plus all the pain, sorrow, and pathos that Stanislavsky felt was in *The Cherry Orchard* and that scholars can still expose. But a reader or viewer of the play need not be quite so myopic. There is sufficient distance from Chekhov's world to free laughter from inhibition, restoring the comic balance that Chekhov felt was somehow missed in his own time.

Source: John Fiero, in an essay for *Drama for Students,* Gale, 1997.

V.S. Pritchett

In the following excerpt from his book, Chekhov: A Spirit Set Free, *Pritchett outlines the historical background of and Chekhov's sources for* The Cherry Orchard, *characterizing the play as "Chekhov's farewell to Russia and his genius."*

Pritchett is an English literary figure, and is considered a modern master of the short story and a preeminent literary critic. He writes in the conversational tone of the familiar essay, approaching literature from the viewpoint of a lettered but not overly scholarly reader.

Chekhov started writing *The Cherry Orchard* in Yalta in February 1903. He wrote to Olga, who was in Moscow and whom he called his "little pony," that a crowd of characters was gathering in his mind but he could only manage to write four lines a day and "even that gives me intolerable pain." His disease was possessing his whole body, moving to his intestines and his bowels. Olga came to Yalta in July, hoping the play would be finished in time for her to take a fair copy back to Moscow in September when the theater season opened. It was not ready because he was continuously revising what he had written, but also because, in his anxiety about money, he had agreed to become the literary editor of a new magazine which had been started by his liberal admirer Lavrov, and he was reading dozens of manuscripts for him. At last the play was finished, "except for difficulties with the second act." Stanislavsky and Nemirovich-Danchenko sent him long and enthusiastic telegrams. There was only one jarring note: Stanislavsky had called the play "a truly great tragedy." Tartly, and fearing Stanislavsky's possessiveness, Chekhov replied that it was not even a drama—"It is a farce."

The central subject of *The Cherry Orchard* seems to have been taken from Chekhov's story *A*

> THE CHERRY ORCHARD IS A FARCE BECAUSE THE PEOPLE ARE A DISORDERED CHORUS WHO HAVE LOST THEIR GODS AND INVENT THEMSELVES "

Visit to Friends, written in 1898, which deals with the bankruptcy of the Kiselev family, with whom he had stayed many times at Babkino. Chekhov did not include the story in the complete edition of his work and it has been suggested that he did not want to offend the family: but the story may very well have been rejected because it is too labored in a novelizing way. In the story, the family have turned cynically to a shrewd and successful young lawyer, hoping against hope that he will find some way of saving them from ruin: he knows so many rich people. The wife thinks the solution lies in getting him to marry their daughter. He *is* sentimentally attracted to her, but self-interest is stronger than sentiment: he simply sneaks away in the night. The young man is ashamed of his behavior.

In *The Cherry Orchard,* Lopakhin, the property speculator, evades all appeals to marry Ranevskaya's ward. He seems to be a new version of the shrewd plain practical railway engineer who appears in *Lights* and more fully in the excellent *My Life,* a man with a businesslike eye for taking over the properties of the feckless landowning families. Chekhov admired this self-made man and he warned Stanislavsky that Lopakhin must not be played as a greedy vulgarian; he saw that Lopakhin's weakness was that he would be too cautious and inhibited in love. Ranevskaya must not be played as an entirely frivolous and irresponsible spendthrift: she is all heart; her sensuality is natural to her and not vicious. In her reckless life in Paris she has nursed a lover who has deceived and robbed her, and she will return to him at the end of the play when he is ill again and appeals to her once more. She is shrewd when she mocks Trofimov, the high-minded and self-absorbed "eternal student" who has been the family tutor, because, at his age, he has never had a mistress. He is, she says, a prig. She may be a victim of what Chekhov called *morbus fraudulentus* when she gazes at her cherry orchard and sees in the white blossoms the symbol of the lost innocence of her girlhood, but the incurable lavishness of her heart is genuine. Lopakhin will not forget the moment she tenderly washed his face when his nose was bleeding when he was a little boy, and called him "little peasant." In Lopakhin, the tongue-tied money-maker, that childhood memory is a genuine grace. What Chekhov brings out, as he makes his people tell their own story without listening to one another, is their absurd pride in their own history and their indifference to everyone else's. Ranevskaya may long for the tongue-tied Lopakhin to propose to her ward, but the girl's real dream is for a life of pious journeys from convent to convent.

The truly desperate character is the bizarre half-German outsider, Sharlotta, who breaks the tension of the play by her mystifying tricks with cards and her ventriloquism. Chekhov had seen such a girl at a fair on one of his trips. She is the daughter of anarchy and is truly frightening. Everyone else knows who they are. She does not know who she is. "I have no proper identity papers and I don't know how old I am. I keep imagining I am young. . . . Where I come from and who I am I do not know." All she knows is that she has traveled, when she was a child, from fair to fair and that her gypsy parents taught her to do card tricks. A German lady rescued her and turned her into a governess. She pulls a cucumber out of her pocket and eats it. "I am so lonely, always so lonely . . . and who I am, what I exist for, nobody knows." Pathos? Not at all—a wild independent native homelessness. In the final scene of the play, in the general good-byes when the house is sold, she picks up a bundle, pretends it is a baby, produces the illusion of a baby crying as she sings "Hush, little baby, my heart goes out to you," and then throws the bundle on the floor and says to them all: "And please find me another job. I can't go on like this."

What about the eloquent speech of Trofimov, the eternal student, sent down twice from the university, working for the "glorious future" in Russia? He attacks the theorizing intelligentsia and proudly refuses a loan from Lopakhin at the end of the play. In Act II he cries out: "The whole of Russia is our orchard." Is he a proud prophet of revolution and reform? Hardly: he is a rootless enthusiastic bookworm.

Objection has been made to the final scene, in which Firs, the sick and rambling old servant, lover of the old days, is left behind when the family leave, locked in by mistake. The family had assumed he

was in the hospital and no one had troubled to find out. Is this eerie or simply anticlimax? It "works," for he is the very conscious historian of the family in a play which is notable for its pairs of matching scenes. For we remember that in the wild ballroom scene in the third act, Chekhov has brought in the local stationmaster, who insists on reciting a notorious poem called "The Sinful Woman." It is dearly directed at Ranevskaya's adultery. He is seemingly unembarrassed by his tactlessness and may even be thinking that he is celebrating her fame in local gossip. No one listens. But it is Firs who enlarges the history of the family. He says:

> We used to have generals, barons and admirals at our dances in the old days, but now we send for the post-office clerk and the stationmaster and even they are not all that keen to come.

He rambles on about the good old days of serfdom:

> I feel frail. The old master, Mr. Leonid's grandfather, used to dose us all with powdered sealing wax no matter what was wrong with us. I've been taking powdered sealing wax for twenty years or more and maybe that is what's kept me alive.

The matching of time present and time past gives the play the density and intricacy of a novel; the play is the most novelized of Chekhov's plays because the people talk it into existence and because no one listens. It *is* a farce because the people are a disordered chorus who have lost their gods and invent themselves. They are a collective farewell, and that is what moves us. As Professor Rayfield has written, the play is also Chekhov's farewell to Russia and his genius.

Source: V. S. Pritchett, in his *Chekhov: A Spirit Set Free*, Hodder & Stoughton, 1988, pp. 220–24.

John Corbin

In the following review, which originally appeared in the New York Times *on January 23, 1923, Corbin praises* The Cherry Orchard, *calling it "the masterpiece of the man who . . . has touched the pinnacle of modern Russian comedy."*

The Moscow players proceeded last night from the lower depths of Gorky to the high comedy of Tchekhoff, revealing new artistic resources. Stanislavsky, Olga Knipper-Tchekhova, Moskvin, Leonidoff and half a dozen others entered with consummate ease into a rich variety of new characterizations. The stage management was less signal in its effects, but no less perfect. Yet for some reason *The Cherry Orchard* failed to stir the audience, even the Russian portion of it, as did *The Lower Depths* and even *Tsar Fyodor.*

This is a play of comedy values both high and light. The milieu is that of the ancient landed aristocracy, beautifully symbolized by an orchard of cherry trees in full bloom which surrounds the crumbling manor house. Quite obviously, these amiable folk have fallen away from the pristine vigor of their race.

The middle-aged brother and sister who live together are unconscious, irreclaimable spendthrifts, both of their shrinking purses and of their waning lives. With a little effort, one is made to feel, even with a modicum of mental concentration, calamity could be averted. But that is utterly beyond their vacuous and futile amiability; so their estate is sold over their heads and the leagues of gay cherry trees are felled to make way for suburban villas.

Beneath the graceful, easy-going surface of the play one feels rather than perceives a criticism on the Russia of two decades ago. Here is a woman of truly Slavic instability, passing with a single gesture from heartbreak to the gayety of a moment, from acutely maternal grief for an only child long dead to weak doting on a Parisian lover who is faithless to her and yet has power to hold her and batten on her bounty. Here is a man whose sentiment for the home of his ancestors breaks forth in fluent declaiming, quasi-poetic and quasi-philosophic, yet who cannot lift a finger to avert financial disaster.

In the entire cast only one person has normal human sense. Lopakhin is the son of a serf who has prospered in freedom. He is loyal enough to the old masters, dogging their footsteps with good advice. But in the end it is he who buys the estate and fells the cherry trees for the villas of an industrial population. It is as if Tchekhoff saw in the new middle class the hope of a disenchanted yet sounder and more progressive Russia. The war has halted that movement, but indications are not lacking that it is already resuming.

With such a theme developed by the subtly masterful art of Tchekhoff there is scope for comedy acting of the highest quality. It is more than likely that the company seized every opportunity and improved upon it. But to any one who does not understand Russian, judgment in such a matter is quite impossible. Where effects are to be achieved only by the subtlest intonation, the most delicate phrasing, it fares ill with those whose entire vocabulary is da, da.

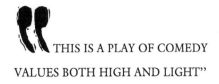
THIS IS A PLAY OF COMEDY VALUES BOTH HIGH AND LIGHT"

As an example of the art of the most distinguished company that has visited our shores in modern memory, this production of *The Cherry Orchard* is abundantly worth seeing. The play in itself is of interest as the masterpiece of the man who, with Gorky, has touched the pinnacle of modern Russian comedy. But if some Moscovite should rise up and tell us that in any season our own stage produces casts as perfect and ensembles as finely studied in detail, it would be quite possible to believe him.

Source: John Corbin, ''Russian High Comedy'' (1923) in *Onstage: Selected Theater Reviews from The New York Times 1920–1970,* edited by Bernard Beckerman and Howard Siegman, Arno Press, 1973, p. 34.

FURTHER READING

Bergson, Henri. ''Laughter,'' in *Comedy,* edited by Wylie Sypher, Doubleday (Garden City, NY), 1956.
Bergson's essay is included with George Meredith's ''An Essay on Comedy'' and appendix essay, ''The Meanings of Comedy,'' by editor Sypher. The collection is an excellent source for ideas on the nature of the comic.

Bruford, W. H. *Chekhov and His Russia: A Sociological Study,* Archon Books (Hamden, CT), 1971.
Relates Chekhov's work to Russia's social structure, with a discussion of the various groups, including the merchants, landowners, intelligentsia, and the peasants; a very useful background study for *The Cherry Orchard.*

Fergusson, Francis. *The Idea of a Theater: A Study of Ten Plays,* Princeton University Press, 1972.
A highly regarded and influential introduction to theater, this study relates the structure of *The Cherry Orchard* to classical tragedy.

Hahn, Beverly. *Chekhov: A Study of the Major Stories and Plays,* Cambridge University Press, 1977.
Although a general study of both fiction and drama, work discusses *The Cherry Orchard* at length to answer critical assaults on Chekhov as ''a melancholy and merely impressionistic dramatist.''

Kirk, Irina. *Anton Chekhov,* Twayne (Boston), 1981.

General introduction to Chekhov. Makes passing mention of Bergson as a relevant theorist for the comic in Chekhov.

Magarshack, David. *Chekhov the Dramatist,* Hill and Wang (New York), 1960.
  Divides Chekhov's plays into two categories: plays of direct and plays of indirect action (plays with significant offstage action), including *The Cherry Orchard.* Stresses comic structure of plays.

Priestley, J. B. *Anton Chekhov,* A. S. Barnes & Co. (Cranbury, NJ), 1970.
  A critical biography in the ''International Profiles'' series, arguing that Chekhov was a better dramatist than fictionist. A good introduction to Chekhov, with illustrations.

Rayfield, Donald. *Chekhov: The Evolution of His Art,* Harper & Row (New York), 1975.
  A critical biography that analyzes the relationship between Chekhov's fiction and his plays, showing how each sheds light on the other.

Styan, J. L. *Chekhov in Performance: A Commentary on the Major Plays,* Cambridge University Press, 1971.
  An act by act interpretation of Chekhov's four major plays, particularly useful for preparing the text for performance.

Valency, Maurice. *The Breaking String: The Plays of Anton Chekhov,* Oxford University Press (New York), 1966.
  Study focuses on Chekhov's plays in the context of the development of modern drama in Europe and the relationship of his plays to his fiction.

SOURCES

Field, Bradford S., Jr., Gilbert, Miriam, and Klaus, Carl H. *Stages of Drama: Classical to Contemporary Theater,* Scott, Foresman, 1981.

Cyrano de Bergerac

EDMOND ROSTAND

1897

When *Cyrano de Bergerac* was first produced at the Porte Saint-Martin Theater in Paris, France, on December 28, 1897, the audience applauded for a full hour after the final curtain was drawn. A classic was created on that night, and an unforgettable hero of literature was born.

The play is based loosely on the life of playwright Savien de Cyrano de Bergerac (1619-1655), Edmond Rostand's favorite writer. Actor Constant-Benoit Coquelin had asked Rostand to write a play to showcase his versatile acting abilities. Rostand, though writing in the 1890's, set his action in the 1640's; during the last two decades of the real de Bergerac's life. This "heroic comedy" uses rhymed Alexandrine verse to combine romance, heroic action, and humor to give life to one of the most enduring characters in modern literature: Cyrano de Bergerac, a hero who is not only a swashbuckler but a poet, using words as effectively as weapons.

Cyrano was first published in France by Charpentier et Fasquelle in 1898; and first translated into English by Howard Thayer Kingsbury for Lamson, Wolfe, and Co. the same year. The play has been produced all over the world. In 1950 it was brought to movie screens in the United States by the United Artists studio with Jose Ferrer starring in the title role. Noted writer Anthony Burgess (*A Clockwork Orange*) translated the play in 1971: this translation was used as the basis for the subtitles for

the 1990 French film version directed by Jean-Paul Rappineau and starring Gerard Depardieu.

A modern interpretation of *Cyrano de Bergerac, Roxanne,* was produced by Columbia Pictures in 1987. This film, loosely based on Rostand's play, was written by and starred comedian Steve Martin as a modern Cyrano. The success of this film was due in part to its loyalty to the central themes of love, loyalty, sacrifice, and independence of Rostand's original classic. The hero, again with a very large nose, woos the woman he loves for another, more "handsome" man.

Edmond Rostand's mix of humor, romance, and heroic action in *Cyrano de Bergerac* has captured audience imagination for almost 100 years. Its recurring themes of love, loyalty, sacrifice, and friendship continue to have resonance for audiences of many generations.

AUTHOR BIOGRAPHY

Edmond (Eugene Alexis) Rostand was born on April 1, 1868 in Marseilles, France. The son of a prominent journalist and economist; Rostand was encouraged to write from a very early age. In his teens he began creating plays for marionette (puppet) theater, and, at the age of sixteen, had several poems and essays published in the literary magazine *Mireille.* At the College Stanislas in Paris he studied literature, philosophy, and history before going on to study law at the local university. Rostand's ambition, however, was to be a writer, and though he completed the coursework, he never practiced law.

Rostand's first play, *Le gant rouge* (1888), and his first book of poetry, *Les musardises* (1890), were largely ignored by both critics and the public. It was *Les romanesques* (*The Romancers,* 1894) which served as his breakthrough. Produced at the Comedie Francaise in 1894, its romantic style stood in contrast to the naturalism and symbolism practiced by many of his contemporaries such as Henrik Ibsen and Maurice Maeterlinck.

On April 8, 1890, Rostand married Rosemonde Gerard, who was herself a poet. Their marriage produced two children, Maurice and Jean.

La princesse lointaine (*The Princess Far-Away,* 1895) solidified Rostand's reputation and its production marked the beginning of his professional alliance with the famous French actress Sarah Bernhardt. Known for her passionate performances, Bernhardt went on to star in several of Rostand's later plays, including *Cyrano de Bergerac.* Though she did not create the role of Roxane, she did portray it on the French stage during its initial run.

It was Rostand's alliance with renowned French actor Constant-Benoit Coquelin, however, which resulted in his masterpiece: *Cyrano de Bergerac* (1897). Coquelin had asked Rostand to write a play that would both challenge and showcase the numerous facets of his acting ability. Rostand delivered a heroic comedy about a swashbuckling poet with an abnormally large nose, a tale based on his own favorite writer. The real-life Cyrano was, like his fictional counterpart, both a soldier and a writer, his famously large nose, however, was Rostand's invention.

Just two years after the critical and popular success of *Cyrano de Bergerac,* illness forced Rostand to move back to his country estate. His last two finished plays: *L'Aiglon* (*The Eaglet,* 1900), and *Chanticler* (1910), were critical disappointments. *L'Aiglon* (about the life of the Duke of Reichstadt, son of Napoleon I) was, according to most critics, considered too simplistic and predictable. *Chanticler* (about a barnyard rooster who defends the importance of his role in the world) had critics divided: while some found it obscure and too long; some found its allegorical verse profound, and view it as a poem to be read and not performed.

Rostand's final play *La derniere nuit de Don Juan* (*The Last Night of Don Juan,* 1922), was left unfinished upon his death in 1918.

Rostand was the youngest member ever elected to the Academie Francaise (one of the highest honors France bestows on scholars of letters) in 1901. He is remembered for his skillful verse and the robust theatricality of his plays, most notably, *Cyrano de Bergerac.*

PLOT SUMMARY

Act I: A Performance at the Hotel de Bourgogne
Act I of *Cyrano de Bergerac* opens at the famous Hotel de Bourgogne in France, where a

troop of actors are setting up for a matinee performance. Joining the actors and stagehands is a cross-section of seventeenth-century Parisian life: cavaliers, pages, pickpockets, peddlers, and even Marquises bustle about the stage. The audience is introduced to Christian de Neuvillette, a handsome young man who has come (with his friend, Ligniere) to catch a glimpse of Roxane, a beautiful woman who may be attending the performance. Christian complains of his inability to speak to her: ''I have no wit,'' he states, and he fears embarrassing himself if he is given the chance to confront her. A greater obstacle, however, is the fact that the Comte de Guiche, who is married to the niece of Cardinal Richelieu, also desires Roxane, and has been pressing her to marry his friend, Valvert, so that he can be near her whenever he wishes. Roxane is, naturally, averse to the idea.

The play truly begins when its title character, the soldier Cyrano, enters and chases Montfleury, an actor whose pomposity and unskilled bombast the swordsman despises, off of the stage. After giving the theatre's manager a purse of gold (to compensate for his closing the play), Cyrano banters with some minor characters—until Valvert, goaded by de Guiche, attempts to mock Cyrano for his most striking feature: his gigantic nose. He taunts Cyrano with, ''your nose is . . . rather large,'' to which Cyrano replies with a fifty-four line oration in which he details all of the insults Valvert *could* have said, had he ''some tinge of letters, or of wit.'' As if this speech is not proof enough of Cyrano's quick mind and sense of humor, he immediately duels Valvert while simultaneously composing a ballad that describes his actions. He states that when he completes his verse, he will strike with his sword, which he does, killing Valvert. Clearly, the ''Performance at the Hotel de Bourgogne'' is Cyrano's own, which the crowd on stage (and in the audience) watch, spellbound. After the hall empties out, Cyrano reveals to his friend, Le Bret, that he is in love with (of course) a woman named Roxane. Like Christian, he is afraid of humiliation, although his problem is not his lack of wit but ''the shadow of my profile on the wall.'' Roxane's lady-in-waiting asks Cyrano if she and Roxane might meet him tomorrow to discuss ''certain things.'' Cyrano agrees and continues his pursuit of making himself ''in all things—admirable.'' He ends the Act by dueling one hundred men to save Ligniere's life, a brave and noble act, although it has already been revealed to the audience that Cyrano's private self is lovelorn and insecure.

Edmond Rostand

Act II: The Bakery of the Poets

The action shifts to Ragueneau's pastry shop, where the baker (and aspiring poet) feeds a host of local artisans in exchange for their verse and conversation. Cyrano enters, for it is here that he will meet Roxane, and he is eager to hear what he hopes will be a pronouncement of her love. Roxane tells him that she *is* in love, with someone ''who does not know,'' who ''loves me too,'' and ''never says one word.'' However, when she describes this man as ''beautiful,'' Cyrano knows that she cannot be speaking of him. Roxane confesses that she loves Christian, and has come to ask Cyrano to watch over him, as he is to enter the Guards (of which Cyrano is a member). Cyrano reluctantly agrees, saying nothing to Roxane about his own feelings.

Cyrano tells Christian of Roxane's love and that she expects a letter from him. Delighted yet distraught, Christian tells Cyrano that he cannot write, for doing so ''would ruin all'': ''I am a fool!/ Stupid enough to hang myself.'' The two men speak of their own deficiencies: Christian, placing his hand on his heart, cries, ''Oh, if I had words/To say what I have here.'' Cyrano wishes he was ''a handsome little Musketeer.'' Finally, Cyrano devises a plan to help Christian: the young soldier can ''borrow'' his wit by allowing Cyrano to write the

A scene from the 1950 film adaptation, starring Jose Ferrer as Cyrano

letter to Roxane. After some prodding, Christian agrees, causing Cyrano to exclaim that, with their combined forces, ''we two'' will ''make one her of romance!''

Act III: Roxane's Kiss

Act III takes place in front of Roxane's house. Cyrano enters and speaks to Roxane about ''Christian's'' letters, which she describes as the work of ''a master,'' but which Cyrano is forced (by virtue of his secret role in their creation) to criticize. De Guiche enters, again asking Roxane to consider his offer; she responds with indifference. When he reveals that the Guards have been ordered to besiege Arras, Roxane's concern for Christian motivates her to trick de Guiche into leaving Cyrano and Christian behind, while the rest of the regiment marches off to glory. He agrees, convinced that this is a sign of Roxane's love. Christian and Cyrano enter and discuss their agreement, which Christian wants to end by speaking freely and openly to Roxane. ''I am no such fool! You shall see,'' the young Cadet promises, only to flounder when he does attempt to speak eloquently to Roxane. She runs into her house, shutting the door in his face and

leaving Christian more heartbroken than before. However, Cyrano again devises a plan: he will stand under Roxane's balcony and pretend that he is Christian; this way, the illusion that they have created will be sustained. Hidden by shadows, Cyrano ''rhapsodizes'' under her window until she begs him to climb the trellis and receive her kiss. Christian does, leaving Cyrano on the ground, comparing himself to Lazarus, the Biblical beggar who waited outside the gates of a rich man who dined on the finest foods.

A Capuchin monk enters with a letter for Roxane from de Guiche, explaining that he has secretly remained in Paris for a day while his regiment is preparing for war. Roxane, however, pretends to read a very different letter to the Capuchin, claiming that she and Christian are to be immediately married by order of Cardinal Richelieu. Roxane and Christian arrive for the ceremony, while Cyrano, again finding himself an outcast, waits outside. When de Guiche enters, Cyrano manages to stall him long enough for the ceremony to conclude; when it does, Roxane and Christian enter and announce their marriage. Furious, de Guiche commands Cyrano and Christian to report to the front. As they leave, Cyrano promises Roxane that ''Christian'' will write her every day.

Act IV: The Cadets of Gascoyne

Act IV occurs at Arras, the front of France's war against Spain. Cyrano has risked his life every day by crossing the battlefield to ensure that Roxane receives her daily letter. All are shocked when a carriage arrives at the camp containing Roxane and Ragueneau; she has come to see Christian, and he has come to supply the hungry men with food and wine. In a conversation with Christian, Roxane asks for his ''forgiveness.'' She feels that she has sinned, that she has fallen in love with him only because he was ''beautiful.'' She tells him that even if he were ''less charming'' or ''ugly even,'' she would still love him. Of course, this is terrible news to Christian, who tells Cyrano that he is ''tired of being/ [His] own rival.'' Christian wants Roxane to know the truth: ''I want her love/For the poor fool I am— or not at all!'' He asks Cyrano to tell Roxane the entire story in the hope that she will choose the man whom she loves more dearly. Christian exits the stage, entering the battle that rages outside.

Cyrano now has the opportunity for which he has been hoping: a chance to reveal himself to Roxane, to show her that it is his soul and his words that she loves. Just as he is about to tell her, however, Christian is brought on stage, mortally wounded. Rather than deny happiness to a dying man, Cyrano tells Christian that Roxane chose him: ''I have told her; she loves you.'' As he watches Roxane weep over Christian's body, Cyrano realizes that he will never be able to tell her the truth: ''I am dead and my love mourns for me/And does not know.'' Inspired to fight, Cyrano rushes to the front, announcing, ''I have two deaths to avenge now— Christian's/And my own!'' The act ends as Cyrano enters the fray.

Act V: Cyrano's Gazette

The scene shifts to fifteen years later. Roxane has entered a convent and is visited by Cyrano every Saturday. During these visits he informs her of the week's events, giving her a dose of the town's gossip. Le Bret tells the nuns that Cyrano is penniless and lonely due to his caustic attacks (''satires'') on hypocrites of all kinds: ''He attacks the false nobles, the false saints,/The false heroes, the false artists—in short,/Everyone!'' De Guiche, whose passion has been cooled by time, visits Roxane to tell her of a rumor he heard at Court concerning the possible murder of Cyrano for offending a ''false noble.'' Ragueneau runs on stage and informs everyone that Cyrano was hit on the head with a log that

''accidentally'' fell from a window. He and Le Bret run off to aid the dying swordsman.

Cyrano, however, appears after they leave to see Roxane before he dies. Although he tries to make jests and tell Roxane the ''gazette'' of news at Court, he is obviously in pain (yet too proud to admit it). Confessing that he is dying, he engages in his last swordfight, a battle with death itself. While his previous clashes with death allowed him escape, this one will not, and he stumbles in exhaustion. Nearing death, Cyrano's last wish is to read the letter that ''Christian'' wrote to Roxane on the day of his death, which she keeps in a locket around her neck. As he reads it aloud, the irony of the situation—and Cyrano's life—intensifies: ''Farewell, Roxanne, because to-day I die . . . and my heart/ Still so heavy with love I have not told,/And I die without telling you!'' When he continues reading the letter after the sun sets, however, Roxane realizes that Cyrano knows the letter by heart; she realizes that it was he, not Christian, who composed the words with which she fell in love. Roxane is so moved by the many sacrifices and selfless acts performed by Cyrano that she professes her love for him. Cyrano thanks her for a life of ''sweetness'' and collapses while offering Roxane ''One thing without stain,/Unspotted from the world, in spite of doom/[His] own!'' As Roxane leans toward him, asking him what he is leaving her, he smiles and says, ''My white plume'': a symbol of his honor in a world that seemed to have little regard for such a quality.

CHARACTERS

Bellerose

The stage manager of the theater where Montfleury was set to perform, he is put in the position of calming the crowd when Cyrano runs Montfleury off the stage. He allows Le Bret and Cyrano to wait in the theater while the mob leaves after the duel with Valvert.

Christian

A handsome but tongue-tied soldier from Touraine; Christian comes to Paris to join the Gascony Guards (Cyrano's regiment) and to find the beautiful Roxane.

So overcome is he with Roxane's beauty that he allows Cyrano to woo Roxane with words when it

MEDIA ADAPTATIONS

- The earliest film adaptation of *Cyrano de Bergerac* is a silent film from 1925 with Pierre Magnier as Cyrano. Available from Kino on Video.

- The most famous film version of *Cyrano de Bergerac* is the one in which Jose Ferrer reprised his famous stage role as the title character. The film was released in 1950 by United Artists and is available on Nostalgia Family Video.

- The Royal Shakespeare Company's 1985 production of the play, with Derek Jacobi as Cyrano, is available on video from Turner Home Entertainment.

- For a newer adaptation of the play, see Jean-Paul Rappeneau's 1990 version of *Cyrano de Bergerac,* starring Gerard Depardieu as Cyrano, a performance for which he won the 1990 Cannes Film Festival's Best Actor award. Available on Orion Home Video.

- Steve Martin's comedy *Roxanne* (1987) tells the story of *Cyrano de Bergerac* in a modern American setting. Starring Steve Martin as C. D. Bales (Cyrano) and Daryl Hannah as Roxanne. Available on Columbia Home Video.

becomes obvious that his good looks are not enough to win her heart. Even after he is married to her, it is Cyrano who continues the relationship, composing moving love letters for Christian. When he finds that the words (Cyrano's heart and soul) are what she loves, the starving and sickly Christian begs Cyrano to tell Roxane the truth. Knowing he cannot continue to dishonestly accept Roxane's love, he seeks death in battle.

Christian is a man with honorable intentions and a good heart. He is also easily led and a victim of his own desires. He willingly allows Cyrano to act as a kind of "emotional surrogate" to make up for the qualities he lacks. He is truly in love with Roxane but knows that her love for him has not been fairly won. He sees an honorable death in battle as the only solution to this problem. It is Christian's hope that, in his absence, Cyrano and Roxane can find true happiness together.

The Citizen

The Citizen is a member of the audience at the theater. An otherwise insignificant character, he serves as a means by which Rostand illustrates his hero's sensitivity regarding his appearance as well as his rapier-sharp wit. The citizen is caught staring at Cyrano's sizable sinuses and subsequently initiates the play's famous "nose tirade."

Cyrano

See Cyrano de Bergerac

Cyrano de Bergerac

Cyrano de Bergerac is a man who excels at poetry and swordsmanship in order to overcome his "physical limitation"—a very large nose. In the words of the character Ragueneau, "there never walked,/stalked rather, strutted, so extravagant, bizzare,/far-fetched, excessive, hyperbolic, droll,/ mad a gentleman-ruffian as this Bergerac."

From the first sight of Cyrano ridiculing the lackluster skills of the actor Montfleury, it is clear that his wit is a weapon as sharp as his sword. When challenged to a duel by the Vicomte de Valvert, he composes a "ballade" (poem) as they fight. He taunts his opponent, "when the poem ends, I hit." It is clear that Cyrano is in complete control, both in the swordfight and in the verbal repartee; as he states, he completes the poem and defeats de Valvert. For Cyrano, composing the poem is an integral part of the fight itself, an illustration that there is little distinction between his mental and physical prowess—and that these powers serve as tools to maintain his individuality and freedom.

Cyrano's dedication to his art (and obsession with independence) is also depicted in his rejection of de Guiche's patronage. His statement, ''I might, (take a patron)/if the thought of anyone's changing a single comma,/didn't make my blood curdle,'' shows his revulsion at the thought of anyone meddling in his affairs. In the end, his insistence on being an independent man brings about his death.

Just as he fights with words, Cyrano can also employ them in the pursuit of love. Believing that his beautiful and intelligent cousin Roxane could not love him because of his looks; he offers to woo her for the handsome but tongue-tied suitor, Christian. It is with Cyrano's words that Roxane is won into marriage, not Christian's looks. Cyrano, his self-esteem so low, cannot believe, even after Roxane's letter to the front in the siege of Arras, that she could love him. For fifteen years he keeps the secret, fearing her rejection, until he is, himself, about to die. Cyrano is a passionate man, whose independence eventually leads to his downfall. He does, however, achieve a bittersweet triumph before his death, learning that Roxane does in fact love him for his soul, not his outward appearance. Cyrano's tale illustrates the concept of true beauty coming from within.

Comte de Guiche

A courtier and somewhat foppish aristocrat; de Guiche, though married to the niece of French leader Cardinal Richelieu, is in love with Roxane. He believes that if he cannot have her he will force her to marry his ally, the Vicomte de Valvert. De Guiche will do whatever is necessary to win Roxane, and is determined to crush whomever stands in his way. When Cyrano thwarts his attempt at a late-night meeting with Roxane and enables her marriage to Christian; he sends Cyrano, Christian, and their regiment, the Gascony Guards, to the siege of Arras in retribution. It is only after many years that de Guiche learns to respect Cyrano for his independence and understands the loyalty of Roxane.

Christian de Neuvillette

See Christian

The Foodseller

The Foodseller is a young woman who shows Cyrano kindness by trying to give him food after he gives his purse to Jodalet at the theater. He refuses her offer but kisses her hand. This illustrates Cyrano's easy and natural charm with women and takes place as he tells Le Bret that no woman will ever want him.

LeBret

LeBret is Cyrano's friend in the Gascony Guards and is the perfect foil (a character who offers complementary—often contrasting—behavior) for Cyrano. He is a staunch supporter and loyal friend to Cyrano, but also reminds Cyrano when he is being reckless (as when Cyrano gives his entire purse to Bellerose, the theater owner). Protective of Cyrano, he tries to keep him safe in the siege of Arras and again at the convent fifteen years later. He has enormous respect and love for Cyrano, and also for Roxane.

Ligniere

A poet and a drunk, Ligniere serves to introduce Christian to all at the theater. De Guiche sends one-hundred ''ruffians'' to kill Ligniere because he wrote a scandalous song about him. Thanks to Christian's warning, Cyrano protects Ligniere, fights off the hundred ruffians, and saves his life. This victory for Cyrano helps solidify his reputation as a fighter at the pastry shop the next day and wins over the crowd until his disagreement with de Guiche over patronage.

Lise

Lise, Ragueneau's wife, has no patience for her husband's love of poetry. She destroys his books to wrap pastries. Irritated by her husband's poet friends, she eventually runs off with a musketeer. Cyrano warns Ragueneau of Lise's friendliness with the musketeer but it is too late.

Magdeleine Robin

See Roxane

Montfleury

Montfleury is a notoriously overweight and very bad actor on the Paris stage. Defying Cyrano's warning to stay off the stage for a month, he finds himself kicked off and run out of town by Cyrano.

Mother Marguerite de Jesus

The Mother Superior of the convent in which Roxane takes refuge after Christian's death, she is an understanding woman, who tells her young sisters Marthe and Claire not to try to convert Cyrano.

She enjoys Cyrano's Saturday visits to Roxane. Her presence serves as a narrative bridge, shading in the events in the fourteen years since the siege of Arras.

Ragueneau

Ragueneau is a baker and would-be poet. A friend to Cyrano, he opens his pastry shop to poets who listen to his verse in exchange for food and drink. He supports Cyrano both in friendship and with food from his shop. He also allows his shop to be used as a meeting place for Cyrano and Roxane. He warns Cyrano of the danger of making too many enemies and tries to help him when he can.

Ragueneau's wife, Lise, leaves him for a musketeer after he bankrupts himself by publishing a book of recipes in verse—"Ragueneau's Rhymed Recipes". By the end of the play he works odd jobs to survive, but he remains a loyal friend to Cyrano until the end.

Roxane

Roxane is one of the most sought after women in Paris. Beautiful, intelligent, and fiercely independent, she lives with her *duenna* (chaperone) in a comfortable home in Paris. She is Cyrano's cousin, and the object of desire for not only Cyrano and Christian, but the Comte de Guiche and the Vicomte de Valvert as well. Described by Rostand as "delicately reared and bookish," she is a lover of words and not men.

While attracted to Christian's good looks, his lack of social skill and clumsy attempts at conversation turn her off. It is only when Roxane hears the words of Cyrano—spoken through Christian—that she is charmed. Convinced that Christian is both handsome and intelligent; it is she that devises a plan to thwart the Comte de Guiche's late-night meeting so that she may marry Christian. It is her quick thinking that convinces the Capuchin (priest) to marry them; despite this cunning, she is nevertheless fooled by Cyrano's ruse.

Roxane proves to be a faithful and loving wife to the end by staying in a convent after Christian's death. She resists the advances of the still-ardent Comte de Guiche, and her only link to the outside world is her faithful cousin Cyrano, who is her regular visitor. It is only when she realizes that the words Christian spoke came from Cyrano that she declares her love for him. Roxane's physical attraction to Christian—and her enduring belief that it

was he who spoke such beautiful words to her—blinds her to Cyrano's deep love. As Cyrano lies dying, however, she realizes her true love in Cyrano.

Roxane's Duenna

The duenna is a chaparone who is easily bribed by Cyrano's cream puffs at Ragueneau's pastry shop. She is at times cynical and sarcastic, yet very protective of her charge, Roxane.

Sister Claire

Counterpart to Sister Marthe, she is concerned about Cyrano and expresses her concern to Mother Marguerite.

Sister Marthe

One of the two sisters at the convent who play out a comic moment as each tells the other's sins to Mother Marguerite. Marthe wishes to convert Cyrano, and Cyrano, before his death tells her to pray for him.

Valvert

See Vicomte de Valvert

Vicomte de Valvert

Valvert is the man de Guiche wishes Roxane to marry in the hopes of keeping her from Cyrano and Christian. Foppish and slightly dim-witted, he provokes Cyrano into a duel in the theater. Unable to come up with a witty retort against Cyrano's torrent of poetry, he enters into the fight. He is slain by Cyrano's sword with the line "the poem ended/ and I hit."

THEMES

Search for Self

Cyrano de Bergerac is a story about fear, beauty, loyalty, friendship, love, and difference. In Cyrano's search for his self—and the conflict between who he is and who he'd like to be—he manages to both gain friends and make enemies. He simultaneously challenges those around him while entertaining others. He must ultimately believe that it is possible for Roxane to love him, and to believe

TOPICS FOR FURTHER STUDY

- Research the life of Cardinal Richelieu (whose niece De Guiche is married to in the play) and explain how a knowledge of Richelieu's role in French history can expand a reader's understanding of De Guiche's character.

- Look in a historical source to discover what life was like in seventeenth-century France. Then, compare and contrast your findings with the presentation of French life in *Cyrano de Bergerac*.

- In the play, Cyrano and the Guards fight the Spanish at the seize of Arras. Investigate the causes and effects of this battle and explain why Rostand would use it in his play.

---

himself worthy of that love, before he can make peace with his enemies. Unfortunately, this realization comes too late for both of them, and he dies as Roxane declares her love for him.

Fear

Cyrano is afraid to declare his love for Roxane, his cousin, because he fears rejection and ridicule—he believes that a woman as beautiful as Roxane could never love a man who is not also physically beautiful. This fear drives him to succeed at swordsmanship, poetry, and scathing wit. He drives the actor Montfleury from the stage, and fights a duel with the Vicomte de Valvert with both his sword and his words. Cyrano fights not only against his foes, but against his own fear of rejection.

Beauty

There is much talk of beauty and and its counterpart ugliness in *Cyrano de Bergerac*. Cyrano believes himself too ugly to be loved by the beautiful Roxane (or any woman). Yet he fails to properly value the more elusive beauty that he possesses in his mind and heart. A beauty that can create his moving poetry and cause Roxane to swoon at his words. Ironically, it is Cyrano's

> This nose precedes me everywhere,/ A quarter of an hour in front, to say, 'Beware,/ Don't love Cyrano' to even the ugliest./ And now Cyrano has to love the best,/ The brightest, bravest, wittiest, the most/ Beautiful!''

Yet Cyrano fails to recognize the source of his own beauty, his heart and mind. With this beauty he creates moving poetry, summons words that cause Roxane to swoon, and rallies the spirits of starving, dejected soldiers.

There are numerous contrasts between beauty and its opposite in the play: with Christian it is his dashing outward appearance against his limited intelligence, with Cyrano it is the direct opposite. It is only when Roxane writes to Christian/Cyrano during the siege of Arras that the two men realize that words mean more to her than looks: "Your beauty is a barrier to you/If you were ugly . . ./ . . . I know I should/Be able to love you more." There lies the notion that Cyrano's beauty comes from within, and has more depth than Christian's. Roxane is in love with the words—Cyrano's words—and not Christian's handsome exterior. The sense that beauty comes from within, from the soul, rather than the body is strong. The play's tragedy comes from its protagonist's failure to recognize this earlier.

Loyalty

Even though aware that it was his words that won the heart of Roxane, Cyrano remains loyal to his friend Christian's memory after the latter's death during the siege of Arras. He does not take the opportunity to romantically pursue Roxane. Christian looks for death in battle rather than struggle on after he realizes that it is Cyrano's soul (his words and feelings) with which his wife is truly in love. Cyrano, still afraid of rejection, keeps this secret for fifteen years. Rather than tarnish the memories Roxane has of Christian, Cyrano remains loyal to his friend and keeps the secret. It is only when he is about to die that he feels that he can reveal to Roxane that it was *he* who wrote all of those letters and wooed her while she was on her balcony. Her declaration of love is what Cyrano wanted more than anything in the world, and he dies finally knowing it was his heart and soul that she truly loved.

Le Bret, Ragueneau, and Roxane are all very loyal to Cyrano. Despite being put into sometimes perilous situations by the poet-hero, they continue to offer support and friendship to him. Le Bret and Ragueneau are there until the end, trying to save him from his enemies, but it is too late. This kind of loyalty is fueled by deep friendship, and that is an important theme in Rostand's work. Those who are friends with Cyrano will defend him to the end.

Difference

Cyrano's markedly different appearance is what drives him and fuels his fear. It is his belief that Roxane could never love him that forges his alliance and friendship with Christian. It is also what drives his bravura and wit. Anyone who mentions his unusually large nose (as the unfortunate citizen in the theater in Act I) is open to attack. The only thing that saves Christian from such an attack in the pastry shop is the love of Roxane. Those who learn to look past the difference—Ligniere, Ragueneau, Le Bret, and eventually Christian and Roxane—realize that Cyrano's true beauty resides within. His difference is merely physical and does not touch his soul. Even the Comte de Guiche sees and understands the "true Cyrano" by the end: "He/Lives his life as he wants, he's one of those/Rare animals that have opted to be free/ . . . Nevertheless,/I think I'd be proud to shake him by the hand."

Freedom

In the end, it is Cyrano's freedom that finishes him. His refusal of the Foodseller's meal in the theater (Act I), de Guiche's offer of Richelieu's patronage at the pastry shop (Act II), and the aid of the Sisters at the convent (Act III): his wish to be free and independent eventually leads to his death. By believing that he cannot be loved, he wishes to be dependent on no one. This fierce thirst for freedom leads him to say and write things that make him many enemies; he is eventually killed because of his words—the words that, ironically, also mirror his inner beauty.

It was Rostand's triumph to create a character so full of bravura, wit, and cunning and yet be so

afraid to declare his love to his beloved. It is his difference that drives his fear, but it also drives his quest for freedom and independence. It is his love and friendship that drive his loyalty; yet it is love that he is afraid to declare. This complex character gives rise to a very simple situation. A love triangle that takes fifteen years to play out. *Cyrano de Bergerac* is about many things: fear of rejection; loyalty, love, and friendship; and freedom and independence. Through Cyrano, all of these themes are realized. Yet, at the end, when our hero dies, the overwhelming feeling is one of vindication: Cyrano triumphed, and, however briefly, knew he was loved.

STYLE

Cyrano de Bergerac is the tale of a man with an abnormally large nose who is in love with his beautiful cousin Roxane. She is, however, in love with the handsome soldier Christian. Cyrano's words work with Christian's good looks to woo Roxane, and it is only upon Cyrano's death that Roxane learns the words she loved so much were Cyrano's. As both poet and swordsman, Cyrano lives out his days independent and free, *"thumbing his nose"* at the conventions of the mid-1600s. The story is a very effective dramatic work, utilizing numerous techniques to convey the emotions and events of Cyrano's life.

Romanticism

Rostand idolized the writer Savinen de Cyrano de Bergerac (1619-1655) and, in creating a fictional account of his life, embellished on one of France's most colorful literary figures. The real de Bergerac was indeed both a soldier and a writer, but Rostand added one distinguishing element: a very large nose. While Cyrano's nose is first seen as a comic prop, his romantic heart and heroic stature quickly change that perception. Those familiar with the play see Cyrano's nose as a symbol of his undying love and devotion.

Cyrano de Bergerac falls very easily into the genre of Romanticism. That term is generally defined as "any work or philosophy in which the exotic or dreamlike figure strongly, or that is devoted to individualistic expression, self-analysis, or a pursuit of a higher realm of knowledge than can be discovered by human reason." Cyrano is, beyond anything else, an individual. From his first appearance in the theater to taunt Montfleury, Cyrano's larger than life personality mirrors his unusually large nose. This physical challenge makes Cyrano an exotic character, one who is more than mere man.

Character

By basing the character of Cyrano on a real historical figure, Rostand was able to use the most interesting aspects of the real de Bergerac and then embellish by adding details such as the incredibly large nose. Rostand created a character that took on a life of his own. Cyrano strives for perfection, both in poetry and in love. The other characters in the play are marvelously written, but it is Cyrano who twists and turns words into tirades and roller coasters. Rostand uses the real de Bergerac's life as a source for some of the verbal virtuosity. Cyrano's speech delaying de Guiche in his late-night meeting with Roxane is based on the real Cyrano's *Histoire comique des etats et empires de la lune et du soleil,* a comic exploration of the "States and Empires of the Moon and the Sun". It is however, the fictional Cyrano's "nose tirade" in Act I that serves to set the stage for his heroic endeavors. This is a man who refuses to lose and refuses to fail. Even in the end he triumphs as he dies. He wins the love of the beautiful Roxane by remaining true to his character.

Repartee

Cyrano engages in witty repartee many times during the play. Repartee is a "conversation featuring snappy retorts and witticisms" (see *DfS* glossary). The repartee between Cyrano and the citizen in the theater leads to the infamous "nose tirade" in which the man is humiliated by Cyrano's rapid fire wit. The comedy that results from this exchange and with his exchange with the Vicomte de Valvert later on in Act I is at the recipients' expense, but it serves to focus our attention on Cyrano and to make him a hero as he defeats his foes with means other than his sword.

Point of View

As with many dramas, *Cyrano de Bergerac* is told with a third person point of view. This presents characters and events from outside any single character, but with no special insights into the thoughts or actions of the characters. We see events from a "spectator" point of view, but we do not hear any of the characters thoughts and feelings other than what they tell each other. Shakespeare often relayed characters' thoughts and interior dialogues through a monologue called a soliloquy, which essentially allows a character to speak his mind out loud.

Rostand eschews this technique in favor of a straight dialogue method, one that places the burden of illustrating his character's feelings on the poetic words they speak to each other.

Heroic Comedy

G. K. Chesterton wrote in his book *Varied Types* that, "heroic comedy is, as it were, a paradise of lovers, in which it is not difficult to imagine that men could talk in poetry all day long." Rostand wrote *Cyrano de Bergerac* in Alexandrine verse: a rhymed verse used by French dramatists and poets. Anthony Burgess, in his English translation in 1971, turned it into Heroic couplets with a rhyming couplet scheme. By writing in verse, Rostand was consciously working against the naturalism and symbolism of his contemporaries Ibsen and Maeterlinck. For Rostand's heroic comedy, he uses poetry to convey the dreamlike, exotic quality of Romanticism. There is no equivalent to Heroic Comedy in English literature. In the English (and American) tradition, comedies should have a happy ending, yet Rostand's ends with the death of his hero. While the ending is sad and somewhat tragic, Cyrano does, in dying, gain his greatest wish: he is loved by the woman he has always worshipped.

HISTORICAL CONTEXT

Seventeenth Century: Thirty Years War

Rostand wrote *Cyrano de Bergerac* in the late 1890s but set it in the mid-1600s. While the late 1890s was a period of great industrial and technological advancement, the mid-1600s (the beginning of the reign of Louis XIV) was a time of political intrigue and artistic intellectualism. It is important to understand both periods to truly understand the effect on Rostand's Heroic Comedy.

France in the 1640s was still feeling the effects of the Thirty Years War (1618-1648). Fought mainly in Germany, the war saw the German Protestant Princes, France, Sweden, Denmark, and England fighting the Holy Roman Empire (including the Catholic Princes of Germany and the countries of Austria, Spain, Bohemia, and Italy). The war was fought primarily over trade, and control over the various trade routes to the east.

The war itself ended for most countries in 1648 with the Peace of Westphalia. Fighting went on between France and Spain, however, and in 1654 the Spanish laid siege to Arras in northwestern

COMPARE
&
CONTRAST

- **1600s:** The real Cyrano de Bergerac writes *Histoire comique des etats et empires de la lune et du soleil,* chronicling his "adventures" on the moon.

  1890s: The atom is discovered to be composed of a nucleus orbited by bodies called electrons. This discovery leads to the advent of space flight and the nuclear age.

  Today: The Space Shuttle makes routine visits to Earth orbit, and there is preparation for a future visit to Mars.

- **1640s:** The Thirty Years War comes to an end for most countries with the Peace of Westphalia, but France and Spain continue to fight over territory until the end of the seventeenth century.

  1890s: European countries continue to pursue colonization of the Third World in order to compete with each other for power. France deposes Queen Ranavalona of Madagascar, while Cuba demands independence from Spain.

  Today: The European Union continues to evolve, making France and Spain member states of a new federation.

- **1600s:** Great plays and books were discussed in the salons of Paris, among the aristocrats and nobles who could afford to spend their leisure time discussing and going to the theater. Most common people did not have this luxury.

  1890s: Through the availability of newspapers and magazines, critics all over the world discussed the great works at the turn of the century. Most people have some access to the arts.

  Today: People from all over the world and of all social classes can read and discuss art and literature over the internet. Information is more widely available than ever before, and it is accessible almost immediately.

- **1640s:** Society was organized into a strict class structure: aristocrats and nobles, the merchant middle-class, and the rural peasants and farmers who worked the land. A great majority of people went uneducated.

  1890s: The Industrial Revolution of the late 1800s drew more people into the cities to work in factories. Society becomes more urbanized, as people leave their jobs in the fields for work these new industries. More and more people are being educated, and there is new emphasis on staying in school.

  Today: The Technological Revolution is producing more and more office jobs as workers are being "downsized" and laid off from their factory positions. As society and industry becomes more mechanized there are fewer jobs for unskilled workers, and there is a great demand for those workers with a college education.

France. The real Cyrano de Bergerac fought in this siege, and Rostand uses this historical fact for the setting of Act II.

Seventeenth Century: Civil Unrest

French nobles, upset with the unreasonable taxation, high tarriffs, and road tolls engaged the aid of Spanish troops and staged a rebellion against Cardinal Mazarin in 1648. The Cardinal was running the government for the eight-year-old Louis XIV. The aristocracy allied with the rising middle class in France to put down the rebellion. The public was outraged that the nobles were allied with France's enemy Spain. The conflict provided the opportunity later on for Louis XIV to consolidate his power over France and become an absolute ruler.

Seventeenth Century: Literature

During the reign of Louis XIV (The Sun King), French literature, arts, and philosophy became the standard for all of Europe. The Academie Francaise, founded by Cardinal Richelieu in 1634, sought to protect the French language by guarding against slang and poor grammar in all art and literature. (Edmond Rostand would become its youngest member ever inducted in 1901.) With a strong monarchy, the French had more leisure time for artistic pursuits than ever before.

The audience for theater in the 1600s tended to be the small elite group of aristocrats who could afford to patronize the arts. The refined style of the time period reflected the lifestyle of the patrons, who could afford to ''keep'' artists in their circle. Writers were generally poor in the seventeenth century and persuaded nobles, landowners, and even Louis XIV to finance their works (an idea which has formed more organized roots in modern drama in the form of government subsidies and grants for the arts and the grants and fellowships awarded to artists by various private and public foundations). Authors often included extreme flattery of their patrons in their books. The real-life Cyrano de Bergerac was sickened by this flattery but eventually was forced to seek the patronage of the Duke of Arpajon. Rostand depicts de Bergerac's feelings in his play, having his fictional Cyrano state: ''Dedicate my works to men of wealth?/ Become a sedulous ape, a fool who waits/For some official's patronizing smile?/No, thank you, . . . I prefer to sing, to dream, to play/To travel light, to be at liberty.''

Seventeenth Century: Salons

Literary works in the seventeenth century were read and discussed in salons. These salons, or *ruelles* as they were called, were often hosted by a French noblewoman who entertained aristocrats, writers, and philosophers while sitting on her bed. Meeting in this situation brought a ''much needed refining influence on both the manners and language'' of the gentlemen in attendance, according to John Lough in his book *An Introduction to Seventeenth-Century France*. Madeleine Robineau, whom Rostand used as a model for Roxane, was an intellectual who was a fixture and frequent hostess of such events.

1890s: Politics

Rostand wrote *Cyrano de Bergerac* in the late 1890s. The year it debuted the French deposed Madagascar's Queen Ranavalona, ending the one hundred year Hova dynasty; a Franco-German agreement defined the boundary between Dahomey and Togoland; and Britain and France inched ever closer to a possible conflict over colonial territories. The United States annexed the Hawaiian Islands much to the dismay of the Japanese; who still had 25,000 nationals there. Also, England's Queen Victoria celebrated her Diamond Jubilee—seventy-five years of rule. Despite the threat of various conflicts, the world was at a time of relative peace.

1890s: Science

In 1897 English physicist Joseph John Thomson proved that an atom was made up of electrons orbiting a nucleus, and that each element had a different number of electrons, and a different weight. The discovery of the atom opened the door to numerous advances in science and, later in the twentieth century, made everything from space travel to nuclear power possible. The malaria parasite was found to be carried by the Amopheles mosquito—a discovery that would lead to the widespread use of insecticides and the draining of wetlands where the insects bred. Also in 1897, the cathode ray tube was invented; which would eventually lead to the development of television and wireless communication.

1890s: Literature

In literature and entertainment, the Library of Congress was completed in Washington D.C. in 1897. *The Invisible Man* by H. G. Wells, *Captains Courageous* by Rudyard Kipling, and *Dracula* by Bram Stoker were all published for the first time in 1897. Other plays that made their debut that year were *John Gabriel Borkman* by Henrik Ibsen, *The Devil's Disciple* by George Bernard Shaw, and *The Liars* by Henry Arthur Jones.

Edmond Rostand wrote *Cyrano de Bergerac* at a time when Naturalism was a major force in the literary world. His heroic comedy was a complete contrast to what most of his contemporaries were writing at the time. While Ibsen was focused on Naturalism and Maeterlinck on Symbolism, de Bergerac used the Romanticism of the 1640's to create a completely different theater experience for his audience. The 1890's was a time of great change in the world, a time of forged alliances, technological and industrial advances, and social, political, and artistic upheaval. By setting *Cyrano* in the seventeenth century and basing the hero on a real-life character, the playwright was free to explore a more exotic and romatic time. As Lionel Strachey wrote in a review of the play in *Lippincott's*, ''Rostand is the preeminent verbalist and sentimentalist of the French drama. He has the perennial talent of the right word in the right place, and that without prejudice to rhyme.'' Rostand's talent was to create a heroic character in Cyrano who transcends time.

CRITICAL OVERVIEW

When *Cyrano de Bergerac* made its debut at the Porte Sainte-Martin Theater in Paris in 1897, it was an instant success. This heroic comedy in Alexandrine verse had won over the sophisticated Parisian public and was on its way to becoming a modern classic. Though Edmond Rostand, the cast, and the producers (the Fleury brothers) were doubtful that the play would be a success, the audience fell in love with the poetry of the play and the beauty of the story. *Cyrano* is acclaimed as a dramatic masterpiece and is renowned for its unforgettable hero and romantic spirit. Though critics have at times labeled the play shallow, most praise its entertaining theatricality and its heroic protagonist who remains loyal to his ideals.

Cyrano *is* the poet turned hero. The verbal virtuosity of the play, from the ''nose tirade'' to Cyrano's admission to Roxane that he is the poet whom she loves, combined with the outbursts and action create a tour-de-force of a play. As William D. Howarth noted in *Reference Guide to French Literature:* ''Despite his extravagance, Cyrano is a human character with whom spectators (the audience) and readers find it by no means impossible to reach the necessary degree of sympathetic identification: not because we ourselves aspire to the same sort of heroics, but because he expresses a Romantic idealism, a nostalgia for absolute values, latent in us all.'' The spectator can relate to Cyrano's dilemma. The insecurities that lead Cyrano to hide his love from Roxane, and to use it to Christian's benefit, are qualities that all humans possess. Rostand's genius was to create a character who is so *human* that he is timeless. Max Beerbohm, writing in his *Around Theatres,* said of Cyrano:

> Cyrano will survive because he is practically a new type in drama. I know that the motives of self-sacrifice-in-love and beauty-adored-by-a-grotesque are as old, and as effective, as the hills, and have been used in literature again and again. I know that self-sacrifice is the motive of most successful plays. But, so far as I know, beauty-adored-by-a-grotesque has never been used with the grotesque as stage-hero. At any rate it has never been used so finely and so tenderly as by M. Rostand, whose hideous swashbuckler with the heart of gold and the talent for improvising witty or

beautiful verses . . . is far too novel, I think, and too convincing, and too attractive, not to be permanent.

As time has passed *Cyrano de Bergerac* has become a beloved play, a classic still performed today in theaters around the world. Critics have, however, found that Rostand as a writer was not a genius as much as a playwright who had a great real-life story to embellish. Beerbohm called Rostand ''a gifted, adroit artist, who does with freshness and great force things that have been done before. . . . It is rather silly to chide M. Rostand for creating a character and situations which are unreal if one examines them from a non-romantic standpoint.'' Beerbohm makes an excellent point: Cyrano must be seen as the *romantic hero* in this heroic-comedy drama. To try to view—or read—*Cyrano de Bergerac* realistically, is to miss the beauty of the play.

Heroic Comedy has no tradition in English Literature. G. K. Chesterton wrote in *Varied Types* that, in today's world, ''the hero has his place in tragedy, and the one kind of strength which is systematically denied to him is the strength to succeed.'' It seemed strange to some critics that a comedy should have a tragic ending. As Chesteron appraised, ''Monsieur Rostand showed even more than his usual insight when he called *Cyrano de Bergerac* a comedy, despite the fact that, strictly speaking, it ends with disappointment and death. The essence of tragedy is a spiritual breakdown or decline. . . . It is not the facts themselves, but our feeling about them, that makes tragedy and comedy, and death is more joyful in Rostand than life in Maeterlinck.''

Though Cyrano dies at the end, he dies loved by his beloved—the beautiful Roxane. It seems appropriate that the hero of a Heroic Comedy should die at the end. Dying for love is one of the most heroic acts a man can commit. Henry James, in the *Critic,* wrote of *Cyrano:* ''The tight-rope in Cyrano is, visibly enough, the question of the hero's facial misfortune, doubly great as opposed to his grand imagination, grand manners, and grand soul, the soul that leads his boisterous personality to run riot, for love and for friendship, in self-suppression, in sentimental suicide.'' As James states, it is the heroism and romanticism that saves *Cyrano de Bergerac* as a play and makes it a masterpiece. James goes on to say: ''I wouldn't, individually, part with an inch of Cyrano's nose. . . . The value of it in the plan, naturally, is that it is liberally symbolic. . . . Cyrano, for a romantic use, had not only to be sensitive, to be conscious, but to be magnificent and imperial; and the brilliancy of the creation of the author's expression of this.''

Writing in *Lippincott's,* Lionel Strachey sums up Rostand's writing ability this way: ''Edmond Rostand's genius is of the highest, but not the highest. . . . And however deeply our aesthetic sense is intoxicated, however we marvel at his nimble scholarship, into whatever ecstasy we go over his perfect expression of exquisite thoughts, our investigating, speculative, deductive, reasoning faculties remain untouched. Our splendid young Frenchman is, indeed, a great poet and little philosopher.'' In all of the criticism one point remains clear: though *Cyrano de Bergerac* has no real philosophical enlightenments, it is nonetheless a masterpiece. The character of Cyrano carries the play—his verbal virtuosity and faithful devotion to those he loved and cared for make him utterly unforgettable and absolutely timeless.

CRITICISM

Daniel Moran

Moran is an author and educator with extensive experience in secondary education. His essay examines Rostand's sharply defined title character and the nature of heroism.

In *As You Like It,* William Shakespeare offers the famous line, ''All the world's a stage,'' an idea that takes on a literal meaning in Rostand's *Cyrano de Bergerac,* his play featuring one of the most theatrical of characters ever created. In the foreword to his translation of the play, Anthony Burgess writes that while ''*Cyrano de Bergerac* may not be the best play ever written,'' its central figure ''is surely one of the great characters in all drama.'' What makes Cyrano such a remarkable and popular character is, primarily, his devotion to his own code of honor, despite the fact that his goals seem unattainable. When asked if he has ever read *Don Quixote,* Cyrano replies, ''I have—and found myself the hero.'' Like Quixote, Cyrano forever chases the ''windmill'' (or unattainable goal) of winning Roxane's heart, and the audience's fascination with this ''bravest soul alive'' resides in his steadfast commitment to this task. When asked if he has ''chosen any plans'' for himself, the flamboyant hero replies that he has decided upon ''The simplest—To make myself in all things admirable!'' How Cyrano struggles with his desire to be ''admi-

rable'' in all things, against his fear of being mocked for his large nose, is the focus of Rostand's ''heroic comedy,'' in which the viewer sees how he plays various roles on the ''stage'' of the world in order to produce what William Lyon Phelps called ''The Triumphant Failure'' in his text *Essays on Modern Dramatists.*

The play begins in the Hall of the Hotel de Bourgogne as various actors and patrons await the day's play. Appropriately subtitled ''A Performance'' by Rostand, the act raises all of the issues of the upcoming play and displays Cyrano (rather than any actor), as the true ''performer.'' First, however, the viewer learns that Ligniere, a friend of Christian, is to be attacked for writing a song that offended someone at court; in addition, Cyrano has commanded that Montfleury, a ''hippopotamus'' of an actor, be forbidden to perform. Clearly, the imaginary seventeenth-century world of *Cyrano de Bergerac,* is one in which art is taken very seriously, as seen later in Ragueneau's trading pastries for sonnets and his setting recipes to rhyme, as well as in the letters that Cyrano will eventually pen to Roxane (in Christian's name).

Cyrano's entrance, however, is when the play really begins, and it is in his entrance that Rostand reveals his hero's character and concerns. After chasing Montfleury off of the stage, Cyrano assumes the spotlight, managing to turn his worst defect into a ''theatrical'' asset. To put Cyrano ''in his place,'' Valvert attempts to insult him, saying, ''Your nose is . . . rather large!'' This lame jibe only proves to be a springboard for Cyrano's wit: he responds with a list of twenty things that Valvert *could* have said in twenty different styles, such as, ''DESCRIPTIVE: 'Tis a rock—a crag—a cape/ A cape? Say rather, a peninsula!'' and concludes his monologue with,

> These, my dear sir, are things you might have said
> Had you some tinge of letters, or of wit To color your
> discourse. But wit—not so, You never had an atom—
> and of letters, You need but three to write you
> down—an Ass.

Cyrano's catalogue of insults shows his own obsession with his ''peninsula,'' his love of language, and his contempt for the tiny minds that surround him. He is ''a soul clothed in armor,'' and his wit is the ''armor'' that defends his often-battered pride. When asked by Valvert to duel, Cyrano again ''performs,'' composing (and reciting) a four-stanza ballad the entire time; his mind and his sword are equally sharp, and his ''thrust-

WHAT DO I READ NEXT?

- Rostand's 1895 play *The Princess Far Away* is his play concerning Joffroy Rudel, a troubadour who travels to see the beautiful Countess of Tripoli before he dies, despite the fact that they have never met. Like Cyrano, Joffroy is an idealist who commits to a plan of action to realize his dream.

- *Chantecler,* Rostand's 1910 play, focuses on a barnyard rooster who, like his counterpart in Chaucer's *Canterbury Tales,* attempts to uphold his dignity among other "animals" of the world.

- Miguel de Cervantes's *Don Quixote* (1605, 1615) is the renowned novel that follows the adventures of an idealist who lashes out at a materialistic world by engaging himself in various chivalric (and delusionary) adventures. When asked if he has ever read *Don Quixote,* Cyrano replies, "I have — and found myself the hero."

---

ing'' at Valvert reflects the "thrusting" of his mind in the previous speech. Imbibing the admiration of the crowd as if it is champagne, Cyrano offers the theater manager a purse of gold in order to compensate for the business he has cost him for this day; when criticized by his friend (and the voice of rationality), LeBret, with, "what a fool," the swordsman rejoins, "but—what a gesture!" This idea, that "gestures" are as important as the day-to-day cares of the world (Cyrano has just given away his month's salary) resurfaces again and again in the play, with Cyrano constantly making "gestures" in which he displays (albeit without her knowledge) his love for Roxane. He displays what Rostand himself described as true "panache": "not greatness . . . but something which . . . stirs above it . . . the spirit of gallantry."

As he leaves the theater to fight the hundred men awaiting Ligniere, he cries, "I want an audience," and as the characters excitedly follow him, Rostand suggests that his play will be one in which various "actors" (such as Cyrano and Christian) perform for an "audience" (Roxane) whose applause they both crave and esteem.

Despite Cyrano's bravado, he does harbor great insecurities about his desire for Roxane. Before he faces (and defeats) his hundred opponents, he tells LeBret that he is afraid to speak to her because "she might laugh," and this "is the one thing in the world" that he fears. Act Two serves as a way for

Rostand to accentuate this fear and intensify the portrait of Cyrano's pride created in Act One. When told by Roxane that she loves a man who "loves me too,/And is afraid of me, and keeps away,/And never says one word," Cyrano (who can always produce a needed remark) can only respond with gasps. When she continues to describe the object of her affections, however, as "beautiful," Cyrano knows that, whoever her love may be, it is not himself. His disappointment grows as he explains to LeBret the reasons for his flamboyance and "growling": "What would you have me do. . .? Eat a toad/ For breakfast every morning. . .? Wear out my belly groveling in the dust?" Rather than live in fear of "the common herd," Cyrano explains that he "is too proud to be a parasite"; thus he will not allow De Guiche to alter "one comma" in his tragedy and is even more committed to a life where he will "stand, not high it may be—but alone!"

Cyrano's problem with Roxane now seems hopeless; however, the plan he hatches with Christian allows him to avoid humility while still proclaiming his love from afar. Their meeting is one in which Rostand invites the viewer to recognize how the deficiencies in each can be filled by the other: when Christian points at his heart and says, "Oh, if I had words/To say what I have here," Cyrano laments, "If I could be/A handsome little Musketeer with eyes!" Their scheme is one in which these deficiencies are combined and "canceled out," for together, Cyrano's mind plus Christian's beauty

---

equals the perfect man. Cyrano tells Christian to "borrow" his wit and asks him, "your beautiful young manhood—lend me that." Together, as a unified force in the battle for Roxane's love, these two will "make one hero of romance!" While Cyrano earlier remarks that he will "render no share to Caesar," that is, not allow anyone else to take credit for his actions, he freely offers his wit (and pen) to Christian, illustrating the play's theme of sacrifice for a higher cause—which reaches its height, of course, when Christian dies and Cyrano does not admit to Roxane (until fifteen years have passed) that it was he who had provided Christian with the words and feelings with which Roxane fell in love.

While such a plan is appealing to Cyrano both practically and aesthetically, Act Three shows the strains of the ruse on the swordsman's noble heart. In an effort to further enrapture Roxane, Cyrano poses as Christian under her balcony, recalling the famous scene from Shakespeare's *Romeo and Juliet*. However, Cyrano is delegated to the role of a "mock-Romeo," duplicating only the Italian hero's emotion and not his rewards. The dramatic irony grows almost oppressive, when phrases like, "My heart/Hides behind phrases," and "It is my voice, mine, my own/That makes you tremble" brings Cyrano closer to Roxane but not vice-versa. After Christian climbs the trellis to receive Roxane's kiss, Cyrano is left alone, resembling Hamlet more than Romeo: "I have won what I have won—/The feast of love—and I am Lazarus!" This Biblical allusion to Lazarus, the beggar who starved at the gate of a rich man who feasted every day, pinpoints Cyrano's anguish and serves as another reminder of the "performance" theme mentioned earlier: Cyrano writes the script, directs the scene, and plays the role—but Christian receives the applause in the form of Roxane's kiss. Earlier in the Act, we learn that Cyrano has won (in a wager) two pages, whom he commands to play "sad" tunes for a man and "merry" ones for a woman. While this music obviously suits Cyrano (sad) and Roxane (merry), there is a second layer of meaning within them: in his ironic position as Roxane's secret admirer and Christian's successful go-between, both tunes apply equally to himself.

In Act Four, the action moves from a domestic to a military setting where Cyrano fights for love and honor more than any political cause. When all of the soldiers complain of their hunger, Cyrano sings to them a song which makes them weep as it

reminds them of their native Gascoyne; his explanation that the men weep "for homesickness—a hunger/More noble than that of hunger of the flesh" raises the issue of the nobility of the spirit when contrasted with that of the body. While this theme has sustained the entire plot, it is emphasized here in several ways. First, we learn that Cyrano has been risking his life "every morning before breakfast" to cross the Spanish lines and deliver one of "Christian's" letters to Roxane. Second, Roxane arrives at the front in order to beg Christian's forgiveness, "for being light and vain" and loving him, as she says, "only because you were beautiful." She, too, has learned the important difference between appearance and reality, between the spirit and the flesh—but, of course, the basis of her knowledge is a falsehood and an even greater example of this difference (Cyrano himself) lies directly in front of her, although she cannot recognize it as such. Christian, like Cyrano before him, now finds himself in an ironic position: feeling guilty about his charade, he urges Cyrano to confess to Roxane. "I am tired of being my own rival," he explains, realizing what Cyrano (and the audience) has known all along about the nobility of the swordsman's heart. However, when Christian dies moments before Cyrano can reveal his true self to Roxane, he forsakes the chance to tell her, highlighting once again his panache in sacrificing his own happiness for hers. He is, essentially, continuing the performance he began when he wrote her his first letter so that Roxane may have the happy memory of Christian as her one true love.

When Act Five begins, the audience learns that Cyrano's nobility has not faded over time: for fifteen years he has visited Roxane (now in a convent) every Saturday, never revealing Christian's secret. LeBret and Ragueneau, however, inform the audience that Cyrano has become embittered, writing satires that attack "the false nobles, the false saints,/The false heroes" and "the false artists." This change can be accounted for by recalling Act Four: nobody knows more than Cyrano what it really means to be "true," and so he attacks hypocrisy in all its forms. The Act is haunted by death: it is autumn, leaves are dying and the sun is setting—and De Guiche informs the others that he heard a rumor at court that "Cyrano may die—accidentally." The world hates a true and noble soul, an idea emphasized when Cyrano later compares himself to Socrates and Galileo. Like Homer's Penelope, Roxane weaves her embroidery—and again like Penelope (although she does not realize this herself), she is awaiting the return of her love, at war not with the Trojans but with the false and ignoble world.

Cyrano's arrival augments the sense of death that pervades the Act and he speaks of "A very old acquaintance" that he dismissed for only an hour so that he could visit the convent; this "most unexpected" visitor is Death himself, and Cyrano's struggle for life is only successful because of the strength of his love for Roxane. She, too, finds herself swept into the tangles of irony that Cyrano and Christian faced earlier: upon discovering that Cyrano wrote all the letters and loved her all the while, she returns his love, saying, "I never loved but one man in my life,/And I have lost him—twice." All of the play's issues now come rushing to the surface for a final examination. For example, when LeBret tells Cyrano that his scene was used by Moliere and that the audience "laughed—and laughed," Cyrano responds, "yes—that has been my life": as before at the balcony, he has seen others take credit for the depth of his mind and soul. The spirit vs. flesh idea is raised again (for the last time) when Cyrano draws his sword to face Death: at the siege of Arras, he expressed his wish to die "by the sword,/The point of honor—by the hand of one/Worthy to be my foeman," but now he is slowly fading out of his life due to a log that someone deliberately let fall onto his head from a window. Clearly, this is *not* the noble and valorous death that the swordsman had envisioned for himself. However, despite this seeming ignominy, Cyrano is allowed to end his performance before his death, saying that he wishes to now die like a leaf, for "they go down gracefully." Struggling, he swings his sword at Death, remarking that although such a fight seems "hopeless," it is "better to know one fights in vain," as he did throughout the play for Roxane's love. The triumph of this French Don Quixote is his refusal to compromise his ideals or spirit for the "falling logs" and "hopeless" battles of the plain and unromantic world. Offering Roxane his white plume, he dies even more spiritually rich than he lived; since he lived the life of the most exaggerated, "admirable" and noble swordsman in French theater, this is no small achievement.

Source: Daniel Moran, in an essay for *Drama for Students,* Gale, 1997.

Poet Lore

In the following essay, an anonymous critic focuses on the irony in Cyrano de Bergerac, *arguing that Rostand intended the play to be a satire, and not, as it was being hailed, as a serious drama.*

I suspect, nay, I believe, that nothing could be aesthetically funnier than [M. Rostand's *Cyrano de Bergerac*] . . . is, save the sentiment, *au grand serieux,* that has been lavished upon it as if it were a real drama instead of a satirical extravaganza. (p. 118)

The rollicking hyperbole, the color far too high for reality with which M. Rostand has heightened the effectiveness of all [the] historic part of his material is alone enough to release him from the imputation of having himself taken his Cyrano as seriously as his public has. He has employed his historic sense in the rehabilitation of seventeenth century Paris; but neither merely as a savant nor merely as a poet, nor even as a dextrous playwright, but rather as all three combined, plus the most important factor of all in the work—namely, as a satirist, has he permeated the whole story with irony. This irony peeping out in his clever manipulation of the historical part of his framework is revealed in all its poignant intentionalness in the invented parts. (p. 119)

It is precisely in these invented parts, which are absolutely unsuited to the seventeenth century character of the real Cyrano, of course, that the design of the playwright can be unquestionably traced. In the balcony scene the sentimentality of the artificial lover of the old school and the exacting whims of a *precieuse* are exquisitely ridiculed. The poses of antiquated romance are recalled to mind and they are re-staged here so as to lay bare before the modern eye their archaic quality. The irony is developed to the point of rendering this lapsed sentimentality not merely comical but at times almost farcical—the levity of the treatment, despite a cleverly contrasting instant or two when Cyrano betrays his own earnestness, being at the opposite pole from the impassioned seriousness of the Shakespearian scene it recalls. To break the fair unity of such a love-passage as the balcony scene in 'Romeo and Juliet,' to cut in two the physical beauty of the youth in Romeo, and the spiritual beauty lent his speeches by the ripe poet, and to personify each of these, is virtually what the French poet has done. He has made of the one half, Christian, the clumsy-tongued, fair and lusty animal, and of the other half, Cyrano, ugly, but mature of phrase if not of mind. Still, further, he has made a Juliet of the Hotel Rambouillet, a *precieuse* enamored not of the artist but of art, hankering rather for the wit which love incites than for love itself. The humor this situation involves is tickling to the last degree. Shall we spoil the comedy by taking it in dead earnest? When Christian utters his bald "I love you!" and on encouragement can but reiterate this trite simplicity, and Roxane, with closed eyes, expecting thrills from the rhapsody that halts, cries out impatiently, "That is the subject, work it up, work it up!" and when she bursts scornfully upon his stammering attempts with her, "Oh! Do labyrinthinize your feelings!" are we not to laugh? Again, when Cyrano, acting as Christian's proxy, pours out his dextrously be-rhymed emotions too successfully, till Roxane, mollified, deceived, makes the proposition to descend to him or for him to ascend to her, and throws him into a panic lest she behold him and his nose, are we not to laugh? And when he is made to ask for a kiss, thanks to Christian's crude desires, interjected in the cooing duet with an unpoetical rushing to the point that again almost threatens to unmask them both and spoil their game, so that Cyrano is forced to ward it off in vain, with outrageous quirks and conceits about a kiss being the rosy dot on the *i* of the verb *aimer,* are we to take this petty prettiness, ... are we to take this burlesque as poetry meant to be genuinely admired? And, finally, when all these fopperies of verse have frittered themselves out to the purpose both of deterring and goading the deluded Roxane till she bids her gallant up to her to take the kiss she never would have given either one of the precious pair without the assistance of the other, and when the acute Cyrano is made to urge the obtuse Christian to climb up, with his "Get up, get up, animal!" are we to believe that the playwright did not choose this most appropriate epithet with malice prepense? In a word, is it really meant that we should be so naive as to take such double-edged fooling as all this for unvarnished tenderness and fresh-born romance?

If so, and this spectacle-bouffe, circling about a nose as its sole dramatic *raison d' etre,* is to be shorn of its irony, it will be left bare of any literary distinction worth mentioning. If it is to be considered as a serious dramatic or poetic work, it must be perceived that its structure is of the slightest and most casual. It has neither motive, progression nor climax, and but little of the most elementary surprise of situation—the general effect being rather that of light opera than of actual comedy. Its acts are not acts, but a succession of well-chosen, effective, spectacular stage-settings loosely incorporating a string of incidents linked together in the most external way. Its characters are not characters having any inherent individuality or capacity for development,

"*CYRANO DE BERGERAC*
MAKES NO PRETENSION TO HIGH
ART, BUT RATHER TO ART SEMI-
CYNICAL*"

or any relationships with one another save of the most accidental sort. Its poetry, as to either imagery or emotional power, is only far-fetched and superficial .... If, on the other hand, it makes no pretension to high art, but rather to art semi-cynical, all these defects as to depth become effective; on that lower plane its buffoonery gains sparkle and significance. (pp. 120–22)

[Instead] of being hailed as this play has been by certain old-fashioned critics as a palpable evidence of the departure of what they call, with reproach, modern "Realism" and the rebirth of the good old "Romanticism" to smother the world in cakes and ale, and crowd out all new aesthetic forces forever, it is rather a token of the shutting of the door of modem life upon a certain phase of Romanticism, as henceforth impossible to be enjoyed quite in the old-world mood or without the assistance of a cultured historic sense—such a sign of the natural close of an epoch in literature and life as 'Don Quixote' was of the close of the epoch of the dominance of chivalry in life and in literature. (p. 123)

Source: "*Cyrano de Bergerac:* What It Is and Is Not," in *Poet Lore,* Vol. XI, No. 1, Winter, 1899, pp. 118–24.

Max Beerbohm

In the following essay, which originally appeared in 1898, Beerbohm predicts that Cyrano will be regarded as one of the most noted romantic heroes of all time, asserting that "Cyrano will survive because he is practically a new type in drama."

M. Rostand is not a great original genius like (for example) M. Maeterlinck. He comes to us with no marvelous revelation, but he is a gifted, adroit artist, who does with freshness and great force things that have been done before; and he is, at least, a monstrous fine fellow. His literary instinct is almost as remarkable as his instinct for the *technique*—the

> CYRANO IS, IN FACT, AS INEVITABLY A FIXTURE IN ROMANCE AS DON QUIXOTE OR DON JUAN, PUNCH OR PIERROT"

pyrotechnique—of the theatre, insomuch that I can read *Cyrano* almost as often, with almost as much pleasure, as I could see it played. . . . It is rather silly to chide M. Rostand for creating a character and situations which are unreal if one examines them from a non-romantic standpoint. It is silly to insist, as one or two critics have insisted, that Cyrano was a fool and a blackguard, in that he entrapped the lady of his heart into marriage with a vapid impostor. The important and obvious point is that Cyrano, as created by M. Rostand, is a splendid hero of romance. If you have any sensibility to romance, you admire him so immensely as to be sure that whatever he may have done was for the best. All the characters and all the incidents in the play have been devised for the glorification of Cyrano, and are but, as who should say, so many rays of limelight converging upon him alone. And that is as it should be. The romantic play which survives the pressure of time is always that which contains some one central figure, to which everything is subordinate— a one-part play, in other words. . . . Cyrano is, in fact, as inevitably a fixture in romance as Don Quixote or Don Juan, Punch or Pierrot. Like them, he will never be out of date. But prophecy is dangerous? Of course it is. That is the whole secret of its fascination. Besides, I have a certain amount of reason in prophesying on this point. Realistic figures perish necessarily with the generation in which they were created, and their place is taken by figures typical of the generation which supervenes. But romantic figures belong to no period, and time does not dissolve them. . . . Cyrano will survive because he is practically a new type in drama. I know that the motives of self-sacrifice-in-love and of beauty-adored-by-a-grotesque are as old, and as effective, as the hills, and have been used in literature again and again. I know that self-sacrifice is the motive of most successful plays. But, so far as I know, beauty-adored-by-a-grotesque has never been used with the grotesque as stage-hero. At any rate it has never been used so finely and so tenderly

as by M. Rostand, whose hideous swashbuckler with the heart of gold and the talent for improvising witty or beautiful verses . . . is far too novel, I think, and too convincing, and too attractive, not to be permanent. (pp. 5–6)

Source: Max Beerbohm, ''*Cyrano de Bergerac*'' (1898) in his *Around Theatres,* Rupert Hart-Davis, 1953, pp. 4–7.

FURTHER READING

Burgess, Anthony. Preface to *Cyrano de Bergerac,* by Edmond Rostand, translation by Burgess, Knopf, 1971, pp. v-xiv.
While much of this essay is an explanation of Burgess's methods as a translator, he does offer some valuable insight into the issues of Rostand's play.

Chesterton, G. K. ''Rostand'' in his *Varied Types,* Dodd, Mead, and Company, 1903, pp. 73-82.
An excerpt from Chesterton's book that characterizes Rostand's work, focusing in particular on *Cyrano de Bergerac* and *L'Aiglon* and their status as heroic comedies.

Phelps, William Lyon. ''Edmond Rostand'' in his *Essays on Modern Dramatists,* Macmillan, 1921, pp. 229-78.
An overview of Rostand's career which traces the theme of the ''Triumphant Failure'' in several of his plays. This is a good source for information about Rostand's thematic concerns.

Spiers, A. G. H., ''Rostand As Idealist'' in *Columbia University Quarterly,* Vol. XX, No. 2, April, 1918, pp. 155-69.
Spiers discusses how several of Rostand's characters (including Cyrano) attempt to fulfill their idealistic goals despite the obstacles with which they are faced. The essay features several passages from Rostand's plays as well as his definition of ''panache.''

SOURCES

Beerbom, Max. ''Cyrano de Bergerac'' in his *Around Theatres,* revised edition, Rupert Hart-Davis, 1953, pp. 4-7.

Howarth, William D. ''Cyrano de Bergerac'' in *Reference Guide to French Literature,* St. Jame's Press, 1992, pp. 165-66.

James, Henry. ''Edmond Rostand'' in the *Critic,* Vol. 29, no. 5, November, 1901, pp. 437-50.

Lough, John. *An Introduction to Seventeenth-Century France,* Longmans, 1960, p. 228.

Strachey, Lionel. Review of *Cyrano de Bergerac* in *Lippincott's,* February, 1899, pp. 264-69.

Death of a Salesman

ARTHUR MILLER

1949

Arthur Miller's *Death of a Salesman* is considered by many to be both the playwright's masterpiece and a cornerstone of contemporary American drama. Subtitled *Certain Private Conversations in Two Acts and a Requiem,* the play was first produced in 1949 and struck an immediate, emotional chord with audiences. The work garnered numerous honors and awards, including the Pulitzer Prize and the New York Drama Critics Circle Award and enjoyed a lengthy run (742 performances) on Broadway. In the decades following its premiere, *Death of Salesman* has become one of the most performed and adapted plays in American theatrical history. Much of this success is attributed to Miller's facility in portraying the universal hopes and fears of middle-class America. Through his main character, Willy Loman, Miller examines the myth of the American Dream and the shallow promise of happiness through material wealth. He uses Willy as an example of how undivided faith in such a dream can often yield tragic results, especially when it goes largely unfulfilled. Audiences have continued to respond to this theme because, in some incarnation, the American Dream has persisted; a viewer can watch *Death of a Salesman* and relate Willy's situation to their own compromised ideals and missed opportunities. More than a cautionary tale, however, Miller's work is also revered for its bold realism and riveting theatricality, a play that deals in weighty emotional issues without descending to melodrama.

AUTHOR BIOGRAPHY

Miller was born in Manhattan, New York, on October 17, 1915. His parents were Jewish immigrants who had come to America in search of prosperity. His father, Isadore, ran a successful garment business for a number of years, while his mother, Augusta, was a schoolteacher. Following the failure of his father's business in 1928, Miller's family moved to Brooklyn, which would serve as the setting for a number of his plays, including *Death of a Salesman.* His father's failure and subsequent withdrawal from the world of business had a profound effect on the young Miller, one that has direct roots in the character of Willy Loman. By the time Miller reached young adulthood, America was in the midst of the Great Depression. He saw firsthand how once-wealthy neighbors were reduced to poverty and the humiliation of menial labor or outright panhandling. Much of the playwright's cynicism regarding wealth and conspicuous consumption can be attributed to his experiences during these years.

Miller followed his high school graduation with two years of work in the hopes of earning enough money to attend college. In 1934 he was admitted to the University of Michigan. His time in college nurtured both his writing skills and his interest in liberal social causes. He studied playwriting under Kenneth Rowe and was twice awarded the Avery Hopwood Award for playwriting. In 1938, the year of his graduation, he won the Theater Guild National Award for his play *They Too Arise;* like many of his early plays, the work features youthful idealogues fighting against social inequity. Following his graduation, Miller returned to New York and began a series of jobs involving playwriting. Near the onset of World War II, he began writing radio scripts for such anthology programs as *The Calvalcade of America* and *The Columbia Workshop.*

During the war, Miller worked on a screenplay for the film *The Story of GI Joe,* a work he envisioned as a realistic portrayal of the average combat soldier. His efforts were overruled by film studio executives, however, who wanted a more palatable, romanticized story to sell the American public. Miller's hunger for realism in drama was not dimmed, however, and he sought out a forum for his art. Unfortunately, the Broadway stage of 1944 would not offer such a forum: Miller's debut with *The Man Who Had All the Luck,* a tale of a man unhappily trapped in his world of wealth, was a failure. Three years later, however, he achieved success on Broad-

way with *All My Sons.* In 1949 he presented *Death of a Salesman,* the work that established him as a major force in American theatre.

Miller's work in subsequent years continued his interest in current events and social injustice, with works such as *The Crucible* (1953) furthering his reputation. By the mid-1950s, however, Miller's personal life began to overshadow his professional. His marriage to film star Marilyn Monroe swept him into a life of celebrity that all but eclipsed his work as a playwright. After his divorce from Monroe, and a lengthy hiatus, he returned to his craft. Not content to rest on the laurels of his past, Miller continued to experiment with forms of drama, crafting a variety of works throughout the 1970s and 1980s. In 1996, at the age of eighty-one, he adapted *The Crucible* for a filmed adaptation starring Daniel Day-Lewis and Winona Ryder.

PLOT SUMMARY

Act I

Death of a Salesman opens with Willy Loman returning to his New York home during the night. Hearing him enter, Linda, his wife, is concerned and gets out of bed to greet him. Although Willy had been on his way to Boston, he reveals that he had made it only to Yonkers before he had decided to return home. During this conversation, the audience discovers that Willy has had several automobile accidents recently and that he seems to be emotionally unstable. Willy and Linda begin arguing about one of their sons, Biff, who has recently returned to New York from the West. Throughout this conversation (as throughout many others), Willy contradicts himself, especially regarding Biff's character.

Upstairs, Biff and his brother, Happy, who are spending the night at their parents' house, wake up and strain to hear the conversation. They reminisce about their childhood and discuss the tensions that have developed between Biff and Willy. Although Biff and Happy are in their thirties, they frequently act much younger—and are treated by their parents as if they are younger. Happy is clearly a womanizer, while Biff is frustrated at his lack of professional success and the conflicts he feels between his own desires and the desires his father has for him. Both men discuss their dissatisfactions with their lives and speculate about their options, though they can't seem to commit to any change. Happy attempts to persuade Biff to move back to New York permanently, especially after they overhear Willy talking loudly to himself. He suggests that Biff visit a man he once worked for, Bill Oliver, and ask for another job.

Much of the action in the play occurs as flashbacks, with Willy responding to the past as if it were the present. Now, Willy remembers buying a much younger Biff and Happy a punching bag; Biff is playing with a football he had stolen from his school. Willy begins bragging about how well-known and well-liked he is in the East coast towns he travels through as a salesman. He makes similar statements frequently throughout the play, though his financial situation belies the success he claims. Within this flashback, Bernard, a cousin of Biff and Happy, enters and urges Biff to come study his math. Biff, a senior in high school at this point, is in danger of failing the course, hence failing to graduate, which would prevent him from accepting an athletic scholarship at the University of Virginia. According to Willy, however, Bernard is the one who will fail at life because he is not popular—a prophecy which will be clearly disproved by the end of the play.

Willy and Linda begin to discuss their financial problems, which have increased because the firm that has employed Willy for decades has taken him off salary and put him entirely on commission. At this point, Willy remembers a woman, apparently a clerk in one of the companies he visits but whose significance will become clear only much later in the play. Willy refers to his Uncle Ben, who ''knew what he wanted and went out and got it,'' who, in other words, became rich.

Linda reveals their financial difficulties to her sons, but when they criticize Willy's firm, Linda claims Biff and Happy are equally neglectful. Linda also reveals that Willy has been trying to kill himself, that his frequent automobile accidents seem to have been intentional, and that she has found a rubber tube near their gas water heater. She suspects that Willy will use the tube to asphyxiate himself with gas.

When Biff tells Willy that he is going to visit his former employer, Bill Oliver, Willy encourages him to ask to borrow $15,000. Simultaneously, he criticizes Biff for lacking a professional or manly demeanor. Happy encourages Biff to get his ''old confidence'' back, though he seems to have lost it years ago, if he ever had it. The Act ends with Linda

Arthur Miller

pleading with Willy to ask for a position that would not require him to travel.

Act II

This Act occurs the following day. At breakfast, Linda assures Willy that Biff had left in a good mood, confident that Bill Oliver will respond to him favorably. She also says that their sons want Willy to meet them for dinner.

Willy talks to his boss, Howard, asking him for a position in New York rather than on the road. Howard declines, claiming to have no position available. Willy begins shouting, citing his early success which exasperates Howard, probably because Willy exaggerates his earlier abilities. By the end of the conversation, Howard has fired Willy entirely. At this point, another flashback occurs, the day of Biff's big high school football game in Ebbets Field. When time shifts back to the present, Willy enters his brother Charley's office. He speaks with Bernard, who has grown into a successful and responsible man. Bernard asks what actually happened to Biff after high school, when he failed math and refused to make the course up over the summer. Willy becomes defensive and loud. As he frequently has, Charley offers Willy a job, but Willy is too proud to accept. Although he is disgusted, Charley continues to lend Willy money.

The scene shifts to the restaurant, where Happy is waiting for Biff and his father. Happy attempts to pick up a woman he assumes is a prostitute. When Biff arrives, he reveals that he had failed with Bill Oliver, who kept him waiting all day and didn't even remember him. Although Biff attempts to have a frank conversation with Willy, both Happy and Willy subvert this effort, cooperating instead with the family's desire to ignore the truth in favor of a mythologized past. Within this conversation, another crucial flashback occurs. When Biff had failed math, he had gone to Boston to persuade Willy to intervene with the teacher. Instead, he discovered Willy in a hotel with another woman and became profoundly disillusioned with both Willy and his own life's possibilities. It was after this discovery, apparently, that Biff refused to attend summer school and hence relinquished his opportunity for an athletic scholarship and a college education.

Biff and Happy leave Willy in the restaurant in order to accompany the prostitute Happy had met earlier. The next morning, Linda asks them both to leave. Willy has clearly become more unstable and thinks more overtly of suicide. The Act ends with Willy speeding off in his car.

Requiem

The last moments of the play occur after Willy's funeral, which has not been well-attended. Biff indicates that he will return to the West, while Happy will remain in business in New York. The play concludes with Linda at Willy's grave, uttering the ironic remark that because their house is finally paid for (with Willy's insurance money), they are now "free."

CHARACTERS

Bernard

Bernard is the son of Charley, Willy's only friend and supporter outside of his family. As a young man he is quiet, dependable, pensive, and a top student; as an adult Bernard remains sensitive and genuine, and displays the intelligence, self-confidence, and perception that have helped him become a successful attorney. Bernard contrasts sharply with Biff and Happy, in a sense serving as the embodiment of the success to which they always aspired but never achieved. When Charley informs Willy that Bernard is going to argue a case before the Supreme Court, Willy communicates that he is impressed, and says "The Supreme Court! And he didn't even mention it." In a line which sharply indicts Willy's habit of chattering endlessly about his own false accomplishments and his dreams, Charley replies, "He don't have to—he's gonna do it."

Charley

Charley is Willy's only friend, and eventually he becomes Willy's sole financial support, "loaning" him fifty dollars a week knowing all the while that his money will never be repaid. Charley is a successful businessman, and is exasperated by Willy's lack of respect for him and his ideals, and by Willy's inability to separate reality and fantasy. Charley tries in vain to dispel Willy's delusions and attempts to save him from financial ruin by offering him a job, and when Willy refuses his offer, Charley exclaims, "You been jealous of me all your life, you damned fool!" When Willy conveys to Charley his disbelief that Howard Wagner has failed to display the gratitude that Willy feels he deserves and has fired him, Charley asks: "Willy, when're you gonna realize that them things don't mean anything? You named him Howard, but you can't sell that. The only thing you got in this world is what you can sell. And the funny thing is that you're a salesman, and you don't know that." Despite his continued arguments with Willy, and despite the feelings of frustration and exasperation Willy arouses in him, Charley cares about his friend and offers him compassion and support.

Miss Forsythe

Miss Forsythe is approached by Happy in the restaurant, and calls her friend, Letta, to come and be a companion for Biff. She is an attractive and sexy woman who conveys the impression that she is highly available.

Miss Francis

See The Woman

Jenny

Jenny is Howard's secretary, and is presented as an efficient, business-like, capable woman who

John Malkovich as Biff and Dustin Hoffman as Willy in the 1985 television adaptation

is annoyed by Willy and considers him a nuisance. Her attitude toward Willy stands in sharp contrast to Linda's admiration of Willy.

Letta

Letta is a friend of Miss Forsythe, and comes to the restaurant to meet Biff after Miss Forsythe calls her. She is a sugary, bubbly young woman, who gives the impression that she has limited intelligence and is extremely available.

Ben Loman

Ben is Willy's older brother, and is, to Willy, the embodiment of true success. He appears in scenes which take place in Willy's imagination, and appears larger-than-life, all-knowing, powerful, a great adventurer; he is everything Willy dreams of becoming. In the play, Ben's primary role is to serve as a sounding board for Willy; Willy conducts imaginary conversations with his brother, who owns timberlands in Alaska and diamond mines in Africa, and it is through these conversations that the audience gains a better understanding of what drives Willy and of his inner thoughts. Ben also represents for Willy the kind of life he dreams of for his sons.

Ben remarks: "William, when I walked into the jungle, I was seventeen. When I walked out I was twenty-one. And, by God, I was rich!" Willy, excited by his brother's stories of adventure, responds enthusiastically: "That's just the spirit I want to imbue them [Biff and Happy] with! To walk into a jungle!"

Biff Loman

Biff is Willy's eldest son; once a high school football idol, he has grown into a man who, in his mid-thirties, displays only a small measure of his youthful confidence, enthusiasm, and affection, and more often appears as a troubled, frustrated, deeply sad man with a tendency to escape into dreams at times. Biff was betrayed by his father at a very young age when he discovered that Willy was having an affair. Biff, who steals things as an adult, blames his father for not giving him the proper guidance when he was caught stealing as a child. Biff also blames his father for instilling in him the belief that success lies in the accumulation of wealth; it is because his father programmed him to think this way, Biff believes, that he is so unhappy and cannot enjoy doing the outdoor labor for which he has a talent. Biff is tortured by his disillusionment with

MEDIA ADAPTATIONS

- *Death of a Salesman* was adapted as a film in 1952. This version was produced by Stanley Kramer and directed by Laslo Benedek. It starred Fredric March as Willy, Mildred Dunnock as Linda, Kevin McCarthy as Biff, and Cameron Mitchell as Happy.

- A made-for-television version was filmed in 1966. Lee J. Cobb plays Willy; David Susskind was the producer.

- A made-for-television version was also filmed in 1986. It stars Dustin Hoffman as Willy and John Malkovich as Biff. It is available through Video Learning Library, Facets Multimedia, and Warner Home Video.

- A documentary, *Private Conversations on the Set of Death of a Salesman,* was also produced based on the 1986 version with Hoffman. Arthur Miller is featured as well as the actors. It is available from Karl-Lorimar Home Video.

- A sound recording of the play was also produced by Decca in 1950.

- Another sound recording is available from Caedmon, which was produced from the 1966 television version with Lee J. Cobb.

Willy, by his failure to live up to his own standards, by his failure to achieve the greatness that Willy dreamed he would, by his desire to get back at his father for what he believes has been done to him, and by his great love for Willy, which creates in him tremendous confusion and emotional turmoil. Biff ultimately decides to try to show Willy that his dreams and fantasies are false, telling his father: "You were never anything but a hard-working drummer who landed in the ash can like all the rest of them! . . . I'm nothing, Pop. Can't you understand that? There's no spite in it any more. I'm just what I am, that's all." In the Requiem scene at the play's end, Biff illustrates that he has truly come to an understanding of his father's failure to achieve success, observing that Willy "never knew who he was" and that he "had the wrong dreams."

Happy Loman

Happy is the younger of Willy's two sons; he has grown up in the shadow of his older brother, and consequently has a hard edge to his personality that the other characters lack. He is a handsome man in his early thirties, who while seemingly even-tempered and amiable, retains an air of hostility that is most apparent in his distinct sexual energy and his womanizing ways. He appears more content than Biff, but at the play's end he is drawn into his father's illusion; he pledges to take up his father's cause and succeed where his father had failed. While after Willy's death Biff recognizes his father's failings, Happy wildly proclaims: "I'm gonna show you and everybody else that Willy Loman did not die in vain. He had a good dream. It's the only dream you can have—to come out number-one man. He fought it out here, and this is where I'm gonna win it for him."

Linda Loman

Linda is Willy's long-suffering, devoted wife, who desperately loves her husband and resents the fact that his sons don't love and appreciate their father as much as she believes they should. She speaks carefully, and has a quiet manner that belies her inner strength. She treads cautiously around Willy, taking care not to raise his temper, and continuously presents a cheerful, hopeful appearance. Linda has tremendous patience, and serves as the family peacemaker. Linda sees through her husbands and sons; she knows that they are deluded, but she continues to bolster their fantasies, believing that she is doing the best, most loving thing for her family. In her essay in the 1991 compilation *Willy Loman,* critic Kay Stanton asserted that "the Loman men are all less than they hold themselves to be, but Linda is more than she is credited to be.... She is the foundation that has allowed the Loman men to build themselves up, if only in dreams, and she is the support that enables them to continue despite their failures.... She represents human dignity and values: cooperative, moral, human behavior as opposed to lawless assertion of self over all others through assumed superiority."

Willy Loman

Willy is the salesman around whom the play is constructed. He is sixty-three years old, desperate to achieve even a small measure of the success to which he has always aspired, and cannot face the reality that he has misdirected his energies and talents chasing a dream that never had any chance of materializing. Willy's flashbacks and fantasies comprise a large part of the play and inform the audience about his past, the histories of the other characters, how he has become what he is in the present, and perhaps most importantly, his ideal self. In the scenes which take place in present time, Willy is highly emotional, unstable, uncertain at times, highly contradictory, and seems worn down by life. In his flashbacks and fantasies, however, Willy is a more loving father and husband, a more capable provider; he is cheerful, light-hearted, and self-assured. Ultimately, because he cannot live with the realization that he has failed to live up to his unrealistic expectations, and because he believes he will finally be able, with his death, to leave his family with a sizable amount of cash, namely a $20,000 life insurance payoff, Willy commits suicide. In an imagined conversation, Willy responds to his brother Ben's admonition that suicide is a "cowardly thing," by asking: "Why? Does it take more guts to stand here the rest of my life ringing up a zero? ... And twenty thousand—that *is* something one can feel with the hand, it is there." Many critics have asserted that Willy is a modern tragic hero, and that his tragedy lies in his belief in an illusory American Dream. In a 1979 interview with Harry Rafsky on the Canadian Broadcasting Company, Miller asserted that after seeing *Death of a Salesman,* the audience members "were weeping because the central matrix of this play is ... what most people are up against in their lives.... they were seeing themselves, not because Willy is a salesman, but the situation in which he stood and to which he was reacting, and which was reacting against him, was probably *the* central situation of

contemporary civilization. It is that we are struggling with forces that are far greater than we can handle, with no equipment to make anything mean anything."

Stanley

Stanley is the waiter who serves Willy, Biff, and Happy during their meeting at the restaurant. He is highly agreeable, helpful, and enthusiastic.

Howard Wagner

Howard is Willy's boss, who rejects Willy and ultimately fires him. Howard, like Charley, is a successful businessman. However, Howard displays none of Charley's kindness or compassion, offering Willy such hollow trade cliches as "It's a business, kid, and everybody's gotta pull his own weight."

The Woman

The Woman is the person with whom Willy has an affair. She appears in flashbacks as a good-natured, fun-loving woman in her forties who appears proper on the surface but displays evidence of a boisterous spirit. Willy gives her an extravagant gift of nylon stockings, which were a rare luxury for women during World War II, and it is the memory of this gift that causes Willy's pangs of guilt and anger when he sees Linda mending her stockings. Her laughter during the flashback scenes serves as a piercing, shrill, painful reminder to Willy and Biff of Willy's infidelity. Willy's affair with the Woman is further evidence of his shortcomings, and illustrates how he has failed to live up to his own image of himself as the ideal husband and father.

THEMES

Appearances vs. Reality

What appears to be true to the characters in *Death of a Salesman* is often a far cry from reality, and this is communicated numerous times throughout the play. Willy's frequent flashbacks to past events—many of which are completely or partly fabricated—demonstrate that he is having difficulty distinguishing between what is real and what he wishes were real. Willy's imagined conversations with his dead brother, Ben, also demonstrate his fragile grip on reality. Willy's mind is full of delusions about his own abilities and accomplishments and the abilities and accomplishments of his sons. Biff and Happy share their father's tendency

TOPICS FOR FURTHER STUDY

- Research the economic growth America experienced during the post-World War II years. What do you feel led people like Willy Loman to expectations regarding success and the ''American Dream.''

- In what ways could the Loman family have avoided their sad situation by the play's end? Consider such elements as communication and compromise.

- Compare and contrast the characters of Willy Loman and Amanda Wingfield (from Tennessee Williams's *The Glass Menagerie*); both of these characters spend much of their time recalling their past, often incorrectly. In what ways does this selective perception of their pasts affect their current situations?

- Miller's play criticizes the false promises of the American Dream. Discuss facets of late twentieth century life that lead people to similar misconceptions of attainable success. Consider the role that advertising, music, television, and films have on this issue.

---

to concoct grand schemes for themselves and think of themselves as superior to others without any real evidence that the schemes will work or that they are, indeed, superior. At the end of the play, each son responds differently to the reality of his father's suicide. Biff, it appears, comes to the sad realization that his father ''didn't know who he was,'' and how his father's unrealistic dreams led him away from the satisfaction he could have found if he had pursued a goal that reflected his talents, such as a career in carpentry. Happy, who had previously given the appearance of being more well-grounded in reality but still hoping for something better, completely falls into his father's thought pattern, pledging to achieve the dream that his father failed to achieve.

Individual vs. Society

Willy is constantly striving to find the gimmick or the key to winning over clients and becoming a true success. He worries incessantly about how he is perceived by others, and blames his lack of success on a variety of superficial personal traits, such as his weight, the fact that people ''don't take him seriously,'' his clothing, and the fact that he tends to talk too much. While all of these concerns are shared by many people, for Willy they represent the reasons for his failure. In reality, Willy's failure is a result of his inability to see himself and the world as they

really are: Willy's talents lie in areas other than sales, and the business world no longer rewards smooth-talking, charismatic salesmen, but instead looks for specially trained, knowledgeable men to promote its products. Willy fails because he cannot stop living in a reality that does not exist, and which dooms him to fail in the reality that does exist.

Individual vs. Self

Willy's perception of what he should be is continually at odds with what he is: A mediocre salesman with delusions of grandeur and an outdated perception of the world around him. He truly believes that he can achieve greatness, and cannot understand why he has not realized what he feels is his true destiny. He completely denies his actual talent for carpentry, believing that pursuing such a career would be beneath him somehow. Willy struggles with the image of his ideal self his entire life, until he can no longer deny the fact that he will never become this ideal self and he commits suicide.

American Dream

Willy's quest to realize what he views as the American Dream—the ''self-made man'' who rises out of poverty and becomes rich and famous—is a dominant theme in *Death of a Salesman*. Willy believed wholeheartedly in this treasured national myth, which began during colonial times, and which was further developed during the 19th century by such industry tycoons as Andrew Carnegie and J.D. Rockefeller. In the 1920s, the American Dream was represented by Henry Ford, whose great success in the automotive industry was achieved when he developed the assembly line.

Also in the 1920s, a career in sales was being hailed as a way for a man without training or education to achieve financial success. Pamphlets, lectures, and correspondence courses promoting strategies for improving the skills of salesmen were widely distributed during this decade. These strategies focused on teaching salesmen how to effectively manipulate their clients. Willy would have begun his career as a salesman in the 1920s, when belief that salesmen adept at manipulation and ''people skills'' were destined for wealth and fame was widespread. However, by the late 1940s, when *Death of a Salesman* takes place, the job market and prevailing belief has changed, and salesmen (and other workers) required specialized knowledge and training in order to succeed. Because he lacks such knowledge or training, Willy is destined to fail in a business world that demands the ability to play a specific part in a large establishment. Willy, of course, does not realize how things have changed, and he continues to try to strike it rich using his powers of persuasion. Willy's personal representations of the American Dream are his brother Ben and the salesman Dave Singleman, and he views the success of these two men as proof that he can indeed attain the success he is so desperate to achieve. According to Willy's version of the American Dream, he is a complete failure.

STYLE

Death of a Salesman is a drama set in 1949, in New York City and Boston. The action of the play takes place largely inside the Loman home in Brooklyn, but other places in New York and Boston are used as well, including hotel rooms, Willy's office, a restaurant, and Willy's gravesite. The play is grounded in realism, which means that it depicts realistically what happens in the lives of its characters, but it also contains elements of expressionism, specifically when it depicts imaginary sequences and portrays for the audience the inner workings of the characters' minds and their emotions. The play is largely a representation of what takes place in the mind of Willy Loman during the last two days of his life.

Willy reminisces about past events and imagines situations, and the audience is able to see his thoughts played out on the stage. The reminiscences and imaginary sequences allow the audience to understand the characters' inner thoughts and provide insight into their behavior during the present-day scenes. For example, the audience learns, during one such reminiscence, that Biff has been tormented for since he was a young child by the discovery that his father had an extramarital affair. This insight helps the audience to better understand both Willy and Biff, explains some of Biff's anger toward his father, and indicates why he is so disillusioned. The instructions for setting in the play provide insight into how Arthur Miller wanted the play to be perceived by the audience. Miller includes instructions that the only substantial part of the set should be the Loman home, and all other locales should be merely hinted at by using changes in lighting or setting up a few chairs or a table. In this way, the audience can clearly see which events on stage are taking place in reality, and which are taking place inside of Willy's mind. Miller originally titled the play *The Inside of His Head,* which illustrates that he intended to show the audience what happens in a man's mind when his dreams are never realized, and when he lives in a world based on illusion. Miller's method of flashing back and forth between the past and the present, and between the imaginary and the realistic, allows the audience to witness how a lifetime of disappointment, delusion, and failure have led to the current situation, and shows facets of each character that would not have been revealed if only the present-day occurrences had been portrayed. Because of the way the play is constructed, the audience can see what the characters have become and what experiences, thoughts, and emotions led them to their present state.

HISTORICAL CONTEXT

When World War II ended in 1945, the United States embarked upon an unprecedented period of economic prosperity, driven by the increase in industrial production markets brought about by the war. Unlike the Great Depression and the war years, Americans had a surplus of goods and services from which to choose, and the money with which to purchase them. Nonfarming businesses grew by one-third, and housing construction became a booming industry. However, the economic situation was not improved for the poorest Americans during this

COMPARE
&
CONTRAST

- **1949:** Post-World War II economic growth combined with advertisements promising the American Dream created widespread optimism among Americans with hopes of attaining material wealth.

   Today: An unpredictable economic climate coupled with a more media-savvy public has created an environment of cynicism and doubt regarding the validity of the American Dream.

- **1949:** The German Federal Republic (West Germany) is established and the German Democratic Republic (East Germany) is established under Soviet control, effectively splitting the country following its defeat during World War II.

   Today: Germany was reunified in 1990, and has shown a steady increase in economic and cultural stature in the world.

- **1949:** The era of smooth-talking sales, when powers of persuasion often overshadowed knowledge and ability, was ending, giving way to careers requiring training and specialized knowledge.

   Today: The advent of ''infomercials'' and multi-media accessibility has sparked a resurgence in slick showmanship and sales techniques reliant on gimmickry.

- **1949:** National Academy of Television Arts and Sciences presents its first Emmy Award ceremony; nine percent of American households own a television set.

   Today: The annual Emmy Awards are a major television event and, like hundreds of other programs, are part of millions of Americans' everyday life; over ninety percent of American households own at least one television set.

---

time. The economic boom brought high inflation, which kept poorer citizens from saving any money, and small farmers faced hard times because of government policies that benefitted larger, corporate farmers. The lowest-paid workers in the country were the migrant farm workers, with sales clerks and unskilled laborers (such as gas station attendants) not far above them. Happy, a sales clerk, and Biff, a farm worker, represent this segment of the American workforce in *Death of a Salesman,* and each of them struggles to retain his dignity in the face of his lowly position in a largely affluent society.

Because Americans felt so secure in their new-found prosperity, they began using credit to purchase the products and services they desired. Although the prices of these goods and services were driven higher and higher by increased demand, Americans continued to purchase them, using credit to buy what they could not otherwise afford. For the first time in history, automobiles were more often purchased on credit than with cash, and the use of long-term credit, such as home mortgages, also rose dramatically. Willy Loman suffers from the effects of relying too much on credit, struggling to keep up his payments while trying to provide the necessities for his family.

The United States emerged from World War II as a ''superpower'' among the world's nations, but this role led to insecurities on the part of the American government and the American people, who suddenly bore the responsibility of retaining their position in the world, ''keeping the world safe for democracy'' by protecting it from the influences of the other world ''superpower,'' the communist Soviet Union. Because of the national pride and feeling of superiority instilled in them by their victories during the war, Americans felt a deep-seated need to prove that capitalism was better than communism during the period that followed World War II, which is known as the Cold War era. Americans felt obligated to achieve financial success, both as a way of defeating the Soviets and as a way to show their gratitude for the freedom they were privileged to possess by virtue of living in a democratic society. Willy's preoccupation with his financial status and his position in society reflect this Cold War attitude.

The Great Depression and World War II led to major changes in the nature of the American government. Beginning with President Franklin D. Roosevelt's New Deal (an economic program that began in response to the Great Depression), government became larger and more influential in the daily lives of American citizens. Furthermore, the growth of large corporations and the spread of such mass communication media as radio and television made Americans feel more like a large, connected society. With this new-found sense of belonging came a new-found desire to conform to the accepted norms and values of the majority. Instead of being a nation of rugged individualists, the United States became a nation of people who wished desperately for acceptance by their peers, which meant that they needed to appear successful in the eyes of society. Willy displays this wish for acceptance in his preoccupation with being ''well liked,'' which he views as the ultimate measure of success. In *The Lonely Crowd,* a book published in 1950, author David Reisman argues that prior to the Cold War era, Americans were motivated by strict morals and rules of conduct, but following World War II they became more motivated by others' perceptions of them, and altered their behavior according to acceptable societal standards. Reisman classified the pre-Cold War behavior pattern as ''inner-directed,'' and the postwar pattern as ''other-directed,'' maintaining that ''other-directed'' people, like Willy Loman, have no established sense of identity because they look to other people to determine their self-image. This idea is reflected in Biff's comment at the end of the play when he says that Willy ''didn't know who he was.''

CRITICAL OVERVIEW

Since its debut performance in 1949, *Death of a Salesman* has brought audiences to tears. Critical debate rages, however, over Willy Loman's stature as a tragic hero. In the classic definition of tragedy, the hero is a person of high stature brought low by an insurmountable flaw in his or her character, known as the ''tragic flaw.'' Some scholars argue

that Willy is pathetic rather than tragic, because he is not a great man who loses his stature because of something he does, but a common man who is largely a victim of a society in which the odds are stacked against him. For instance, Eric Mottram contended in *Arthur Miller: A Collection of Critical Essays* that Willy represents ''what happens to an ordinarily uneducated man in an unjust competitive society in which men are victimized by false gods. His fate is not tragic. There is nothing of the superhuman or providential or destined in this play. Everyone fails in a waste of misplaced energy.'' Others have suggested that Willy cannot be considered a tragic hero because he never confronts his faulty values. In his *Arthur Miller: Portrait of a Playwright,* Benjamin Nelson asserted: ''Although the play's power lies in its stunning ability to elicit . . . sympathy, the intensely idiosyncratic portrait of Willy Loman is a constant reminder that the meaning of his drama depends upon our clear awareness of the limitations of Willy's life and vision.'' Conversely, *College English* contributor Paul Siegel compared Willy Loman to William Shakespeare's great tragic hero King Lear, asserting: ''The cause of the catastrophe of the king of ancient Briton and that of the salesman of today is the same: each does not know himself and the world in which he is living.'' In his introduction to *Arthur Miller's Collected Plays,* Miller commented on his character's inherent tragedy: ''Willy Loman has broken a law without whose protection life is insupportable if not incomprehensible to him and to many others; it is the law which says that a failure in society and in business has no right to live. . . . The law of success is not administered by statute or church, but it is very nearly as powerful in its grip upon men.''

Because Willy struggles for money and recognition and then fails to gain either, some critics see *Death of a Salesman* as a condemnation of the American system. In *Newsweek,* Jack Kroll suggested that the drama is ''a great public ritualizing of some of our deepest and deadliest contradictions. It is a play about the misplaced energy of the basic human material in American society.'' However, many critics have offered differing opinions on the message Miller sends in the play. For example, Stephen A. Lawrence in an essay in *College English,* suggested: ''Perhaps what is wrong with the society is not that it has implanted the wrong values in [Willy], . . . but that it has lost touch with values which should never be relegated only to the personal sphere or the family unit. . . . Willy's problem is that he is human enough to think that the same things that matter in the family—especially his love for his son—matter everywhere, including the world of social success.'' *Catholic World* contributor Sieghle Kennedy offered another view, maintaining: ''With Charley living next door, economics can hardly be termed the nemesis of Willy's life. His failure as a man is the cause, rather than the effect, of his economic failure.'' Willy's decline is made more pathetic by the suggestion that he might have become an expert carpenter if he had not pursued the fantasy of wealth and popularity.

On one point most critics agree: *Death of a Salesman* is one of the significant accomplishments of modern American literature. In *The Forties: Fiction, Poetry, Drama,* Lois Gordon called it ''the major American drama of the 1940s'' and added that it ''remains unequalled in its brilliant and original fusion of realistic and poetic techniques, its richness of visual and verbal texture, and its wide range of emotional impact.'' *New York Times* columnist Frank Rich concluded that *Death of a Salesman* ''is one of a handful of American plays that appear destined to outlast the 20th century. In Willy Loman, that insignificant salesman who has lost the magic touch along with the shine on his shoes after a lifetime on the road, Miller created an enduring image of our unslaked thirst for popularity and success.'' According to John Gassner in the *Quarterly Journal of Speech,* Miller ''has accomplished the feat of writing a drama critical of wrong values that virtually every member of our middle-class can accept as valid. It stabs itself into a playgoer's consciousness to a degree that may well lead him to review his own life and the lives of those who are closest to him. The conviction of the writing is, besides, strengthened by a quality of compassion rarely experienced in our theatre.''

CRITICISM

L. M. Domina

An educator and author, Domina discusses the themes of failure and delusion that pervade Miller's landmark work.

Arthur Miller's classic American play, *Death of a Salesman,* exposes the relationship between gender relationships and dysfunctional family behaviors. In this play, the themes of guilt and innocence and of truth and falsehood are considered through the lens of family roles. Willy Loman, the salesman whose death culminates the play, is an anti-hero, indeed the most classic of anti-heroes. According to an article on the play in *Modern World Drama,* Willy is ''a rounded and psychologically motivated individual'' who ''embodies the stupidity, immorality, self-delusion, and failure of middle-class values.'' While his self-delusion is his primary flaw, this characteristic is not necessarily tragic since Willy neither fights against it nor attempts to turn it toward good. Dennis Welland in his book, *Miller: The Playwright* summarized this view, critiquing critics who believe that ''Willy Loman's sense of personal dignity was too precariously based to give him heroic stature.'' Although he is ordinary and his life in some ways tragic, he also chooses his fate. The article in *Modern World Drama* confirmed that ''considerable disputation has centered on the play's qualification as genuine tragedy, as opposed to social drama.''

Although Willy is dead by the end of the play, that is, not all deaths are truly tragic. The other characters respond to Willy's situation in the ways they do because they have different levels of access to knowledge about Willy and hence about themselves. An analysis of the relationships among these characters' insights and their responses will reveal the nature of their flawed family structure.

According to conventional standards, Biff, the older son of Willy and Linda, is the clearest failure. Despite the fact that he had been viewed as a gifted athlete and a boy with a potentially great future, Biff has been unable as an adult to succeed or even persevere at any professional challenge. Before the play opens, he had been living out west, drifting from one low-paying cowboy job to another, experiencing neither financial nor social stability. Back in New York, he is staying with his parents but seems particularly aimless, although he does gesture toward re-establishing some business contacts. Although one could speculate that the Loman family dynamics in general have influenced Biff toward ineffectuality, as the play progresses readers understand that one specific biographical moment (and his willingness to keep this moment secret) provides the key to his puzzling failure.

Near the end of the play, Bernard, Willy's nephew, asks Willy about this crucial incident. Although Biff had already accepted an athletic scholarship to the University of Virginia, he failed math his last semester in high school; his best option was to make the course up during summer school. Before he makes this decision, Biff visits Willy,

WHAT DO I READ NEXT?

- *King Lear,* a play by William Shakespeare written in approximately 1605 is a classic tragedy which also concerns generational discord, this time between a father and his daughters. The play confronts the difficulty of interpreting events and the actions of others with accuracy.

- *The Bell Jar* by Sylvia Plath, published in 1963, concerns a young woman's psychological instability and her eventual suicide.

- *The Crucible,* a play Arthur Miller wrote in 1953, has a multi-layered plot. On the surface, it concerns the Salem witch trials, while the subtext concerns the U.S. Senate's investigation into alleged communist activity in Hollywood.

- *Necessary Losses* by Judith Viorst, published in 1986, is a psychological study which concerns how people negotiate loss in order to reach greater maturity. She argues that people must give up some expectations as well as suffer loss through death and physical separation.

- *Making a Living While Making a Difference,* published by Melissa Everett in 1995, is a career guide for people who desire a profession which is socially meaningful. This book is designed for people who want to be financially successful without undermining their own ethics.

who is in Boston on business. According to Bernard, Biff ''came back after that month and took his sneakers—remember those sneakers with 'University of Virginia' printed on them? He was so proud of those, wore them every day. And he took them down in the cellar, and burned them up in the furnace. We had a fist fight. It lasted at least half an hour. Just the two of us, punching each other down the cellar, and crying right through it. I've often thought of how strange it was that I knew he'd given up his life. What happened in Boston, Willy?'' Willy responds defensively: ''What are you trying to do, blame it on me?''

What had happened, of course, as Willy subsequently remembers and as he has probably remembered frequently during the intervening years, was that Biff had discovered Willy in the midst of an extramarital affair. In contrast to Linda, who frequently appears with stockings that need mending, this other woman receives gifts of expensive stockings from Willy. The existence of this woman (and perhaps others like her) is one factor contributing to the financial strain of the Loman family. Biff understands this instantly, and he also understands the depth of Willy's betrayal of Linda—and the family as a whole. The trust Biff had given Willy now

seems misplaced. Indeed, according to the flashbacks within the play, the young Biff and Happy had nearly idolized Willy, so this betrayal while Biff is yet an adolescent is particularly poignant. As Biff is about to make a momentous life decision, in other words, he is confronted with duplicity from the man he had looked to as a role model. Yet Biff shares this knowledge with no one; instead this secret becomes the controlling element of his own life.

When Biff does attempt to tell the truth, not about Willy's affair but about his own life, Willy and Happy both resist him. ''Let's hold on to the facts tonight, Pop,'' Biff says, indicating that ''the facts'' are slippery in their hands. The outright lies members of the Loman family tell, that is, come more easily because they also exaggerate some facts and minimize others. Although many of their stories may be eventually founded in truth, that truth is so covered with their euphemistic interpretations that it is barely recognizable. The stories the family has told have become nearly indistinguishable from the real circumstances of their lives. Trying to separate reality from fantasy, Biff says, ''facts about my life came back to me. Who was it, Pop? Who ever said I was a salesman with Oliver?'' But Willy refuses to acknowledge the substance of the question: ''Well,

A scene from the 1979 production at the National Theatre in London

you were.'' Biff contradicts him, as determined to acknowledge the truth as Willy is to deny it: "No, Dad, I was a shipping clerk.'' Willy still declines to accept this fact without the gloss of embellishment: "you were practically'' a salesman.

Later, the conversation among the three men reveals that similar embellishments continue to characterize their lives. "We never told the truth for ten minutes in this house!'' Biff proclaims. When Happy protests that they "always told the truth,'' Biff cites a current family lie: "You big blow, are you the assistant buyer? You're one of the two assistants to the assistant, aren't you?'' But Happy continues the family habit: "Well, I'm practically . . .''

This inability to acknowledge the truth affects the family on many levels but most particularly in terms of their intimacy with one another and their intimate relationships with others. Biff hasn't dated anyone seriously, and Happy is most comfortable with prostitutes. While waiting for Willy at a restaurant, Happy assures Biff that a woman at another table is "on call'' and urges her to join them, especially if she "can get a friend.'' Although Happy is clearly a participant in this encounter, he says, "Isn't that a shame now? A beautiful girl like that? That's why I can't get married. There's not a

good woman in a thousand.'' Although Happy and Biff would probably classify their mother as a "good woman,'' they follow their father's example in seeking out women they won't marry to gratify their egos and then in treating those women as disposable.

Linda eventually responds to her sons with scathing disrespect in part because of the way they respond to other women, but primarily because she assumes they chose to accompany prostitutes rather than to fulfill their dinner plans with their father. "You and your lousy rotten whores!'' she says. "Pick up this stuff, I'm not your maid any more,'' she continues, and then asserts, "You're a pair of animals!'' Linda, of course, doesn't realize that Willy, too, whom she accuses her sons of deserting, is guilty of infidelity. Willy's emotional stability is threatened, she believes, in part because of the way his sons respond to him. She fails to consider the possibility that Biff's instability and the immaturity of both Biff and Happy has been affected by Willy's model.

The most profound secret of the play, however, is of course Willy's apparent obsession with suicide. He has been involved in several inexplicable automobile accidents, and he has perhaps planned to asphyxiate himself by attaching a rubber tube to their gas water heater. Linda has discovered this tube and has revealed her discovery to her sons, but she forbids them from addressing the subject directly with Willy, for she believes such a confrontation will make him feel ashamed. This secret is hence ironically acknowledged by everyone except the one whose secret it is—Willy. When he does finally succeed in killing himself, his act can be interpreted as a culmination of secrets, secrets which are compounded through lies because they have been created through lies. Welland suggested that Willy's suicide results from his affair—"To argue that in these days of relaxed social morals one minor marital infidelity hardly constitutes grounds for suicide is, paradoxically, to add weight to the theme in the context of this play: for Willy Loman it *is* enough." His affair is certainly one factor in his decision, but it is a factor because he had been found out by his son, and because others are now starting to question him. So although these secrets include his affair(s) and Biff's knowledge of this aspect of his life, they also include his failure as a salesman and the subsequent failures of his sons.

Source: L. M. Domina, in an essay for *Drama for Students*, Gale, 1997.

Sister M. Bettina

In the following essay, Sister Bettina examines the function of the character of Ben in Death of a Salesman, *arguing that Ben is an extension of Willy's own consciousness, and that "through [Ben] Miller provides for the audience a considerable amount of the tragic insight which, though never quite reaching Willy, manifests itself to them in the dramatic presentation of the workings of his mind."*

In the thirteen years since Arthur Miller's *Death of a Salesman* had its spontaneous Broadway success, critics have often cited as a deficiency in it the lack of tragic insight in its hero, Willy Loman. "He never knew who he was," says his son Biff at Willy's grave; and by a like judgment critics can substantially discount the play's tragic claims.

But Biff's choric commentary on his father, like many other very quotable remarks in the scene of Willy's "requiem," is not quite true. Willy did struggle against self-knowledge—trying not to know "what" he was; but he had always a superb consciousness of his own individual strength as a "who." "I am not a dime a dozen!" he shouts in the play's crisis; "I am Willy Loman. . .!" And it is this very sense of his personal force and high regard for it which qualify him as a hero.

What turns this self-esteem into something tragic and self-destructive is his contrasting awareness that, in spite of his powers, he is not what he wants to be. Himself partially unaware that he actually desires simple fulfillment as a father, Willy dreams of being an important businessman, greatly admired by his two sons. He has misconstrued the ideal of fatherhood, confusing it with the ability to confer wealth and prestige. Because of this misplaced idealism—and his related commitment to the economic delusion known as "the American dream" —he seems not to have the stature of the traditional tragic hero.

That, as his son Biff says, Willy has "the wrong dreams" is certainly true. What criticism has to decide, in the light of the play's dramatic structure, is whether this common human defect does not increase rather than weaken his effectiveness as tragic hero.

Because playwright Miller has buttressed the basic realism of *Salesman* with strongly expressionistic elements, analysis of his play has to be made carefully. Willy's stage presence does not equal his characterization, as it would in a more conventional play. Instead of simply appearing in the events on stage, he himself—or rather, his confused mind—is the scene of much of the dramatic action.

Consideration of tragic insight in Willy, then, leads one to notice an expressionist device which reappears with the regularity of a motif in episodes taking place in Willy's consciousness. This is the stylized characterization of Willy's rich brother Ben who, when closely observed, takes shape less as a person external to Willy than as a projection of his personality. Ben personifies his brother's dream of easy wealth.

Ben is the only important character not physically present during Willy's last day. He is on stage only as he exists in Willy's mind. But he is the first person whom Willy asks in his present distress, "What's the answer?"; and in the end it is Ben's answer which Willy accepts. As one critic summarizes it:

> Ben "walked into the jungle and three years later came out with a million"; Ben shot off to Alaska to "get in on the ground floor"; Ben was never afraid of new territories, new faces, no smiles. In the end, Ben's last territory—Death—earns Willy Loman's family $20,000 insurance money, and a chance for them finally to accomplish his dream: a dream of which they have never been capable, *in* which they also can only be buried: the old "million" dream. [Kappo

"WILLY, WHO WILL GIVE UP HIS LIFE RATHER THAN HIS CHOSEN IMAGE OF HIMSELF, REPRESENTS THE FOOL IN EACH OF US"

Phelan, "Death of a Salesman," *Commonweal* XLN, 1949, p. 520]

Although Ben is dead before the play begins, the force which he symbolizes draws Willy to suicide.

Ben also stands out as the play's only predominantly formalized characterization. That in him Miller combines realism with expressionism in a ratio inverse to that of the rest of the play seems another indication of his distinctive symbolic function.

The audience first sees him when memories of a visit paid by him some twenty years before push themselves into Willy's consciousness. "William," he boasts, "when I walked into the jungle, I was seventeen. When I walked out I was twenty-one. And, by God, I was rich!" This is the first insinuation of what may be called Ben's theme—the going into a strange country and emerging with its wealth. Willy, who in this scene is a young father, triumphantly concurs: ". . . was rich! That's just the spirit I want to imbue them with! To walk into a jungle! I was right!" Ben, whom he has presented to his sons as "a great man," has confirmed his ambitions for them.

At his second appearance in Willy's memory, Ben again exults over his wealth, but this time he puts his brother on the defensive. He is now making money in Alaska and wants Willy to come into his business. Willy does find the offer attractive, and he hesitates before deciding that, after all, he is "building something" here in the States. "And that's the wonder, the wonder of this country," he goes on to exclaim, "that a man can end with diamonds here on the basis of being liked!" Ben repeats, "There's a new continent at your doorstep, William. You could walk out rich. Rich!" But Willy insists, "We'll do it here, Ben! You hear me? We're gonna do it here." He is still calling this when Ben, for the second time, abruptly disappears into darkness.

Willy next sees his brother after he has finally admitted to himself that he is a business failure. And from this point in the play Ben functions as a symbol of Willy's dream. He no longer is a memory; instead he has become a force working in the present.

Willy has lost his job, is thoroughly defeated, and wants to talk over with his brother a "proposition" of suicide. At first seeming to dissuade Willy, making reluctant appeals to his pride, Ben gradually comes to admit that Willy's insurance indemnity is worth suicide: "And twenty thousand—that *is* something one can feel with the hand, it is there." Willy becomes lyrical: "Oh, Ben, that's the whole beauty of it! I see it like a diamond, shining in the dark, hard and rough, that I can pick up and touch in my hand." Ben's motif, riches waiting in darkness, is working in Willy's mind. He no longer believes he can make money in another way.

The play's crisis ensues and Willy comes to see that his son Biff loves and forgives him. More than before he yearns to give his son something, and Ben immediately reappears to recall the suicide plan. The idyllic leitmotif which accompanies Ben starts up in accents of dread. "The jungle is dark but full of diamonds, Willy. . . . One must go in to fetch a diamond out." Slowly he moves into the offstage darkness. "Ben! Ben, where do I. . .?" Willy pleads. "Ben, how do I. . .?" Finally he rushes off after him; seconds later he is dead.

Ben's one-dimensional character becomes a facet of the intimate psychological portrayal of Willy just as expressionism fuses with realism in *Salesman* a whole. Miller uses Ben—along with the more conspicuous devices of skeletal setting, nonrealistic lighting, free movement in space and time, and musical leitmotifs—to provide a deeper realism than conventional dramatic form would have allowed.

Traditional drama implements audience-insight into the hero's problem by his own voluble awareness of it; tragic figures are more or less poetically articulate about their destinies, desires, and mistakes. *Death of a Salesman,* however, forces a question as to whether insight in the hero is a dramatic end in itself or only insofar as it heightens audience-consciousness. For, in spite of its hero's foolish commitment to something so hollow that he will not even admit it to himself, the play's structure permits its audience to follow in the very action on stage the inexorable working of his mind. Thus Willy emerges as more than a pathetic victim of American society. Miller employs expressionism precisely to show Willy's struggle against self-knowledge, thereby pointing up his personal responsibility for refusing to estimate himself sincerely.

What Miller believes to be the basic impetus of any tragic hero—the supreme importance of his self-respect, even when he must lie to himself to preserve it—is, structurally and otherwise, the main concern of his play. *Salesman* studies the break-up of an ideal rather than of a man. But Willy's collapse will follow inevitably that of his self-image. His existence has come to depend upon belief in his ideal. Symbolically speaking, he has become his delusion.

Functioning in Willy's consciousness as a personification of this dream, Ben is a most important ''minor'' character, a projection of his brother's personality rather than an individual human force. Through him Miller provides for the audience a considerable amount of the tragic insight which, though never quite reaching Willy, manifests itself to them in the dramatic presentation of the workings of his mind.

In one way Willy's commitment to his dream typifies a necessary breaking of the laws of reality by all men: their construction of the tenuous ideals of themselves which truth by its very nature has to destroy. Willy, who will give up his life rather than his chosen image of himself, represents the fool in each of us. By that very fact, he must go the way of the tragic hero.

Source: Sister M. Bettina, ''Willy Loman's Brother Ben: Tragic Insight in *Death of a Salesman*'' in *Modern Drama,* Vol. 4, no. 4, February, 1962, pp. 409–12.

Brooks Atkinson

In the following excerpt from his review of Death of a Salesman, *which originally appeared in the* New York Times *on February 11, 1949, Atkinson declares that the play, which he calls ''a superb drama,'' ''has the flow and spontaneity of a suburban epic that may not be intended as poetry but becomes poetry in spite of itself because Mr. Miller has drawn it out of so many intangible sources.''*

As drama critic for the New York Times *from 1925 to 1960, Atkinson was one of the most influential reviewers in America.*

Arthur Miller has written a superb drama. From every point of view *Death of a Salesman,* which was acted at the Morosco last evening, is rich and memorable drama. It is so simple in style and so

> MR. MILLER HAS NO MORAL PRECEPTS TO OFFER AND NO SOLUTIONS OF THE SALESMAN'S PROBLEMS. HE IS FULL OF PITY, BUT HE BRINGS NO PIETY TO IT''

inevitable in theme that it scarcely seems like a thing that has been written and acted. For Mr. Miller has looked with compassion into the hearts of some ordinary Americans and quietly transferred their hope and anguish to the theatre. Under Elia Kazan's masterly direction, Lee J. Cobb gives a heroic performance, and every member of the cast plays like a person inspired.

Two seasons ago Mr. Miller's *All My Sons* looked like the work of an honest and able playwright. In comparison with the new drama, that seems like a contrived play now. For *Death of a Salesman* has the flow and spontaneity of a suburban epic that may not be intended as poetry but becomes poetry in spite of itself because Mr. Miller has drawn it out of so many intangible sources.

It is the story of an aging salesman who has reached the end of his usefulness on the road. There has always been something unsubstantial about his work. But suddenly the unsubstantial aspects of it overwhelm him completely. When he was young, he looked dashing; he enjoyed the comradeship of other people—the humor, the kidding, the business.

In his early sixties he knows his business as well as he ever did. But the unsubstantial things have become decisive; the spring has gone from his step, the smile from his face and the heartiness from his personality. He is through. The phantom of his life has caught up with him. As literally as Mr. Miller can say it, dust returns to dust. Suddenly there is nothing.

This is only a little of what Mr. Miller is saying. For he conveys this elusive tragedy in terms of simple things—the loyalty and understanding of his wife, the careless selfishness of his two sons, the sympathetic devotion of a neighbor, the coldness of his former boss' son—the bills, the car, the tinkering around the house. And most of all: the illusions by which he has lived—opportunities missed, wrong formulas for success, fatal misconceptions about his place in the scheme of things.

Writing like a man who understands people, Mr. Miller has no moral precepts to offer and no solutions of the salesman's problems. He is full of pity, but he brings no piety to it. Chronicler of one frowsy corner of the American scene, he evokes a wraithlike tragedy out of it that spins through the many scenes of his play and gradually envelops the audience. . . .

Source: Brooks Atkinson, in a review of *Death of a Salesman* (1949) in *On Stage: Selected Theater Reviews from The New York Times, 1920–1970,* edited by Bernard Beckerman and Howard Siegman, Arno Press, 1973, pp. 298–99.

FURTHER READING

Carson, Neil. *Arthur Miller,* Grove, 1982.
This book offers an overview of Miller's major works, with an emphasis on their status as theater.

Corrigan, Robert W. *Arthur Miller: A Collection of Critical Essays,* Prentice-Hall, 1969.
An excellent resource for critical information on Miller and his work. *Death of a Salesman* is discussed at length.

Matlaw, Myron, editor. *Modern World Drama,* Dutton, 1972, pp. 194-96.
This is primarily a plot summary with introductory comments situating the play within dramatic literary tradition.

Murray, Edward. *Arthur Miller, Dramatist,* Ungar, 1967.
Provides analysis of Miller's major works with respect to structure, dialogue, and theme. While not overtly negative, Murray shows distaste for Miller's use of language, calling it unpoetic.

Welland, Dennis. ''Death of a Salesman'' in his *Miller: The Playwright,* Methuen, 1979.
This book considers much of Miller's work. Welland considers the views of several other critics while coming to a positive evaluation of the play.

Doctor Faustus

CHRISTOPHER MARLOWE

1594

Christopher Marlowe based his play *Doctor Faustus* on stories about a scholar and magician, Johann Faust, who allegedly sold his soul to the devil to gain magical powers. Born in 1488, the original Faust wandered through his German homeland until his death in 1541. In 1587, the first story about his life appeared in Germany, translated into English in 1592 as *The History of the Damnable Life and Deserved Death of Doctor John Faustus.*

Exactly dating Renaissance texts can be difficult, but *Doctor Faustus* poses particular challenges. Scholars believe Marlowe heard or read the story of Johann Faust and composed *Doctor Faustus* sometime between 1588 and 1592. London's Stationer's Register entered the play into the official records in 1601, but in 1602, at least two other writers were paid for additions to the text. (Most critics believe that Marlowe wrote the play's tragic beginning and end, while his collaborators wrote much of the comical middle sections.) A theatrical company named the Earl of Nottingham's Men (commonly known as the Admiral's Men) performed the play twenty–four times between its opening in 1594 and 1597. Thomas Busshell published the play in 1604, though John Wright published a different version in 1609. Editors generally combine parts of these and other versions of the text to create the play as it is widely read today.

Contemporary theatre records indicate that in early performances, Faustus may have worn the

cloak of a scholar, decorated with a cross, while the devil Mephistopheles appeared in the costume of a dragon. It has been said that performances of the play were so terrifying that during the 17th century audiences believed that the devil actually appeared among them.

In spite of a literary career prematurely shortened by his violent life, Marlowe profoundly influenced English literature. In particular, scholars credit his play *Tamburlaine* with successfully introducing blank verse into English drama and with developing the Elizabethan concept of tragedy as a way of exploring key moral issues of the Renaissance. Although not a favorite with early audiences, today critics and theatre-goers alike consider *Doctor Faustus* Marlowe's masterpiece.

AUTHOR BIOGRAPHY

Born in 1564, the same year as fellow playwright William Shakespeare, Christopher Marlowe's great dramatic achievements appeared on London's stage a few years before Stratford's favorite son (Shakespeare wrote and worked in Stratford) came to dominate the English stage. In their day, Marlowe's plays marked a highpoint in English drama, particularly because he first successfully introduced blank verse into tragedy. Blank verse is written in poetic stanzas marked by Iambic Pentameter (each line has ten syllables with accents on every second beat); the verse is composed without rhyme. In addition, Marlowe's characterization helped develop the Elizabethan concept of tragedy as a way of exploring key moral issues of the Renaissance.

A native of Canterbury, England, and the son of a successful shoemaker, Marlowe received a scholarship enabling him to attend Corpus Christi College, Cambridge, and prepare for a church career. He resided at Cambridge from 1581 to 1587, receiving his B.A. in 1584 and his M.A. in 1587. Throughout his life, however, Marlowe provoked controversy. Initially, Cambridge sought to prevent Marlowe from receiving his M.A. after hearing that he had traveled to France with plans to seek ordination as a Catholic priest. Significantly, however, the Privy Council contradicted these reports, stating that Marlowe's travels had been in the service of Queen Elizabeth's government and that he should therefore receive his degree. Though hard evidence does not exist, these circumstances have led some critics to speculate that Marlowe had been engaged by the

government as a spy, on this and subsequent occasions.

Marlowe's wild lifestyle challenged social conventions. Arrested for his involvement in a brawl that led to his opponent's death, Marlowe spent time in Newgate prison. His release followed a legal ruling of the fight as self-defense. In May, 1593, officials arrested Marlowe's roommate, playwright Thomas Kyd for possession of heretical writing. (Kyd wrote *The Spanish Tragedy,* believed to be the first English revenge tragedy.) Kyd insisted the papers involved belonged to Marlowe. The Privy Council issued an arrest warrant for Marlowe, but before the case could proceed, Marlowe died in another fight. The dispute arose over an argument concerning a bill at a local tavern. Officials ruled the death self-defense, though some speculate that Marlowe's companions assassinated him for political or religious reasons.

Despite his short and violent life, Marlowe produced a significant amount of work, much of it of high quality. In addition to *Doctor Faustus* (1594), Marlowe's other famous plays include *Tamburlaine, Parts I and II* (1587- 88), *The Jew of Malta* (c. 1590), and *Edward II* (1592-3).

Two related themes run through his works: ambition and Machiavellianism, the latter based on popular interpretations of Niccolo Machiavelli's *The Prince* (1513), which outlines how monarchs can gain and maintain power by acting with cunning and ruthlessness.

PLOT SUMMARY

Prologue
The chorus enters, explaining that the play tells the story of a scholar named Faustus, who, like Icarus, ''his waxen wings did mount above his reach.''

Act I, Scene i
Faustus contemplates his accomplishments and plans his future endeavors. He considers, then rejects, philosophy, medicine, law, and theology before deciding to study magic. Significantly, Faustus rejects theology because of a misunderstanding of the relationship between divine justice and Christian mercy.

A good and bad angel appear, urging Faustus to resist and indulge in temptation, respectively. Two magicians, Valdes and Cornelius, enter, offering Faustus books of spells and agreeing to instruct him in the black arts.

Act I, Scene ii

Two scholars, who wonder what has become of Faustus, ask his assistant, Wagner. He chides the scholars about the logic of their conversation, then informs them that Faustus dines with Valdes and Cornelius. The scholars suspect that Faustus has ''fall'n into that damned art.''

Act I, Scene iii

Lucifer and four devils appear as Faustus chants his spells. When he asks them if his chants commanded them to appear, they reply that was merely accidental, that they appear whenever anyone ''abjures the scriptures and his savior Christ.'' Faustus asks about the nature of hell but ignores the devil Mephistopheles's reply and agrees to exchange his soul for twenty–four years of ''voluptuousness'' and power.

Act I, Scene iv

Wagner and the clown Robin joke about what they would do with Faustus's powers.

Act II, Scene i

As Faustus prepares to sign in blood a contract giving Lucifer his soul, the Good and Bad Angels appear, offering advice. After Faustus signs, devils dress him in rich robes and dance around. Again, Faustus asks Mephistopheles about hell, then refuses to believe the devil's honest reply, insisting that ''hell's a fable.''

Faustus asks and receives from Mephistopheles several books of spells to bring riches, control the elements, and provide knowledge of nature.

Act II, Scene ii

Faustus tells Mephistopheles that when he sees the heavens, he considers repenting. The Good Angel appears, urging Faustus to repent and take advantage of God's mercy, while the Bad Angel tells him he will never repent. Faustus agrees that he cannot ask for forgiveness.

Faustus asks Mephistopheles who made the world, but rather than answer and introduce the subject of God, the devil offers a morality play

Christopher Marlowe

showing the seven deadly sins: Pride, Covetousness, Envy, Wrath, Gluttony, Sloth, and Lechery.

Act II, Scene iii

Robin and Dick joke about the power of magic.

Chorus

The Chorus tells us of Faustus learning the secrets of nature and travelling to Rome.

Act III, Scene i

Bruno, supported as Pope by German Emperor Charles V, is brought before Roman Pope Adrian, to be condemned for heresy. As a joke, Faustus and Mephistopheles put the cardinals to sleep, then impersonate them, telling Pope Adrian they have decided to punish Bruno severely. Delighted, Pope Adrian orders a banquet to be prepared.

Act III, Scene ii

Faustus and Mephistopheles free Bruno, who returns to Germany. When the real cardinals awake, they tell Pope Adrian they had not yet delivered their verdict, and when Pope Adrian learns that Bruno has escaped, he imprisons the cardinals.

Faustus, now invisible, accompanies the Pope, archbishop, and friars to the banquet, stealing food and drink from the Pope's hand. The clergy damn the soul responsible for this mystical behavior.

Act III, Scene iii

Robin and Dick have stolen a cup from the Vintner; when he comes to reclaim it, they conjure up Mephistopheles. Angry at being disturbed, the devil transforms Dick into an ape and Robin into a dog.

Chorus

The Chorus explains that Faustus has arrived at the court of the Emperor.

Act IV, Scene i

The Emperor requests that Faustus conjure up Alexander the Great and his paramour. Skeptical of Faustus's power, Benvolio, a knight with a hangover, insists that if Faustus can bring back Alexander, he will become Actaeon and turn himself into a stag. After Alexander appears, Faustus grows horns on Benvolio's head, which the Emperor, pleading leniency, asks Faustus to remove.

Act IV, Scene ii

Two knights, Martino and Frederick, help Benvolio in a vengeful attack on Faustus. When the magician appears, they cut off his head, but he rises again, telling them he cannot die before his contract expires in twenty-four years. They plead for mercy but various devils punish them and their soldiers.

Act IV, Scene iii

Benvolio, Frederick, and Martino enter, bloody, with horns on their heads. Embarrassed, they decide to hide in Benvolio's castle.

Act IV, Scene iv

Faustus sells his incredible horse to the Horse-courser (dealer) for 40 dollars, but warns the dealer not to ride it through water.

Alone, Faustus, "a man condemn'd to die," remembers that divine mercy led Christ to forgive one of the thieves with whom he was crucified. Still, the thief had repented, and Faustus does not. Instead, he falls asleep.

The Horse dealer returns, wet. His curiosity led him to ride the horse through water, and the animal has turned into a little wet straw. He comes upon the sleeping Faustus and demands his money back. When he pulls Faustus's leg to wake him, the leg comes off in his hand. Faustus screams murder, and the Horse dealer runs off, holding the leg.

Wagner enters to tell Faustus that the Duke of Vanholt seeks his company.

Act IV, Scene v

In a tavern, Robin, Dick, the Horse-courser, and the Carter (a driver) drink beer, swapping stories about Faustus's tricks. The Carter explains how Faustus came upon him and, claiming to be hungry, asked if he could eat some of the hay the Carter hauled. The Carter said yes, knowing that an ordinary person could eat very little hay, but Faustus consumed the entire wagon-load! The Horse-courser then told how the horse he bought turned into hay when ridden in the water, but how he was revenged on the magician by stealing his leg.

Act IV, Scene vi

The Duke of Vanholt thanks Faustus for erecting an enchanted castle in the air. The pregnant Duchess requests a dish of ripe grapes. As it is January, Faustus sends Mephistopheles to the East to bring the fruit.

The Carter, Horse dealer, and others come to settle accounts with the magician. When they demand beer and question Faustus about his missing leg, he teases them, then sends them off.

Act V, Scene i

Faustus raises the spirit of Helen of Troy for a group of scholars. When the scholars leave, an Old Man appears, urging Faustus to repent. Faustus, believing himself damned, contemplates suicide, and Mephistopheles hands him a dagger. The Old Man advises repentance, but Faustus asks the demon for Helen. Faustus then makes redemption impossible by kissing her spirit, asking as he does, for Helen, not God, to make him immortal.

Act V, Scene ii

Lucifer, Beelzebub, and Mephistopheles come to claim Faustus, whose time has run out. Various scholars, seeing Faustus's sad demeanor, wonder if physicians might cure his ill, but he informs them that his powers came, not from himself, but because he sold his soul to the devil. The scholars advise him to repent, but Faustus says if he thinks of God, the devil will tear his body to pieces. The Good Angel appears, telling Faustus that the time for repentance is past, while the Bad Angel gloats over the damnation of the magician's soul. The Bad Angel tells Faustus, who refused to repent because his fear of physical pains exceeded his fear of spiritual pain, about the exquisite torments that await him in hell.

As the clock strikes eleven, Faustus wishes he could stop time, then wishes he were not immortal and doomed to suffer for eternity, but still he fails to repent. Finally, as the clock strikes twelve, he wishes his soul could be turned into drops of water which disappear into an ocean, but still, repentance eludes him as he exits with Mephistopheles.

Act V, Scene iii
The scholars discover Faustus's body torn to pieces. In spite of his end, they agree to give him a proper funeral because of his great learning.

Epilogue
The Chorus tell us that while Faustus was a branch that "might have grown full straight," instead he yearned to learn "unlawful things . . . [and] to practice more than heavenly power permits."

CHARACTERS

Archbishop of Rhelms
When an invisible Faustus creates a stir at Pope Adrian's banquet, all present wonder about the cause. The Archbishop suggests that perhaps a soul, which escaped from Purgatory and wishes the Pope's prayers, causes the disturbance. Ironically, Faustus's contract with the devil has placed him in need of prayers, though the spiritual power of the worldly pope remains in doubt.

Benvolio, Frederick, and Martino
When Faustus arrives at the court of Emperor Charles V to display his magic, Benvolio, a knight, seems too hungover to witness the performance. When the Emperor requests that Faustus conjure up Alexander the Great and his paramour, Benvolio is skeptical of the magician's power and insists that if Faustus can bring back Alexander, he will become

MEDIA ADAPTATIONS

- Actor Richard Burton directed and starred in a 1968 adaptation of *Doctor Faustus*. The film is available on videotape from Columbia.
- *Marlowe Leads the Way.* A filmstrip about the life and works of Christopher Marlowe, distributed by Eye Gate House, 1967.

the mythological character Actaeon and turn into a stag. After Alexander appears, Faustus grows horns on Benvolio's head, which the Emperor, pleading leniency, asks Faustus to remove.

Humiliated by these horns, Benvolio plans revenge against Faustus for his trick, and, helped by Martino and Frederick, tries to ambush and kill the magician. When Faustus appears, they cut off his head, but he rises again, telling them he cannot die before the term of his twenty-four-year contract. They plead for mercy, but he has various devils punish them and their soldiers. Later, Benvolio, Frederick, and Martino enter, bloody and muddy from their struggle against the devils. All have sprouted horns on their heads. They agree to hide away from the world at Benvolio's castle while they wait, hoping that in time, their horns will disappear and people will forget their disgrace.

Bruno
Bruno, a rival pope supported by German Emperor Charles V, appears before Roman Pope Adrian, to be condemned for heresy. Conversation between the popes reveal them to be political, rather than spiritual leaders. Faustus and Mephistopheles put the Cardinals to sleep, then free Bruno, who returns to Germany.

Cardinals of France and Padua
The Cardinals must determine the punishment for Bruno, a papal rival supported by German

Emperor Charles V, whom Pope Adrian has condemned for heresy. As a joke, Faustus and Mephistopheles put the Cardinals to sleep, then impersonate them, telling Pope Adrian they have decided to punish Bruno severely. Faustus and Mephistopheles then free Bruno, who returns to Germany. The Cardinals wake and tell Adrian they had not yet delivered a verdict. Adrian learns that Bruno has escaped and imprisons the Cardinals.

Carter

In a tavern, with Robin, Dick, and the Horse-courser, the Carter (a cart driver) explains the trick Faustus played on him. Faustus approached him and, claiming to be hungry, asked if he could eat some of the hay the Carter hauled. The Carter said yes, knowing that an ordinary person could eat only a little hay, but Faustus consumed the entire wagon-load.

Later, the Carter and others confront Faustus at the Duke of Vanholt's palace, only to be humiliated, silenced, and ejected.

Charles V, Emperor of Germany

At a meeting of the Senate, Faustus meets Charles V, Emperor of Germany. The Emperor thanks Faustus for freeing the German supported rival pope Bruno, then asks the magician to conjure up Alexander the Great and his paramour. Skeptical of Faustus's power, Benvolio insists that if Faustus can bring back Alexander, he will become Actaeon and turn into a stag. After Alexander, Darius, and Alexander's Paramour appear, Faustus grows horns on Benvolio's head, which the Emperor, pleading leniency, asks Faustus to remove.

Chorus

The Chorus appears four times, first to establish the heroic nature of the play. Later, the Chorus identifies the places and times of the action. It also judges or comments on that action. As Renaissance texts should ''teach and delight,'' the Chorus ensures that the audience understands the lesson.

In the final scene, the Chorus implies that there are permissible limits for human knowledge, describing Faustus as a branch that ''might have grown full straight;'' instead, he yearned to learn ''unlawful things. . . . To practice more than heavenly power permits.''

Duchess of Vanholt

Faustus provides the Duchess, who is pregnant, with a dish of ripe grapes, which Mephistopheles brings from the East.

Duke of Vanholt

Faustus entertains the Duke of Vanholt by erecting an enchanted castle in the air and supplies the pregnant Duchess with a dish of ripe grapes. As it is January, Faustus sends Mephistopheles to the East to bring the fruit.

They are interrupted by a crowd, including the Carter and Horse-courser, come to settle accounts with the magician. When they demand beer and question Faustus about his missing leg, he teases them, then sends them off. As the scene ends, the Duke says that Faustus's ''artful sport drives all sad thoughts away.'' Ironically, however, the audience knows that Faustus cannot drive away his own sad thoughts.

Faustus

See Dr. John Faustus

Dr. John Faustus

A Wittenberg scholar who sells his soul to the devil in exchange for twenty-four years of power. The Faust myth originates in the story of a 14th century German scholar and magician, Johann Faust, who allegedly sold his soul to the devil.

In many ways, Faustus typifies the Renaissance hero, for this can be seen as the age of the overachiever typified by warrior poet-courtiers like Sir Philip Sidney or Sir Walter Raleigh. Such Renaissance individuals strove for and sometimes attained ambitious military or navigational goals; Faustus sought ultimate power and forbidden knowledge. Overachieving Renaissance individualists like Faustus play significant roles in all Marlowe's dramas.

Faustus's damnation results from his failure to reconcile divine justice with divine mercy. Ironically, this scholar and student of logic ultimately falls because of his over-reliance on logic and his failure to account for empirical evidence. This becomes evident in Faustus's considerations of sin, mercy, and hell.

Good Angel and Bad Angel

Throughout the play, the Good Angel urges Faustus to acknowledge his error and plead for divine mercy, which repentance would make forthcoming. The Good Angel chastises Faustus for going beyond appropriate boundaries of human knowledge.

The Bad Angel tells Faustus that he has no hope of mercy or forgiveness, that he faces inevitable damnation.

Helen of Troy

Faustus conjures Helen's spirit to impress the Scholars, then later, urges Mephistopheles to bring her back. Faustus kisses her, asking her to "make me immortal." Her lips "suck forth . . . [his] soul," thereby damning Faustus to hell.

Horse-courser

The Horse-courser (or dealer) agrees to buy Faustus's incredible horse for 40 dollars. Faustus warns the Horse-courser that though he may ride the horse over hedges and ditches, he must not ride it through water.

The Horse-courser returns, wet. His curiosity led him to ride the horse through water, and the animal has turned into a wet straw. He comes upon the sleeping Faustus and demands his money back. When he pulls Faustus's leg to wake him, the leg comes off in his hand. Faustus screams murder, and the Horse- courser runs off, holding the leg.

Later, the Horse-courser accompanies the Carter and others to the palace of the Duke of Vanholt to confront Faustus. He finds that Faustus has not lost a leg at all but again played a joke on him. Then, the magician makes of fool of them all before silencing them and having them ejected.

Lucifer

The chief devil and Mephistopheles's master, to whom Faustus agrees to give up his soul in exchange for twenty four years of "voluptuousness" and power. Lucifer entertains Faustus with the Seven Deadly Sins and claims his soul at the play's end.

Mephistopheles

The devil who primarily serves Faustus, doing his bidding and debating, theological, philosophical, and scientific issues. He entertains and distracts Faustus when he seems to be reconsidering his deal and repenting.

Old Man

The Old Man represents positive spiritual power. He rescues Faustus from his temptation to commit suicide and urges the scholar to repent. After the magician kisses the spirit of Helen of Troy, the Old Man returns, informing Faustus that his actions have made his damnation inevitable.

Pope Adrian

Pope Adrian, the pope of Rome, confronts Bruno, a papal rival supported by German Emperor Charles V. Adrian condemns Bruno for heresy and demands that the Cardinals determine his sentence. As a joke, Faustus and Mephistopheles put the Cardinals to sleep, then impersonate them, telling Pope Adrian they have decided to punish Bruno severely. Delighted, Pope Adrian orders a banquet to be prepared.

Faustus and Mephistopheles then free Bruno, who returns to Germany. When they wake, the real Cardinals tell Adrian they had not yet delivered their verdict. When Adrian learns that Bruno has escaped, he imprisons the Cardinals.

Faustus, now invisible, accompanies Adrian, the Archbishop, and friars to the banquet, stealing food and drink from the Pope's hand. The clergy decide to damn the soul responsible for this behavior—essentially a moot point given Faustus's inevitable fate.

Scholars

In the first act, Wagner teases the Scholars about their understanding of logic. Later, several Scholars ask Faustus to show them Helen of Troy.

In the last act, Faustus confesses to a group of Scholars that his powers come from a Satanic pact. Finally, they discover the remains of Faustus's dismembered body, and agree to hold a proper funeral for him because of his former standing as a great scholar.

Valdes and Cornelius

Two magicians who help instruct Faustus in the dark arts.

Wagner, Dick, and Robin

Faustus's servant Wagner, like Dick and the clown Robin, serves as one of the play's comic characters. In the first act, Wagner teases students about the inadequacy of their logic, introducing the theme of skepticism toward reason. As the play ends, Wagner, the primary beneficiary of Faustus's will, inherits all his worldly possessions.

Wagner and Robin, a clown, joke about what they would do with Faustus's powers. Generally, these and subsequent comic scenes ridicule the arrangement Faustus has made. Robin and Dick steal a cup from the Vintner, and when he comes to reclaim it, they conjure up Mephistopheles. Angry at being disturbed, the devil transforms Robin into a dog and Dick into an ape.

THEMES

As might be expected, a play in which the main character makes a pact with the devil, exchanging his soul for earthly power, raises many interrelated themes. These issues resonate with readers today, though they become more complex when they are situated within the Renaissance, a time in many ways different from contemporary life.

Individualism

The status of the individual during the Renaissance is central enough to have its own name: "Renaissance Individualism." This comes about for a variety of reasons. Most importantly perhaps, during the Medieval Period, the largely church-dominated society attended primarily to things of the next world. The Renaissance, though still spiritual, brought with it a new focus on seeking happiness and fulfillment in this world. Society's secularization and the invention of printing enhanced people's literacy and political and economic changes made entirely new ways of life possible.

The Renaissance applauded those people—explorers, courtiers, traders—who successfully took advantage of these opportunities. This was also the age of the "Renaissance Man," a person who could succeed in a variety of seemingly unrelated projects. Think of men like Sir Philip Sidney and Sir Walter Raleigh, who were warriors, diplomats, courtiers, and poets. Remember that even the king and queen pursued a variety of interests: Henry VIII wrote music, and Elizabeth wrote poetry.

Finally, the Renaissance was an age in which people who had read Machiavelli's *The Prince* and Castiglione's *The Courtier* knew that the image people created for themselves also contributed significantly to their success. In that sense, *Doctor Faustus* illustrates the negative side of Renaissance Individualism, for he gains power but uses it foolishly.

Good and Evil

Ethical issues are central to *Doctor Faustus*. Even Faustus knows that justice demands he be punished for selling his soul to the devil, though his pride blinds him to the fact that divine mercy could in time forgive his transgression. After all, aside from his demonic exchange (admittedly, a big exception) Faustus does not do anything truly evil. He plays a few cruel jokes, but he does not really cause any permanent damage or harm. In Christian terms, Faustus confuses the Old Testament God of justice with the New Testament God of mercy. Faustus experiences a moral corruption and misunderstands that it is possible for him to repent, seek atonement, and earn forgiveness.

Another way to see Faustus's actions is in Platonic terms. Plato believed that, although people obviously did evil, they always believed their actions were for good. This is not to say that they did not know the difference between right and wrong but that they acted out of a mistaken idea of good. This describes Faustus's behavior. In the entire play, though he plays a few cruel pranks, he never

TOPICS FOR FURTHER STUDY

- Characters who sell their souls to the devil are a common plot device in stories such as Nathaniel Hawthorne's ''Young Goodman Brown,'' novels like William Faulkner's *The Hamlet,* and movies from *Rosemary's Baby* to *Angel Heart.* Compare and contrast the themes raised by these works with themes from Marlowe's play. Despite similar plot element, the significance of these stories differs. What do those different stories say about the societies which produced them?

- Anyone who has spent time with children knows one reason they get into mischief is because of what might be called their natural curiosity. Some thinkers believe curiosity forms the basis of our humanity. What is it that makes people wonder and want to know more? In Marlowe's *Doctor Faustus,* the desire for knowledge fails to produce happiness. Do you believe that limits should be placed on the pursuit of knowledge? Are there some things people were not meant to know? The Angels and Chorus in Marlowe's play seem to think so—do you? You might study the issues surrounding free speech and censorship, or controversial scientific research, exploring what kinds of things society believes should and should not be thought and communicated.

- Most readers of Marlowe's play feel that Doctor Faustus wastes a wonderful opportunity. We condemn his selling his soul to the devil, of course, but we also condemn the fact that he fails to make significant use of his infinite power. If you had Faustus's power, what would you do?

- Ethicists examine the rights and wrongs of human behavior. One question that comes up relates to goals (ends) and the actions necessary to accomplish them (means). For example, stealing is wrong, but do we condemn stealing from the rich to feed the poor, as Robin Hood did? Wounding someone is wrong, but surgeons ''wound'' people every day in efforts to heal them. In both these cases, we might be tempted to say the ends justify the means. If you could do infinite good for all the world, would you sell your soul to the devil? Before you answer, read the works of several ethical philosophers. They may help you answer, or they may make your answer even more difficult.

---

performs any truly evil actions against other people. He does do evil, of course, when he renounces God and embraces Lucifer, but while he knows this is wrong, he acts based on a mistaken understanding of scripture. Believing himself to be damned and alienated from God, aligning himself with the devil seems the best remaining alternative. In that sense, Faustus acts out of a mistaken idea of good.

Knowledge and Ignorance

The issue of knowledge occupied a central place during the Renaissance: what kinds of knowledge should be pursued, how far, by whom, and for what purposes? Faustus seeks knowledge—something we might see as good—though that knowledge only leads him to destruction; this is not the fault of the knowledge but of the knower. Marlowe partially implies, however, that there should be limits to human knowledge. Both the Bad Angel and the Chorus at the play's end seem to suggest that man can only know so much without falling to evil, but other voices in the play suggest that knowledge is good if it is understood and used within proper contexts. The issue seems to be not what should be known but how one distinguishes valuable, accurate knowledge from useless error. Ironically, Act I suggests that Faustus's theological misunderstandings stem from misreading the bible. Faustus's pride prevents him from learning. Instead, he concentrates on what he already knows—or believes he knows—rather than what he has to learn—from the

Bible, from the devil, and from the Good Angels who hope to save him.

Choices and Consequences

Faustus makes one of the most famous choices in literary history—to sell his soul to the devil. He chooses freely, though with faulty knowledge of both his options and the consequences (at one moment in the play, Faustus suggests that the "stars" have caused his downfall, but this seems difficult even for Faustus himself to accept). Failing to see repentance as an option, Faustus misunderstands the nature of hell, which he believes is physical instead of psychological. Actually, though not technically "damned" until the play's end, he seems in hell right from the moment he separates himself from the divine. Of this, he remains unaware; it is part of his tragedy.

Faustus makes a second choice. Right up to the play's penultimate act, he has the option of repenting, but because of pride and ignorance, as well as fear of physical punishment, he fails to do so and damnation results. Faustus seems to take responsibility for his actions, though in the final scene, he desperately wishes he had never existed—or existed in a different way that might mitigate his punishment. Right up to the very end, he tries to argue or reason his way out of a situation from which only repentance can save him.

Appearance and Reality

If Faustus learns one lesson before his tragic end, it is that things are not always what they seem. This theme is treated seriously and comically throughout the play.

Faustus's problem with appearance and reality begins with his basic assumption that he can use magic—something inherently not real—to go beyond appearance and gain true understanding of the natural world. Faustus's magic makes things happen but nothing true arises from it. When Faustus shows Alexander the Great to the Emperor, Faustus admits that he is not real, but spirit. The Emperor wants to see a mole on Helen of Troy's neck, to see if the "real" Helen had one. This attention to specific detail creates a kind of "reality-effect," but the fact is, as they both know, she is not real but a spirit. Faustus's warning to the Emperor not to touch her suggests the danger of the products of magic and suggests that the natural knowledge and worldly good that Faustus seeks are not permanent but illusory.

In a broadly comical scene in Rome, Faustus makes himself invisible and interrupts the papal banquet. The scene's comedy depends on confusion between what is and what appears to be. The popes and cardinals appear to be religious figures but are in reality political ones concerned more with temporal than spiritual power. Faustus appears to be an otherworldly spirit with magical powers, but he actually only controls the powers of Mephistopheles or in a broader sense, hell. The scene comically reveals temporal power to be insubstantial.

Finally, when Faustus makes love with the spirit of Helen at the play's end, he knows that she is not real and that contact with a spirit will damn him. This comments on the nature of love and symbolizes the absolute lack of substance involved in sex without emotional and psychological contact.

After Faustus has magically entertained the Duke, he says that Faustus's "artful sport drives all sad thoughts away." Faustus appears to have everything. Ironically, however, the audience knows that Faustus cannot drive away his own sad thoughts.

Human Condition

In several scenes, discussions between Faustus and Mephistopheles address the central issues of the human condition: who made the world? What is the purpose of human life? Why does evil exist? The devil's replies fail to satisfy Faustus, who only wants to hear what he already believes to be true. Those who will not learn cannot be taught, and Faustus learns the truth about the spirituality which underlies the human condition too late to avoid destruction.

Meaning of Life

Throughout the play, Faustus searches for the meaning of life, but his search is inhibited because he believes he knows what life is all about. His search for the truth fails because of his own incorrect preconceptions and beliefs.

Pride

As the world's greatest scholar, Faustus believes he has nothing to learn from other people and little to learn even from the devil to whom he has sold his soul. When Mephistopheles tells Faustus about the nature of hell, he does not believe him. Because of pride, Faustus cannot learn from others. Pride in his own knowledge prevents him from evaluating the world around him in a meaningful manner. When he does act, he bases his decisions on prejudice rather than objective and empirical data.

Finally, everything Faustus does is egocentric: he performs no altruistic deed, no humanitarian gesture. His pride motivates him only to seek admiration from others but never to really deserve it—from them or from himself.

Success and Failure

Faustus's experiences illustrate the maxim: be careful what you wish for—you just might get it. He successfully obtains his desires. Ironically, however, his power over the devils and material world leaves him unfulfilled and empty. His material success fails to make him happy, and his pact with the devil makes spiritual happiness impossible. His is an empty success, based on actions which are selfish and immature.

STYLE

Christopher Marlowe's *Doctor Faustus,* a tragedy in five acts, tells the story of the title character's agreement to sell his soul to the devil in exchange for twenty-four years of absolute power.

Chorus

In drama, a chorus is one or more actors who comment on and interpret the action unfolding on stage. In Marlowe's *Doctor Faustus,* the chorus appears four times. First, it introduces the play's theme. Later, it provides the where and when in the narrative action. Finally, it relates the moral and helps the audience understand the significance of the closing scene.

Allegory

In an allegory, characters represent abstract ideas and are used to teach moral, ethical, or relig-

ious lessons. Marlowe's play contains a Morality Play, in which Mephistopheles orders a parade of the seven deadly sins to entertain Faustus. Sins like Pride, Envy, and Lechery are deadly, according to Christian religions, because committing one of them damns a person to hell.

Antithesis

The antithesis of something is its direct opposite. One example is the Good and Bad Angels who appear to save and tempt Faustus, though other figures which appear to be antithetical are God and Lucifer, Helen and the Old Man, and Faustus and Mephistopheles.

Elizabethan Drama

Elizabethan Drama are English comic and tragic plays produced during the Renaissance, or written during the reign of Queen Elizabeth of England, who ruled from the late-sixteenth to early-seventeenth century. Christopher Marlowe's *Doctor Faustus* was first produced in 1594.

Comic Relief

The use of humor to lighten the mood of a serious story. In this work, while Faustus has sold his soul to the devil in order to accomplish great things, the comic relief involves Wagner, Robin, and Dick, who use magic mostly for tricks and practical jokes. While not strictly comic, it is a wry irony that Faustus also wastes his powers performing tricks, rather than accomplishing anything worthwhile.

Tragedy

Elizabethan Drama is defined by an adherence to a specific structure—in the case of *Doctor Faustus,* a tragedy. Some critics see the structure of Marlowe's *Doctor Faustus* as flawed and not conforming to that of a pure tragedy. They believe that, while the play has a tragical beginning and an ending, it fails to have a true middle in which the protagonist grows, changes, or learns something. According to Aristotle's famous treatise on drama, *Poetics,* a tragedy must have a beginning, middle, and end. Some scholars attribute *Doctor Faustus*'s lack of a significant middle to the work of coauthors, who, it is speculated, filled in the space between Marlowe's beginning and ending.

By definition, a tragedy is a drama about an elevated hero who, because of some fatal character flaw or misdeed (also known as a hamartia), brings ruin on himself. Marlowe's *Doctor Faustus* tells the story of a famous scholar who due to hubris (pride) sells his soul to the devil and ends up damned to hell.

Hamartia

In a tragedy, the event or act that causes the hero's or heroine's downfall. In Marlowe's *Doctor Faustus,* that act is the contract he makes with the devil, exchanging his soul for worldly power.

Catharsis

At the end of a tragedy, the audience is supposed to experience a release of energy, because they have felt pity and fear; pity for the person suffering the tragic fate, then fear that a similar fate might happen to them. In many instances, playwrights will attempt to evoke catharsis in their audiences as a way of cautioning them, a means of instructing them to avoid the unfortunate fate of their protagonists.

Suspense

Marlowe maintains the audience's attention by making them wonder when, if ever, Faustus will repent and what consequences his actions will have. Until the last act, there is still a possibility that Faustus will appeal to God for forgiveness. This ''will he or won't he'' scenario—combined with the question of whether God would actually accept the Doctor's penance were it offered—keeps the viewer guessing.

HISTORICAL CONTEXT

In many ways, Marlowe's *Doctor Faustus* reflects the extensive intellectual, economic, and political changes taking place in sixteenth century England, changes sparked by the Renaissance and the Reformation.

The Renaissance began in Italy during the 14th century, and in the next two centuries, spread new ideas throughout Europe. Generally, this intellectual and aesthetic rebirth resulted from the recovery and translation of many lost ancient Greek and Roman texts and from the new ideas which people developed after studying the work of earlier thinkers.

Politics and religion came to be intricately interwoven with national identity because of the association between the Protestant Reformation and England's Renaissance culture. Exploration of Asia, Africa, and the Americas, pioneered by Spain, led to changes in Europe's political and social structure. Imperial economies developed that linked European nations with their colonies, contributing to the rise of the modern nation state by creating a heightened sense of national identity.

During the reign of Henry VII as king of England, which began in 1485, government centralization and efficient bureaucracy brought England political stability. This allowed Renaissance ideas to flourish.

Henry VIII became king in 1509. His inability to conceive a male heir with his wife Catherine of Aragon led him to demand a divorce. When Pope Leo X refused that demand, largely due to the political pressure of Spain, Henry broke with the Roman Catholic Church. The Act of Supremacy in 1534 established the Church of England, with the monarch as its head. This initiated in England an era of serious religious strife, though not as bloody as similar struggles in other parts of the world. After Henry VIII's death, Edward VI, who continued England's Protestant course, ruled for a short period. At his death, Mary Tudor, a half-Spanish Catholic became queen and attempted to return England to Catholicism. Religious persecution earned her the name ''Bloody Mary,'' and her marriage to her cousin Philip II of Spain raised concerns about England coming under the political and religious influence of Catholic Spain. Mary's death led to the crowning of Queen Elizabeth, who reversed England's Catholic drift but maintained a largely centrist position regarding religion and politics. Spain's preeminent role on the world stage, fueled by gold from its conquest of the Americas, led to England's continued anxiety about that country's Catholicism and the effects it might have on England. This concern was eased by a large military failure incurred by the Spanish Armada in 1588.

Readers of Marlowe's plays may want to keep this history in mind, for it helps to explain Faustus's

COMPARE
&
CONTRAST

- **1590's:** People were anxious about the "New Science" of Galileo, Copernicus, and Bacon. They also were intrigued by the explorations of the "New World" of the Americas by Christopher Columbus and by the discoveries of maritime adventurers like Sir Frances Drake.

  Today: Scientific advances in genetic engineering and cloning both intrigue and frighten people, as does the discovery of possible life in new worlds in space.

- **1590's:** People feared those who were different from them. Protestants feared Catholics; Catholics feared Protestants, and both feared Jews and Muslims.

  Today: In spite of advances in education and literacy, people today remain anxious of those who are of different races, creeds, and colors.

- **1590's:** Theatre audiences respond to plays that take them to magical places or allow them to meet incredible beings like the demons in *Doctor Faustus*.

  Today: Modern audiences are bored by straight narrative tales; they now demand spectacles such as the prop- and effect-heavy *Phantom of the Opera*. Special effects play a significant role in most successful Broadway shows and in many

films. The advent of computer generated animation—which created life-like dinosaurs in the films *Jurassic Park* and *The Lost World*—has upped the ante on what constitutes entertainment.

- **1590's:** Audiences respond positively to plays about heroes like kings and warriors, and enjoy plays like *Doctor Faustus* which poke fun at academics.

  Today: Then as now, people admire those who achieve great things—especially when they must also overcome adversity—such as the title character in the film *Forrest Gump*. Films such as *Back to School* and television shows like *3rd Rock from the Sun* satirize inflexible, "by the book" teachers and academics.

- **1590's:** Monarchy is the dominant form of government throughout the world. Though some monarchies have legislative branches that allow group decision-making, most of the power is concentrated in the executive branch.

  Today: Very few absolute monarchs exist today, though several constitutional monarchies (such as England) function with royal figureheads and government power concentrated in the hands of a legislature and ministry.

---

mockery of the Pope and even Faustus's damnation. Remember that, as the play begins, Faustus contemplates pursuing the black arts. He rejects study of theology instead of magic because of his reading of Jerome's bible, a much-revised edition negatively identified with Catholicism by England's Protestant majority. Reading the "wrong" version of the bible contributes to Faustus making his fatal decision.

The Renaissance placed a new focus on Humanism. Generally, medieval religious attitudes emphasized the next, spiritual world instead of this, the material world. Medieval society prized collective values over those of the individual. The Renais-

sance changed this way of thinking, validating individual worth and emphasizing the potential for happiness and accomplishment in this world.

Several factors contributed to the rise of Humanism. First, Martin Luther and the Protestant reformation weakened the hold Roman Catholicism held over European religion during the middle ages. Translations of rediscovered classical texts as well as contemporary continental writers increased the general trend toward secularization. Previously, books were hand copied, but the invention of printing by Johann Gutenberg in 1445 and its introduction into England by William Caxton in 1476 made books more readily available. The style and content of education also changed. Tutors and universities added the study of newly recovered classical texts to the subjects taught during the medieval period. Students read these texts not only to improve language skills but also to understand their ethical, social, and political content. Classical values influenced English society, as did those of contemporary Italian texts like Niccolo Machiavelli's 1513 *The Prince* and Baldassare Castiglione's 1528 *The Book of the Courtier.* Not only the elite but professionals, artisans, and merchants recognized the value of education, both for its personal and economic value. Literacy increased.

By freeing intellectual inquiry from the confines of theology, a scientific revolution known as the "New Science" began to take place. In the wake of astronomical discoveries by Galileo and Copernicus, thinkers like Francis Bacon privileged observation of nature over the study of traditional writings about nature, developing what we recognize today as the scientific method. Marlowe's *Doctor Faustus* satirizes both the New Science and Humanism, which lie behind Faustus's unquenchable desire to know more about the natural world. The play questions what limits, if any, should be set on human knowledge and scientific inquiry.

Columbus's travels to the Americas late in the 15th century inaugurated an age of maritime exploration among Spain, France, Portugal, and England. The demand for financing to support this exploration and trade led to the beginnings of modern banking and commerce, particularly crown-supported monopolies. Organizations like the Senegal Adventurers (1588) and the East India Company (1600) enabled entrepreneurs to sell stock to finance various businesses, in particular trade with Asia, African, and the Americas.

Political and economic changes affected not only how but where people lived. The industrial and agricultural revolutions that came to fruition during the eighteenth century have their roots in the Renaissance. Under Queen Elizabeth, the enclosure movement led to more efficient agriculture, but it displaced rural workers, who migrated from the city. England, up to this point a wool exporting country, began manufacturing and exporting cloth. Increases in trade drew people to urban population centers, where trade- related industries flourished. Such commerce enriched the country as a whole,

and city dwellers who provided these goods and services became increasingly prosperous. That prosperity sped the growth of England's professional and artisan-based middle classes that began in the late middle ages and that Geoffrey Chaucer represented in his *Canterbury Tales.* In addition to being a political and economic center, London became a cultural center as well, providing the necessary ingredients for great theatre like Marlowe's: patrons, artists, and audiences.

Students of Marlowe must pay particular attention to these shifting social structures, which allowed people without titles or inherited wealth to advance to prominence. Increased social mobility, coupled with renewed emphasis on secular education, led to the rise of the strong, ambitious personality type that exemplifies Renaissance Individualism. Marlowe's heroes epitomize this type, aspiring to greatness in the military, political, or spiritual realm. In *Tamburlaine,* for example, a shepherd becomes a warrior-king. Not all shepherds became kings, but economic opportunities broadened horizons for many people. The over- reaching of Marlowe's characters, often combined with the ruthlessness of their efforts, leads to their downfall. In that sense, their personal ambitions reflect those of society at large and serve as a warning not to sell one's soul for material advancement.

CRITICAL OVERVIEW

When Christopher Marlowe's *The Tragical History of the Life and Death of Doctor Faustus* appeared on the London stage in 1594, audiences did not name it an overwhelming success. Today, however, critics and theatre-goers alike consider it Marlowe's masterpiece. Contemporary critical debate focuses on several, related critical issues: what motivates Faustus's character? When does his damnation occur? And does the play have a "middle?"

Critics interested in assessing the play's quality consider the unity of *Doctor Faustus*'s structure to be central. For some, it has a beginning—Faustus's contract with the devil—and an end—Faustus's damnation—with little of consequence in between. The frivolous ways Faustus uses his powers supports this position, suggesting that the hero learns or changes little as the narrative action progresses. As Wilbur Sanders wrote in *Shakespeare's Contemporaries: Modern Studies in English Renaissance Drama,* the "unity of *Doctor Faustus* is . . . something that we have to create for ourselves."

The play's complex textual history further complicates the issue. Two different published versions of the play appeared in 1604 and 1616, and theatre manager Philip Henslowe contracted revisions from other writers. This leaves the authorship of the play's middle sections open to debate, though Marlowe certainly wrote the play's beginning and end. Few believe Marlowe wrote the middle of *Doctor Faustus* alone, and some believe he had little part in it at all.

Audiences and critics agree that Faustus seems an essentially selfish, superficial man who uses infinite power foolishly. In *Further Explorations,* L. C. Knights saw Faustus's motivations as essentially immature, driven by "the perverse and infantile desire for enormous power and immediate gratifications." This does not trivialize that desire, however, for "we should see the pact with the devil and the magic . . . as dramatic representations of the desire to ignore that 'rightness of limitation', which, according to Whitehead, 'is essential for the growth of reality' [from *Religion in the Making*]." While Faustus's efforts to transcend limits distract him from understanding reality, the audience gains insight from the magician's errors. Faustus's excessive ambition must be condemned, whether in terms of Renaissance Aristoteanism, which validates moderate behavior, or Freudian psychoanalytic theory, in which the ego's reality principle must negotiate between the pure desire of the "id" and the absolute law of the "superego." The audience learns to question immoderate behavior, but the play leaves a viewer unsatisfied about Faustus's motivation. Perhaps Faustus will realize what the audience already knows, that eternal suffering is a high price to pay for the power to perform a few, trivial practical jokes.

If Faustus's agonizing over whether or not to repent forms the play's dramatic middle, the play's dramatic unity depends on the timing of his damnation. If he can seek mercy until the last moment—an option open to him theologically, though one he fails to see—then the play has suspense until the end as audiences wonder if Faustus will see his error

and repent. If, on the other hand, Faustus seals his fate in the first act, when signing the deed, then, as Cleanth Brooks wrote in *A Shaping of Joy: Studies in the Writer's Craft,* all that follows would be merely "elegiac." The play falls flat, absent of actual dramatic conflict.

Pinpointing the exact moment of Faustus's damnation can be difficult. Some believe that his damnation follows his signing the deed, uttering as he does the same words that Christ said before he died: "*Consummatum est*"; it is finished. "On a purely legalistic basis, of course, Faustus's case *is* hopeless," wrote Brooks. "He has made a contract and he has to abide by it."

The play offers other options, however, and Brooks notes that even after Faustus has signed the bond, the Good Angel appears, urging him to "Repent, yet God will pity thee." Also, at various points in the play, it seems important to Mephistopheles to distract Faustus from repenting, so some form of reconciliation between Faustus and God must be possible. Finally, the Old Man appears just in time to prevent Faustus from committing suicide, at Mephistopheles's instigation, and he too holds out the possibility of mercy. In each case, though, Faustus fails to believe that mercy can mitigate his offence, which he realizes deserves punishment.

According to Peter Davison, the exact moment of Faustus's damnation comes as he kisses the spirit of Helen of Troy. When Faustus first conjures up her spirit, he warns the spectators neither to speak with nor touch her, for, as Davison noted in *International Dictionary of Theatre-1: Plays,* "verbal or physical intercourse with spirits is unforgivable." Later, however, Faustus makes his redemption impossible by kissing the spirit of Helen. As he does, he asks Helen, not God, to make him immortal. As they kiss, he says, "Her lips suck forth my soul." By doing so, Faustus exchanges the "heaven" of Helen's lips for the heaven of spiritual delight. Davison wrote: "Faustus has triumphed in going beyond man's terrestrial limits, but he has been simultaneously damned and it is as a damned soul that he will be 'eternalized.'" The Old Man appears before Faustus kisses Helen still holding out the possibility of salvation, but when the Old Man returns after the kiss, he says: "Accursed Faustus, miserable man/That from thy soul excludest the grace of heaven."

Like the Renaissance itself, which mixed ancient and modern ideas, Marlowe's *Doctor Faustus* constructs desire in ways both medieval and modern. The morality play in which Faustus sees the parade of the Seven Deadly Sins presents a medieval notion of sin. For Sanders, "Marlowe's introduction of devils who are medieval in temper . . . [revives] the earlier psychomachia form (the 'battle for a soul' of which *Everyman* is the best example)." The more modern idea that punishment may be psychological comes from Mephistopheles's description of hell as not a place but a state of mind. According to Brooks, Marlowe's use of demonic apparatus to externalize emotional states—and in that sense, his model of temptation—seems essentially modern and psychological. Brooks wrote: "the devils . . . are always in some sense mirrors of the inner states of the persons to whom they appear." These two positions share common ground, however. Brooks would no doubt agree with Sanders when he wrote: "Marlowe is studying the collision between the old wisdom of sin, grace and redemption, and the new wisdom of humanist perfectibility."

CRITICISM

Arnold Schmidt

Schmidt holds a Ph.D. from Vanderbilt University and is an author and educator. His essay discusses Marlowe's play as both entertainment and edification.

Most people have wanted something so badly that, in moments of desperation, they imagined they would do anything to have it. Most learn to balance their desires with reality while a few people act on those desperate imaginings. Still, drama offers the possibility of exploring the implications of such impetuous actions, at least as experienced by characters in the play. In Marlowe's *Doctor Faustus,* the main character decides to sell his soul to the devil in exchange for twenty-four years of absolute power. Part of the pleasure of reading or seeing the play comes from the viewer putting themselves in Faustus's predicament and imagining how they would respond to similar temptations. Marlowe's story also illustrates the Renaissance's prevalent belief that art should "teach and delight," that is, be entertaining while simultaneously presenting a morale.

Stories of people who bargain with the devil in exchange for worldly goods abound. These can be literal exchanges, such as Nathaniel Hawthorne's short story "Young Goodman Brown" or W. B. Yeats's *The Countess Cathleen.* This concept can also be treated thematically, as it is in such works as William Shakespeare's *Macbeth,* Mary Shelley's *Frankenstein,* and Herman Melville's *Moby Dick.* These tales illustrate, without evoking supernatural deals, characters whose obsessions drive them to sacrifice all the goodness in their lives.

In many ways, Marlowe's plays typify attitudes in Renaissance England. The intellectual and aesthetic rebirth known as the Renaissance began in Italy during the 14th century and, in the next two centuries, spread new ideas throughout Europe. Three aspects of Renaissance culture—Humanism, Individualism, and the New Science—figure as prominent themes in Marlowe's play.

Rejecting medieval social and religious attitudes, Renaissance Humanists privileged individual over collective values. Humanism encouraged people to realize their happiness and potential in this, the material world, rather than focusing solely on eternal happiness in the afterlife. By freeing intellectual inquiry from the confines of theology, a scientific revolution known as the "New Science" took place. The influence of Galileo and Copernicus spread. Thinkers like Francis Bacon, who emphasized the observation of nature over study of traditional writings about nature, developed what we recognize today as the scientific method.

Finally, the era's social, political, and economic changes meant that even people without a title or inherited wealth could advance in society. This led to the rise of the strong, ambitious personality type that characterized an upwardly mobile Renaissance individual. Marlowe's heroes epitomize this character type, aspiring to a greatness that extends beyond their current status. This overzealous ambition often results in ruthless and irrational actions; they have the power to make their own choices, yet those choices lead to their downfall. In this sense, Marlowe's work serves to caution the viewer against this kind of behavior.

In many ways, the Renaissance can be seen as a period of the over-achiever, of individuals who aspire for great things which they then struggle to reach. Consider men like Sir Philip Sidney or Sir Walter Raleigh, admired by their age as courtiers, warriors, and poets. Renaissance individuals strove for and sometimes attained ambitious goals: Sir

WHAT DO I READ NEXT?

- Perhaps the most natural play to read next would be Johann Wolfgang von Goethe's *Faust,* published in two parts in 1808 and 1828. If Marlowe's play epitomizes Renaissance ideals Goethe's represents the unique values of the Romantic period. While both plays tell broadly similar stories, they have very different endings which warrant comparison.

- In general, any works by Nathanial Hawthorne would make compelling follow-up reading to *Doctor Faustus,* but several short stories seem particularly appropriate. In ''Young Goodman Brown,'' a newlywed walks off into the forest to discuss selling his soul to the devil. Though he decides against consummating the deal, he fears his wife has and spends the rest of his life unhappily aware of the corruption that seems to surround him.

- Two other Hawthorne short stories raise the theme of forbidden knowledge, suggesting that the blind sacrifice of everything of value for science resembles a compact with the devil. In ''The Birthmark,'' a man causes the destruction of his beloved by endeavoring to remove a tiny imperfection from her otherwise perfectly beautiful body. In ''Rapaccini's Daughter,'' a father's efforts to create a daughter who is beautiful but poisonous also leads to the downfall of all involved.

- In one of the first gothic novels, Matthew Lewis's *The Monk,* the main character completes a deal with the devil, exchanging his soul for escape from the Inquisition, though not escaping eternal punishment. Scandalous when published during the eighteenth century, in part because of its for-the-time explicit sex and violence, in part because Lewis was at the time a sitting member of Parliament and indicated so on the book's title page. Overall, fast-paced and suspenseful reading.

- *Macbeth* by William Shakespeare. In plotting to kill their king, Macbeth and his wife metaphorically ''sell their souls'' in exchange for political power. Both *Doctor Faustus* and this play successfully explore the psychology of transgression, guilt, and punishment. Students also might compare the images of Shakespeare's witches with Marlowe's representations of sorcery.

- In Mary Wollstonecraft Shelley's novel *Frankenstein,* scientist Victor Frankenstein's search for the secret of human life leads to his destruction at the hands of the creature he creates. Here too, Victor exchanges everything of value in his life—friends, family, fiance—in a figurative deal with the devil that grants him the secrets of life.

- In *The Countess Cathleen,* the title character exchanges her soul with the devil for food to feed the starving Irish. This short play by William Butler Yeats raises intriguing ethical issues. After all, a person who sacrifices all for humanity is a saint, not a sinner—but what if that sacrifice involves selling one's soul to the devil? In the end, despite Cathleen's bargain, heaven intervenes, and she ultimately eludes the devil's grasp.

Francis Drake sailed around the world and returned with abundant riches. The period was the first to advance the concept of the self-made man; a person could achieve considerable status through his actions, could raise his social standing through ability and determination. When readers of Machiavelli's *The Prince* and Castiglione's *The Book of the Cour-* *tier* realized the important role a person's image played in attaining success, they sought to fashion impressive images for themselves either through actions or fabrication. If Faustus typifies the Renaissance hero, *Doctor Faustus* shows the problems with unbridled individualism. Though Faustus has unlimited power, his actions are juvenile and selfish. He does no good deed, no charitable action, no feat for the good of his fellow human.

Marlowe's first stage success, the two-part *Tamburlaine,* probably appeared on the London stage in 1587 or 1588. It relates the story of the rise to power of a shepherd who uses military and political strength to dominate an empire. *Tamburlaine* personifies a Renaissance ideal. The play recounts the story of a self-made man who achieves greatness not through a birthright or inheritance but through skill, determination, and character. The shepherd Tamburlaine's success also stems from his Machiavellian attitudes, however. Though the first part of the play ends with him triumphant, the second part concludes with the hero paying the price for his pride. Still, as an individual, Tamburlaine embodies the expansive optimism of Renaissance society, offering a heroism that fails to acknowledge limitation.

Marlowe's next major play, *The Jew of Malta,* appeared in 1593. Barabas, the protagonist, resembles Tamburlaine in his intense desire for wealth and revenge. In representing the struggle between Barabas, a wealthy Jew, and Malta's Catholic elite, Marlowe offers a world in which values are corrupted by materialism and a ruthless, scheming manner of human relations. In Marlowe's day, religious conflict permeated English society, which viewed Catholics and Jews with suspicion. Though the two plays differ, scholars believe that *The Jew of Malta* influenced Shakespeare's treatment of similar themes in *The Merchant of Venice.*

Marlowe continued to blend ambition and Machiavellianism in *Edward II,* recognized by many as the first great history play written in English. Different from earlier works, the play shifts focus from a single character to several complex relationships, a sign of Marlowe's advancing skill at weaving numerous plot threads. Marlowe telescopes more than two decades of history into the play, which alternates tragedy with comedy and lyricism. Echoes of *Edward II* appear in Shakespeare's *Richard II.*

Marlowe based *Doctor Faustus* on tales of a scholar and magician, Johann Faust, who allegedly sold his soul to the devil so that he might gain immense power. Marlowe found in this tale a parallel to the themes he explores in his previous three plays. In Faustus, however, he found a character whose thirst for power results in the most terrible price—the loss of his eternal soul. The story also

offered Marlowe a framework with which to examine the society in which he lived.

During the Renaissance, people realized that education offered economic opportunities. Still, then as now, professors and pedants were often sources of comedy, and some critics see *Doctor Faustus* as a satire of popular images of Humanist scholars. In some ways, Faustus's strengths as a scholar actually contribute to his downfall as a man. In that sense, the play can be seen not only as a critique of Humanism, but also of empiricism and the New Science generally.

Ironically, the fall of Faustus, a scholar and student of logic, comes in the end from his narrow understanding of logic in general and of the syllogism in particular. A syllogism consists of two statements which, if both true, make a third true. The most famous syllogism is ''Socrates is a man; all men are mortal; therefore, Socrates is mortal.'' If either of the first two statements is not universally true, the conclusion must be false.

In the play's first act, as Faustus plans future subjects for study, he rejects several—philosophy, law, medicine—before considering theology. He quotes the scripture of John, which indicates that the wages of sin is death (damnation), then realizes that all people sin and therefore that damnation is inevitable. ''We must sin, and so consequently die./Ay, we must die an everlasting death.'' He terms this ''hard,'' and then decides, if damnation cannot be avoided, to seek power from the devil.

Logically, Faustus's thoughts construct a syllogism. His two general statements—''sin leads to damnation'' and ''all people sin''—leads to his third—''all people are damned.'' Faustus has read the quote from John about the wages of sin out of context, however, for the rest of the quote promises mercy for those sinners willing to repent. Further, Faustus is reading (as he notes) Jerome's bible. Protestant Elizabethan England saw this edition, associated with Catholicism, as an erroneous text that altered or eliminated key elements of the Bible. Ironically, then, Faustus, the world's greatest scholar, comes to ruin because of faulty research methods: he misreads an important quote from a source that is untrustworthy.

As the narrative unfolds, Faustus's demands for learning teach him little, and his failure to reconcile empiricism with faith precipitates his downfall. *Doctor Faustus* is a play about an individual's

Scene from a 1974 production at London's Aldwych Theatre

knowledge of the world and how it relates to his knowledge of himself; it examines knowledge that serves as a means to an end and knowledge that is an end unto itself. This concept can be explained in two parts.

First, Marlowe's play is about knowledge of the world and of the self. For example, Faustus repeatedly demands from Mephistopheles information about natural and spiritual phenomenon, from facts about the planets to facts about hell. *Doctor Faustus* becomes a play about self-knowledge when the viewer considers Faustus's responses to Mephistopheles's lessons. When Faustus says, "First I will question thee about hell," Mephistopheles defines hell not as physical but psychological, not as a place but "a state of mind." Although Faustus receives this information from an authority (a devil of Hell), he refuses to believe Hell exists, clinging to the notion that Hell is an "old wives' tale." The devil gives Faustus a lesson in the scientific method, which emphasizes learning through direct experience. When Faustus clings to his existing prejudices, Mephistopheles replies, "Ay, think so still, till experience change thy mind."

Secondly, the play can be thought of as being about knowledge as a means to an end and knowledge that is an end. Here too, Faustus's understand-

ing is flawed. Faustus's questions of means—such as how the planets move?—lead him to inquire about ends—who created the planets and for what purpose? But when Faustus demands, "Now tell me, who made the world?" Mephistopheles replies, "I will not." Faustus knows the answer and says, "Think, Faustus, upon God, that made the world." Try as he might, though, Faustus cannot repent to this God. Consequently Mephistopheles's information regarding nature cannot give Faustus answers about God that are any different from what he already knew before selling his soul. Faustus's fixation with amassing as much knowledge as he can is not in the service of any goal; he is not learning to accomplish anything.

As a failed practitioner of the scientific method, Faustus refuses to evaluate evidence and experience objectively and instead relies on the prejudices of traditional, and in a sense superstitious, medieval religion. Just as medieval scholars resisted questioning Aristotle's natural science, so Faustus relies on medieval church doctrine. Faustus seeks a physical hell rather than taking Mephistopheles at his word that hell is psychological. If knowledge comes from observation, however, the devil's empirical evidence should be superior to Faustus's book learning. Still, he does not believe.

Source: Arnold Schmidt, in an essay for *Drama for Students,* Gale, 1997.

W. W. Greg

In the following essay, Greg examines several aspects of the hero's downfall in Doctor Faustus, *particularly how Faustus's pact with Mephistopheles leads not to a rise in grandeur and power, but to mere worldly gratification. Ultimately, the critic claims, Faustus ''commits the sin of demonality, that is, bodily intercourse with demons.'' The quotations are taken from Greg's own collation of the 1604 and 1616 quarto editions of* Doctor Faustus.

An English literary scholar and librarian, Greg was a pioneer in establishing modern bibliographical scholarship. Combining bibliographical and critical methods, he developed an approach to editing Shakespeare and other Elizabethan dramatists.

When working lately on the text of *Doctor Faustus,* I was struck by certain aspects of the story as told in Marlowe's play that I do not remember to have seen discussed in the editions with which I am familiar. I do not pretend to have read more than a little of what has been written about Marlowe as a dramatist, and it may be that there is nothing new in what I have to say; but it seemed worth while to draw attention to a few points in the picture of the hero's downfall, on the chance that they might have escaped the attention of others, as they had hitherto escaped my own.

As soon as Faustus has decided that necromancy is the only study that can give his ambition scope, he seeks the aid of his friends Valdes and Cornelius, who already are proficients in the art—

Their conference will be a greater help to me/Than all my labours, plod I ne'er so fast.

Who they are we have no notion: they do not appear in the source on which Marlowe drew— 'The historie of the damnable life, and deserved death of Doctor John Faustus . . . according to the true Copie printed at Franckfort, and translated into English by P. F. Gent.'—and Cornelius is certainly not the famous Cornelius Agrippa, who is mentioned in their conversation. But they must have been familiar figures at Wittenberg, since on learning that Faustus is at dinner with them, his students at once conclude that he is 'fallen into that damned art for which they two are infamous through the world'. The pair are ready enough to obey Faustus' invitation, for they have long sought to lead him into forbidden ways. 'Know', says Faustus—

Know that your words have won me at the last/ To practise magic and concealed arts

At the same time, though they are his 'dearest friends', he is anxious not to appear too pliant, adding, a little clumsily (if the 1604 text is to be trusted)

Yet not your words only, but mine own fantasy,

and he makes it plain that he is no humble seeker after instruction, but one whose personal fame and honour are to be their main concern—

Then, gentle friends, aid me in this attempt,
And I, that have with concise syllogisms
Gravelled the pastors of the German church,
And made the flowering pride of Wittenberg
Swarm to my problems, as the infernal spirits
On sweet Musaeus when he came to hell,
Will be as cunning as Agrippa was,
Whose shadows made all Europe honour him.

His friends are content enough to accept him on these terms. Valdes, while hinting that common contributions deserve common rewards—

Faustus, these books, thy wit, and our experience
Shall make all nations to canonize us—

paints a glowing picture of the possibilities before them, adding however—in view of what follows a little ominously—

If learned Faustus will be resolute.

Reassured on this score, Cornelius is ready to allow Faustus pride of place—

Then doubt not, Faustus, but to be renowned,
And more frequented for this mystery
Than heretofore the Delphian oracle—

but only on condition that the profits of the enterprise are shared—

Then tell me, Faustus, What shall we three want?

However, it soon appears that for all their sinister reputation the two are but dabblers in witchcraft. They have, indeed, called spirits from the deep, and they have come—

The spirits tell me they can dry the sea
And fetch the treasure of all foreign wracks,
Yea, all the wealth that our forefathers hid
Within the massy entrails of the earth—

but they have made no use of this knowledge, they have never become the masters—or the slaves—of the spirits. Even to raise them they must, of course, have run a mortal risk—

Nor will we come unless he use such means/Wherby he is in danger to be damned—

but they have been careful not to forfeit their salvation for supernatural gifts; they have never succumbed to the temptation of the spirits or made proof of their boasted powers. Nor do they mean to put their own art to the ultimate test. When Faustus eagerly demands,

> Come, show me some demonstrations magical,

Valdes proves himself a ready teacher—

> Then haste thee to some solitary grove,
> And bear wise Bacon's and Albanus' works,
> The Hebrew Psalter, and New Testament;
> And whatsoever else is requisite
> We will inform thee ere our conference cease—

and guarantees to make him proficient in the art—

> First I'll instruct thee in the rudiments,/And then wilt thou be perfecter than I.

Knowing the depth of Faustus' learning, and satisfied of his courage and resolution, they are anxious to form a partnership with one whose potentialities as an adept so far exceed their own. But Cornelius leaves us in no doubt of their intention to use Faustus as a cat's-paw rather than run into danger themselves—

> Valdes, first let him know the words of art, /And then, all other ceremonies learned, /Faustus may try his cunning by himself.

The precious pair are no deeply versed magicians welcoming a promising beginner, but merely the devil's decoys luring Faustus along the road to destruction. They serve their purpose in giving a dramatic turn to the scene of his temptation, and except for a passing mention by the students, we hear no more of them.

Faustus goes to conjure alone, and alone he concludes his pact with the devil. What use will he make of his hazardously won powers? His dreams, if self-centred, are in the heroic vein:

> Oh, what a world of profit and delight,
> Of power, of honour, and omnipotence,
> Is promised to the studious artizan!
> All things that move between the quiet poles
> Shall be at my command; emperors and kings
> Are but obeyed in their several provinces,
> But his dominion that exceeds in this
> Stretcheth as far as doth the mind of man:
> A sound magician is a demi-god!

More than mortal power and knowledge shall be his, to use in the service of his country:

> Shall I make spirits fetch me what I please?
> Resolve me of all ambiguities?
> Perform what desperate enterprise I will? . . .
> I'll have them read me strange philosophy
> And tell the secrets of all foreign kings;
> I'll have them wall all Germany with brass, . . .
> And chase the Prince of Parma from our land . . .

Whatever baser elements there may be in his ambition, we should, by all human standards, expect the fearless seeker after knowledge and truth, the scholar weary of the futilities of orthodox learning, to make at least no ignoble use of the power suddenly placed at his command.

Critics have complained that instead of pursuing ends worthy of his professed ideals, Faustus, once power is his, abandons these without a qualm, and shows himself content to amuse the Emperor with conjuring tricks and play childish pranks on the Pope; and they have blamed this either on a collaborator, or on the fact of Marlowe's work having been later overlaid and debased by another hand.

The charge, in its crudest form, involves some disregard of the 1616 version, which is not quite as fatuous as its predecessor, but in broad outline there is no denying its justice. As to responsibility: it is of course obvious that not all the play as we have it is Marlowe's. For my own part, however, I do not believe that as originally written it differed to any material extent from what we are able to reconstruct from a comparison of the two versions in which it has come down to us. And while it is true that the middle portion, to which objection is mostly taken, shows little trace of Marlowe's hand, I see no reason to doubt that it was he who planned the whole, or that his collaborator or collaborators, whoever he or they may have been, carried out his plan substantially according to instructions. If that is so, for any fundamental fault in the design Marlowe must be held responsible.

The critics' disappointment is quite natural. Although it is difficult to see how any dramatist could have presented in language and dramatic form the revelation of a knowledge beyond the reach of human wisdom, there is no question that much more might have been done to show the wonder and uphold the dignity of the quest, and so satisfy the natural expectation of the audience. Marlowe did not do it; he deliberately turned from the attempt. Instead he showed us the betrayal of ideals, the lapse into luxury and buffoonery.

And what, in the devil's name, would the critics have? I say 'in the devil's name', because all that happens to Faustus once the pact is signed is the devil's work: 'human standards' are no longer relevant. Who but a fool, such a clever fool as Faustus, would dream that any power but evil could be won by a bargain with evil, or that truth could be wrung from the father of lies? 'All power tends to corrupt, and absolute power corrupts absolutely,' is indeed an aphorism to which few Elizabethans would have subscribed; but Marlowe knew the nature of the power he put into the hands of his hero and the inevitable curse it carried with it.

Of course, Faustus' corruption is not a mechanical outcome of his pact with evil. In spite of his earnest desire to know truth, and half-hidden in the Marlowan glamour cast about him, the seeds of decay are in his character from the first—how else should he come to make his fatal bargain? Beside his passion for knowledge is a lust for riches and pleasure and power. If less single-minded, he shares Barabbas' thirst for wealth—

> I'll have them fly to India for gold,
> Ransack the ocean for orient pearl,
> And search all corners of the new-found world
> For pleasant fruits and princely delicates . . .

Patriotism is a veil for ambition: he will

> chase the Prince of Parma from our land
> And reign sole king of all our provinces . . .
> I'll join the hills that bind the Afric shore
> And make that country continent to Spain,
> And both contributary to my crown:
> The Emperor shall not live but by my leave,
> Nor any potentate in Germany.

His aspiration to be 'great emperor of the world' recalls Tamburlain's vulgar desire for

> The sweet fruition of an earthly crown.

But Faustus' ambition is not thus limited; the promptings of his soul reveal themselves in the words of the Bad Angel:

> Be thou on earth, as Jove is in the sky/Lord and commander of these elements.

If there is a sensual vein in him, it is hardly seen at this stage; still his demand to 'live in all voluptuousness' anticipates later desires—

> Whilst I am here on earth let me be cloyed
> With all things that delight the heart of man;
> My four and twenty years of liberty
> I'll spend in pleasure and in dalliance—

and it may be with shrewd insight that Valdes promises 'serviceable' spirits,

> Sometimes like women or unwedded maids/Shadowing more beauty in their airy brows /Than in the white breasts of the Queen of Love.

But when all is said, this means no more than that Faustus is a man dazzled by the unlimited possibilities of magic, and alive enough to his own weakness to exclaim:

> The god thou serv'st is thine own appetite . . .

After Faustus has signed the bond with his blood, we can trace the stages of a gradual deterioration. His previous interview with Mephostophilis struck the note of earnest if slightly sceptical inquiry with which he entered on his quest:

> This word Damnation terrifies not me,/ For I confound hell in Elizium: /My ghost be with the old philosophers!

He questions eagerly about hell, and the spirit replies:

> Why, this is hell, nor am I out of it:
> Think'st thou that I who saw the face of God
> And tasted the eternal joys of heaven,
> Am not tormented with ten thousand hells
> In being deprived of everlasting bliss? . . .
> FAU.: What, is great Mephostophilis so passionate
> For being deprived of the joys of heaven?
> Learn thou of Faustus manly fortitude,
> And scorn those joys thou never shalt possess.

After the bond is signed the discussion is renewed, but while the devil loses nothing in dignity of serious discourse, we can already detect a change in Faustus; his sceptical levity takes on a more truculent and jeering tone. Asked 'Where is the place that men call hell?' Mephostophilis replies:

> Within the bowels of these elements,
> Where we are tortured and remain for ever.
> Hell hath no limits, nor is circumscribed
> In one self place, but where we are is hell,
> And where hell is, there must we ever be:
> And to conclude, when all the world dissolves
> And every creature shall be purified,
> All places shall be hell that is not heaven.
> FAU.: Come, I think hell's a fable.
> MEPH.: Ay, think so still, till experience change thy mind. . . .
> FAU.: . . . Think'st thou that Faustus is so fond to imagine
> That after this life there is any pain?
> Tush! these are trifles and mere old wives' tales.
> MEPH.: But I am an instance to prove the contrary;
> For I tell thee I am damned and now in hell.
> FAU.: Nay, and this be hell, I'll willingly be damned:
> What? sleeping, eating, walking, and disputing!

In the next scene there follows the curiously barren discussion on astronomy. It has probably been interpolated and is not altogether easy to follow, but the infernal exposition of the movements of the spheres calls forth an impatient,

> These slender questions Wagner can decide

and at the end Mephostophilis' sententions

> Per inaequalem motum respectu totius

and Faustus' half-satisfied

> Well, I am answered!

leave in the mouth the taste of dead-sea fruit. The quarrel that follows on the spirit's refusal to say who made the world leads to the intervention of Lucifer and the 'pastime' of the Seven Deadly Sins. There seems to me more savour in this than has sometimes been allowed; still it is a much shrunken Faustus who exclaims:

Oh, this feeds my soul!

He had been no less delighted with the dance of the devils that offered him crowns and rich apparel on his signing the bond: we do not know its nature, but from his exclamation,

Then there's enough for a thousand souls!

when told that he may conjure up such spirits at will, we may perhaps conclude that it involved a direct appeal to the senses. That would, at least, accord with his mood soon afterwards; for while it would be rash to lay much stress on his demanding 'the fairest maid in Germany, for I am wanton and lascivious' (this being perhaps an interpolation) we should allow due weight to Mephostophilis' promise:

I'll cull thee out the fairest courtesans
And bring them every morning to thy bed;
She whom thine eye shall like, thy heart
    shall have,
Were she as chaste as was Penelope,
As wise as Saba, or as beautiful
As was bright Lucifer before his fall.

So far Faustus has not left Wittenberg, and emphasis has been rather on the hollowness of his bargain in respect of any intellectual enlightenment than on the actual degradation of his character. As yet only his childish pleasure in the devil-dance and the pageant of the Sins hints at the depth of vulgar triviality into which he is doomed to descend. In company with Mephostophilis he now launches forth into the world; but his dragon-flights

To find the secrets of astronomy /Graven in the book of Jove's high firmament,

and

to prove cosmography,/ That measures coasts and kingdoms of the earth,

only land him at last in the Pope's privy-chamber to

take some part of holy Peter's feast,

and live with dalliance in

the view /Of rarest things and royal courts of kings . . .

It is true that in the fuller text of 1616 the rescue of 'holy Bruno', imperial candidate for the papal throne, lends a more serious touch to the sheer horse-play of the Roman scenes in the 1604 ver-

sion, and even the 'horning' episode at the Emperor's court is at least developed into some dramatic coherence; but this only brings out more pointedly the progressive fatuity of Faustus' career, which in the clownage and conjuring tricks at Anhalt sinks to the depth of buffoonery.

If, as may be argued, the gradual deterioration of Faustus' character and the prostitution of his powers stand out less clearly than they should, this may be ascribed partly to Marlowe's negligent handling of a theme that failed to kindle his wayward inspiration, and partly to the ineptitude of his collaborator. But the logical outline is there, and I must differ from Marlowe's critics, and believe that when he sketched that outline Marlowe knew what he was about.

Another point to be borne in mind is that there is something strange and peculiar, not only in Faustus' situation, but in his nature. Once he has signed the bond, he is in the position of having of his own free will renounced salvation. So much is obvious. Less obvious is the inner change he has brought upon himself. Critics have strangely neglected the first article of the infernal compact: 'that Faustus may be a spirit in form and substance'. Presumably they have taken it to mean merely that he should be free of the bonds of flesh, so that he may be invisible at will, invulnerable, and able to change his shape, ride on dragons, and so forth. But in this play 'spirit' is used in a special sense. There is, of course, nothing very significant in the fact that, when the 'devils' dance before him, Faustus asks:

But may I raise such spirits when I please?

  that he promises to

make my spirits pull His churches down

  and bids Mephostophilis

Ay, go, accursed spirit to ugly hell!

  or that the latter speaks of the devils as

Unhappy spirits that fell with Lucifer—

though it is noticeable how persistently devils are called spirits in the play, and it is worth recalling that in the *Damnable Life* Mephostophilis is regularly 'the Spirit'. What is significant is that when Faustus asks 'What is that Lucifer, thy lord?' Mephostophilis replies:

Arch-regent and commander of all spirits

which Faustus at once interprets as 'prince of devils'; and that the Bad Angel, in reply to Faustus' cry of repentance, asserts:

Thou art a spirit; God cannot pity thee

—a remark to which I shall return. And if there could be any doubt of the meaning of these expressions, we have the explicit statement in the *Damnable Life* that Faustus' 'request was none other than to become a devil'. Faustus then, through his bargain with hell, has himself taken on the infernal nature, although it is made clear throughout that he still retains his human soul.

This throws a new light upon the question, debated throughout the play, whether Faustus can be saved by repentance. Faustus, of course, is for ever repenting—and recanting through fear of bodily torture and death—and the Good and Bad Angels, who personate the two sides of his human nature, for are ever disputing the point:

FAU.: Contrition, prayer, repentance: what of these?

GOOD A.: Oh, they are means to bring thee vnto heaven.
BAD A.: Rather illusions, fruits of lunacy

and again:

GOOD A. Never too late, if Faustus will repent.
BAD A. If thou repent, devils will tear thee in pieces.
GOOD A. Repent, and they shall never raze thy skin.

There are two passages that are particularly significant in this respect: and we must remember, as I have said, the double question at issue—Faustus' nature, and whether repentance can cancel a bargain. First then, the passage from which I have already quoted:

GOOD A.: Faustus, repent; yet God will pity thee.
BAD A.: Thou art a spirit; God cannot pity thee.
FAU.: Who buzzeth in mine ears, I am a spirit?
Be I a devil, yet God may pity me;
Yes, God will pity me if I repent.
BAD A.: Ay, but Faustus never shall repent.

The Bad Angel evades the issue, which is left undecided. Later in the same scene, when Faustus calls on Christ to save his soul, Lucifer replies with admirable logic:

Christ cannot save thy soul, for he is just:/ There's none but I have interest in the same.

Thus the possibility of Faustus' salvation is left nicely poised in doubt—like that of the archdeacon of scholastic speculation.

It is only when, back among his students at Wittenberg, he faces the final reckoning that Faustus regains some measure of heroic dignity. Mar-

lowe again takes charge. But even so the years have wrought a change. His faithful Wagner is puzzled:

I wonder what he means; if death were nigh,
He would not banquet and carouse and swill
Among the students, as even now he doth . . .

This is a very different Faustus from the fearless teacher his students used to know, whose least absence from the class-room caused concern—

I wonder what's become of Faustus, that was/ wont to make our schools ring with *sic probo.*

One good, or at least amiable, quality—apart from a genuine tenderness towards his students—we may be tempted to claim for him throughout: a love of beauty in nature and in art:

Have not I made blind Homer sing to me
Of Alexander's love and Oenon's death?
And hath not he that built the walls of Thebes
With ravishing sound of his melodious harp
Made music—?

and the climax of his career is his union with the immortal beauty of Helen, to measures admittedly the most lovely that flowed from Marlowe's lyre. Is this sensitive appreciation something that has survived uncorrupted from his days of innocence? I can find no hint of it in the austere student of the early scenes. Is it then some strange flowering of moral decay? It would seem so. What, after all, is that 'ravishing sound' but the symphony of hell?—

Made music—with my Mephostophilis!

And Helen, what of her?

Here we come, if I mistake not, to the central theme of the damnation of Faustus. The lines in which he addresses Helen are some of the most famous in the language:

Was this the face that launched a thousand ships
And burnt the topless towers of Ilium?
Sweet Helen, make me immortal with a kiss! . . .
Here will I dwell, for heaven is in these lips,
And all is dross that is not Helena
I will be Paris, and for love of thee
Instead of Troy shall Wittenberg be smoked;
And I will combat with weak Menelaus,
And wear thy colours on my plumed crest:
Yes, I will wound Achilles in the heel,
And then return to Helen for a kiss.
Oh, thou art fairer than the evening's air
Clad in the beauty of a thousand stars,
Brighter art thou than flaming Jupiter
When he appeared to hapless Semele,
More lovely than the monarch of the sky
In wanton Arethusa's azured arms;
And none but thou shalt be my paramour!

In these lines Marlowe's uncertain genius soared to its height, but their splendour has obscured, and was perhaps meant discreetly to veil, the real nature of the situation. 'Her lips suck forth my soul', says Faustus in lines that I omitted from his speech above. What is Helen? We are not told in so many words, but the answer is there, if we choose to look for it. When the Emperor asks him to present Alexander and his paramour before the court, Faustus (in the 1604 version) laboriously explains the nature of the figures that are to appear:

> My gracious lord, I am ready to accomplish
> your request so far forth as by art and power of
> my spirit I am able to perform. . . . But, if it
> like your grace, it is not in my ability to present
> before your eyes the true substantial bodies of
> those two deceased princes, which long since are
> consumed to dust. . . . But such spirits as can
> lively resemble Alexander and his paramour
> shall appear before your grace in that manner
> that they best lived in, in their most flourishing
> estate . . .

He adds (according to the 1616 version):

> My lord, I must forewarn your majesty
> That, when my spirits present the royal shapes
> Of Alexander and his paramour,
> Your grace demand no questions of the king,
> But in dumb silence let them come and go.

This is explicit enough; and as a reminder that the same holds for Helen, Faustus repeats the caution when he presents her to his students:

> Be silent then, for danger is in words.

Consider, too, a point critics seem to have overlooked, the circumstances in which Helen is introduced the second time. Urged by the Old Man, Faustus has attempted a last revolt; as usual he has been cowed into submission, and has renewed the blood-bond. He has sunk so low as to beg revenge upon his would-be saviour—

> Torment, sweet friend, that base and aged man,/ That
> durst dissuade me from thy Lucifer, /With greatest
> torments that our hell affords.

And it is in the first place as a safeguard against relapse that he seeks possession of Helen—

> One thing, good servant, let me crave of thee
> To glut the longing of my heart's desire;
> That, I may have unto my paramour
> That heavenly Helen which I saw of late,
> Whose sweet embraces may extinguish clear
> Those thoughts that may dissuade me
>   from my vow,
> And keep mine oath I made to Lucifer.

Love and revenge are alike insurances against salvation. 'Helen' then is a 'spirit', and in this play a spirit means a devil. In making her his paramour Faustus commits the sin of demoniality, that is, bodily intercourse with demons.

The implication of Faustus' action is made plain in the comments of the Old Man and the Angels. Immediately before the Helen episode the Old Man was still calling on Faustus to repent—

> Ah, Doctor Faustus, that I might prevail/To guide thy
> steps into the way of life!

(So 1604:1616 proceeds:)

> Though thou hast now offended like a man,
> Do not persever in it like a devil:
> Yet, yet, thou hast an amiable soul,
> If sin by custom grow not into nature . . .

But with Faustus' union with Helen the nice balance between possible salvation and imminent damnation is upset. The Old Man, who has witnessed the meeting (according to the 1604 version), recognizes the inevitable:

> Accursed Faustus, miserable man, /That from thy
> soul exclud'st the grace of heaven/ And fliest the
> throne of his tribunal seat!

The Good Angel does no less:

> O Faustus, if thou hadst given ear to me/ Innumerable
> joys had followed thee . . ./ Oh, thou hast lost celestial
> happiness . . .

And Faustus himself, still haunted in his final agony by the idea of a salvation beyond his reach—

> See, see, where Christ's blood streams in the firma-
> ment! /One drop would save my soul

— shows, in talk with his students, a terrible clarity of vision:

> A surfeit of deadly sin, that hath damned both
> body and soul. . . . Faustus' offence can ne'er
> be pardoned: the Serpent that tempted Eve may
> be saved, but not Faustus.

and Mephostophilis echoes him:

> Ay, Faustus, now hast thou no hope of heaven!

It would be idle to speculate how far the 'atheist' Marlowe, whom gossip accused of what we call 'unnatural' vice, may have dwelt in imagination on the direst sin of which human flesh is capable. But in presenting the fall and slow moral disintegration of an ardent if erring spirit, he did not shrink from depicting, beside Faustus' spiritual sin of bartering his soul to the powers of evil, what is in effect its physical complement and counterpart, however he may have disguised it in immortal verse. (pp. 97–107)

Source: W. W. Greg, ''The Damnation of Faustus,'' in the *Modern Language Review*, Vol. XLI, No. 2, April, 1946, pp. 97–107.

Brooks Atkinson

In the following review of a 1937 production of The Tragical History of Dr. Faustus, *which origi-*

DR. FAUSTUS HAS THE
VITALITY OF A MODERN PLAY"

nally appeared in The New York Times *on January 9, 1937, Atkinson illustrates how the manner in which the play is staged enhances its effectiveness. Atkinson maintains that the result of the masterful staging in this production "is a* Dr. Faustus *that is physically and imaginatively alive, nimble, active— heady theatre stuff."*

As drama critic for The New York Times *from 1925 to 1960, Atkinson was one of the most influential reviewers in America.*

Although the Federal Theatre has some problem children on its hands, it also has some enterprising artists on its staff. Some of them got together at Maxine Elliott's Theatre last evening and put on a brilliantly original production of Christopher Marlowe's *The Tragical History of Dr. Faustus,* which dates from 1589. If that sounds like a schoolbook chore to you, be disabused, for the bigwigs of the Federal Theatre's Project 891 know how absorbing an Elizabethan play can be when it is staged according to the simple unities that obtained in the Elizabethan theatres. Every one interested in the imaginative power of the theatre will want to see how ably Orson Welles and John Houseman have cleared away all the imposing impedimenta that make most classics forbidding and how skillfully they have left *Dr. Faustus ,* grim and terrible, on the stage. By being sensible as well as artists, Mr. Welles and Mr. Houseman have gone along way toward revolutionizing the staging of Elizabethan plays.

Although *Dr. Faustus* is a short play, consuming hardly more than an hour in the telling, it is not a simple play to produce. It is the story of the eminent German philosopher who sold his soul to the devil in exchange for universal knowledge. Like most Elizabethan plays, it has an irresponsible scenario; it moves rapidly from place to place, vexing the story with a great many short scenes; it includes several incidents of supernaturalism and, of course, it is written in verse.

If the directors had tried to stage *Dr. Faustus* against descriptive backgrounds it would be intolerably tedious to follow. But they have virtually

stripped it of scenery and decoration, relying upon an ingenious use of lights to establish time and place. In the orchestra pit they have built an apron stage where the actors play cheek by jowl with the audience. The vision of the seven deadly sins is shown by puppets in the right-hand box. Upstage scenes are unmasked by curtained walls that can be lifted swiftly. Entrances are made not only from the wings, but from the orchestra pit and from trap doors that are bursting with light and that make small incidents uncommonly majestical.

The result is a *Dr. Faustus* that is physically and imaginatively alive, nimble, active—heady theatre stuff. As the learned doctor of damnation Orson Welles gives a robust performance that is mobile and commanding, and he speaks verse with a deliberation that clarifies the meaning and invigorates the sound of words. There are excellent performances in most of the parts, notably Jack Carter's Mephistopheles, Bernard Savage's friend to Faustus and Arthur Spencer's impudent servant. There are clowns, church processionals and coarse brawls along the street. Paul Bowles has composed a score which is somewhat undistinguished in itself, although it helps to arouse the illusion of black magic and diabolical conjuration.

Not that Elizabethan dramas have never been staged before under conditions approximating the conventions of Elizabethan theatres. Most of those experiments have a self-conscious and ascetic look to them. But Mr. Welles and Mr. Houseman have merely looked to the script and staged it naturally. In the first place, it is easy to understand, which is no common virtue. In the second place, it is infernally interesting. *Dr. Faustus* has the vitality of a modern play, and the verse sounds like good, forceful writing. For this is a simple experiment that has succeeded on its merits as frank and sensible theatre, and a good many people will now pay their taxes in a more charitable frame of mind.

Source: Brooks Atkinson, "*Faustus* Put On by the Federal Theatre" (1937) in *On Stage: Selected Theater Reviews from The New York Times, 1920–1970,* edited by Bernard Beckerman and Howard Siegman, Arno Press, 1973, pp. 185–86.

FURTHER READING

Brooks, Cleanth. "The Unity of Marlowe's *Doctor Faustus*" in *A Shaping of Joy: Studies in the Writer's Craft,* Harcourt Brace Jovanovich, 1972, pp. 367-80.

Brooks responds to those critics who fail to see the unity of *Doctor Faustus*. Brooks realizes that if Marlowe's agreement with the devil damns his soul to hell, then the play, in structural terms, has no conflict, offers no possible dramatic development, and becomes merely "elegiac." Admitting the weakness of the play's middle section, Brooks believes that the sheer force of Marlowe's poetry holds the play together. Thematically, Brooks sees the play as exploring various types of knowledge: of the self, of the natural world, and of the divine. While Marlowe's treatment of this theme has medieval elements, Brooks describes his use of demonic apparatus in essentially psychological terms, noting that "the devils . . . are always in some sense mirrors of the inner states of the persons to whom they appear."

Davison, Peter. "Doctor Faustus" in *International Dictionary of Theatre-1: Plays*, edited by Mark Hawkins-Dady, St. James Press, 1992, pp. 187-89.

In a short but focused commentary, Davison identifies the exact moment of Faustus's damnation as that in which he kisses Helen of Troy. Davison also usefully discusses the role of the Good and Bad Angels and of the Old Man.

Keeble, N. H. In *Reference Guide to English Literature*, edited by D. L. Kirkpatrick, St. James Press, 1991, pp. 1548-49.

Keeble provides background on the historical origins of the Faustus myth and shows how Marlowe may have been introduced to the original German story. Agreeing with critics who believe that Marlowe did not write the play's comic interludes (the middle acts), Keeble sees the subplots as the work of another writer, most likely Samuel Rowley. Keeble perceives as mistaken those who read *Doctor Faustus* as an anti-Christian play and views Faustus's self-deception as his tragic flaw. The play's fine ending contains Faustus's final soliloquy, which Keeble sees as "one of the most powerful in all Renaissance drama."

Knights, L. C. "The Strange Case of Christopher Marlowe" in *Further Explorations*, Chatto & Windus, 1965, pp. 75-98.

Knights sees Marlowe's *Doctor Faustus* essentially as a play about desire and limitation. These can be destructive, as they are for Faustus himself but balanced properly, they result in a true understanding of reality. Knights describes Faustus's motivations as essentially immature, driven by "the perverse and infantile desire for enormous power and immediate gratifications." Knights does not trivialize this desire nor see it as inherently evil, for when it leads to a recognition of human limitation, this balance of desire and limit produces a mature understanding of reality. Faustus's fall results not from his desire, but from his refusal to accept human limitation.

Maxwell, J. C. Introduction to *Complete Plays and Poems of Christopher Marlowe*, Everyman, 1996, pp. vii-xxvi.

In a short but thorough overview of Marlowe's writings, Maxwell presents biographical information, as well as thematic analyses of the author's work.

Sanders, Wilbur. In *Shakespeare's Contemporaries: Modern Studies in English Renaissance Drama*, edited by Max Bluestone and Norman Rabkin, second edition, Prentice-Hall, 1970, pp. 112-27.

Sanders sees Marlowe's *Doctor Faustus* as a great, though flawed play with structural, aesthetic, and thematic inconsistencies. The "unity of *Doctor Faustus* is . . . something that we have to create for ourselves," wrote Sanders, who has difficulty reconciling the play's strong opening and closing sections with its formless middle. Audiences must appreciate the magnificent poetic moments, which overlooking other poetry of "baffling banality, if not naivety." Finally, Sanders believes that the play mixes without successfully blending medieval and modern theological elements, particularly in regard to its conflicting images of Hell.

A Doll's House

HENRIK IBSEN

1879

A Doll's House was published on December 4, 1879, and first performed in Copenhagen on December 21, 1879. The work was considered a publishing event and the play's initial printing of 8,000 copies quickly sold out. The play was so controversial that Ibsen was forced to write a second ending that he called ''a barbaric outrage'' to be used only when necessary. The controversy centered around Nora's decision to abandon her children, and in the second ending she decides that the children need her more than she needs her freedom. Ibsen believed that women were best suited to be mothers and wives, but at the same time, he had an eye for injustice and Helmer's demeaning treatment of Nora was a common problem. Although he would later be embraced by feminists, Ibsen was no champion of women's rights; he only dealt with the problem of women's rights as a facet of the realism within his play. His intention was not to solve this issue but to illuminate it. Although Ibsen's depiction of Nora realistically illustrates the issues facing women, his decision in Act III to have her abandon her marriage and children was lambasted by critics as unrealistic, since, according to them, no ''real'' woman would ever make that choice. That Ibsen offered no real solution to Nora's dilemma inflamed critics and readers alike who were then left to debate the ending ceaselessly. This play established a new genre of modern drama; prior to *A Doll's House,* contemporary plays were usually historical romances or contrived comedy of manners. Ibsen is known as the

"father of modern drama" because he elevated theatre from entertainment to a forum for exposing social problems. Ibsen broke away from the romantic tradition with his realistic portrayals of individual characters and his focus on psychological concerns as he sought to portray the real world, especially the position of women in society.

AUTHOR BIOGRAPHY

Ibsen was born March 20, 1828, in Skien, Norway, a lumbering town south of Christiania, now Oslo. He was the second son in a wealthy family that included five other siblings. In 1835, financial problems forced the family to move to a smaller house in Venstop outside Skien. After eight years the family moved back to Skein, and Ibsen moved to Grimstad to study as an apothecary's assistant. He applied to and was rejected at Christiania University. During the winter of 1848 Ibsen wrote his first play, *Catiline,* which was rejected by the Christiania Theatre; it was finally published in 1850 under the pseudonym Brynjolf Bjarme and generated little interest. Ibsen's second play, *The Burial Mound,* was also written under the pseudonym Brynjolf Bjarme, and became the first Ibsen play to be performed when it was presented on September 26, 1850, at the Christiania Theatre.

In 1851 Ibsen accepted an appointment as an assistant stage manager at the Norwegian Theatre in Bergen. He was also expected to assist the theatre as a dramatic author, and during his tenure at Bergen, Ibsen wrote *Lady Inger* (1855), *The Feast at Solhoug* (1856), and *Olaf Liljekrans* (1857). These early plays were written in verse and drawn from Norse folklore and myths. In 1857 Ibsen was released from his contract at Bergen and accepted a position at the Norwegian Theatre in Christiania. While there, Ibsen published *The Vikings at Helgeland* and married Suzannah Thoresen in 1858. The couple's only child, Sigurd, was born the following year.

By 1860, Ibsen was under attack in the press for a lack of productivity—although he had published a few poems during this period. When the Christiania Theatre went bankrupt in 1862, Ibsen was left with no regular income except a temporary position as a literary advisor to the reorganized Christiania Theatre. Due to a series of small government grants, by 1863 Ibsen was able to travel in Europe and begin what became an intense period of creativity. During

Henrik Ibsen

this period, Ibsen completed *The Pretenders* (1863) and a dramatic epic poem, "Brand" (1866), which achieved critical notice; these works were soon followed by *Peter Gynt* (1867). The first of Ibsen's prose dramas, *The League of Youth,* published in 1869, was also the first of his plays to demonstrate a shift from an emphasis on plot to one of interpersonal relationships. This was followed by *Emperor and Galilean* (1873), Ibsen's first work to be translated into English, and *Pillars of Society* (1877). *A Doll's House* (1879), *Ghosts* (1881), and *An Enemy of the People* (1882) are among the last plays included in Ibsen's realism period. Ibsen continued to write of modern realistic themes in his next plays, but he also relied increasingly on metaphor and symbolism in *The Wild Duck* (1884) and *Hedda Gabler* (1890).

A shift from social concerns to the isolation of the individual marks the next phase of Ibsen's work. *The Master Builder* (1892), *Little Eyolf* (1894), *John Gabriel Borkman* (1896), and *When We Dead Awaken* (1899) all treat the conflicts that arise between art and life, between creativity and social expectations, and between personal contentment and self deception. These last works are considered by many critics to be autobiographical. In 1900, Ibsen suffered his first of several strokes. Ill health ended his writing career, and he died May 23, 1906.

Although Ibsen's audiences may have debated the social problems he depicted, modern critics are more often interested in the philosophical and psychological elements depicted in his plays and the ideological debates they generated.

PLOT SUMMARY

Act I

The play opens on the day before Christmas. Nora returns home from shopping; although her husband is anticipating a promotion and raise, he still chides her excessive spending. In response, Nora flirts, pouts, and cajoles her husband as a child might, and, indeed, Torvald addresses her as he might a child. He hands her more money but only after having berating her spending. Their relationship parallels that of a daughter and father and, indeed, is exactly like the relationship Nora had with her father. Early in this act the audience is aware that the relationship between the Helmers is based on dishonesty when Nora denies that she has eaten macaroons, knowing that her husband has forbidden her to do so.

Nora is visited by an old friend, Kristine Linde. Mrs. Linde tells Nora that she has had some difficult problems and is seeking employment. Nora confesses to Mrs. Linde that she, too, has been desperate and recounts that she had been forced to borrow money several years earlier when her husband was ill. The money was necessary to finance a trip that saved her husband's life, but Nora forged her father's signature to secure the loan and lied to Torvald that her father had given them the money. Thus, she has been deceiving her husband for years as she worked to repay the loan. She tells this story to Mrs. Linde to demonstrate that she is an adult who is capable of both caring for her family and conducting business. Unfortunately, Nora's secret is shared by Krogstad, an employee at Torvald's bank. After a confrontation with Krogstad, Torvald decides to fire Krogstad and hire Mrs. Linde in his place.

Krogstad threatens Nora, telling her that if he loses his job he will reveal her earlier dishonesty. Krogstad fails to understand that Nora has no influence with her husband, nor does he appreciate the level of dishonesty that characterizes the Helmer marriage. For her part, Nora cannot believe that forging her father's signature-an act that saved her husband's life-could lead to a serious punishment.

She cannot conceive that she could be held accountable and has an unrealistic appreciation for how the law and society functions. Still, she is concerned enough to plead Krogstad's cause with Torvald. Torvald refuses to reconsider firing Krogstad and forbids Nora to even mention his name.

Act II

Mrs. Linde stops by to help Nora prepare for a costume ball. Nora explains to Mrs. Linde that Krogstad is blackmailing her about the earlier loan. After Nora again begs Torvald not to fire Krogstad, her husband sends Krogstad an immediate notice of his dismissal. Nora is desperate and decides to ask help of Dr. Rank, a family friend. Before she can ask him for his help, Dr. Rank makes it obvious that he is in love with her and Nora determines that because of this it would be unwise to ask his help. Krogstad visits Nora once again and this time leaves a letter for Torvald in which Nora's dishonesty is revealed. To divert Torvald's attention from the mailbox, Nora elicits his help with her practice of the dance she is to perform, the tarantella. Finally, Nora asks Torvald to promise that he will not read the mail until after the party.

Act III

Krogstad had years earlier been in love with Mrs. Linde. At the beginning of this act they agree to marry, and Krogstad offers to retrieve his letter from Torvald. However, Mrs. Linde disagrees and thinks that it is time that Nora is forced to confront the dishonesty in her marriage. After the party, the Helmers return home and Torvald reads the letter from Krogstad. While Torvald reads in his study, Nora pictures herself as dead, having committed suicide by drowning in the icy river. Torvald interrupts her fantasy by demanding that she explain her deception. However, he refuses to listen and is only concerned with the damage to his own reputation. Torvald's focus on his own life and his lack of appreciation for the suffering undergone by Nora serve to open her eyes to her husband's faults. She had been expecting Torvald to rescue her and protect her, and instead he only condemns her and insists that she is not a fit mother to their children. At that moment another letter arrives from Krogstad telling the Helmers that he will not take legal action against Nora. Torvald is immediately appeased and is willing to forget the entire episode. But having seen her husband revealed as a self-centered, selfish, hypocrite, Nora tells him that she can no longer live as a doll and expresses her intention to leave the

Alan Hale and Alla Nazimova in a scene from a 1922 production

house immediately. Torvald begs her to stay, but the play ends with Nora leaving the house, her husband, and her children.

CHARACTERS

Nora Helmer

Nora is the "doll" wife of Torvald. She is sensitive, sensible, and completely unaware of her own worth until the last act of the play. She initially appears flighty and excitable. Nora is most concerned with charming her husband and being the perfect wife; she is also secretive and hides her thoughts and actions from her husband even when there is no real benefit in doing so. Rather, deception appears to be almost a habit for Nora. Her husband constantly refers to her with pet names, such as "singing lark," "little squirrel," and "little spendthrift." He pats her on the head much as one would a favorite puppy. She forges her father's signature on a loan, lies to her husband about the source of the money, lies about how she spends the household accounts, and lies about odd jobs she takes to earn extra money. She is viewed as an object, a toy, a child, but never an equal. Her problem is that she is totally dependent upon her husband for all her needs; or she deceives herself into thinking so until the end of the play.

Torvald Helmer

Torvald is a smug lawyer and bank manager who represents a social structure that has decreed an inferior position for women. He is a symbol of society: male dominated, authoritative, and autocratic. He establishes rules for his wife, Nora. Some of the rules, such as no eating of macaroons, are petty and demeaning. He refers to his wife in the diminutive. She is always little, a plaything, a doll that must be occasionally indulged. He treats Nora just as her father did. Torvald has established a system of reward for Nora that responds to her subservient and childlike behaviors. If she flirts and wheedles and begs, he rewards her with whatever she asks. Torvald is critical of Nora when she practices her dance because he wants to keep her passion under control and he is concerned with propriety. He is completely unaware that Nora is capable of making serious decisions and is baffled at the play's conclusion when she announces that she is leaving him. He has failed to consider that she might have any serious needs or that her desires may contradict his own. Torvald is not a Neanderthal or a villain, but he often presents a challenge to students who can find little that is positive in his characterization.

Nils Krogstad

Krogstad is desperate and so initially he appears to be a villain; in fact, he has been trying to remake his life after having made earlier mistakes. He has also been disappointed in love and is bitter. His threats to Nora reflect his anger at being denied the opportunity to start over and his concerns about supporting his dependent children. Accordingly, he is not the unfeeling blackmailer he is presented as in the first act. Once he is reunited with his lost love, Mrs. Linde, he recants and attempts to rectify his earlier actions.

Kristine Linde

Mrs. Linde is a childhood friend of Nora's. She functions as the primary means by which the audience learns of Nora's secret. Mrs. Linde is a widow and quite desperate for work. At one time she was in love with Krogstad, but chose to marry for money so that she could provide support for her mother and

MEDIA ADAPTATIONS

- *A Doll's House* was adapted for television for the first time in 1959. The adaptation starred Julie Harris, Christopher Plummer, Jason Robards, Hume Cronyn, Eileen Heckart, and Richard Thomas. Sonny Fox Productions. Available on videotape through MGM/UA Home Video, black and white, 89 minutes.

- *A Doll's House* was adapted for film for the second time in 1973. This version stars Jane Fonda, Edward Fox, Trevor Howard, and David Warner. The screenplay was by David Mercer. World Film services. Available on videotape through Prism Entertainment/Starmaker Entertainment, color, 98 minutes.

- *A Doll's House* was adapted for film again in 1977. This film stars Claire Bloom. Paramount Pictures.

- *A Doll's House* was adapted for film again in a 1989 Canadian production. Starring Claire Bloom, Anthony Hopkins, Ralph Richardson, Denholm Elliott, Anna Massey, and Edith Evans, this is

considered a superior adaptation of the play. Elkins Productions Limited. Available on videotape through Hemdale Home Video, color, 96 minutes.

- *A Doll's House* was adapted for film most recently in 1991. This cast includes Juliet Stevenson, Trevor Eve, Geraldine James, Patrick Malahide, and David Calder. This is an excellent adaptation with some insightful commentaries by Alistair Cooke. PBS and BBC.

- In *A Doll's House, Part 1: The Destruction of Illusion*, Norris Houghton helps the audience explore the subsurface tensions of the play. Britannica Films, 1968.

- In *A Doll's House, Part II: Ibsen's Themes*, Norris Houghton examines the characters and the themes of the play. Britannica Films, 1968.

- *A Doll's House,* audio recording, 3 cassettes. With Claire Bloom and Donald Madden. Caedmon/Harper Audio.

---

younger brothers. At the end of the play, she and Krogstad are reconciled, but it is Mrs. Linde who decides that Nora and Torvald must face their problems. Thus, she stops Krogstad from retrieving his letter and moves the play toward its conclusion.

Dr. Rank

Dr. Rank is a family friend of the Helmers, who is secretly in love with Nora. Dr. Rank has been affected by his father's corruption; he suffers from syphilis inherited from his father and he is dying. When Nora finally realizes that Rank loves her, she decides that she cannot ask him for help. Rank's treatment of Nora contrasts sharply with Torvald's. Rank always treats Nora like an adult. He listens to her and affords her a dignity missing in Torvald's treatment. He tells Nora that when he is near death he will send her a card. It arrives in the same mail as

Krogstad's letter and receives little attention in the ensuing melee.

THEMES

Nora Helmer, the "doll" wife, realizes after eight years of marriage that she has never been a partner in her marriage. At the play's conclusion, she leaves her husband in order to establish an identity for herself that is separate from her identity as a wife and mother.

Appearances and Reality

On the surface, Nora Helmer appears to be the ideal wife her husband desires. Torvald sees a

TOPICS FOR FURTHER STUDY

- Feminists are often bothered by the reconciliation between Kristine and Krogstad. Just as Nora is breaking free of the confines of her marriage, Kristine is embracing marriage. Do you agree with some feminists critics that Kristine's decision to reunite with Krogstad negates Nora's flight to personal freedom? Investigate the role of women in late nineteenth-century marriage and compare the two different ways that Nora and Kristine seek to define their identity within the social convention of marital life.

- In a second ending that Ibsen was forced to write, Nora looks at her sleeping children and realizes that she cannot leave them. Instead of seeking her freedom and discovering her identity, she decides to remain in the marriage. Compare the two endings offered for this play. Given the social and cultural context in which the play is set, which ending do you think best reflects the realities of nineteenth-century European life?

- The Helmer's marriage can best be described as a marriage of deception. Torvald has no idea who Nora really is and is in love with the wife he thinks he possesses. Nora is also in love with a vision rather than reality. During the course of the play, these deceptions are stripped away and each sees the other as if for the first time. The audience also sees the reality of Victorian life. The ideal family and house, the decorated tree and the festivities of the holidays also perpetuate the Victorian myth; but is it a myth? Investigate the economic and social conditions of the nineteenth century. Charles Dickens's view of this society predates Ibsen's by less than half a century, and yet Dickens's view of the social condition is often regarded as especially bleak and pessimistic. Would you agree or is the artificiality of the Helmer household just as bleak as that outlined in any Dickens novel?

---

woman who is under his control; he defines her every behavior and establishes rules that govern everything from what she eats to what she buys. The reality is that Nora has been maintaining a secret life for seven years, and that Torvald and Nora maintain a marriage that is a fiction of suitability and trust. Torvald has a public persona to maintain and he views his marriage as an element of that public need. When the fiction is stripped away at the play's conclusion, both partners must confront the reality of their marriage.

Betrayal

Betrayal becomes a theme of this play in several ways. Nora has betrayed her husband's trust in several instances. She has lied about borrowing money, and to repay the money she must lie about how she spends her household accounts and she must lie about taking odd jobs to earn extra money. But she also chooses to lie about eating sweets her

husband has forbidden her. However, Nora trusts in Torvald to be loyal to her and, in the end, he betrays that trust when he rejects her pleas for understanding. Torvald's betrayal of her love is the impetus that Nora requires to finally awaken to her own needs.

Deception

Deception is an important theme in *A Doll's House* because it motivates Nora's behavior, and through her, the behavior of every other character in the play. Because Nora lied when she borrowed money from Krogstad, she must continue lying to repay the money. But, Nora thinks she must also lie to protect Torvald. Her deception makes her vulnerable to Krogstad's blackmail and casts him in the role of villain. And although Nora does not lie to Mrs. Linde, it is Mrs. Linde who forces Nora to confront her deceptions. Dr. Rank has been deceiving both Nora and Torvald for years about the depth of his feelings for Nora. Only when she attempts to seek his help does Nora finally see beneath the surface to the doctor's real feelings. Torvald, who has been deceived throughout most of the play, is finally revealed in the final act to have been the one most guilty of deception, since he has deceived Nora into believing that he loved and cherished her, while all the while he had regarded her as little more than his property.

Growth and Development

In Act I, Nora is little more than a child playing a role; she is a "doll" occupying a doll's house, a child who has exchanged a father for a husband without changing or maturing in any way. Nevertheless, through the course of the play she is finally forced to confront the reality of the life she is living. Nora realizes in the final act of *A Doll's House* that if she wants the opportunity to develop an identity as an adult that she must leave her husband's home. When Nora finally gives up her dream for a miracle and, instead, accepts the reality of her husband's failings, she finally takes her first steps toward maturity.

Honor

Honor is of overwhelming importance to Torvald; it is what motivates his behavior. Early in the play, Torvald's insistence on the importance of honor is the reason he offers for firing Krogstad, asserting that because he once displayed a lack of honor means that Krogstad is forever dishonored. When he learns of his wife's mistake, Torvald's first and foremost concern is for his honor. He cannot appreciate the torment or sacrifice that Nora has made for him because he can only focus on how society will react to his family's shame. For Torvald, honor is more important than family and far more important than love; he simply cannot conceive of anyone placing love before honor. This issue exemplifies the crucial difference between Nora and Torvald.

Identity and Search for Self

In the final act of *A Doll's House,* Nora is forced to acknowledge that she has no identity separate from that of her husband. This parallels the reality of nineteenth century Europe where a wife was regarded as property rather than partner. Torvald owns Nora just as he owns their home or any other possession. Her realization of this in the play's final act provides the motivation she needs to leave her husband. When Nora realizes the inequity of her situation, she also recognizes her own self worth. Her decision to leave is a daring one that indicates the seriousness of Nora's desire to find and create her own identity.

Pride

Like honor, pride is an important element in how Torvald defines himself. He is proud of Nora in the same way one is proud of an expensive or rare possession. When her failing threatens to become public knowledge, Torvald is primarily concerned with the loss of public pride. Nora's error reflects on his own sense of perfection and indicates to him an inability to control his wife. Rather than accept Nora as less than perfect, Torvald instead rejects her when she is most in need of his support. His pride in himself and in his possessions blinds him to Nora's worth. Because she has always believed in Torvald's perfection, Nora is at first also unaware of her own strengths. Only when she has made the decision to leave Torvald can Nora begin to develop pride in herself.

Sexism

Sexism as a theme is reflected in the disparate lives represented in this play. Nora's problems arise because as a woman she cannot conduct business without the authority of either her father or her husband. When her father is dying, she must forge his signature to secure a loan to save her husband's life. That she is a responsible person is demonstrated when she repays the loan at great personal sacrifice. In the nineteenth century women's lives were limited to socially prescribed behaviors, and women were considered to be little more than property; Nora embodies the issues that confronted women during this period. Torvald's injustice cannot be ignored and Nora's sympathetic loss of innocence is too poignant to be forgotten. Thus, the controversy surrounding sexual equality becomes an important part of the play.

STYLE

This is a three act play with prose dialogue, stage directions, and no interior dialogue. There are no soliloquies, and thus, the thoughts of the characters and any action off stage must be explained by the actors. The actors address one another in *A Doll's House* and not the audience.

Acts

Acts comprise the major divisions within a drama. In Greek plays the sections of the drama were signified by the appearance of the chorus and were usually divided into five acts. This is the formula for most serious drama from the Greeks to the Romans, and to Elizabethan playwrights like William Shakespeare. The five acts denote the structure of dramatic action; they are exposition, complication, climax, falling action, and catastrophe. The five act structure was followed until the nineteenth century when Ibsen combined some of the acts. *A Doll's House* is a three act play; the exposition and complication are combined in the first act when the audience learns of both Nora's deception and of the threat Krogstad represents. The climax occurs in the second act when Krogstad again confronts Nora and leaves the letter for Torvald to read. The falling action and catastrophe are combined in Act Three when Mrs. Linde and Krogstad are reconciled but Mrs. Linde decides to let the drama play itself out and Torvald reads and reacts to the letter with disastrous results.

Naturalism

Naturalism was a literary movement of the late nineteenth and early twentieth centuries, and is the application of scientific principles to literature. For instance, in nature behavior is determined by environmental pressures or internal factors, none of which can be controlled or even clearly understood. There is a clear cause and effect association: either the indifference of nature or biological determinism influences behavior. In either case, there is no human responsibility for the actions of the individual. European Naturalism emphasized biological determinism, while American Naturalism emphasized environmental influences. Thus, Torvald's accusation that all of her father's weakest moral values are displayed in Nora is based on an understanding that she has inherited those traits from him.

Realism

Realism is a nineteenth century literary term that identifies an author's attempt to portray characters, events, and settings in a realistic way. Simply put, realism is attention to detail, with description

intended to be honest and frank at all levels. There is an emphasis on character, especially behavior. Thus, in *A Doll's House,* the events of the Helmers's marriage are easily recognizable as realistic to the audience. These are events, people, and a home that might be familiar to any person in the audience. The sitting room is similar to one found in any other home. Nora is similar to any other wife in nineteenth-century Norway, and the problems she encounters in her marriage are similar to those confronted by other married women.

Setting

The time, place, and culture in which the action of the play takes place is called the setting. The elements of setting may include geographic location, physical or mental environments, prevailing cultural attitudes, or the historical time in which the action takes place. The location for *A Doll's House* is an unnamed city in nineteenth-century Norway. The action begins just before Christmas and concludes the next evening, and all three acts take place in the same sitting room at the Helmers's residence. The Helmers have been married for eight years; Nora is a wife and mother, and her husband, Torvald, is a newly promoted lawyer and bank manager. They live in comfortable circumstances during a period that finds women suppressed by a social system that equates males with success in the public sphere and females with domestic chores in the private sphere. But this is also a period of turmoil as women demand greater educational opportunities and greater equality in the business world. Accordingly, *A Doll's House* illuminates many of the conflicts and questions being debated in nineteenth-century Europe.

HISTORICAL CONTEXT

Women's Rights

In 1888, married women in Norway were finally given control over their own money, but the Norway of Ibsen's play pre-dates this change and provides a more restrictive environment for women such as Nora Helmer. In 1879, a wife was not legally permitted to borrow money without her husband's consent, and so Nora must resort to deception to borrow the money she so desperately needs. Ibsen always denied that he believed in

COMPARE & CONTRAST

- **1879:** Congress gives women the right to practice law before the United States Supreme Court.

  Today: Women attorneys are as common as men in all areas of the law. Acceptance for women in the upper echelons of corporate law proved to be a bigger hurdle than practicing before the Supreme Court. Despite all of the advances made in the area of gender equality, women still earn less than seventy cents for every dollar earned by men.

- **1879:** Edison announces the success of his incandescent light bulb, certain that it will burn for 100 hours. Arc-lights are installed as streetlights in San Francisco and Cleveland.

  Today: Electric lights illuminate theatres, businesses, and homes in all areas of the industrialized world and have become a part of the human environment that is so accepted as to go largely unnoticed and often unappreciated.

- **1879:** In Berlin, electricity drives a railroad locomotive for the first time. George Seldon files for a patent for a road vehicle to be powered by an internal combustion engine.

  Today: Transportation based on the earlier combustion engine has been greatly refined and is easy, accessible, and fast. But it is only now that electricity is being researched seriously as a power source for more ecologically prudent transportation.

- **1879:** A woman's college, Radcliffe, is founded by Elizabeth Cary Agassiz in Cambridge, Massachusetts.

  Today: The opportunity for an education has ceased to be a novelty for women in the United States and most of Europe. Yet even in the late 1990s legal battles are waged over a woman's right to enter a male-only federally subsidized school, the Citadel.

- **1879:** The multiple switchboard invented by Leroy B. Firman is invented; it will help make the telephone a commercial success and dramatically increase the number of telephone subscribers.

  Today: Telephone lines are no longer used only for transmitting conversations, as communications have expanded to include computers and multimedia technology. The video phone and computers that permit visual connection in addition to vocal are now a reality and will likely become common and more affordable for much of the industrialized world.

---

women's rights, stating instead that he believed in human rights.

The issue of women's rights was already a force in Norway several years before Ibsen focused on the issue, and women had been the force behind several changes. Norway was a newly liberated country in the nineteenth century, having been freed from Danish control in 1814; therefore, it is understandable that issues involving freedom—both political and personal freedom—were important in the minds of Norwegians. Poverty had already forced women into the workplace early in the nineteenth century, and the Norwegian government had passed laws protecting and governing women's

employment nearly five decades before Ibsen's play. By the middle of the century women were granted the same legal protection as that provided to male children. Women were permitted inheritance rights and were to be successful in petitioning for the right to a university education only three years after the first performance of *A Doll's House*. But many of the protections provided to women were aimed at the lower economic classes. Employment opportunities for women were limited to low-paying domestic jobs, teaching, or clerical work. Middle-class women, such as Nora, noticed few of these new advantages. It was the institution of marriage itself that restricted the freedom of middle-class women. Although divorce was available and inexpensive, it was still socially stigmatized and available only if both partners agreed. The play's ending makes clear that Torvald would object to divorce and so Nora's alienation from society would be even greater. There was no organized feminist movement operating in Norway in 1879. Thus Nora's exodus at the play's conclusion is a particularly brave and dangerous act. There was no army of feminist revolutionaries to protect and guide her; she was completely alone in trying to establish a new life for herself.

Christmas Celebrations

Christmas was an important family holiday in Norway and was viewed as a time of family unity and celebration. Thus it is ironic that the play opens on Christmas Eve and that the Helmer family unity disintegrates on Christmas Day. Christmas Day and the days following were traditionally reserved for socializing and visiting with neighbors and friends. Costume parties such as the one Nora and Torvald attend were common, and the dance Nora performs, the tarantella, is a dance for couples or for a line of partners. That Nora dances it alone signifies her isolation both within her marriage and in the community.

Sources

Nora's forgery is similar to one that occurred earlier in Norway and one with which Ibsen was personally connected. A woman with whom Ibsen was friendly, Laura Kieler, borrowed money to finance a trip that would repair her husband's health. When the loan came due, Kieler was unable to repay it. She tried to raise money by selling a manuscript she had written and Ibsen, feeling the manuscript was inferior, declined to help her get it published. In desperation, Kieler forged a check, was caught, and was rejected by her husband who then sought to gain custody of their children and have his wife committed to an asylum. After her release, Kieler pleaded with her husband to take her back, which he did rather unwillingly. Ibsen provides Nora with greater resilience and ingenuity than that evidenced by Kieler. Nora is able to earn the money to repay the loan, and her forgery is of her father's signature on a promissory note and not of a check. Lastly, Nora is saved by Krogstad's withdrawal of legal threats and so is not cast out by her husband. Instead, she becomes stronger and her husband is placed in the position of the marital partner who must plead for a second chance. Ibsen provides a careful reversal of the original story that strengthens the character of the ''doll'' wife.

CRITICAL OVERVIEW

In Norway, *A Doll's House* was published two weeks before its first performance. The initial 8,000 copies of the play sold out immediately and so the audience for the play was both informed, excited, and eagerly anticipating the play's first production. The play elicited much debate, most of it centered on Nora's decision to leave her marriage at the play's conclusion. Reaction in Germany was similar to that in Norway. Ibsen was forced to provide an alternative ending by the management of its first German production, since even the actress playing Nora refused to portray a mother leaving her children in such a manner. Ibsen called the new ending, which had Nora abandoning her plans to leave upon seeing her children one last time, ''a barbaric outrage to be used only in emergencies.'' The debate was focused not on women's rights or other feminist issues such as subordination or male dominance; instead, people were consumed with the question, ''What kind of a wife and mother would walk out on her family as Nora does?'' The play's reception elsewhere in Europe mirrored that of Norway and Germany with the debate still focused largely on social issues and not on the play's challenge to dramatic style.

Another issue for early reviewers was Nora's transformation. Many critics simply did not accept the idea that the seemingly submissive, flighty woman of the first two acts could display so much resolve and strength in the third act. According to Errol Durbach in *A Doll's House: Ibsen's Myth of Transformation,* one review of the period stated that Ibsen had disgusted his audience by ''violating the unconventional.'' Many reviewers just could not visualize any woman displaying the kind of behavior demonstrated by Nora. It was beyond their comprehension that a woman would voluntarily choose to sacrifice her children in order to seek her own identity. Durbach argued that the audience and the critics were accustomed to social problem plays, but that Ibsen's play presented a problem without the benefit of a ready or acceptable solution. In fact, the critics identified with Torvald and saw his choice of so unstable a wife as Nora as his only real flaw. In 1879 Europe, *A Doll's House* was a problem play, but not the one Ibsen envisioned. Instead, the problem resided with the critics who were so consumed with the issue of Nora's decision that they ignored the deeper complexities of the play. Early in the first act it becomes clear that Nora has a strength and determination that even she cannot acknowledge. When her eyes are opened in Act III, it is not so much a metamorphosis as it is an awakening.

In England, the play was embraced by Marxists who envisioned an egalitarian mating without the hierarchy of marriage and an end to serfdom when wives ceased to be property. But many other Englishmen were more interested in the aesthetics of the play than in its social content. Bernard Shaw embraced Ibsen's dramatic poetry and championed the playwright's work. Since the first performance of *A Doll's House* in England occurred ten years after its debut in Norway, the English were provided with more time to absorb the ideas presented in the play. Thus the reviews of the period lacked the vehemence of those in Norway and Germany. Rather, according to Durbach, Ibsen was transformed into a liberal championed by English critics more interested in his dramatic poetry than the nature of his argument. In her 1919 book, *Ibsen in England,* Miriam Alice Franc declared that Ibsen "swept from the stage the false sentimentality and moral shams that had reigned there. He emancipated the theatre from the thraldom of convention."

Initial responses in America were even less enthusiastic then in Europe. Many critics dismissed Ibsen as gloomy and pessimistic and as representing the "old world." But by 1905, a production starring Ethel Barrymore was embraced by early feminists. Durbach noted that Barrymore's performance occurred within the context of the American woman's efforts at emancipation, and Ibsen became an "Interpreter of American Life." In his introduction to *The Collected Works of Henrik Ibsen,* which was published between 1906 and 1912, William Archer remarked: "It is with *A Doll's House* that Ibsen enters upon his kingdom as a world-poet." Archer added that this play was the work that would carry Ibsen's name beyond Norway. In a 1986 performance review, *New York Times* contributor Walter Goodman declared that *A Doll's House* is "a great document of feminism, and Nora is an icon of women's liberation."

CRITICISM

Sheri Metzger

Metzger is an adjunct professor at Embry-Riddle University. In this essay she discusses Ibsen's contributions to drama as a forum for social issues.

Henrik Ibsen elevated theatre from mere entertainment to a forum for exposing social problems. Prior to Ibsen, contemporary theatre consisted of historical romance or contrived behavior plays. But with *A Doll's House,* Ibsen turned drama into a respectable genre for the examination of social issues: in exposing the flaws in the Helmer marriage, he made the private public and provided an advocacy for women. In Act III, when Nora slams the door as she leaves, she is opening a door into the hidden world of the ideal Victorian marriage. In allowing Nora the right to satisfy her need for an identity separate from that of wife and mother, Ibsen is perceived as endorsing the growing "women question." And although the play ends without offering any solutions, Ibsen has offered possibilities. To his contemporaries, it was a frightening prospect.

Bjorn Hemmer, in an essay in *The Cambridge Companion to Ibsen,* declared that Ibsen used *A Doll's House* and his other realistic dramas to focus a "searchlight" on Victorian society with its "false morality and its manipulation of public opinion." Indeed, Torvald exemplifies this kind of community. Of this society, Hemmer noted: "The people who live in such a society know the weight of 'public opinion' and of all those agencies which keep watch over society's 'law and order': the norms, the conventions and the traditions which in essence belong to the past but which continue into the present and there thwart individual liberty in a variety of ways." It is the weight of public opinion that Torvald cannot defy. And it is the weight of public opinion that condemns the Helmer's marriage. Because Torvald views his public persona as more important that his private, he is unable to understand or appreciate the suffering of his wife. His reaction to the threat of public exposure is centered on himself. It is his social stature, his professional image, and not his private life which concern him most. For Nora to emerge as an individual she must reject the life that society mandates. To do so, she must assume control over her life; yet in the nineteenth century, women had no power. Power resides with the establishment, and as a

WHAT DO I READ NEXT?

- Joyce Carol Oates's short story, ''The Lady With The Pet Dog,'' offers an interesting contrast to the way Nora chooses to deal with her marriage. This is the retelling of the Chekhov story, only from the woman's point of view. The theme of deception is also important in this story, since Anna chooses to keep secret important events in her life. Her efforts to escape her marriage and establish a new identity are different from Nora's because she internalizes the changes and so is not forced to confront her husband in the same manner that Nora must.

- In both William Shakespeare's *Hamlet* and Henrik Ibsen's *A Doll's House*, there is a huge disparity between image and reality. If a character is known by what he/she says or he/she does or by what others say about him/her, then both these plays offer interesting opportunities to compare how the differing perspectives of personality affect the outcome of each play.

- Susan Glaspell's *Trifles* was written almost forty years after *A Doll's House*. In Glaspell's play, the relationship between men and women is certainly as oppressive as in Ibsen's. The differ-

ences in setting, notably the dirt and poverty of the Wrights' home, serve as an interesting contrast to the decor of the Helmers'. Still, the female inhabitants face similar struggles and Mrs. Wright's chosen method of escape offers an interesting opposition to Nora's.

- James Joyce's short story ''The Dead'' can be compared to Ibsen's *A Doll's House*. Both depict a woman's struggle to become emotionally independent of the husband who seeks to control her. In both cases, there are secrets and deception involved in the wife's past. Both also feature Christmas as a background for some of the play's events.

- In Ibsen's *Ghosts*, the author further explores the ramifications of a father's actions on his family. As in *A Doll's House*, this play embraces naturalism as an explanation for human behavior. In the play, the sins of the father become manifest in the son when the son discovers he has inherited his father's venereal disease and that he is in love with his illegitimate half-sister. In *A Doll's House*, Dr. Rank, too, inherits the venereal disease of his father.

---

banker and lawyer, Torvald clearly represents the establishment.

Deception, which lies at the heart of *A Doll's House,* also provides the cornerstone of Victorian life, according to Hemmer. Hemmer maintained that it is the contrasts between reality and fiction that motivated Ibsen to tackle such social problems as marriage. Victorian society, Hemmer stated, offered a ''clear dichotomy between ideology and practice.'' The facade of individuality was buried in the Victorian ideal of economics. In the hundred years since the French Revolution, economic power had replaced the quest for individual liberty, and a married woman had the least amount of economic power. When Nora rejects her marriage, she is also rejecting bourgeois middle-class values. In this

embracing of uncertainty rather than the economic guarantee of her husband's protection, Nora represents the individual, who, Hemmer asserted, Ibsen wanted to make ''the sustaining element in society and [who would] dethrone the bourgeois family as the central institution of society.'' Nora's rebellion at the play's conclusion is a necessary element of that revolution; it is little wonder that Ibsen was no disgusted at the second conclusion he was forced to write. In making Nora subordinate her desires as an individual to the greater need of motherhood, Ibsen is denying his reason for creating the conflict and for writing the play.

The question of women's rights and feminist equality is an important aspect of understanding *A Doll's House*. Ibsen himself stated that for him the issue was more complex than just women's rights and that he hoped to illuminate the problem of human rights. Yet women have continued to champion both Ibsen and his heroine, Nora. Social reform was closely linked to feminism. In her discussion of the role Ibsen played in nineteenth-century thought, which appeared in *The Cambridge Companion to Ibsen,* Gail Finney explained: "The most prominent socialist thinkers of the day, male and female, saw that true sexual equality necessitates fundamental changes in the structure of society." Thus, in embracing women's equality in *A Doll's House,* Ibsen is really arguing for social justice. Ibsen supported economic reform that would protect women's property and befriended a number of notable Scandinavian feminists. Finney argued that Ibsen's feminist wife, Suzannah, provided the model for Nora as a strong-willed heroine.

Finney devoted part of her essay to the feminist reception of early stage productions of *A Doll's House,* which Finney maintained, "opened the way to the turn-of-the-century women's movement." Nineteenth-century feminists praised Ibsen's work and "saw it as a warning of what would happen when women in general woke up to the injustices that had been committed against them," according to Finney. Finney indicated that in Ibsen's own notes for this play the playwright asserted that "a mother in modern society is 'like certain insects who go away and die when she has done her duty in the propagation of the race.'" That the prevailing view is that women have little worth when their usefulness as mothers has ended is clear in Torvald's repudiation of Nora when he discovers her deception; she can be of no use to her children if her reputation is stained. That he wants her to remain under his roof—though separate from the family—defines his own need to protect his reputation within the community. Her use, though, as a mother is at an end. Until, that is, Torvald discovers that the threat has been removed. If Nora wants to define her worth, she can only do so by turning away from her children and husband.

Finney refutes early critical arguments that Nora's transformation in Act III is unbelievable or too sudden. Nora's childlike response to Torvald in which she states "I would never dream of doing anything you didn't want me to" and "I never get anywhere without your help" contrast sharply with the reality of her situation, which is that she has forged a signature and saved her husband's life and has also shown herself capable of earning the money necessary to repay the loan. Thus Nora's submis-

siveness is as much a part of the deception as other elements of Nora's personality. Finney also argued that Nora's repeated exclamations of how happy she is in Act I and her out-of-control practice of the tarantella are indicative of a woman bordering on hysteria. This hysteria further demonstrates that Nora is a more complicated woman than the childlike doll introduced at the beginning of Act I. Finney noted that Ibsen stated late in his life that "it is the women who are to solve the social problem. As mothers they are to do it. And only as such can they do it." Finney posited that rather than arguing that women are suited only for motherhood, Ibsen really saw motherhood as a vocation that women perform best when it is offered as a choice. When Nora states that she must leave to find her identity because she is of no use to her children as she is, she is giving voice to Ibsen's premise: Nora must have the right to choose motherhood and she cannot do that until she has the freedom to choose.

Errol Durbach was also concerned with Nora's role of mother. In a discussion in his *A Doll's House: Ibsen's Myth of Transformation* that focuses on the critical reception that greeted Nora's decision to leave her children, Durbach offered the review of Clement Scott, an Ibsen contemporary. Scott held that Nora "committed an unnatural offense unworthy of even the lower animals: 'A cat or dog would tear anyone who separated it from its offspring, but the socialistic Nora, the apostle of the new creed of humanity, leaves her children without a pang.'" But Durbach maintained that for Nora to subordinate her own needs to the function of motherhood would be a greater offense, and cited Ibsen's own words to support his claim: "These women of the modern age, mistreated as daughters, as sisters, as wives, not educated in accordance with their talents, debarred from following their mission, deprived of their inheritance, embittered in mind—these are the ones who supply the mothers for the new generation. What will be the result?" Nora's decision, then, can be described not as an offense, but as a display of strength. Rather than take the easy path, she recognizes that to be a good mother requires more than her presence in the home; she cannot be a model for her children, especially her daughter, if she cannot claim an identity as an individual. Clearly this principle exemplifies Ibsen's stated position that if women are to be mothers of a new generation, they must first achieve a measure of equality as human beings.

Of Ibsen's approach to marriage, Durbach asserted it would be a mistake to read *A Doll's House* and extrapolate from the play that Ibsen was striking a ''militant blow against the institution of marriage.'' For although Nora slams the door on marriage, Kristine opens the same door. In the same way that a mirror reverses a reflection, Kristine reflects the opposite of Nora. Kristine has already suffered in marriage and has been provided with a second opportunity with the death of her husband. She has the freedom that Nora now seeks. Where Nora has known security and happiness, Kristine has known deprivation and a loveless marriage. As Durbach illustrated, Kristine is clearly a non-doll to Nora's doll. Durbach argued that if feminists want to embrace Ibsen's Nora as a symbol for women's equality, they must also address the problem of Kristine; her choice is the opposite of Nora's and coming to terms with that choice only reveals the complexities of Ibsen's play. As nineteenth-century critics noted, Ibsen presents no solutions, only questions.

Source: Sheri Metzger, in an essay for *Drama for Students*, Gale, 1997.

W.E. Simonds

In the following excerpt, Simonds calls A Doll's House *''one of the strongest plays that Ibsen has produced,'' praising the playwright's ability to create a narrative that grows in intensity and captivates its audience. Simonds also examines the pivotal role of Nora Helmer in communicating the play's themes and tone to the audience.*

The Doll's House is one of the strongest plays that Ibsen has produced. In the way of character-painting, and artful and artistic handling of the situations, he has done nothing better. It is a pity that we could not have had *The Enemy of Society,* with its strong autobiographic suggestiveness, first; but there is no more characteristic play upon the list, nor one more indicative of the author's mind and power—if only it be read with fairness and appreciation,—than the one selected. The heroine of *The Doll's House* is its light-hearted pretty little mistress, Nora Helmer. She has been eight years the wife of Torvald Helmer, and is the mother of three bright vigorous children. She is her husband's doll. Torvald Helmer calls her his little lark, his squirrel, provides for her every fancy, hugely enjoys her charms of person, forgets that she has a soul—and is sure he loves her most devotedly. Nora has always been a child; her father, a man of easy conscience, has brought her up entirely unsophisticated. She knows nothing of the serious side of life,—of its privileges, its real

> THE DOLL'S HOUSE IS ONE OF THE STRONGEST PLAYS THAT IBSEN HAS PRODUCED. IN THE WAY OF CHARACTER-PAINTING, AND ARTFUL AND ARTISTIC HANDLING OF THE SITUATIONS, HE HAS DONE NOTHING BETTER"

opportunities—nothing of the duties of the individual in a world of action. Nora is passive, she submits to be fondled and kissed. She is happy in her ''doll-house,'' and apparently knows nothing outside her home, her husband, and her children. Nora loves her family with an ideal love. Love, in her thought, is an affection which has a right to demand sacrifices; and in turn is willing to offer up its own treasures, whether life, honor, or even its soul, be the stake. She is not merely ready for such a sacrifice—poor sentimental Nora!— she has already, though in part ignorantly, made it, and has committed a crime to save her husband's life.

There is much machinery to carry on the plot; but in spite of the abstract nature of the theme, the episodes are so dramatic and the dialogue so brisk and natural that the drama moves without perceptible jar, and our interest intensifies and the suspense increases until the *denouement* occurs. Herein lies the secret of the success of this and all the other of Ibsen's kindred dramas. Along with the poet's insight and the cold clear logic of the philosopher, he possesses in an eminent degree the secret of the playwright's art, and knows well how to clothe his abstract dialogue on themes philosophical or psychological, so that the observer follows every incident and every word with an interest that grows more and more intense.

It is impossible to tell all of Nora's story here. Miss [Henrietta Frances] Lord's translation will do that best, if only curiosity may be aroused concerning it. Suffice it to say that the catastrophe falls in a situation characteristically dramatic. The curtain descends just as Nora, the wife and mother, turns her back upon husband and children, and passes, by her own free choice, nay, in accord with her relentless insistence, out from her doll-home into the

> **NO WORK OF IBSEN'S HAS EXCITED SO MUCH CONTROVERSY AS *A DOLL'S HOUSE.*"**

night, and— whither? This is the question that all the hosts of Ibsen's censors are repeating. Whither? And did she do right to leave her children and her husband? And what a revolutionary old firebrand Ibsen must be to teach such a moral, and proclaim the doctrine that all those unfortunate mismated women who find themselves bound to unsympathetic lords may, and should, turn their back on the home and abandon their offspring to the mercies of strangers! But alack! this isn't the moral of Nora Helmer's story. It was the doll-marriage and the relation between Torvald Helmer and his doll-wife that was at fault. Nora's abandonment was an accidental, though a necessary, episode. It is the *denouement* of the play, to be sure; but the end is not yet. There is an epilogue as well as a prologue to the drama, though both are left to the reader's imagination to perfect. "A hope inspires" Helmer as he hears the door close after Nora's departure; and he whisperingly repeats her words—" the greatest of all miracles!"

This particular phase of wedded life—and perhaps it is becoming not so very infrequent a phase even on this side the water—is a problem which confronts us in society. Is this your idea of marriage? demands Ibsen. Is it a marriage at all? No; he declares bluntly. It is a cohabitation; it is a partnership in sensuality in which one of the parties is an innocent, it may be an unconscious, victim.

Nora goes forth, but we feel she will one day return; her children will bring her back. Neither she nor Torvald could have learned the bitter lesson had Nora remained at home. It is the wife at last who makes the sacrifice. How strange it is that so many of the critics fail to see that Nora's act is not selfishness after all! There is promise of a splendid womanliness in that "emancipated individuality" that Ibsen's enemies are ridiculing. There will be an ideal home after the mutual chastening is accomplished: an ideal home—not ideal people necessarily, but a home, a family, where there is complete community, a perfect love.

Source: W. E. Simonds, "Henrik Ibsen" in the *Dial,* Vol. X, No. 119, March, 1890, pp. 301–03.

Edmund Gosse

In the following excerpt, Gosse speculates that A Doll's House *aroused controversy because the play features a female protagonist seeking individuality.*

Gosse was a prominent English man of letters during the late nineteenth century. A prolific literary historian, biographer, and critic, he is best known for his work Father and Son: A Study of Two Temperaments *(1907), an account of his childhood that is considered among the most distinguished examples of Victorian spiritual autobiography. Gosse was also a major translator and critic of Scandinavian literature, and his importance as a critic is due primarily to his introduction of Ibsen to an English-speaking audience*

No work of Ibsen's, not even his beautiful Puritan opera of *Brand,* has excited so much controversy as *A Doll's House.* This was, no doubt, to a very great extent caused by its novel presentment of the mission of woman in modern society. In the dramas and romances of modern Scandinavia, and especially in those of Ibsen and Bjornson, the function of woman had been clearly defined. She was to be the helper, the comforter, the inspirer, the guerdon of man in his struggle towards loftier forms of existence. When man fell on the upward path, woman's hand was to be stretched to raise him; when man went wandering away on ill and savage courses, woman was to wait patiently over her spinning-wheel, ready to welcome and to pardon the returning prodigal; when the eyes of man grew weary in watching for the morning-star, its rays were to flash through the crystal tears of woman. But in *A Doll's House* he confronted his audience with a new conception. Woman was no longer to be the shadow following man, or if you will, a *skin-leka* attending man, but an independent entity, with purposes and moral functions of her own. Ibsen's favourite theory of the domination of the individual had hitherto been confined to one sex; here he carries it over boldly to the other. The heroine of *A Doll's House,* the puppet in that establishment *pour rire* ["not to be taken seriously"], is Nora Helmer, the wife of a Christiania barrister. The character is drawn upon childish lines, which often may remind the English reader of Dora in *David Copperfield.* She has, however, passed beyond the Dora stage when the play opens. She is the mother of children, she has been a wife for half a dozen years. But the spoiling of injudicious parents has been succeeded by the spoiling of a weak and silly husband. Nora remains childish, irrational, concentrated on tiny cares and empty interests, without self-control or self-respect. Her doctor and her husband have told her not to give way to her passion for "candy" in any of its seductive forms; but she is introduced to us greedily eating macaroons on the sly, and denying that she has touched one when suspicion is aroused.

Here, then in Nora Helmer, the poet starts with the figure of a woman in whom the results of the dominant will of man, stultifying the powers and gifts of womanhood, are seen in their extreme development. Environed by selfish kindness, petted and spoiled for thirty years of dwarfed existence, this pretty, playful, amiable, and apparently happy little wife is really a tragical victim of masculine egotism. A nature exorbitantly desirous of leaning on a stronger will has been seized, condemned, absorbed by the natures of her father and her husband. She lives in them and by them, without moral instincts of her own, or any law but their pleasure. The result of this weakness—this, as Ibsen conceives, criminal subordination of the individuality—is that when Nora is suddenly placed in a responsible position, when circumstances demand from her a moral judgment, she has none to give; the safety, even the comfort, of the man she loves precede all other considerations, and with a light heart she forges a document to shield her father or to preserve her husband's name. She sacrifices honour for love, her conscience being still in too rudimentary a state to understand that there can be any honour that is distinguishable from love. Thus Dora would have acted, if we can conceive Dora as ever thrown into circumstances which would permit her to use the pens she was so patient in holding. But Nora Helmer has capacities of undeveloped character which make her far more interesting than the, to say the truth, slightly fabulous Dora. Her insipidity, her dollishness, come from the incessant repression of her family life. She is buried, as it were, in cotton-wool, swung into artificial sleep by the egotistical fondling of the men on whom she depends for emotional existence. But when once she tears the wrappings away, and leaps from the pillowed hammock of her indolence, she rapidly develops an energy of her own, and the genius of the dramatist is displayed in the rare skill with which he makes us witness the various stages of this awaking. At last, in an extraordinary scene, she declares that she can no longer live in her doll's house; husband and wife sit down at opposite ends of a table, and argue out the situation in a dialogue which covers sixteen pages, and Nora dashes out into the city, into the night; while the curtain falls as the front door bangs behind her.

The world is always ready to discuss the problem of marriage, and this very fresh and odd version of *L'ecole des Femmes [The School for Wives]* excited the greatest possible interest throughout the north of Europe. The close of the play, in particular, was a riddle hard to be deciphered. Nora, it was said, might feel that the only way to develop her own individuality was to leave her husband, but why should she leave her children? The poet evidently held the relation he had described to be such an immoral one, in the deepest and broadest sense, that the only way out of the difficulty was to cut the Gordian knot, children or no children. In almost Nora's very last reply, moreover, there is a glimmer of relenting. The most wonderful of things may happen, she confesses; the reunion of a developed wife to a reformed husband is not, she hints, beyond the range of what is possible. We are left with the conviction that it rests with him, with Helmer, to allow himself to be led through the fires of affliction to the feet of a Nora who shall no longer be a doll. (pp. 113–15)

Source: Edmund Gosse, "Ibsen's Social Dramas" in the *Fortnightly Review,* Vol. XLV, No. CCLXV, January 1, 1989, pp. 107–21.

FURTHER READING

Magill, Frank N., editor. *Masterpieces of World Literature,* Harper & Row, 1989, pp. 203-206.
   This book compresses literary works into easily understood summaries. In addition to plot summaries and character reviews, the editor also addresses historical context and critical interpretations. The Magill compilations provide a reliable, accessible means for students to review texts.

Meyer, Michael, editor. *The Compact Bedford Introduction to Literature,* 4th Edition, St. Martin's Press, 1996, pp. 1128-1136.
   This anthology encapsulates several brief approaches to the study of this play. Excerpts from psychological, Marxist, and feminists readings are provided to assist students with a comparison of the different critical readings possible.

Rickert, Blandine M., editor. *Major Modern Dramatists,* Volume 2, pp. 1-32.

This work provides an introduction to Ibsen drawn from reviews and critical interpretations of his work. Excerpts date from late in the nineteenth century to the late twentieth century. Compiling this information allows students of Ibsen to see how his plays have influenced succeeding generations.

SOURCES

Archer, William. Introduction to *The Collected Works of Henrik Ibsen,* edited and translated by Archer, Scribner, 1906-1912.

Durbach, Errol. *A Doll's House: Ibsen's Myth of Transformation,* Twayne Masterworks Studies, Twayne Publishers, 1991.

Finney, Gail. "Ibsen and Feminism," in *The Cambridge Companion to Ibsen,* edited by James McFarlane, Cambridge University Press, 1994, pp. 89-105.

Franc, Miriam Alice. *Ibsen in England,* The Four Seas Co., 1919, pp. 131-33.

Goodman, Walter. Review of *A Doll's House, The New York Times,* May 14, 1986.

Hemmer, Bjorn. "Ibsen and the Realistic Problem Drama," in *The Cambridge Companion to Ibsen,* edited by James McFarlane, Cambridge University Press, 1994, pp. 68-88.

The Glass Menagerie

TENNESSEE WILLIAMS

1944

The Glass Menagerie was originally produced in Chicago in 1944 and then staged in New York on Broadway in 1945. The text was also published in 1945. This play was the first of Williams's to win the New York Drama Critics Circle Award, an honor he was given four times. Although *The Glass Menagerie* also received much popular acclaim, some critics believe that the thematic devices that Williams relies on, such as the legends on the screen, are too heavy-handed.

The Glass Menagerie is autobiographical in its sources. In some ways, this is a coming of age story, with both Tom Wingfield and Laura Wingfield negotiating their roles as young adults. Like many coming of age stories, the major conflicts in this play are both internal and external; Tom cannot choose both the future he desires for himself and the future his mother, Amanda Wingfield, desires for him and for Laura. Emerging through this major conflict between Tom and Amanda are the themes of alienation and loneliness, duty and responsibility, and appearances and reality.

Through its poetic structure and reliance on stage technology, *The Glass Menagerie* has had a significant impact on later twentieth century drama. Tom serves as both narrator and character, dissolving the present into the past; Williams signals this by exploiting lighting and sound, especially music—technologies which were less available to

earlier playwrights. In this sense, the themes of the play are inseparable from its production values.

AUTHOR BIOGRAPHY

Tennessee Williams was born in Mississippi in 1911. His given name was Thomas Lanier Williams. His family lived in Mississippi and Tennessee until 1918, when they moved to St. Louis, Missouri, where Williams's father, Cornelius, worked as a shoe salesman. This move to a metropolitan area was difficult for both Williams and his sister, Rose. Williams's family was Episcopalian and his grandfather a minister, although Williams himself converted to Roman Catholicism in 1969. As an adult, he moved frequently, living in such cities as St. Louis and New York. Many critics base their interpretation of *The Glass Menagerie* as autobiographical in part because of the similarities between the Wingfield family and Williams's own. Williams's mother, Edwina, was a Southern belle, and his older sister, Rose, to whom Williams was close, suffered from schizophrenia as an adult.

Williams attended the University of Missouri from 1931 until 1933 and Washington University in St. Louis from 1936 until 1937 before earning his A.B. degree from the University of Iowa in 1938. He began publishing his work in magazines when he was only twelve years old and decided to become a playwright at the age of twenty, although he also wrote short stories, poems, novels, and memoirs. As a young man, he supported himself with various jobs, including waiter, teletype operator, and theater usher.

After *The Glass Menagerie* was produced on Broadway in 1945, however, Williams consistently had his new work produced in various New York theaters, often averaging one play every other year. He was not only prolific but also successful. His plays won many honors, beginning with the Group Theatre Award in 1939. This was followed by a Rockefeller Foundation fellowship. He won the New York Drama Critics Circle Award four times, and he won the Pulitzer Prize for *A Streetcar Named Desire,* his other most well-known play, in 1948. Williams was the first recipient of the centennial medal from New York's Episcopal Cathedral of St. John the Divine in 1973. During the last decade of his life, he received a Kennedy Honors Award and was elected to the Theatre Hall of Fame.

Williams's most popular plays were also produced as movies, and he frequently served as screenwriter, sometimes with a collaborator. His later work continues the themes of his early plays, and he is sometimes accused of failing to develop further. In part because of this, his audience began to drift away near the end of his life.

Tennessee Williams died by choking in a hotel in New York City in 1983.

PLOT SUMMARY

Scene I

The Glass Menagerie opens with some fairly elaborate stage directions which serve both to describe the setting and to introduce themes and symbols through their tone. For example, the apartments in the Wingfields' neighborhood are described as ''warty growths'' and the people as ''one interfused mass of automatism.'' Tom Wingfield is the first character on stage, and he functions here as both narrator and interpreter. In this role, Tom exists several years after the primary action of the play. He introduces the other characters, and his presence in this role guides the audience in the direction of the play.

The action begins with Amanda, Tom's mother, calling him to the supper table. Throughout the meal, Amanda instructs and criticizes Tom in his eating habits, until Tom responds with disgust. At once, the audience realizes that Tom and Amanda live in a state of tension. The other character present at this meal is Laura, Tom's sister, who wears a brace on her leg. When Laura offers to serve the dessert, Amanda says that she wishes Laura to ''stay fresh and pretty—for gentlemen callers!'' Amanda will remain concerned with the possibility of ''gentlemen callers'' for Laura throughout the play, and here she reminisces about her own youthful days. When Laura indicates that she's not expecting any gentlemen callers, Amanda appears to be astonished, although this conversation seems to be a frequent one. Laura explains that ''I'm not popular like you [Amanda] were.''

Scene II

As this scene begins, Laura is sitting alone in the living room, washing the animals in her glass

Tennessee Williams onstage during rehearsals for one of his plays

collection. Amanda enters, clearly upset. Their conversation reveals that although Laura has been enrolled in a typing course, and although she has left the apartment every day as if to attend her class, she has in fact not been going. Amanda had stopped by to speak with Laura's teacher, who revealed that Laura had become ill during a typing test and had not returned. Laura admits that she simply goes to the zoo nearly every day.

Amanda is concerned about Laura's future because she has no prospective husband, nor does she have any skills by which she could make a living. Laura says that she had like a boy once, while she was in high school, although she is now twenty-three years old. This boy's name was Jim, and he was very popular then and predicted to be very successful. Jim had called Laura by the nickname "Blue Roses" because he had misunderstood her when she had said she'd been sick with pleurosis.

Scene III

This scene opens with Tom again functioning as narrator and describing the changes that occurred in the family over the next several weeks. Amanda became even more concerned with "gentlemen callers." Because she believes that the apartment will have to be redecorated if gentlemen callers

begin to arrive, she takes a job selling magazine subscriptions.

The major portion of this scene consists of an argument between Tom and Amanda. Amanda has thrown away some of Tom's books because they were written by D. H. Lawrence, a British writer some people considered scandalous. The argument continues when Tom says he is going out to the movies, although Amanda replies that no one can go to as many movies as Tom claims to. She implies that Tom is lying, especially since he often comes home late and apparently drunk. She is worried that he will lose his job because he so frequently goes to work when he has had only three or four hours of sleep. She urges him to think of the good of the family rather than only himself. Tom replies by emphasizing how much he hates his job and slams out of the apartment after calling Amanda an "ugly—babbling old—witch."

Scene IV

Tom arrives home much later. Laura lets him in, apparently believing that he really has been to the movies. Laura asks Tom to apologize to Amanda at breakfast, which he eventually does. Amanda sends Laura out to buy some butter so that she can have a few words alone with Tom. She explains that she is worried that Tom is becoming like his father, who had abandoned the family. Amanda assures Tom that he will be able to go wherever and do whatever he wants as soon as Laura is secure in a future. She asks Tom to bring home an acquaintance from the warehouse where he works to meet Laura, though Tom does not respond enthusiastically to the prospect.

Scene V

Tom and Amanda argue about whether he smokes too much. Eventually, Tom reveals that he has invited someone home to dinner, and that he's coming tomorrow. Amanda panics because of all of the preparations that will have to be made. Tom says that the man's name is James Delaney O'Connor and that he works as a shipping clerk, making approximately eighty-five dollars per month (Tom makes sixty-five dollars per month). Tom urges Amanda not to anticipate too much, since Laura is ''crippled,'' a word she reprimands him for using, and ''peculiar.'' The scene ends with Tom once again leaving for the movies.

Scene VI

The scene begins with Amanda and Laura preparing supper. Laura is extremely nervous and becomes even more upset when she discovers that the visitor's name is Jim O'Connor, since that was the name of the boy she liked in high school. Tom and Jim arrive, and Jim discusses his future he hopes for in public speaking. Tom reveals that he has joined The Union of Merchant Seamen and has paid his dues with the money he was supposed to use for the electric bill. Amanda enters wearing an old dress from her youth and acting extremely coy. Amanda claims that Laura has prepared the supper, but when it is time to eat, Laura is so nervous that she becomes ill. She rests on the sofa throughout dinner.

Scene VII

As Tom, Amanda, and Jim are eating, the lights go out. Amanda assumes they have blown a fuse, though Jim says none of the fuses look faulty. Amanda urges Jim to keep Laura company in the living room. Laura reveals that she had known Jim in high school, and he eventually remembers who she is. She says that she had always felt conspicuous because of her brace, but Jim assures her that it was

hardly noticeable. Laura has kept a program from a play Jim had starred in, and he autographs it for her. He reveals that he broke up with his high school girlfriend. When he asks Laura what she has done since high school, she states that her glass collection keeps her very busy.

Jim suggests that she simply needs more self confidence and begins talking about inferiority complexes. Laura shows him her favorite glass animal, a unicorn. Because music is audible from the dance hall across the alley, Jim asks Laura to dance. While they dance, they bump the table; the unicorn falls off and breaks its horn, though Laura says now he's like the other horses rather than being ''feakish.'' Telling Laura that she is pretty, Jim kisses her. A few minutes later, though, he confesses that he is engaged, and that he hadn't realized Tom had invited him home in order to meet Laura. She gives him the broken unicorn. Amanda serves lemonade, and Jim tells her also that he is engaged. Embarrassed, Amanda assumes that Tom had been playing a mean-spirited joke on them. Tom leaves again, though this time his departure is permanent. The play concludes with Laura blowing out the candles.

CHARACTERS

Blue Roses
See Laura Wingfield

Jim O'Connor

Jim is the gentleman caller Tom invites home for dinner. Although he also works at the warehouse, he makes more money than Tom and has greater aspirations—even if they are somewhat conventional ones. Yet, his situation reveals that dreams are often not achieved, for in high school Jim had been predicted to become very successful. He treats Laura kindly, but during their conversation he reveals that he too is not entirely realistic, for he discounts the severity of Laura's problem and assures her that all she needs is more confidence.

Amanda Wingfield

Amanda is the mother of Tom and Laura. She has difficulty facing reality, though by the end of the play she does acknowledge Tom's desire to

Laurette Taylor and Julie Haydon in a scene from a stage adaptation.

leave and Laura's uncertain future. She frequently fantacizes about the past, probably exaggerating her own popularity then. Her relationship with Tom is conflicted, most prominently when she criticizes his minor habits.

Laura Wingfield

Laura is the daughter of Amanda and sister of Tom. She is extremely shy, even emotionally disturbed, and she wears a brace on her leg which makes her feel conspicuous. Her collection of glass animals gives the play its title. She does not work, and she has been unable to complete a typing class because of her nervousness. Although she says she had once liked a boy in high school, she has never had and is unlikely to have any kind of romantic relationship.

Tom Wingfield

Amanda's son and Laura's brother, Tom is the protagonist of the play. He dreams of abandoning the family, as his father had done. He feels trapped in his job, where he often neglects his duties in order to write poetry, and in his home, where he is reprimanded for reading some modern literature which was considered scandalous at the time. Al-

though he claims to go to the movies every night, he also probably goes to a bar, since he sometimes comes home drunk. Eventually, he agrees to bring a "gentleman caller" home to meet Laura, but he leaves the family that night. Although Tom appears to genuinely care for Laura, his greater desire is to relieve his frustration at his confining situation. When he functions as narrator at a time several years after the action of the play, readers understand that he has escaped physically but not emotionally.

THEMES

Appearances and Reality

Throughout this play, emerging in every scene and through the actions of every character is the theme of Appearances vs. Reality. Characters believe in a future and a past which are not realistic, and these beliefs affect the decisions they make regarding their relationships with each other. For example, Amanda frequently describes the days of her youth, when she claims she received "seventeen!—gentlemen callers!" during one Sunday afternoon. Although she describes these men as if

MEDIA ADAPTATIONS

- *The Glass Menagerie* was released as a film by Warner Brothers in 1950. This black and white version was produced by Jerry Wald and Charles K. Feldman and directed by Irving Rapper. It starred Jane Wyman as Laura Wingfield, Kirk Douglas as Jim O'Connor, Gertrude Lawrence as Amanda Wingfield, and Arthur Kennedy as Tom Wingfield. It also included roles for several characters who are only referred to in the play.

- Another version of *The Glass Menagerie* was filmed by Cineplex Odeon and released in 1987. It was produced by Burtt Harris and directed by Paul Newman. Newman's wife, Joanne Woodward played Amanda; John Malkovich played Tom; Karen Allen played Laura; and James Naughton played the gentleman caller. It is available on video through MCA/Universal Home Video.

- A television adaptation also aired on CBS in 1966. This version starred Shirley Booth as Amanda, Hal Holbrook as Tom, Barbara Loden as Laura, and Pat Hingle as Jim. David Susskind was the producer and Michael Elliott the director.

- Another television version was broadcast on ABC in 1984.

- A sound recording has also been produced by Caedmon. This two-cassette version was released in 1973; the cast consists of Montgomery Clift, Julie Harris, Jessica Tandy, and David Wayne.

they either are wealthy or have died a tragic/heroic death, the man she married was apparently both unsuccessful and irresponsible. And despite all evidence to the contrary, Amanda seems to believe that Laura, too, will one day be visited by similar gentlemen callers.

Rather than fantasizing about his past, Tom believes that his future holds excitement, if he can only escape his family. Yet he fails to escape completely even though he does leave. In his last monologue, Tom reveals that he is not running toward something but away from his past: "I was pursued by something." And although he travels continually, he fails to find the excitement he longs for, as the "cities swept about me like dead leaves."

Even Jim O'Connor, the most conventional character, continues to believe in unattainable dreams. Although he apparently is talented, he has been unable to make choices that will guarantee him professional success. He refers enthusiastically to his public speaking class, but readers understand that Jim is attributing more significance to this course than it perhaps deserves.

Laura, however, is the character who is most obviously detached from reality. She cannot have normal interactions with other people without becoming ill. Her emotional energy is invested in her collection of glass animals, which may be exotic and delicate but are nevertheless "unreal," especially the unicorn she claims is her favorite. For the unicorn doesn't even represent a realistic animal. Even the nickname Jim once gave her, Blue Roses, is a flower that doesn't exist. By the time the play ends, Laura seems to be more detached from reality rather than able to adjust.

Coming of Age

Although most pieces of literature which have "coming of age" as a major theme discuss younger characters, in some ways *The Glass Menagerie* also considers this theme. While all of the characters are technically adults, they do not relate to each other as adults. Amanda instructs Tom about his eating habits as if he is still a child, and he reacts to her with the resentment of an adolescent. In this regard, Tom is in a double bind, for he cannot simultaneously exercise all of the qualities of an adult in his

TOPICS FOR FURTHER STUDY

- Although *The Glass Menagerie* is set in the 1930s, many critics describe it as timeless. Describe the historical changes you would have to make if you were to set the play today.

- Research the financial situation of single mothers today and compare their options to those of Amanda.

- Examine the catalogs of several business or technical schools in your area and compare their curricula to the apparent curriculum of Rubicam's Business College, where Laura has been attending typing classes.

- Interview someone in your school who has worked on the production of a play. Focus your questions especially on the technical aspects of stage craft so that you can discover how the screens, lighting, etc. would work in *The Glass Menagerie.*

---

situation. If he is to fulfill his family obligations, obligations Amanda has thrust upon him rather than ones which he has voluntarily assumed, he will have to relinquish his independence. If he is to act independently, he will have to forsake his family responsibilities. Although Tom does eventually assert his independence, he does not seem to ever become fully mature. Rather, he is compared to his father, who also abandoned the family, though he had presumably chosen that responsibility by getting married. It is his father's desertion which places Tom into such an oppressive situation. Because Tom is so clearly compared to his father, readers can easily forget this primary difference between them.

Duty and Responsibility

Woven into the coming of age theme is the issue of duty and responsibility. While Amanda insists that Tom's primary duty is to her and Laura, Tom resents this responsibility because it presents him with so few options. On the other hand, Tom also has a responsibility to himself, one he might say he exercises precisely by attempting to abandon his family. By the end of the play, however, we see that Tom is both irresponsible and a failure in attaining his goals. Yet, the responsibilities of a son are different from those of a father. Although Amanda, in some ways, wants Tom to be a surrogate husband—she holds him responsible for supporting the family although she does not permit him

the authority of a head of a household—Tom's action, while being objectively similar to his father's, might not be identical morally.

STYLE

Conflict

Although the action in *The Glass Menagerie* occurs over only a couple of days, nearly every scene is laden with overt conflict. The most obvious conflict occurs between Tom and Amanda, since Tom needs to remove himself from the family in order to achieve his goals, while Amanda needs him to stay. This conflict is most evident during their frequent bickering about the way Tom chews his food or the number of cigarettes he smokes. A more significant conflict, however, occurs within Tom's character. In order to follow his dream, vague as it is, he will have to abandon not only Amanda but also Laura.

Narrator

Although most plays do not rely on a narrator, *The Glass Menagerie* is structured so that Tom can fulfill two roles. He is both a character in the play and the person who, at times, tells the story directly to the audience. This occurs particularly at the beginning of the play, when Tom summarizes the events that have preceded the action and describes the setting, and at the end of the play, when Tom reveals what has happened to him during the intervening years.

Protagonist

The protagonist of a literary work is the main character, who must change in some way during the course of the events, even if the change is entirely internal. Tom is clearly the protagonist of *The Glass Menagerie*. Although he is not heroic and will probably never triumph over his obstacles, he does take action by the end of the play.

Setting

The broad setting of *The Glass Menagerie*—as described in Williams's stage directions—is "one of those vast hive-like conglomerations of cellular living-units that flower as warty growths in overcrowded urban centers of lower middle-class population." In other words, it is a fairly large apartment house in a comparatively poor neighborhood. The specific city is unnamed, as if details are unnecessary since these neighborhoods so closely resemble each other. All of the action occurs within the living room and dining room of the Wingfield's apartment; the primary importance of the setting is to reinforce the cramped feeling the characters struggle against. The time is also vague. Obviously, the play is set several decades ago, since Tom can support (although inadequately) a family of three on sixty-five dollars a month; yet, were it not for details such as these, the play could easily be set in the current generation.

Symbolism

The Glass Menagerie achieves part of its effect through the prominent display of symbols. The father's portrait looms above the family on their wall, although he has been absent for years; obviously, he remains psychologically present and significantly affects the attitudes of the other characters. The candles also function symbolically. When Tom fails to pay the light bill, Amanda lights the apartment with candles, suggesting that this will lend a more romantic atmosphere to their home. The last action of the play is when Laura blows the candles out, as if this will erase her from Tom's memory in a death-like moment.

The primary symbol in this play, however, is Laura's glass menagerie, particularly the unicorn.

The glass animals are fragile, as Laura is both emotionally and physically. Although they might imitate reality, they are not in themselves real, and their primary value lies in Laura's imagination. When the unicorn's horn breaks off, Laura describes him as now like the other horses, as if one must be broken in order to be normal. Laura is already "broken," however, and has never had the mythic status of a unicorn; she will never attain normalcy.

HISTORICAL CONTEXT

World War II

Although the setting of *The Glass Menagerie* is the 1930s, during the Great Depression and slightly before the beginning of World War II, Williams wrote the play after America had entered the war but before a decisive victory had been achieved. After being produced in Chicago in 1944, the play arrived in New York in 1945, the year the war ended. For Americans, the most significant historical event of the first half of the 1940s was the entry of the United States into World War II. Although the United States had not been eager to enter this war, Japan bombed Pearl Harbor on December 7, 1941, making U.S. participation inevitable on the side of the Allies—primarily England, France, and Russia. In addition to Japan, the Allies fought against Germany, led by Adolf Hitler, and Italy, led by Benito Mussolini. Through most of the war, Franklin Roosevelt was President of the United States, until he died on April 12, 1945; he was succeeded by his vice president, Harry S. Truman. The European phase of the war ended in May 1945, and the Pacific phase ended with the dropping of nuclear bombs on Japan (in Hiroshima and Nagasaki) in August of 1945.

Women in the Workforce

Among the American ramifications of World War II was the sudden increase of women in the workplace. Primarily because so many men were serving in the armed forces, women began performing jobs that had not previously been open to them, in factories for example; such work was now considered patriotic. "Rosy the Riveter" is a famous character who represents this trend. When the war ended and men returned home, however, women were expected to leave their jobs so that the men might find employment. Women did not enter

COMPARE & CONTRAST

- **1930s:** Adolf Hitler begins to achieve power in Germany. Some Americans fought in the Spanish Civil War, although the United States did not officially participate. World War II began in Europe in 1939, but the United States declared its neutrality.

  1940s: During World War II, most men served in the military, unless they were exempt for health or other reasons. Because so many people were affected, this war received prominent attention both in politics and in individual daily lives.

  Today: Although The United States has engaged in comparatively minor military engagements during the last generation, no given war has become a cultural obsession since the Vietnam War ended in the mid-1970s. While men must register for the draft when they reach the age of 18, no one is currently drafted, and the military consistently speaks of "down sizing."

- **1930s:** The major economic event was the Great Depression, which lasted most of the decade. Unemployment reached 13.7 million in the United States in 1932. Although men were considered the family's primary breadwinner when possible, women were also grateful for and sought out work.

  1940s: During the war women entered the workforce but returned to homemaking when the war ended. They worked in factories and other places formerly identified with men in order to patriotically support the men who were overseas fighting.

  Today: Many women work outside the home, even those with young children. They often do so in part because one salary can no longer adequately support a family. Another factor is the women's movement which has argued for equal treatment of men and women in politics and business and which has provided more diverse opportunities for women.

- **1930s and 1940s:** Works of literature could be easily censored when they were considered obscene, even if the material was subtle. Writers such as James Joyce and D. H. Lawrence often received a scandalized response from the general public.

  Today: Artistic merit and censorship remain an issue today. Although the works that were considered pornographic in the 1940s are frequently taught in high schools today, other works continue to be attacked. This is most evident when Congress considers the budget for the National Endowment for the Arts.

- **1930s and 1940s:** Romantic interactions between men and women were often formal and constrained. Men were expected to initiate dating situations and were also expected to introduce themselves to the woman's parents. A woman generally lived with her parents until she got married.

  Today: Although some relationships are "conventional," the range of acceptable behavior between men and women is quite broad. Gender roles are no longer as rigid, although women still do the vast majority of housework and child care. In part because the age of marriage has risen, women as well as men often live independently before they get married, and couples frequently live together before they get married. Simultaneously, women can remain single if they choose without being considered "old maids."

- **1930s and 1940s:** Women seldom attended college or received any higher education. (Even for men, college was generally restricted to those who were financially comfortable.) If women attended a business school, they studied such subjects as typing and shorthand and prepared to be secretaries for bosses who would not have such skills.

  Today: The percentage of women and men attending college is nearly equal, although some fields, such as technology and engineering continue to be dominated by men. A person who aspires to work in an office, however, needs many more sophisticated skills. Shorthand, for example, is an outdated practice, and a person who can type is often not employable unless he or she also knows one or more computer programs.

the workforce in significant numbers again until the 1970's.

The Boom Years

Another effect of returning soldiers was the passage of the G.I. Bill of Rights which provided education benefits and home loans for many veterans. As a result, college enrollment increased substantially and began to become more available to middle and lower class students. New home construction and suburban development also expanded. This meant that many middle-class people moved out of major cities. On the other hand, because of work available in factories, this decade also saw mass migration from rural areas into cities.

Technological innovations also occurred, although contemporary standards make them seem decidedly dated. In 1944, the first general-purpose digital computer began to operate at Harvard University—although it needed four seconds to perform multiplication problems and eleven seconds to perform division! This computer had been built with 760,000 parts and 500 miles of wire—clearly neither a desktop nor a laptop version. Although its inventors might not have anticipated the electronic age of the late twentieth century, they clearly initiated a technological revolution.

More pertinent to average Americans was the development of Kodacolor, a color film marketed by Eastman Kodak. This film permitted individuals to take color pictures with inexpensive cameras.

The Growth of Post-War Arts

Within the arts, Tennessee Williams worked in a rich context. Other plays performed in New York or major European cities included *The Searching Wind* by Lillian Hellman, *No Exit* by Jean-Paul Sartre, and *I Remember Mama* by John Van Druten, which included Marlon Brando in its cast. W. Somerset Maugham published his novel, *The Razor's Edge,* in 1944. Stephen Vincent Benet won the Pulitzer Prize for Poetry that year, and T. S. Eliot published his *Four Quartets.* Such well-known and talented painters as Pablo Picasso, Georgia O'Keeffe, and Frida Kahlo produced much of their work during this period. Cole Porter, Judy Garland, Rita Hayworth, and Gene Kelly were popular entertainers. On a more humorous note, 1944 also saw the introduction of the Chiquita Banana song, which encouraged consumers to identify the fruit with a particular brand name-a trend that reached mammoth proportions by the late twentieth century.

CRITICAL OVERVIEW

When *The Glass Menagerie* reached the New York stage in 1945, it was a resounding success. A year earlier, it had also been successful in Chicago, despite poor weather which initially deterred the audience. According to Felicia Hardison Londre, writing in *American Playwrights since 1945,* "a crusade by the warmly enthusiastic Chicago critics" was launched to keep the play in production. It has remained popular, with staged as well as filmed versions appearing frequently, and it is considered to be one of Williams's most successful works. Indeed, writing in *The Christian Century* in 1964 while Williams was still alive, critic William R. Mueller stated that Williams "is the greatest living American playwright and ranks next to [Eugene] O'Neill in the history of American theater."

Critics almost inevitably remark on the poetic structure and language of *The Glass Menagerie.* As evidenced by the success with which his plays have been filmed, Williams brought a "cinematic concept of dramatic action to the American stage," according to Londre. She continued, describing Williams's work as characterized by "a harmonious blending and mutual reinforcement of dialogue, character, symbols, scenic environment, music, sound effects, and lighting." In his article Mueller stated that a "common denominator of Williams's plays is the quality of their poetry." Mueller defined this "poetry" not in terms of conventional poetic devices such as rhyme and meter, but as language "suffused with imagery and so phrased as to create a dreamlike state." In *Tennessee Williams: A Tribute,* S. Alan Chesler credited Williams with creating "a new poetic drama. . . . Williams has employed visual and auditory effects to previously unattempted extents by emphasizing color, music and scenic devices."

Yet poetry is far from the only characteristic for which critics have praised Williams and his plays. Although many of the stage directions in this play are almost novelistic in their detail, his work is also discussed in terms of its theatricality. Contrasting Williams with William Shakespeare, Mueller argued that "Shakespeare *can* be played without setting, lighting, costume, music; Williams cannot. He makes fullest use of the craft of the stage: scenic effects, lighting, color, music are of vast importance in evoking from the audience the desired emotional response." The use of a scrim between the audience and the actors at the beginning of the play would be one example of this. Another would be the frequency with which scene changes are signaled through fading music.

Critics also frequently comment on the psychological complexity of Williams's work, especially addressing the autobiographical roots of *The Glass Menagerie.* In part because of his success in creating characters who evoke empathy, even if they are not entirely typical, *The Glass Menagerie* and plays which soon followed appealed to an exceptionally broad audience, from high school students to professional critics. In the words of Foster Hirsch in *A Portrait of the Artist: The Plays of Tennessee Williams,* "Williams creates driven characters who are unlike anyone most of us are ever likely to meet and yet they are almost all convincing and recognizable." In an article published in *Players,* Gerald Berkowitz analyzed these characters in terms of the setting Williams has created for them: "as we discover each aberration or peculiarity in their [the Wingfields'] characters, we also discover that it is benign or even appropriate to their setting. Laura's pathological shyness does not stifle her at home; she is even able to overcome her fear of Jim when talking of her glass animals. Her lameness, which so embarrassed her in high school, becomes irrelevant when she is sitting in the apartment."

In addition to the number of awards Williams won during his lifetime, another way to measure his critical success, and the critical success of *The Glass Menagerie,* is through the professional attention he continues to receive. Books and articles continue to be written about this play as the thematic, literary, and theatrical issues it raises continue to be debated. Within the last generation, these publications include not only a wide range of American and Canadian periodicals but also journals published in Brussels, France, Brazil, The Netherlands, Germany, and South Africa. This play, in other words, has achieved not only significant popular success but international critical success.

CRITICISM

L. M. Domina

Domina is an author and educator. This essay examines William's use of modern theatrical technology as an essential element of his drama.

Tennessee Williams is admired for the theatricality of his plays and for introducing liter-

ary, specifically poetic, devices into the theater. In *The Glass Menagerie* particularly, he relies on the craft of modern theater—on such devices as lighting and sound techniques—to enhance the effectiveness of his themes, themes which are not difficult to recognize

Throughout this play, the characters are tempted toward illusion when they find reality too painful. Although the illusions of some characters are more socially acceptable, even typical, than others, Williams suggests that the "American dream" is as illusory as more overt psychological illnesses and that any given manifestation of illusion is as understandable, even acceptable, as any other one. Even Jim O'Connor, the character an audience would likely describe as closest to "normal," in other words, does not distinguish between reality and fantasy. Jarka M. Burian, writing in *International Dictionary of Theatre-1: Plays,* stated that each of the Wingfields "has a secret life and dream that inherently has little likelihood of actualization." Furthermore, in this play Williams suggests that the most specific arena of confinement, the family, is also the primary motivation for fantasy. Freedom equals freedom from familial responsibilities; yet since each character either attempts to achieve conventional family relations or obsessively to deny them, Williams indicates that such freedom is at best a vain hope.

This tendency to resist reality is most obvious in the female characters. Amanda Wingfield, the mother of Tom and Laura, is an abandoned wife who longs for a stable family structure, that is, a stable means of support, for her daughter. Amanda does not rely on her own experience as a cautionary device—or her experience cautions her toward conservatism. Her husband, who had left the family years ago, remains present in the "warty growth" of the Wingfield apartment; his photograph, "the face of a very handsome young man in a doughboy's First World War cap . . . gallantly smiling, ineluctably smiling," dominates the living room. Rather than suggest that Laura should not depend on a husband to support her (as difficult as this choice would have been during the 1930s), Amanda desires instead that Laura find a suitable husband, one who will not drink excessively, who will find excitement enough in a conventional career and family.

Yet although she has kept her husband's photograph on her wall, Amanda sometimes seems to forget that she chose to marry a less-than-ideal man. She speaks frequently, almost obsessively, of

WHAT DO I READ NEXT?

- Tennessee Williams wrote *A Streetcar Named Desire* in 1947. It features another frustrated family, though here the interactions become violent.

- Eugene O'Neill is also considered a major American playwright. He published *Long Day's Journey into Night* in 1956. It also features a family within which tensions are obvious, in part because of the alcohol abuse present in the characters.

- *A Raisin in the Sun,* written by Lorraine Hansberry and first produced in 1959 presents the situation of a black family, each of whose members attempts to exercise choice for the good of the family and themselves indivually.

- *The Bluest Eye* published by Toni Morrison in 1970 concerns a young African American girl who loses touch with reality because of her life circumstances.

- Elizabeth Bishop's poem, "In the Waiting Room," (1976) tells the story of a young girl at the moment when she realizes she is both an individual and part of a community.

the Sunday afternoon when she received "*seventeen!*—gentlemen callers! Why, sometimes there weren't chairs enough to accommodate them all." And each of these men was special: "Among my callers were some of the most prominent young planters on the Mississippi Delta—planters and sons of planters! . . . There was young Champ Laughlin who later became vice president of the Delta Planters Bank. Hadley Stevenson who was drowned in Moon Lake and left his widow one hundred and fifty thousand in Government bonds. . . . That Fitzhugh boy went North and made a fortune—came to be known as the Wolf of Wall Street! He had the Midas touch." In continually reliving this Sunday afternoon, Amanda is able to retain a sense of her own popularity, a sense of success rather than of the failure that accompanies the marriage she did make. The unstated question is, of course, why she married the man "who fell in love with long distances" rather than one of these other implausibly successful beaux.

Simultaneously, however, because she lives more energetically in the past than in the present, she appears rather foolish when a gentleman caller does accompany Tom home for dinner. Although she does desire that Laura find a suitable husband, Amanda dresses and acts as if the gentleman is calling for her: "She wears a girlish frock of yellowed voile with a blue silk sash. She carries a bunch of jonquils—the legend of her youth is nearly revived." This dress is not only "girlish," but is precisely the one "in which I led the cotillion" over twenty years earlier. But the intervening time has collapsed; Amanda's girlhood merges with her middle age.

Although Laura remembers liking only one boy rather than receiving seventeen gentlemen callers and although she knew this boy approximately five rather than twenty-five years ago, Laura's romantic life initially seems as decidedly over as Amanda's. While Amanda's illusions lead her to act foolishly, to become coyly extraverted, Laura's function with opposite results. Laura's fantasies are not simply a preference but a need; they incapacitate her. Laura's fantasies, that is, don't merely supplement reality but *become* reality. More specifically, her glass menagerie which gives the play its title resembles Laura in disturbingly accurate detail. Even the stage directions instruct us to interpret Laura as more similar to these delicate glass objects than to any of the other human characters: "A fragile, unearthly prettiness has come out in Laura: she is like a piece of translucent glass touched by light, given a momentary radiance, not actual, not lasting." Laura describes the unicorn with similar language: "he loves the light! You see how the light shines through him?" In the *Reference Guide to American Literature,* Christian H. Moe supported this view. Laura, he argued, "reveals herself as too fragile ... to pursue outside reality and thus becomes instead its victim retreating into her own fantasy world." This glass collection constitutes Laura's community, for she indicates that she devotes most of her time, and implicitly her emotional energy, to it. She personifies the animals, creating lives for them that reflect her own. When the unicorn's horn breaks, for example, Laura speculates that "The horn was removed to make him feel less—freakish! ... Now he will feel more at home with the other horses."

By this point, Laura has revealed why she also feels "freakish." The brace on her leg "clumped so loud" according to her memory, drawing everyone's attention, she believes, to her disability. Yet the one time Tom uses the word "crippled" to describe Laura, Amanda reprimands him—demanding that her fantasy take precedence over the family's reality. One could argue that when the unicorn's horn breaks, he becomes "crippled" rather than "less—freakish." For it is his horn that grants him individuality. Laura, of course, longs to be more similar to others rather than so distinct from them.

In his willingness to be honest about Laura, Tom is perhaps the only character who can see Laura simultaneously as "peculiar" and as beautiful; a person so delicate that light can shine through her. Because he acknowledges that his life is frustratingly dull and confining, Tom fantasizes about the future. If he can leave the family, he believes, if he can imitate his father and simply follow his desires for long distance, he will have opportunity rather than responsibility. He will be able to write poetry rather than sell shoes. Tom does leave, of course, after he loses his job selling shoes because he was writing poetry. But though he does join the merchant marine and though he does abandon the family physically, he discovers that memory can haunt him. He can never leave them emotionally. The future becomes as oppressive as the past, for the "cities swept about me like dead leaves, leaves that were brightly colored but torn away from the branches." Rather than live merrily in the past as Amanda does, Tom is haunted by it. "I was pursued by something," he says. Try as he might to escape, "all at once my sister touches my shoulder. I turn around and look into her eyes. Oh, Laura, Laura, I tried to leave you behind me, but I am more faithful than I intended to be!"

Even Jim O'Connor, the most conventional of these characters, is nagged by his past. In an article

Jane Wyman and Kirk Douglas in the 1950 film adaptation.

published in *Players,* Gerald Berkowitz critiqued Jim for his own fantasies: "His dreams and values, as practical and, realistic as they may be, sound shallower and more comical than Amanda's ... and his disquisitions on the art and etiquette of its [a pack of chewing gum] use sound far more odd and foolish than Laura's fantasies about the animals' feelings." While he may not be as obsessed as any of the others, he has discovered that the present has not lived up to his hopes. In high school, he had been extremely popular and had been expected to succeed at whatever he attempted. Yet, even if he makes somewhat more money, he nevertheless works in the same warehouse as Tom. Rather than surrender to disappointment, however, Jim continues to invest his hope in the future. Although he acknowledges that he had "hoped when I was going to high school that I would be further along at this time," he is currently studying public speaking because he believes it will suit him for "executive positions." It will give him "social poise," the one characteristic that will make him more successful, although the image he presents of himself in high school would indicate that he had been poised then. Like Tom, Jim continues to believe that the life he desires is possible. He lives with the illusion that if he simply tries harder, if he alters the details of his circumstances without altering their substance, then his search for excitement will be validated. Jim claims that "being in love has made a new man of me!" but he provides no evidence for this outside of rhetoric.

Although we don't discover what occurs to Jim in the future, the desolation of the play's conclusion indicates that disappointment is the inevitable outcome. In the words of Benjamin Nelson in his book, *Tennessee Williams: The Man and His Work,* these characters are "doomed to failure because of their inability to do more than dream." Whether these characters attempt to achieve freedom through a family or detached from one, the play indicates that such freedom is the stuff of which dreams are made.

Source: L. M. Domina, in an essay for *Drama for Students,* Gale, 1997.

John Mason Brown

In the following excerpt, Brown offers a mixed assessment of The Glass Menagerie, *maintaining that while the play is "blessed with imagination" and "is the work of a mind both original and sensitive. . . . Mr. Williams's drama sometimes proves empty." Brown also speculates that the play suffers from a plot that is too loosely constructed and dialogue that provides little action and thus fails to hold the audience's interest.*

A lady, obviously no psychologist, once encountered William Lyon Phelps on the street in New Haven. "I hope you won't mind my telling you how much I enjoyed your lecture yesterday?" she asked. "Madam," beamed Professor Phelps, "you misunderstand me entirely. I am glutton for praise."

All of us are. Praise has never made anyone unhappy. We like it even when we do not believe it. We tire of it only when it is bestowed too long on other people. It is a music we do not object to having played off-stage. Although it may shame our consciences and insult our minds, it does no damage to our ears. So long as we remember that it sings the song not of what we are but of what we wish we were, it probably does not hurt us.

But the advance praise we hear of a book we have not read or a play we have not seen is another matter. Genuine and well meant as it is, if too unstinted it can do harm. Not to us, but to what it has been lavished upon. We take such praise seriously. It sends our hopes skyrocketing. It prepares us for a miracle in a world where miracles are infrequent.

To the book or play in question it presents a challenge few works can survive. Critics (and what playgoer or reader is not one?) are never more gluttonous than when it comes to *giving* praise. When disappointed because of the praise bestowed by others, we forget our own guilt in anticipating reactions or, worse still, raising expectations. We remember only our present disappointment. At such moments we are tempted to understand why managers employ, ungratefully, though not unreasonably, the word "raves" to describe reviews which find hats tossed so far in the air that their owners' heads are lost sight of.

I raise these general questions with a specific instance in mind. Recently I had the good fortune to see *The Glass Menagerie* but the bad fortune to see it after reading the reviews and hearing ecstatic reports about it from Chicago. Although Tennessee Williams's fantasy is a play I would not have missed, I wish I had missed both the reviews and the advance reports. At least until later. I wish I had missed them because Mr. Williams's play was forced to live them down. It was compelled to struggle against them much as a joke, however good, is condemned to a harder hearing when introduced by some witless fellow who insists upon laughing first, and then saying, "Oh, that reminds me of a very funny story."

A play would have to be a master piece indeed to compete with what has been said about *The Glass Menagerie* both in Chicago and New York. Mr. Williams's script, I am afraid, is not that masterpiece.

It has its high, its shimmering virtues. It is blessed with imagination. It has its many lovely moments. It is the kind of play one is proud to have the theatre produce, and pleased to sit before even when disappointed in this scene or in that. In any season it would be uncommon; in this season it is outstanding. It is the work of a mind both original and sensitive. Although it follows trails blazed by Thornton Wilder and William Saroyan, it manages to walk down them with a gait of its own.

It is as promising a first play as has been seen hereabouts in many a year.

Mr. Williams's is a play of moods; a study in frustration. Its plot is nonexistent, at least so far as plotting is ordinarily understood. It is too close to the heart of life to bother about story-telling merely for the sake of telling a story. To attempt to suggest its qualifies by outlining its actions would be as unfair to *The Glass Menagerie* as it would be to try to suggest the qualities, say, of *The Three Sisters* in terms of a synopsis. No one can deny that *The Three Sisters* is about three Russian women who want to go to Moscow and never get there. Yet to say—this and only this—is to omit the wit, wisdom, perception, and autumnal radiance which make Chekhov's play one of the wonders of the modern stage.

Mr. Williams bases his drama upon an incident rather than a plot. The only story he tells is how an impoverished Southern mother has her hopes dashed when she learns that the Gentleman Caller, who has at last come to see her crippled daughter, is already engaged. But Mr. William's interest does not stop with this story. His concern is what lies under the surface of events. He deals with those small happenings which can loom so large in the lives of unhappy people. He shows us the hopes such happenings can quicken, the memories they stir, the transformations they are able to effect, and the despair they often evoke.

His drama is projected as a memory, seen at moments not only through the actual gauzes provided by set designer Mr. Mielziner, but in flashes through the thicker curtain of time itself. Mr. Williams's is the simplest kind of make believe. The narrator he employs is the crippled girl's brother. The scenes we are invited to share are this brother's recollections. They are recalled to him when, as a merchant sailor in a foreign port, he sees objects in a store window which remind him of his sister's glass menagerie at home.

We move back in the sailor's life until we encounter the nagging the dulness which drove him to seek the release of the sea. We learn of his hatred of the factory in which he worked; of his need for escape; of his incessant movie-going when (as Mr. Williams puts it), in the company of millions of other Americans sitting in darkened theatres in the pre-war years, he let a few Hollywood actors have all his adventures for him.

With this sailor brother we enter the poor home his memory has recreated. We inhale the honeysuckle of his mother's Southern recollections. We overhear her steady, soft-voiced scoldings, and understand her exasperation. We meet the crippled sister too. She is a girl who lives in the dreams summoned by the music of her Victrola records and the small glass animals in her collection to which she has given her heart. This sister is painfully shy. She is denied life by the selfconsciousness her

braces have forced upon her. In an overstressed moment of symbolism Mr. Williams insists that, because of her deformity, she is as out of place among her healthy contemporaries as is the glass unicorn in her menagerie among the commoner animals.

We learn how this girl blooms under the attentions of a happy extrovert who cannot marry her. We also eavesdrop on her when, at last, she consents to face the boy her brother has asked home from the factory for a humbler version of the "Alice Adams" dinner party. Above all, we understand the decision of the brother, being what he was, to go to sea.

Mr. Williams writes about his characters warmly, with a sympathy that is constant and yet probing. He knows how to etch them in line by line, so that before the evening is over we know them well. We are on intimate terms even with the hard-drinking father who has deserted them and is represented only by a shoddy photograph on the wall. But, in spite of Mr. Williams's perceptions and the quality of his play, his writing lacks the impact of Clifford Odets's phrasing and the ultimate radiance of William Saroyan's feeling.

Full though his heart is, Mr. Williams's drama sometimes proves empty. I found that it lost my interest even while it held my admiration. Fascinated as I remained by the way in which its lines were spoken, it became difficult for me to keep my mind (in the second act) on every line that was being spoken. I was certain of my respect for the play in general, but increasingly aware of Mr. Williams's uncertainties.

Perhaps this was because, unlike Chekhov, Mr. Williams permits us to become uncomfortably conscious of how slight is the incident upon which he has based his play. Perhaps it is because his dialogue is not always active enough to compensate for the lack of action in his story. Perhaps it is because he allows us to know too much too early about all his characters except the charmingly written and played Gentleman Caller. Perhaps it is because Miss Taylor is off-stage for so long a scene in the second act. Or Perhaps, as I have hinted, it is because the praise the play had won in advance had led me to expect that miracle which is every critic's hope.

Source: John Mason Brown, "Miss Taylor's Return" in the *Saturday Review,* Vol. 28, no. 15, April 14, 1945, pp. 34–36.

MR. WILLIAMS BASES HIS DRAMA UPON AN INCIDENT RATHER THAN A PLOT"

Lewis Nichols

In the following excerpt from a review that originally appeared in the New York Times *on April 2, 1945, Nichols assesses a production of* The Glass Menagerie, *praising the actors' performances and noting that while the play has some flaws, "Mr. Williams has a real ear for faintly sardonic dialogue, unexpected phrases and an affection for his characters."*

The theatre opened its Easter basket the night before and found it a particularly rich one. Preceded by warm and tender reports from Chicago, *The Glass Menagerie* opened at the Playhouse on Saturday, and immediately it was clear that for once the advance notes were not in error. Tennessee Williams' simple play forms the framework for some of the finest acting to be seen in many a day. "Memorable" is an overworked word, but that is the only one to describe Laurette Taylor's performance. March left the theatre like a lioness.

Miss Taylor's picture of a blowsy, impoverished woman who is living on memories of a flower-scented Southern past is completely perfect. It combines qualities of humor and human understanding. The Mother of the play is an amusing figure and a pathetic one. Aged, with two children, living in an apartment off an alley in St. Louis, she recalls her past glories, her seventeen suitors, the old and better life. She is a bit of a scold, a bit of a snob; her finery has worn threadbare, but she has kept it for occasions of state. Miss Taylor makes her a person known by any other name to everyone in her audience. That is art.

In the story the Mother is trying to do the best she can for her children. The son works in a warehouse, although he wants to go to far places. The daughter, a cripple, never has been able to finish school. She is shy, she spends her time collecting glass animals—the title comes from this—and playing old phonograph records. The Mother thinks it is time she is getting married, but there has never

been a Gentleman Caller at the house. Finally the son brings home another man from the warehouse and out comes the finery and the heavy if bent candlestick. Even the Gentleman Caller fails. He is engaged to another girl.

Mr. Williams' play is not all of the same caliber. A strict perfectionist could easily find a good many flaws. There are some unconnected odds and ends which have little to do with the story: Snatches of talk about the war, bits of psychology, occasional moments of rather flowery writing. But Mr. Williams has a real ear for faintly sardonic dialogue, unexpected phrases and an affection for his characters. Miss Taylor takes these many good passages and makes them sing. . . .

Source: Lewis Nichols, in a review of *The Glass Menagerie* (1945) in *On Stage: Selected Theater Reviews from The New York Times, 1920–1970,* edited by Bernard Beckerman and Howard Siegman, Arno Press, 1973, p. 260.

FURTHER READING

Berkowitz, Gerald. "The 'Other World' of *The Glass Menagerie*" in *Players,* Vol. 48, no. 4, April-May, 1973, pp. 150-53.
> Berkowitz argues that the setting or "locus" of *The Glass Menagerie* as well as of other of Williams's plays influences perceptions of the characters to the extent that they seem "normal," while the "normal" people seem outsiders.

Burian, Jarka M. "The Glass Menagerie" in *International Dictionary of Theatre-1: Plays,* edited by Mark Hawkins-Dady, St. James Press, 1992, pp. 187-89.
> Burian provides several character analyses, focusing especially on Tom.

Chesler, S. Alan. "Tennessee Williams: Reassessment and Assessment" in *Tennessee Williams: A Tribute,* edited by Jac Tharpe, University Press of Mississippi, 1977, pp. 848-80.
> Chesler describes Williams's characteristics as a playwright and contextualizes his career in terms of his affect on American drama.

Hirsch, Foster. *A Portrait of the Artist: The Plays of Tennessee Williams,* Kennikat Press, 1979.
> Hirsch analyzes Williams's plays according to their autobiographical influences.

Londre, Felicia Hardison. ''Tennessee Williams'' in *American Playwrights since 1945: A Guide to Scholarship, Criticism, and Performance,* edited by Philip C. Kolin, Greenwood, 1989, pp. 488-517.

> Londre provides a thorough discussion of Williams's work and reputation, including a production history of several of his plays.

Moe, Christian H. ''The Glass Menagerie'' in *Reference Guide to American Literature,* edited by James Kamp, third edition, St. James Press, 1994.

> Moe traces the development of this play from a short story and describes the plot.

Mueller, William R. ''Tennessee Williams: A New Direction?'' in *The Christian Century,* Vol LXXXI, no. 42, October 14, 1964, pp. 1271-72.

> Mueller traces Williams's career, describing characteristics common to several plays. He suggests that Williams's earlier work was more successful, artistically, than his later plays.

Nelson, Benjamin. *Tennessee Williams: The Man and His Work,* Ivan Obolensky, 1961.

> Nelson critiques the body of Williams's work, evaluating the plays in terms of each other.

The King and I

RICHARD RODGERS AND OSCAR HAMMERSTEIN, II

1951

In this romantic musical, the boy-meets-girl plot is woven into the historical context of British Imperialism in Asia. Thus it is also the story of a clash between cultures and the dynamics between Great Britain and "oriental" peoples. The King of Siam invites an English governess to come to his country and teach the children of his many wives about the modern world. Yet he himself resists changing his traditional role as benevolent patriarchal dictator until the attractive and bold young governess wins his heart and his respect. It is his son Prince Chulalongkorn who will carry on the King's program of scientific modernization of Siam after the King's death in the final scene. Oscar Hammerstein based the play on a novel by Margaret Landon, *Anna and the King of Siam.* He and composer Richard Rodgers transformed it into one of the most memorable musicals they produced in their long association together, departing from the more typical "musical comedy" with a more serious treatment of their subject. Yul Brynner played the king in the Broadway production and then in the film version with co-star Deborah Kerr, whose singing was dubbed. Over the years Brynner performed the role over 4,000 times. The film was a box-office success and is still considered one of the better musical films of the twentieth century. The play's enduring popularity was verified in 1996, when film star Lou Diamond Phillips assumed the title role for a successful Broadway revival.

AUTHOR BIOGRAPHY

While both Rodgers and Hammerstein are credited as the authors of *The King and I,* there was a distinct division of labor in the writing of the play-as there was with all of their collaborations. Technically, Rodgers is the author of the music and Hammerstein the author of the lyrics and book (or story). This section focuses on Hammerstein's background, as he is the author of the material this entry will examine.

Oscar Hammerstein II was born July 12, 1895, in New York City to a family with deep roots in the theatre. Although the Hammerstein family myth holds that Oscar was discouraged from going into the theater, he could have heard of little else at family gatherings. His grandfather and namesake Oscar Hammerstein spent the fortune he made on cigar-rolling inventions building new theaters in New York City and investing in the staging of operas. He passed his interest on to his two sons, Willy and Arthur. Oscar II's father Willy Hammerstein managed a highly successful vaude-ville house and his uncle Arthur was the producer who gave Oscar his first theater job—assistant stage manager, which he began at the age of twenty-two. Oscar's decision to take the theater job ended his plans to finish law school at Columbia University. Not that his heart was in the law anyway—he decided to attend Columbia more for dramatic activities such as its annual varsity show than its law program. Once launched into the world of the theater, he stayed there for the rest of his life.

By the time he teamed up with Richard Rodgers in 1942 to work on *Oklahoma!,* he had already collaborated on forty-five musicals, including the groundbreaking *Show Boat* with Jerome Kern. Together, Rodgers and Hammerstein would set the standard for the ''musical play'' for the next two decades, churning out nine memorable productions for the stage (in addition to *Oklahoma!* they wrote *Carousel, Allegro, South Pacific, The King And I, Me and Juliet, Pipe Dream, Flower Drum Song,* and *The Sound Of Music*), the film musical *State Fair,* and the television production *Cinderella.* Hammerstein's lyrics are known not for their clever wit but for their simplicity and directness, their sincere emotion. He took great pains to make smooth transitions between the spoken dialogue of his plays and the songs. Sometimes Rodgers would write the music first and Hammerstein fit the lyrics to it, and at other times Hammerstein created the mood and

Oscar Hammerstein II, author of book and libretto

rhythm in his lyrics and then Rodgers, always one who composed quickly, would in a day or so compose the music for it. Their partnership was known for its compatibility and fertile productivity and for their congeniality toward their casts. Oscar Hammerstein II died in 1960, Richard Rodgers in 1979.

PLOT SUMMARY

In Bangkok, Siam (which would later come to be known as Thailand), in 1862 a strong-willed, widowed schoolteacher, Anna Leonowens, arrives at the request of the King of Siam to tutor his many children. Anna's young son, Louis, fears the severe countenance of the King's ''Prime Minister'' the Kralahome, but Anna refuses to be intimidated. She teaches her son to ''Whistle a Happy Tune'' whenever he is afraid. The Kralahome escorts them to the palace; he rides on a carried chair, while Anna and her son follow on foot behind him. Anna is bristling to confront the King about his broken promise regarding a house for Louis and herself outside of the palace walls. As they await an audience, the King receives a gift from the king of Burma, a

Richard Rodgers, composer

lovely girl named Tuptim. The King sends her off to his harem of wives, dismissing the young man who delivered the gift, Lun Tha, who has fallen deeply in love with Tuptim. The King turns to go, so Anna marches up to him, demanding to be heard. She is taken aback by the King's dominance, as he claps his hands and orders her to ''stand here'' to meet the royal children. Anna plans to depart on the waiting ship if she does not get what has been promised to her, but she is so taken with the children that she decides she will stay. She announces that she will pursue the topic of the house later.

For the next several weeks, Anna proceeds to teach the children songs, proverbs, and poems all having to do with longing for a home. The King recognizes her subterfuge and refuses to supply the house. The handful of wives who also have been allowed to partake of Anna's teaching continually refer to Anna as ''Sir.'' When she asks them why, Lady Thiang, the King's number one wife, explains ''because you scientific, not lowly like woman.'' Tuptim reveals her secret love for Lun Tha to Anna, and Anna sings ''Hello, Young Lovers,'' in sympathy for the star-crossed couple.

The King is quite pleased with Anna's teaching. His eldest son Prince Chulalongkorn has some concerns, however. The young prince asks his fa-

ther when he will know he knows everything and thus be ready to rule. This prompts the King to sing ''A Puzzlement,'' in which he expresses his own doubts about how best to bring justice and knowledge to his people. In the meantime, Anna confirms that she loves the children, singing to them ''Getting to Know You,'' a song about the joys of new friendship. Then she launches into a new lesson— geography—having just received a more accurate map from England. The new map shows Siam in its proper size in relation to other countries. She has to end her lesson prematurely, though, when Prince Chulalongkorn refuses to believe that Siam is so small and that there is such a substance as snow. His father rescues Anna by ordering the children to believe her.

The Kralahome demands that Anna cease encouraging the King to modernize; he foresees danger ahead because he thinks that the King will not be able to lead effectively if he loses his authoritarian style. When Anna disregards this warning, the Kralahome retorts by predicting she'll become the King's slave. As if to confirm this, the King sends for Anna in the middle of the night and demands that she take a letter. During this menial task, to which Anna submits because she is charmed by the King's desire to write to Abraham Lincoln, the King extracts from Anna the promise that she will conform to the tradition of never letting her head be higher than the King's. In spite of her scientific and liberal beliefs, Anna promises to comply.

During another confrontation between Anna and the King, he finally articulates the phrase that Anna least wants to hear, ''You are my servant!'' Now Anna can no longer pretend to herself that she has not submitted to the King's will, and she threatens to leave, saying ''I cannot stay in a country where a promise has no meaning.'' Anna is awaiting the next available ship when Lady Thiang comes to seek Anna's help in advising the King on a new matter of great urgency. She sings ''Something Wonderful,'' expressing her way of loving a man who is both brutal and unexpectedly generous. Anna recognizes the wisdom and grace of Lady Thiang's kind of love.

Anna agrees to go to the King and to protect his male ego by acting as though she is not there to help him. The problem is that rumors have reached Queen Victoria that the King of Siam is a barbarian. If that is the case, or even if the perception is generally accepted, then the Queen will have little

Yul Brynner as the King and Deborah Kerr as Anna in the film adaptation

trouble making a protectorate of Siam. The King cleverly demands that Anna ''guess'' what he should do, thus opening the door for her to give him some much-needed advice. She guesses that he will entertain the British Ambassador and the prominent British citizens of Bangkok, to demonstrate his civility. The King is elated and he rushes all of his women, Anna included, off to the Buddhist in order to pray for success. Amid his wishes and demands that Anna supervise sewing European dresses for each of his many wives, he at last promises to give Anna her house.

The European style dinner and entertainment have the desired effect. Tuptim has written a play for the entertainment of the notables, an Asian-style version of Harriet Beecher Stowe's 1852 novel, *Uncle Tom's Cabin.* The guests find the King witty, love Tuptim's play, and toast the continued sovereignty of Siam. The King has won. However, he is disturbed by the note of rebellion he and Anna each have detected in Tuptim's play. The cruel Simon Legree, whom Tuptim has transformed into a King rather than the plantation owner he was in Stowe's novel, drowns in the pursuit of the escaped slave Eliza. The King knows that Tuptim is unhappy in his court and resents her expressing rebellion in this way. He initiates a search of the palace so that he

may reprimand her, but she has fled with Lun Tha. As the guards continue their search, the King and Anna celebrate their victory by dancing a polka together. They are abruptly interrupted by the guards carrying a screaming Tuptim. The King furiously prepares to beat her himself, but Anna appeals to him to contain his anger and refuses to leave the room. The King cannot bring himself to whip the girl in front of Anna and runs offstage. The Kralahome snarls at Anna that she has destroyed the King. At this painful moment more bad news arrives—the guards have found Lun Tha's drowned body in the river.

Once again Anna is awaiting the arrival of a ship to take her home to England. Lady Thiang once again arrives to plead with Anna to overcome her pride and visit the King. This time the situation is more grave; he is dying, having refused nourishment for many weeks. Lady Thiang hands Anna a letter that the King has managed to write her. In it he declares his admiration for Anna, who has been ''much trouble'' but who has affected him greatly. She runs to his side.

The children are brought in to their father. One child recites a letter to Anna begging her not to leave. Anna decides to send Louis to the ship to retrieve their luggage—she will stay after all.

Young Prince Chulalongkorn fears being made King before he is ready. The dying King asks him what he would do first as a ruler. As the prince explains his proclamation abolishing the traditional groveling bow, an idea clearly influenced by Anna, the King dies. Anna reverently kisses the hand of the dead king.

CHARACTERS

British Ambassador

The British Ambassador comes to the royal palace in Bangkok expecting to confirm the rumors of the King's barbarity. He is delighted to find him a civilized and learned man. The Ambassador declares in a toast to the King that he will carry the message to Queen Victoria that Siam is quite capable of remaining a sovereign nation.

Eliza

Eliza plays the runaway slave in the play-within-a-play written by the slave Tuptim. In traditional Asian dress Eliza dances and pantomimes scenes of escape from wicked Simon Legree.

Keeper of the Dogs

The Keeper of the Dogs dances a ballet chase of Eliza, across the frozen river, which miraculously melts and drowns him, his dogs, and Simon Legree.

Simon Legree

Wicked Simon Legree is a plantation slave owner in Harriet Beecher Stowe's novel. Tuptim converts him to a king in her adaptation, a more direct reference to the King of Siam, who angrily recognizes himself in the portrayal of the tyrannical ruler.

Anna Leonowens

Anna, a British governess has come to Siam at the request of the King. She is to teach his many young children about the world. She brings with her Louis, her nine- or ten-year-old son and a photograph of her beloved dead husband, Tom. Anna is a strong-willed woman who shows her character immediately by demanding that the King provide her with the house outside the palace walls that she had stipulated in her negotiations with him. She is also a warm-hearted woman, however, and the instant she meets the King's charming children, she submits to live in the palace "for now." She makes it clear, however, that the issue of the separate home is not over. In other ways, too, Anna defies the authority and machismo of the King, as when she deliberately orders a new map to replace the King's map that showed Siam in exaggerated proportions. She is, as the King wanted her to be, a "scientific person" which is why the King's many wives and children insist on calling her "Sir." Lady Thiang explains that they call her this because she is "scientific, not lowly like woman." Throughout the play, Anna's soft-hearted, womanly side vies with her precise, rational side in dealing with the King's traditional, chauvinistic attitude toward all women, even her. She finally wins her battle with the King for a house, but she does so through womanly charm rather than through scientific logic.

Louis Leonowens

Louis is the nine- or ten-year-old son of Anna. He plays a rather small role in the play, mostly serving as the civilized and rather timid counterpart to the more robust and feisty Prince Chulalongkorn. In the first scene Louis expresses fear for the severe-looking, "half-naked" Kralahome, so his mother shows him her method for overcoming fear—to "Whistle a Happy Tune"; at the end of the play Louis worries about missing the boat home. He's a typical British schoolboy of the upper class.

Lun Tha

Lun Tha is a Burmese man charged with delivering the Burmese King's gift to the King of Siam—a beautiful and intelligent young woman named Tuptim. He makes his delivery, but not before falling completely in love with Tuptim. He risks his life just for moments with her and later runs away with her when the palace is occupied with the British visitors. After Tuptim is captured by the angry King, Lun Tha is found drowned in the river.

The King

The King of Siam is a study in nineteenth-century contrasts. He is at once the patriarchal and despotic leader, unused to being defied and quick to anger; yet he is also a budding cosmopolitan leader, eager to learn the ways of the "scientific" modern world he wants his country to join. He thinks of

MEDIA ADAPTATIONS

- A 1946 black and white film starring Rex Harrison and Irene Dunne and produced by John Cromwell was adapted from Margaret Landon's novel *Anna and the King of Siam* before Hammerstein undertook the musical version of the work.

- Charles Brackett produced the famous film version with Yul Brynner and Deborah Kerr (1956); it is available on videotape from CBS/Fox Video.

- A sound recording featuring Julie Andrews, Ben Kingsley, and Marilyn Horne is available on Philips records (1992). A 1989 disc includes selections from various Rodgers and Hammerstein musicals sung by Samuel Ramey (available from EMI). Decca carries the sound track of the original Broadway cast with Gertrude Lawrence, while RCA carries one made in 1977 with Yul Brynner and Constance Towers (who took over the role of Anna in the original Broadway production after Gertrude Lawrence died of cancer). Capital Records carries the 1956 motion picture sound track recording as well as a disc of musical excerpts from the film.

---

himself as an innovative and open-minded leader, but, as Anna finds, he is blindly tied to traditional ways of thinking and acting. He is intelligent enough to read the Bible and find parallels between the words of Moses and new scientific thinking, but also brutal enough to want to beat an unhappy slave for running away. His chauvinism prevents him from directly seeking the advice he knows that Anna can provide him, so he cleverly challenges her to ''guess'' what he plans to do to impress the British Ambassador, and then implements her ideas as his own. The King proves that he does, after all, have a heart, when he allows himself to waste away and die after Lun Tha drowns. He cannot manage to cross the chasm between his traditional, outmoded oriental world and the new, scientific world that Anna represents. He has to die so that his son, Prince Chulalongkorn, can take Siam into its future.

Kralahome

The Kralahome is the Siamese version of a Prime Minister—the King's most trusted advisor. The Kralahome greets Anna's ship and escorts her and her son to the palace. Anna quickly learns the station of women in Siamese society because he rides in a slave-carried chair while she walks behind. The Kralahome's severe demeanor and looks frighten young Louis, but Anna refuses to be bullied by him, even when he demands that she stop encouraging the King to become something he is not—a cosmopolitan and egalitarian leader. When the king falls ill, Kralahome blames Anna for destroying him.

Prince Chulalongkorn

The young Prince is a wonderful combination of his father's self-assured leadership and his mother's careful wisdom. Prince Chulalongkorn brings to Anna's classroom a healthy skepticism and a junior version of his father's arrogance. Prince Chulalongkorn bridles at the geography lesson which reveals Siam to be smaller than he'd thought, then rebels and refuses to believe in snow, turning the classroom to pandemonium until his father orders the children to believe the schoolteacher. While the king is dying, the young prince makes his first proclamations, one of which is to abolish the established tradition of bowing low to the ground ''like a toad''; instead, he wants his people to show their respect with straight backs and a confident look in their eyes. His display of command and concern for his people demonstrate his readiness to rule as well as his successful assimilation of modern Western thought.

George Ramsay

George Ramsay accompanies the British Ambassador on his fact-finding mission because he once loved Anna Leonowens and hopes to win her back. He had proposed marriage to her once in London; now he is prepared to renew his offer. He accepts Anna's rebuff with the dignity of an Englishman and the resignation of a man who does not love intensely enough to feel much regret.

Ship's Captain

The Ship's Captain helps to set the scene of *The King and I* by warning Anna Leonowens about the unnamed dangers that an Englishwoman alone with her young son may face in Siam. He tells her that the Kralahome (the Siamese ''Prime Minister'') who has been sent to escort Anna to the palace, is a powerful man of whom she must beware. The Captain several times offers to take Anna back with him, but his chauvinistic concerns and patronizing attitude do not faze Anna.

Lady Thiang

Lady Thiang is the King's ''number one wife.'' She is the mother of Prince Chulalongkorn, the heir to the throne, and the most dignified, poised, well-educated, and wise of his many wives. She forms a fast friendship with Anna. Lady Thiang is a ready pupil for Anna's teaching, but she, like the King, has many traditional ways and views that clash with Anna's modern ideas. By the end of the play, she teaches the worldly schoolteacher about her way of loving—to accept the faults of her husband and to love him because of the moments when he is ''wonderful''—and because he needs her.

Tuptim

Tuptim is the beautiful gift that the king of Burma has delivered to the King of Siam, who makes her his newest wife. She is mocked by the other wives, who cannot understand how she could possibly be unhappy in the king's luscious palace. Tuptim, however, loves Lun Tha. She tries not to fall in love with him, knowing she is fated to be given away, but she cannot help herself. She befriends Anna and receives comfort from her, as well as English books to read. One of these is Harriet Beecher Stowe's *Uncle Tom's Cabin.* The story of the runaway slave appeals to Tuptim, and she writes an adaptation of the story for presentation after dinner to the King's important British dinner guests.

The guests love her saucy blend of American ideology with Asian culture and style, but the King perceives the note of rebellion in the death of the wicked King Simon Legree. Under cover of the evening's festivities, Tuptim runs away with Lun Tha, but she is quickly caught and brought to the king. Only the intervention of her friend Anna prevents her from being cruelly beaten for her insubordination. The news of Lun Tha's death crushes her.

THEMES

Custom and Tradition

The King of Siam announces from the very beginning of *The King and I* that he wants to lead Siam into the modern world. He says ''Siam is to be modern, scientific country.'' However, when it comes to renouncing traditional attitudes in order to replace them with modern thinking, the King himself is the last to change. He maintains a chauvinistic posture toward women and his subjects, snapping his fingers to call them to attention or to do his bidding. He might admire Abraham Lincoln and express agreement with abolishing slavery, but he is blind to the slavery in his own palace. Anna chides the King for treating Tuptim like a possession, just ''a bowl of rice.'' Then she realizes that he treats her, an English schoolteacher, in the same way, presumptuously demanding that she ''take a letter'' for him and ordering her about as though she were one of his wives or slaves. Anna tolerates his behavior because she understands that habits are difficult to change, even when one wants to embrace new ideas. She also understands that her modern attitude about women threatens his sense of manhood. The King respects Anna and recognizes the value of her opinions, but he refuses to ask for them, for to do so would raise a woman to equal status with him. When considering how to resist England's making a protectorate of Siam, he cannot bring himself to ask Anna for advice. Instead he pretends to have her play a guessing game so that he can adopt her guess as his plan. To combat the sense that Anna is indeed gaining in status with him, he demands that she follow the custom never to let her head be higher than his. He tests her by dropping nearly prostrate on the floor, and when she hesitates he reminds her that ''a promise is a promise.'' The custom and traditions of old Siam are so deeply

TOPICS FOR FURTHER STUDY

- Is Anna a feminist? What are the principles of feminism that she upholds, and how does she demonstrate her interest in the rights of women? Where and how does she depart from your idea of feminism?

- How is "orientalism" portrayed in *The King and I?* What role do you think "orientalism" played in the British Commonwealth's interest in Siam in the nineteenth century? What role does this play indicate that it had?

- What effect on the meaning of the story would occur in adapting *The King and I* to a dramatic play with no music or songs?

- How would the story of *The King and I* be different if Anna were happily married when she took the assignment to act as governess to the King's children? Is this play a love story?

embedded in the ambitious King that his death is a necessity to allow his more flexible young son to carry Siam the next step forward.

Culture Clash

The Ship Captain warns Anna of the unnamed dangers that threaten an Englishwoman alone in Bangkok. He expects harm to come of this confrontation between Western and Eastern cultures. Of course, the King himself has arranged for it by bringing Anna to his palace to teach his children about the world outside of Siam. What he does not realize is how difficult it will be for him to adapt to Western culture and how much he will have to sacrifice to do so. The play overtly assumes that in this encounter Siam stands to gain in modernity, while England generously and paternalistically contributes values to be adopted. Underlying the culture encounter is an issue of economics. Lady Thiang tells Anna that because of a rumor saying that the King is a barbarian, Queen Victoria may make Siam into a protectorate. The King understands that he would lose his kingdom under a British protectorateship. His goal conflicts with the goal of the British Queen. Queen Victoria wants to develop trade routes and to establish a foothold in Siam. The King wants to take advantage of British interest in his country to develop Siam into a modern country with a place in world trade but to do so as a sovereign nation that keeps its profits in his

coffers, not in England's. These larger issues at stake beneath the culture clash compromise the relationship between Britain and Siam so that they cannot confront each other as equals. Anna acts intellectually and morally superior to the King, proffering advice on how to impress the British government and congratulating him for reading the Bible. She barely tolerates being in the Buddhist temple, as though it was a profane place and not a religious sanctum. The British see the Siamese as culturally inferior but also enticing—a possession to be captured and controlled. This enticement is almost sensual, especially in scenes such as when the wives throw their skirts over their heads to run away from the British Ambassador because he "looks like a goat" and when Anna dances with the King with his hand on her waist. Hammerstein's play seems to suggest that if only Siam would submit to the teachings of modern British people like Anna, it would be taken seriously among the world powers. It could always save its cultural heritage in the form of entertainment such as Tuptim's orientalized version of Western ideology.

Knowledge and Ignorance

With very few exceptions the characters in *The King and I* can be ranked in prestige according to their relative knowledge and ignorance— of Western culture. For instance, Tuptim ranks very high because she speaks and reads English;

hers is a courageous spirit. She even writes her own play, although she bases it on an American (Western culture) novel. The wives who do not take their learning as seriously as Tuptim behave in a silly, ''womanly'' manner and ignorantly make fun of Tuptim for her unhappiness. They irresponsibly paw through Anna's clothing and assume that her body is shaped like her hoop-skirted dresses, while Tuptim politely asks for English books. The Kralahome ranks low because he resists Anna's teaching, even reveals his ignorance by suggesting that the young Prince should not waste his time learning about Western culture because it will make him a less effective leader. The King ranks high because he reads the great books of Western culture, such as the Bible. Anna stands on the pinnacle of knowledge because she dispenses knowledge to others and seldom appears ignorant or in need of teaching herself. Lady Thiang ranks fairly high because she has the most education of all the wives, and she is entrusted by Anna to teach a lesson now and then. Even more importantly, Lady Thiang actually teaches something to Anna. When Lady Thiang comes to convince Anna to help the King strategize how to avoid the protectorateship of Siam, she sings a song about her tolerant love for the imperfect but admirable king. Although Thiang does not impart factual knowledge to Anna, she does impart her special kind of wisdom about love.

STYLE

Musical

Together Richard Rodgers and Oscar Hammerstein produced eleven musicals. *The King and I* was one of their most popular. A musical is a drama with singing, music, and spoken dialogue. The songs express the sentiments of one or more characters and may be addressed directly to other characters in the play. For example, Anna sings ''Whistle a Happy Tune'' in direct address to her son Louis, and Lady Thiang sings ''Something Wonderful'' to Anna. Sometimes the song is simply an expression of a character's state of mind, as when the King sings ''A Puzzlement.''

In the case of some musicals, existing songs are worked into a storyline. The lyrics (by Hammerstein) and music (by Rodgers) for *The King and I* were written specifically for the play, so the songs corre-spond seamlessly with the narrative. The songs enhance the richness of the action, they are part of the dialogue that moves the plot along, although the songs, dance, and music of *The King and I* could be removed without disrupting the plot line altogether. A musical differs from an opera in this respect, for an opera contains little or no dialogue and limited action, thus the songs must carry the weight of advancing the plot. Musicals such as *Jesus Christ Superstar* and The Who's *Tommy,* works with little or no spoken dialogue, are called ''rock operas,'' not musicals. The musical enjoyed its heydey between 1920 and 1950, when producers and writing teams such as Rodgers and Hammerstein created dozens of musicals to showcase the talents of such dancing and singing stars as Judy Garland, Fred Astaire, Gene Kelly, and Ginger Rogers. Rodgers and Hammerstein's musicals, beginning with their first work together, *Oklahoma,* undertake a more serious topic than the musical comedies of the 1920s and 1930s, and their songs and music are more integrated with the plot. Musicals ''came of age'' with the work of Rodgers and Hammerstein. The successful 1996 revival of *The King and I,* starring Lou Diamond Phillips as the King, demonstrates that the musical still continues to enjoy great popularity.

Play within a Play

The slave girl Tuptim creates a Siamese version of a book she admires, *Uncle Tom's Cabin* by Harriet Beecher Stowe. This book would have been making a stir in America in 1862 (the year portrayed in *The King and I*) because it championed the cause of the abolition of slavery, an issue over which American president Abraham Lincoln was waging war with the American South (the Civil War) at the time of Anna's visit to Siam. The King admires the self-taught Lincoln and his principles of freedom, so it is ironic that Tuptim's play should offend him. It does, because the King has not recognized the suffering his own brand of slavery inflicts on his wives and subjects. Tuptim intends to shock the King. Hers is a rebellious spirit, and she not only wants to escape, she wants to confront the King's hypocrisy as well. Hammerstein has Tuptim use the same technique as Shakespeare does his title character in *Hamlet,* although her purpose differs. Hamlet uses his play to ''catch the conscience of the king'' in order to entrap Claudius and justify murdering him. Tuptim's motives are less clear. She may not have had any particular plan of reprisal in mind nor realized the power of her creation until she saw the King's face. When Tuptim sees that her play has affected the King, she begins urgently to plead the cause of unhappy slaves everywhere, but the King's quick temper immediately cuts her off. The effect of the play within a play in *The King and I* underscores the theme of culture clash and the irony of a leader who wants to modernize his country but cannot bear to modernize himself.

HISTORICAL CONTEXT

British Imperialism

In the nineteenth century, the British held the point of view that trade was "the true herald of civilization" and that Great Britain's expertise in commerce gave it the right to its leadership role in international trade (Great Britain controlled forty percent of the world's manufactured trade in 1860). The Great Exhibition of 1851 in London showcased the world's fascination for technology and trade in a gigantic structure of glass and iron called the Crystal Palace. It housed exotic booty harvested from Britain's colonies and overseas trade—inventions, consumer products, and the contributions of many other countries, all crammed on over eight miles of display shelves. Queen Victoria visited the stunning Crystal Palace nearly every day, joined by throngs of pride-filled British subjects, to view the exhibits and to reinforce a sense of manifest superiority in technology and trade.

The Great Exhibition helped to allay any disquiet over the aggressive expansion of the British Empire. And there were reasons for disquiet. Just prior to Anna Leonowen's visit to Siam, the two "Opium Wars" (1839-1842 and 1856-1860) were fought in China to secure Britain the dubious right to export opium from India (a colony of the British Empire) into China and to establish British-governed trade posts in China's most active ports. The "treaty-port system" became Great Britain's mode of dominating Chinese trade for the next forty years; it was also used in many other countries not officially colonized into the Empire. In 1855, Siam ceded to diplomatic pressure to sign the Bowring Treaty, which added Siam to Great Britain's extensive "informal empire," by granting Great Britain certain trade advantages as well as the rights to establish a consulate in Bangkok and to try its people in British and not Siamese courts. This agreement granted economic power over Siam and also provided Britain a buffer zone between its South Asian holdings (Malaya and Burma) and the holdings of the French (Indochina), thus making it easier for competing colonizers to cohabitate South Asia. Siam, unlike India, New Zealand, and Burma, retained its sovereign status; however, as Margaret Marshall wrote in the *Nation*, "the divide between empire and influence was often indistinct," and British predominance in education, religion, the economy, and politics took the form of a cultural authority that would change Siam irrevocably.

Orientalism

Besides the obvious naval and trade superiority of nineteenth century Great Britain, cultural stereotyping of non-European peoples contributed to the building of the British Empire upon the backs of Asian, African, and Arab nations. The *Nation*'s Marshall wrote that "there can be little doubt that, as British acquaintance with the non-European world grew in the nineteenth century, so did a readiness to be highly critical and even totally dismissive of alien cultures as well as a view that Britain had a mission or national duty to spread the benefits of its civilization, economy, and religion as widely as possible overseas." Since the eighteenth century, the term "Orientalism" had referred to a negative perception of Asia, which Edward Said summarized in *Orientalism* as "its eccentricity, its backwardness, its silent indifference, its feminine penetrability, its supine malleability."

This culturally annihilative description in turn justified the Western colonizing agenda, because it made the Orient into "a locale requiring Western attention, reconstruction, even redemption." With the justification of this cultural bias in hand, colonizing "oriental" nations became a gift of civilization granted by British colonizers. It also blinded British subjects to the true nature of Britain's interest in the Orient—to establish advantageous trade relationships, obtain inexpensive products and labor, and to hold the Asians in thrall. A more fundamental reason for Orientalism also existed. Often humans make use of foreign "others" as repositories of projected "bad" traits so that the subject's identity remains "clean." Literary critic Said asserted that "European culture gained in strength and identity by setting itself off against the Orient as a sort of surrogate and even underground self." Orientalism, then, is a construction of the other that is used to bolster the identity of the

COMPARE
&
CONTRAST

- **Nineteenth-century:** In Anna Leonowens's day, women were expected to show respect for men by not challenging their authority. They were to be demure and beautiful, not strong and self-willed. Few career opportunities existed for women who had no husbands to provide for them.

  1950s: World War II necessitated women joining the work force to replace the men who were fighting overseas. By the 1950s, women had a secure place in the work force, although their career options were usually limited to clerical functions.

  Today: Women can choose from almost unlimited career possibilities and are no longer expected to appear subservient to men.

- **Nineteenth-century:** Europeans looked down on "Orientals" as backward, morally inferior people who could only benefit from an encounter with Western culture, an encounter that would place the Asian countries in a socially and economically dependent position.

  1950s: World War II interrupted the establishment of trade practices between Asian and European/American countries. The American internment of Japanese-American citizens during the war years proved that the specter of Orientalism still persisted.

  Today: Trade with Asian countries is more equitable and fair; however, vestiges of racism against Asians persists in many places and is still slow to disappear.

---

speaker—the real identity of the subject, the Siamese in the case of Rodgers and Hammerstein's play—becomes lost in translation.

American Musicals

The King and I produced in 1951 by Richard Rodgers (music) and Oscar Hammerstein (book, libretto, and lyrics) was part of a new tradition of musical drama. Up until 1927 when Jerome Kern and Hammerstein's *Show Boat* broke the mold of the musical comedy by blending music, lyrics, dance, and libretto, staged musical productions typically consisted of a series of unrelated songs, dances, and comic routines loosely clustered around a simple, even inane, boy-meets-girl plot. With *Show Boat,* the musical came of age. Now songs were integrated into the plot and advanced the action in the same manner that operatic arias did. It took a few years for audiences to appreciate the transformation, but by 1951, the form had sophisticated to the point that most critics were on the lookout for songs that *didn't* have a place in the narrative, although a few still longed nostalgically for the more comedic elements of musical comedies typi-

cal of the Ziegfeld Follies days. Rodgers and Hammerstein together would create eleven memorable "musicals" to join the ranks of the dozens of artistic and commercial successes produced by George Gershwin, Cole Porter, Stephen Sondheim, Kurt Weill, and others, as well as the twenty-four musicals Rodgers had created in his partnership with Larry Hart.

CRITICAL OVERVIEW

Expectations were high for the latest production by the team of Richard Rodgers and Oscar Hammerstein when *The King and I* opened at the St. James Theater in New York City in 1951. It earned mostly favorable reviews, with only a few being less than enthusiastic. The lavish sets by Jo Mielziner and costumes by Irene Sharaff created a glamorous backdrop; As David Ewen quoted an admirer in *New Complete Book of American Musical Theater,* the work represented "a flowering of all the arts of the theater with moments that are pure genius."

However, some critics found fault with the boyscout-ish seriousness of the play, especially its melodramatic ending. The *New Yorker* reviewer John Lardner liked the exotic touches, but found the play ''a little too unremittingly wholesome'' and the lyrics too ''corny.'' Lardner disliked the ''touch of Walt Disney in all the recent Rodgers and Hammerstein shows.'' *Nation* reviewer Margaret Marshall lamented that the play took all of actress Gertrude Lawrence's showmanship to prevent the play's drawn-out plot from ''sagging too often'' but added that ''even Miss Lawrence [could] do little with the last scene.'' A reviewer for *Time* found the ''battle of sexes, collision of races and conflict of ideas sometimes touching, and far less insipid than the usual musicomedy romance.''

Other reviewers struggled to find words to describe this new musical form that departed from musical comedy in its seriousness of plot and theme. A critic writing in *Harper's* noted that *The King and I* was not billed as a musical comedy but as a ''musical play,'' and suggested that ''it might better have been billed as 'a sentimental fantasy with music and a message thrown in.''' Later in the article, the reviewer's distaste gathers steam: ''Mr. Hammerstein has got his mediums mixed up. He wants to perform the function of the serious problem-drama (that is, to provide searching insight into the psycho-philosophical stresses of individuals and of society) with the light, but not too light touch. The theater provides two established methods for such delving: the serious drama and high comedy.'' Rodger's and Hammerstein had introduced this a form of musical back in 1927 with the groundbreaking *Show Boat,* which, like *The King and I* has a more fully developed plot and songs that advance the story along. *The King and I* also tackled a more serious topic, and reviewers had not yet developed a critical vocabulary for evaluating this new form of ''musical'' (as opposed to the ''musical comedy'') on its own terms. Nevertheless, the 1951 stage production with Gertrude Lawrence and Yul Brynner received Antoinette Perry (also called Tony) Awards for best musical of the year, and the play was the first musical to win the Theater Club Award.

By the time of the release of Twentieth Century-Fox's film of adaptation of *The King and I*—with Brynner reprising his stage role and starring Deborah Kerr as Anna (her singing was dubbed by Marni Nixon), critics had accepted Rodgers and Hammerstein's new form, but some still rankled at the melodrama of the King's death at the end. A

Time reviewer found that the film ''moves along satisfactorily from spectacle to spectacle until the conclusion, when it's message (democracy is good; slavery is bad) gets a truly pedestrian delivery at Yul Brynner's deathbed.'' On the other hand, a critic for *Commonweal* called the film a ''magnificent production'' and actually praised the finale, calling it ''joyful and tearful.'' Former musical conductor turned critic Lehman Engel writing in 1967 also found the end fitting; he pointed out in his book *The American Musical Theater,* that in comparison to the original story by Leonowens and its adaptation by Margaret Landon in which the King does not die, Hammerstein's decision to have the King die is ''a far more effective (and conclusive!) piece of dramaturgy.'' The film received nine Academy Award nominations and won five, including one for Yul Brynner's performance and one for the musical score. It also won two Golden Globe Awards for best film and best actress in a musical/comedy (for Deborah Kerr).

A spate of six new or revived musicals competed for New York theatregoers' attentions in 1996, among them a revival of *The King and I* starring Lou Diamond Phillips (best known for his portrayal of Ritchie Valens in the film *La Bamba*) as the King and Donna Murphy as Anna with direction by Christopher Renshaw. In spite of trepidation over whether anyone could erase the memory of Yul Brynner in the role that seemed custom designed for him, the revival enjoyed ecstatic reviews on its debut. As a *Newsday* reviewer noted, Lou Diamond Phillips ''was the wild card when he dared to step into Yul Brynner's footsteps,'' and while a *People* reporter found that he fails to bring Brynner's ''heft or authority to the role,'' a critic writing in *Time* agreed with the majority of critics who commended Phillips because he ''eventually shrugs off the shroud of Yul Byrnner'' to create a his own memorable version of the Siamese king. New York audiences, hoping for an evening of nostalgia, got even more than they could imagine from the $5.5 million-dollar production. The staging was so successful that it catapulted the musical into a new realm of legitimacy; *New York* magazine critic John Simon found himself comparing it to opera: ''I never thought I would say this about a musical, but in a production such as this, *The King and I* is the equal of all but the supreme operatic masterpieces.'' Perhaps the musical has, indeed, come of age—*Time* concluded that ''Rodgers and Hammerstein songs are secular hymns—liturgical music for the American mid-century.''

CRITICISM

Carole L. Hamilton

Hamilton is an instructor at Cary Academy. Her essay examines the themes of subservience prevalent in the play.

Over the years, many reviewers of Rodgers and Hammerstein's musical *The King and I* have complained about the ending of the musical, in which the king dies. Critics have called his deathbed scene too solemn and melodramatic—simply not in keeping with the musical comedy tone of the rest of the play. What these reviewers fail to recognize is that *The King and I* is not simply a "love" story between people of different cultures; the story is actually an analogy for a political relationship between their two countries. It is this political analogy underlying the relationship between Anna and the Oriental King that gives weight to the death scene (which Hammerstein added to the narrative when he adapted the story from Margaret Landon's *Anna and the King of Siam*). The deathbed scene resolves both of the central conflicts in the play—both the one between Anna and the King and the larger national conflict. The King's death resolves the first issue by removing the potential of an interracial union; it resolves the second by removing the King's backward politics from Siam's foreign policy, allowing his more modern—and anglicized—son to rule the country with better diplomacy.

The conflict between Anna and the King resides in the hierarchy of their relationship—who will rule, who will decide, and whose influence will predominate the lives of the King's children, and his subjects. The conflict between Great Britain and Siam is essentially the same. The presence of the British Ambassador in the plot attests to the economic and political context within which the schoolteacher and the King both operate. The British Ambassador may report the rumor that the King is a barbarian, precipitating the Queen's decision to make Siam a protectorate. Thus the political analogy of the variation of boy-meets-girl plot in *The King and I* is the ascension of unofficial British domination over Siam (later known as Thailand), a domination that will transform the economic, political, and ideological Siamese culture. By the same token, Anna's presence will transform the King's children, and ultimately his kingdom, in a similar manner. Great Britain's relationship with Siam was not destined to be an official political colonization such as the kind achieved in Malaysia, Burma,

Africa, and Hong Kong; in Siam Great Britain pursued more of an unofficial alliance. Just as the courting between Anna and the King results in a kind of marriage (one that affords Anna some of the privileges of being a King's wife), Britain's courting of Siam ended not with an official colonization but with an agreement that gave Great Britain trade advantages with Siam.

The British actively sought trade advantages in Oriental nations, but this self-serving aspect of their interest was conveniently subsumed under the more commendable label of colonial development. It was in the interest of cultural development that Anna embarked on her program to educate and Westernize the royal children. To the British, the Siamese—as well as Africans, Indians, and Arabs—desperately needed exposure to Western religion, economic practices, and culture; and it just so happened that the British economy could use Siamese goods and services as well. Great Britain undertook the monumental task of civilizing "Oriental" nations and, in the process, wove their economies into these countries.

To accomplish this act of cultural dominance required an attitude of superiority over Oriental peoples-in much the same manner that men were once thought to be superior to women. Social Darwinism was invoked to explain why the Asians (another non-whites) had not advanced as far as Western nations, and the word "oriental" came to be associated with backwardness and moral corruption, thus justifying the British program of anglicizing Oriental people. The "Orientalism" of Asian countries consisted of the imposition of a negative stereotype (immoral, inferior, and backward) that filtered actual observations. It is a form of racism that persisted for many centuries and still has residual effect on modern Western/Asian relations. In her book *The English Governess at the Siamese Court: Being Recollections of Six Years in the Royal Palace at Bangkok,* the original Anna Leonowens tells of falling prey to cultural bias toward Orientals. She describes the Siamese people as "apt to be indolent, improvident, greedy, intemperate, servile, cruel, vain, inquisitive, superstitious, and cowardly." Her terms coincide with the accepted sentiment that Orientals were morally inferior, child-like people whose culture would not progress without the intervention of their Western neighbors. As Edward Said commented on this relationship in *Orientalism:* "Orientals were rarely seen or looked at; they were seen though, analyzed not as citizens, or even people, but as problems to be solved or

WHAT DO I READ NEXT?

- The real Anna Leonowens wrote two books about her adventures in Siam teaching the children of King Mongkut. Her books, *The English Governess at the Siamese Court* (1870) and *The Romance of the Harem* (1873), were renounced by Mongkut's biographer, who claimed that her accounts grossly misrepresented the Siamese king as a tyrant and that her description of the court was inaccurate.

- Margaret Landon wrote a popular novel based on Leonowens's books, called *Anna and the King of Siam* (1944). It was also the basis for a 1946 film, starring Rex Harrison and Irene Dunne, before Hammerstein adapted it to the stage play.

- Maxine Hong Kingston's novels *China Men* and *The Woman Warrior: Memoirs of a Girl among Ghosts* discuss the situation of contemporary Chinese Americans in California.

- *Farewell to Manzanar* by Jeanne Wakatsuki Houston portrays the experience of Japanese-American citizens in internment during World War II.

---

confined or . . . taken over." Sometimes the takeover was overt, as it was in India in the eighteenth century, when Great Britain replaced the fragmenting political structures in Bengal and elsewhere with its own governors. But in Siam, as well as in some other Asian countries, the defeat of the sovereign body was accomplished from within—through education.

The King of Siam himself (the real King Mongkut as well as the Hammerstein character) played into the British imperialist hand and conveniently asked for Ms. Leonowens's teaching services. The King had already been brainwashed to value Western culture over his own. He viewed his world as substandard, in need of an infusion of Western culture that could be introduced through the education of his children. Unfortunately, he himself was unable to make the leap to the "scientific" and "modern" Western stereotype. He sings a song in which he expresses his doubts and insecurities; he finds leading his people "A Puzzlement," and the implication is that Anna can help him to sort out his confusion. Lady Thiang corroborates this view of the King, singing about his limitations and his many dreams that will never unfold, adding the faint praise that "at least he tries." His inability to suit the values of the new society he himself wants to impose upon his kingdom necessitates his death, to

make room for young Prince Chulalongkorn to complete the transformation of Siam from a "backward" country to a modern one.

In the analogy between the human relationship and the political one, the courtship and ritual marriage (in which the King gives Anna a ring and demands that she place it on her finger) corresponds to the courtship and unofficial alliance between Great Britain and Siam. The King invites Anna to his palace, hoping to benefit from her teaching while controlling her as a "servant." On a political level, he invites Great Britain to create an economical presence in Bangkok, while hoping to prevent the British from taking over the country. But the King cedes more than he plans to in both arenas. He refuses at first to give Anna the house she bargained for, but eventually he gives in and offers to build her one that adjoins the palace. Granting her the right to own property and build a proper English home is equivalent to offering her the right to colonize, and she jumps at the chance. On the political level, the King's first reaction to the threat of being made a protectorate is to send the British Ambassador packing, but Anna convinces him to put on a show of Westernization instead. Just as the show of "whistling a happy tune" ends up restoring confidence to Anna and her son, preparing for a display of Western culture has the ultimate effect of actually West-

Yul Brynner in a 1985 revival of The King and I

ernizing the King's palace. In the process of sewing European dresses and learning to use European eating implements, the King's court is transformed into a quasi-European court, displaying many of the earmarks of British civilization. This is precisely where Great Britain wants Siam—eager to adopt to Western customs.

Giving Anna a home and adopting Western customs for an evening represents the King's hand in the colonizing of his culture. The Kralahome sees the imminence of assimilation more clearly than does the King, and he fears it. On two occasions he warns Anna not to "ruin" the King or the Prince with her Western ideas, but he soon he realizes his own impotence in resisting her. The Kralahome represents a throwback to old Siamese culture. His role in the new Siam is left undefined at the play's end. He has tried to arrest the inevitable union between the King and Anna and between Great Britain and Siam, but he has failed.

There are several moments in the play that reinforce the symbolism of a ritual marriage between the King and Anna. Her elaborate preparations for the entertainment of the British Ambassador place her in the role of "first lady" of the house—ordering the King's wives about, deciding on decor, going into dinner on his arm, and engineering the conversation to display his scholarship. These are the tasks of the wife, and she reaps her rewards after the guests have departed in an intimate dance with the King and in the gift of a ring. To further underscore her status, Lady Thiang on two occasions begs Anna to go to the King, at one point telling her that she herself cannot meet the King's "special needs," that only Anna can. Lady Thiang, the King's number one wife, also releases her son to Anna's teaching, recognizing that Anna can provide the young man with instruction that she cannot.

The King's death scene is unusual in that the focus rests not on the dying King but on Anna's decision to stay in Siam. The children certainly show more interest in that outcome than in the death of their imperious father. Anna stands at center stage during most of this scene, with the King dying on a divan on one side and Prince Chulalongkorn addressing the wives and other children on the other. Besides Anna's decision, the other business to be accomplished here is the transfer of power from the King to the prince. This is duly accomplished and then the final conflict of the play is happily resolved—the Prince's second proclamation proves that Anna's teachings have taken hold, for he proclaims that no longer will his subjects have to bow in the lowly position of a toad but will stand erect and look him in the eye with confidence. He will be a King who values his subjects as people. The Prince has shown his mettle in Anna's classroom—challenging her authority at times but also displaying an appreciation for pragmatism and the demands that the modern world will make of him. At the time of his ascension to the throne, he is still a child—still in need of a governess, and still malleable. Anna's decision to stay assures that the young prince will complete his Westernization and, more importantly, not forsake his humanity in a quest for power. In addition to fulfilling this political task, Anna's continued presence will also serve the personal relationship she had with the King; she will continue to be a loving, guiding force in the children's lives.

Source: Carole L. Hamilton, in an essay for *Drama for Students,* Gale 1997.

Steven Erlanger

In the following article, Erlanger examines the differences between the original Broadway production of The King and I *and the 1996 revival of the play, illustrating how the later production places more emphasis upon historical and cultural accura-*

cy. Erlanger provides historical background for the play.

The new $5.5 Million Broadway revival of *The King and I,* the 1951 Rodgers and Hammerstein musical that Yul Brynner built a carrer on, lavishes enormous attention and money on constructing a sumptuous and remarkably authentic stage version of Thailand in the last century.

But the concentration on esthetic authenticity begs the question of whether the show, which opens on Thursday at the Neil Simon Theater and stars Donna Murphy and Lou Diamond Phillips, reflects a historical authenticity. The team of Australian designers involved has labored mightily to create the look of a Thailand that never existed.

The King and I, after all, is a romantic entertainment, much better known for its songs (''Shall We Dance'' ''I Whistle a Happy Tune,'' ''Getting to Know You'') than for its story. The musical, which starred Gertrude Lawrence and Yul Brynner, opened soon after World War II. Three years later, the French defeat at Dien Bien Phu would begin to pull the United States into what became the Vietnam quagmire. But at that time, Thailand was about as far from America, and about as exotic, as Oscar Hammerstein or anyone else could have imagined.

The original show (and the popular 1956 film version with Brynner and Deborah Kerr) employs a form of pan-Asianness that derives from a variety of sources: a generic restaurant in a shopping mall, say, with a bit of Japanese kabuki thrown in, along with white face to hide Western facial features and a peculiar, even eccentric vision of Buddhism.

The current version, based largely on a 1991 Australian production starring the English actress Hayley Mills, was first licensed by the Rodgers and Hammerstein Organization and then embraced by it. This *King and I* seems to struggle hard to present a Thailand that a more sophisticated audience today would accept as truthful.

Indeed, the sets aim for the spectacular, with 2,000 square feet of gold leaf, majestic thrones and shimmering headdresses. The stage curtain—six panels depicting traditional costumed dancers—is flanked by the profiles of 30-foot elephants with gilt-edged trunks and jeweled eyes. Incense wafts from altars built over the box seats on either side of the stage, and before the curtain goes up, the audience can watch saffron-robed monks at prayer.

THE KING AND I IS AN OUTPOURING OF AMERICAN INNOCENCE, LIKE SO MUCH OF RODGERS AND HAMMERSTEIN, SUGGESTING THAT A PURE AMERICAN LIBERALISM WILL LEAD, IF NOT ALWAYS TO HAPPY ENDINGS, THEN TO A BETTER CIVILIZATION THAN THE BARBARITY OF THE PAST''

Brian Thomson, the set designer, has used the color deep burgundy to frame authentic Thai murals and designs taken from the Grand Palace in Bangkok, from old photographs and paintings, and even from a richly lacquered, elephant-legged coffee table that he bought in northern Thailand.

The costume designer, Roger Kirk, also an Australian, has used Thai materials and clothing making sure that some of Anna's hoop-skirted dresses are of Thai silk and that the royal dancers (in numbers originally choreographed by Jerome Robbins, with added choreography by Lar Lubovitch) wear Thai sarongs and use Thai masks. Some of the ''gold-bullion'' embroidery and beadwork was done in India to keep down costs.

''For Australians, Thailand is next door,'' Mr. Kirk said ''So a cheap sarong won't wash.'' The glittering outfits that Mr. Phillips wears as the King are based on old photographs of the real monarch, as is the actor's haircut.

The striving for authenticity has also meant putting Asian faces in Asian roles. And even the accent of the actors as they speak English is as Thai-like as possible, with help from a dialect coach and a Thai waiter at a Bridgeport, Conn., restaurant named, implausibly. *The King and I.* The waiter was found after an appeal on the Internet, said the show's director, Christopher Renshaw:

Dodger Productions, one of the producers, and Wendy's International, the hamburger chain, in its first association with Broadway production, are helping to market the musical as family entertainment. But Mr. Renshaw and his Australian team are more subversive than that.

They are modernizing this musical, and not only through the lavishness of the sets, the vast computerized lighting system designed by the other Australian on the team; Nigel Levings, and the sheer busyness of 54 actors: they are seeking to stress the deeper, even darker themes of colonialism, slavery, feminism and cultural ambiguity that they believe are buried in the text.

"To do it just as an entertainment, that's been done before," declared Mr. Renshaw, an Englishman who said that he reveres Thailand. Living there for a time, he added, made him question some of his Western assumptions about what it is to be civilized, and ultimately it changed him profoundly.

"If you're doing a piece that is 40 years old," he said, "you have to come in with a viewpoint. If you take all this new understanding on board, it shifts emphasis and changes the show, so it's worth doing."

The show itself, however, is viewed with displeasure—even banned, in fact—in the relatively easygoing, unpuritanical Thailand, largely because it treats one of the country's most enlightened monarchs, king Mongkut, as a vaguely silly barbarian who is introduced to "civilization" (and the polka) by a Western governess. For many Thais, *The King and I* diminishes both the terror of a truly omnipotent monarchy and the importance of the complex culture that produced it.

The musical tells the story of Anna Leonowens, a supposedly Welsh-born woman who was said to have served as a governess to the children of the King of Siam, as Thailand was known, in the 1860's.

The show's script, however, is based on a 1943 best-selling novel, *Anna and the King of Siam,* by Margaret Landon, which itself was loosely based on Anna Leonowens's two books. *The English Governess at the Siamese Court,* (1870) and *The Romance of the Harem* (1873). Both are full of historical errors, beginning with the title of governess, since the King's diaries make clear that Anna was hired only as a teacher of English.

William Warren, a longtime American scholar of Thailand, said Anna's worst errors were in the second book, when her need to publish began to outrun her experiences. She asserts that the King threw wives who displeased him into dungeons and that he ordered the public torture and burning of a

consort and the monk with whom she had fallen in love, an incident that Anna claims to have witnessed and which serves as the model for the Tuptim episode in the musical.

But Bangkok's Watery soil could support no dungeons or even basements, nor, Mr. Warren notes, is there mention of a public burning in domestic or foreign accounts of the time. As one of the king's biographers, Alexander Griswold wrote about Anna, "Virtue was not unknown in Siam before her arrival, and a cool assessment suggests that she did not loom very large in the life of King Mongkut or his children."

Anna's version of her own life was just that: a version. She was not born in Wales and brought up in a middle-class English family; she was born Ann Edwards and brought up in India. Her father was not a high-ranking British officer but a soldier who died before her birth. She grew up in an army barracks, where blankets served as walls to separate families and her mother found another man. Anna's own husband, Thomas Leon Owens, was a clerk in the army pay office at Poona. When he died, she was left with two children to support. She altered her name to the more exotic Leonowens and taught in the British community of Singapore before hearing of — and landing — a job as teacher to the many children (and many wives) of King Mongkut.

The musical, then, is a confection built on a novel built on a fabrication. It is an outpouring of American innocence, like so much of Rodgers and Hammerstein, suggesting that a pure American liberalism will lead, if not always to happy endings, then to a better civilization than the barbarity of the past.

American influence on Southeast Asia was apparent soon enough, and to their credit, Rodgers and Hammerstein, for all the conventional fantasies of *The King and I,* toy with some of the paradoxes. Even Anna starts to understand that her effect is helping to destroy the king she loves, let alone Tuptim, the Burmese slave she teaches. And as she tries to bring Western "enlightenment" to Siam, while protecting it from British colonialism, she begins to sense the strain and damage she has caused.

"We blunder into cultures other than our own and we do such terrible damage," Mr. Renshaw said of Anna. But did she ever feel that way? "I don't think she ever felt it," he said slowly. "But it's in the text; there's more in it than they wrote." Similarly, he said, King Mongkut seems to understand in the script that he must modernize Siam if it is to survive and escape colonialism, ''but he knows that change will be tainted and destroy him.''

The oddest part of the musical is the bizarre ballet ''The Small House of Uncle Thomas,'' enacted for the King and his British guests. It is the story of *Uncle Tom's Cabin,* narrated by the slave Tuptim, which Anna suggests to show the British how civilized Siam really is. Under Anna's influence and teaching, Tuptim turns it into a parable about her own subjugation and that of the King's other women.

In America, at roughly the same historical moment, there was a civil war about slavery of a far harsher kind than the servitude then practiced in Thailand. Rodgers and Hammerstein seem, at least, to be warning their audiences not to be too smug in their attitudes toward this ''barbarian'' king.

Theodore S. Chapin, president of the Rodgers and Hammerstein Organization, which licenses 2,500 R&H productions annually, said, ''In any given year, every producer in Australia asks us about *The King and I.*'' But Richard Rodger's daughter, Mary Rodgers Guettel, was especially taken with this Australian production and its sets and thought it would do well on Broadway.

Five years later, with more money and two actors who are under contract for a year, Mr. Renshaw and his team believe they can pull off their real vision of the play.

''We've given them lots of leeway,'' Mr. Chapin said, from using lines about Abraham Lincoln in early rehearsal scripts to lots of ''soundscape''— music, much of it Thai — to carry the action and make the show more like a film. ''You can add music,'' Mr. Chapin recalled telling Mr. Renshaw, ''but remember, there's a polka in this score.''

He paused, and added with a hint of irony: ''I don't think they've pulled it too far toward authenticity to keep it from being an American musical.''

Before King Mongkut becomes too romanticized through revisionism, however, it should be noted that he did speak a remarkably embellished and florid English and had added to the Grand Palace a clock tower modeled after Big Ben in London. According to Mr. Warren, the King also provided his favorite artists with scenic photographs sent to him by President Franklin Pierce. The result was some startling glimpses of Mount Vernon

and Monticello in traditional murals on the walls of one temple, Wat Bovorn-nives.

And it was King Chulalongkorn, Mongkut's son (whom Anna most influences in the show), who traveled widely and built the Throne Hall, a strange Italianate structure that still stands in the Grand Palace complex, with its Thai-style roofs instead of the planned domes.

''I would hope,'' said Mr. Thompson, the set designer, ''that in this production the story comes across that it isn't the Thais who are the strangers but Anna herself; that Anna, being a woman of that period needing to wear those garments and needing to have those beliefs, is the real stranger in that court.''

Source: Steven Erlanger, ''A Confection Built on a Novel Built on a Fabrication,'' in the *New York Times,* April 7, 1996, pp. 4, 23.

Brooks Atkinson

In the following review, which originally appeared in the New York Times *on March 30, 1951, Atkinson argues that while* The King and I *is a less innovative, accomplished musical than Rodgers and Hammerstein's* Oklahoma! *or* South Pacific, *it ''is an original and beautiful excursion into the rich splendors of the Far East, done with impeccable taste by two artists and brought to life with a warm, romantic score, idiomatic lyrics and some exquisite dancing.''*

As drama critic for the New York Times *from 1925 to 1960, Atkinson was one of the most influential reviewers in America.*

Nearly two years having elapsed since they invaded the South Pacific, Richard Rodgers and Oscar Hammerstein II have moved over to the Gulf of Siam. *The King and I,* which opened at the St. James last evening, is their musical rendering of Margaret Landon's *Anna and the King of Siam.* As a matter of record, it must be reported that *The King and I* is no match for *South Pacific,* which is an inspired musical drama.

But there is plenty of room for memorable music-making in the more familiar categories. Strictly on its own terms, *The King and I* is an original and beautiful excursion into the rich splendors of the Far East, done with impeccable taste by two artists and brought to life with a warm, romantic score, idiomatic lyrics and some exquisite dancing.

As the English governess who comes out from England in the Eighteen-Sixties to teach the King's

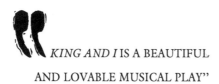

KING AND I IS A BEAUTIFUL AND LOVABLE MUSICAL PLAY"

children, Gertrude Lawrence looks particularly ravishing in some gorgeous costumes and acts an imposing part with spirit and an edge of mischief. Yul Brynner plays the King with a kind of fierce austerity, drawn between pride of office and eagerness to learn about the truth of the modern world from a "scientific foreigner." Apart from the pleasures of the musical theater, there is a theme in *The King and I,* and, as usual, Mr. Rodgers and Mr. Hammerstein have developed it with tenderness as well as relish, and with respect for the human beings involved.

Part of the delight of their fable derives from the wealth of beauty in the Siamese setting; and here Jo Mielziner, the Broadway magnifico, has drawn on the riches of the East; and Irene Sharaff has designed some of her most wonderful costumes. As a spectacle, *The King and I* is a distinguished work. In the direction, John van Druten has made something fine and touching in the elaborate scene that introduces the King's charming children to their English school marm. Jerome Robbins, serving as choreographer, has put together a stunning ballet that seasons the liquid formalism of Eastern dancing with some American humor. Yuriko, the ballerina, is superb as the Siamese notion of Eliza in *Uncle Tom's Cabin.*

Mr. Rodgers is in one of his most affable moods. For Miss Lawrence he has written several pleasant and ingratiating numbers which she sings brightly—"Hello, Young Lovers!" "The Royal Bangkok Academy" and "Shall I Tell You What I Think of You?" Dorothy Sarnoff does something wonderful with "Something Wonderful," which is one of Mr. Rodgers' most exultant numbers. Probably the most glorious number is "I Have Dreamed," which Doretta Morrow and Larry Douglas sing as a fervent duet. Mr. Brynner is no great shakes as a singer, but he makes his way safely through a couple of meditative songs written with an agreeable suggestion of Eastern music.

Say a word of thanks to Russell Bennett for his colorful orchestrations that make a fresh use of individual instruments and that always sound not only interesting but civilized. His orchestration should be especially appreciated in the long and enchanting scene that brings on the children one by one.

Don't expect another *South Pacific* nor an *Oklahoma!* This time Mr. Rodgers and Mr. Hammerstein are not breaking any fresh trails. But they are accomplished artists of song and words in the theatre; and *King and I* is a beautiful and lovable musical play.

Source: Brooks Atkinson, in a review of *The King and I* (1951) in *On Stage: Selected Theater Reviews from The New York Times, 1920–1970,* edited by Bernard Beckerman and Howard Siegman, Arno Press, 1973, pp. 333–34.

FURTHER READING

Engel, Lehman. *The American Musical Theater,* Macmillan, 1975.
   A narrative history of musical theater in America that describes the form and conventions of various forms of musicals: musical comedy, operetta, reviews (revues), and others.

Ewen, David. *New Complete Book of American Musical Theater* Holt, Rinehart, and Winston, 1970.
   A useful compendium of musical plots and brief biographies of composers, lyricists, and producers.

Fordin, Hugh. *Getting to Know Him: A Biography of Oscar Hammerstein II,* Random House, 1996.
   An in-depth biography of the life and works of Oscar Hammerstein.

Jackson, Arthur. *The Best Musicals: From* Show Boat *to* A Chorus Line *Broadway, Off-Broadway, London,* Crown Publishers, 1977.
   A coffee-table book of photographs and text chronicling the history of musicals from 1866 to 1977.

Landon, Margaret. *Anna and the King of Siam,* The John Day Company, 1943, 1944.
   A faithful prose rendition of Anna Leonowen's book about her exploits as governess in Siam.

James, Lawrence. *The Rise and Fall of the British Empire,* St. Martin's Press, 1996.
   An objective and scholarly look at the causes and consequences of the extensive empire England built and then had to disband.

Marshall, P. J. *The Cambridge Illustrated History of the British Empire,* Cambridge University Press, 1996.
      This illustrated text adopts a neutral position regarding the impact of the British Empire on its colonies and on its own national development.

Mast, Gerald. *Can't Help Singin': The American Musical on Stage and Screen,* Overlook Press, 1987.
      An in-depth review of the most popular musicals in America, with photographs.

McConache, Bruce. "The 'Oriental' Musicals of Rodgers and Hammerstein and the U. S. War in South East Asia" in *Theater Journal,* Volume 3, October, 1994, pp. 385-98.
      Compares narrative patterns of musicals with patterns of foreign policy. Asserts that three Rodgers and Hammerstein musicals helped draw the United States into the Vietnam War.

Said, Edward. *Orientalism,* Penguin, 1995.
      Using Egypt and the Arab nations as examples, Said asserts that "orientalism" is a form of identifying the "other" in stereotypical terms as a means of bolstering the national identity of European countries and of justifying their domination of the Asian countries.

Time, Volume 57, number 78, April 9, 1951).
      A positive theater review of the stage debut of *The King and I.*

SOURCES

"After Hours" in *Harper's,* Volume 203, September, 1951, pp. 99-100.

"Getting to Know Lou" in *People,* Volume 45, June 3, 1996, p. 100.

Lardner, John. "The Surefire Boys in Siam" in the *New Yorker,* Volume 27, April 7, 1951, pp. 70-71.

Marshall, Margaret. Review of *The King and I* in the *Nation,* Volume 172, April 14, 1951, p. 353.

Review of *The King and I* in *Newsday,* April 25, 1996.

Simon, John. Review of *The King and I* in *New York,* Volume 29, number 16, April 22, 1996, p. 34.

"A Stately Pleasure Dome" in *Commonwealth,* Volume 64, July 20, 1956, pp. 396-97.

Time 68:90 (July 16, 1956).

Time 147 (April 29, 1996): 84.

The Little Foxes

LILLIAN HELLMAN

1939

Lillian Hellman's cynical play of family greed and revenge, *The Little Foxes,* is her most popular piece of drama, and it is the one most frequently revived. It was acclaimed an instant hit after a hugely successful opening night in 1939, even though drama and literary critics then, as now, disagreed over whether the melodramatic story of the greed-driven Hubbard family succeeds either as a morality play or as a satire. Certainly moral dissembling lies at the heart of the play: the Hubbard siblings steal, deceive, and plot against each other in their efforts to invest in one of the first cotton mills to industrialize the New South, a plan that stands to win them millions of dollars. Regina, temporarily cheated out of her share by her brothers, even ''murders'' her sick husband by refusing to fetch his medicine when he threatens to obstruct her from taking part in the investment. Their daughter serves as a moral standard who dislikes the family machinations. Unfortunately, Alexandra is too young to defy them. Nor can her Aunt Birdie, who drinks to anesthetize the pain of having married a bully and lost her family's plantation to the rapacious Hubbards. The satiric element of the play consists of its condemnation of the Hubbards's crimes against society. The Hubbards are a family prone to deceit, caught in a cycle of revenge not unlike Greek classical tragedies. The family forbears harvested their merchant profits by overcharging the newly freed slaves, and now the Hubbards will create a larger dynasty on the toil of poor workers, who will flock to the cotton mill for

its paltry wages. The play voices Marxist disapproval of the Hubbard form of capitalism.

AUTHOR BIOGRAPHY

Until she was 16, Lillian Hellman lived half of her time in the South—New Orleans, Louisiana, where she was born in 1906—and half in New York City. Once she married and began her career as a writer, she never returned to the South, which housed the rapacious immorality she denounced in *The Little Foxes,* its "prequel," *Another Part of the Forest,* and *Toys in the Attic.* Nor did she reserve her harsh moralizing for the South—most of her plays attack universal moral faults. Hellman's repulsion against the profiteering of people like the Hubbard family of *The Little Foxes* perhaps began as she listened to the scheming of her mother's side of her family, the Marxs. They were a wealthy and elegant family who had risen from immigrant poverty to make their fortune in merchandising in the South, and who later succeeded in banking. Hellman is quoted in William Wright's 1986 book, *Lillian Hellman: The Image, The Woman* as asserting that the Marx family grew "rich from the 'borrowings' of poor Negroes," and that this heritage fueled her lifelong radicalism. She further revealed that great-uncles Max and Isaac Marx and great-aunt Sophie Newhouse Marx served as models for the Hubbard family. When Lillian was five, her father contributed to Hellman's lifelong obsession with the power of money—his shoe business went bankrupt, forcing the comfortable family to move in with poorer relatives, the Hellmans, who ran a boarding house. During Max Hellman's entrepreneurial ups and downs, the Marx family wealth was always available for comparison, since each family maintained a home both in New York City and New Orleans.

From an early age, Hellman had a "wild" nature: she skipped school, smoked, and told people exactly what she thought of them. As an adult she had numerous love affairs, including a 30-year relationship with detective fiction author Dashiell Hammett. Her politics were equally scandalous. Disgusted with the alarming growth of fascism she found in Germany in 1929, Hellman, along with many other writers, academics, and intellectuals, became involved in the communist party. For this ideological experimentation, she found herself blacklisted by the film industry in 1948 and was required to appear before the McCarthy subcommittee on

Lillian Hellman in 1966

communist activity, the House Un-American Activities Committee, in 1952. On the stand Hellman stoutly denied being a member of the communist party, although recent biographer Carl Rollyson has confirmed that she was. However, a (HUAC) party member who was briefly Hellmmann's lover has explained that what really mattered was whether or not the party controlled you and that Hellman was entirely independent. Independent Hellman certainly was—throughout her life she voiced her opposition to what she considered wrong, and she used her influence as an American intellectual and public figure to persuade others of her view. Unlike Alexandra in *The Little Foxes,* who does no more than threaten to find out the truth, Hellman wrote plays that made the truth stare her American audiences in the face. She died in 1984.

PLOT SUMMARY

Act One
The Little Foxes takes place in the living room of the Giddens house, in a small town in the deep South in 1900. At curtain rise, the black maid Addie is tidying up and Cal, the black porter, is setting out a bottle of the best port. Birdie Hubbard, a well-

bred but faded woman enters from the dinner party offstage, obviously tipsy. Her husband Oscar follows, scolding her for boring their special guest. His sister Regina Giddens and brother Ben enter with Mr. William Marshall of Chicago, enjoying light-hearted banter after closing a deal to build a new cotton mill that will make all of them wealthy. Marshall is pleased by the Hubbards's promise to prevent labor problems, a ''certain benefit'' of the southern locale. One family member who stands to gain from the transaction is missing—Horace Giddens, Regina's husband, a banker. He is in Baltimore under the care of specialists for a heart condition. Leo, Oscar's toady son, has been ''keeping an eye on things'' at his bank. Mr. Marshall and Regina flirt openly, and she promises to visit him in Chicago. Apparently her brothers approve of this potential affair, as it cements the business deal.

After Mr. Marshall leaves, the Hubbard family members speculate about how they will spend their millions. Birdie wants two things: to restore to its pre-Civil War elegance her family plantation Lionnet, now under the ownership of her husband and for Oscar to stop shooting the game their black neighbors need for sustenance. Oscar scornfully hushes her. Regina's grand plan is to move to Chicago and become a member of high society. Ben interrupts the wish-making to suggest they assume a fifty-one percent controlling interest, with an investment of $225,000. Ben and Oscar pressure Regina to get her third of the investment money from Horace, who has not responded to Regina's letters. Regina shrewdly manages to turn their skepticism to her benefit by fabricating that Horace is holding out for a larger share. The brothers grant their sister this coup just to keep the deal in the family; the difference will come out of Oscar's share. In return Oscar wants Regina's daughter Alexandra (Zan) to marry his son. Regina promises only to think about it.

Birdie promises Alexandra that she will not allow the family force her to marry Leo, and this earns her a slap on the face from her husband, which Birdie conceals from Zan. Regina announces that Alexandra is to leave the next morning to bring her father home. The curtain closes on Alexandra looking puzzled and frightened.

Act Two

One week later, the family nervously awaits Horace's arrival. Cal makes an offhand remark about the meat Oscar is wasting, but Oscar cuts him off with an ominous threat. Leo and Oscar concoct a scheme to ''borrow'' $88,000 worth of Union Pa-

cific bonds from Horace's safe deposit box, giving them two-thirds of the investment, thus turning the tables on Ben. They would replace the bonds before Horace discovers them missing. Ben arrives and the siblings discuss Horace's delay over breakfast offstage.

Addie rushes hopefully to the door at the sound of voices; it is Horace, looking completely exhausted, and Alexandra, covered in soot from the trip. Alexandra asks not for her mother, but for Aunt Birdie. Addie and Horace happily reminisce for a moment, then Horace asks her why he has been called home. She tells him about the plan to become ''high-tone rich'' and to marry Zan to Leo, muttering ''over my dead body.'' Sobered, Horace is announced. The family rushes to him, Regina greeting him with a warm kiss. It isn't long, however, before the problems between Horace and Regina emerge again. Regina wonders if his ''fancy women'' caused his bad heart. She then forces a discussion of the investment, in spite of his obvious fatigue. Horace discovers that the Hubbards have promised Marshall low wages and no strikes; he dryly observes that Ben will certainly accomplish this by playing the workers off against each other. Horace intends to obstruct the Hubbards: by not allowing Leo to marry Zan and not giving Regina his money. Regina pursues him as he retires upstairs, even though Ben urges her to wait, to use ''softness and a smile.'' With their angry voices audible, Oscar puts forth his plan to circumvent Horace and Regina by ''borrowing'' $88,000 from ''a friend'' of Leo's. Ben, guessing the friend's identity, encourages them to proceed but refuses to shake Leo's hand good-bye. Regina returns downstairs unsuccessful and barely acknowledges Alexandra's plea to stop causing stress to her father. Regina turns instead to Ben, who shocks her with the news that everything is settled and that Oscar is going to Chicago. When Horace comes downstairs to relish the Hubbards's dispute, Regina cruelly accuses him of wishing her ill because of his own impending death. Horace responds that he refuses to help the Hubbards ''wreck the town and live on it.''

Act Three

On a rainy afternoon two weeks later, Birdie and Alexandra contentedly play a piano duet while Horace is nearby. Abruptly, Horace tells Cal to run to the bank with a puzzling message meant for Leo's ears—that he has received the safe deposit box and now wants the manager to bring an attorney over that evening. Birdie's indulgence in elderberry wine causes her to reminisce about the happy days when Horace used to play the fiddle. In her inebriated gaiety, Birdie relates that her mother would never associate with the Hubbards. She explains that she married Oscar because Ben wanted the Lionnet cotton, so Oscar "married it." Birdie hopes Zan will not turn out like herself, unhappily trailing after the power holders. Addie's remark sums up the play's moral: "Well, there are people who eat the earth and eat all the people on it. . . . Then there are people who stand around and watch them eat it."

When Regina comes in, Horace announces that they have, after all, invested in the cotton mill. At first she thinks that Horace has decided to join her and she feels triumphant, but she has misunderstood. Horace will let the brother keep the stolen money, her only legacy in the new will he is about to write. In retaliation, she tells him that she has never loved him, that his impending death pleases her. This shocks Horace enough that he reaches for his heart medicine, but he drops the bottle and it breaks. He cannot even call to Addie for another bottle, and Regina makes no move to help him. He falls and is carried upstairs. When the brothers and Leo arrive, Regina divulges that she knows of their crime, and Ben and Oscar let Leo take the blame. Now she and Ben seem almost to relish fencing for the upper hand. If Horace lives, Ben and Oscar will "win," but if he dies, Regina will triumph and send her brothers to jail. Betting that Horace will die, Regina blackmails them for a seventy-five percent share. Ben and Oscar are ready to give it to her to save themselves when Zan comes downstairs. Her posture indicates that Horace is dead; Regina has won. Regina reminds them of her sway over Mr. Marshall, who will abort the deal rather than risk a scandal—the brothers had better behave. Ben and Regina make amends, being cut of the same cloth. Only after Oscar departs does Ben deal his final blow: he shares Zan's suspicions about Horace's death. After Ben leaves, Regina commands Zan to accompany her to Chicago, then relents, not wanting to force her. She almost timidly inquires if Zan would like to sleep in her room. Zan, seeing a new side of her mother, asks, "Are you afraid, Mama?" Addie comforts Zan as the curtain falls.

CHARACTERS

Addie

Addie is the Hubbards's black maid and Alexandra Hubbard's nanny; she has a keen sense

Tallulah Bankhead in the first New York production (1939) of The Little Foxes

of justice and she tries to protect Alexandra from the rapacity of the Hubbard family. She considers Ben, Oscar, Regina, and Leo a scourge on humanity, "eaters of the earth," and she scorns those who are too feeble or too uncommitted to stand up to them, saying: "Well, there are people who eat the earth and eat all the people on it. . . . Then there are people who stand around and watch them eat it. . . . Sometimes I think it ain't right to stand and watch them do it." She herself lacks the social status to fight them effectively. Her comments serve as a moral compass for the audience.

Ben

See Benjamin Hubbard

Cal

Cal is a slightly bumbling and mild-mannered black servant who very indirectly protests Oscar's monopolization of the area's hunting rights by offhandedly mentioning how his friends would "give anything for a little piece of that meat."

Alexandra Giddens

Seventeen-year-old Alexandra Giddens, or Zan, adores her father Horace Giddens and her Aunt

MEDIA ADAPTATIONS

- Lillian Hellman adapted *The Little Foxes* into a screenplay in 1941 that starred Bette Davis as Regina and won critical acclaim for director William Wyler and cameraman Gregg Toland, later famed for his deep-focus camerawork in *Citizen Kane*. The black-and-white film was nominated for nine Academy Awards, but received none.

- In 1949 Marc Blitzstein premiered an opera adaptation called *Regina* with original libretto and music. Although it ran for only a few months, it fared better than the usual Broadway opera.

- An NBC television drama based on the play was broadcast in 1956, and starred Greer Garson. It was produced by George Schaefer, with a screenplay by Robert Hartung, and was broadcast as an episode of ''The Hallmark Hall of Fame'' series.

Birdie but mistrusts and, by the end of the play, actively dislikes her mother, Regina. Addie has protected Zan from her family, allowing youthful idealism to carry Zan along, but Horace wants her to ''learn to hate and fear''—the Hubbard way of life—so that she will get away from them. She grows up suddenly after Horace's murder, but it remains unclear in what way she will fulfill her promise to ''be fighting ... some place where people don't just stand around and watch.''

Horace Giddens

Horace Giddens, Regina's husband, is a man of moral conviction who lacks the physical and emotional fortitude to honor his conviction by fighting the Hubbards. Instead he takes refuge in a Baltimore hospital, nursing a heart ailment and ''thinking about'' about his unhappy life with Regina. Alexandra fetches him home for his final showdown, wherein he shows some mettle in his elaborate scheme to obstruct Regina's access to his money; nevertheless, when Regina strips away that last shred of his defenses by admitting that she married him only for money, has always held him in contempt, and cannot wait until he dies, the shock kills him. He dies having done nothing to deter the Hubbards.

Regina Giddens

Regina Giddens, born Regina Hubbard, handsome sister to Ben and Oscar, wife to Horace, and mother of Alexandra, is the central character in *The Little Foxes*. In the first stage production Tallulah Bankhead portrayed her as an inherently evil villainess, but in the 1941 film version Bette Davis created a more sympathetic character who gradually becomes evil.

Regina's flirtation with Mr. Marshall is done as much to seal a business deal as it is to secure a stepping stone into the high society of Chicago she wants to join. She is sexually cold, having scornfully banned her husband from her bed for the last ten years. Money and power are her loves, and she resorts to an unusual method of murder to get them: she shocks Horace, who has a weak heart, with the news that she has never loved him and that she will relish his death, then she fails to aid him when he predictably has an attack. While he lies dying upstairs, she coolly savors a familiar game of blackmail, fencing with her brothers for the stakes of the ultimate control of the family power.

Benjamin Hubbard

Ben Hubbard, eldest brother to Regina and Oscar, is the soft-spoken but callous ringleader of the Hubbard family and one of the predatory capitalists of the New South. Unmarried, he shows no interest in human relations beyond the use he makes of them to achieve financial domination of the ''small unnamed town in the south'' where he was born. He has built his local empire by cheating and overcharging black customers in his drygoods store and he can guarantee Chicago investor Mr. Marshall low wages and no strikes in their new cotton mill because he knows how to play his workers against each other. Ben vies for power with the cool precision of a chess player who holds a grudging respect for his primary opponent, Regina.

Birdie Hubbard

Birdie Hubbard is a timid, well-bred, but aging Southern belle, a nervous and flighty woman abused and completely dominated by her bullying husband Oscar. She once innocently enjoyed coming-out parties at her parents' plantation, Lionnet, but now she has not had a day of happiness in twenty-two years. A weak woman, she has not prevented her son from becoming even worse than his father, and she drowns her misery in a ''secret'' drinking habit that the family cloaks under the euphemism of ''her headaches.'' Her only salvation is music and her relationship with her niece, who, she hopes, will avoid her fate.

Leo Hubbard

Leo is the son of Birdie and Oscar Hubbard, a lying toady with all of the greed and deceitfulness of his father and none of his mother's cultural refinement, but having ''a weak kind of good looks.'' His own mother detests him. He foolishly reveals to his father that he has taken an illicit look into his uncle Horace's safe deposit box and tries to blame it on others, but his intimate knowledge of the box's contents and the whereabouts of the keys give away his culpability. Ben can barely conceal his contempt for Leo and makes him take the full blame for the theft when it is discovered. Leo is apparently too stupid to save himself.

Oscar Hubbard

Oscar Hubbard is the sharp-tempered, mean-spirited brother of Regina and Ben who kowtows to his older and more powerful brother, bullies his wife Birdie, and goes hunting daily, only to throw out the precious game he kills, ignoring Cal's hints to share it. He is clever enough to develop a scheme to steal Horace's money but he slavishly hands it over to Ben without realizing that Ben will not let himself be implicated. Although he presumably wants to make millions for his son's sake, he and Ben let Leo take the blame when the theft is discovered. He treats his cultivated wife, Birdie, with disdain, having married her solely to help Ben take over her family's cotton plantation. He advises his son: ''It's every man's duty to think of himself.''

William Marshall

William Marshall, a Chicago businessman, wants to invest in the industrialization of the New South by building a cotton mill but needs local partners to manage the mill and keep the workers in hand. Although married, he flirts openly with Regina during the one scene in which he appears.

Zan

See Alexandra Giddens

THEMES

Greed

Greed drives the Hubbards—Regina, Ben, Oscar, and Leo—to seek more and more wealth, beyond the very comfortable financial stability they have already secured from their drygoods business. Each of them sacrifices integrity to achieve it. The allure of wealth is a primary force that offers something slightly different to each of them. The expected millions will catapult Regina beyond the domain of the small town in the deep south into the glittering international social life of Chicago and Paris, but she kills her husband to get there and thereby loses the love of her daughter; thus she will go to Chicago utterly alone. Ben lost his integrity long ago; as Regina reminds him, ''You couldn't find twelve men in this state you haven't cheated and hate you for it.'' Ben treats negotiating with his siblings like a game of chess, where the pawns are the future mill workers whom he will play off against each other in order to keep the cotton mill wages low. His greed is an end in itself. Oscar lacks Ben's mastery and Regina's coolness under fire, and therefore exists on a lower level of the family hierarchy. He lets his son steal Horace's bonds, and then has no qualms about letting Leo take the full blame for the theft when Horace discovers them missing. Oscar enjoys his daily game hunt, blithely discarding his catch in spite of the fact that the poor black residents of the town need the meat. Furthermore, he refuses to allow them to hunt in the area. He kills for the sheer pleasure of killing, owns for the pleasure of denying ownership to others.

Hellman warns her audience that not only are the Hubbards destined to flourish, but that they are not alone. According to Ben: ''There are hundreds of Hubbards sitting in rooms like this throughout the country. All their names aren't Hubbard, but they are all Hubbards and they will own this country

TOPICS FOR FURTHER STUDY

- Investigate the Northern interest in the industrialization of the New South. Is William Marshall a ''carpetbagger''? Explain your answer.

- How did the Antebellum South differ economically, socially, and politically from the South before the Civil War? In what ways do the characters in Hellman's play reflect these changes?

- Does *The Little Foxes* conform to the conventions of the melodrama or the well-made play? In what ways does it conform to these archetypes and in what ways does it differ?

- What were some of the differences in wage and labor conditions between the North and the South at the turn of the 20th century, and what led workers to form labor unions?

- What were some of the factors that kept African Americans like Addie and Cal in subservient and essentially powerless positions twenty-five years after emancipation?

---

some day.'' Greed underlies the mentality of unscrupulous industrialists who infiltrated the New South and nourished a form of predatory capitalism that Hellman considered a threat to the American ethic.

Apathy and Passivity

Hellman's herself was an activist who constantly signed petitions and joined committees bent on political change. She deplored passivity in the face of malice and she has the erstwhile heroes of *The Little Foxes* express their disdain for it as well. Addie, who serves a moral compass in the midst of the evil machinations of the Hubbards, expresses more concern about the passivity that allows them to continue than about what they actually do, saying, ''Well, there are people who eat the earth and eat all the people on it.... Then there are people who stand around and watch them eat it.... Sometimes I think it ain't right to stand and watch them do

it.'' To Addie the Hubbards are like an impersonal and inevitable plague, a scourge on humanity, and whether one fights them or stands by in apathy, permitting them to feed off of others, is a test of character that most of the others in the play fail. Addie fails too, since, being black, she lacks the social status to fight them effectively. She nurtures Alexandra in the hope that the young girl will one day escape the Hubbard sphere of influence. Horace also hopes Alexandra will leave; he wants her to ''learn to hate and fear'' the Hubbards's mean-spirited avarice. Horace himself gets away for a few peaceful months at a hospital in Baltimore. He returns too weak, physically and emotionally, to fight the Hubbards, and the shock of hearing that his wife hates him and wishes him dead kills him. Thus Hellman demonstrates that apathy exacts a price—those who fail to strive against evil are devoured from inside. Horace's heart weakens, Birdie resorts to alcohol, and both of their lives are ruined by the Hubbards. Furthermore, their weakness perpetuates the evil they cannot stop. Hellman was surprised that audiences sympathized with Birdie's defeated, drunken passivity. She expected them to scorn her as much as she did: ''I just meant her to be . . . a lost drunk,'' Hellman said in a 1958 interview quoted in *Conversations with Lillian Hellman.*

Revenge

If audiences find anything to admire in the detestable maneuverings of the Hubbards's rivalry over money and power, it is in the vengeance one evil character wreaks upon another. This play does not offer the grand satisfaction of a strong and good hero winning retribution for harm done in a dramatic moment of victory. Rather, it displays a series of tiny victorious moments wherein one villain wrests control away from the others, only to lose it again in the next scene. In the climax of the action, Regina steps carefully around what she does not know for sure, hinting that she can put Ben, Oscar, and Leo into jail for stealing the bonds. That she puts her winning hand together while her husband dies upstairs proves her to be an evil villainess; but her cool command and deft strategizing make her a very smart villainess, one who commands a measure of respect. She also provides the vicarious pleasure of defeating scoundrels—her criminally scheming brothers. The heroic figures in the play are too weak to obtain recompense for their injuries and do little more than irritate the Hubbards—Horace dies almost unnoticed before he can have his showdown, Birdie no longer cares, Addie knows better than to step out of her subservient role, and Alexandra chooses to fight elsewhere. Thus the only pleasure of victory available is in the shifting of power amongst the evil characters as the losers seek revenge, prevail, and then are overturned. The viewer sympathizes with these repellent characters long enough to enjoy their moment of vengeance and their prowess in achieving it. One might wonder why Regina and her brothers have developed their contentious relationship in the first place. Hellman wrote another play to answer that question. *Another Part of the Forest* goes back twenty years to reveal a father who cheats and betrays his neighbors and humiliates his children. Ben blackmails his father for his estate, leaving Regina and Oscar at Ben's beck and call, thus beginning the Greek cycle of revenge that continues in *The Little Foxes* and would have evolved in a third play had Hellman completed the trilogy.

STYLE

Symbolism

The symbolism in this play about the greed and revenge that destroys the Hubbard family and everyone associated with them is subtle but effective. Oscar, the least clever of the three siblings, enjoys his daily sport of hunting wastefully discarding his bounty. He completely monopolizes the local hunting area, thus denying the black population much-needed access to meat. His pastime has symbolic resonances to the "hobby" he and his siblings make of their struggle for power and wealth; both endeavors involve killing for the sheer pleasure of killing and a drive to dominate others and monopolize resources beyond what is needed. Oscar's pillage is an outgrowth of his underdog status—since he cannot make his siblings do his bidding, he resorts to pillage of the animal world and bullying men of lesser social status. In another instance of symbolism, Horace has what is loosely termed a "bad heart," a weakened physical condition that presumably results from emotional deprivation. His heart "ache" and a broken violin in his safe deposit box, combined with the fact that he has not slept with Regina in ten years, suggest that Horace cannot thrive in his wife's presence, and he retreats to Baltimore where he lives under the care of doctors. Back home, a few caustic words from Regina push him beyond medical aid and he dies, having failed to stop or even slow down the Hubbards's rapacity. His "bad" or weak heart carries symbolic significance: his association with th Hubbards has ruined

him both physically and morally. In other words, Horace "lacks the heart" to fight, an implication that it takes moral strength, or "heart" to combat evil successfully.

The Well-made Play

Some controversy exists over whether or not *The Little Foxes* is what is called a well-made play. A well-made play normally contains a plot based upon a withheld secret, steadily mounting suspense relying on precise timing, a climax in which the secret is revealed, and a logical denouement or resolution of all loose ends. Certainly the central story line here—the need for Regina's share of the investment, Horace's refusal, Oscar's secret plan to steal the needed funds from him, and the resolution in which Horace permits the theft as penance to Regina—moves to fulfillment with remarkable clarity and speed. However, the play leaves a number of enormous loose ends untied, and these unresolved plot details throw into question the applicability of the label, well-made play. At the final curtain it remains unclear whether Ben will pursue with any success his threat to expose Regina's complicity in Horace's death. (Perhaps Hellman left this open in order to provide closure in the third play of the trilogy, which she never completed.) Other unresolved plot details also belie the category of the well-made play—an important character, William Marshall, appears only in Act 1 and never returns to the stage; Leo's culpability in the theft remains officially undisclosed, and Horace never rewrites his will or has his triumphant moment of confrontation over the Hubbard's crimes. Taken together, these loose ends contribute to a sense that the evil of the Hubbards remains unchecked, a sense that Hellman clearly meant to convey, since it corresponds to her oblique accusation that those who only "stand and watch" are complicitous in the designs of the evil. Hellman concerned herself very little about the applicability of labels to her work, saying, as quoted in *Conversations with Lillian Hellman:* "It's newspaper idiots who make these distinctions between well-made plays, or magazine idiots. It seems to be a very dull idea to worry about."

Melodrama

Throughout its stage life, *The Little Foxes,* full of high intensity and the relentlessly malicious Hubbards, has withstood the charge that it is a melodrama, that is, a play in which emotional sensation holds more importance than character motivation and psychological depth. At the end of a typical melodrama, good characters are duly rewarded while bad characters are punished for their foul deeds. Of course, the purposely unresolved ending of *The Little Foxes,* which was to be followed by a third play in the planned trilogy, does not suit the dictionary definition of a melodrama. Critics have also debated over whether *The Little Foxes* is "serious theater" or mere melodrama, the distinction being that serious theater causes the characters and the audience to reflect on the larger philosophical implications of the central conflict whereas melodrama simply presents the struggle between good and evil as pure entertainment. The extent of introspection inspired by this play is limited to the charge that "it ain't right to stand and watch" the eaters of the earth (i. e., the Hubbards and their like), a criticism vaguely directed at the audience. On the other hand, *The Little Foxes* takes the genre of melodrama to a new dimension with its witty dialogue and taut plotting. Hellman uses all of the stock-in-trade of the melodramatist to expose a social problem, that to ignore the doings of social malefactors is a destructive form of passivity. If this is melodrama, it is socially responsible melodrama.

HISTORICAL CONTEXT

The Industrialization of the New South

By the turn of the 20th century in the American South, the period and setting of Hellman's *The Little Foxes,* the Civil War had taught Southerners the wisdom of industrialization and a diversified economy, and now planting was taking second place to merchandising and factory building. The economy was slowly emerging from the depression that followed the war. Cotton was strong in the South because of international trade with the Far East, although the Boxer Rebellion (1898-1900) slowed exports temporarily, recovering just about the time that the Hubbard and Williams cotton mill would have gone into production. Williams's interest in this investment can be explained by the situation in the North, where mill owners were suffering from a decline in the domestic textile market coupled with rising labor agitation for better wages. At first, Northern politicians attempted to chip away at the Southern market advantage by promoting new legislation against abusively long working hours and low wages and by sponsoring bills to guarantee better education for workers, realizing that a more intelligent work force would

demand better working conditions and higher pay. But failing to equalize the labor force, Northern investors, like Hellman's Williams, began to build mills in the South, joining ranks with Southern cotton producers to compete more effectively with European manufacturers. At the same time, Southern financiers, from the wealthiest landowners to the family with just a few hundred dollars to spare, conducted fund-raisers to construct mills in almost every town, in an effort "to bring the cotton mills to the cotton." With money coming in from both sides, mills sprang up all over the South, along with other kinds of factories. Factory and mill jobs were highly desirable to poor whites and blacks because the wages, although lower than those in the North, were high in comparison to Southern rural standards. Often mills reserved labor jobs for poor whites, causing competition with the black population; mill owners like Ben played one group against another to keep wages low. Ben knew that the situation in the South almost guaranteed that he would be able to keep his promise to Williams regarding low wages and no labor problems. Although no one mentions convict leasing in Hellman's play, its presence in the South in the early 1900s would have bolstered an unscrupulous mill owner's ability to hold wages at a minimum and prevent labor problems. Convict leasing consisted of hiring out prison inmates as strikebreakers and railroad workers, and since African Americans received the longest sentences, they filled the prisons and became, essentially, another form of slave labor in the South, without the paternalism of plantation owners who cared about the welfare of their slaves. Northern versions of convict leasing existed, but as with other forms of unfair labor practices, the North ended them long before their Southern counterparts did, and it was easy for certain investors to take advantage of this lag in order to make a profit.

CRITICAL OVERVIEW

New York theater critics gave enthusiastic reviews to *The Little Foxes,* and Tallulah Bankhead's portrayal of Regina still ranks high on the list of the most brilliant performances on Broadway. The smash hit opening of *The Little Foxes* in 1939 followed Hellman's highly successful *The Children's Hour* (1934) and *Days to Come* (1936), a failure that closed after a handful of performances. Her third effort catapulted her into the New York theater limelight, a status she enjoyed for the rest of her life,

COMPARE
&
CONTRAST

- **1900s:** During the industrialization of the New South, Southern labor laws and practices were more exploitative of workers than those in the North, giving owners of Southern factories and mills a decided profit advantage over their Northern counterparts.

  1939: After 1935, the National Labor Board assured that workers had the right to organize, a national minimum wage was established by the Wages and Hours Act of 1938, and the Congress of Industrial Organizations (CIO) organized workers by industries, giving workers stronger bargaining power with employees; however to many Americans alarmed by the continued intolerable conditions for factory and migratory workers, socialism became an attractive political option.

  Today: Union membership is in decline since widespread labor issues no longer exist. However, in spite of vigilance over the enforcement of fair labor laws, inequities still exist for hundreds of illegal immigrants secretly confined to ''sweatshops'' where they work long hours in substandard conditions at below-minimum wages.

- **1900:** In spite of emancipation in 1865, African Americans were actively disenfranchised by Jim Crow Laws in the South that prevented them from voting or receiving fair trials, and schools and public places were legally segregated. 115 lynchings were recorded in this year.

  1939: Some Southern African Americans migrated north to escape Jim Crow laws, where they met with resistance from European immigrants threatened by this new source of cheap labor; those who stayed in the South continued to experience the oppression of the Ku Klux Klan and segregationist policy.

  Today: The Civil Rights Acts of the 1960s ensure voting rights to people of any race or color and schools and workplaces are becoming more racially diverse, although the effects of long-term oppression continue to plague contemporary African Americans.

---

even though she wrote only five more original plays. In spite of strong competition from hit plays running at the same time—*The Philadelphia Story* with Katherine Hepburn, a Cole Porter musical called *Leave it to Me* that made Mary Martin a star, Laurence Olivier playing in *No Time for Comedy,* and the record-breaker *Life with Father,* a play that would see over 3,000 performances—*The Little Foxes* was hailed as ''the year's strongest play'' by a *Life* magazine critic and ran for 410 performances. The taut engineering of the plot garnered immediate attention. A *Time* critic described it best, saying that Hellman made ''her plot crouch, coil, dart like a snake.'' Over the years, Hellman's deliberate plot craftsmanship has brought reproach as well as praise; in a review of a 1967 Lincoln Center revival, *New York Review of Books* critic Elizabeth Hardwick faulted the play for failing to do justice to the

complexities of its underlying story and condemned the plot's intricate construction as ''quite awkwardly managed.'' Hardwick's comments included the accusation that the play lacked the elements of a true tragedy, galvanizing Richard Poirier, Edmund Wilson, and other notable critics to write eloquent rebuttals in the next issue. Hellman's play has been alternatively condemned and lauded as representative of the genre of the well-made play, meaning a play whose tight plot structure leaves no loose ends, where each and every event contributes to steadily mounting tension that is resolved at the unveiling of an important secret. Those critics who dub *The Little Foxes* a well-made play cite the relentless, chess-like move and countermove of the Hubbards's game of blackmail and revenge that cumulates in Regina's apparent triumph over her brothers at the end of Act Three. However, the play leaves some untidy loose ends that push it out of the neat category of the well-made play, such as the hovering threat that Ben may find proof of Regina's agency in Horace's death. A paradigmatic well-made play would not leave such matters unresolved. Critics have also debated whether the well-made play itself represents good or bad drama, a debate that Hellman chose to ignore; in response to an interviewer's query on the prognosis of the well-made play, Hellman quipped, as quoted in *Conversations with Lillian Hellman:* "Survival won't have anything to do with well-made or not well-made . . . I don't like labels and isms. They are for people who raise or lower skirts because that's the thing you do for this year." The other criticism leveled at Hellman is equally ephemeral, namely that *The Little Foxes* is pure melodrama, that is, a play more concerned with emotional sensationalism than with reflective thought. That the play addresses social issues through the genre of melodrama led one critic to call it a "social melodrama." More recently, Mark Estrin took all of these critics to task for failing to notice the satiric humor of the play; he claimed that early reviewers "tended to take the works too seriously." Hellman admits that humor was her intent, saying in one interview quoted in *Conversations with Lillian Hellman:* "I think Regina's kind of funny" and "the brothers amuse me." The play has certainly withstood the test of time, having frequent revivals to showcase reigning stars such as Elizabeth Taylor (1981).

Over time, critical opinion has shifted from focusing upon the evil inherent in the industrialization of the New South to the more general view of the themes of greed and revenge and the sin of idly standing by as they go unchecked. Literary scholar Warren French wrote that neither *The Little Foxes* nor Hellman's earlier dramatic success, *The Children's Hour,* would ever "become period pieces as long as malice and greed make the world wobble round."

CRITICISM

Carole L. Hamilton

Hamilton is an educator with significant experience in drama and secondary curricula. In this essay she compares Hellman's play to classic Greek drama.

In interviews Hellman has acknowledged her debt to Henrik Ibsen and Anton Chekhov as models of dramatic structure (she even edited an anthology of Chekhov's letters), but she never articulated her ties to classic Greek theater, the ultimate source of the genre called tragedy. Yet the two plays of her planned but uncompleted trilogy, *The Little Foxes* and its "prequel," *Another Part of the Forest,* show considerable resemblance to classic Greek tragedy, especially to Aeschylus's trilogy, the *Orestiea.* At the same time, Hellman's plays truly represent their time period, the modernist era, in their cynicism and their lack of a true heroic figure. On top of that, the quietly disturbing condemnation of passivity in the face of social ills move the play beyond the realm of pure tragedy to a unique dramatic genre that combines the best of classic tragedy with the best of the morality play.

As in Greek staging, what Aristotle termed the three unities of time, place, and action are respected in *The Little Foxes:* all of the events take place in one setting, over a short three-week period, and no extraneous incidents mar the relentless action of the lean plot. Hellman's trilogy contains a father's betrayal of his children, interference in betrothals, deceit, and murder, all themes common to Greek mythology and drama. There is cyclical revenge whose stoppage is central to the trilogy, and there is at least one character who wishes to end the familial cycle of revenge. But, unlike the typical classic Greek story, no character appears capable of ending generations of deception and revenge.

In the Greek myth that most closely resembles the structure and story of Hellman's planned trilogy, Orestes and his sister Electra put a stop to several generations of vengeance murders in their family, the House of Atreus, by themselves murdering their own mother and her lover. Aeschylus dramatized their story in the *Oresteia,* which begins with the murder of Agamemnon by his wife Clytemestra and her paramour, Aegisthus. Their motive is not to rid themselves of an unwelcome spouse, but revenge for Agamemnon's sacrifice of his daughter Iphigenia, an act that her mother Clytemestra never forgave. Child killing goes back to Agamemnon's paternal ancestors, when a father killed his son and served him at a banquet. In another case Atreus (Agamemnon's father) serves his brother a dish of his own children as an act of revenge. In a slight departure from this motif, Agamemnon kills his daughter to solicit the gods' help in the Trojan War. He tells Iphigenia she is setting sail to marry Achilles, but she is bound for a

WHAT DO I READ NEXT?

- In *Another Part of the Forest*, the "prequel" to *The Little Foxes*, Hellman jumps back 20 years to show the genesis of the family revenge cycle. It portrays a dominating father (Marcus) whom Ben blackmails (with evidence of Marcus's betrayal of neighbor soldiers during the Civil War) to obtain full ownership of his estate, leaving Regina and Oscar virtually penniless.

- Henrik Ibsen's play *A Doll's House* (1879) was a model of social realism for Hellman. In it a dutiful wife leaves her husband when she discovers that he has never seen her as a human being, but as little more than a doll.

- *All My Sons,* the 1947 play by Hellman's contemporary and rival Arthur Miller, portrays Joe Keller, a manufacturer who knowingly ships defective airplane parts that kill twenty—two American pilots in World War II, and lets his partner take the jail sentence for it.

- In Arthur Miller's play *Death of a Salesman* (1949), Willie Loman sacrifices his integrity for expected riches.

- The son of Big Daddy, the wealthy cotton plantation owner of Tennessee Williams's *Cat on a Hot Tin Roof* (1955), turns to alcoholism rather than follow in his father's footsteps in this intense drama.

- Aeschylus's *Orestiea*, a Greek trilogy concerning a family's heritage of malice and revenge is a fine representative of Greek tragic theater.

- Historian Edward L. Ayers's *Southern Crossing: A History of the American South, 1877-1906* (Oxford University Press, 1995), is a concise account of the daily, public, and cultural life in the South during the years from post-Reconstruction into the Progressive period, including the turn of the century portrayed by Hellman's play.

---

sacrificial, not a wedding altar. The cycle of betrayal, child murder, and revenge ends when Orestes and Electra avenge their father Agamemnon's murder through matricide.

The story of the House of Atreus and the plays of Aeschylus would have been familiar to well-educated writers like Hellman. Just a few years before Hellman began to design her Southern tragic trilogy, Eugene O'Neill reworked the last part of this myth into a New England setting. O'Neill's *Mourning Becomes Electra* (1931) is also a dramatic trilogy, and it contains a virtuous character named Lavinia, who, like the Lavinia in Hellman's *Another Part of the Forest,* helps a family avenger. Hellman apparently decided to make her affinities to Greek tragedy more clear when she wrote *Another Part of the Forest,* because she includes numerous references to Aristotle, father of literary criticism about tragedy. She also alluded to her essential departure

from Greek purism when she described the Marcus Hubbard mansion as "something too austere, too pretended Greek," in *Another Part of the Forest.*

Hellman's malovolent Hubbard family is a veritable House of Atreus when it comes to revenge and intrigue. However, in place of corporal murder of child or parent, Hellman substitutes financial and emotional "murder," a topic more in keeping with the modernist period in which she wrote. As in the Greek myth, the curse is patrilineal, coming from the line of the father. Marcus, like a depraved king, rules and dominates his Southern domain, which he has won through a relentless siege upon his neighbors' money and land. His worst sin (betraying the location of confederate troops and lying about it) is revisited upon his offspring, who vie with each other over who will prevail as the most devious backstabber. Hellman makes other adjustments to the Greek model of tragedy as well. In her modern story characters seek after power as did Greek characters, but they do so by waging economic war as predatory capitalists cheating the poor, not by conquering lands as mighty warriors battling equally mighty foes. In addition, sacrifice has evolved from a religious sacrament to an empty habit. Animals are "sacrificed" in *The Little Foxes,* not to appease the gods but for base entertainment. Birdie tells Oscar, "I don't like to see animals and birds killed just for the killing. You only throw them away." The theme of a marriage derailed also appears in Hellman's two plays, but, again, with a difference. A father (Marcus) obstructs the marriage of his daughter, but whereas Agamemnon offers his daughter to the gods, she (Regina) performs her own "sacrifice," offering herself to a man she cannot love (Horace) in order to gain access to his money.

In Hellman's play, money is a source of wealth and also a marker of power. As Hellman said, in an interview reprinted in *Conversations with Lillian Hellman:* "Money's been the subject of a great deal of literature because it . . . isn't only money, of course, it's power, it's sex; it's a great many other things." To Regina money equals mobility—with the profits from the cotton mill, she will escape the stifling Southern town to Chicago and belong to a smarter social circle, one that measures the status of its members by the clothes and jewels they wear. To her brother Oscar, money is a way to reclaim power from Ben, the older and shrewder brother who pauperized his siblings and their father in *Another Part of the Forest* using blackmail. Power is important to Oscar; he compensates for his submission to his father and Ben by bullying economically and socially stymied black people. Money in and of itself does not answer any of Ben's needs; he intends to remain a bachelor and already owns more than he spends. To Ben, money is an end in itself, and his form of depraved capitalistic dynasty-building is the ultimate target of the Marxist criticism Hellman levels in this play.

The correspondences between Hellman's Hubbard family and Greek myths about the family Atreus drift apart when the last generations are compared. Orestes and Electra are heroes who dare to put a stop to generations of revenge through their courage and perseverance. In *The Little Foxes,* Alexandra corresponds to Electra; however, Alexandra does not live up to Electra's courageous moral standards. At the end of the play, Alexandra threatens to fight the "eaters of the earth," but her threat is aimed vaguely and indirectly "some place"

instead of right here where the eaters have taken hold. Alexandra mumbles her suspicion that Regina killed Horace, but has led too sheltered a life to stand up to Regina in court, or impede her from going to Chicago, nor can she stop her uncle Ben from continuing to cheat the townspeople. Alexandra expresses Hellman's Marxist philosophy, but she lacks the vitality to achieve a revolution. Hellman said of her, in an interview in *Conversations with Lillian Hellman:* "She did have courage enough to leave, but would never have the force or vigor of her mother's family." Even more significantly, there is no corresponding Orestes figure in *The Little Foxes* to avenge Horace's death and end the cycle for good. Alexandra she has no siblings to assist her as did Electra, because Regina has not slept with Horace in 10 years. That Hellman deprives her audience of a strong avenging figure suggests a cynical attitude toward the state of affairs in the South of 1900, the year of the play's setting, an attitude one may easily extend to include the present of 1939 when the play opened, as well as the present of the 1990s. As Ben says early in the play, "Cynicism is an unpleasant way of saying the truth."

The single remaining male Hubbard heir is Leo, son of Oscar and Birdie, who combines the weaknesses of his mother and the lost Southern aristocracy (ineffectiveness in a ruthless world) with the grasping rapacity of his father and the rising class of capitalist merchants (who compromise ethics for wealth). Leo may exceed his father in evilmindedness, but he lacks the family shrewdness and vitality necessary for financial success in the New South. It appears that the family vigor, though dissipated, will not disappear, however, since Leo enjoys his "elegant worldly ladies" in Mobile, and through whoring will populate a world of Hubbards. Even without Leo's contribution, the Hubbard syndrome is already pervasive in the world portrayed by Hellman in *The Little Foxes.* Ben warns that "there are hundreds of Hubbards sitting in rooms like this throughout the country. All their names aren't Hubbard, but they are all Hubbards and they will own this country some day." The Hubbards are like an impersonal scourge on the earth that Addie compares to the locusts of the Bible, and she wonders whether one can consider oneself virtuous while ignoring their presence. She concludes: "Well, there are people who eat the earth and eat all the people on it. . . . Then there are people who stand around and watch them eat it. . . . Sometimes I think it ain't right to stand and watch them do it." The passivity Addie deplores but shares is a theme that

Hellman will return to again and again in later plays. In *The Little Foxes* a moral message quietly threads its way through the spectacle of the Hubbards' acts of deceit and revenge. In this respect Hellman's work seems more aligned with the morality play than tragedy. In a morality play, allegorical figures representing human vices such as greed and malice struggle for possession of a human soul. To the extent certain Hellman's characters are categorically evil, they fit the description of the flat, one-dimensional characters of the morality play.

The title of Hellman's play comes from the Bible, an idea consistent with a pervasive moralizing tone expressed mostly by Addie. Hellman includes in the inscription the whole passage from the Song of Solomon: "Take us the foxes, the little foxes, that spoil the vines; for our vines have tender grapes." The lines imply that if no one catches them, the little foxes will despoil the newly budded vines of precious grapes. In Hellman's play, the Hubbards are "little foxes" despoiling the lost glory of the New South in their greedy rise to power, and they are poised to rise even further on the wave of industrialization that swept over the New South in 1900. *The Little Foxes* is what one critic has called a social melodrama, a tragedy with a moral. Aristotle defined tragedy as a dramatic action that excited and then purged pity and fear, a spectacle that cleansed the audience of these emotions. But *The Little Foxes* provides no such service. It contains all of the elements of classic tragedy, but instead of a cathartic action, the play leaves the audience with a nagging sense of unfulfilled moral obligation. Critic Louis Kronenberger's 1939 review in *Stage* magazine said that the play "denies us all sense of tragedy," leaving the audience feeling "not purged, not released, but still aroused and indignant." It leaves audiences feeling sullied, fearing that they, like the latent and unprovidential heroes Horace, Addie, and Alexandra, lack the fortitude to involve themselves in stopping the plundering of the "little foxes" of the world, and can only stand idly by, being entertained by the spectacle of their rapacity. Herein lies the power of *The Little Foxes,* a play that concerns an age 100 years past and that is formatted in a dramatic structure, the tragedy, that predates Christ. This social melodrama, or whatever term one applies to it, continues to captivate audiences no longer enmeshed in the debate between Marxism and capitalism. The underlying themes of greed and revenge continue to strike a responsive chord in audiences whenever the play is revived, and its terse, witty

dialogue and tense, streamlined plot draw each new audience under its remarkable power.

Source: Carole L. Hamilton, in an essay for *Drama for Students,* Gale, 1997.

Ritchie D. Watson

In the following essay, Watson analyzes Hellman's portrayal of the South in The Little Foxes, *examining the varied critical commentary on the subject. Some critics argue that Hellman's play romanticizes the Old South, while others contend that the author offers a realistic and entirely unsentimental portrayal of the South.*

If one looks for a copy of Lillian Hellman's *The Little Foxes* in a chain or suburban mall bookstore he is not likely to find it. More often than not, however, the clerk will produce one of the author's memoirs, such as *Pentimento* or *An Unfinished Woman.* The ready availability in bookstores of what critic John Lahr describes as Hellman's "quasi autobiography" testifies to the success with which, beginning in the late 1960s, she transformed herself from a playwright into a prose writer, thus gaining in the final stage of her career "both a new public and new fame." By contrast, the relative scarcity of her plays reflects the decline of her reputation in this genre during the 1970s and 1980s. In recent years there has been a modest resurgence of interest in Hellman's plays. For example, during its 1993–94 season, the Royal National Theater in England mounted a very successful production of *The Children's Hour.* Still Lillian Hellman's reputation as a playwright in the 1990s remains markedly lower than it was in the late sixties, when she abandoned Broadway and its increasingly dismissive critics and launched into her thoroughly successful autobiographical venture.

Robert Heilman, in his analysis of *Tragedy and Melodrama on the Modern Stage,* represented a substantial body of scholarly opinion in 1973 when he observed that *The Little Foxes,* Hellman's most acclaimed and most frequently revived play, "teeter[ed] between the slick and the substantial," with the slick ultimately predominating. Elizabeth Hardwick, however, mounted the most provocative and stimulating, as well as the most damaging, critique of Hellman's plays. In a brief but powerful essay for the *New York Review of Books,* Hardwick used the occasion of the 1967 Lincoln Center revival of *The Little Foxes* for nothing less

HELLMAN WAS PROBABLY ABLE TO LOOK WITH CLEAR AND UNDISTORTED VISION AT THE SOUTH AND ITS CHERISHED MYTHS BECAUSE SHE WAS NEITHER FULLY NORTHERN NOR FULLY SOUTHERN IN HER TEMPERAMENT"

than a complete reassessment of its author's place in the hierarchy of modern American drama.

In her essay Hardwick observed that Hellman's plays exhibited "an unusual mixture of the conventions of fashionable, light, drawing room comedy and quite another convention of realism and protest." She judged this combination of conventional dramatic technique and equally modish 1930s radicalism to be awkward and unfortunate. Turning to a more specific examination of *The Little Foxes,* Hardwick argued that over the years the play had metamorphosed from a melodrama attacking the rapaciousness of capitalism into a melodrama concerned with "a besieged Agrarianism, a lost Southern agricultural life, in which virtue and sweetness had a place, and more strikingly, where social responsibility and justice could, on a personal level at least, be practiced." In Hardwick's view, a play that in the 1930s had seemed to strike a stylishly leftist pose now evoked in the 1960s a more fundamental, if subtle, nostalgia for an idealized Southern past, a past rooted ultimately in the antebellum plantation system.

Although Hardwick's observations on the conventional nature of Hellman's dramatic approach are apt and penetrating, there is good reason to question her contention that the interpretation of the South's past conveyed in *The Little Foxes* is essentially sentimental, pervaded by nostalgia for a plantation golden age. Indeed, as her research notes for the play clearly indicate, Hellman was concerned almost to the point of obsession with the factual accuracy of her dramatic portrayal of the turn-of-the-century South. She compiled over 100 pages of amazingly detailed material covering every conceivable aspect of both American and Southern

economic and social history between 1880 and 1900, with particular emphasis on the South's agricultural and economic development during these decades.

In compiling her notes Hellman drew from period descriptions and commentaries on the South, such as Julian Ralph's *Dixie or Southern Scenes and Sketches* (1896), Philip Alexander Bruce's *The Rise of the New South* (1905), and Clifton Johnson's *Highways and Byways of the South* (1913). She also culled information from more contemporary and more leftist works, such as Howard Odom's *An American Epoch* (1930), T. S. Stribling's *The Store* (1932), and Matthew Josephson's *The Robber Barons* (1934). From these sources she compiled information of a general social nature, including the observation that in the South when travelling away from home the mother "must accompany her young lady everywhere." Though this brief social observation may seem inconsequential, Hellman would put it to good dramatic use in delineating Regina Hubbard's materialistic and decidedly unsouthern-lady-like character when, at the end of Act I, she sends her daughter Alexandra unchaperoned to Baltimore to retrieve her ailing husband, despite the obvious disapproval of the black servant Addie. She also collected in her research notes remarkably precise economic data, such as the price for a dozen eggs in the South in the 1890s (10 cents); and she even found a few direct quotes in her sources, most notable Henry Frick's observation that "railroads are the Rembrandts of investments," which were apposite enough to be incorporated into the text of *The Little Foxes.*

If Lillian Hellman was, as Elizabeth Hardwick contends, partially motivated by a compulsion to romanticize the Old South in *The Little Foxes,* the playwright provides absolutely no evidence for this thesis in her research notes. What these pages of detailed observations and facts reveal is a passion for historical accuracy in her depiction of her characters and setting that suggests the saturation realism technique of fellow American writers Theodore Dreiser and Sinclair Lewis.

Turning from Hellman's research notes to the text of *The Little Foxes,* a reader finds plentiful evidence of the uncompromising realism and the sharp irony in which the author took justifiable pride. Moreover, the play's historical sensibility, viewed from the perspective of the 1990s, seems anything but antiquated, sentimental, or nostalgic. A careful reading of the opening act reveals a subtle, unsentimental, and complex understanding of the South's postbellum history well removed from the naively romantic historical vision that Hardwick claimed to have encountered in the play. Far from using *The Little Foxes* to purvey an anachronistic agrarianism, the drama's introductory act reveals a sharp understanding of the paradoxical role that the myth of the plantation South played in establishing a new commercial-industrial order below the Mason-Dixon line.

The Little Foxes opens at the Giddens's house, where Regina Giddens and her brothers, Ben and Oscar Hubbard, are entertaining Chicago plutocrat William Marshall, hoping to attract his Northern capital to establish a textile mill in their Alabama town. Oscar's wife, Birdie, excited by Marshall's interest in music, is sending a servant to bring back her album, a record of her parents' musical trips to Europe which includes a program signed by the great Wagner. Birdie is checked, however, by her husband, who scolds his wife for chattering to Marshall "like a magpie" and who observes that he can't imagine that the industrialist "came South to be bored with you." Birdie's hurt and bewildered protest that she talked to Marshall simply because "some people like music and like to talk about it" is confirmed soon after when Marshall asks again to see the Wagner autograph and insists that Birdie play the piano.

It is evident that Hellman is setting up, with considerable dramatic economy, what at first glance may seem a too-obvious contrast between her grasping Hubbards and the genteel Birdie. The Hubbards—Regina, Ben, and Oscar—are the foxes of the play's title. Rapacious and unscrupulous, they easily crush the fragile Birdie, the delicately nurtured flower of antebellum plantation society. Like Faulkner's Snopes family, they give their allegiance to no creed and serve no interest but their own. As *Another Part of the Forest* later reveals, they not only have not served, but have actively collaborated against their native region's sacred cause during the Civil War. Birdie, in contrast, reflects the breeding and cultivation that has been popularly ascribed to the Southern plantation aristocracy, a cultivation that the wealthy and sophisticated Marshall recognizes and admires.

Given this vivid contrast between Birdie, originally of Lionnet Plantation, and her pile-driving Hubbard in-laws, one may well be surprised when Marshall opines that the Hubbards represent the remarkable capacity of "Southern aristocrats" for having "kept together and kept what belonged to you." It is perhaps the remarkable social opacity which Marshall seems to betray in his observation that prompts Ben Hubbard to reply: "You misunderstand, sir. Southern aristocrats have *not* kept together and have *not* kept what belonged to them." Ben proceeds to explain in some detail the distinction between the Hubbards and the planter-aristocracy that dominated Alabama before the Civil War. Ben observes that Birdie's family, bound as it was to the land, lacked the capacity for adapting to the profound changes brought about by the Civil War. To Marshall's observation that it is difficult to learn new ways, Ben responds in a distinctly hard-bitten manner:

> You're right, Mr. Marshall. It is difficult to learn new ways. But maybe that's why it's profitable. *Our* grandfather and *our* father learned the new ways and learned how to make them pay. (Smiles) *They* were in trade. Hubbard Sons, Merchandise. Others, Birdie's family, for example, looked down on them. To make a long story short, Lionnet now belongs to *us*. Twenty years ago we took over their land, their cotton, and their daughter.

Interest in this scene falls especially on William Marshall. Not only is he willing to accord the Hubbards the status of aristocrats, he seems neither pleased nor overly interested in hearing Ben's cataloguing of the reasons his family fails to measure up to the standards of this exalted class. He ironically observes—"*a little sharply*" in Hellman's stage direction—that, in emphasizing the difference between Birdie and the Hubbards, Ben makes "great distinctions." Apparently the social differences Ben describes between the old landed aristocracy and the new commercial plutocracy are picayune and irrelevant to Marshall. Though he clearly sympathizes with Birdie, who is the agonized victim of Ben's gloating, his sensitivity to her humiliation does not lead to any doubts about the wisdom of his business association with the Hubbard clan.

A careful analysis of this scene suggests that Marshall is neither so socially opaque nor so naive as his original remark about the Hubbards being "Southern aristocrats" might have suggested. He is astute, sophisticated, and cultivated enough to recognize the difference between the delicately bred Birdie and the rather crass Hubbards; but he is obviously a man who, like his new business partners, allows himself few illusions. Responding in amusement to Ben's piously hypocritical assertion that "a man ain't only in business for what he can get out it," Marshall confesses that "however grand [Ben's] reasons are, mine are simple: I want to make money and I believe I'll make it on you." This brief speech expresses a sentiment worthy of the foxiest Hubbard.

William Marshall associates his new business partners with the old Southern aristocracy, not because he erroneously assumes that they are the real things, but because it suits his economic purpose to label them aristocrats. His impatience with Ben's detailed explanation of the rise of the postbellum Southern nouveau riche comes in part from the fact that Ben is explaining social nuances that Marshall undoubtedly has detected but that, to suit his business aims, he would rather not have articulated. As he tells the Hubbards, they need not labor to justify themselves to him: "Now you don't have to convince me that you are the right people for the deal. I wouldn't be here if you hadn't convinced me six months ago."

If Hellman's opening scene reveals anything, it reveals the irony that the trappings of the aristocratic plantation myth can be manipulated to further the most antithetical of designs. This irony acquires added depth when one realizes that it is the Northern industrialist who invests his partners with the mantle of Southern aristocrat. Yet Hellman demonstrates that the Hubbards are also quite capable of utilizing the Old South myth to advance their ambitions. Regina's Southern belle exterior gracefully masks a savage heart. Marshall's prediction that in Chicago the ladies will "bow to your manners and the gentlemen to your looks" is probably not mere flattery.

It is Ben's farewell toast to Marshall, however, which most effectively illustrates the ability of the Hubbards to use and manipulate Southern traditions with which they have essentially no temperamental identification. Ben explains to Marshall that in the South "we have a strange custom. We drink the *last* drink for a toast. That's to prove that the Southerner is always on his feet for the last drink." Ben's toast is to Southern cotton mills, which "*will be* the Rembrandts of investment," and to "the firm of Hubbard Sons and Marshall, Cotton Mills...." Only later does he confess to his brother that the Southern custom he evoked is non-existent. "I already had his signature. But we've all done business with men whose word over a glass is better than a bond. Anyway it don't hurt to have both." One imagines that the only gentlemen in this play whose word over a glass would constitute their bond are Birdie's ancestors, the vanished sires of Lionnet Plantation.

Examining the earliest manuscript version of *The Little Foxes* in which the cast of characters and the plot of the play are definitively established, one is impressed by the numerous minor revisions Hellman made in later versions of her work to heighten its suggestiveness and sharpen its focus. In the early version, for example, Ben responds to Marshall's impatient assertion that Hubbard makes "great distinctions" by countering: "Why not? They are important distinctions." Ben's reply in Hellman's final version is both more subtle and more suggestive: "Oh, they have been made for us. And maybe they are important distinctions."

A similar thickening of dramatic texture and sharpening of focus is achieved a few lines later when Birdie rises to the defense of her family against Ben's implied charge of reckless extravagance. In the early version she responds to Ben's observation that Birdie's family had "niggers to lift their fingers" by sharply interjecting: "We were good to our Negroes. Everybody knew that." In the final version she adds an additional comment: "We were good to our people. Everybody knew that. We were better to them than...." At this point Regina quickly interrupts her sister-in-law by observing, "Why, Birdie. You aren't playing." The audience should have little trouble imagining to whom Birdie was about to compare her family's benevolent treatment of their "people." Hellman's slightly revised exchange works more elliptically and more skillfully to suggest the cruelty and the intelligence of the Hubbard clan as well as Birdie's impotence in the face of their common malice.

If a reader is impressed by the thoroughness and the subtlety of Hellman's revisions of her opening act, he will be equally impressed by the firmness with which Hellman had obviously grasped her Hubbard characters from the earliest version of *The Little Foxes,* by the completeness with which she understood from the very beginning the irony of their role in linking the South's plantation past with its industrial future. In both early and final drafts Marshall has no illusions about his Southern business partners, but he is convinced that the Hubbards are the right people for his purposes. In neither early nor final draft is he interested in fine Southern social distinctions. In both versions his purpose is boldly stated: "I want to make money and I believe I'll make it on you."

In both early and final drafts, Birdie offers her plaintive wish that Lionnet be restored. In both versions Ben indulgently labels her dream a "pretty picture.'' In both, Birdie goes on to dream of a lost Eden where nobody loses his temper or is "nasty-spoken or mean." In both, the futility of her first wish is matched by the pathetic quality of her second—that her husband Oscar stop shooting "animals and hinds." And in both, Oscar brings an abrupt halt to her distracting chatter. In the early manuscript he impatiently and somewhat querulously observes: "Very well. We've all heard you. Now don't excite yourself further. You will have one of your headaches again." In the final version his sentence is shorter and more brutal. "Very well. We've all heard you. That's enough now." Birdie's fragile dreams of an idealized Old South have been casually smashed by the Hubbards, New South apostles who brush the concerns of this pathetic relic of Southern ladyhood aside so that they can snarl and squabble over the spoils of their prospective partnership with Yankee capital.

From her earliest to her final draft of *The Little Foxes* Lillian Hellman maintained a fine and subtle understanding of the profoundly ironic way that the Edenic myth of the plantation South had come to serve in the promulgation of a new and fundamentally antithetical Southern economic order. Indeed, her play can fairly claim to be prescient in its historical understanding, anticipating by more than three decades the ideas of historian Paul Gaston in *The New South Creed: A Study of Southern Mythmaking.* In his book Gaston investigates the way Southern advocates of a New South sought to tie the articles of their creed (reconciliation between sections, racial peace, and a new economic and social order founded on industry, scientific research, and modern farming methods) with the values of the old plantation South. His book makes clear that during the postbellum Southern economic revival both the mythic Old South creed and the New South creed flourished side by side and that a Northern industrialist and a native New South spokesman alike not only tolerated the romantic view of antebellum Dixie but embraced and promoted it, along with their visions of a new economic order. The explanation of this strange exercise in double-think is not as recondite as one might assume. In the words of Gaston, "the romance of the past was used to underwrite the materialism of the present."

Gaston's book examines in impressive detail the Southern paradox that C. Vann Woodward had wittily and succinctly expressed in 1951: "One of the most significant inventions of the New South was the 'Old South'." But even earlier, as the text of *The Litte Foxes* makes abundantly clear, this Old South/New South paradox had been intellectually apprehended and dramatically examined by Lillian Hellman. She understood as a playwright what historians Woodward and Gaston would also come to understand, that the vision of an orderly postbellum South dominated by a strong and enduring antebellum aristocracy provided the sort of picture of traditional social stability that appealed to the conservative temperaments of Northern businessmen like William Marshall and that encouraged the southward flow of Yankee capital to sharp and often unscrupulous Southern entrepreneurs like the Hubbards.

Hellman was probably able to look with clear and undistorted vision at the South and its cherished myths because she was neither fully Northern nor fully Southern in her temperament. As biographer William Wright has explained, her ancestors represented "a fascinating yet little known aspect of American history: the quick rise during the nineteenth century in the deep South of a number of Jewish families from immigrant poverty to mercantile power." Hellman's Marx and Newhouse relations were wealthy Southerners, but they were Southern Jews who had established their fortunes not as slave-owning planters but as merchants. As transplanted Alabamians living in New York, they combined Southern inflected manners and tastes with a ruthlessly pragmatic personal style. Hellman eventually intuited the deep discrepancy between their polished exteriors and the baldly materialistic content of their Sunday dinner conversations, "full of open ill will about who had the most money, or who spent it too lavishly, who would inherit what, which had bought what rug that would last forever, who what jewel she would best have been without" (*Unfinished Woman*). She would eventually employ this understanding of her relatives in creating the Hubbard clan, characters who achieve both a universally human dimension and a specific social identification as representatives of a new postbellum Southern class of ambitious and opportunistic nouveau riche.

But even though Hellman had no illusions about her grasping apostles of a modern industrial South, she refused to buy into the counter myth of an idyllic plantation past. Katherine Lederer is correct when she argues that there is a marked degree of ironic detachment in Hellman's characterizations which critics such as Elizabeth Hardwick have been unwilling to recognize. Rather than seeing Birdie as a nostalgic symbol of "besieged Agrarianism" Lederer describes her more accurately as "a silly, lost, pathetic woman, representative of a class that learned nothing from the Civil War, that felt that being 'good to their people' made them superior to William Faulkner's Snopeses and the Hubbards.'' Hellman's unique position as a not-quite-Southern offspring of a Deep South Jewish mercantile family made it possible for her as a dramatist to look with equal irony and dispassion on both the South's rage for progress and its infatuation with a hopelessly romanticized aristocratic past.

Lillian Hellman is guilty, as Elizabeth Hardwick persuasively argues, of her share of melodramatic contrivances of plot and hackneyed leftist postures in *The Little Foxes.* The tone with which she develops characters such as Alexandra and Horace Giddens seems uncertain and unresolved. But Hellman's play also demonstrates considerable dramatic strength and toughness of spirit. There is no reason for burdening it with the charge of historical sentimentality. Far from being intellectually naive, *The Little Foxes* conveys, among other insights, an astute understanding of the way the moonlight-and-magnolia vision of a dead Southern past was used in postbellum Dixie to validate a fundamentally restructured but equally sterile Southern present.

Source: Ritchie D. Watson, Jr., ''Lillian Hellman's *The Little Foxes* and the New South Creed: An Ironic View of Southern History'' in the *Southern Literary Journal,* Vol. XXVIII, no. 2, Spring, 1996, pp. 59–68.

Brooks Atkinson

In the following excerpt from his review of The Little Foxes, *Atkinson calls the play ''a deliberate exercise in malice,'' and asserts that ''Miss Hellman has made an adult horror-play. Her little foxes are wolves that eat their own kind.''*

As drama critic for the New York Times *from 1925 to 1960, Atkinson was one of the most influential reviewers in America.*

As a theatrical story-teller Lillian Hellman is biting and expert. In *The Little Foxes,* which was acted at the National last evening, she thrusts a bitter story straight to the bottom of a bitter play. As compared with *The Children's Hour,* which was her first notable play, *The Little Foxes* will have to take second rank. For it is a deliberate exercise in malice—melodramatic rather than tragic, none too fastidious in its manipulation of the stage and presided over by a Pinero frown of fustian morality. But out of greed in a malignant Southern family of 1900 she has put together a vibrant play that works and that bestows viable parts on all the members of the cast. None of the new plays in which Tallulah

> *THE LITTLE FOXES IS SO CLEVERLY CONTRIVED THAT IT LACKS SPONTANEITY. IT IS EASIER TO ACCEPT AS AN ADROITLY DESIGNED THEATRE PIECE THAN AS A DOCUMENT IN THE STUDY OF HUMANITY''*

Bankhead has acted here has given her such sturdy support and such inflammable material. Under Herman Shumlin's taut direction Miss Bankhead plays with great directness and force, and Patricia Collinge also distinguishes herself with a remarkable performance. *The Little Foxes* can act and is acted.

It would be difficult to find a more malignant gang of petty robber barons than Miss Hellman's chief characters. Two brothers and a sister in a small Southern town are consumed with a passion to exploit the earth. Forming a partnership with a Chicago capitalist, they propose to build a cotton factory in the South, where costs are cheap and profits high. The Chicago end of the deal is sound. But Miss Hellman is telling a sordid story of how the brothers and the sister destroy each other with their avarice and cold hatred. They crush the opposition set up by a brother-in-law of higher principles; they rob him and hasten his death. But they also outwit each other in sharp dealing and they bargain their mean souls away.

It is an inhuman tale. Miss Hellman takes a dextrous playwright's advantage of the abominations it contains. Her first act is a masterpiece of skillful exposition. Under the gentility of a social occasion she suggests with admirable reticence the evil of her conspirators. When she lets loose in the other two acts she writes with melodramatic abandon, plotting torture, death and thievery like the author of an old-time thriller. She has made her drama air-tight; it is a knowing job of construction, deliberate and self-contained. In the end she tosses in a speech of social significance, which is no doubt sincere. But *The Little Foxes* is so cleverly contrived that it lacks spontaneity. It is easier to accept as an adroitly designed theatre piece than as a document in the study of humanity. . . .

As for the title, it comes from the Bible: "Take us the foxes, the little foxes, that spoil the vines; for our vines have tender grapes." Out of rapacity, Miss Hellman has made an adult horror-play. Her little foxes are wolves that eat their own kind.

Source: Brooks Atkinson, in a review of *The Little Foxes* in the *New York Times*, February 16, 1939, p. 16.

FURTHER READING

Adler, Jacob. *Lillian Hellman*, Steck-Vaughn, 1969.
    A biographic monograph that contains the first detailed analysis of Hellman's plays. Adler praises Hellman as an important American follower of the Ibsenite tradition.

Bills, Steven. *Lillian Hellman: An Annotated Bibliography*, Garland, 1979.
    One of three annotated bibliographies of Hellman's work.

DISCovering Authors, Gale, 1995.
    A cd-rom reference source containing an overview of Hellman's works and career.

Estrin, Mark W. *Lillian Hellman: Plays, Films, Memoirs*, G. K. Hall & Co., 1980.
    Estrin's annotated bibliography is the most recent and the most complete one available.

French, Warren. *The Thirties: Fiction, Poetry, Drama*, Everett/Edwards, 1969.
    A scholarly work that analyzes the key contributions in three genres produced by American writers in the 1930s.

Goodman, Charlotte. "The Fox's Cubs: Lillian Hellman, Arthur Miller, and Tennessee Williams," in *Modern American Drama: The Female Canon*, Fairleigh Dickinson University Press, 1990.
    Makes a strong case that Hellman's *The Children's Hour* and *The Little Foxes* influenced Miller and Williams, who were coming of age in the 1930s when those plays came out.

Kronenberger, Louis. "Greed," in *Stage*, April 1, 1939, pp. 36-37, 55.
    A positive review typical of those that greeted the triumphant opening of *The Little Foxes* on Broadway.

Lederer, Katherine. *Lillian Hellman*, Twayne, 1979.
    An early study of Hellman's life, completed before her death in 1984.

MacNicholas, Carol. "Lillian Hellman," in *Dictionary of Literary Biography*, Volume 7: *Twentieth-Century Dramatists*, edited by John MacNicholas, Gale, 1981, pp. 276- 94.
    A biographical entry with summaries and critical analyses of Hellman's plays.

Riordan, Mary Marguerite. *Lillian Hellman, A Bibliography: 1926-1978*, Scarecrow Press, 1980.
    An annotated bibliography.

Rollyson, Carl. *Lillian Hellman: Her Legend and Her Legacy*, St. Martin's Press, 1988.
    Rollyson's unauthorized biography traces links between Hellman's plays and her life, some of which had not been noted by earlier critics. Reports the finding that Hellman had been a member of the Communist party, a fact she denied throughout her life.

Turk, Ruth. *Lillian Hellman: Rebel Playwright*, Lerner, 1995, 128 p.
    A biography written for the young adult reader. Contains photographs.

SOURCES

Bryer, Jackson R. *Conversations with Lillian Hellman*, University Press of Mississippi, 1986.

Estrin, Mark W. *Critical Essays on Lillian Hellman*, G. K. Hall & Co., 1989.

Hardwick, Elizabeth. "The *Little Foxes* Revived," *New York Review of Books*, December 21, 1967, pp. 4-5.

Life, March 6, 1939.

Time, February 27, 1939, pp. 33, 38.

Wright, William. *Lillian Hellman: The Image, the Woman*, Simon and Schuster, 1986.

Medea

EURIPIDES
431, B.C.

Euripides's *Medea* (431 B.C.) adds a note of horror to the myth of Jason and Medea. In the myth, after retrieving the golden fleece Jason brings his foreign wife to settle in Corinth. There Jason falls in love with the local princess, whose status in the city will bring Jason financial security. He marries her without telling Medea. Medea takes revenge by killing the new bride and her father, the King of Corinth. One variation of the myth says that Medea then accidentally kills her two sons by Jason while trying to make them immortal. Euripides takes the myth into a new direction by having Medea purposely stab her children to death in order to deprive Jason of all he loved (as well as heirs that would carry on his name). In one of literature's most intensely emotional scenes, Medea debates with herself whether to spare her children for her own love's sake or to kill them in order to punish her husband completely. A chorus of Corinthian women sympathize with Medea but attempt to dissuade her from acting on her anger. However, her need for revenge overpowers her love for her children, and she ruthlessly kills them. Euripides introduced psychological realism into ancient Greek drama through characters like Medea, whose motives are confused, complex, and ultimately driven by passion. Although the tetralogy that included this play did not earn Euripides the coveted prize at the Dionysus festival in which it debuted, *Medea* has withstood the test of time to become one of the great tragedies of classical Greece.

AUTHOR BIOGRAPHY

Although historians can only piece together the biography of a man who lived before detailed biographical information was reliably recorded, certain "facts" about Euripides's life are generally accepted. Euripides was born around 480 B.C. to parents who were presumably affluent, considering that the playwright obtained a good education and owned a library of philosophical works. Euripides knew the philosopher Anaxagoras, entertained the Sophist Protagoras in his home, and could count on the philosopher Socrates attending his plays. Although no evidence exists that Euripides conversed with Socrates, the latter's influence is apparent in the playwright's skepticism. Euripides's life was deeply affected by the Peloponnesian Wars, which ultimately ended the Golden Age of Athens; the scars of a life plagued by war are evident in the mood of pessimism and uncertainty that permeates his works of tragedy. Euripides's characters have more psychological depth than those found in the works of his dramatic predecessors, Aeschylus and Sophocles. Euripides broke with traditional theater and chose to examine the motivations of realistic humans instead of the acts of gods, heroes, and stock characters. He championed the underdog and challenged traditions through his radical ideas regarding the gods and society. Some called him an atheist, but he did not reject religion-he merely identified and denounced its shortcomings.

In all, there are references to ninety-two plays by Euripides; of these, only nineteen are known to have survived the centuries. Most of these plays were more than likely altered as a result of the common practice of oral storytelling, in which tales were verbally passed from town to town, generation to generation. It was not until a century after their author created them that most of these works were actually written down. After his death, Euripides's plays enjoyed more popularity than they had during his lifetime. One measure of his renown is that Aristophanes wrote three plays that lampoon Euripides. In the *Frogs,* Euripides is portrayed as a radical who taught the Athenians to "think, see, understand, suspect, question, everything," according to Edith Hamilton in her book *The Greek Way.* In his later years Euripides withdrew from public society and spent most of his time in a cave, working on his plays. The Peloponnesian Wars, in their final throes, were destroying the city and society which he so loved; Athens was collapsing. Finally, at age seventy Euripides left Athens for

A bust of Euripides

Macedonia, to help that city's king establish a cultural center to rival Athens. He died there in 406 B.C.

PLOT SUMMARY

Euripides's play takes place in Corinth, where Jason had settled with his Colchian wife Medea after his adventure in pursuit of the Golden Fleece (in Greek mythology, a rare garment made from the wool of a magical flying ram). The scene opens with a prologue spoken by Medea's nurse. She summarizes what has led to her lady's current state of grief and rage: her husband Jason has married the daughter of the local king, Creon. The nurse recounts how Medea aided Jason in his exploits, even killing her own brother to help Jason escape. The nurse knows the many moods that Medea is capable of and fears that her rage may settle on her two children by Jason. When the attendant appears with the boys, the nurse warns him to keep them away from their angry mother.

Next is heard Medea herself chanting a savage curse at her husband, the children, and the whole family. The chorus of Corinthian women interpose

Legendary actress Sarah Bernhardt as Medea

comments of sympathy for the "sad wife" with Medea's anguished cries and the nurse's fearful warnings. Finally, Medea herself appears to plead for empathy from the chorus in a long monologue. At its end, Creon enters with more bad news for Medea: because he fears Medea may harm his daughter, the new wife of Jason, he banishes her from the land of Corinth. Medea hypocritically assures him she would not do such a thing and in an extended duet of dialogue (or duologue), begs for just one day to find living arrangements for her sons. Won over, Creon grants her wish, but threatens to kill her if she does not depart the next day.

Now Medea considers how to obtain revenge upon Jason, for she abhors the thought of being a laughing-stock in her loss. The chorus encourages her. Next Jason encounters Medea, with words seemingly calculated to offend her. She reminds him that she saved his life, slew a dragon, left her father's home and killed her brother Pelias, all for the love of him. Jason plays the sophist ("as for me, it seems I must be no bad speaker"), arguing petty points against her valid complaint. His suggestion that he is marrying the princess so that Medea and her children may live in comfort incenses the chorus so much that they defy discretion and accuse Jason

of sinning. To appease Medea, Jason merely offers her money; he refuses to help Medea convince Creon to let her stay. Medea scornfully dismisses Jason. The chorus judiciously comments upon the need to moderate passion, thus for the first time indirectly finding fault with both parties. The chorus ends, however, on a note of sympathy for Medea.

The next scene offers another perspective on Medea and underscores the importance of children to a royal family. The ruler of a neighboring city, Aegeus, confides to Medea that he has just visited the oracle to learn how he might reverse his childless life. In a marked shift of mood, Medea calmly and professionally offers advice and promises to cast a potent spell to help him, asking only for asylum in return. Upon learning of her distress, Aegeus offers her sanctuary in his city with the caveat that she must find her own passage there as he does not want to incur the anger of his allies, Creon and Jason.

With a means of escape well in hand, Medea unveils her evil plan for revenge. Not only will she kill princess Creusa and her father Creon, but she will slay her own children, in order to destroy Jason's life completely—because she cannot abide the thought of being mocked for her downfall, and because she knows that the Corinthians will kill the children anyway, in retaliation for her murder of Creusa and Creon. The chorus tries to dissuade her from including the children in her murderous rampage, for her own safety and for the sake of respecting the law. When Medea remains unmoved, the chorus warns her that no city would pollute itself with her presence. Thus is introduced the theme of pollution, a concern that underlies the whole play. Jason returns at Medea's bidding. She shrewdly begs his pardon for her angry words and shares with him her "plan" to ply Creusa with gifts and then request that they be allowed to remain in Corinth. Jason blesses his two children with the wish for long life, bringing unexpected tears to Medea who masks her real reason for sadness with the explanation that she will miss them when she goes.

Thoroughly appeased, Jason departs with the sons and their attendant to deliver Medea's gifts, a robe of gold and a diadem (crown) of gold. The chorus laments the forthcoming death of the young bride and realizes that the two children are doomed as well.

The attendant returns with the simple news that the gifts have been delivered. He is surprised by Medea's tears at this announcement. The appearance of the children causes Medea to dispute her resolve, but she is overcome by her desire for revenge and bids the children leave her. The chorus acclaims that it would be better never to have children at all than suffer the grief of losing them. A messenger rushes in, warning Medea to flee. He recounts in gruesome detail how the princess, at first irritated by the presence of Medea's children, gleefully dons the robe and crown which almost instantly begin to eat her flesh. Embracing her, Creon becomes entangled in the trap and they die together. The chorus, still in league with Medea against Jason, laments that Medea has '' gone away to the house of Hades'' as the price of her marriage to Jason.

The children's screams are now heard, as they fruitlessly seek to escape their murderous mother. The chorus now accuses Medea of having a heart of stone. Jason rushes in to save his children from Medea, but the chorus informs him that he is too late. In the final scene Jason and Medea hurl stinging reproaches at each other. Jason reminds her that she too suffers from her crime, but Medea still claims that vengeance was worth the pain. In a final act of insult, she carries the children's dead bodies away on her chariot drawn by dragons, refusing Jason even one last touch of their skin. The chorus quickly closes the play with the warning that one never knows how things will turn out.

CHARACTERS

Aegeus, King of Athens

Aegeus, with his dilemma of childlessness, reinforces the importance of children (heirs) to royal leaders, making doubly hurtful Jason's loss. Aegeus follows the conventional means of solving his problem—consulting an oracle for advice. Aegeus is obviously a kind man. He recognizes that Medea is downcast and asks tactful questions; then gives her his complete sympathy. His accepting attitude toward Medea and his offer to give her shelter in his city elevate her in the eyes of the audience. His refusal to help her travel to Athens because it would offend his allies shows that he is a careful leader—it also reinforces the danger of Medea's situation.

Children's Attendant

The attendant discourses with the nurse in the opening scene to further reveal the nature of Jason's

break with his wife. The attendant also displays the cynical attitude for which Euripides was known—rebuking the nurse that every man cares for himself first and for others when it profits himself, only rarely from honest motives.

Chorus of Corinthian Women

The chorus of Corinthian women at first shows a great deal of sympathy for Medea, who is rejected by her heroic husband for the young princess of Corinth. But at the same time, the chorus honors the laws of its city and therefore tries to persuade Medea to control her anger. Occasionally the leader of the chorus interacts with the players, as when the leader criticizes Jason, telling him that he has in fact sinned against his wife. When Medea seems at last determined to kill her children, the chorus pleads with her, suggesting that she will not be able to look upon their faces and do the deed. Thus the chorus represents a more moderate kind of woman than Medea—these women of Corinth show anger at Jason's betrayal but advise control in the retaliation; they even express pity for Jason's downfall. The chorus insists that all women are capable of wisdom. They serve as an antidote to the devastating events of the play, reminding the audience of the broader concepts being enacted. The final lines of the chorus fall short of the intensity of its other songs, however, saying something to the effect of, ''what will be, will be.'' Their explanations ultimately leave the audience unable to transcend the horror of the final scene.

Creon

Creon is King of Corinth and father to Creusa, whose marriage to Jason so infuriates Medea. Creon is well aware of Medea's bloody reputation; fearing that Medea might, in her rage, harm Creusa, he bans the rejected woman. A soft heart causes the King to allow Medea into the city for one day. His love for his daughter brings about his own death. Creon is portrayed as a weak, indecisive man whom Medea easily persuades to allow her another day in Corinth—a day that proves fatal to Creon. He is also ambivalent at his daughter's corpse, first saying he wants to die with her, yet when her poisoned garment ensnares him, he struggles to escape.

Jason

Jason, the Argonaut who retrieved the golden fleece, was a well-known character to Athenian audiences and a significant hero in Greek mytholo-gy. However, Euripides's portrayal casts him in a

MEDIA ADAPTATIONS

- Medea's anguished story has been transformed into film, music, opera, art, poetry, prose, and drama. In the early years of the first century A.D., the Spanish Roman, Seneca, wrote a melodramatic version of *Medea* that portrays Medea as a witch and Jason as being relatively innocent of causing her anger. Ianni Xenakis, a Greek born in Rumania, wrote music for Seneca's version of *Medea* in 1967.

- In 1946, French playwright Jean Anouilh adapted the play to serve as an analogy for modern life. American poet Robinson Jeffers produced a singular Broadway stage production of *Medea*, a work that Jeffers loosely adapted from Euripides's play and that bears Jeffers's trademark stamp of nihilism and destructive passion. A sound recording is available on Decca Records. Maxwell Anderson, an American contemporary of Jeffers, placed the story in the contemporary United States and named his piece *The Wingless Victory*.

- A 1959 film version was directed by Jose Quintero and starred Colleen Dewhurst and Zoe Caldwell.

- A 1971 Italian film version of the play stars opera diva Maria Callas in her only screen appearance. The adaptation by late eighteenth-century composer Luigi Cherubini follows the basic structure of the Euripidean plot line.

- A one-act musical interpretation called *Medea in Corinth* was written by Benjamin Lees in 1985 and is available through Boosey and Hawkes.

- A Kabuki Japanese version was produced in 1984 by Shoca Sato, with traditional Kabuki music and costume and called *Kabuki Medea* (available on Illinois Video).

- An African version of *Medea* was created in 1968 by J. Magnuson.

- Samuel Barber wrote ballet music for *Medea* in 1949. A different ballet version of the play was produced in the Soviet Union in 1979 and videotaped; it is available from Kultur Video Distributors.

- John Gardner, whose other classical adaptation, *Grendel,* is better known, also adapted the story of Jason and Medea into a long (354 pages) epic poem, *Jason and Medeia*; his version contains a modernistic twist on Euripides's theme. Countee Cullen's translation of ''The Medea'' can be found in his collection, *The Medea and Some Poems.*

rather negative light. Medea catches him lying when he tells her he is marrying Creusa simply to increase their fortune, and he never accepts responsibility for his new love alliance. Medea has a valid complaint, yet Jason attributes her anger to a ''stubborn temper'' and blames her banishment on her inability to submit to Creon's will. Jason is made even less sympathetic when he minimizes Medea's role in helping him obtain the golden fleece (a feat that involved killing her own brother so that Jason could escape) and suggesting that Medea is merely jealous and not legitimately hurt. Jason almost deserves the punishment Medea serves him.

Medea

Courageous, powerful, and reckless, Medea left her father's home without his blessing to accompany Jason to the land of Corinth, after using her magic powers to slay the dragon that guarded the golden fleece. She also killed her own brother to slow Jason's pursuers. A foreigner to Corinth, Medea nevertheless found favor with the Corinthians and all of Hellas because of her cleverness. For a while she and Jason were in harmony and her life with him and their two sons was blissful. However, when Jason takes as wife the daughter of Creon, king of Corinth, Medea is both grief-stricken at her loss and rage-filled at Jason's betrayal. As her nurse explains during the prologue, ''she'll not stop raging until she has struck at someone'' and the fact that Medea now says she hates the sight of her own children by Jason leads the nurse to fear for them.

Alone in a foreign land, rejected by her beloved husband, and unable to return to her homeland, Medea goes mad, going to great extremes in exacting her revenge for Jason's infidelity. When faced with their presence, Medea spends a few moments debating the wisdom of murdering those she loves, yet her desire for revenge fully outweighs her mother's heart. Even after she has accomplished the deed her rage outstrips her better nature, for she will not allow Jason to bury or even kiss the children farewell. She claims that the price she has paid is worth the harm she has caused Jason.

In his book *The Poetry of Greek Tragedy,* Richard Lattimore speculated on Medea's motives for murdering her own children: ''We are given, not one compelling motive but a whole assortment of motives. She kills them because she hates them, because she loves them, to spite and hurt Jason, to leave him without posterity, to vindicate the rights and prestige of herself and her country, to save them from the Corintihians who, she supposes, would kill them if she did not. In the end she does not know why she kills them and neither do we.''

Messenger

The messenger has only one scene to act—he delivers to Medea the news that her gifts smeared with poison have had their desired effect on Creusa and Creon. His is a storytelling role and he is given gruesome details to spin out to Medea's delight.

Nurse

The Nurse opens the play with her prologue, reciting Medea's reasons for rage and grief and generally providing a sympathetic first appraisal of her mistress. She also warns of Medea's ''wildness and bitter nature,'' saying that she fears some harm will come to the children Medea now claims to hate. The nurse herself demonstrates more resolve; she catches herself cursing Jason and stops herself because he is still her master. The implication is that Medea cannot so successfully contain her anger, both because the harm is hers and because of her savage nature.

Sons of Medea and Jason

Medea and Jason's two sons participate in only four scenes, but the entire action of the play revolves around their victimhood. They appear initially with their attendant, immediately drawing audience sympathy, and are sent inside by the nurse to protect them from their raging mother. When they innocently bear Medea's gifts to Creusa, they garner even more audience sympathy because she at first becomes irritated at the sight of them. Later their sweet smiles cause Medea to pause in her resolve to kill them. Their pitiful screams as she pursues and then slays them are finally heard offstage.

THEMES

Revenge

In Euripides's *Medea,* revenge—its necessity, its causes, and its price—is the central to the drama. Euripides makes Medea's desire for revenge plausible. Not only has her husband Jason wronged her by marrying the king of Corinth's beautiful young daughter, but the king of Corinth has banished her from the city to prevent her from avenging herself on his daughter. Medea can no longer return to her father's home because she left without his blessing upon her marriage to Jason. Thus she is unlawfully abandoned, emotionally wounded, and legitimately outraged. She bridles at the idea that she might be the laughing-stock of Corinth. Even when Aegeus offers her a secure future in Athens, Medea remains unsolaced—she now only seeks revenge.

The chorus of Corinthian women legitimize her outrage, sympathizing with her grief as well as her desire for revenge. But Medea takes revenge that goes far beyond the conventionally accepted forms of retribution. Euripides altered the traditional myth to include Medea murdering her own children to avenge her errant husband. Her act represents a form of revenge that is shocking to today's audiences. The excess of her revenge can be measured by the reaction of the Chorus: the women of Corinth exhibit no surprise that Medea might want to kill Jason's new bride, nor do they try to dissuade Medea from murdering the king of their city simply because it was his daughter whom Jason loved; but the idea of killing her own children alarms these women. They ask Medea how she will be able to look upon her own children and murder them simply to hurt Jason. When Medea commits her horrendous crime the chorus withdraws its alliance. The

TOPICS FOR FURTHER STUDY

- What kind of revenge would the Chorus of Corinthian woman have approved? Why do they object to Medea's revenge?

- It has been said that the first song of the chorus could well be a feminist's theme song. How so?

- What effect might the Peloponnesian War have had on Euripides's writing, and why?

- How does Medea's reaction to being rejected by her husband for another woman compare with similar contemporary situations? What are some of the ways spouses exact revenge upon each other for marital indiscretions? What is the impact of these actions and how do they compare to the impact of Medea's revenge?

women of Corinth also recognize that this act will hurt not just her erring husband Jason but, in a much deeper way, hurt Medea herself. Jason too recognizes her self-inflicted pain and demands that she acknowledge her error. In a final, shocking outburst of hatred, Medea retorts that her pain is worth the price of avenging herself upon him. Medea's revenge is excessive, perverse, and nihilistically potent.

Passion

In a way, the theme of passion that overcomes one's better sense lies behind the theme of revenge in Euripides's provocative play. The ancient Greeks considered passion dangerous, and the chorus expresses this in the song that follows Medea scornful rejection of Jason's offer of money. The chorus sings that love in excess brings neither glory nor repute, though love in moderation is blissful. Medea's problem is that she loved Jason so much that she left behind her homeland and family—and even killed her brother to slow their pursuers. Medea loved not in moderation but in excess.

Then, when Jason removed himself from her love, her passion turned to anger and since hate is the nearest thing to passionate love, she also hated in excess. It is as though Medea goes mad with the urgent need to punish her husband for his betrayal. The nurse suggests that Medea enrages herself, goading herself to greater heights of fury. In a state of self-aggravated wrath, Medea is immune to the warnings of the chorus of Corinthian women who, although sympathizing with her, warn her not to break the law. But the law is meaningless to Medea;

she tells the chorus that its words are wasted. For it is Medea's tragic flaw to succumb to her own fury, a passion that imprisons her better self, and to goad herself into a heedless frenzy of anger that brings her to the point of murdering her own children.

From the very beginning, the nurse warns that Medea is not to be trifled with, that "she'll not stop raging until she has struck at someone." It had been Medea's reckless heart that drove her to leave her father's home to take up with Jason. And yet, in the exchange with Aegeus Medea behaves perfectly rationally. Smoldering with rage within, she is capable of convincing Creon to allow her to stay another day and of charming Jason into taking her gifts to Creusa. These moments complicate the question whether Medea could have controlled her passion enough to spare her children. Typically of Euripides, he leaves the question unanswered.

Euripides fabricated the murder of the two children—in variations of the myth they are either killed by accident or not involved at all. Euripides's invention pushes Medea's need for vengeance beyond the bounds of normalcy, thus underscoring that destructive passion reigns in her heart.

STYLE

Chorus

Taking his cue from Sophocles, who demoted the chorus from primary character status to that of a speaking spectator, Euripides reduced this dramatic device even further. In *Medea* the chorus appears less often than it would have in Sophocles or Aeschylus's plays; its time on stage is limited to mere moments between scenes. At the same time, the acting characters now have chanting parts (a move that eventually led to the development of opera)—further eroding the unique contribution of the chorus. Euripides also reduced the interaction between chorus and characters. Euripides's reduced use of the chorus ultimately led it is eventual disappearance from ancient Greek theater.

In its modified role, Euripides's chorus of Corinthian women is a kind of precursor to the modern theater's narrator (such as the one employed in Thornton Wilder's *Our Town*). The chours in *Medea* goads the consciences of the audience while it sympathizes with, pleads to, and chides Medea. The chorus follows a clear progression of observations that influence and validate the reactions of the audience. At first the women completely sympathize with Medea as an honest woman wounded by an errant husband, and they concur with her desire for revenge (''You are right, Medea, in paying your husband back.''). In fact, D. J. Conacher, in his *Euripidean Drama: Myth, Theme, and Structure,* has called the first choral stanza (lines 410-445) a virtual theme ''song for feminists.'' The chorus even goes so far as to accuse Jason of sinning in his betrayal of Medea. The women shift their attitude, however, as soon as they learn that Medea intends to murder her own children. As the play progresses, the chorus moves from sympathy to horror, interacting less with the characters and turning to address the gods of nature and, late in the play, the audience. The chorus does not simply condemn Medea, however. It complicates a too-easy judgement of Medea by showing pity for her throughout the play. When Medea puts her plan into action, the chorus expresses pity for the children, Creusa, Jason, and Medea in turn—in order, apparently, from innocence to guilt. In this crime, all parties deserve pity, even the perpetrator, because the perpetrator had a reasonable cause for anger. The chorus' list blurs Medea's liability by including her as one deserving compassion.

The Euripidean chorus also reminds the audience of the larger issues involved in the action of the play. It evokes the concept of pollution, warning Medea that no city will want to be polluted by her presence if she should commit the deed she threatens. Here the purpose of the chours is to place Medea's deed into the larger context of society, to suggest the greater implications of her personal crime. The Euripidean chorus frequently reminds the audience of ideal values, such as in the second choral stanza when it expounds on the virtues of moderate love and fidelity and proclaims the misery of the loss of fatherland to elicit sympathy for Medea. In *Medea,* as in most of Euripides's work, the chorus chants poetic asides on the themes raised by the action. This was the typical role of the chorus—to express the ultimate emotion or beauty of even the most painful event, ''to translate the particular act into something universal,'' as Gilbert Murray noted in *Euripides and His Age.* The action of the play consists of the here and now, while the choral odes consists of the eternal. However, some Euripidiean choral odes, including those in *Medea,* seem only slightly connected with the events of the play, and it was this innovation that led to the elimination of the chorus altogether. The final lines of the chorus, something on the order of ''whatever happens, happens,'' are so far removed from the actions that have just unfolded that they do nothing to dispel the uneasiness the final scene elicits. The same stock ending appears in three other Euripidean plays that have survived. The effect is a rather abrupt return to reality.

Deus ex Machina

In the final scene, Medea rides off with the corpses of her murdered sons in a chariot pulled by dragons. On the ancient Greek stage, this stage effect would have been accomplished by means of a large crane that would permit the contraption to ''fly.'' The ''deus ex machina,'' literally ''god from a machine,'' was a common closing device in ancient Greek theater. Normally, a god would descend from the heavens to bring the action to a close and ordain the ritual the play celebrates. In *Medea,* no god appears, although the chariot has been supplied by Medea's grandfather, the sun god, thus weakening considerably the invocation of the gods. Perhaps this slight derives from Euripides's skepticism about religious rituals. In any event, the scene is glaringly inconsistent with the realism of the rest of the play. But considering that Medea is now guilty of multiple murders, it seems one of a very few possible means of escape available to her.

Prologue and Duologue

The prologue precedes the action of the play. Before Euripides's time, the prologue was spoken, chanted, or sung by a chorus, but it had evolved into a presentation by the actors by the time he began writing dramas. Euripides's plays often begins with a single actor who addresses the audience directly, explaining the background of the story to be told (even though his Athenian audience would already be quite familiar with the myth upon which the play would, by convention, be based). *Medea* opens with a monologue by the nurse, who recounts the cause of Medea's grief. The nurse is joined by the attendant, and together, in *duologue* (a dialogue among two actors) they discuss the implications and extent of Medea's rage, foreshadowing the murder and mayhem that will come. The duologue between Jason and Medea is called the *agon,* an intense argument between powerful antagonists.

HISTORICAL CONTEXT

The End of the Golden Age of Athens

The year Euripides produced *Medea,* the devastating Peloponnesian War (431-404 B. C.) began. The tensions which precipitated this conflict between Athens and its neighbors on the Peloponnesian peninsula, primarily the cities of Sparta and Corinth certainly existed before the first recorded battle and possibly led Euripides to set his play in Corinth. Thucydides (c.460-400 B.C.) claims that the true cause of the war was Athen's rise to greatness, which made Spartans fearful. However, trade rivalry with Corinth may also have fueled the conflict. At any rate the Peloponnesian War was to last the next thirty years, with great losses suffered by both winners and losers. Ultimately, after a victory at Aegospotami, Sparta forced Athens—decimated in money and ships, emotionally enervated, and without allies—to submit to its terms. The Golden Age of Athens had come to an end. Herodotus (480-425 B.C.), writing during the early years of the war, hints that Athens had become a tyrant city, and Thucydides records its further corruption as the war progressed. Euripides's life spanned the peaceful years before the Peloponnesian War through the imminent end, although he died before Athens's final defeat. By the time of his death, Euripides had fled his beloved city to take refuge in calmer Macedonia. The sense of uncertainty and adversity that pervade Euripidean tragedy stem at least partially from the anguished, extended demise of the greatness that was Athens.

Women and Marriage in Ancient Greek Culture

Medea's complaint that Jason married another might have carried less weight had Jason followed the conventional method of divorce in Athens. Although women could only under exceptional conditions obtain a divorce, any Athenian man could rid himself of a wife simply by publicly renouncing his marriage. Marriages were arranged by the parents with no input from the daughter; thus Medea's flight with Jason was scandalous impertinence. The daughter came with a dowry, a substantial one if the family was wealthy. Once married, the woman served her husband by caring for the children and slaves, who legally belonged to her husband. *Medea* accurately describes the conditions of married life for women in lines 231-251. Athenian women never experienced independence during their lives. They received no education, lived in separate quarters from their husbands, and seldom went out. The ideal woman was "spoken of as little as possible among men, whether for good or for ill" according to the historian Thucydides (c. 460-400 B.C.). Athenian law forbade Athenian men to marry any but Athenian women, but it was not uncommon for Athenian men to keep foreign concubines, who often had more education than their Athenian rivals. However, the children of these unions were not official citizens of Athens, just as the children of Jason and Medea would not be official citizens of Corinth, while Creusa's offspring by Jason would enjoy the full benefits of Corinthian citizenship.

Greek Theater

Greek theater evolved from rituals in honor of Dionysus. Three playwrights would each present three tragedies and one satyr play that burlesqued one of the tragedies. To be invited to produce a tetralogy was a significant honor; to win the coveted prize of the festival was a cherished one. Although the dramas belonged to a religious festival, the audience was by no means solemn. In Euripides's time, Dionysus was still carried into the theater in procession and was revered as the god of wine, who inspires music and poetry. It was his festival, conducted in March over a three-day period, that hosted the competition in which *Medea* was performed, the first play of the conventional tetralogy.

Euripides's other two tragedies and satyr play have been lost. His tetralogy containing *Medea* placed last in the competition.

COMPARE
&
CONTRAST

- **5th century B.C.:** In Greece, humans are considered part of the vast web of life; what was important about any individual is the way in which he or she is like all others and connected to them through society. Thus art, philosophy, and religion sought to explain and represent the whole order of things and not the individual within that order, with fate ultimately in control of human events.

  Today: Humans are seen as unique individuals and contemporary art, philosophy, and religion conform to a world view in which the individual is central—and responsible.

- **5th century B.C.:** Women in Ancient Greece essentially lived in a separate society from their husbands and fathers, and they held few rights. Women kept quarters and ate apart from men; they seldom went out and never walked in public without a male escort. They did not own property or money, did not choose their own husbands, did not receive an education, and could only terminate a marriage under extreme conditions.

  Today: Women have equal rights to men and, in most fields, equal opportunities in the workplace.

- **5th century B.C.:** Thousands of Greek city-states (*polis* in Greek) practiced a wide range of different governing systems during this period of fertile political experimentation. In Athens, a form of radical democracy promised equality

among Athenian citizens (meaning adult males born of two Athenian parents); these citizens participated freely in the governing of the city and ardently defended the city's political system. The philosopher Aristotle called Athenian democracy "a common life for a noble end."

  Today: the very different form of democracy that exists today in many developed nations has little in common with Athenian democracy, for the simple reason that modern democracies serve larger and more diverse populations and extend their ideals to all.

- **5th century B.C.:** Greek tragic theater was produced in March for the ritual celebration of Dionysus, the god of wine. Everyone in the city attended the festival and the overall mood was festive—but also serious—this was a religious festival and the outcome of the competition was a matter of civic pride. It took place in the heart of the city at the altar of Dionysus and was at the center of Greek culture as well.

  Today: The Modern theater no longer has ties to religion, although dramas for religious rituals are produced in some organized religions for important holidays. In the public theater, the sense of solemn ritual as experienced by the Athenians has no counterpart today. Theater is a form of entertainment and diversion that holds a rather peripheral status in today's societies.

The center of the theater, or orchestra (literally, "dancing-place") in which Euripides's plays were produced consisted of a circle sixty feet in diameter, with an altar to Dionysus at its center. On the South side, a stage building served as backdrop (scene or "skene") and as a place for players to make their entrances and exits. A crane provided the means for gods to drop in from the heavens for the *deus ex machina* (literally, "god from a machine"). In a horseshoe around the other sides ranged rows of stone seats fitted into a natural hill slope. Because of

the bowl-shaped site, acoustics were excellent for the 14,000 or so spectators the theater would accommodate. Unlike modern theatre, Greek dramatic presentations were more like readings. Different characters were represented by masks that the actors would wear. Usually only a handful of actors would enact a play, with one actor often performing multiple roles (or wearing multiple masks). Another difference from modern dramatic performance is the manner in which the actors read their lines. Where contemporary actors emote or "act out" their parts, their Greek counterparts would most often impassively read their lines.

CRITICAL OVERVIEW

When Euripides's *Medea,* along with three other tragedies and a satyr play (a tetralogy), were presented at the annual March festival of Dionysus, Euripides did not win the coveted prize; in fact, his tetralogy came in last of the three tetralogies performed that day. This initial reaction, however, has not affected *Medea*'s reputation over the centuries. Euripides's contemporaries did not consider him a master tragedian, and he won only four prizes during his lifetime, although his elder, Sophocles, regarded him as a master playwright and ordered that the participants in the next Dionysian festival after Euripides's death dress in mourning out of respect for him.

A tendency to revive fifth-century plays during the fourth century led to a revised judgment of Euripides. His reputation grew significantly during this period, so much so that Aristophanes (448-380 B.C.) dedicated three plays to ridiculing his style. This is not to suggest that Aristophanes admired Euripides—far from it. But burlesque presumes an audience familiar with the original; Athenian audiences must have known enough about Euripides to make Aristophanes's jibes recognizable. Euripides was considered a fine poet with a misguided message. As Philip Vellacott, one of his many recent translators, explained in *Ironic Drama: A Study of Euripides's Method and Meaning:* "As a poet he was revered; in his function as a teacher of citizens' he was misunderstood."

During the century following Euripides's death, Aristotle (384-322 B.C.) called Euripides "with all his faults the most tragic of the poets" and used four of his works to illustrate various concepts of tragedy in his *Poetics.* When Greek culture fell into decline, Euripides's fame went to Alexandria, and then on to Rome and the Byzantine culture. Plutarch (c.46-120 A.D.) tells three historical anecdotes of escapes made good because of an ability to recite Euripidean poetry, suggesting that Euripides's reputation, at least as a poet, persisted in Greece as well.

Euripides was the youngest of the three Greek tragedians (along with Aeschylus and Sophocles) whose plays were required reading for the classical education valued during the Renaissance and Romantic periods, among others. Scholarly writings of the Middle Ages and of the Renaissance cite Euripides more often that his contemporaries: Italian poet Dante Alighieri mentions him in his masterwork the *Divine Comedy* and seventeenth-century English poet Ben Jonson used one of his plays as a model. Also in the seventeenth century, Jean Racine adapted many of his plays and considered Euripides his master. Poet John Milton, author of *Paradise Lost,* was also an admirer.

The eighteenth century lost interest in Euripides because his work was too innovative for the classical revival then in progress. Then German author Johann Wolfgang von Goethe (whose work would greatly influence European literature of the nineteenth and twentieth centuries), paid him the ultimate Romantic period compliment by calling his work "sublime." It was of Euripides that Goethe wrote his oft-adapted expression: "Have all the nations of the world since his time produced one dramatist who was worthy to hand him his slippers?" In the nineteenth century, English poet Robert Browning make conspicuous allusions to his plays, and Euripides was once again central to a good, classical education. Gilbert Murray's translation in the early twentieth century once again revived interest in him.

The twentieth century literary criticism holds a reserved judgment about Euripides. Modern critics appreciate his championing of the underdog—slaves, women, the elderly, and children—and his lampooning of religious and secular hypocrisy. But he remains a shadowy figure whose actual political and religious beliefs have been lost. Lacking sufficient evidence to say with certainty how his philosophy manifested itself in his life, many critics have turned to focusing on his dramatic technique and structure. In this context Euripides does not quite measure up to Sophocles or Aeschylus—the poetry of *Medea* does not reach the heights of beauty that Sophocles achieved in *Antigone.* Euripides's forte is irony, and he finds a ready audience in the modern period, as Vellacott explains: "Our present generation responds readily to irony, revels in it; therefore we should have the better chance of understanding Euripides." Literary criticism devoted to his play, *Medea* appears only occasionally nowadays. Writers and artists ranging in cultural background continue to reinterpret Euripides's version of Medea, but they never overshadow Euripides's.

CRITICISM

Carole L. Hamilton

In this essay Hamilton contrasts modern audience reaction to Euripides's play with fifth-century Greek perceptions of the drama.

Euripides's psychologically realistic portrayal of Medea, who indulges in an excessive form of revenge-the murder of her own children. This is a fascinating study of motivation, yet it is a topic safely distant to modern audiences. The people and society in *Medea* are part of ancient history. Today's audiences can consider and understand Medea's motivation while simultaneously dismissing it as both a work of fiction and as part of a past culture. However, to Euripides's fifth-century Athenian audience, Medea's act would, under the circumstances, make perfect sense. These Athenians, congregated in the temple of Dionysus to celebrate an annual ritual of dramatic performances, would give no more than a moment's thought to Medea's motivations. Instead, the significance of Medea's act would lie in the consequences to her society and in the larger philosophical question "is revenge effective?" The fifth-century Greeks would not see Medea as an isolated fictional character but as part of a grander scheme that was part of their everyday lives. According to historian Edith Hamilton in *The Greek Way,* "Greeks always saw things as parts of a whole." Medea's story was not an isolated act of uncontrolled passion but a reminder that things are not always what they seem and that contact with someone tainted with evil represents danger to the whole society.

A fifth-century Greek citizen was only important insofar as his or her connection to society. The ancient Greeks thought of the individual not as a unique entity but as a component in the larger organism of society. The Greek view of the individual differed from the modern view, as Hamilton wrote: "To the Greeks [character] was a man's share in qualities all men partake of; it united each one to the rest. We are interested in people's special characteristics, the things in this or that person which are different from the general. The Greeks, on the contrary, thought what was important in a man were precisely the qualities he shared with all mankind." Thus the Athenian audience would consider Medea's resemblance to themselves, her place in society, and her effect upon it. Furthermore, the citizen wholly belonged to the city, sharing in the

city's well-being, beliefs, and laws. Religion especially was, according to E. R. Dodds in *The Greeks and the Irrational,* a "collective responsibility." If one person committed an act of sacrilege, the gods might punish the whole city. Therefore, each citizen had a moral obligation and civic duty to obey the religious customs and honor its gods. To do otherwise was dangerous: during the final thirty years of the fifth century B.C., intellectuals whose ideas threatened tradition were successfully prosecuted on the grounds of disbelieving in the gods. At the same time, there was no separation between religion, law, and customs—rites, prayers, recipes, and legislature peacefully coexisted. All were civic obligations to which the citizens submitted willingly. "The citizen was subordinate in everything, and without any reserve, to the city; he belonged to it body and soul," wrote Numa Denis Fustel de Coulanges in *The Ancient City: A Study on the Religion, Laws, and Institutions of Greece and Rome.*

Rather than feeling bound by confines of a restrictive society, the ancient Greeks valued their membership in a society; it was critical to them. That is why Jason's comment, that Medea had found favor among her new neighbors, was not as trivial as it sounds to the modern ear, and why Medea shows so much dismay at having nowhere to go after Creon banishes her. The fact that Medea left her own city to run off with Jason was, to ancient Greek audiences, evidence of a flaw in Medea's ability to remain connected to her society. The chorus' reminder, "there is no sorrow above the loss of a native land," would only confirm what the audience already knew.

Beyond the perimeter of the city or community, humans were connected in other ways. The emotions and drives that lie behind actions and feelings were not simply common sensations but palpable forces that flowed through all humankind. Fate both surrounded the individual and society and also ran through them, moving individuals to act in a prescribed manner. The impulses which tempted humans to misdeeds were considered outside of human control, and "endowed with a life and energy of their own," according to Dodds. Epidemics and famines were "demons" just as were urges toward sinful acts. Fate was fused with the will of the gods; Dodds quoted Pindar, who put it this way: "the great purpose of Zeus *directs* the daemon [demon] of the men he loves." Medea realizes, "The gods and I, I in a kind of madness, have contrived all this." Against these forces, humans were helpless to defend themselves; they would be foolish to defy

WHAT DO I READ NEXT?

- Euripides's *Phaedra* and Jean Racine's seventeenth-century version of it, *Phedre,* portray a woman who immorally falls in love with her step-son and in retaliation against his rebuff claims that he tried to dishonor her. The works examine similar moral ground to that examined in *Medea.*

- Toni Morrison's moving novel *Beloved* (1987) revolves around a historical incident of infanticide performed by a slave mother who is moved to this tragic act by the horrors of slavery—she murders her child to remove it from the life of toil, shame, and pain that she has led. Her act haunts characters through several generations of her family.

- In Shakespeare's *Macbeth* (c. 1605) Lady Macbeth pushes her husband to commit murder and then goes mad from the guilty thoughts that plague her. Indirectly, her ambition is responsible for a series of murders, including some innocent children, that Macbeth commissions in his vain efforts to obscure their crime.

- George Eliot's *Adam Bede* (1859) centers on the relationship between Adam Bede and Hetty Sorrel, who becomes pregnant by a local nobleman and abandons her baby to die.

- *The Lion in Winter,* a 1968 film directed by Anthony Harvey and starring Katherine Hepburn as the powerful Eleanor of Acquitaine, concerns the tense interplay between her and Henry II as he chooses between her and his lover's brother for a successor to the throne. Eleanor and Henry's three sons side with her in rebelling against the unfaithful king.

the gods. The ancient Greeks had no concept of "will" in the sense of "freedom of choice" but rather felt at the mercy of sensations moving through them. Passions could overwhelm them and obscure their ability to make rational decisions. These passions might come from the gods, from inherited guilt, or from *hubris*—excessive arrogance. When Medea argues with herself, she confronts her demon, the irrational force demanding the deaths of her two sons. She acknowledges the wickedness of this act but finds no power to escape the emotions that will force her to act: "Stronger than all my afterthoughts is my fury, fury that brings upon mortals the greatest of evils." The chorus acknowledges Medea's powerlessness to free herself from the grip of such a force: "Medea, a god has thrown suffering upon you in waves of despair." Fate possesses Medea, and it becomes Medea's fate to murder her own children. The concept of Medea having a "motive" or "choosing" to kill her sons would not have made sense to Euripides's audience.

The Greek rationalists Aristotle and Plato argued that humans did not have to fall prey to the demons of passion but could, with training and resolution, endeavor to maintain their rationality in the face of these demons. Euripides pits the rationalists against the fatalists in *Medea* in the form of the chorus who consistently represent the voice of quiet rationalism. The Corinthian women sympathize with Medea's grief and outrage, but they counsel moderation in seeking revenge: "I both wish to help you and support the normal ways of mankind, and tell you not to do this thing." However, their counsel proves impotent in the face of the forces driving Medea. She tells them that no compromise is possible and turns her attention to calling Jason back. Euripides's audience would have pondered the question whether Medea had the capacity for rational behavior under the circumstances of Jason's betrayal and Creon's decree of banishment. Yet, the question would not have been cast in terms of the conflict between Medea and Jason, two individuals, but of the conflict within Medea, between her rational mind and the fates driving her.

To complicate matters, the Greeks considered guilt a kind of contamination that spread through contact or through inheritance. The Corinthians might indeed have killed Medea's children to eliminate the danger they represented. Although innocent in their youth, Medea's offspring would surely manifest her evilness when they grew up because they were polluted through inheritance. All of Medea's descendants would carry her curse. In a way, her murdering the children and ending her lineage saves Corinth the trouble of either killing them or suffering the consequences of harboring them, for any contact with them was potentially dangerous. The city that hosted them would bring down upon itself the wrath of the gods. Medea's killing the children while they are still innocent, then, serves as a kind of sacrificial act that purifies the city of Corinth.

The chorus recognizes that Medea, already banished from Corinth, will make herself an outcast by committing her horrendous crime. The women tell Medea that she "is not pure with the rest" and ask her what city could accept a woman who murdered of her own children. The pollution of guilt can result from contact as well as inheritance. Corinth may unwittingly have brought disaster upon itself for welcoming Medea into their society in the first place, falling prey to her charm in spite of knowing that she had abandoned her family and city and had killed her own brother to facilitate Jason's escape. Or perhaps Jason brought on the disaster by his ambition to marry the King's daughter and secure a place in Corinthian society; his *hubris* put his adopted city into danger. Either or both of these contaminating factors led to the disaster of Medea murdering the King and Princess of Corinth. Jason and Medea sinned against each other, but they also sinned against the city of Corinth—their sin was that of profane contact. Jason and Medea are foreigners who entered the city and covertly brought pollution in their wake.

The year that Euripides presented his play, the devastating Peloponnesian War was being waged. This was the first major war the Greeks had fought against people of their own ethnic background, introducing a new difficulty in identifying the enemy. *Medea* contains a sub-theme concerning the danger of mistaken appearances. When Medea's sons deliver her gifts to Creon's daughter, she at first is irritated by their presence—she mistakenly takes them for enemies. Ironically, her first reaction was the more accurate one. But seeing the bright gifts, she welcomes them and completely accepts the pretext of their visit, as Medea hoped she would. The young princess is tricked by appearances, just as were the Trojans when the Greeks presented a

"gift" horse that secretly harbored Odysseus and his best warriors. That night the Greek warriors burst out of the horse's belly and slaughtered the sleeping Trojans. Likewise, the poison in Medea's gifts takes effect the moment Jason's new wife innocently dons the robe and crown. Euripides plays on the anxieties of his audience over their ability to recognize enemies and to know when and when not to trust others. Effectively, the King's daughter was polluted through unknown and dangerous contact with Medea via poisoned gifts. Nor does the cycle end with the young princess. Creon becomes enmeshed in his daughter's poisoned embrace and dies with her, despite his efforts to disentangle himself. This gruesome detail, related by the messenger in almost lyrical prose, demonstrates how even the desire for contact with a known loved one can bring about disaster.

Creon's fate most aptly fulfills the closing lines of the chorus: "What we thought is not confirmed and what we thought not god contrives." This is the Euripidean version of "expect the unexpected," a stock phrase with which a number of his plays abruptly end. Euripides suggests that ironically, passion—the same force that drives humans to desire contact with others—has the capacity to destroy. Jason is guilty of misdirected passion on several counts. He initially brought his fate upon himself by marrying a foreign wife, a known sorceress, and then betraying her. He also allowed his ambitious desire for connection with Corinthian society to turn him away from a faithful, loving wife and their two sons. Medea's culpability is thus compromised by Jason's. Medea herself has a passionate, reckless nature, which makes her a perfect medium for the expression of the forces of passion orchestrated by the gods. Whether Medea or the gods are to blame for the infanticide she commits, her act, as far as Euripides's Athenian audience would have been concerned, would generate a civic disaster. She became a danger for Corinth, and banishing her made her all the more dangerous. Euripides's deeply pessimistic and fatalistic play would have been disturbing to his Athenian audience; perhaps that is why his tetralogy-which include *Medea*—failed to win the festival prize.

Source: Carole L. Hamilton, in an essay for *Drama for Students,* Gale, 1997.

D. J. Conacher

In the following excerpt, Conacher provides an in-depth analysis of the Medea, *outlining each*

The intense centripetal focus of this tragedy begins
in the prologue. Its three parts, monologue, dialogue
and a frightened anapaestic series punctuated by
Medea's off-stage cries, produce their complementary effects in an ascending scale of excitement. The
first speaker is the Nurse, and so our earliest impression of Medea comes through an intimate and
sympathetic witness. Her news, that Jason has deserted Medea for the daughter of King Creon, is
enclosed by accounts of the past services of Medea
to Jason and to the city which has sheltered him,
and, hideous as these services have been, they are
presented in the light of Medea's passionate devotion to her husband. The description of Medea's
mood suggests a savage, wounded animal and in the
Nurse's apprehension of some monstrous deed (perhaps against the children, whose sight Medea now
abhors) we get our first warning, from the one who
knows her best, of what Medea can become,
when wronged.

Enter the Tutor, leading the children of Medea.
As the bearer of fresh news—that Creon is about to
exile Medea—and more particularly as the guardi-
an of the children, he increases the sense of apprehension and makes it more specific. The Nurse
redoubles her worried chatter:

> O keep the children from her . . . for even now I saw
> her glaring at them like an angry bull. . . . She'll not
> leave this fit, too well I know it, till she has charged at
> someone. May it be enemies, not friends, she chooses!

Two savage cries, off-stage, provide the final
impact of this prologue: Medea screams her wrongs
and curses husband, children, "all the house." The
brief intensity of these cries, contrasted with the
Nurse's long-winded moralizing, brings the prologue to a chilling climax. The series of emotions
traversed—sympathy, apprehension, horror—anticipates in a few rapid strokes the responses which,
in the same sequence, the coming action will evoke.

This sinister blend of effects is repeated, in
choral terms, in the *parodos,* where the brief songs
expressing sympathy and fear are harshly punctuated by Medea's off-stage cries. The direction of this
tragedy requires that the Chorus should *begin* by
feeling sympathy for Medea. Thus, singing as wom-
en rather than as Corinthians, they remind us that it
was Jason's vows, by which Medea now curses him,
which first induced her to take her ill-starred
voyage to Greece.

The contrast between the fury of Medea's initial cries and the controlled and calculated rhetoric
of her opening address to the Corinthian women has
already been compared with the presentation of
Phaedra in the *Hippolytus.* The same dramatic purpose is served in both cases: that of showing in
striking contrast the most elemental and the most
civilized or even sophisticated aspects of the same
personality. What difference there is between the
two contrasts is due to the difference between the
two women. Even in hysteria, Phaedra seeks to
cloak her naked passion (this impulse is, indeed, the
cause of her hysteria); later, in her discourse on
human frailty (her own included) one feels that she
expresses her own character more truthfully than
does Medea in *her* official bid for sympathy.
Freudians, no doubt, could express these same
distinctions more accurately in terms of the *ego,* the
super ego and the *id.*

Medea's purpose in her opening speech is,
purely and simply, to win the Chorus of female
citizens to her side. As a piece of rhetoric (this time
needing no apology for dramatic relevance) the
speech is one of the poet's finest passages. It begins
on a note of specious but ingratiating familiarity,
moves on to the briefest possible indication ("I'm
finished, good women, my husband has betrayed
me!") of the speaker's plight, and then concentrates
with a wealth of poignantly familiar detail on "woman's lot," a trouble which the Chorus shares. "We
women are a timid lot . . . but wronged in marriage,
there's none more murderous!" All Medea has
asked is silent co-operation. By the end of her
speech, the Chorus, to a woman regards her vengeance as its own.

The poet's purpose in this passage is, perhaps,
more complex than Medea's, though it has much in
common with it: we, too, like the Chorus, are
destined to begin in pity then to move through fear
to horrified revulsion. But to see the larger dramatic
purpose of the speech we must consider it in relation
to the whole presentation of Jason's barbarian wife.

Prior to this speech, Medea is known to us only
as the terrifying witch whom the dramatist has
received from the tradition; even if we have no
direct knowledge of that tradition, both deeds and
character of *that* Medea have been emphatically
made known to us in the opening portions of the
play. Now, for the first time, we are introduced to
another Medea: a woman and a foreigner who can
move the Greeks of the Chorus, and perhaps of the

audience, with that disciplined compound of passion and reason which the Greeks called rhetoric. Despite her outlandish background, this Medea manages to strike a common chord in people who (as Jason so tactfully reminds her later) regarded their own society as a privilege which a barbarian must enjoy on sufferance. Thus it is that the dramatist begins, at least, to endow his folk-tale witch with something of the stature which a tragic heroine requires: here and in subsequent encounters with Creon, with Jason and with Aegeus, the many aspects of Medea's powerful personality—eloquent and cunning, wise and passionate by turns—are gradually revealed.

In facing Creon, Medea must play the fawning hypocrite to win at least a day's reprieve from exile. With nice irony, the dramatist endows her with the insight and skill to twist what should most tell against her—her reputation as "a wise one" and Creon's protective love for his own daughter—to serve her purpose. The exchange with Creon has other qualities as well. Medea's appeal "for her children's sake" to Creon's paternal instincts keeps the "children theme" before our minds, while the passage in which Medea allays Creon's fears about her special powers allows Euripides a sly, contemporary aside on the slander which clever people must suffer in society.

While something of Medea's power appears even in the scene with Creon, the full force of her personality is necessarily muted by the situation. This briefly *piano* effect is more than redressed by her next and most dramatic encounter. Here Medea's greatest advantage is achieved at the expense of, and in contrast to, the traditionally "epic" figure of Jason, for the hero of the good ship Argo cuts a very sorry figure in her presence. Generosity, absolute loyalties, action and feeling on the grand scale, are the hallmarks of the heroic character. Jason's quibbling rationalization of his actions Medea answers with the single word . . . ("O utter shameless brazenness!"), as she launches into an impassioned account of all that she has done for him. Consistently, Jason plays the sophist to a heroic Medea: for past favours, he has really Cypris to thank, not her; besides, for a barbarian, life and fame among the Greeks is more than just requital of her service. Previously, horror may have been our main reaction to Medea's deeds for Jason. Now, confronted by Jason's niggling sums in settling the accounts of love, we are impressed by the wild generosity of passion which made them possible.

> TO GRASP THE NATURE OF THIS STRUGGLE, WE MUST SEE THE GOOD IN MEDEA BEFORE WE SEE HER AT HER WORST"

The effect of the Aegeus scene on the "public image" of Medea seems often to have been missed by the critics, distracted, no doubt, by arguments concerning its allegedly "episodic" nature. Surely we must be impressed by Aegeus' respect for Medea's advice and the readiness with which he confides in her. Nor does he speak in the tone which one reserves for one's witch-doctor: rather, they converse on terms of mutual regard—witness the warmth of their greetings and the exchange of confidence and sympathy with one another's plight. It should be noted, too, that Medea's utterances acquire a sort of brisk professionalism, completely different in tone from other speeches in the play, as soon as Aegeus begins his consultation; this is our only actual view in the play of Medea as a specialist, a professional "wise woman." And the readiness with which Aegeus accepts Medea's offer to put an end to his childlessness in return for future sanctuary at Athens shows a confidence in her powers at least equal to that which he feels in Apollo's oracle or in the wise and pious Pittheus of Trozen. In general, this treatment from the King of Athens does as much as anything to establish Medea in our minds as a "personage" not to be disposed of as a mere gypsy baggage from barbarian lands.

The Aegeus episode is, of course, important for other reasons as well; it heralds, as we shall see, a turning-point in Medea's career of vengeance and in the sympathy which the Chorus has hitherto afforded her.

In her encounters with Creon and Aegeus, Medea has assumed soft-spoken roles which circumstances have forced upon her. After both these encounters, the essential single-minded Medea reappears in impassioned outbursts alone with the Chorus. ("Do you think," she reassures the Chorus. . . , about her attitude to Creon, "that I'd have ever fawned on *that* one, if I'd not been weaving wiles to serve my ends?") There is, however, a terrible difference in the content of these two speeches, and this gulf is marked by the sharp contrast in tone between the earlier and later choral lyrics of the play. In the first of these speeches, Medea shows, it is true, a sinister delight in pondering the different routes—poison or the knife—by which her enemies may be despatched, but however much her oath "by Hecate, the sharer of my hearth" may chill us, it is still her enemies she speaks of killing.

In the lyric (almost "a song for feminists") which follows this speech, the Chorus is still full of sympathy for Medea. As often in Euripides, the first strophe and antistrophe generalize on the situation (here, "the injustice done to women") while the second strophic pair applies the theme directly to the tragic sufferer:

> Now rivers flow upstream and the established course of justice is reversed—for now 'tis *men* who are unjust and laugh at oaths. . . .

> Through the ages, man-made songs show women faithless, but if we women had the gift of song, we'd sing a different tune. . . . (paraphrase)

> So with you, Medea. Love brought you across the seas to Greece. But now, abandoned (for no longer do Greeks reverence marriage oaths) you have no refuge, no paternal home, as a royal rival destroys your marriage bed. (paraphrase)

The chorus which follows the encounter with Jason is not, however, quite as single-minded in its championship of women and Medea. The first strophe, praising moderate love, decries that excessive passion which ruins judgment and virtue; the answering antistrophe, which praises self-control (*sophrosyne*), decries the adulterous love which causes strife. Thus, in the generalizing part of this lyric, the Chorus glances at the faults of both Medea and Jason in turn. In the second half, however, nothing distracts attention from sympathy for the deserted and homeless foreigner.

The decisive change in the dramatic action and in the attitude of the Chorus occurs after the scene with Aegeus, for it is then that Medea announces the awful means by which she plans to take vengeance on her husband. The excellence of the play's structure is well illustrated by the placing of this crisis and by the kinds of effect which precede and follow it. The gradual revelation of Medea's personality has now been completed, save for one essential feature which is to give the *agon* its tragic meaning. The "children theme," so essential to this meaning, has been kept constantly before our minds: in the frightened premonitions of the Nurse and in Me-

dea's own off-stage curses; in Medea's exploitation of Creon's paternal instincts, and, ironically enough, in Jason's own claim that *he* is acting for his family's sake: "For what need have *you* of children?" he asks Medea. The Aegeus episode itself is, of course, vital both to this theme and to the mechanics of the plot. Aegeus' own royal trouble, childlessness, and the lengths to which he goes to cure it, is our most forcible reminder of a king's essential need of sons. Again, in promising the outcast sanctuary in Athens, Aegeus unwittingly removes the only barrier to Medea's plans and her last reticence in revealing them to the Chorus.

Medea's three addresses to the Chorus follow an ascending scale in keeping with the gradually increasing impetus in plot and theme. In the first and most rhetorical of these, Medea's passion is rigorously subordinated to her immediate purpose of winning the Chorus to her side. The second speech with its curse by Hecate and its pondering of the various means of murder, is both more savage and more sinister, but it tells us little of Medea's actual intentions. Only after the scene with Aegeus does she shout for all to hear the full horror of the vengeance which she plans.

One of the most shocking effects of this speech comes from the lack of horror which Medea displays herself. The plan to send her children to the princess bearing poisoned robes is told with hideous matter-of-factness, and only an occasional word or phrase suggests any hesitation at the awful plan of slaying her children for the sake of vengeance on their father. All this suggests that the hints given in the prologue told the truth, that Medea has from the start been determined on this course of action. The main emphasis of the speech is that laughter from one's enemies is not to be endured and the cry, "grievous to my enemies and kindly to my friends" serves as a grim reminder of the accuracy of the Nurse's description (at v. 38) of Medea's spirit.

It is in the ode immediately following these dreadful revelations that the Chorus begins to withdraw its allegiance from Medea. The first strophe and antistrophe deal, in highly poetic terms, with the purity and beauty of Athens. Euripides may well have enjoyed pleasing his fellow citizens and himself with such idealized pictures of his city, but here he does not do so at the expense of the dramatic situation. The point of the description appears in the second strophic pair: "How," asks the Chorus, "will such a city ever welcome you, Medea, a child-murderer polluting all you meet?" Now the respect and chivalrous treatment which Medea had won from the King of Athens has been one of the most impressive features of her earlier presentation; the immediate effect of that treatment, however, has been to confirm Medea in her secret and terrible decision. Thus to dwell as the Chorus does on the hideous uncongeniality between Medea the child-murderer and the pure and serene haven which she has chosen in an effective way of expressing the self-destruction which her plans involve. The terms in which Athens is described are admirably suited to this purpose: it is the physical serenity of the place which is stressed, for this is the aspect which is particularly vulnerable to the pollution with which Medea threatens it. Thus, Athens is "the sacred, unplundered land—where golden Harmonia produced the Muses nine"; the land whose children "ever culling illustrious wisdom, stride spendidly under skies of glorious brightness." What sharper contrast to the black deeds of Medea could we find than all this bright serenity? Even Cypris, so dread a goddess in Medea's case, "breathes moderate, pleasure-wafting breezes on this land."

The actual execution of Medea's plot against the Princess needs little comment. It provides, of course, one of the most exciting and theatrical of the playwright's intrigues and suggests, perhaps, at least one reason why the *Medea,* of all Greek drama, has survived most successfully as a play which is still presented on the stage. The gulling of the pompous Jason, unaware as ever of his wife's true nature; the contrast between the children's innocence and the glittering fatality of the gifts they bear; the suspense, heightened by the vivid anticipations of the Chorus, as to whether the Princess will yield to the "heavenly charm" of these adornments; the gruesome account, in the messenger's speech, of the switch from delight to anguish, then all the gory details of the deaths themselves: all this provides many opportunities (and none is missed) for melodrama and irony of the more obvious sort. Such effects are legitimate enough in themselves, particularly in view of the sort of creature which Medea is to become before the last scene is ended; nevertheless, a tendency to overplay this aspect of the drama, from the second scene with Jason to the murder of the children, has sometimes obscured certain more subtly tragic effects with which it is combined. Thus far the dramatist has presented a Medea who combines the elemental passion of the folk-tale witch with certain qualities of mind, emotion and personality which let her tower above the several royal and (conventionally) heroic char-

acters who appear beside her on the stage. Now, in her last speech to the Chorus this human and potentially tragic Medea vanishes: instead we hear an embodiment of the *alastor* (the avenging spirit from Hades) coldly announcing child-murder as a necessary part of her revenge. If this is the Medea which we are to watch without relief to the play's end, then both the Chorus and ourselves have been the dupes, both of the "heroine" and of the dramatist, for yielding our sympathy and interest. Fortunately, however, it is the air of cold inflexibility which is false: a cloak of desperate resolution hiding the maternal anguish as well as a device by which the dramatist may, in the end, present that anguish more effectively.

The agony of Medea begins quietly and unexpectedly in the scene with Jason. The "reconciliation speech," the apology to Jason, Medea accomplishes with all her usual aplomb. The first onset of grief suddenly occurs at the entry of the children, summoned to heal the reconciliation, when Jason thus addresses them: "Only grow up! Your father and whatever gods are kindly will assure the rest! Soon may I see you glorying in the strength of youth. . . ." In each instance, the effect of Medea's tears is so veiled by her ambiguous explanations, so muted by her resourceful ironies, that some critics have taken the tears themselves as a calculated device for securing Jason's sympathy. But Medea's dissimulation only shows us the measure of her will in masking, with characteristic ingenuity, the anguish which, for a moment, overcomes her. So viewed, this scene anticipates, in miniature, the major struggle to come.

The alternation of the human and the fiendish Medea in the following scenes corresponds to the curious interweaving of the tragic and the macabre elements in the double catastrophe. The chorus which follows the despatch of the children with the gifts heralds both deeds of violence: the first strophe and antistrophe anticipate, with sinister vividness, the temptation of the Princess and its fatal results, while the concluding strophic pair expresses grief for the woes of Jason and Medea, respectively, in the coming murder of the children. The report of what has happened at the palace is divided, most remarkably, into two parts. The Tutor's announcement that the children and their gifts have been accepted is, to his surprise, greeted with sullen gloom by Medea; on the other hand, the Messenger's announcement in the following episode, of the deaths which the gifts have caused is received with hideous joy. In between these two reports comes the most crucial passage in the play: that agonizing self-debate in which Medea twice revokes and twice confirms her decision to slay her children. After the Messenger Speech, lengthy . . . with all the harrowing details, we are brought with the speed of necessity to the final catastrophe for, Medea argues desperately, if their mother does not kill the children now, some hostile hand may do so . . . the beginning of the speech reminds us of the truth of the matter: the original decision to slay the children was a part, perhaps the major part, of the original plan, before the fatal gifts were sent. Medea utters her final determination with the grim conviction that for her a life of misery must now begin: ''Steel your heart for one brief day—then mourn thereafter!''

A final brief and despairing lyric precedes the off-stage murder. It is significant that now the Chorus no longer addresses its pleas to Medea but to the ''nature'' deities, Earth and Sun (Medea's grandsire) to restrain this unnatural murderess, this embodiment of a vengeance-driven Erinys, which Medea has become. For Medea herself they have only despairing questions and equally dismal prophecies.

Why are the two deeds of violence, in many ways so different, presented in this interwoven fashion? Partly, no doubt, for the practical reason that the poet does not wish to lose dramatic impetus by having to work up two separate crises. But there are, I think, reasons more significant than this.

From her folk-tale chrysalis, Medea has emerged, in this play, as a human heroine with the power to achieve her ends in a highly civilized social context (as Jason reminds her) against all odds. So far, however, save for a few hints in the second scene with Jason, her passion for vengeance has been tempered by no redeeming emotion: though human, she is not sympathetic (the Chorus sympathizes with her situation rather than with her): we cannot achieve any degree of identification with her. Again, so far there has been no essential conflict in this play. True, Medea, abandoned and alone in a hostile state, has had to bend two kings, a Chorus of Corinthian women and an ambitious husband to her will, but this achievement is only the measure of her greatness: in this play, Medea herself is really the only one capable of resisting Medea. Regarded as a tragic figure, the Medea of the earlier scenes corresponds to a hate-ridden Philoctetes as yet undisturbed by the friendship of Neoptolemus, or to a stubbornly resentful Achilles, untried by the loss of Patroclus.

Medea's first full statement of her plans (in the last of her three addresses to the Chorus) has shocked us by its coldness. More recently, in the second scene with Jason, we have seen signs that this frozen determination does not represent the whole Medea. Now, when the child-murder suddenly becomes imminent with the success of the first phase of the plan, Medea's resolution falters for the first time. Thus the great speech at 1019 ff. is essential to the characterization of Medea and to the meaning of the play.

If Medea's sudden flood of emotion, her passionate regrets for lost maternal joys, should strike us as commonplace, let us remember that that is just its purpose. We are meant, simply, to realize that Medea loves her children as deeply as any woman does. So, too, the sudden effects of the children's smiles, and of Medea's lightning switches from ''I cannot do it'' to ''I must,'' and back again, far from being bathetic melodrama, are essential to the realistic presentation of the struggle in Medea's soul. Without this scene, what Medea eventually becomes would indeed smack of melodrama. That monstrous figure attains tragic significance only when we see it as the result of a conflict—of a victory, as Medea herself expresses it—of her all-consuming passion for vengeance over her better counsels. To grasp the nature of this struggle, we must see the good in Medea before we see her at her worst. The plot requires that something of her lethal savagery should appear before the ultimate horror of the child-murder, but had we already seen her gloating over the details of her palace butchery the sympathetic presentation of her own agony would have been impossible. So it is that the *first* news from the palace, that the children and their gifts have been accepted, is greeted sadly by Medea, and that the horrible sequence to this news is postponed till after the emotional climax at vv. 1019–80. By the time that the second bulletin, showing the first results of Medea's cruelty, arrives from the palace, Medea's self-debate concerning her children, and with it the dramatic need for our sympathy, is over; indeed, the wholehearted gloating over the Messenger's hideous account, contrasting so sharply with her despondent reception of the Tutor and his news, may be meant to illustrate the new Medea, now totally committed to evil, who emerges only after the completion of her interior struggle.

In the concluding passages of the play, after the murder of the children, the monstrous and inhuman aspects of Medea are played up in a variety of ways. The Chorus by its reference to Ino, intimates that no human mother could bear to live after slaying her children and Jason echoes this thought when he cries, "Can you still look upon the sun and earth, after enduring such an impious deed?" And yet Medea lives and flourishes. More significant, perhaps, is Jason's bitter reference to the unnatural deeds of Medea—deeds from which *he* took the profit—against her own family in Colchis. During the very human action of this play, little has been made of these dark deeds, save as examples of Medea's devotion to the ingrate Jason, but now that "Medea the fiend" has triumphed over the human heroine this reminder of the barbarous, magic-working Medea of the folk tale is all too apposite. Jason complains that the *Alastor* which should pursue Medea for these deeds is pursuing him instead, but we who have witnessed the moral destruction of Medea in the preceding episode are all too well aware that the *alastor* has not missed its mark. As for the murderess herself, Medea the avenger, in the final scene with Jason, has quite defeated Medea, the tortured mother: ". . . Call me lioness or Scylla, as you will . . . as long as I have reached your vitals. . . ." "My grief is solaced if *you* cannot mock!"

The "improbable" and inorganic ending of the play—Medea's departure in the Sun-god's fiery chariot—is a feature of the play which appears to have irritated Aristotle. (*Poetics* 1454b 1–2) However, such macabre touches, such departures from the real world of tragedy, if they serve some purpose, are surely permissible when the tragic meaning has already been expressed. That, in this instance, the supernatural intervention is not meant to intrude on the real action of the play has already been shown by the fact that, earlier, the human and the tragic Medea has been concerned with such practical matters as the arrangement for asylum at Athens and the impossibility of escaping with her children from the vengeful Corinthians. (See, for example, lines 1236–41). Thus the only point of interest in the *deus-ex-machina* ending lies in the symbolic purpose which this device fulfils. This has been variously expressed by critics in accordance with their different views of Euripides' "Medea theme." Kitto finds in the device the poet's answer to the Chorus's and Jason's idea that "Sun and Earth, the most elemental things in the Universe, have been outraged by these terrible crimes," while Lesky and M. P. Cunningham both regard the chariot scene as marking the fundamental, qualitative change which her awful deed has effected in Medea. In terms of the present study, it seems fair to

suggest that by this final macabre touch of symbolism, the poet is once again expressing the transformation of a human heroine back to the folk-tale fiend of magic powers.

Source: D. J. Conacher, in his *Euripidean Drama: Myth, Theme, and Structure,* University of Toronto Press, 1967, pp. 187–98.

Brooks Atkinson

In the following review, which originally appeared in the New York Times *on October 21, 1947, Atkinson offers praise for Robinson Jeffers's adaptation of Euripedes's* Medea. *His review illustrates how ancient Greek dramas can be altered slightly or extensively without changing the messages intended by the original authors. Such adaptations can make these dramas more accessible to modern audiences.*

As drama critic for the New York Times *from 1925 to 1960, Atkinson was one of the most influential reviewers in America.*

If Medea does not entirely understand every aspect of her whirling character, she would do well to consult Judith Anderson. For Miss Anderson understands the character more thoroughly than Medea, Euripides or the scholars, and it would be useless now for anyone else to attempt the part. Using a new text by Robinson Jeffers, she set a landmark in the theatre at the National last evening, where she gave a burning performance in a savage part.

Mr. Jeffers' "free adaptation," as it is called, spares the supernatural bogeymen of the classical Greek drama and gets on briskly with the terrifying story of a woman obsessed with revenge. His verse is modern; his words are sharp and vivid, and his text does not worship gods that are dead.

Since Miss Anderson is a modern, the Jeffers text suits her perfectly and releases a torrent of acting incomparable for passion and scope. Miss Anderson's Medea is mad with the fury of a woman of rare stature. She is barbaric by inheritance, but she has heroic strength and vibrant perceptions. Animal-like in her physical reactions, she plots the doom of her enemies with the intelligence of a priestess of black magic—at once obscene and inspired. Between those two poles she fills the evening with fire, horror, rage and character. Although Miss Anderson has left some memorable marks on great women in the theatre, Medea has summoned all her powers as an actress. Now everyone realizes that she has been destined for Medea from the start.

The general performance and the production are all of a piece. As the nurse, Florence Reed is giving an eminent performance that conveys the weariness and apprehensions of a devoted servant who does not quarrel with fate. John Gielgud's Jason is a lucid, solemn egotist well expressed in terms of the theatre. As Creon, Albert Hecht has the commanding voice and the imperiousness of a working monarch. The chorus of women, which has been refreshingly arranged in Mr. Gielgud's unhackneyed direction, is well acted by Grace Mills, Kathryn Grill and Leone Wilson. The parts of the two young sons are disarmingly represented in the guileless acting of Gene Lee and Peter Moss. Hugh Franklin as Aegeus and Don McHenry as the Tutor give agreeable performances, innocent of the stuffiness peculiar to most classical productions.

Ben Edwards' setting of the doorway to a Greek house is no more than pedestrian designing, although Peggy Clark has lighted it dramatically, and Castillo has dressed the characters well. Your correspondent could do very well without the conventional theatrical effects—the lightning and the surf especially, for, unlike the acting, they derive from the old-fashioned theatre of rant and ham.

Out of respect for Miss Anderson's magnificent acting in this incarnadined drama, they ought to be locked up in the lumber room. For she has freed Medea from all the old traditions as if the character had just been created. Perhaps that is exactly what has happened. Perhaps Medea was never fully created until Miss Anderson breathed immortal fire into it last evening.

Source: Brooks Atkinson, in a review of *Medea* (1947) in *On Stage: Selected Theater Reviews from The New York Times, 1920–1970,* edited by Bernard Beckerman and Howard Siegman, Arno Press, 1973, pp. 282–84.

FURTHER READING

Barlow, S. A. *The Imagery of Euripides,* Methuen, 1971.
A scholarly examination of the images and devices in Euripidean drama, finding Euripides thin in metaphoric images but rich in visual detail.

Conacher, D. J. "The Medea," in his *Euripidean Drama: Myth, Theme, and Structure,* University of Toronto Press, 1967.

An analysis of the motivations and psychological forces driving Medea and the intertwining of folk motifs with the familiar myth of Jason and Medea as well as deviations Euripides's from the prevailing mythical versions.

Dodds, E. R. *The Greeks and the Irrational,* University of California Press, 1951.
A convincing argument that irrationalism played as much of a role in ancient Greek culture as did rationalism.

Easterling, P. E. "The Infanticide in Euripides's *Medea,*" in *Yale Classical Studies,* Vol. 25, 1977.
A scholarly examination of Euripides's decision to have Medea murder her own children, a departure from the Greek myth as his audience would have known it.

Ferguson, John. *Euripides, Medea & Electra: A Companion to the Penguin Translation,* Bristol Classical Press, 1987.
A handy guide to the language and structure of two of Euripides's plays designed for use with the Penguin translation of the works by Philip Vellacott.

Foustel De Coulanges, Numa Denis. *The Ancient City: A Study on the Religion, Laws, and Institutions of Greece and Rome,* Johns Hopkins University Press, 1980, 1956.
A nineteenth-century work of scholarship that describes the life of the ancients in glowing detail; although dated, this work is still respected for its insights and depth.

Grene, David, and Richard Lattimore, Editors. *The Complete Greek Tragedies,* Vol. III: *Euripides,* University of Chicago Press, 1992.
An anthology of Euripides's plays, including the Rex Warner translation of *The Medea.*

Grube, G. M. A. *The Drama of Euripides,* Methuen, 1961.
Explores the role of the gods in the works of Euripides and his contemporaries. Euripides, sometimes accused of being an atheist, did not portray the gods as infallibly rational, but rather as bound by the same passions as humankind.

Hamilton, Edith. *The Greek Way,* W. W. Norton, 1993, 1930.
In her inimitable style, Edith Hamilton describes the mind and spirit of ancient Greek culture and includes a brief chapter on Euripides.

Kitto, H. D. F. *Greek Tragedy: A Literary Study,* Methuen, 1961.
Kitto suggests that Euripides built his tragedies around a central theme or idea, not a plot line, and that this choice explains his loose dramatic structure.

Lattimore, Richard. *The Poetry of Greek Tragedy,* Johns Hopkins Press, 1958.
Lattimore remains the foremost translator of Greek classic, and his commentary on poetic structure is insightful. Includes a chapter on Euripides.

Lattimore, Richard. *Story-Patterns in Greek Tragedy,* University of Michigan Press, 1964.
Another useful resource from Lattimore.

Lucas, F. L. *Euripides and His Influence,* Marshall Jones, 1923.

Lucas describes some of the innovations of Euripides's plays and how his work influenced later generations of writers.

Murray, Gilbert. *Euripides and His Age,* Oxford University Press, 1955.
 A landmark work describing the historical context of Euripides's Athens, including the Peloponnesian War and the rise of the Sophists. Also includes critical treatments of the major plays of Euripides.

Vellacott, Philip. *Ironic Drama: A Study of Euripides's Method and Meaning,* Cambridge University Press, 1975.
 In this work, Vellacott explains how Euripides uses ironic reversals of expectations in many of his plays.

Vickers, Brian. ''Myths in Tragedy'' in his *Towards Greek Tragedy: Drama, Myth, Society,* Longman, 1973, pp. 268-343.
 An essay emphasizing the importance of the oath and its betrayal by Jason in *Medea.*

Oedipus Rex

SOPHOCLES

c. 430, B.C.

Sophocles's *Oedipus Rex* is probably the most famous tragedy ever written. It is known by a variety of title (the most common being *Oedipus Rex*), including *Oedipus the King* and *Oedipus Tyrannus.* Sophocles, first produced the play in Athens around 430 B.C. at the Great Dionysia, a religious and cultural festival held in honor of the god Dionysus, where it won second prize. In the play Oedipus, King of Thebes, upon hearing that his city is being ravaged by fire and plague, sends his brother-in-law Creon to find a remedy from the Oracle of Apollo at Delphi. When Creon returns Oedipus begins investigating the death of his predecessor, Laius, and discovers through various means that he himself was the one who had unknowingly killed Laius and then married his own mother, Jocasta. Jocasta commits suicide, Oedipus blinds himself, takes leave of his children, and is led away. Aristotle praises the play in his *Poetics* for having an exemplary, well- constructed plot, one which is capable of inspiring fear and pity not only in its audience but especially in those who have merely heard of the story. Following Aristotle's appraisal, many prominent authors including Voltaire, Frederich Nietzsche, and Sidmund Freud reacted at length to the play's themes of incest and patricide. In the twentieth century, the most influential of these thinkers, Freud, showed that Oedipus's fate is that of every man; the "Oedipus Complex" is the definitive parent-child relationship. Throughout history, writers have drawn upon the myth of Oedi-

pus, and dramatists, composers, and poets, including Pierre Corneille, Fredrich von Schiller, Heinrich von Kleist, William Butler Yeats, Ezra Pound, Igor Stravinsky, and Jean Cocteau, have both written on, translated, and staged the tragedy; contemporary filmmakers such as Pier Paolo Pasolini and Woody Allen have directed self-consciously autobiographical versions of *Oedipus Rex.*

AUTHOR BIOGRAPHY

Sophocles was born in Colonus, Greece, c. 496 B.C. and died in Athens c. 406 B.C. The son of an armor manufacturer, he was a member of a family of considerable rank, was well-educated, and held a number of significant political positions in addition to being one of the best dramatists in his age—an age in which his dramatic peers included the famed playwrights Euripides and Aeschylus. Sophocles studied under the musician Lampras and under Aeschylus, later becoming his rival. He lived and wrote during an era known as the Golden Age of Athens (480-406 B.C.); in 480 and 479 B.C. the city had won the battles of Salamis and Plataea against Persian invaders, thereby inaugurating what would become a definitive period in the history of Western literature and society, famed for its flourishing political and cultural life. The Golden Age lasted until Athens's humiliating defeat to Sparta in 404 B.C., after 27 years of war between the two city-states (commonly referred to as the Peloponnesian War).

In many ways, the dramatic arts stood at the center of the cultural achievements of the Golden Age, and the popularity and success of the plays of Sophocles were evident in his own day. His works were produced at the Great Dionysia in Athens, an annual festival honoring the god Dionysus and culminating in the famous dramatic competitions. Sophocles won first prize over twenty times in the competition, beginning with *Triptolemos* in 468 B.C., the first year that Aeschylus lost the contest to him. Euripides lost to Sophocles in 438 B.C. Unfortunately, *Triptolemos* is one among many of Sophocles's lost plays. He is purported to have written over one hundred tragedies yet only seven have survived to the modern era: *Ajax* (c. 450 B.C.); *Antigone* (c. 442 B.C.); *Ichneutai* (translated as *The Trackers,,* c. 440 B.C.); *The Trachiniae* (c. 440-430 B.C.); *Oedipus The King* (c. 430-426 B.C.); *Electra*

Sophocles

(c. 425-510 B.C.); *Philoctetes* (409 B.C.); and *Oedipus at Colonus* (c. 405 B.C.).

While there is some dispute among scholars as to their actual relationship, three of Sophocles's surviving works are thought to comprise a trilogy. Known as the Theban Trilogy the plays are *Antigone, Oedipus The King,* and *Oedipus at Colonus.* All of these plays draw upon the ancient story of Oedipus, King of Thebes. The sources for Sophocles's version of this legendary tale are thought to include Book XI of Homer's *Odyssey,* two ancient epic poems entitled the *Oedipodeia* and the *Thebais,* and four plays by Aeschylus, including *Seven against Thebes.*

In addition to being a dramatist and a public official, Sophocles also was a priest of the god Amynos, a healer. He married a woman named Nicostrata and had two sons, Iophon and Agathon.

PLOT SUMMARY

Prologue
Oedipus Rex begins outside King Oedipus's palace, where despondent beggars and a priest have gathered and brought branches and wreaths of olive

leaves. Oedipus enters and asks the people of Thebes why they pray and lament, since apparently they have come together to petition him with an unknown request. The Priest speaks on their behalf, and Oedipus assures them that he will help them. The Priest reports that Thebes has been beset with horrible calamities—famine, fires, and plague have all caused widespread suffering and death among their families and animals, and their crops have all been destroyed. He beseeches Oedipus, whom he praises for having solved the riddle of the Sphinx (an action which justified his succession to King Laius, as Jocasta's husband and as king) to cure the city of its woes. Oedipus expresses his profound sympathy and announces that he sent Creon, the Queen's brother, to Delphi to receive the Oracle of Apollo, in order to gain some much-needed guidance.

Creon arrives and Oedipus demands, against Creon's wishes, that he report the news in front of the gathered public. Creon reports that the gods caused the plague as a reaction against the murder of their previous king, Laius, and that they want the Thebans to ''drive out pollution sheltered in our land''; in other words, to find the murderer and either kill or exile him (Laius had been killed on the roadside by a highwayman). Oedipus vows to root out this evil. In the next scene, the chorus of Theban elders calls upon the gods Apollo, Athena, and Artemis to save them from the disaster.

Act I

Declaring his commitment to finding and punishing Laius's murderer, Oedipus says that he has sent for Teiresias, the blind prophet. After much pleading and mutual antagonism, Oedipus makes Teiresias say what he knows: that it was Oedipus who killed Laius. Outraged at the accusations Oedipus calls him a ''fortuneteller'' and a ''deceitful beggar-priest.'' Both are displaying what in Greek is called *orge,* or anger, towards each other. Oedipus suspects the seer of working on Creon's behalf (Creon, as Laius's brother, was and still is a potential successor to the throne). Teiresias thinks the king mad for not believing him and for being blind to his fate (not to mention ignorant of his true parentage). Oedipus then realizes that he does not know who his real mother is. Teiresias is led out while saying that Oedipus will be discovered to be a brother as well as a father to his children, a son as well as a husband to the same woman, and the killer of his father. He exits and the Chorus enters, warning of the implications of the decisive, oracular charges against Oedipus.

Act II

Creon expresses great desire to prove his innocence to Oedipus, who is continues to assert that Creon has been plotting to usurp the throne. Creon denies the accusations, saying he is quite content and would not want the cares and responsibilities that come with being king. Oedipus calls for his death. Jocasta, having heard their quarrel, enters and tries to pacify them, and the Chorus calls for proof of Creon's guilt before Oedipus punishes him. Jocasta reminds Oedipus of Apollo's oracle and also of the way Laius died. She recounts the story as it was told to her by a servant who was there at the crossroads where a charioteer and an old man attacked a man who in turn killed them. Hearing the tale, Oedipus realizes that he was the murderer and asks to consult the witness, the shepherd, who is sent for. The Chorus expresses its trust in the gods and prays to Heaven for a restoration of faith in the oracle.

Act III

Jocasta prays to Apollo to restore Oedipus's sanity, since he has been acting strange since hearing the manner in which Laius's died. A messenger tells her that King Polybos (the man Oedipus believes to be his father) has died and that the people of Isthmus want Oedipus to rule over them. Oedipus hopes this news means that the oracle is false (he hasn't killed his father since Polybos has died of old age), but he still fears that he is destined marry his mother. The messenger tells him that Polybos was not his father and that he, a shepherd, had been handed the child Oedipus by another shepherd, one of Laius's men. Jocasta tries to intervene and stop the revelations, but Oedipus welcomes the news.

Act IV

The shepherd enters and tells Oedipus, after a great deal of resistance, that he is Laius's son and that he had had him taken away to his own country by the messenger so as to avoid his fate. The chorus bewails the change in Oedipus from revered and fortunate ruler to one who has plunged into the depths of wretchedness.

Act V

A second messenger reports that Jocasta has just committed suicide, having realized that she was married to her son and thus had given birth to his children. He also reports that the king, suffering intensely upon hearing the news of his identity, blinded himself with the Queen's brooches. Oedipus has also requested that he be shown to the people of Thebes and then exiled; he comes out, bewildered and crying, asking for shelter from his painful memory, which cannot be removed as easily his eyes could be.

In the darkness of his blindness he wishes he were dead and feels the prophetic weight of the oracle. His blindness will allow him to avoid the sight of those whom he was destined to wrong and toward whom he feels immense sorrow and guilt. He asks Creon to lead him out of the country, to give Jocasta a proper burial, and to take care of his young daughters, Antigone (who comes to play a central role in the play named after he) and Ismene. In an extremely moving final moment with his children (who, he reminds himself, are also his siblings), Oedipus hears them and asks to hold their hands for the last time. He tells them they will have difficult lives and will be punished by men for sins they did not commit; for this reason he implores Thebes to pity them. He asks Creon again to exile him, and in his last speech he expresses regret at having to depart from his beloved children. The Chorus ends the play by using Oedipus's story to illustrate the famous moral that one should not judge a man's life until it is over.

CHARACTERS

Chorus of Theban Elders

Unlike the chorus in *Antigone,* whose Ode on Man historically has been regarded as a model expression of Athenian individualism, the chorus in this play has no famous statement, though its role is not insignificant. The Theban elders of the chorus are considered to be fairly representative men of Thebes who honor and respect the king and the gods; their odes reveal both a strong attachment to the king as well as a grounding in religious culture. In *The Idea of a Theater,* Francis Fergusson likens the chorus' role to that of a character who provides a broader context for the action of the play as a whole: "the chorus' action is not limited by the sharp, rationalized purposes of the protagonist; its mode of action, more patient, less sharply realized, is cognate with a wider, if less accurate, awareness of the scene of human life.''

Creon

Creon is the brother of Laius. Before the play begins Oedipus sent him on a mission to receive the Oracle of Apollo at Delphi, and he returns with its news during the prologue. With great hesitation he reports that "The god commands us to expel from the land of Thebes/An old defilement we are sheltering.'' He says that in order to rid the city of its woes, Oedipus must find the murderer of King Laius, his predecessor. Oedipus feels threatened by Creon and believes that he covets the throne (by some accounts Creon was to have been the next ruler following his brother's death, and he is thus filled with resentment).

When Teiresias tells the unbelieving Oedipus what he will come to know his true identity and responsibility for his father's murder, Oedipus immediately assumes that Teiresias is working for Creon, trying to get him the throne. Creon takes these accusations seriously and wishes to clear his name: "The fact is that I am being called disloyal/To the State, to my fellow citizens, to my friends.'' Creon defends himself to Oedipus in the next scene, saying that he has no desire to become king and that Oedipus harms himself and the state in leveling such accusations. Oedipus grows more incensed and calls for Creon's death; only the pleading of Jocasta and a member of the chorus prevent him from acting. At the end of the play, after Oedipus has blinded himself, Creon becomes king and acts with compassion towards the repentant Oedipus, leading him into the palace and then, as Oedipus requests—and Apollo has ordained— into exile.

Jocasta

Jocasta is Oedipus's wife and mother; she is also the mother of his children. Her first entrance onstage occurs when Oedipus and Creon are in the midst of arguing; Jocasta storms in and demands that they resolve their petty personal dispute because the country's troubles are far more urgent: "Poor foolish men, what wicked din is this?/With Thebes sick to death, is it not shameful/That you should rake some private quarrel up?'' She pleads

MEDIA ADAPTATIONS

- There is an outstanding sound recording from 1974 of the opera-oratorio adaptation of *Oedipus Rex* by Igor Stravinsky and Jean Cocteau; the text is translated by e. e. cummings. It is available from Columbia Music.

- *Oedipus Rex* was adapted as a film by Tyrone Guthrie, starring Douglas Campbell, Donald Davis, Eleanor Stuart, and Douglas Rain, Motion Pictures, 1957. The translation is by poet William Butler Yeats.

- The play was also adapted for film by Pier Paolo Pasolini, starring Franco Citti, Silvano Mangano, Julian Beck, and Pasolini himself as the High Priest, Euro International Films, 1967. This epic film was shot in Morocco. Its interpretation of the Oedipus story is bleak, emotionally demanding, and self-consciously autobiographical.

- Another film version from the 1960s is that of Philip Saville, starring Christopher Plummer, Lilli Palmer, Orson Welles, and Donald Sutherland, Universal, 1968.

- Rainer Simon, a German filmmaker, directed *Der Fall Dipus,* or *The Oedipus Case.* Set in summertime Greece when a foreign military detachment camp out near Thebes and film the Oedipus story, the film stars Sebastian Hartmann, Tatiana Lygari, and Jan-Josef Liefers, 1990, Toro Film.

- The British Broadcasting Corporation (BBC) adapted the play for film, starring Michael Pennington, Claire Bloom, and John Gielgud, 1991, Films for the Humanities, British Broadcasting Corporation. Excellent performances from the principal actors as well as from the chorus; staging is minimal but sufficient.

- *Oedipus Rex* was adapted as a film for the *Living Literature: The Classics and You* series, Lesson No. 5., 1994, available from RMI Media Productions.

- Two half-hour, made-for-video stage performances of the play are available from Children's Television International (The Play Series, volume 2) and Encyclopedia Britannica Educational Corporation (The EBE Humanities Program, Drama Series).

- Far from a literal translation of the play is Woody Allen's *Oedipus Wrecks,* a short comedy about a Jewish New York attorney, Sheldon Mills, who is constantly being nagged, followed, and publicly humiliated by his overbearing mother, Sadie Millstein. The film stars Allen, Julie Kavner, Mia Farrow, and Mae Questel, 1989, Touchstone Pictures; it is the third segment in an anthology film entitled *New York Stories.*

---

with Oedipus to believe Creon's good intentions towards him and their hostilities momentarily abate. She assures Oedipus that the oracle proclaiming Laius's murder by his own son was false, since Laius was killed by highwaymen and his son had been left "to die on a lonely mountainside." Rather than placating Oedipus, her words haunt him, he recalls "a shadowy memory," and asks her to give details about Laius's death. The surviving witness to the crime, tells Jocasta, had come to her when Oedipus was made king and asked her if he could be sent far away; she granted him his wish and now is asked by Oedipus to recall this witness—a shepherd—to the palace to testify about the murder.

Jocasta tells Oedipus not to trust in the truth of oracles. When the messenger arrives to tell of Polybos's death, Jocasta is hopeful that she can allay Oedipus's fears about fulfilling the prophecy. Later in the same scene she tries to stop him from questioning the messenger regarding his true father: "May you never learn who you are!" In her final speech she calls Oedipus "miserable" and says she will have no other name for him. Towards the end of the play a second messenger reports that she has hanged herself, giving a moving account of her wailing and physical expressions of grief during her last moments. Thornton Wilder, the American playwright, eloquently described Sophocles's artistry in portraying Jocasta in *American Characteristics and Other Essays:* "The figure of the Queen is drawn with great precision, shielding her husband form the knowledge she foresees approaching; alternately condemning and upholding the authority of the oracles as best suits the direction of the argument at the moment, and finally giving up the struggle."

Messenger

The messenger enters in Scene III and tells Oedipus that King Polybos of Corinth, who Oedipus had believed to be his father is dead. Oedipus also learns from this messenger that Polybos was not his father; the messenger himself had been given Oedipus as an infant by one of Laius's men and that he had untied Oedipus's bound ankles. He causes the shepherd who left Oedipus to die (having been given him by Jocasta, his mother) to come in and testify that Oedipus is Laius's son.

Messengers were common devices used in Greek drama. They were often used to relate action that occurred offstage or to summarize events that have taken place between acts or scenes.

Oedipus

Oedipus, the title character, is the protagonist of the play. His name means "swell-foot" or "swollen-foot." One of the most famous dramatic characters in the history of Western literature, he was singled out by Aristotle in his *Poetics* as the right kind of protagonist because he inspires the right combination of pity and fear. "This is the sort of man who is not pre-eminently virtuous and just, and yet it is through no badness or villainy of his own that he falls into the misfortune, but rather through some flaw in him; he being one of those who are in high station and good fortune, like Oedipus and Thyestes and the famous men of families such as these." Oedipus's fatal flaw, the technical Greek term for which is *hamartia,* can be thought of as a character fault or a mistake, or more like an Achilles heel rather than a flaw for which he can be held directly responsible. A hereditary curse has been placed on his family, and he unknowingly has fulfilled the terms of the prophecy that Laius's son would kill him and marry his wife.

The play's action is concerned with the gradual and delayed revelation of the fulfillment of this oracle. It specifically focuses on Oedipus's quest for knowledge, on the one hand, and, on the other, the other characters' resistance to discovering the truth; Jocasta tries to protect her husband/brother from the facts and the shepherd cannot be forced to speak until his life is at stake. Oedipus impatiently confronts Creon and Teiresias with their hesitation to answer his summons to the palace to share their knowledge with him and the public. Connected with this frustration is a feature of Oedipus's personality for which he is somewhat more responsible; Oedipus is also said to suffer from a character flaw known as *hubris,* or pride, and his cruel treatment of Creon and Teiresias in the aforementioned situations evidences this trait. He insists on hearing the truth, again and again, in the face of reluctant tellers who are scared for their lives, for his life, and for the future of Thebes.

Perhaps it is Oedipus's pride which rounds him out and allows Aristotle to hold him up as a well-fashioned character, since without it he would seem too virtuous and the tragedy would be too "unlikely." Oedipus's speech is also given a good dose of irony in the play. For example, when he calls for an investigation of Laius's murder and says "then once more I must bring what is dark to light," he is also foreshadowing his future blinding, since his investigation will reveal the dark secret of his parentage, metaphorically enlightened by the truth but literally blinded by it as well. When he curses the murderer of Laius he is cursing himself and predicts his own exile and consequent life of "wretchedness." Oedipus is wise (he has solved the riddle of the Sphinx), revered by his subjects, and dedicated to the discovery of truth. He wants to rid Thebes of the plague (pollution, a common theme in Greek drama) that is decimating its population. Fate and the gods, however, have other things in store for Oedipus, and his helplessness and utter ruin at the play's conclusion are a painful spectacle.

Priest

After Oedipus's opening lines, the Priest of Zeus is the next character in the play to speak, and he does so as a religious leader and elder representative of the people of Thebes. Standing before the king's palace, surrounded by the Theban people, the priest informs Oedipus (and the audience) of the misery-laden condition of Thebes: a plague is killing many of the city's human and animal populations and fires are destroying the lands and its crops.

He praises Oedipus, who has solved the riddle of the Sphinx, for his wisdom and ability to improve their lives, and asks of him, on behalf of the people, swiftly and decisively to act and end the suffering.

Second Messenger

The second messenger appears in the last scene to announce and describe Jocasta's suicide. He also relates Oedipus's discovery of her body and his subsequent blinding. He predicts future sorrows for a people whose kings descend from this polluted line. The second messenger also announces Oedipus's entry onstage after his self-mutilation: "You will see a thing that would crush a heart of stone."

Shepherd of Laius

The old shepherd is summoned by Oedipus so that he can discover his true parentage. The shepherd reveals his information only after Oedipus threatens his life if he remains silent. He admits to receiving the infant he gave to Polybos's messenger from Laius and Jocasta. Oedipus realizes his identity and his crimes of patricide and incest after hearing the shepherd's story.

Teiresias

Teiresias, a blind prophet and servant of Apollo, twice was asked by Oedipus to come to the palace to discuss the crisis in Thebes. In the first act of the play he finally appears, revealing the reasons for the city's devastation, knowledge that he is reluctant to reveal to Oedipus for fear of making him miserable. Oedipus, feeling himself to be betrayed by the prophet's resistance, verbally abuses Teiresias ("You sightless, witless, senseless, mad old man!") and accuses him of working on behalf of the "usurper" Creon.

Reluctantly, Teiresias tells Oedipus that he should not mock him so quickly; in a famous moment of foreshadowing, he tells the king that it is he who is blind: "But I say that you, with both your eyes, are blind:/You cannot see the wretchedness of your life,/Nor in whose house you live, no, nor with whom." Significantly, Teiresias is also the first character in the play to question Oedipus's assumption that he knows his parentage and to tell him that he has committed atrocities that he does not yet know are his own. He tells Oedipus that he will become blind and poor, that Oedipus is himself Laius's murderer, and that he will learn that he has fathered children with his mother. While Teiresias's presence on stage is brief, as a prophet representing the god Apollo he remains one of the most powerful

characters in the play; in addition, the Athenian audience would have recognized him from Homeric mythology (in *The Odyssey* the title character must go down into the underworld to gain information from the dead prophet).

THEMES

Oedipus Rex is the story of a king of Thebes upon whom a hereditary curse is placed and who therefore has to suffer the tragic consequences of fate. During a time of plague, fires, and other forms of decimation, Oedipus decides to take action to restore life and prosperity to his kingdom, only to discover through this quest that his identity is not what he thought. He learns that he has killed his father, married his mother, and had children with her; his wife-mother Jocasta kills herself and Oedipus blinds himself and goes into exile; his uncle Creon becomes King of Thebes.

Knowledge and Ignorance

Oedipus's desire to gain knowledge that will help to rid Thebes of its pollution is evident from the beginning of the play. When the priest comes to him to ask for help, Oedipus has already begun the process of searching for solutions; he has sent Creon to Delphi to learn from Apollo what measures should be taken. When Creon enters, Oedipus begins questioning him intensely, declares a search for Laius's murderer, and asks for Teiresias's assistance as well as that of others; when a member of the chorus offers information Oedipus says "tell me. I am interested in all reports." His strong belief that the search for the truth will lead to a successful cleansing of Thebes is juxtaposed with the reluctance on the part of other characters to deliver their knowledge. Most fear retribution, since their knowledge points to Oedipus as the source of Thebes's troubles. This belief should also be understood in the context of Oedipus's ignorance and final, tragic discovery of his identity; by demanding that others tell him all they know he is forced to confront the hideous facts of his patricide and incest.

Choices and Consequences

Another theme in the play is the distinction between the truthfulness of oracles and prophecies of the gods (fate), as opposed to man's ability to influence his life's trajectory through his own actions (free will or self-determinism). While argu-

TOPICS FOR FURTHER STUDY

- In his *Third Letter on Oedipus,* Voltaire, a French Enlightenment philosopher and writer, expressed incredulity at the fact that Oedipus, upon discovering that the shepherd who witnessed Laius's murder was still alive, decides to consult an oracle rather than actively to seek the testimony of this witness. How does Voltaire's questioning of Oedipus's decision-making reveal the differences in religious belief between Athenian society in the fifth century B.C. and the Enlightenment? Research the status of belief in oracles in Athenian culture and compare it to the debates between the Jesuits and Jansenists in Voltaire's France. Discuss this difference in the context of *Oedipus Rex.*

- During the fifth century in Athens, the skill of *sophistry*—the ability to be a rhetorically persuasive public speaker, and to gain political power through the effectiveness of one's speech performances—was becoming an increasingly important aspect of civic culture. One of the most famous sophists, Protagoras, is famous for saying "Man is the measure of all things," and this statement is indicative of the sophists' attitude toward man's potential to learn to excel at rhetoric and thereby win court cases, for example, even if their causes are unjust. Research this aspect of Athenian society, and juxtapose the powers of rhetorical persuasion with the treatment of fate in *Oedipus Rex.* You might wish to start by looking at the well-known first choral ode in *Antigone,* which warns against the kind of over-confidence in man's abilities that Athens was famous for. How does Sophocles use oracular knowledge to comment on man's belief that he can master the universe through knowledge?

- *Oedipus Rex* was written in Athens shortly after its war with Sparta—commonly referred to as the Peloponnesian War—broke out in 431 B.C. Investigate the war-torn environment in Athens during Sophocles's day by reading Book II of Thucydides's *History of the Peloponnesian War,* paying close attention to Pericles's funeral oration in the middle of the book. Imagine what it would have been like to have been an audience member for opening night, 426 B.C., of *Oedipus Rex,* and write a journal entry from the perspective of such a person.

- Were a person in contemporary America to unwittingly commit the crimes of Oedipus, to what kind of moral scrutiny would they be subjected? Do you think it's fair that a person is punished for a crime they did not realize they were committing? How might contemporary society (as opposed to Athenian culture) deal differently with this issue?

ments exist regarding the predominance of these schools of thought, *Oedipus Rex* emphasizes the eventual and tragic triumph of the former over the latter. Despite his best efforts to be a good and wise king and to substantiate his claims about the evil machinations of Creon and Teiresias, fate works against him and finally shows that he was wrong to believe in a conspiracy. For example, when Oedipus wishes to punish Creon, he expresses to a member of the chorus his intention to shape his policy in forcefully self-determining language: "Would you have me stand still, hold my peace, and let this man win everything, through my inaction?" Again, Oedipus struggles against the oracle that predicts his hand in his father's death and boldly asserts that it is wrong when Polybos's death is reported: "Polybos/ Has packed the oracles off with him underground./ They are empty words." But the oracle remains true, and Oedipus is helpless in the face of its powerful prophecy.

Public vs. Private Life

The extent to which Oedipus desires public disclosure of information is particularly striking in the play's first scenes. He asks the priest and Creon to speak publicly about the troubles of Thebes and to offer possible clues and solutions in front of his subjects, in spite of their reservations. Creon asks: ''Is it your pleasure to hear me with all these/ Gathered around us? I am prepared to speak,/But should we not go in?'' Oedipus consistently refuses to hide any knowledge he will receive and wants his informers to adopt a similar attitude. When Teiresias refuses to answer Oedipus's call and later resists revealing the king's dark truth, Oedipus grows impatient, hostile, and abusive. Teiresias would like to keep his information to himself, as will the shepherd in a later scene, but Oedipus will hear nothing of it. In addition, Jocasta is inclined to evade or gloss over the truth as it is about to be revealed from various people. She views the matter a private one and tries to protect Oedipus from the disastrous disclosures. Oedipus, however, refuses to tolerate a world in which secrets exist. He publicly learns the truth—at the expense of his sanity and happiness. His desire for a Theban society that fosters truth and openess is an admirable one, one that albeit contributes to his demise.

STYLE

The Genre of Greek Tragic Drama

Ever since Aristotle's high praise regarding its structure and characterization in his *Poetics, Oedipus Rex* has been considered one of the most outstanding examples of tragic drama. In tragedy, a protagonist inspires in his audience the twin emotions of pity and fear. Usually a person of virtue and status, the tragic hero can be a scapegoat of the gods or a victim of circumstances. Their fate (often death or exile) establishes a new and better social order. Not only does it make the viewer aware of human suffering, tragedy illustrates the manner in which pride (*hubris*) can topple even the strongest of characters. It is part of the playwright's intention that audiences will identify with these fallen heroes-and possibly rethink the manner in which they live their lives. Theorists of tragedy, beginning with Aristotle, have used the term *catharsis* to capture the sense of purgation and purification that watching a tragedy yield in a viewer: relief that they are not in the position of the protagonist and awareness that one slip of fate could place them in such circumstances.

Structure

The dramatic structure of Greek drama is helpfully outlined by Aristotle in the twelfth book of *Poetics.* In this classical tragedy, a Prologue shows Oedipus consulting the priest who speaks for the Theban elders, the first choral ode or Parodos is performed, four acts are presented and followed by odes called *stasimons,* and in the *Exodos,* or final act, the fate of Oedipus is revealed.

Staging

Tragedies in fifth-century Athens were performed in the marketplace, known in Greek as the *agora.* The dramatic competitions of the Great Dionysia, Athens's annual cultural and religious festival, were held in a structure made of wood near the Acropolis. The chorus performed on a raised stage. There were no female actors, and it is still unknown (though much speculated upon) whether women attended these performances. It is also noteworthy that the performance space was near the Pnyx, the area in which the century's increasingly heated and rhetorically sophisticated political debates took place—a feature of Athenian cultural life that suggests the pervasive nature of spectacles of polished and persuasive verbal expression.

The Chorus

The Greek chorus, like the genre of tragedy itself, is reputed to be a remnant of the ritualistic and ceremonial origins of Greek tragedy. Sophocles added three members of the chorus to Aeschylus's twelve. In terms of form, the choral ode has a tripartite structure which bears traces of its use as a song and dance pattern. The three parts are called, respectively, the strophe, the antistrophe, and the epode; their metrical structures vary and are usually very complex. If the strophe established the dance pattern, in the antistrophe the dancers trace backwards the same steps, ending the ode in a different way with the epode.

With respect to content, the choral odes bring an additional viewpoint to the play, and often this perspective is broader and more socio-religious than those offered by individual characters; it is also conservative and traditional at times, potentially in an effort to reflect the views of its society rather than the protagonist. The Chorus's first set of lyrics in *Oedipus Rex,* for example, express a curiosity about

A scene from an Indonesian production of Oedipus Rex

Apollo's oracle and describes the ruinous landscape of Thebes. Its second utterance reminds the audience of the newness of Teiresias's report: ''And never until now has any man brought word/Of Laius's dark death staining Oedipus the King.'' The chorus reiterates some of the action, expressing varying degrees of hope and despair with respect to it; one of its members delivers the play's final lines, much like the Shakespearean epilogue. Sometimes the chorus sings a dirge with one or more characters, as when it suggests to Oedipus not to disbelieve Creon's protestations of innocence.

Setting

The play's action occurs outside Oedipus's palace in Thebes. Thebes had been founded, according to the myth, by Cadmus (a son of Agenor, King of Phoenicia) while searching for his sister Europa, who had been abducted by Zeus in the form of a bull. A direct line of descent can be traced from Cadmus to Oedpius; between them are Polydorus, Labdacus, and, of course, Laius.

Imagery and Foreshadowing

Associated with knowledge and ignorance are the recurring images of darkness and light in the play, and these images work as examples of a kind of foreshadowing for which the play is justly famous. When the play begins, the priest uses this set of contrasts to describe the current condition of Thebes: ''And all the house of Kadmos is laid waste/All emptied, and all darkened.'' Shortly after this moment, Oedipus promises Creon: ''Then once more I must bring what is dark to light,'' that is, the murder of Laius will out and Oedipus will be responsible for finding and exposing the culprit(s). Metaphorical and literal uses of darkness and light also provide foreshadowing, since it is Oedipus's desire to bring the truth to light that leads him to a self-knowledge ruinous and evil enough to cause him to blind himself. After the shepherd reveals his birth he declares, ''O Light, may I look on you for the last time!'' In saying this he sets up for the audience, who are, presumably, familiar with the legend of Oedipus, his subsequent actions. The second messenger describes his command to himself as he proceeds to perform the gruesome task: ''From this hour, go in darkness!'' thereby enacting both a literal and metaphorical fall into the dark consequences of his unbearable knowledge. These are but a few examples of how imagery and foreshadowing as techniques can meet, overlap, and mutually inform one another in the play; through subjective interpretation, many more may be found.

HISTORICAL CONTEXT

Sophocles lived and worked in a time of great cultural significance, not only in the history of Athens but the greater sense of Western democratic culture. Wars with Persia and Sparta, the development of democratic culture, public architectural projects, and theatrical entertainments, as well as the rise of a distinctively rhetorical culture (a culture based on the strength of language and writing) are important features of the Athens during Sophocles's life, known as the Golden Age of Athens.

Soon after Cleisthenes established democracy in Athens in 507 B.C., Athens was threatened by outside enemies. At the beginning of the fifth century B.C., the Persians, led by Darius, crossed the Aegean to conquer Athens. After its triumph over Miletos in 494, the Persian army began to be defeated, with Athens winning the decisive victory at Marathon in 490. The battles of Salamis, Platea, and Mycale in 480-79 were also won by Athens, and the Persian forces (led by Xerxes I) finally lost the war. The Athenians prided themselves on their victory over Xerxes; roughly fifteen years after Sophocles's birth, Athens had become an Empire in its own right, forming the Delian League in 478-77. From 492-60 the city-state was led by Pericles, a populist leader who is famous today for his military skill, his rhetorical prowess, and his public building projects—including the Parthenon. Sophocles himself took part in some of Pericles's projects and in the city's military life, aiding Pericles in the Samian war (441-39), becoming an ambassador some years later, and joining the ruling council in 413.

Although the Persian threat had subsided, a new threat arose: the Peloponnesian War with Sparta and other states under their leadership began in 432. Thucydides, an Athenian general and historian noted for his impartiality and accuracy, tells the story of this war in his *History of the Peloponnesian War*. Athens, defeated in Sicily in 413, surrendered to Sparta (which was being supported by Persia) in 404, the year after Sophocles died.

In the midst of all this war, Athenian democracy flourished during Sophocles's lifetime, its commercial enterprises along the eastern Mediterranean coastline were successful and its cultural life enjoyed immense nourishment and development. Greek religious life centered around the shrines frequented by worshippers of Apollo at Delphi, Apollo and Artemis at Delos, and Zeus at Olympia. Festivals were often held at the shrines and athletic competi-

tions, dance, song, and theatrical performances also took place. Intellectually, Athens was thriving—its mathematicians and scientists, after the work of Pythagoras and Xenophanes during the previous century, began to make new discoveries in arithmetic and geology; Pericles, who studied sophistry with Zeno, brought the skill of oratory to new, unprecedented heights, and his support of the plastic and literary arts allowed Athenians to enjoy the lasting achievements of their contemporaries. While public building was interrupted by the Persian war, it resumed with vigor in the latter half of the fifth century, with the Temple of Zeus at Olympia and, in Athens, the Temple of Athena Nike, as well as the Parthenon, Propylaea, and the Erechtheum. Pericles saw to it that elaborate public building projects motivated artists of his time to achieve greatness for their city.

Greek drama also flourished. Pericles provided entertainments and pageantry, granting allowances for public festivals so that all men could attend them. Aeschylus, Sophocles, and Euripides were the three great dramatists of the age; Sophocles competed successfully with both his teacher Aeschylus and with his contemporary, Euripides, in the annual tragic competitions of the Great Dionysia. Some of the drama of this period concerned specific political issues, such as Phrynichos's *Capture of Mileros* (493) and Aeschylus's *Persians* (472). Other plays, like Aeschylus's *Oresteia* and *Oedipus Rex* address broader questions about mythological leaders and their relationships to the gods, fate, and their native Greek cultural heritage. While critics have argued that readers are not meant to draw any parallels between the plague-ridden Thebes in which *Oedipus Rex* takes place and the plague in Athens in 430-29 B.C., it is not difficult to surmise that an audience for whom the experience of such devastation was familiar would have felt particular connections with their own situation.

CRITICAL OVERVIEW

The history of the critical reception to *Oedipus Rex* begins with Aristotle (384-322 B.C.), who in his *Poetics* inaugurated the history of formalist and structural analysis of literature, two important cornerstones for the enterprise of the critical interpretation of literature. In some ways it can be regarded as the first book of literary criticism, and its significance for the subsequent study of the works of

COMPARE
&
CONTRAST

- **Fifth Century B.C.:** The development of trial by jury in the law courts and the art of sophistry as practiced by philosophers such as Zeno, led to the creation of the first hired lawyers. The ability to persuade a public audience was an important feature of cultural life, and philosophers tutored leaders such as Pericles in oratorical skills.

  Today: Rhetorical efficacy remains the chief attribute of today's courtroom lawyers. The public has limited access to these trials unless they garner media attention, as, for example, did the infamous trial of former football star O. J. Simpson, who was accused of murdering his ex-wife Nicole Simpson and her acquaintance Ronald Goldman.

- **Fifth Century B.C.:** In one of many bids for popularity, Athens ruler Pericles spent extraordinary sums of money to support the arts through pageants, processions, public banquets, and monetary allowances for theatrical performances. The theater was associated with the cultural and religious festivals of the Great Dionysia, in whose annual competitions Sophocles won over twenty first-place awards.

  Today: Public funding for the arts constitutes less than one percent of the federal budget, and the Republican leaders in Congress have proposed to eliminate this public source of support in favor of a privatized system of grants generated by donations from actors and other private citizens. While the theater continues to be a popular form of entertainment, the festivals surrounding public performances are rarely state-funded.

- **Fifth Century B.C.:** There was a great conflict leading to a long war between Athens and Sparta, the most powerful city-states, and the two supported radically different governmental structures—Athens was a democracy; Sparta, an oligarchy (absolute rule by a committee).

  Today: Until the early 1990s, the two largest global powers, the capitalist, democratic United States and the communist U.S.S.R., were fighting the Cold War, with both sides building up conventional weaponry and nuclear arms. The U.S.S.R. fell because of inner strife, and the Cold War mentality gave way to an understanding of the potential for global peace, on the one hand, and the escalation of more localized, civil strife, on the other.

- **Fifth Century B.C.:** Scientific advancement and great progress in mathematics coincided with a belief, in the words of Protagoras, that "man is the measure of all things," and that people can control their own destinies, mastering the universe through the power of knowledge.

  Today: Developments in artificial intelligence and bioengineering lead to difficult, controversial issues about the potential for computers and robots to "think," and about the ethics of such techniques as cloning.

Sophocles in general and *Oedipus Rex* in particular is enormous, due to the exemplary status he granted the play, as the greatest tragedy ever written. He gave it high praise for its outstanding fulfillment of the requirements he set out for tragedy, including reversal of situation, characterization, well-constructed plot, and rationality of action.

Oedipus Rex contains an excellent moment of "reversal" in the scene in which the messenger comes to tell Oedipus of the death of Polybos, whom he believes to be Oedipus's father. According to Aristotle, because Oedipus learns from him inadvertently that Polybos is not his father, "by revealing who he is, he produces the opposite effect." Aristotle also praised the play for its characterization of the hero, who causes the audience to feel the right mixture of "pity and fear" while observing his actions. The hero should not be too

O e d i p u s   R e x

virtuous, nor should he be evil: "there remains, then, the character between these two extremes—that of a man who is not eminently good and just, yet whose misfortune is brought about not by vice or depravity, but by some error or frailty. He must be one who is highly renowned and prosperous—a personage like Oedipus, Thyestes, or other illustrious men of such families."

The plot receives commendation by Aristotle for its ability to stir the emotions of not only its audience members but, even more significantly, those who merely hear the story: "he who hears the tale told will thrill with horror and melt to pity at what takes place." In addition, *Oedipus Rex* succeeds in shaping the action in such a way that its ramifications are unknown until after the event itself occurs: "the deed of horror may be done, but done in ignorance, and the tie of kinship or friendship be discovered afterwards . . . here, indeed, the incident is outside the drama proper." Lastly, Aristotle remarks that he prefers the role of the chorus in Sophocles to that of Euripides, and that the *Oedipus Rex* excludes from the play proper any irrational elements, such as Oedipus's ignorance of the mode of Laius's death. This last point is taken up by Voltaire, who subjected the play to intense questioning on the basis of the improbability of aspects such as this one.

After Aristotle, the major figures who have analyzed the play include those dramatists, from antiquity to the present, such as Seneca, Corneille, Dryden, and Hofsmannsthal, who respectively translated the play into Latin, French, English, and German. Poets and dramatists are themselves acting as critics when they embark on projects of translation, even if they have not given explicit accounts of how and why they have proceeded. Implicitly, these works ask their readers to attempt to answer these questions for themselves, and a short list of the variations on Sophocles's play should begin to generate such study. In 50 A.D, the Roman writer Seneca, for instance, decided to add an unseen episode narrated by Creon in which the ghost of Laius identifies his murderer to Teiresias.

In the 1580s in England the Tudor university dramatist William Gager sketched out five scenes for an unfinished version of the play, combining elements of Seneca's *Oedipus* and his *Phonecian Women* with scenes of his own creation; the first original scene is a lament of a Theban citizen for his dead father and son, to whom he seeks to give a proper burial in the midst of the plague-ridden city. His Jocasta kills herself because of her sons' fratricidal struggle for power. In 1659 Corneille prefaced his neo-Classical version of the play with a notice that he has reduced the number of oracles, left out the graphic description of Oedipus's blinding because of the presence of ladies in the audience, and added the happy love story of Theseus and Dirce in order to satisfy all attendees. He keeps Seneca's additional scene but makes Laius's speech more vague. Dryden, two decades later, self-consciously drew upon Corneille's subplot but changing its ending to an unhappy one. Like Corneille he laments the fact that audiences demand such light entertainment accompanying their experience of great tragic drama.

In the next century, translators and commentators in England and France beginning with Voltaire and including Pierre Brumoy, Thomas Maurice, and R. Potter brought unique perspectives to the play. Voltaire believed the play to be defective in ways that many scholars expected from the Enlightenment thinker. Following Aristotle and going much further in his skeptical stance, in 1716 Voltaire criticized the lack of plausibility in Oedipus's ignorance of the manner of Laius's death: "that he did not even know whether it was in the country or in town that this murder was committed, and that he should give neither the least reason nor the least excuse for his ignorance, I confess that I do not know any terms to express such an absurdity." Another famous criticism of his concerns the fact that Oedipus, upon learning that the shepherd who knows his origins is still alive, chooses to consult the oracle "without giving the command to bring before him the only man who could throw light on the mystery." In contradistinction to Voltaire, in the middle of the eighteenth century Brumoy movingly expressed his satisfaction with the play. Of the opening scene he wrote: "This is a speaking spectacle, and a picture so beautifully disposed, that even the attitudes of the priests and of Oedipus express, without the help of words, that one relates the calamities with which the people are afflicted, and the other, melted at the melancholy sight, declares his impatience and concern for the long delay of Creon, whom he had sent to consult the Oracle." Brumoy also recognizes that the play's values are pagan rather than Christian, and specifically he emphasizes the influential classical notion of destiny; after him, the English translators Thomas Maurice (1779) and R. Potter (1788) did the same.

German authors, including Johann Wolfgang von Goethe, dominate the reception history of *Oedipus* in the nineteenth century.

CRITICISM

Jennifer Lewin

In this essay Lewin argues that the story of Oedipus qualifies as the greatest of all tragedies.

Oedipus Rex is arguably the most important tragedy in all of classical literature. Ever since Aristotle used it in his *Poetics* in order to define the qualities of a successful tragedy, its strengths have been emphasized again and again by countless notable authors whose remarks illuminate the play's historical reception as much as they help us to understand the broader critical climate in which they wrote. When Freud, for example, helped to shape the direction of twentieth-century thought with his 1900 *The Interpretation of Dreams,* his coinage of the term ''Oedipal Complex'' was an integral part of his definition of dreams and imaginative literature as representations of wishes that usually remain hidden during normal social interaction. For Freud, then, Oedipus's predicament dramatizes the desire of every man to marry his mother and kill his father, but whereas most people tend to harbor or hide these feelings, Oedipus unknowingly acts them out. While still remaining extremely controversial, his theory's suggestive placement of Oedipus in closer psychological proximity to his readers throughout history raises fundamental questions about possible relationships between literature and reality. Other twentieth century scholars have occupied themselves less with these issues than with local readings of the play's characters, its plot, structure, and, finally, what it can teach its readers about religious values and human knowledge in fifth-century Athenian culture, a moment of great historical importance for its artistic achievements as well as its political culture.

The character of Oedipus has historically inspired a combination of fascination and repulsion. It is generally acknowledged, however, that he is to be admired for many reasons, and especially for demonstrating, as a responsible leader, his desire—from the very opening lines of the play—for honesty and directness in approaching the problem of Thebes's plague. In the Prologue, when he asks the priest to speak for the petitioners before him, he does so with majestic generosity: ''Tell me, and never doubt that I will help you/In every way I can; I should be heartless/Were I not moved to find you suppliant here.'' The Priest responds to him with equal magnanimity, praising Oedipus for his past achievements (he solved the riddle of the Sphinx, sent to Thebes as divine punishment for Laius's sins) and pleading for the help that the capable Oedipus has proven he can provide. Oedipus's position of power in relation to the Priest is extraordinary; as C. H. Whitman pointed out in *Sophocles: A Study of Heroic Humanism,* pagan culture customarily reversed those roles: ''The appeal of the priest, with its moving yet dignified description of the general suffering, is especially remarkable in that it is an inversion of the usual situation, in which the secular ruler consults the priest or seer about divine things, as Oedipus later consults Teiresias.''

The scene establishes Oedipus as a ruler not with divine intuition (the Priest also says ''You are not one of the immortal gods, we know'') but with the intellectual prowess to ameliorate Thebes's grave situation. A later exchange between Creon and Oedipus and the first scene's dialogue between Teiresias and Oedipus, in which Oedipus presses both figures publicly to utter the oracular knowledge they possess (but are extremely reluctant to offer) show Oedipus as extremely eager to gain the knowledge that will help to rid Thebes of its ills. In her recent study of Sophocles, *Prophesying Tragedy Tragedy: Sight and Voice in Sophocles's Theban Plays,* Rebecca Bushnell agrees that the play establishes Oedipus as someone ''who believes in speaking freely . . . but he is not content merely to speak himself; he also forces others to speak.'' Oedipus shows fearlessness in the face of turmoil, and his unstoppable quest for public utterance of the truth of the oracle leads him, tragically, to the knowledge that he has fulfilled its terms. His perception of his responsibilities as king, however, have led him to be compared to Pericles, the ruler when Sophocles lived and wrote, remembered for heroically facing the most famous epoch of war and civil strife in Athenian history.

Oedipus has also been noted for possessing a less desirable quality related to his desire for disclosure, and that quality, *hamartia,* is an ancient Greek concept that E. R. Dodds, in *Greece and Rome,* classified as ''sometimes applied to false moral judgments, sometimes to purely intellectual error.'' *Hamartia* can be understood to refer to the all too human limitations possessed by the tragic hero, his faults that make him less than perfect but not

WHAT DO I READ NEXT?

- Sophocles's *Oedipus at Colonus,* produced posthumously by his grandson in 401 B.C., tells the story of Oedipus's wanderings after going into exile. He was attended by Antigone, his daughter, to Colonus, and there Theseus protected him until he died. Before he died he cursed his sons Eteocles and Polyneices that they should kill each other, and after Eteocles had ruled for a time he refused to surrender the throne to his brother, who gathered seven champions known as the Seven against Thebes. They attacked the city at each of its seven gates. The brothers died in battle. *Oedipus at Colonus* is the second play in the trilogy of Theban plays, which also includes *Antigone* (the final play) and *Oedipus Rex.*

- In *Antigone,* the title character (Oedipus's daughter) and her uncle, Creon the king of Thebes, quarrel because the king will not permit the burial rite to be performed for her brother, Polyneices, who was condemned as a traitor. Creon punishes Antigone for her attempts to bury her brother by sealing her alive inside a stone tomb. She hangs herself, and her husband-to-be Haemon, Creon's son, stabs himself next to her body.

- *The History of the Peloponnesian War,* by the Athenian citizen and general Thucydides (c. 460-400 B.C.), is a careful, compelling, and often first-hand account of the war between Athens and Sparta (431-404 B.C.), which occurred during the heyday of Sophocles's career.

- Written in the first century A.D., the lives of Athenian leaders presented in Plutarch's *The Rise and Fall of Athens: Nine Greek Lives* include Theseus, Pericles, Alcibiades, and Lysander;

these last three figures played key roles in Athens during the Peloponnesian War, and their lives provide an instructive political and cultural context for Sophoclean drama.

- *Democracy, Ancient and Modern* (1973), by M. I. Finley, traces the history of democratic culture from fifth-century Athens to the present day. It compares the political, social, and economic structures as well as the role of the arts and literature in different historically significant democracies.

- Shakespeare's *Hamlet,* written c. 1600, recounts the story of a young man whose father has died and his brother Claudius has assumed the throne, marrying his widow Gertrude. The ghost of king appears to his son, Hamlet, and urges him to avenge his death; Hamlet is obsessed with the memory of his father's death and is repulsed at the thought and sight of his mother's hasty remarriage; he wants to kill his uncle, Claudius, but does not succeed in finding the right opportunity until the final scene, when most of the main characters die in the tragedy's final blood bath. Since Freud, the mother-son relationship in the play has been historically considered to be driven by the son's Oedipus complex.

- *My Oedipus Complex,* a short story by Frank O'Connor (published in 1956), sets the Oedipus story in Ireland during World War I. While his father is away fighting in the war, a young boy, the first-person narrator, develops a misunderstood attraction toward his mother, a situation which becomes complicated by his father's return home and the parents' decision to have another child. An ironic but very touching version of the myth, complete with a happy ending.

---

blameworthy in any moral sense. While he may have flaws (like the heel of Achilles), we cannot attribute his downfall to them. Oedipus's impatience with Teiresias's attempt to withhold the

contents of the oracle, for example, led him to suspect the prophet of conspiring against him on behalf of Creon. He calls Teiresias a "sightless, witless, senseless, mad old man."

A. J. A. Waldock related Oedipus's *hamartia* to his approach to oracular knowledge. In his *Sophocles the Dramatist,* Waldock wrote: "he was in fault for not perceiving the truth, now he is in fault because he is too urgent to see it." In other words, Oedipus's eagerness to use his mind to act upon and thereby to solve every problem he encounters, when taken to its logical extreme, leaves no room for the gods' influence over the fate of man, an idea considered somewhat heretical in a culture which places much emphasis on and had faith in the role of the gods in shaping man's destiny. Readers such as W. P. Winnington-Ingram, in *Sophocles: An Interpretation,* have criticized Oedipus because he "trusts his intellect too much and must learn how fallible it is."

Ultimately, while we can regard Oedipus as both admirable for his leadership skills and noble intentions and imperfect for his overconfidence and harsh treatment of others, he is a figure whose fate inspires pity and terror because of his ability to endure misfortune. He blinds himself in an act of self-punishment and self-protection, since he is deeply horrified by his own crimes and unwilling to face others' gazes: "After exposing the rankness of my own guilt,/How could I look men frankly in the eyes?" Rather than ending his life, Oedipus lives to bear the weight of two curses, one imposed on his family line by the gods and the other self-imposed when he announces his intention to send Laius's murderer into exile. Dodds nicely captured the pathos of his suffering: "Oedipus is great, not in virtue of a great worldly position—for his worldly position is an illusion which will vanish like a dream—but in virtue of his inner strength: strength to pursue the truth at whatever personal cost, and strength to accept and endure it when found."

Notably, the end of the play does not show Oedipus leaving Thebes; although we see him ask Creon again and again to lead him into exile, the play ends with him being led into the palace, into a private space and away from a public domain polluted by his presence. In a detailed discussion of the last scene, M. Davies wrote in an issue of *Hermes* that it leaves our vision of Oedipus as a commanding figure very much intact: it "shows him still acting spontaneously like a king, in the old imperious manner, although the once equivalent temporal power has now fallen away."

In order to understand both the protagonist and the play itself in the larger context of fifth-century Greece, it is important to consider the conflicting roles of oracular knowledge and Athenian self-confidence in their culture's perception of man's place in the universe. At the time of the Peloponnesian War, oracular knowledge was often doubted because the oracles came from Apollo's shrine at pro-Spartan Delphi; the messages often reflected an anti-Athenian bias. In an essay on *Oedipus Rex* in *Homer to Brecht: The European Epic and Dramatic Traditions,* Paul Fry noted that "around 427 B.C., when the play was first acted, the priests of Apollo were out of favor because Apollo's oracles considering the Peloponnesian War were all pro-Spartan."

While this historical fact does not mean that the Priest and Teiresias would have been ridiculous figures for the play's first audiences, it does mean that Oedipus's skepticism would have been understood and sympathized with. In the context of the very different times of turmoil that the play depicts, however, Oedipus's disbelief may have appeared slightly more threatening, since, as Bushnell argued, Oedipus has no system of belief other than his own intellectual power with which to replace oracular knowledge: "Tiresias's arrival initiates the conflict between Apollo's signs and Oedipus's voice— a conflict that strikes at the roots of the city's order, which is based on the cooperation between sacred and secular interests . . . Oedipus seems to threaten directly the stability that the fulfillment of oracles represents, without establishing any new structure." In the plot thus conceived, Apollo's oracle is truth and Oedipus chastises himself for having believed otherwise: "Oedipus, damned in his birth, in his marriage damned,/Damned in the blood he shed with his own hand!" As an efficacious tool by which to shape human destiny, the power of oracular knowledge is retained by the gods, while Oedipus is able to reach lyrical heights in expressing the tragic consequences of being confined in such a world.

In ancient Athens, dissatisfaction with oracular knowledge was coupled with a growing sense that, in the words of Protagoras, "man is the measure of all things." Self-confidence in man's ability to order and rule his world reached even new heights under the leadership of Pericles, whose extensive training in sophistry and lack of fear in the gods led him to be a highly persuasive thinker who inspired in his subjects a sense of man's ability to accomplish limitless goals. For Sophocles's contemporaries, Oedipus's intellectual prowess was probably strongly reminiscent of Pericles—his eloquence and devotion to his country in a time of upheaval were legendary, and his investment in public building projects (the Parthenon among them) employed laborers and inspired artists to create beautiful memorials to their epoch.

While Oedipus's affection for Thebes is of a very different nature, his expression of care is moving: "Let me purge my father's Thebes of the pollution/Of my living here, and go out to the wild hills,/To Kithairon, that has won such fame with me,/The tomb my mother and father appointed for me,/And let me die there, as they willed I should." His desire to "purge [his] father's Thebes" and move mentally and physically towards death provides a powerfully cathartic closure for the play. In *The Birth of Tragedy,* the philosopher Nietzsche wrote of the spirituality of this final scene, its ability to leave audiences with a sense of rejuvenation: "Sophocles understood the most sorrowful figure of the Greek stage, the unfortunate Oedipus, as the noble human being who, in spite of his wisdom, is destined to error and misery but who eventually, through his tremendous suffering, spreads a magical power of blessing that remains effective even beyond his disease."

Source: Jennifer Lewin, in an essay for *Drama for Students,* Gale, 1997.

Janet M. Green

In this essay, educator and critic Green discusses symbolism in Oedipus Rex *and offers her interpretation of the play's climactic scene.*

In the fall 1992 issue of *The Explicator,* Bernhard Frank presented an unusual interpretation of the dramatic climax of Sophocles' *Oedipus Rex* In the scene, reported by the Second Messenger, Oedipus, horrified by the truth and distraught by his discovery that Jocasta has hanged herself, first lowers his queen/mother/wife to the ground and then plunges the long pins of her robe's brooches into his eyes. Professor Frank suggests that Jocasta's rope is an umbilical cord, that here we have a "role reversal," in which Jocasta becomes "the dead infant Oedipus should have been, if the tragedy was to have been averted." Then, in "another stage of the role reversal," he blinds himself. He is not castrating himself—a Freudian theory that Frank rightly rejects—but in the persona of Jocasta he "rapes his own eyes with her 'phalluses'."

It is sometimes tempting in literary criticism to seek in a thrusting instrument a sexual parallel, but one should carefully base such a parallel on hints and statements in the text. I do not find suggestions in *Oedipus Rex* for Frank's interpretation of the blinding scene, which raises several difficulties. For example, there are many nonsexual references to "eyes" and "sight" in the play. In fact, "seeing" could be called a unifying metaphor. Why should this passage, with no hint from the translators, be read as having such powerful sexual meaning? Oedipus's beard, into which the blood gushes, is identified as "the pubic region, as it were, of his pierced eyes. It is Jocasta's twofold revenge, reciprocating his off—repeated coital act." This reading poses considerable anatomical difficulties. Then, too, how can Jocasta at one moment represent her dead son and at the next a raging rapist? What is one to make of the blood that gushes forth? (Herman Melville symbolizes a bloody beard successfully in his poem, "The Portent," about the mutilation of John Brown's corpse.)

The Frank essay also considers the use of the brooches highly significant, inasmuch as Oedipus could have used "any nearby object for the purpose." But not just "any nearby object" is agreeable for blinding oneself, and probably weapons did not lie scattered about a queen's apartment as part of the decor. When Oedipus asks the Chorus for a sword with which to pursue Jocasta, the Frank essay concludes that in his frenzy, Oedipus "intends to thrust his sword into her offending womb, which ironically would emulate the sexual act one last time." What the text really says, however, is this: "From one to another of us he went, begging a sword, / Hunting the wife who was not his wife, the mother / Whose womb had carried his own children and himself."

Across the fiery enthusiasms of Professor Frank fall the long and soothing shadows of Aristotle and Sophocles. Aristotle's famous definition of tragedy, in *The Poetics,* stresses that pity and fear will be evoked by action of "a certain magnitude." His frequent praise of *Oedipus Rex* proves that Sophocles' masterpiece met his highest standards. We can therefore safely conclude that the emotions Aristotle thought that the play produced were pity and fear—not disgust and revulsion, which would be our more likely reactions to the interpretation that Professor Frank suggests.

Sophocles' treatment of blindness in the drama accords with Aristotle's reading of the play. It has far greater meaning than that of a symbolically achieved sexual act. Spiritual blindness is equated with obduracy and arrogance—hubris—and towards the end of *Oedipus Rex,* the physical blinding is already encouraging new insight, awareness, and compassion. When Oedipus could see, he beheld the piercing light of Greece, but he had then less understanding of his fate, less inner vision, and less humility than he is beginning to achieve after he loses that flooding, outer light. The resemblance between Oedipus and the blinded Gloucester in *King Lear* often comes to mind. Gloucester says, ''I stumbled when I saw.'' And when Lear observes, ''[Y]et you see how this world goes,'' Gloucester answers, ''I see it feelingly.''

Light, to the ancient Greeks, was beauty, intellect, virtue, indeed represented life itself. The Choragos asks Oedipus, ''What god was it drove you to rake black / Night across your eyes?'' And Oedipus replies in anguish:

> Apollo, Apollo, Dear
> Children, the god was Apollo.
> He brought my sick, sick fate upon me.
> But the blinding hand was my own!
> How could I bear to see
> When all my sight was horror everywhere?

We have in the drama, then, not just bitter irony played out by incredible coincidence, nor the story of a proud man rightly humbled. We have a powerful statement that the inscrutable gods exert extreme power over the unjust and the just, who suffer alike from their mysteriously random power. We do not need to make Oedipus's self-blinding into a sexual symbol or allegory to feel his baffled woe. Surely, enough sorrow is here to achieve the effect that Aristotle underlines so often and Sophocles creates with such skill.

Source: Janet M. Green, review of *Oedipus Rex,* in the Explicator, Vol. 52, no. 1, Fall, 1993, pp. 2–3.

Martin Kallich

In this excerpt, Kallich explains the myth of Oedipus and how it is represented in Sophocles's dramatic work.

In Sophocles' *Oedipus Tyrannus* [*Oedipus Rex*](c. 427 B.C.) . . . the supernatural agency that dominates the action is Apollo. Unfortunately, however, there is no certainty concerning meaning of the role of the Apollonian god in Sophocles' work. Apollo appears to use a man of noble, innocent, and pious nature to undermine social and religious values, despite his horror of sinning against them. But it is obvious that interpretations of this fundamental conflict between the irresistible power of destiny and the sacredness of natural ties will vary, depending upon what tone is read into the richly human and

> " WE DO NOT NEED TO MAKE
> OEDIPUS'S SELF-BLINDING INTO A
> SEXUAL SYMBOL OR ALLEGORY TO
> FEEL HIS BAFFLED WOE"

ambiguous lines. Here a representative selection from the vast resources of Sophoclean scholarship, particularly the work of modern American and English scholars, will made in order to illustrate the diversity of interpretation and provide a basis for understanding the adaptations of the creative writers.

Sir Richard Jebb, taking the traditional position in the nineteenth century, sees in Oedipus a symbol of modern man facing a religious dilemma. Both Oedipus and Jocasta, he points out, do not reject the gods—both are reverent, both believe in the wise omnipotence of the gods. But, on the other hand, both also reject the gods' moral ministers—Oedipus the prophet Tiresias, and Jocasta the priests at Delphi. Oedipus, Jebb states, is a rationalist, intellectually self-reliant; Jocasta, likewise, is a sceptic who questions the reliability of the oracles. Considering their views, Jebb feels that they represent a ''spiritual anarchy'' that not only unbalances the ''self-centered calm'' of Sophocles' mind but also endangers ''the cohesion of society.'' Thus, through their experience, ''a note of solemn warning, addressed to Athens and Greece, is meant to be heard.'' But Jebb concludes by reading into the drama the nineteenth-century problem of adjusting religious faith to the findings of science: ''It is as a study of the human heart, true to every age, not as a protest against tendencies of the poet's own, that the *Oedipus Tyrannus* illustrates the relation of faith to reason.'' Jebb's view is interesting because it illustrates in scholarship the possibility of accommodating the myth to changing life—in general, the attitude of the later imaginative critics of the myth. The modern trend in Sophoclean scholarship, however, is historical in orientation, for the scholars look at Sophocles' work not in the light of universal values but in the light of the ancient Greek past, particularly that of Sophocles himself in the Periclean Athens of the fifth century.

For example, Sir John Sheppard, the first to demonstrate carefully the possibility of presenting

"OEDIPUS SUFFERS NOT BECAUSE OF HIS GUILT, BUT IN SPITE OF HIS GOODNESS"

Sophocles' opinions in fifth-century terms, relates ancient Greek meanings given to the maxims of the Delphic oracle, "Know Thyself" and "Nothing Too Much," to an understanding of Oedipus' character, and concludes that they provide the final moral of the play. Sheppard interprets the philosophical theme of Sophocles' play as a mild agnosticism or neutral fatalism. Oedipus, he declares, behaves normally, commits an error in ignorance, and brings suffering upon himself. "Sophocles justifies nothing. . . . His Oedipus stands for human suffering. His gods . . . stand for the universe of circumstances as it is. . . . He bids his audience face the facts. . . . Oedipus suffers not because of his guilt, but in spite of his goodness."

Sir Maurice Bowra also synthesizes the two Delphic maxims, his point being that Oedipus has learned that he must do what the gods demand, and in his life illustrates what the Platonic Socrates means when he says the commands "Know Thyself" and "Be Modest" are the same. Oedipus finds modesty because he has learned to know himself: "So the central idea of a Sophoclean tragedy is that through suffering a man learns to be modest before the gods." Bowra argues that Sophocles' *Oedipus,,* reflecting such tragic contemporary events (noted by Thucydides) as a catastrophic plague in Athens and an unsuccessful war with Sparta, as well as a current disbelief in the oracles, dramatizes a conflict between gods and men. He concludes that "Sophocles allows no doubts, no criticism of the gods. . . . If divine ways seem wrong, ignorance is to blame. . . . For this conflict the gods have a reason. They wish to teach a lesson, to make men learn their moral limitations and accept them" (*Sophoclean Tragedy,* [Oxford], 1944). But Bowra appears to be too committed to supporting the religious establishment, and as a result misses the subtle and humane questioning suggested in the dramatic situation. For example, is not a very critical irony intended by the dramatist when Jocasta's offering at the altar of Apollo on center stage is seen still smoking at the time the messenger inform us of

her suicide by hanging? Another such irony may be intended in the *epilogos* when Oedipus, blind and polluted, craves to be sent out of the land as an outcast only to have Creon reply that Apollo must first pronounce. This need not only suggest respect for the power of the god; it may also suggest the god's failure at empathy. For it is as if the dramatist were asking Apollo to show a little charity, love, and forbearance towards erring man.

On the basis of such evidence, Cedric H. Whitman takes issue with Bowra. He states that the picture of a pure and pious Sophocles never questioning the oracles and serenely supporting the traditional belief in the Greek theodicy is completely wrong. Sophocles, Whitman believes, appears in the *Tyrannus* to have suffered a loss of faith; he is bitter, ironic, and pessimistic because of the irrational evil perpetrated by unjust gods on a morally upright man who wishes to be and do good. Whitman's point is that the ancient Greeks used the gods to explain where evil came from, especially that irrational evil which seemed to have no cause or moral meaning. Thus Sophocles was doubting the moral trustworthiness of the Greek gods: "The simple fact is that for Sophocles, the gods, whoever they are, no longer stand within the moral picture. Morality is man's possession, and the cosmos—or chaos—may be what it will." Sophocles dramatizes the theodicy "with a kind of agnostic aloofness. Sophocles was religious rather than pious" (*Sophocles: A Study of Heroic Humanism,* [Cambridge], 1951).

Such, briefly, are a few of the more significant prevailing views in American and English scholarship concerning Sophocles' handling of the myth in his masterpiece. They demonstrate, despite differences of opinion about Athenian life and Sophocles' character, that the meaning of the myth in the *Tyrannus* derives from the society and culture of Athens during the fifth century, and that Sophocles accommodates the basic story not only to his own time but also to his personal ideological and spiritual needs. So, depending upon how critic reads the complexities and ambiguities of Athenian culture and the author's tenuous character, Sophocles, in this play about King Oedipus, is impious or pious. But whatever the stand on Apollo and his oracles that Sophocles has really taken, there is no doubt about the depth, conviction, and art with which he expresses his credo. These qualities have always been admired, and, as a result, the form in which Sophocles has cast the myth has often been imitated.

Source: Martin Kallich, "Oedipus: From Man to Archetype" in *Comparative Literature Studies,* Vol. 3, no. 1, 1966, pp. 33–35.

FURTHER READING

Aristotle. *The Poetics,* translation by W. Hamilton Fyfe, Heinemann (London), 1927.

Aristotle's important discussion of effective tragic form includes many references to the exemplarity of Sophocles's play, and provides a useful understanding of classical poetic theory.

Bates, William Nickerson. *Sophocles: Poet and Dramatist,* Oxford University Press (London), 1940.

In a chapter on Oedipus, Bates summarizes the plot and offers general, laudatory remarks on Sophoclean tragedy, followed by discussions of the protagonist and Jocasta.

Bowra, C. M. *Sophoclean Tragedy,* Clarendon Press (Oxford), 1944.

Bowra's focus is on the role of Apollo and the gods in the play, offering a historical reading that contextualizes the oracle in Athenian society.

Bushnell, Rebecca W. *Prophesying Tragedy: Sight and Voice in Sophocles's Theban Plays,* Cornell University Press, 1988.

Bushnell compellingly argues that Oedipus's desire to speak and his aversion to silence together create a character whose faith in the efficacy of human words unsuccessfully challenges oracular knowledge.

Davies, M. "The End of Sophocles's O.T." in *Hermes,* Vol. 110, 1982, pp. 268-77.

Davies argues that the last scene of the play, in which Creon ushers Oedipus into the palace but does not send him into exile as some have assumed, shows us that neither character has changed psychologically as a result of the reversals of fortune in the play. Oedipus still understands himself in the majestic terms of a king, and Creon remains cautious and concerned.

Dawe, R. D., editor. *Sophocles: The Classical Heritage,* Garland (New York), 1996.

This collection of criticism of the play includes excerpts for the works of Aristotle, Corneille, Voltaire, and modern theorists as well. Also contains a few discussions of performances of the play from the Italian Renaissance to the present day.

Dodds, E. R. "On Misunderstanding the Oedipus Rex" in *Greece and Rome,* Vol. 13, 1966, pp.37-49.

Dodds's famous and generous account of three popular but misguided undergraduate interpretations of the play is extremely useful in helping to sort out the play's attitudes towards oracular knowledge and human culpability.

O'Brien, Michael J., editor. *Twentieth Century Interpretations of Oedipus Rex,* Prentice-Hall, 1968.

O'Brien's indispensible collection of essays includes notable excerpts from the work of Francis Fergusson, Bernard Knox, Richard Lattimore, and Victor Ehrenberg, as well as a smattering of quotations from Plutarch, Longinus, Freud, and Marshall McLuhan.

Fry, Paul H. *Homer to Brecht: The European Epic and Dramatic Traditions,* edited by Michael Seidel and Edward Mendelson, Yale University Press, 1977, pp. 171-90.

Fry's introductory lecture for undergraduates focuses on the riddle of the Sphinx, Oedipus, and the problem of knowledge, and the pathos generated by the punishment of the gods.

Sophocles. *Oedipus Rex,* translation by Dudley Fitts and Robert Fitzgerald, [New York], 1949.

This volume also contains *Oedipus at Colonus* and *Antigone;* all three translations are considered standard ones.

Waldock, A. J. A. *Sophocles the Dramatist,* Cambridge University Press, 1951.

Waldock challenges Bowra's discussion of the play, claiming that its plot does not center around the role of the gods in human life but rather the consequential pain of ambitious desires to gain knowledge.

Whitman, C. H. *Sophocles: A Study of Heroic Humanism,* Harvard University Press, 1951.

Whitman compares Oedipus to Pericles, the Athenian leader and general, and also discusses the play in general terms. A balanced though dry antidote to the polemical tones of Bowra and Waldock.

Wilder, Thornton. *American Characteristics and Other Essays,* Harper and Row (New York), 1979.

Wilder provides learned reflections on the play's treatment of the oracle and discusses the attractiveness of myth-making for Western writers.

Winnington-Ingram, W. P. *Sophocles: An Interpretation,* Cambridge University Press, 1980.

Offers detailed account of the second choral ode, or second "stasimon," in order to demonstrate the usefulness of close attention to commonly neglected aspects of the play.

SOURCES

Nietzsche, Friedrich. *The Birth of Tragedy,* Macmillan, 1907.

Our Town

THORNTON WILDER

1938

Grover's Corners, New Hampshire. Small, rural, out-of-the-way fictional town. 1901 to 1913. Life is pretty much the same for small towns in America. There is no apparent threat of global conflict or war. Such is the setting of Thornton Wilder's play, *Our Town.*

Received with mixed reviews at its premiere in 1938, but awarded the Pulitzer Prize, *Our Town* has become one of the most popularly produced plays of the twentieth century. It is quite possible that on almost any given day of the year, somewhere in the world, *Our Town* is being performed by either a professional company or an amateur troupe of actors.

There are echoes of classic Greek drama: the Stage Manager as Chorus and the three-act structure as trilogy. Like its Greek ancestors, *Our Town* concerns itself with the continuing cycle of life, humankind's nearest understanding of eternity.

The central values of the play—Christian morality, community, the family, appreciation of everyday pleasures—are traditional. Yet, Wilder's methods of presenting these values on the stage are anything but. No scenery, few props, mimed actions, a *dramatis persona* who fluidly travels both in and out of the action of the play—all these make for a radically innovative way of presenting a drama. This was certainly a risk at a time when theater productions were known for their lavish costumes and scenery. However, these ''experimental techniques'' allow the audience to focus on the charac-

ters themselves rather than on their location and how they related to objects that surrounded them.

In *Our Town,* Thornton Wilder artfully manipulates time and place and relates the here-and-now of a small, New England village to the timeless concerns of all humankind. He builds the action of the play toward the dramatic revelation that human life, however painful, dreary, or inconsequential its daily events, is both a precious gift in its own right as well as a portion of the mysterious plan that rests in the "Mind of God."

AUTHOR BIOGRAPHY

The surviving member of a pair of twin boys, Thornton Niven Wilder was born on April 17, 1897, in Madison, Wisconsin, where his father owned and edited a local newspaper. In 1906, his father, Amos Parker Wilder, relocated the family to Hong Kong after accepting a post as the U. S. Consul General. As a result, Wilder's early formal education took place in German schools in Hong Kong and Shanghai, the China Inland Mission School at Chefoo, and public schools in California. He graduated from high school in Berkeley, California, in 1915, and then, at the insistence of his father, attended Oberlin College.

After two years, Wilder, again at the insistence of his father, transferred to Yale and graduated in 1920. As a student, Wilder began writing short plays and essays for publication in the *Yale Literary Review* and had hoped to pursue writing as a career after earning his degree. But Amos Wilder intervened again and found young Thornton a teaching position at Lawrenceville School, a preparatory school for boys near Princeton, New Jersey. While at Lawrenceville, Wilder earned his master's degree from Princeton University.

In 1927, Wilder published *The Bridge of San Luis Rey,* a critical and popular success which earned him the Pulitzer Prize and gave him the financial security to resign his position at Lawrenceville and pursue writing as a full-time career. While teaching comparative literature at the University of Chicago, Wilder became increasingly involved with theater and in some of its more experimental aspects. He continued to write and published *The Angel That Troubled the Waters, and Other Plays* (1928), a collection of short scenes with stage directions considered virtually impossi-

Thornton Wilder

ble to accomplish in the theater, a novel, *The Woman of Andros* (1930) and *The Long Christmas Dinner and Other Plays in One Act* (1931).

Through his friendship with *New York Times* critic Alexander Wolcott, Wilder gained entry into New York theatrical circles. In 1938, *Our Town* brought Wilder both financial success and his second Pulitzer Prize. It ran for 336 performances on Broadway and established Wilder's reputation as a major dramatist. Wilder's reputations as a playwright also rests on two comedies, *The Matchmaker,* (1955, originally performed as *The Merchant of Yonkers,* 1938) and *The Skin of Our Teeth* (1943). *The Matchmaker* was adapted by Michael Stewart and Jerry Herman as their popular musical *Hello, Dolly!,* and *The Skin of Our Teeth* earned Wilder his third Pulitzer Prize.

Wilder's other prominent works include *The Ides of March* (1948), a historical novel about the last days of Julius Caesar, and *The Eighth Day* (1967), a novel dealing with the effects of an act of violence on a growing number of people.

In 1963 Thornton Wilder received the United States Presidential Medal of Freedom and in 1965 he was honored with the first National Medal of Literature. He died on December 7, 1975, in Hamden,

Connecticut, widely recognized as an accomplished dramatist and man of letters whose innovative works remain central to discussions of the American theater.

PLOT SUMMARY

Act One: Daily Life

The title for Act One is ''Daily Life,'' the Stage Manager tells the audience. *Our Town* begins at daybreak in Grover's Corners, New Hampshire, in the year 1901. The Stage Manager points out some of the geographical features of the town and indicates the houses of the two families who provide much of the action of the play, the Webb and Gibbs families. Dr. Gibbs is returning home from delivering twins, Joe Crowell delivers the morning newspaper, and Howie Newsome makes his rounds delivering milk.

The children of the two central families (Emily and Wally Webb and George and Rebecca Gibbs) appear for breakfast in their houses and get themselves ready for school. After the Doctor has retired for a nap and the children are on their way to school, Mrs. Gibbs and Mrs. Webb stop for some gossip while they string beans. The Stage Manager interrupts the women and calls on Professor Willard for a scientific report on Grover's Corners and on Editor Webb for a social and political report. As Editor Webb leaves, children return home from school and Emily promises to help George with his homework. The Stage Manager returns with brief biographies of Joe Crowell and Howie Newsome.

Evening falls on Grover's Corners and the Congregational Church choir, under the direction of Simon Stimson, begins its practice. George and Emily discuss Algebra. Dr. Gibbs and George have a ''serious'' talk about allowances and responsibility. Mrs. Webb and Mrs. Soames gossip about Simon Stimson's drinking problem. George and Rebecca chat at the window. Mr. Webb talks to his daughter, who is enjoying the moonlight at her bedroom window. The constable makes his rounds to ensure that all is well, and the Stage Manager calls an end to this typical day in Grover's Corners.

Act Two: Love and Marriage

The Stage Manager informs the audience that Act Two will be called ''Love and Marriage.'' It isn't much of a surprise to discover that George and Emily are the central figures for this part of the play.

Three years have passed since Act One and it is now early on the morning of July 7, 1904. George attempts to see Emily, but Mrs. Webb won't let him see his bride on their wedding day.

The Stage Manager interrupts to present a scene from the past when George and Emily first became aware of their love for each other. The Stage Manager calls on Dr. and Mrs. Gibbs to explain to the audience how the parents reacted to the engagement. They know that the young couple will have their share of trouble, but, since they know the pain is worth enduring, they agree to the marriage.

While the actors set up chairs to be pews for the wedding scene, the Stage Manager talks to the audience about the importance of marriage. Mrs. Webb expresses sudden concern for Emily. George has some momentary doubts and is comforted by his mother. Emily arrives dressed in white, doubtful and very frightened. Her father tries to comfort her, but without success. He calls George over, the doubts and fears are overcome, and the wedding begins with the Stage Manager as the clergyman. The words of the service are overwhelmed by the shrill comments of Mrs. Soames on the loveliness of marriage and the ''perfectly lovely wedding.'' George and Emily run off joyously at the end of the ceremony, and the Stage manager announces the end of the second act.

Act Three: Death

Act Three opens in a graveyard. The Stage Manager tells the audience that nine years have passed. He talks briefly about death and what death means to the people of Grover's Corners, but is interrupted by Joe Stoddard, the undertaker, and Sam Craig, a Grover's Corners native who moved away but has returned for the funeral. The graves of Mrs. Gibbs, Mrs. Soames, Mr. Stimson, and others are represented by rows of chairs in which the occupants are quietly sitting. When the funeral procession enters, Mrs. Soames asks Mrs. Gibbs who is coming, and Mrs. Gibbs replies that it is her daughter-in-law, Emily.

When Emily appears from the umbrellas of the funeral procession, the dead greet her, but she is still restless, talking about the new barn and George's new Ford. Despite the warnings from Mrs. Gibbs, Mrs. Soames, and even the Stage Manager, Emily decides to return to the happiest moment of her life: her twelfth birthday. She sees the town as it was then, but it is just too painful. She can't stand watching everyone pay so little attention to life while it is being lived, so she returns to her place among the dead.

As the Stage Manager draws a black curtain over this quiet scene, he tells the audience that almost everyone is asleep in Grover's Corners. ''You get a good rest, too,'' he advises the audience as the play ends.

CHARACTERS

Constable Warren

There seems to be little in the way of crime in Grover's Corners, so Constable Warren has to watch over the safety of the townspeople. He rescues a man who has fallen drunk into a snowbank and tries to make sure that the young boys, like Wally Webb, don't start smoking. He also ensures, when Simon Stimson is wandering around town at night, drunk, that he gets home safely.

Sam Craig

Like the Crowell brothers and Howie Newsome, Sam Craig and Joe Stoddard bring news, but instead of bringing news of life, they bring news of death. Through them the audience learns of recent deaths and how they have affected the town.

Joe Crowell

Joe Crowell and his brother Si, are the town's newspaper boys. They are up early making their rounds before the town wakens. As the play progresses, the Stage Manager reveals that Joe was bright, but died in France during World War I.

Si Crowell

Si Crowell and his brother Joe are the town's newspaper boys. Neither one has a positive opinion of marriage; Si and his Grover's Corners teammates lose ''the best baseball pitcher Grover's Corners ever had'' when George Gibbs decides to marry Emily Webb and settle down to farming.

Dr. Frank Gibbs

Frank Gibbs is a loving father and a kind husband. He knows just about everything about everybody in town, and he is perfectly content to live his life in Grover's Corners. Although there are differences that distinguish him from the character

of Charles Webb, the two characters share similar roles and functions in the play.

George Gibbs

George Gibbs is the All-American boy, or, more appropriately, what some people think of as the typical boy—nice and polite, but not very good at book and school learning; loving, but not very good at expressing those emotions; and perfectly happy to stay on the farm.

George is sincere, though just a bit tongue-tied when it comes to telling Emily that he loves her in Act Two. He is not a rebel and he doesn't want to change the world. He just wants to fall in love, marry, and live happily until ''death do us part.'' And, even though the living happily part didn't last as long as he wanted it to, that's exactly what happens to George and Emily.

In Act Three, George doesn't utter a single word, but, when he throws himself on Emily's grave, his actions speak volumes.

Julia Hersey Gibbs

Mrs. Gibbs, a wife and a mother, can be viewed as interchangeable with the character of Myrtle Webb. Each worries about her husband and her children. Each seems content with life in Grover's Corners, although Mrs. Gibbs does express a desire to take the money received by selling an antique piece of furniture and convince her husband to take a vacation to Paris, instead of their usual excursion to visit Civil War battlefields. But, instead, she holds onto the money and leaves it in her will to the married George and Emily, who use the funds to improve the farm.

Rebecca Gibbs

Rebecca is the younger sister of George Gibbs. She is presented, with Wally Webb, as a child squabbling with an older sibling in the family scenes, especially in Act One. The Stage Manager informs the audience in Act Three that Rebecca has married and moved to Ohio.

Howie Newsome

Howie Newsome, the milkman, is one of the town's early risers. A friendly and chatty man,

MEDIA ADAPTATIONS

- *Our Town* was brought to the big screen in 1940 by producer Sol Lesser and director Sam Wood. Thornton Wilder received a writing credit for the screenplay. Frank Craven played the Stage Manager and also contributed to the screenplay. The film was nominated for Best Picture (losing to *Rebecca*). Ninety minutes, black & white, available from Nostalgia Home Video.

- In September, 1955, NBC-TV Producers Showcase brought *Our Town* to the small screen with Frank Sinatra in the Stage Manager role, and Eva Marie Saint and Paul Newman as Emily and George. This production introduced the song ''Love and Marriage'' [''go together like a horse and carriage'']. Earlier appearances of *Our Town* on television were as part of these anthology series: *Robert Montgomery Presents* (NBC, April, 1950) with Burgess Meredith as the Stage Manager, and *Pulitzer Prize Playhouse* (ABC, December, 1950) with Edward Arnold as the Stage Manager. Not available on video.

- A second adaptation of *Our Town* appeared on NBC in November, 1959, with Art Carney in the Stage Manager role. Not available on video.

- NBC presented a third special adaptation of *Our Town* in May, 1977, with Hal Holbrook as the Stage Manager and Glynnis O'Connor and Robby Benson as Emily and George. 120 minutes, color, available from Mastervision.

- The most recent adaptation available on video is a 1989 TV version of the Tony Award-winning Lincoln Center production of *Our Town*. Spaulding Gray stars as the Stage Manager with Penelope Ann Miller and Eric Stolz as Emily and George. 104 minutes, color, available from Mastervision.

- Britannica Films has two half-hour films, *Our Town and Our Universe, I* and *Our Town and Ourselves, II*. These films discuss the unusual conventions of the play and Wilder's use of music, light motif, and the condensed line or word. 1959, Britannica Films.

Howie delivers the local gossip with his milk and cream every morning to the residents of Grover's Corners.

Louella Soames

Mrs. Soames is the town chatterbox. She always has something to say, even when she's dead. It is Mrs. Soames who reveals Simon Stimson's drinking problem, and it is Mrs. Soames who gushes about the wedding. In death, it is Mrs. Soames who observes that life was both awful and wonderful.

Stage Manager

The most important character in the play has no name and little importance in the story's action. But, he has the longest part, more speeches than any other character, and is always on the stage. Some critics have commented that he is like the omniscient narrator encountered in fiction. Often it appears that he simply chats with the audience, dispensing folksy wisdom and sounding like the embodiment of common sense.

In classical Greek theater, the chorus served an important function. As a group of neutral observers, the chorus commented on the play's action and advised the audience how they should respond to the events of the drama. The nineteenth century's fascination with representing ''reality'' on the stage did away with the use of asides (comments made by stage performers that are intended to be heard by the audience but not by other characters). Wilder returns to that convention and uses the Stage Manager as a chorus figure to halt the action, intervene in the story, move back and forth in time, and make it clear that the representation on the stage is not ''reality'' in the naturalistic sense.

In addition to his duties as the ''chorus,'' the Stage Manager also plays prim Mrs. Forest, old-fashioned and conservative Mr. Morgan, and the solemn minister.

Simon Stimson

Stimson is the church organist who has a drinking problem and is the focus of much of the gossip of Grover's Corners. The conversation between the undertaker and Emily's cousin reveals that Stimson committed suicide and, instead of a epitaph on his grave stone, there are just notes of music. Stimson is the only character in the play who is unhappy. Other characters, such as Doc Gibbs, refer to Stimson's sorrows in general terms but never indicate specifically what they are. Even in death, Simon Stimson is a bitter man.

Joe Stoddard

Like the Crowell brothers and Howie Newsome, Joe Stoddard and Sam Craig bring news, but instead of bringing news of life, they bring news of death. It is through them that the audience learns of recent deaths and how they have affected the town.

Charles Webb

Like the character of Dr. Frank Gibbs, Charles Webb is a loving father and a kind husband with a sense of humor that survives the strain of their children's marriage. While each man has some interest that differentiates him from the other (Civil War battlefields for Doc Gibbs; Napoleon for Editor Webb), the speeches delivered by these two could be spoken by the other without any loss of importance.

Emily Webb

Emily Webb might be called ''the All-American girl.'' She is bright, articulate, and, despite the anxiety she shares with her mother, a beautiful creature. She is the focus of the action of the play. In Act One, Emily is the naive schoolgirl, in Act Two, the maturing young woman, and in Act Three, the mother who has died in childbirth. It is through Emily that time of the play can be tracked.

Emily exhibits emotions that are familiar to the audience. From the unsure adolescent looking at the

moonlight to the bride with a moment of last-minute panic on her wedding day, the audience connects with these feelings. It is also through Emily that Wilder presents his central life-affirming idea—''Oh, earth, you're too wonderful for anybody to realize you.''

Myrtle Webb

Myrtle Webb and Julia Hersey Gibbs, like their husbands, are two characters that can be viewed as virtually interchangeable. Content with life in Grover's Corners, each is a wife and a mother whose life focuses on her husband and her children.

Wally Webb

As the younger brother of Emily Webb, Wally is seen throughout the play as child squabbling with his older sibling, especially in Act One. In this, his character is a parallel to that of Rebecca Gibbs. At the beginning of Act Three, the Stage Manager informs the audience that Wally Webb, who died of a ruptured appendix on a camping trip, is one of those in the cemetery.

THEMES

Cycle of Life

Our Town begins at daybreak with the birth of twins in a Polish town and ends at night with the death of Emily Webb Gibbs in childbirth. As one life ends, another begins. Throughout the play, Wilder (through the Stage Manager—a role Wilder himself once played) directs the attention of the audience to the repetition of the cycle of life. In his opening monologue, he points out that the names on tombstones in the graveyard that date back to the 1600s are ''the same names that are around here now.'' As Act Two opens, the Stage Manager talks about the sun having ''come up over a thousand times,'' the growing up and the slowing down of some of the town's residents, and the millions of gallons of water [that have gone] by the mill.'' His comments about marriage are particularly interesting:

> I've married over two hundred couples in my day. Do I believe in it? I don't know. M. . . . marries N. . . . millions of them. The cottage, the g-cart, the Sunday-afternoon drives in the Ford, the first rheumatism, the grandchildren, the second rheumatism, the deathbed,

TOPICS FOR FURTHER STUDY

- Some other American writers did not look as kindly on the village in their works as Thornton Wilder did in *Our Town*. Look at the poems of Edgar Lee Masters and Edwin Arlington Robinson, the short stories of Sherwood Anderson, and the novels of Sinclair Lewis for different views of life in small town America.

- Research the Progressive Movement in American politics at the turn of the century. Investigate the links between the Progressives and the Women's Suffrage Movement.

- Many small towns in New Hampshire were thriving manufacturing centers during the 19th century. Research what life might have been like for the average 16-year-old in one of those towns at the turn of the century.

- Some critics have complained that Wilder oversimplified life in turn-of-the-century America, depicting an idealized society that never existed in reality. What do you think Wilder's motivations were for creating such a town?

---

the reading of the will,. . . Once in a thousand times it's interesting.

Meaning of Life

Thornton Wilder is often considered to be a religious writer and *Our Town* is often considered to be a religious play. Yet, there is little mention of heaven or God or any of those subjects often thought of as being religious. The Stage Manager muses aloud about the word eternal at the beginning of Act Three.

> Now there are some things we all know, but we don't take'm out and look at'm very often. We all know that *something* is eternal. And it ain't houses and it ain't names, and it ain't earth, and it ain't even the stars . . . everybody knows in their bones that *something* is eternal, and that something has to do with human beings. All the greatest people ever lived have been telling us that for five thousand years and yet you'd be surprised how people are always losing hold of it. There's something way down deep that's eternal about every human being.

Love and Passion

The characters in *Our Town* mention love often and Wilder provides the audience with many illustrations. The major characters all love one another, and throughout the play the audience is given examples of different types of love. In Act One, family

love and friendship predominate. Parents and children love each other, and neighbors love one another as well. In Act Two, romantic love blossoms into marriage. In Act Three, spiritual, selfless love, the love that expects nothing in return, is shown.

STYLE

Experimental Techniques

When *Our Town* was first performed in 1938, Thornton Wilder was better known as the Pulitzer prize-winning (1927) author of a novel, *The Bridge of San Luis Rey.* Unhappy with most of what he was seeing on the American stage, Wilder decided to introduce a different approach to theater. He explains his idea in the preface to *Three Plays by Thornton Wilder* (Bantam, 1958):

> Toward the end of the twenties I began to lose pleasure in going to the theater. I ceased to believe in the stories I saw presented there. . . . I felt that something had gone wrong with it [the theater] in my time and that it was fulfilling only a small part of its potentialities.

Our Town was considered innovative for its time because of the experimental techniques Wilder incorporated into the play. The Stage Manager, a character both inside and outside the play, narrates the action. He comments to the audience on the present, the past, and the future. He is bounded by the limits of time, and, yet, he stands both beyond and outside it. In addition, there are no props, background scenery, or designed sets—just chairs, two tables, two step ladders, and two trellises ("scenery for those who think they have to have scenery," as Wilder explained). Action that normally would involve the use of props is mimed by the actors. This approach carried a great deal of risk at a time when theatrical productions were trying to outdo each other in terms of costumes and scenery. Wilder's use of these experimental techniques forced the audience to focus more on the characters than on what they were wearing and what objects surrounded them. In her book, *Currents in Contemporary Drama,* Ruby Cohn explains Wilder's approach: "The Stage Manager in *Our Town* functions much like an omnipresent author in a novel, but he does not suggest that his characters are actors. . . . On the contrary, the characters are more real than things, because they are present on stage whereas things are not."

Homage to Classical Drama

Thornton Wilder was educated in what is called "the classical tradition." *Our Town* includes several influences from classical Greek drama. The Stage Manager functions as a sort of Greek chorus. He is a neutral character who comments on the action and tells the audience about events that happen offstage. He advises the audience how they should (or should not) react to events on stage, and he reinforces the moral message of the play. Additionally, Wilder does not divide the acts into scenes, but does try, in a way, to follow the three unities of Greek drama: unity of time, unity of place, and unity of action.

Unity of time usually means that the entire action of the play occurs within a single twenty-four hour period. In a strict counting of time, the action of *Our Town* spans much more than a single day, including shifts both forward and backward. But, in a different reading, the action of *Our Town* all takes place in one day. The play begins at daybreak and ends at night—a single day of life. Unity of place demands that the action of the play occur in a single location. As the stage directions state, "the entire play takes place in Grover's Corners, New Hampshire." There is also unity of action. *Our Town* focuses on one story with no subplots to complicate things.

HISTORICAL CONTEXT

Invention and Growth

During the time period of the play, 1901 to 1913, America saw many industrial advances. One that features prominently in the play itself is the introduction in 1908 of Henry Ford's Model T automobile. The Stage Manager, in his opening speech in Act Three, mentions that "farmers are coming to town in Fords." The horse and buggy days are gone, even for the fictional town of Grover's Corners.

Organized baseball had its first World Series in 1903 and the sport soon earned the nickname of "The National Pastime." Scouts from the professional teams would travel to rural areas looking for talented athletes. Though none of these scouts appear in the play, much mention is made of George Gibbs's skill as a pitcher.

The Progressive Movement

When Theodore Roosevelt became president of the United States after the assassination of William McKinley in 1901, The Progressive Era in American society began. The Progressives believed that the irresponsible actions of the rich were corrupting both public and private life in the country. In order to change this, regulations had to be instituted to create a more balanced and efficient society. Even though the country was relatively stable economically, the social spectrum ranged from the opulently wealthy to the tragically poor. Jacob Riis, a photographer, documented the plight of these disenfranchised Americans. In an effort to eliminate child labor, Lewis Hine photographed young children working in factories. Other Progressives fought for new laws that would break up large monopolies or trusts. (They were called "Trust Busters.") These reformers called for regulation of the railroads, the opportunity for people to vote on laws themselves through referendum, a graduated income tax where people who earned more money would pay higher taxes, and better conservation of natural resources. The "Belligerent Man" who questions Mr. Webb in Act One may be Wilder's nod to the Progressives.

Childbirth

Emily dies in childbirth, a common occurrence during this time period. Causes of death ranged from infection due to unsanitary conditions to the

Thornton Wilder (center) during rehearsals for a run of 1938 performances in which he played the role of Stage Manager

transfer of disease into the household. Most births occurred at home, not in a hospital, and many babies were delivered by midwives and not doctors. In rural areas, especially farms with cattle, sheep, pigs, and other animals, germ-free conditions were hard to come by. Sometimes people were infected by doctors and midwives who cared for both people and animals. By the early 1900s, the practice of providing antiseptic environments had still not been adopted in all rural areas.

The Turn of the Century and the Industrial Revolution

Our Town's action occurs at the turn of the twentieth century, a time of great societal change in America. By this time the industrial revolution, which would forever change the work environment of America, was well underway. Despite mention of such technical advancements as the automobile, life in Grover's Corners is relatively unaffected by the great changes that were sweeping most of the country. Most people in the town earn their livings the way that their predecessors did for much of the nineteenth century; they are milkmen, newspaper editors, doctors, and farmers. In this sense, Grover's Corners represents an American way of life that is

fading; the play freezes this simpler time, preserving it for future generations.

CRITICAL OVERVIEW

Our Town's off-Broadway warm-up shows met with cool reception in 1938, but New York critics, spearheaded by Brooks Atkinson, built up a favorable response that was matched by public enthusiasm and a run of 336 performances. It is, without question, the most produced play in American theater. Scarcely a day has passed since its opening in 1938 that *Our Town* has not been performed somewhere in this country—in productions from professional revivals to community theaters to colleges and high schools. Why? There is no scenery; the actors dress in everyday clothing for the early 1900s; there is no sex or violence; there's not even any harsh language. Yet there is something in this play that draws people to it year after year.

John Mason Brown remarked in his *Dramatis Personae: A Retrospective Show* that ''Mr. Wilder's play involves more than a New England town-

COMPARE & CONTRAST

- **Turn of the Century:** Most schoolteachers were women. If they wanted to marry (like Joe Crowell's teacher in Act One), they had to resign their teaching positions. In rural communities, teachers often lived with local families during the school year.

  1930s: As the country struggled with unemployment during the Great Depression, teaching positions were prized jobs for both single and married women. More men joined the ranks of teachers, mostly at the upper grade levels. Rural areas still had one- and two-room schoolhouses.

  Today: Women still outnumber men in the teaching profession. Salaries have increased and people can support families on teachers' wages. In many rural areas, towns have been forced to give up their own schools and join with other towns to create a single regional school.

- **Turn of the Century:** People lived and worked in the same location. No place was too far away that a person couldn't walk to it. Horse and buggy was the principal transportation.

  1930s: Automobiles replaced the horse and buggy as the primary mode of transportation. The Great Depression forced mills and factories that once thrived in small New England towns to shut their doors, forcing people to either move away or to travel elsewhere to seek work.

Today: Thousands of people commute into Boston everyday from small towns in southern New Hampshire. Some drive their cars on mutli-lane highways for nearly two hours each way, while others travel to an outlying train station and finish their commute into the city by rail.

- **Turn of the Century:** Women rarely worked at a job outside the home. As the Stage Manager says in his opening monologue to Act Two: "both those ladies cooked three meals a day—one of 'em for twenty years, the other for forty—and no summer vacation. They brought up two children apiece, washed, cleaned the house—and *never a nervous breakdown.*"

  1930s: Most women were mothers and housewives, but the economic realities of the Great Depression dictated that whoever could, worked. When the country entered World War II just three years after *Our Town* opened, thousands of women took factory jobs while men went off to war.

  Today: Women are in the workforce in larger numbers than ever before. Families juggle work schedules of the father, the mother, and the children. Take-out food has replaced the traditional family dinner, and eating in front of the television has replaced conversation at the dinner table.

---

ship. It burrows into the essence of the growing-up, the marrying, the living, and the dying of all of us who sit before it and are included by it. . . . It is not so much of the streets of a New England Town he writes as of the clean white spire which rises above them." This is the kind of play, Brown continued, that "[makes] us weep for our own vanished youth at the same time we are sobbing for the short-lived pleasures and sufferings which we know await our children." Wilder gives his audience precise geographical coordinates, as well as an entire Venn diagram of its imaginary location. But "Mr. Wild-

er's place is laid in no imaginary place. It becomes a reality in the human heart."

Reknowned dramatist Arthur Miller remarked in *The Atlantic Monthly* that *Our Town* is a play that is "poetic without verse," and that uses traditional family figures as a prism through which is reflected the author's basic idea—"the indestructibility, the everlastingness, of the family and the community, its rhythm of life, its rootedness in the essentially safe cosmos despite troubles, wracks, and seemingly disastrous, but essentially temporary, dislocations."

Arthur H. Ballet argued in an essay in *English Journal* that *Our Town* is a carefully constructed drama, actually a trilogy. Like its Greek predecessors, *Our Town* is concerned with the great and continuing cycle of life; out of life comes death and from death comes life. This cycle is man's closest understanding of eternity, his finest artistic expression of what he senses to be a mission and a purpose. The fears and faith of the play "ring true" because they are common experiences. *Our Town* brilliantly shows that life is a paradox, and that human beings retain their faith that in death, too, there is life and a greater understanding.

CRITICISM

William P. Wiles

Wiles is a teacher with more than twenty years of experience in secondary education. His essay examines why Wilder's play continues to be so popular.

No scenery. Not even a curtain hides the back wall of the stage. A few chairs; two tables; two stepladders. No props, except for the Stage Manager's pipe. No breathtaking special effects; no stirring musical score. Just a few recorded sounds and some hymns. Why, then, has *Our Town* not only endured since 1938, but prospered as America's most often produced play?

Thornton Wilder shows human beings as they believe in their hearts they live. Life in this play seems simple. Nearly everyone is happy and good-natured. Only one, Simon Stimson the church organist, appears to be truly unhappy, but, other than some gossip, the audience never gets to know him as a developed character.

By setting the play in the not too distant past, Wilder strikes a responsive chord with feelings of nostalgia. The past, the way things used to be, seems better than the present, the way things are. The combination of life as people would like it to be set in a less complicated (and better) time than the present day creates enormous appeal. If Wilder explored the darkness of Simon Stimson's life, that would detract from the innocence of George and Emily. If Wilder had set the play in the nineteenth century instead of at its end, there would be difficulty relating to the characters. Instead of dealing with the particular aspects of a small New England Town and its inhabitants, Wilder focuses attention on the bigger picture—the universality of events, emotions, and responses.

In the classic film *Casablanca,* Humphrey Bogart's character, Ric Blaine, says to Ilsa (Ingrid Bergman), "[T]he problems of three little people don't amount to a hill of beans in this crazy world." Thornton Wilder would not agree. By using the ordinary, everyday events of people from a town off the beaten path, Wilder argues that it is precisely the problems of the common people that make life interesting and worth examining. The focus of *Our Town* is two events which are common to every single human who has ever lived, who lives now, and who will live long after the current population has turned to dust: birth and death. A third event, love and marriage, is so much a part of people's lives that it receives equal billing. Everyone who watches the play can identify with some part of what is going on and can probably name a counterpart from their own real world for each of the characters.

Act One, called "Daily Life," introduces this concept of the particular representing the universal. The inhabitants of Grover's Corners go about their routines: delivering milk and newspapers and babies in the early morning hours; preparing breakfast; getting ready for school; feeding chickens; stringing beans with a neighbor; chatting about a dream; worrying about looks; gossiping about the town drunk; walking home from choir practice. Those in the audience are drawn into this world because, even though it is set in the recent past, it is familiar territory; these events are part of the audience's experiences too. Thus, a bond between actors and audience is established.

Thornton Wilder points out in the preface to a 1957 collection that includes *Our Town* that "the recurrent words in this play (few have noticed it) are 'hundreds,' 'thousands,' and 'millions.'" How can people comprehend such vast numbers? Wilder maintains that they do not—"each individual's assertion to an absolute reality can only be inner, very inner." The only way to make sense, then, of this "crazy world" is to look at those things that are real and important, those that happen on the inside. The actions on the stage are not important in and of themselves; what becomes important, then, is how the individual responds to them. And, because the actions of the play are part of the overall human experience, the response becomes one of connectedness and not alienation.

WHAT DO I READ NEXT?

- Also by Thornton Wilder and included with *Our Town* in *Three Plays by Thornton Wilder* are *The Skin of Our Teeth* and *The Matchmaker. The Skin of Our Teeth* focuses on the Antrobus family from Excelsior, New Jersey. Together they endure the Ice Age and the Great Flood, as well as the malicious acts of son Henry, whose name is changed to Cain after the "accidental" death of his brother. This play earned Wilder his third Pulitzer Prize. *The Matchmaker* had an earlier life as *The Merchant of Yonkers: A Farce in Four Acts* (1938). The title character of the play is Dolly Levi, a worldly-wise widow who attempts to dissuade an uncharitable merchant from opposing the marriage of his niece to an impoverished artist. In 1964, Michael Stewart and Jerry Herman adapted *The Matchmaker* as the popular musical *Hello, Dolly!*

- *Spoon River Anthology* by Edgar Lee Masters is a collection of poems that detail thoughts of residents of the fictional town of Spoon River, Illinois, who speak from the grave. Instead of the very brief comments of the dead from Act Three of *Our Town,* Masters presents free verse epitaphs from the inhabitants of the graveyard on the hill. The Stage Manager himself refers to this work in the opening monologue to Act Two: "It's like what one of those Middle West poets said: You've got to love life to have life, and you've got to have life to love life." This line comes form "Lucinda Matlock," one of the epitaphs of Spoon River.

- *Main Street* by Sinclair Lewis presents a completely different portrayal of small town life than does *Our Town.* A good choice for contrast.

- *Shoeless Joe,* a novel by W. P. Kinsella that was later made into the film *Field of Dreams,* and the book *Baseball* that accompanies the PBS series of the same name by filmmaker Ken Burns, provide some insight into the popularity of the game of baseball before it became a business. Both film projects are worthwhile as well, even though the *Baseball* series is nine hours long (9 one-hour episodes or "innings"). These works, like *Our Town,* evoke a more innocent and simpler time in America's past.

In Act Two, "Love and Marriage," Wilder, through the Stage Manager, manipulates time so that the audience can not only participate in the wedding of George and Emily, but also see how and when this romance began in earnest. "I'm awfully interested in how big things like that begin," the Stage Manager declares. Throughout this act we are reminded of the vast continuum not only of human existence, but of the residents of Grover's Corners. In three years since Act One, the sun has "come up over a thousand times." The mountain has eroded ever so slightly and "millions of gallons of water [have gone] by the mill." Babies aren't babies any longer, and some inhabitants have grown older. Other residents have fallen in love. It is against this vast backdrop that Morgan's drugstore becomes the focal point for the moment when George declares

his affection for Emily in the halting shy way that countless others have attempted to express their deepest feelings.

In his descriptions at the beginning of Act Three of those who rest in the cemetery on a hilltop in Grover's Corners, the Stage Manager comments on the beauty of the setting. He also points out that these people were both silly *and* noble, Wilder's reminder that the human race is not an either/or proposition—it contains *all* possibilities.

At the beginning of the play, the Stage Manager mentioned the death of Mrs. Gibbs, but it was simply a statement of fact. Now, to learn that Mrs. Gibbs has died and is buried in the cemetery along with Wally Webb and Mrs. Soames and Simon Stimson strikes a responsive chord. These are no longer just names; the audience has met them and the characters they represent have become real. Death becomes less of an abstraction and more a part of the universal experience. Everyone—the characters in the play, the author, the audience, the reader, the critic—is going to die. That is part of what it means to be human, and one of the two events that all humans share no matter what their station, background, or ability.

The dead in the Grover's Corners cemetery are waiting, says the Stage Manager, for the earth part of them to be burned away and for the "eternal part in them to come out clear." It is this idea that the dead hardly remember what it was like to be alive that Wilder seeks to emphasize here. It is this movement toward the "eternal" rather than an emptiness or void that Emily joins but is not yet ready to accept. When she realizes that she can return to earth to relive her life, she persists in making it happen, even though the dead and the Stage Manager strongly advise against it.

It is when Emily relives her twelfth birthday (her happiest memory) that she comes to realize that the living don't appreciate being alive. "They're sort of shut up in little boxes," she says. With her knowledge of past, present, and future time, she becomes overwhelmed at the realization that the tiniest moments of everyday life are full of the essence of being alive. "Oh earth, you're too wonderful for anybody to realize you."

As the Stage Manager draws a black curtain across the scene, the cycle is complete. The play began at daybreak and ends at night. It began with birth and ends with death. It began with the particulars of daily life and ends with eternity.

Source: William P. Wiles, in an essay for *Drama for Students*, Gale, 1997.

Winfield Townley Scott

In this excerpt, Scott examines the bittersweet nostalgia that pervades Wilder's play.

Ten minutes up the road from where I live in Connecticut there is a town called Brooklyn, and when I go there or while I read the play I always see it as the scene of Thornton Wilder's Grover's Corners in *Our Town*. Which of course it is not. And it is even a smaller town—there is no high school, no railroad—than Wilder's imaginary New Hampshire one. Further, unlike Grover's Corners, Brooklyn has been touched a little with remarkability: a huge equestrian statue of General Israel Putnam

holds down his Revolutionary bones not far from the town's crossroads; in pre-Civil War days Prudence Crandall was jailed at Brooklyn for admitting Negro youngsters to her school over the hills in Canterbury, and until her death a surprisingly few years ago old Mrs. Theodore Roosevelt spent her summers in a square white house, now gone into tenements, alongside the Putnam monument. Wilder's point, on the contrary, is that Grover's Corners is not in the least exceptional: William Jennings Bryan once spoke from the Town Hall steps, the Stage Manager tells us, but very soon he assures us of his beloved place that "Nobody very remarkable ever come out of it, —s' far as we know."

Nevertheless, I "see" Brooklyn as Wilder's typical New England small town: its few stores, the clapboard houses set comfortably apart across lawns and under maples and elms, the schoolhouse with the flagpole in the yard near the crossroads and flanking the crossroads the village green, the Congregational, Baptist, Episcopal, and Catholic churches, the post office, the roofed town pump, the farms off from the outskirts, and over it all a simple air of living that is neither rich nor poor, neither distinguished nor negligible, neither large nor shallow.

This I believe is the associational power of reading which Gertrude Stein warred against: if she wrote "brook," she wanted it new, abstract, a Platonic "brook"; and she did not wish you to call up at her word a particular brook familiar to you. But how futile! This is merely the habit of the mind. It is not at all a narrowing sentimentality, it is one of the warmest responses to be got from reading. Again and again we do not construct, as the novelist is allegedly doing, an invented scene: as he constructs it he *reminds* us, reading, of something we know—and, hardly conscious of the process, we adapt our memory to his text at once.

It may be that we most generally do this over books which are themselves soaked with a sense of time and place: that is, not over the vastest things— the "King Lear," the "War and Peace"—but over lesser literatures intensely regional and profoundly native; for example, *Tom Sawyer, Spoon River Anthology, Winesburg, Ohio*. These are some of the masterpieces in a genre which even in minor instances such as Whittier's *Snow-Bound*, Sarah Orne Jewett's *Country of the Pointed Firs*, and many more, is curiously evocative and durable. *Our Town* has in this genre a high position, perhaps among the highest. It is narrower, less colorful, and sweeter than the best of the books I have mentioned, but it is a more intelligently managed work of art than any of them; it is not lacking in the instinctiveness which makes those other books great primitives—that is to say, it is not lacking in poetry—though no doubt it is more self-conscious and literary; yet in the very skillful construction of the play is the secret of why *Our Town* does rank as one of the most moving and beautiful of American books.

This construction, or this method, comes to its apotheosis almost at the very end of *Our Town* with the shattering scene in which the dead Emily wills her own return to a day in her childhood; actually the double point of view, an intermeshing of past and present, runs throughout the play and accounts for its peculiar poignancy. It is as though the golden veil of nostalgia, not stretched across stage for us to see through, bisects the stage down center: it glows left and right upon past and present, and the players come and go through its shimmering summer haze, now this side of it, now that; but the audience sees both sides of it. And so too of course does that deus ex machina of the entire play, the Stage Manager (whom, I have heard, Mr. Wilder himself can act very well). . . .

Emily appears, to take her place with the dead. Already she is distant from the mourners, but her discovery that she can ''go back'' to past time seduces her despite the warnings of the older dead. The ubiquitous Stage Manager, too, can talk with Emily, and what he says to her introduces the summation scene with the keynote of the entire play: ''You not only live it,'' he says, ''but you watch yourself living it.'' Now Emily, in the yet more poignant way of self-involvement, will achieve that double vision we have had all along; and now we shall be burdened also with her self-involvement.

''And as you watch it,'' the Stage Manager goes on, ''you will see the thing that they—down there—never know. You see the future. You know what's going to happen afterwards.''

Then perfectly in key comes Mrs. Gibbs' advice to Emily: ''At least, choose an unimportant day. Choose the least important day in your life. It will be important enough.'' There sound the central chords of the play: the common day and the light of the future.

Emily chooses her twelfth birthday and the magic begins to mount to almost unbearable tension. Now the Stage Manager repeats his enriched gesture as he announces that it is February 11, 1899,

> THE APTEST THING EVER SAID ABOUT *TOM SAWYER* WAS SAID BY THE AUTHOR HIMSELF AND APPLIES AS NICELY TO *OUR TOWN*. MARK TWAIN SAID HIS BOOK WAS "A HYMN."

and once again, as we saw him summon it in the same casual way so many years before, the town of Grover's Corners stirs, awakens; a winter morning—Constable Warren, Howie Newsome, Joe Crowell, Jr., making their appearances along Main Street, Mrs. Webb firing the kitchen stove and calling Wally and Emily to breakfast. The little daily rhythms recur, now more touching for the big wheel has become vaster. Now *we* are taken back with Emily's double-awareness accenting our own. Though the then-living are unaware as always, now the golden veil shines everywhere, even all around us ourselves. It is a terrific triumph of dramatic method.

''Oh, that's the town I knew as a little girl. And, look, there is the old white fence that used to be around our house. Oh, I'd forgotten that! . . . I can't look at everything hard enough,'' Emily says. ''There's Mr. Morgan's drugstore. And there's the High School, forever and ever, and ever.'' For her birthday young George Webb has left a postcard album on the doorstep: Emily had forgotten that.

The living cannot hear the dead Emily of fourteen years later, her whole lifetime later. Yet she cries out in the passion, which the play itself performs, to realize life while it is lived: ''But, just for a moment now we're all together. Mama, just for a moment we're happy. Let's look at one another.'' And when offstage her father's voice is heard a second time calling, ''Where's my girl? Where's my birthday girl?'', Emily breaks. She flees back through the future, back to the patient and disinterested dead: ''Oh,'' she says of life, ''it goes so fast. We don't have time to look at one another.''

Here if the play is to get its proper and merited response there is nothing further to say of it: one simply weeps.

> "BY STRIPPING THE PLAY OF
> EVERYTHING THAT IS NOT
> ESSENTIAL, MR. WILDER HAS GIVEN
> IT A PROFOUND, STRANGE,
> UNWORLDLY SIGNIFICANCE"

It is thus, finally, that Emily can say farewell to the world—that is, to Grover's Corners. Night, now; the night after Emily's burial. The big wheel of the mutable universe turns almost alone. The Stage Manager notices starlight and its "millions of years," but time ticks eleven o'clock on his watch and the town, though there, is mostly asleep, as he dismisses us for "a good rest, too."

The aptest thing ever said about *Tom Sawyer* was said by the author himself and applies as nicely to *Our Town*. Mark Twain said his book was "a hymn."

Source: Winfield Townley Scott, "*Our Town* and the Golden Veil" in *Virginia Quarterly Review,* Vol. 29, no. 1, Winter, 1953, pp. 103–5, 116–17.

Brooks Atkinson

In this review, which originally appeared in the New York Times*'s February 5, 1938, edition, Atkinson praises* Our Town *as a moving evocation of the beauty and simplicity of ordinary life in America.*

Considered one of the most influential theatre reviewers in America, Atkinson served as drama critic for the New York Times *from 1925 to 1960.*

Although Thornton Wilder is celebrated chiefly for his fiction, it will be necessary now to reckon with him as a dramatist. His *Our Town,* which opened at Henry Miller's last evening, is a beautifully evocative play. Taking as his material three periods in the history of a placid New Hampshire town, Mr. Wilder has transmuted the simple events of human life into universal reverie. He has given familiar facts a deeply moving, philosophical perspective. Staged without scenery and with the curtain always up, *Our Town* has escaped from the formal barrier of the modern theatre into the quintessence of

acting, thought and speculation. In the staging, Jed Harris has appreciated the rare quality of Mr. Wilder's handiwork and illuminated it with a shining performance. *Our Town* is, in this column's opinion, one of the finest achievements of the current stage.

Since the form is strange, this review must attempt to explain the purpose of the play. It is as though Mr. Wilder were saying: "Now for evidence as to the way Americans were living in the early part of the century, take Grover Corners, N.H., as an average town. Mark it 'Exhibit A' in American folkways." His spokesman in New Hampshire cosmology is Frank Craven, the best pipe and pants-pocket actor in the business, who experimentally sets the stage with tables and chairs before the house lights go down and then prefaces the performance with a few general remarks about Grover Corners. Under his benign guidance we see three periods in career of one generation of Grover Corners folks—"Life," "Love" and "Death."

Literally, they are not important. On one side of an imaginary street Dr. Gibbs and his family are attending to their humdrum affairs with relish and probity. On the opposite side Mr. Webb, the local editor, and his family are fulfilling their quiet destiny. Dr. Gibbs's boy falls in love with Mr. Webb's girl—neighbors since birth. They marry after graduating from high school; she dies several years later in childbirth and she is buried on Cemetery Hill. Nothing happens in the play that is not normal and natural and ordinary.

But by stripping the play of everything that is not essential, Mr. Wilder has given it a profound, strange, unworldly significance. This is less the portrait of a town than the sublimation of the commonplace; and in contrast with the universe that silently swims around it, it is brimming over with compassion. Most of it is a tender idyll in the kindly economy of Mr. Wilder's literary style; some of it is heartbreaking in the mute simplicity of human tragedy. For in the last act, which is entitled "Death," Mr. Wilder shows the dead of Grover Corners sitting peacefully in their graves and receiving into their quiet company a neighbor's girl whom they love. So Mr. Wilder's pathetically humble evidence of human living passes into the wise beyond. Grover Corners is a green corner of the universe.

With about the best script of his career in his hands, Mr. Harris has risen nobly to the occasion. He has reduced theatre to its lowest common denominator without resort to perverse showmanship.

As chorus, preacher, drug store proprietor and finally as shepherd of the flock, Frank Craven plays with great sincerity and understanding, keeping the sublime well inside his home-spun style. As the boy and girl, John Craven, who is Frank Craven's son, and Martha Scott turn youth into tremulous idealization, some of their scenes are lovely past all enduring. Jay Fassett as Dr. Gibbs, Evelyn Varden as his wife, Thomas W. Ross and Helen Carew as the Webbs play with an honesty that is enriching. There are many other good bits of acting.

Out of respect for the detached tone of Mr. Wilder's script the performance at a whole is subdued and understated. The scale is so large that the voices are never lifted. But under the leisurely monotone of the production there is a fragment of the immortal truth. *Our Town* is a microcosm. It is also a hauntingly beautiful play.

Source: Brooks Atkinson, review of *Our Town* (1938) in *On Stage: Selected Theater Reviews from the New York Times, 1920–1970,* edited by Bernard Beckerman and Howard Siegman, Arno Press, 1973, pp. 198–200.

FURTHER READING

Ballet, Arthur H. "In Our Living and In Our Dying" in *English Journal,* Vol. XLV, no. 5, May, 1956, pp. 243-49.
    In this essay, Ballet considers *Our Town* in terms of its affinity with classical tragedy.

Brown, John Mason. "Wilder's 'Our Town'" in his *Dramatis Personae: A Retrospective Show,* Viking, 1963, pp.79-84.
    A highly respected drama critic and editor for the *Saturday Review* during the 1940s, Brown wrote several critical studies of the American theater. In this assessment of *Our Town,* written in 1938 and later included in his *Dramatis Personae* (1963), he supports Wilder's rejection of contemporary political and social issues while praising his portrayal of such fundamental human concerns as death, love, and the passage of time.

DISCovering Authors: Modules, Gale, 1996.
    A CD-ROM and online publication that contains biographical and critical information for Thornton Wilder (and hundreds of other authors). Particularly useful were hypertext links to critical articles.

Johns, Sally. "Thornton Wilder" in *Dictionary of Literary Biography,* Volume 7: *Twentieth Century American Dramatists,* edited by John MacNicholas, Gale, 1981, pp. 304-19.
    This article presents an overview of Wilder's career, concentrating on his contributions to American theater.

Miller, Arthur. "The Family in Modern Drama" in the *Atlantic Monthly,* Vol. 197, no. 4, April, 1956, pp. 35-41.
    The author of *Death of a Salesman* (1949), *The Crucible* (1953), and numerous other dramatic works, Miller is ranked among the most important and influential American playwrights since World War II. In his essay, he praises *Our Town* as a poetic work that effectively links daily life to "the generality of men which is our society and our world."

Pygmalion

GEORGE BERNARD SHAW

1914

Pygmalion is a comedy about a phonetics expert who, as a kind of social experiment, attempts to make a lady out of an uneducated Cockney flower-girl. Although not as intellectually complex as some of the other plays in Shaw's "theatre of ideas," *Pygmalion* nevertheless probes important questions about social class, human behavior, and relations between the sexes.

Hoping to circumvent what he felt was the tendency of the London press to criticize his plays unfairly, Shaw chose to produce a German translation of *Pygmalion* in Vienna and Berlin before bringing the play to London. The London critics appreciated the acclaim the play had received overseas, and, after it opened at His Majesty's Theatre on April 11, 1914, it enjoyed success, firmly establishing Shaw's reputation as a popular playwright.

Accompanying his subterfuge with the London press, Shaw also plotted to trick his audience out of any prejudicial views they held about the play's content. This he did by assuming their familiarity with the myth of Pygmalion, from the Greek playwright Ovid's *Metamorphoses,* encouraging them to think that *Pygmalion* was a classical play. He furthered the ruse by directing the play anonymously and casting a leading actress who had never before appeared in a working-class role. In Ovid's tale, Pygmalion is a man disgusted with real-life women who chooses celibacy and the pursuit of an ideal woman, whom he carves out of ivory. Wishing the

statue were real, he makes a sacrifice to Venus, the goddess of love, who brings the statue to life. By the late Renaissance, poets and dramatists began to contemplate the thoughts and feelings of this woman, who woke full-grown in the arms of a lover. Shaw's central character—the flower girl Liza Doolittle—expresses articulately how her transformation has made her feel, and he adds the additional twist that Liza turns on her ''creator'' in the end by leaving him.

In addition to the importance of the original Pygmalion myth to Shaw's play, critics have pointed out the possible influence of other works, such as Tobias Smollett's novel *The Adventures of Peregrine Pickle* (which similarly involves a gentleman attempting to make a fine lady out of a ''coarse'' working girl), and a number of plays, including W.S. Gilbert's *Pygmalion and Galatea* and Henrik Ibsen's *A Doll House.* Shaw denied borrowing the story directly from any of these sources, but there are traces of them in his play, as there are of the well-known story of Cinderella, and shades of the famous stories of other somewhat vain ''creators'' whose experiments have unforeseen implications: Faust, Dr. Frankenstein, Svengali.

The play was viewed (thankfully, by many critics) as one of Shaw's less provocative comedies. Nevertheless, *Pygmalion* did provoke controversy upon its original production. Somewhat ironically, the cause was an issue of language, around which the plot itself turns: Liza's use of the word ''bloody,'' never before uttered on the stage at His Majesty's Theatre. Even though they were well aware of the controversy from its coverage in the press, the first audiences gasped in surprise, then burst into laughter, at Liza's spirited rejoinder: ''Not bloody likely!''

AUTHOR BIOGRAPHY

George Bernard Shaw was born into a poor Protestant family in Dublin, Ireland, on July 26, 1856. Despite childhood neglect (his father was an alcoholic), he became one of the most prominent writers of modern Britain. His mother introduced him to music and art at an early age and after 1876, when he moved to London to continue his self-education, she supported him for nine more years. During this period Shaw wrote five unsuccessful novels, then,

in 1884, he met William Archer, the prominent journalist and drama critic, who urged him to write plays. Through Archer, Shaw became music critic for a London newspaper. With a strong background in economics and politics, Shaw rose to prominence through the socialist Fabian Society, which he helped organize in 1884. He also established himself as a persuasive orator and became well known as a critic of art, music, and literature. In 1895 he became the drama critic for the *Saturday Review.*

Shaw's socialist viewpoint and penetrating wit show through in his journalism, economic and political tracts, and his many plays. An articulate nonconformist, Shaw believed in a spirit he called the Life Force that would help improve and eventually perfect the world. This hope for human and social improvement gave a sense of purpose to much of Shaw's work and had a broad range of effects across many facets of his life, from his vegetarian diet to his satirizing of social pretensions. It also led to his rebellion against the prevailing idea of ''art for art's sake'' (that is, works of art that did not also have an explicit social purpose).

Shaw's plays were frequently banned by censors or refused production (both their themes and their expansive scope made them difficult to stage), so he sought audiences through open readings and publication. He published his first collection, *Plays Pleasant and Unpleasant,* in 1898, which included the combative, ''unpleasant'' works *Widowers' Houses* (his first play), *Mrs. Warren's Profession,* and *The Philanderer ;* and the milder, more tongue-in-cheek plays *Arms and the Man, Candida, The Man of Destiny,* and *You Never Can Tell.* Also in 1898, Shaw married the wealthy Charlotte Payne-Townsend. The year was a turning point in Shaw's life, after which he was centrally associated with the intellectual revival of the English theatre.

After the turn of the century, Shaw's plays gradually began to achieve production and, eventually, acceptance in England. Throughout his long life, his work expressed a mischievous delight in outstripping ponderous intellectual institutions. His subsequent plays include *Man and Superman* (written from 1901 to 1903), a complex idea play about human capability; *John Bull's Other Island* (1904), a satire of British opinions concerning his native Ireland; *Major Barbara* (1905), a dazzling investigation of social conscience and reform; *Pygmalion* (1914); *Heartbreak House* (1920), an anguished allegory of Europe before the First World War;

George Bernard Shaw

Back to Methuselah (1922), a legend cycle for Shaw's "religion" of creative evolution; *Saint Joan* (1923), a startling historical tragedy; *The Apple Cart* (1929), one of three later plays Shaw termed "political extravaganzas"; and *Buoyant Billions* (1948), his last full-length play.

Shaw received the Nobel Prize for literature in 1925, which was considered to be the high point of his career (although he was still to write seventeen more plays). In later life, he remained a vigorous symbol of the ageless superman he proclaimed in his works, traveling extensively throughout the world and engaging in intellectual and artistic pursuits. In September, 1950, however, he fell from an apple tree he was pruning, and on November 2 of that year died of complications stemming from the injury.

PLOT SUMMARY

Act I

The action begins at 11:15 p.m. in a heavy summer rainstorm. An after-theatre crowd takes shelter in the portico of St. Paul's Church in Covent Garden. A young girl, Clara Eynsford Hill, and her mother are waiting for Clara's brother Freddy, who looks in vain for an available cab. Colliding into flower peddler Liza Doolittle, Freddy scatters her flowers. After he departs to continue looking for a cab, Liza convinces Mrs. Eynsford Hill to pay for the damaged flowers; she then cons three half-pence from Colonel Pickering. Liza is made aware of the presence of Henry Higgins, who has been writing down every word she has said. Thinking Higgins is a policeman who is going to arrest her for scamming people, Liza becomes hysterical. Higgins turns out, however, to be making a record of her speech for scientific ends. Higgins is an expert in phonetics who claims: "I can place any man within six miles. I can place him within two miles in London. Sometimes within two streets." Upbraiding Liza for her speech, Higgins boasts that "in three months I could pass that girl off as a duchess at an ambassador's garden party." Higgins and Pickering eventually trade names and realize they have long wanted to meet each other. They go off to dine together and discuss phonetics. Liza picks up the money Higgins had flung down upon exiting and for once treats herself to a taxi ride home.

Act II

The next morning at 11 a.m. in Higgins's laboratory, which is full of instruments. Higgins and Pickering receive Liza, who has presented herself at the door. Higgins is taken aback by Liza's request for lessons from him. She wants to learn to "talk more genteel" so she can be employed in a flower shop instead of selling flowers on the street. Liza can only offer to pay a shilling per lesson, but Pickering, intrigued by Higgins's claims the previous night, offers to pay for Liza's lessons and says of the experiment: "I'll say you're the greatest teacher alive if you make that good." Higgins enthusiastically accepts the bet, though his housekeeper, Mrs. Pearce, pleads with him to consider what will become of Liza after the experiment. Liza agrees to move into Higgins's home and goes upstairs for a bath. Meanwhile, Higgins and Pickering are visited by Liza's father, Doolittle, "an elderly but vigorous dustman." Rather than demanding to take Liza away, Doolittle instead offers to "let her go" for the sum of five pounds. Higgins is shocked by this offer at first, asking whether Doolittle has any morals, but he is persuaded by Doolittle's response, that the latter is too poor to afford them. Exiting quickly with his booty, Doolittle does not at first recognize his daughter, who has re-entered, cleaned up and dressed in a Japanese kimono.

Act III

The setting is the flat of Mrs. Higgins, Henry's mother. Henry bursts in with a flurry of excitement, much to the distress of his mother, who finds him lacking in social graces (she observes that her friends "stop coming whenever they meet you"). Henry explains that he has invited Liza, taking the opportunity for an early test of his progress with Liza's speech. The Eynsford Hills, guests of Mrs. Higgins, arrive. The discussion is awkward and Henry, true to his mother's observations, does appear very uncomfortable in company. Liza arrives and, while she speaks with perfect pronunciation and tone, she confuses the guests with many of her topics of conversation and peculiar turns of phrase. Higgins convinces the guests that these, including Liza's famous exclamation "not bloody likely!" are the latest trend in small talk. After all the guests (including Liza) have left, Mrs. Higgins challenges Henry and Pickering regarding their plans; she is shocked that they have given no thought to Liza's well-being, for after the conclusion of the experiment she will have no income, only "the manners and habits that disqualify a fine lady from earning her own living." Henry is characteristically flip, stating "there's no good bothering now. The thing's done." Pickering is no more thoughtful than Higgins, and as the two men exit, Mrs. Higgins expresses her exasperation.

A following scene, the most important of the "optional" scenes Shaw wrote for the film version of *Pygmalion* —and included in later editions of the play—takes place at an Embassy party in London. Higgins is nervous that Nepommuck, a Hungarian interpreter and his former student, will discover his ruse and expose Liza as an aristocratic imposter. Nepommuck, ironically, accuses Liza not of faking her social class, but her nationality. He is convinced Liza must be Hungarian and of noble blood, for she speaks English "too perfectly," and "only foreigners who have been taught to speak it speak it well." Higgins is victorious, but finds little pleasure in having outwitted such foolish guests.

Act IV

Midnight, in Henry's laboratory. Higgins, Pickering, and Liza return from the party. Higgins loudly bemoans the evening: "What a crew! What a silly tomfoolery!" Liza grows more and more frustrated as he continues to complain ("Thank God it's over!"), not paying attention to her or acknowledging her role in his triumph. Complaining about not being able to find his slippers, Higgins does not observe Liza retrieving them and placing them directly by him. She controls her anger as Higgins and Pickering exit, but when Higgins storms back in, still wrathfully looking for his slippers, Liza hurls them at him with all her might. She derides Higgins for his selfishness and demands of him, "What's to become of me?" Higgins tries to convince her that her irritation is "only imagination," that she should "go to bed like a good girl and sleep it off." Higgins gradually understands Liza's economic concern (that she cannot go back to selling flowers, but has no other future), but he can only awkwardly suggest marriage to a rich man as a solution. Liza criticizes the subjugation that Higgins's suggestion implies: "I sold flowers. I didn't sell myself. Now you've made a lady of me I'm not fit to sell anything else." Liza infuriates Higgins by rejecting him, giving him back the rented jewels she wears, and a ring he had bought for her. He angrily throws the ring in the fireplace and storms out.

In the next important "optional scene," Liza has left Higgins's home and comes upon Freddy, who, infatuated with the former flower girl, has recently been spending most of his nights gazing up at Liza's window. They fall into each other's arms, but their passionate kisses are interrupted first by one constable, then another, and another. Liza suggests they jump in a taxi, "and drive about all night; and in the morning I'll call on old Mrs Higgins and ask her what I ought to do."

Act V

Mrs. Higgins's drawing room, the next day. Henry and Pickering arrive and while they are downstairs phoning the police about Liza's disappearance, Mrs. Higgins asks the chambermaid to warn Liza, taking shelter upstairs, not to come down. Mrs. Higgins scolds Henry and Pickering for their childishness and the careless manner in which they treated another human. The arrival of Alfred Doolittle is announced; he enters dressed fashionably as a bridegroom, but in an agitated state, casting accusations at Higgins. Doolittle explains at length how by a deed of Henry's he has come into a regular pension. His lady companion will now marry him, but still he is miserable. Where he once could "put the touch" on anyone for drinking money, now everyone comes to him, demanding favors and monetary support. At this point, Mrs. Higgins reveals that Liza is upstairs, again criticizing Henry for his unthoughtful behavior towards the

A scene from the original 1914 production

girl. Mrs. Higgins calls Liza down, asking Doolittle to step out for a moment to delay the shock of the news he brings. Liza enters, politely cool towards Henry. She thanks Pickering for all the respect he has shown her since their first meeting: calling her Miss Doolittle, removing his hat, opening doors. "The difference," Liza concludes, "between a lady and a flower girl is not how she behaves but how she's treated."

At this point, Doolittle returns. He and Liza are re-united, and all the characters (excepting Henry) prepare to leave to see Doolittle married. Liza and Higgins are left alone. Higgins argues that he didn't treat Liza poorly because she was a flower girl but because he treats everyone the same. He defends his behavior by attacking traditional social graces as absurd: "You call me a brute because you couldn't buy a claim on me by fetching my slippers," he says. Liza declares that since Higgins gave no thought to her future, she will marry Freddy and support herself by teaching phonetics, perhaps assisting Nepommuck. Higgins grows furious at Liza and "lays his hands on her." He quickly regrets doing so and expresses appreciation of Liza's new-found independence. At the play's curtain he remains incorrigible, however, cheerfully assuming

that Liza will continue to manage his household details as she had done during her days of instruction with him.

CHARACTERS

Clara
See Miss Clara Eynsford Hill

Doolittle
See Alfred Doolittle

Alfred Doolittle
Alfred is Liza's father, whom Shaw describes as "an elderly but vigorous dustman.... He has well marked and rather interesting features, and seems equally free from fear or conscience. He has a remarkably expressive voice, the result of a habit of giving vent to his feelings without reserve." Doolittle describes himself as the "undeserving poor," who need just as much as the deserving but never get anything because of the disapproval of middle-class morality. Nevertheless, he is a skilled moocher who is capable of finessing loans from the most miserly of people. He is miserable when he comes into money during the course of the play, however, because people then come with hopes of borrowing money.

Eliza Doolittle
A cockney flower girl of around 18 or 20 years of age, Eliza is streetwise and energetic. She is not educated by traditional standards, but she is intelligent and a quick learner. As she presents herself in her "shoddy coat" at Higgins's laboratory, Shaw describes the "pathos of this deplorable figure, with its innocent vanity and consequential air." She learns a genteel accent from Higgins and, washed and dressed exquisitely, passes in society for a Duchess. In this transformed state, she is shown to be capable of inspiring awe in the observer. While she wins Higgins's wager for him, she is shocked to find him lose interest in her once the experiment is complete; she cannot believe that he's given no thought to her future well-being. Pickering, by having been polite to her from the very beginning, provides a contrast, from which Liza is able to realize that "the difference between a lady and a

MEDIA ADAPTATIONS

- *Pygmalion* was adapted as a film produced by Gabriel Pascal, directed by Anthony Asquith and Leslie Howard, starring Howard and Wendy Hiller; Metro-Goldwyn-Mayer, 1938. The film received Academy Awards for Shaw's screenplay and for the adaptation by Ian Dalrymple, Cecil Lewis, and W. P. Lipscomb.

- *Pygmalion* was also filmed for American television, directed by George Schaefer for the Hallmark Hall of Fame series, starring Julie Harris and James Donald, adapted by Robert Hartung; Compass, 1963.

- The play has also been produced in audio recordings. In 1972 Peter Wood directed a recording starring Michael Redgrave, Donald Pleasence, and Lynn Redgrave (Caedmon TRS 354). In 1974, the play was recorded in association with the British Council, starring Alec McCowen and Diana Rigg (Argo SAY 28).

- *Pygmalion* was also adapted into the musical *My Fair Lady* by Alan Jay Lerner and Frederick Loewe. An original cast recording was released in 1959, starring Rex Harrison, Julie Andrews, and Stanley Holloway (CK 2015 Columbia).

- *My Fair Lady* was made into a film in 1964, produced by Jack L. Warner and directed by George Cukor, starring Audrey Hepburn as Liza with Rex Harrison reprising his stage role of Higgins. The film was nominated for twelve Academy Awards and received eight. It is considered a film classic in the musical genre.

---

flower girl is not how she behaves, but how she's treated.'' She learns from Higgins's behavior an even deeper truth, that social graces and class are not the true measure of a person's worth.

Miss Doolittle
See Eliza Doolittle

Freddy
See Frederick Eynsford Hill

Henry Higgins
Henry Higgins is an expert in phonetics and the author of ''Higgins's Universal Alphabet.'' Shaw describes him as ''a robust, vital, appetizing sort of man of forty or thereabouts. . . . He is of the energetic, scientific type, heartily, even violently interested in everything that can be studied as a scientific subject, and careless about himself and other people, including their feelings. . . . His manner varies from genial bullying . . . to stormy petulance . . . but he is so entirely frank and void of malice that he remains likeable even in his least reasonable mo-

ments.'' In his book *Shaw: The Plays,* Desmond MacCarthy observed that ''Higgins is called a professor of phonetics, but he is really an artist—that is the interesting thing about him, and his character is a study of the creative temperament.''

For many, this temperament is a difficult one. His housekeeper, Mrs. Pearce, observes of Higgins that ''when you get what you called interested in people's accents, you never think of what may happen to them or you.'' Certainly, Higgins gives no thought to Liza's future after his experiment, and when he gradually loses interest in it, he seems, at least from her perspective, to have disposed of her as well. He is shaken by the independence Liza demonstrates and thus by the end of the play is able to show a kind of respect to her. It is on such terms and presented in such a way, however, that a romantic ending between himself and Liza is never really feasible.

Mrs. Higgins
Henry's mother, a generous and gracious woman. She is frequently exasperated by her son's lack

of manners and completely sympathizes with Liza when the girl leaves Higgins and takes shelter with her. She is perceptive and intelligent, and capable of putting Henry in his place. It is indicative of Mrs. Higgins's character that after the conflict between her son and Liza, both characters choose to come to her for guidance.

Frederick Eynsford Hill

Freddy is an upper-class young man of around 20, somewhat weak although eager and good-natured. Proper and upstanding, he is infatuated with Liza and thoroughly devoted to her both before and after she takes shelter with him in an all-night cab after leaving Higgins. Liza claims to be going back to him at the end of the play, an idea which Higgins finds preposterous. Freddy does not have the money to support them both (and from Liza's perspective seems unfit for difficult work), which prompts her idea to earn a living by teaching phonetics.

Miss Clara Eynsford Hill

A pampered socialite of around 20, she is somewhat gullible and easily disgusted. Shaw writes that she "has acquired a gay air of being very much at home in society; the bravado of genteel poverty." Her social position is not secured, however, and this anxiety drives much of her behavior.

Mrs. Eynsford Hill

The middle-aged mother of Freddy and Clara, whom Shaw describes as "well-bred, quiet" and having "the habitual anxiety of straitened means." She is acutely aware of social decorum and highly invested in finding proper spouses for her two children.

Liza

See Eliza Doolittle

Nepommuck

Higgins's first pupil and later his dupe, a Hungarian of around 30. The mustachioed interpreter, according to Higgins, "can learn a language in a fortnight—knows dozens of them. A sure mark of a fool. As a phonetician, no good whatever." He is completely fooled by Liza's performance as a lady of high society and declares that she must be a European duchess.

Mrs. Pearce

Higgins's middle-class housekeeper. Very practical, she can be severe and is not afraid of reproaching Higgins for his lack of social graces. She is conscious of proper behavior and of her position, and quite proud. She is taken aback by the seeming impropriety of Liza coming into the Higgins household but quickly develops a bond with the girl, often defending her from Higgins.

Pick

See Colonel Pickering

Pickering

See Colonel Pickering

Colonel Pickering

A phonetics expert like Higgins, this "elderly gentleman of the amiable military type," meets the latter in a rainstorm at the St. Paul's Church. The "author of Spoken Sanskrit," Pickering excels in the Indian dialects because of his experience in the British colonies there. Courteous and generous, as well as practical and sensible, he never views Liza as just a flower girl and treats her with the respect due a lady of society. "I assure you," he responds to a challenge by Mrs. Higgins, "we take Eliza very seriously." Open-hearted, he finds it easy to sympathize with others and, decidedly unlike Higgins, is conscience-stricken when he fears he's hurt Liza.

THEMES

Appearances and Reality

Pygmalion examines this theme primarily through the character of Liza, and the issue of personal identity (as perceived by oneself or by others). Social roles in the Victorian era were viewed as natural and largely fixed: there was perceived to be something inherently, fundamentally unique about a noble versus an unskilled laborer and vice versa. Liza's ability to fool society about her "real" identity raises questions about appearances. The importance of appearance and reality to the theme of *Pygmalion* is suggested by Liza's famous observation: "You see, really and truly, apart from the things anyone can pick up (the dressing and the proper way of speaking, and so on), the difference

TOPICS FOR FURTHER STUDY

- Research the history of phonetics and speech as a subject of study; does Shaw's depiction of the scientific interests of his character Higgins seem to have been well-grounded in historical precedent?

- Compare and contrast the ways in which both Liza and her father are thrust into the middle class (she through learning to speak "properly," he through obtaining money), and why each is not comfortable in it. Through these characters, what does Shaw seem to be saying about class distinctions?

- Contrast Colonel Pickering and Henry Higgins in terms of manners and behavior. What are the implications of their very different treatments of Liza?

- Research the social position of women in early twentieth-century Britain (economic opportunities, cultural conventions, legal rights), and use this information to explain further why Liza is so concerned about her future following the conclusion of Higgins's "experiment."

---

between a lady and a flower girl is not how she behaves, but how she's treated."

Beauty

In *Pygmalion,* Shaw interrogates beauty as a subjective value. One's perception of beauty in another person is shown to be a highly complex matter, dependent on a large number of (not always aesthetic) factors. Liza, it could be argued, is the same person from the beginning of the play to the end, but while she is virtually invisible to Freddy as a Cockney-speaking flower merchant, he is totally captivated by what he perceives as her beauty and grace when she is presented to him as a lady of society.

Change and Transformation

The transformation of Liza is, of course, central to the plot and theme of *Pygmalion.* The importance at first appears to rest in the power Higgins expresses by achieving this transformation. "But you have no idea," he says, "how frightfully interesting it is to take a human being and change her into a quite different human being by creating a new speech for her. It's filling up the deepest gulf that separates class from class and soul from soul." As the play unfolds, however, the focus shifts so that the effects

of the change upon Liza become central. The truly important transformation Liza goes through is not the adoption of refined speech and manners but the learning of independence and a sense of inner self-worth that allows her to leave Higgins.

Identity

The indeterminacy of appearance and reality in *Pygmalion* reveals the significant examination of identity in the play. Shaw investigates conflicts between differing perceptions of identity and depicts the end result of Higgins's experiment as a crisis of identity for Liza. Liza's transformation is glorious but painful, as it leaves her displaced between her former social identity and a new one, which she has no income or other resources to support. Not clearly belonging to a particular class, Liza no longer knows *who she is.*

Language and Meaning

In an age of growing standardization of what was known as "the Queen's English," *Pygmalion* points to a much wider range of varieties of spoken English. Shaw believed characteristics of social identity such as one's refinement of speech were completely subjective ones, as his play suggests. While Shaw himself hated poor speech and the varieties of dialect and vocabulary could present obstructions to conveying meaning, nevertheless the play suggests that the real richness of the English language is in the variety of individuals who speak it. As for the dialect or vocabulary of any one English variety, such as Cockney, its social value is determined in *Pygmalion* completely by the context in which it is assessed. While Liza's choice of words as a Cockney flower merchant would be thought as absurd as her accent, they are later perceived by the mannered Eynsford Hill family to be the latest trend, when they are thought to emanate from a person of noble breeding.

Sex Roles

Sex and gender have a great deal to do with the dynamics between Liza and Higgins, including the sexual tension between them that many audience members would have liked to see fulfilled through a romantic union between them. In Liza's difficult case, what are defined as her options are clearly a limited subset of options available to a woman. As Mrs. Higgins observes, after the conclusion of the experiment Liza will have no income, only "the manners and habits that disqualify a fine lady from earning her own living." To this problem Higgins can only awkwardly suggest marriage to a rich man as a solution. Liza makes an astute observation about Higgins's suggestion, focusing on the limited options available to a woman: "I sold flowers. I didn't sell myself. Now you've made a lady of me I'm not fit to sell anything else."

Ubermensch ("Superman")

Shaw's belief in the Life Force and the possibility of human evolution on an individual or social level led him to believe also in the possibility of the Superman, a realized individual living to the fullest extent of his or her capacity. (The naming of the concept is credited to the influential German philosopher Friedrich Wilhelm Nietzsche, 1844-1900). Shaw addresses the topic explicitly in his play *Man and Superman* and in many other works, but he also approaches it in *Pygmalion*. Higgins, for example, represents the height of scientific achievement in his field, though he may be too flawed as an individual to continue evolving towards a superhuman level. Liza, proving herself capable of one type of transformation, also makes an important step towards self-awareness and self-realization, which for Shaw is the beginning of almost endless possibilities for personal development.

Wealth and Poverty

One of the many subjects under examination in *Pygmalion* is class consciousness, a concept first given name in 1887. Shaw's play, like so many of his writings, examines both the realities of class and its subjective markers. The linguistic signals of social identity, for example, are simultaneously an issue of class. Economic issues are central to Liza's crisis at the conclusion of Higgins's experiment, for she lacks the means to maintain the standard of living he and Pickering enjoy. Doolittle's unforeseen rise into the middle class similarly allows Shaw to examine wealth and poverty. Though Doolittle fears the workhouse he's not happy with his new class identity, either; Shaw injects humor through Doolittle's surprising (according to traditional class values) distaste for his new status.

STYLE

Plotting with a Purpose

In *Pygmalion*'s plot, Higgins, a phonetics expert, makes a friendly bet with his colleague Colonel Pickering that he can transform the speech and manners of Liza, a common flower girl, and present her as a lady to fashionable society. He succeeds, but Liza gains independence in the process, and leaves her former tutor because he is incapable of responding to her needs.

Pygmalion has a tightly-constructed plot, rising conflict, and other qualities of the "well-made play," a popular form at the time. Shaw, however, revolutionized the English stage by disposing of other conventions of the well-made play; he discarded its theatrical dependence on prolonging and then resolving conflict in a sometimes contrived manner for a theater of ideas grounded in realism. Shaw was greatly influenced by Henrik Ibsen, who he claimed as a forerunner to his theatre of discussion or ideas. Ibsen's *A Doll House,* Shaw felt, was an example of how to end a play indeterminately, leading the audience to reflect upon character and theme, rather than simply entertaining them with a neatly-resolved conclusion.

Intellect vs. Entertainment

Shaw broke both with the predominant intellectual principle of his day, that of "art for art's sake," as well as with the popular notion that the purpose of the theatre was strictly to entertain. Refusing to write a single sentence for the sake of either art or entertainment alone, Shaw openly declared that he was for a theater which preached to its audience on social issues. Edward Wagenknecht wrote in *A Guide to Bernard Shaw* that Shaw's plays "are not plays: they are tracts in dramatic form." He further reflected a popular perception of Shaw's plays as intellectual exercises by stating that Shaw "has created one great character—G.B.S. [George Bernard Shaw]—and in play after play he performs infinite variations upon it." Thus, in his day Shaw was viewed as succeeding *despite* his dramatic technique rather than because of it. Wagenknecht again: "it is amazing that a man whose theory of art is so patently wrong should have achieved such a place as Shaw has won."

Though his plays do tend towards ideological discussion rather than dramatic tension, Shaw succeeded because he nevertheless understood what made a play theatrical, wrote scintillating dialogue, and always created rich, complex characters in the center of a philosophically complex drama. Among his character creations are some of the greatest in the modern theatre, especially the women: Major Barbara, Saint Joan, Liza Doolittle. Also, Shaw's deep belief in the need for social improvement did not prevent him from having a wry sense of humor, an additional component of his dramatic technique which helped his plays, *Pygmalion* most predominantly, bridge a gap between popular and intellectual art.

Romance

In calling *Pygmalion* a *romance* (its subtitle is "A Romance in Five Acts"), Shaw was referencing a well-established literary form (not usually employed in theatre), to which *Pygmalion* does not fully conform. (Shaw was aiming to provoke thought by designating his play thusly.) The term romance does not imply, as it was misinterpreted to mean by many of Shaw's contemporaries, a romantic element between Liza and Higgins. Since the middle ages, romances have been distinguished from more realistic forms by their exotic, exaggerated narratives, and their idealized characters and themes. Shaw playfully suggests *Pygmalion* is a romance because of the almost magical transformations which occur in the play and the idealized qualities to which the characters aspire.

HISTORICAL CONTEXT

World War I

Nineteen-fourteen, the year of *Pygmalion*'s London premiere, marked tremendous changes in British society. On July 28, the Austrian archduke Franz Ferdinand and his wife were assassinated in Sarajevo, Bosnia, setting off an international conflict due to a complicated set of alliances which had developed in Europe. Within two weeks, this conflict had erupted into a world war (known in Britain at the time as the "Great War"). By the end of World War I (as it came to be known later), 8.5 million people had been killed and 21 million wounded, including significant civilian casualties. The war constituted the most intense physical, economic and psychological assault on European society in its history; Britain was not alone in experiencing devastating effects on its national morale and other aspects of society.

It is ironic, Eldon C. Hill wrote in *George Bernard Shaw,* that *Pygmalion,* "written partly to demonstrate that language (phonetics particularly) could contribute to understanding among men, should be closed because of the outbreak of World War I." The war brought out Shaw's compassion, as well as his disgust with the European societies that would tolerate the destruction of so many lives. When the actress Mrs. Patrick Campbell informed Shaw of the death of her son in battle, he replied that he could not be sympathetic, but only furious: "Killed just because people are blasted fools," Hill quoted the playwright saying. To Shaw, the war only demonstrated more clearly the need for human advancement on an individual and social level, to reach a level of understanding that would prevent such tragic devastation.

Colonialism and the British Empire

In 1914 Great Britain was very much still a colonial power, but while victory in the First World War actually increased the size of the British Empire, the war itself simultaneously accelerated the development of nationalism and autonomy in the provinces. Even before the war, British pride in its Empire had reached a climax prior to the death of Queen Victoria in 1901, and the brutalities of the Boer War (1899-1902), fought to assert Britain's authority in South Africa. Still, British society proudly proclaimed that "the sun never sets on the British Empire" and believed in Britain's providential mission in geographies as widely diverse as Ireland, Australia and New Zealand, India, Burma, Egypt,

COMPARE
&
CONTRAST

- **1910s:** Women in Britain do not have the right to vote, and their opportunities for education and employment remain limited.

  Today: Since 1928, all women over the age of 21 have had the right to vote in Britain. The direct participation of women in government continues to be more limited than that of men, although the election of Margaret Thatcher as Prime Minister in 1979 set an important precedent. Women were admitted to full admission at Oxford in 1920 and to Cambridge University in 1948. Women make up a much larger portion of the work force than they did at the turn of the century, and although their compensation and employment opportunities continue to lag behind those of men, the Equal Pay Act of 1970 and other measures have addressed this issue. It is no longer the case that a women's natural role is widely assumed to be limited to domestic work.

- **1910s:** With industrialization and legislative reform beginning a process of diversification, Britain's society is still rigidly hierarchical, with a tradition of a landed aristocracy and a pyramid of descending ranks and degrees. In 1911, the power of the royally-appointed House of Lords in Parliament to veto the legislation of the democratically-elected House of Commons is reduced to a power to delay legislation.

  Today: The political power of royalty and the nobility has been greatly reduced through a process of legislative reform. While titles of nobility remain, Britain's society remains stratified primarily by wealth rather than rank. While the middle class grew considerably throughout the century and there was significant growth in economic indicators such as owner-occupation of homes, sharp divisions between rich and poor persist in Britain. With the growth of the technical institutes, the "polytechnics," the expansion

  of the university system after World War II greatly increased opportunities for higher education in the country.

- **1910s:** Despite the promotion of a standard "Queen's English," beginning in the Victorian era, the British Isles—even London itself—is marked by a wide diversity of spoken English. The diversity of British population (including its varieties of English) was further shaped by large-scale immigration, by Irish beginning in the 1830s, Germans in the 1840s, Scandinavians in the 1870s, and Eastern Europeans in the 1880s.

  Today: The diversity of English culture—especially in London and the major cities—has been further increased, along with the diversity of English dialects, by twentieth-century immigration from Britain's colonies and former colonies in Africa, the Caribbean, the Indian subcontinent, and the Far East.

- **1910s:** Europe is devastated by the 8.5 million dead and 21 million wounded in "the Great War" (World War I), including unprecedented levels of civilian casualties. Britain was not alone in experiencing the most intense physical, economic, and psychological assault in its history.

  Today: The specter of civilian death leads to a realization that modern warfare potentially endangers the future of the entire nation. This feeling has been accentuated since the end of World War II by the threat of nuclear destruction. Much more so than at the beginning of the century, citizens have come to perceive war and the necessity of avoiding it as their business, and they often try to impact their government's policies to this end. Shaw's position against war, still somewhat radical in his day, has become much more common.

the Sudan, South Africa, Nigeria, Guyana, Honduras, Jamaica, and numerous other islands throughout the Caribbean, and Canada.

In addition to providing a symbolic unity to the Empire, the long reign of Queen Victoria (1837-1901) also gave coherence to British society at home, through a set of values known as Victorianism. Victorian values revolved around social high-mindedness (a Christian sense of charity and service), domesticity (most education and entertainment occurred in the home, but children, who ''should be seen and not heard,'' were reared with a strict hand) and a confidence in the expansion of knowledge and the power of reasoned argument to change society. By the time of Victoria's death, many of the more traditional mid-Victorian values were already being challenged, as was the class structure upon which many of these values depended. Victorianism, however, survived in a modified form through the reign of Victoria's son, Edward. 1914, the year of *Pygmalion* and the onset of the Great War, constituted a much different kind of break, symbolic and social.

Industrialization

The growth of industrialization throughout the nineteenth century had a tremendous impact on the organization of British society, which had (much more so than the United States) a tradition of a landed aristocracy and a more hierarchical class system—a pyramid of descending ranks and degrees. Allowing for the growth of a merchant middle class, industrialization changed British society into a plutocracy—an aristocracy of money more than land. Social mobility, however, still did not widely extend into the lower classes, propagating a lack of opportunity reflected in Liza's anxiety over what is to happen to her following Higgins's experiment.

Industrialization brought about a demographic shift throughout the nineteenth century, with more and more agricultural laborers coming to seek work in the cities. Unskilled laborers like the Doolittles competed for limited employment amid the poverty of the inner city and were largely at the mercy of employers. Increased health standards combated urban crises like tuberculosis and cholera, but slum conditions and rampant urban poverty remained a major social problem after the turn of the century. *Pygmalion* suggests the subjectivity of class identity, and the rapid deterioration of many pre-industrial social structures, but strict class distinctions of another kind nevertheless persisted. This fact is

suggested by the severely disproportionate distribution of wealth in Britain at the time: during the years 1911-1913, the top 1% of the population controlled 65.5% of the nation's capital. The poorest of the poor, meanwhile, were often forced into workhouses, institutions which had been developed in the 17th century to employ paupers and the indigent at profitable work. Conditions in the workhouses differed little from prisons; they were deliberately harsh and degrading in order to discourage the poor from relying upon them. Conditions in the workhouses improved later in the 19th century but were still unpleasant enough that fear of going to one, for example, causes Doolittle in *Pygmalion* to accept his new position in the middle class even though it is displeasing to him for other reasons.

The Rise of Women and the Working Classes

During the decade which produced *Pygmalion,* the political power of the working class increased greatly, through massive increases in trade union membership. Bitter class divisions gave rise to waves of strikes and disturbances, including a major railway strike in 1911, a national miners' strike in 1912, and the ''Triple Alliance'' of miners, railway, and transport workers in 1914. A new political party, Labour, came into existence in 1893, advancing an eight-hour work day and other workplace reforms. Meanwhile, reforms to laws concerning suffrage, the right to vote, further brought men (and later, women) of the working class into Britain's ever-more participatory democracy. Suffrage (the right to vote) had in Britain always been based on requirements of property ownership, reflecting the contemporary idea that only landowners were considered reasoned and informed enough to vote but also that they would do so in the best interest of those in the classes below them. These property requirements were gradually relaxed throughout the nineteenth century, gradually increasing the size of the male electorate.

Only after many years of political struggle by organizations of women known as ''suffragettes'' did women achieve the right to vote: first in 1918 for women over 30 who also met a requirement of property ownership, then extended in 1928 to all women over the age of 21 (as was already the case for men). Increased political participation further prompted a shift in sex roles: British society had already noted the phenomenon of ''the new woman,'' and was to see further changes such as increasing numbers of women in the work force, as well as reforms to divorce laws and other impacts upon domestic life.

CRITICAL OVERVIEW

Building upon the acclaim *Pygmalion* had received from German-language production and publication, the original English production of the play at His Majesty's Theatre was likewise a success, securing Shaw's reputation as a popular playwright. Still, contemporary reviews of *Pygmalion* are mixed, revealing the somewhat prejudicial views English critics continue to hold towards Shaw's work. For example, an unsigned review in the *Westminster Gazette,* reprinted in *Shaw: The Critical Heritage,* criticized many aspects of the production but had qualified praise for the play, "a puzzling work." Aware that Shaw usually "does not use the drama merely as a vehicle for telling stories," the critic expressed a curiosity about what "the foundation idea" of *Pygmalion* might be. "Curiosity, in the present instance," however, "remains unsatisfied. There are plenty of ideas, but none is predominant."

Alex M. Thompson, meanwhile, wrote in a review in the *Clarion* that "Britain's most famous playwright has won his place at last on the stage of Britain's most famous playhouse" but regretted that "while the great playwright's really significant plays" were wasted through production elsewhere, "the play admitted to our classic shrine is one whose purpose, according to the author himself, is 'to boil the pot.'" H. W. Massingham, in a review for the *Nation,* declared that "there is a fault in the piece as well as in its production," namely that Shaw "observes too coldly": in pursuing the clash of wits, the excitement of argument, he obscures real beauty and affection. Shaw, somewhat like Higgins, "hides his spirituality or his tenderness under a mask of coarseness," to the extent that he "has failed to show his audience precisely what he meant."

The sensation caused by Shaw's use of the mild profanity "bloody" (breaking with tradition at His Majesty's Theatre) went a long way to ensure the publicity for *Pygmalion,* but many critics found the language of the play shocking. T. F. Evans commented in his notes for *Shaw: The Critical Heritage,* that "[it] is almost impossible . . . to assess accurately the critical response to the play itself because of the totally disproportionate amount of space, time and attention that was given to the use

by Shaw . . . of the word 'bloody'. . . . Some critics who might have been expected to give largely favourable comments on the play seem to have allowed the use of the adjective to affect them." By 1938, however, the year *Pygmalion* was made into a movie, Shaw's text was still dramatic and challenging but much of the shock had faded. Of the film version, Desmond MacCarthy observed in *Shaw: The Plays* that "'bloody' still gets its laugh, but it no longer releases the roar that greets the crash of a taboo."

In his 1929 study *A Guide to Bernard Shaw,* Edward Wagenknecht demonstrated the delicate balance many critical interpretations of Shaw in that era tried to maintain, explaining how Shaw had succeeded despite breaking many established conventions of dramatic art. Shaw "revolted" against deeply-held ideas that literature is writing which supersedes a specific purpose other than to communicate life experience, and is not didactic. "It is amazing," Wagenknecht wrote, "that a man whose theory of art is so patently wrong should have achieved such a place as Shaw has won."

By the end of Shaw's life, his status as perhaps the greatest single English dramatist since Shakespeare was secure, but nevertheless critical opinion on him appeared mixed and in many cases prejudiced. Eric Bentley wrote in his book *Bernard Shaw, 1856-1950,* that in reviewing the already voluminous writing on Shaw, "I found praise, but most of it naive or invidious. I found blame, but most of it incoherent and scurrilous." Perhaps Shaw's complexity of thought provoked these mixed (and largely unsatisfying) critical assessments, to the extent that to some critics "Shaw, the champion of will and feeling, is an arch-irrationalist," but to others "Shaw, the champion and incarnation of intellect, is the arch-rationalist." In *Pygmalion* Bentley found a play of "singularly elegant structure . . . a good play by perfectly orthodox standards" needing "no theory to defend it."

In his summary of the play's merits, Bentley avoided the tendency of earlier critics to distinguish sharply between various aspects of Shaw's work, instead celebrating the intimate connection between them. *Pygmalion,* he wrote, "is Shavian, not in being made up of political or philosophic discussions, but in being based on the standard conflict of vitality and system, in working out this conflict through an inversion of romance, in bringing matters to a head in a battle of wills and words, in having an inner psychological action in counterpoint to the outer romantic action . . . in delighting and surprising us with a constant flow of verbal music and more than verbal wit.'' Bentley's modern assessment of the complexity of Shaw's political thought and dramatic method established a precedent for much Shavian criticism of the last fifty years.

Beginning immediately with the first English production of *Pygmalion,* a popular debate developed as to whether there should have been a romantic ending between Higgins and Liza. Shaw insisted that such an ending would have been misery for his characters but producers and audiences nevertheless tended to prefer a romantic ending. MacCarthy expressed the sentiments of many when he wrote about the original production ''when the curtain fell on the mutual explanations of this pair [Higgins and Liza] I was in a fever to see it rise on Acts VI and VII; I wanted to see those two living together.''

When the play was first published in 1916, Shaw added an afterword which recounted what Liza did after leaving Higgins and was intended to show to audiences that there was to be ''no sentimental nonsense'' about the possibility of Higgins and Liza being lovers. The English-language film of *Pygmalion* gave Shaw another opportunity to remove ''virtually every suggestion of Higgins's possible romantic interest in Liza.'' He was to discover, however, at a press show two days before the film's premiere, that the director had hired other screenwriters who added a ''sugar-sweet ending'' in which Higgins and Liza are united as lovers. MacCarthy commented in 1938 that the effect of the changes in the film version ''is merely that of a wish fulfillment love story of a poor girl who became a lady and married the man who made her one.'' He observes that the difference is ''due to a peculiarity inherent in the art of cinema itself'' (a need for closure), and that the changed ending is no doubt what accounts for the film's ''immense popularity.''

CRITICISM

Christopher Busiel

Busiel is an English instructor at the University of Texas. His essay considers Shaw's play within the context of his other great works.

Like all of Shaw's great dramatic creations, *Pygmalion* is a richly complex play. It combines a central story of the transformation of a young wom-

an with elements of myth, fairy tale, and romance, while also combining an interesting plot with an exploration of social identity, the power of science, relations between men and women, and other issues. Change is central to the plot and theme of the play, which of course revolves around Higgins's transformation of Liza from a flower-girl who speaks a coarse Cockney dialect (a manner of speech which he says will ''keep her in the gutter to the end of her days'') into a lady who passes as a duchess in genteel society. The importance of transformation in *Pygmalion* at first appears to rest upon the power Higgins expresses by achieving his goal. ''But you have no idea,'' he says, drawing attention to his talent, ''how frightfully interesting it is to take a human being and change her into a quite different human being by creating a new speech for her.''

But where does the real transformation occur in Liza? Much more important than her new powers of speech, ultimately, is the independence she gains *after* the conclusion of Higgins's ''experiment.'' Charles A. Berst noted in his study *Bernard Shaw and the Art of Drama* that Shaw omitted from *Pygmalion* the scene of the ball at the Ambassador's mansion where Liza shows herself as the triumph of Higgins's art. The reason Shaw does so is ''because the emphasis here is not on the fairy-tale climax of the triumphant 'test' . . . but on the social and personal ramifications of the real world to which Eliza must adjust after the test.'' In short, Liza realizes Higgins's lack of concern at her unsure future, and she turns on her ''creator,'' leaving him.

Higgins's successful transformation of Liza contradicts the class rigidity of Victorian and Edwardian society, demonstrating Shaw's belief in the highly subjective construction of social identities. A proponent of a school of thought known as Fabianism, Shaw believed firmly in the power of individuals to transform, to improve themselves. Drawing on a power Shaw called the Life Force, human beings could both evolve to the full extent of their capabilities and collectively turn to the task of transforming society. Eric Bentley wrote in *Bernard Shaw, 1856-1950* that ''Fabianism begins and ends as an appeal—emotionally based—for social justice.'' In the Fabian perspective, social systems are changeable and need to change. Shaw introduced his *Intelligent Woman's Guide to Socialism and Capitalism* by encouraging the reader to ''clear your mind of the fancy with which we all begin as children, that the institutions under which we live, including our legal ways of distributing income and allowing people to own things, are natural, like the

WHAT DO I READ NEXT?

- *Major Barbara,* another of Shaw's plays, first produced in 1905, and considered his first major work. It explores the ideological conflict between "Major" Barbara Undershaft, who strives to lift up the poor through her untiring effort with the Salvation Army, and her father, Sir Andrew Undershaft, a fabulously wealthy arms manufacturer. Both achievers represent Shaw's theory of the Life Force, or human advancement through "creative evolution." The play explores the question of whose actions better serve society, Barbara's or those of her father, who provides a comfortable existence for his employees but can only do so through his profiting by the destruction of human life. Similar to *Pygmalion* (and many of Shaw's other plays), the action revolves around a strong, independent female character and explores issues of class, social identity, and human worth.

- *The Intelligent Woman's Guide to Socialism and Capitalism.* A significant example of Shaw's political writing, one which examines many themes central to *Pygmalion.* The text demonstrates Shaw's firm, lifelong belief that only members of a socialist society—with collective ownership of wealth and equal opportunity for all—could look forward to the future with hope. Writing ten years after the Bolshevik revolution in Russia, Shaw viewed that experiment as a failure (recognizing the developing trend towards totalitarianism in the Soviet state). In general, Shaw looked with hope not to revolution but to a democratic transition to socialism, a truly collective evolution towards an equitable society. That "the intelligent woman" was his audience for the work was a deliberate choice; Shaw was particularly concerned with the exploitation of women, both through their unpaid but crucial domestic labor and their limited and underpaid positions in the work force. "Our whole commercial system," he wrote, "is rooted . . . in cheap female labour." Shaw perceived the special need during his era to increase educational and employment opportunities for women. This text is of a significant length but has an encyclopedic structure.

- *Plays and Players: Essays on the Theatre,* edited by A. C. Ward (Oxford University Press, 1952); and *Shaw on the Theatre,* edited by E. J. West (Hill and Wang, 1958). These volumes compile a number of Shaw's extensive writings on the theatre (commenting on both the plays and productions of his own career, as well as on other playwrights such as Shakespeare and Ibsen.)

- *Bernard Shaw and Mrs. Patrick Campbell: Their Correspondence,* edited by Alan Dent (Knopf, 1962). The compiled correspondence between Shaw and the actress who created the part of Liza in the English premiere. Shaw also wrote *Caesar and Cleopatra* for her and the actor Johnston Forbes-Robertson, though she never performed in it. *Pygmalion* is discussed extensively.

- *The Story of English* by Robert McCrum, William Cran, and Robert MacNeil (Viking Penguin, 1986; revised, 1992). A companion book to a public-television series (available on video at most libraries) about the history of English: its historical development out of Germanic, Celtic, and Anglo-Saxon roots; its transition from an early, to a middle and then a modern form; and its unprecedented spread throughout the world through British colonialism and emigration (approximately 1 billion people worldwide speak it as a first or second language). Students interested in Shaw's exploration of issues of speech and dialect in *Pygmalion* will be especially interested in this book, which further examines the seemingly innumerable varieties of spoken English throughout the world. This text examines how standards of "the Queen's English" developed in the Victorian era, and how social identities were constructed based on variations from this standard. The Cockney of Liza Doolittle, among numerous varieties in the British Isles, is given close attention. *The Story of English* provides the basis of valuable discussion on topics such as: what constitutes "Standard" English? What is a dialect? An accent? In what ways is dialect still a mark of social position?

weather. They are not. . . . They are in fact transient makeshifts; and many of them would not be obeyed, even by well-meaning people, if there were not a policeman within call and a prison within reach. They are being changed constantly by Parliament because we are never satisfied with them.''

As a Fabian, Shaw believed in human improvement and evolution as the key to social transformation. What Liza learns by breaking free of Higgins's influence is an independence of thought Shaw believed was a crucial component of personal evolution. Berst emphasized the importance of this process by which ''a soul awakens to true self-realization.'' Having shown that there are no hard and fast rules for social identity, Shaw does not allow his leading character to remain limited within a society in which she can only marry for money. Liza identifies such an arrangement as a kind of prostitution, an explicit example of how, as Bentley summarized, in a culture built around ''buying and selling the vast mass of the population has nothing to sell but itself.'' Instead, Shaw has Liza break free—into an uncertain future to be sure but one in which she will work, struggle, and, hopefully, prosper as an independent woman.

Shaw did not believe in the sense of innate inequality which dominated British society around the turn of the century, in the supposedly natural divisions between classes based on built-in qualities of character. Instead, he believed in the power of ''nurture'' over ''nature,'' and the ''conditioning effects of social circumstance,'' as discussed by Lynda Mugglestone in the *Review of English Studies*. Though Liza appears rough on the edges to the standards of Edwardian society, she has self-respect, pride, ambition, and a sense of humor—all qualities which help her mature to the independence she achieves by the play's end. That Liza has such great success mastering the speech of a duchess suggests that all people are fundamentally of equal worth, that the social differences between them are merely the result of different levels of opportunity (financial and otherwise). In Shaw's view, meanwhile, a Socialist society would mean ''equal rights and opportunities for all,'' a definition he gave in a Fabian pamphlet published in 1890.

As Mugglestone wrote, Eliza's education in the ways that the English upper classes act and speak provides an opportunity for the playwright to explore ''the very foundations of social equality and inequality.'' What we discover in *Pygmalion* is that phonetics and ''correct'' pronunciation are systems of markers superficial in themselves but endowed with tremendous social significance. Higgins himself observes that pronunciation is ''the deepest gulf that separates class from class and soul from soul.'' Playwright and character differ, however, in that instead of criticizing the existence of this gulf, Higgins accepts it as natural and uses his skills to help those who can afford his services (or are taken in as experiments, like Liza) to bridge it.

Act III of *Pygmalion* highlights the importance of Liza's double transformation, by showing her suspended between the play's beginning and its conclusion. At Mrs. Higgins's ''At Home'' reception, Liza is fundamentally the same person she was in Act I, although she differs in what we learn to appreciate as ''superficialities of social disguise'' (according to Mugglestone): details of speech and cleanliness. ''In modern society, however, as Shaw illustrates, it is precisely these superficial details which tend to be endowed with most significance.'' Certainly the Eynsford Hills view such details as significant, as Liza's entrance produces for them what Shaw's stage directions call ''an impression of . . . remarkable distinction and beauty.'' Ironically, however, Liza's true transformation is yet to occur. She experiences a much more fundamental change in her consciousness when she realizes that Higgins has more or less abandoned her at the conclusion of his experiment.

At first, Liza experiences a sense of anxiety over not belonging anywhere: she can hardly return to flower peddling, yet she lacks the financial means to make her new, outward identity a social reality. ''What am I fit for?'' she demands of Higgins. ''What have you left me fit for? Where am I to go? What am I to do? What's to become of me?'' Berst wrote that ''while Pickering is generous, Eliza is shoved into the wings by Higgins. The dream has been fulfilled, midnight has tolled for Cinderella, and morning reality is at hand.'' Liza must break away from Higgins when he shows himself incapable of recognizing her needs. This response of Higgins is well within his character as it has been portrayed in the play. Indeed, from his first exposure to Liza, Higgins denied Liza any social or even individual worth. Calling Liza a ''squashed cabbage leaf,'' Higgins states that ''a woman who utters such depressing and disgusting sounds has no right to be anywhere—no right to live.'' While treated primarily with humor, Higgins is a kind of anti-hero in Shaw's dramatic universe, because he accepts as natural the divisions among the classes. Assuming that Liza has no inherent worth, Higgins believes only he can bestow worth upon her, by helping her pass in society as a lady.

A romantic union between Liza and Higgins is impossible primarily because unlike her, he is incapable of transformation. He remains the confirmed bachelor that he has always been, an unsuitable Prince Charming denying either a fairy-tale ending to *Pygmalion* or a satisfactory marriage to its "Cinderella." Nowhere is Higgins shown more strongly to be incapable of change than in his response to Liza's challenge to him. Liza has thrown his slippers at him out of frustration with his lack of concern for her. "I'm nothing to you," she observes, "not so much as them slippers." Higgins instantly corrects her with "those slippers," a mechanical response which shows him clinging to the externals of his trade, incapable of recognizing the importance of the change which has come over Liza.

The response of audiences and actors alike was strongly in favor of a romantic liaison between Higgins and Liza, but such a future for the characters would depend upon a transformation in Higgins which he is incapable of making. Indeed, Berst ventured, a "close examination of Higgins's character and comments cannot support a romantic conclusion. He is by nature celibate and self-centered, slightly perverse in both respects." Shaw altered the play's ending to make his point more explicit, and when the play was first published in 1916, he added an afterword which recounted what Liza did after leaving Higgins. This was intended to show to audiences that there was to be "no sentimental nonsense" about the possibility of Higgins and Liza being lovers.

Source: Christopher Busiel, in an essay for *Drama for Students,* Gale, 1997.

Stanley J. Solomon

Solomon addresses the controversy surrounding the ending of Shaw's Pygmalion *in this essay. Examining the play's action, he concludes that the playwright's original denouement is the only appropriate one.*

Solomon is an educator and critic who specializes in film theory.

Pygmalion is one of Shaw's most popular plays as well as one of his most straightforward ones. The form has none of the complexity that we find in *Heartbreak House* or *Saint Joan,* nor are the ideas in *Pygmalion* nearly as profound as the ideas in any of Shaw's other major works. Yet the ending of

Pygmalion provokes an interesting controversy among critics. Higgins and Eliza do not marry at the end of the written text, while the play as it is usually produced often does reconcile the two main characters. Obviously many directors and many readers feel that the apparent unromantic ending is an arbitrary bit of sarcasm appended to the play merely for spiteful humor.

It is my contention that the only valid approach to the problem of *Pygmalion*'s ending is to analyze the structure of the dramatic movement. In examining the play, I will consider the central situation and the dramatic problem it raises in preparation for the ending, which is the solution to that problem. All other critical approaches applied to the ending have tended to introduce extraneous information and lead to inconclusive suppositions about which of the possible endings is to be preferred. For instance, in evaluating the ending, one would probably be wise to pass over two extremely interesting but contradictory pieces of evidence which, at first, seem to bear directly on the matter. On the one hand we have the postscript which Shaw added to the published version of *Pygmalion.* In it he explains vehemently and reasonably why Eliza will not *marry* Higgins. On the other hand there is the movie version ending which Shaw rewrote so that it becomes clear to the audience that Eliza *will* marry Higgins. We can speculate about Shaw's real intention, but lacking conclusive external evidence we should justify or condemn the ending of the stage play only in relation to the text itself.

The controversy over the ending deserves some scrutiny, however, because the criticism represents a good many different approaches to Shaw's work. One approach is the "instinctive" method, a method which is outside the realm of literary criticism but is certainly of value in judging a play, since Shaw or any good dramatist realizes that during a performance the spectators will intuitively "feel" that an action is right or wrong without bothering to analyze their feelings. After considering the structure of *Pygmalion,* Milton Crane, in an often-quoted article, concludes that Shaw was either wrong or not serious in his ending. But Professor Crane gives no objective reason for his point of view, nor does he tie it in with his analysis of structure. A similar view is expressed by St. John Ervine concerning the denouement:

> [The ending] convinces nobody who reads it . . . the facts of the play cry out against its author. The end of the fourth act as well as the end of the fifth act deny . . . [the postscript], and assure all sensible people that

she married Henry Higgins and bore him many vigorous and intelligent children (*Bernard Shaw: His Life, Work, and Friends,* [New York], 1956).

The trouble with such opinions is that a great many people may instinctively feel that the play ends correctly. We cannot depend too much on a director's view of the text, for if the play in production has been interpreted romantically, the ending of the stage version seems inappropriate; on the other hand, if the play is produced "anti-romantically," the ending of this version is necessary.

Two directly opposing interpretations of the ending can be based on an analysis of character and situation. In one view, Eliza, a representative of Shavian vitality, is in the vitalistic sense superior to Higgins who is "the prisoner of 'system,' particularly of his profession" (Eric Bentley in his *Bernard Shaw,* [Norfolk], 1957). Higgins and Eliza are unsuited for one another since their temperaments are totally dissimilar. Another interpretation places emphasis on the growth of Eliza's character to the point where she is able, at the end of the play, to rid herself of her fear of the rich (her middle-class morality); thus, no longer the intimidated flower girl, Eliza has no need to bargain for Higgins' affection. On the other hand, Eliza may be considered as less than a match for Higgins, for her desires are the commonplace ones of marriage and security. Higgins, then, is the representative of Shavian vitality, the true superman, and as such he is superior to Eliza. In each interpretation, the Shavian denouement is justified by the critics' belief that a marriage between the two characters would be a misalliance; or, as Eric Bentley has said, "Eliza's leaving Higgins is the outcome of the realities of the situation" (*Modern Drama,* September, 1958).

The criterion of realism is of questionable value here. Shaw is a realist— if we must classify him at all—but dramatic realism does not always call for a "realistic" (that is, "true-to-life") ending. After all, Shaw often does marry off his heroine and hero (e.g. *Arms and the Man, Man and Superman, The Millionairess, Buoyant Billions*), and when he does so, it is not because he is particularly concerned with "true-to-life" probabilities, but because he is doing the correct dramatic thing. Furthermore, even if the criterion of realism were valid, we would face a difficult task in trying to prove that a marriage between Higgins and Eliza is hopelessly unrealistic. The two have existed in the same environment for a long time, they have grown used to one another— even reliant on one another, and they are no longer very far apart in social position. The fact is, as Shaw

PYGMALION IS ONE OF SHAW'S BEST-CONSTRUCTED PLAYS, AND THIS IS AN IMPORTANT REASON FOR ITS REPEATED SUCCESS IN PRODUCTION."

himself points out and as Professor Bentley notes, such a marriage would be a bad one. But what is more realistic than a bad marriage! It happens so often in real life that one can hardly accuse an author of being a romanticist if he includes it in his play. It is not quite right dramatically, but for critics to attribute Shaw's ending to "the realities of the situation" is to evince a rather unnecessarily limited view of what reality is.

An examination of the structure of *Pygmalion* can leave little doubt that Shaw's ending is the only logical one. The most direct way to approach the structure is to discern what the dramatic problem of the plot is. Some possibilities that might come immediately to mind concern the superficiality of class distinctions, the inability of Higgins to dominate Eliza's spirit, and the satire on middle-class morality. All of the preceding are aspects of the play, but further thought on the matter of what happens in *Pygmalion* will eventually lead us to some statement about Higgins' making Eliza into a "lady." Indeed, it would be difficult to avoid the conclusion that this is just what the play is about since the action, obviously, is mainly taken up with the development of Eliza from Act I through Act V. Furthermore, the play is concerned not only with the fact of her development but with the peculiar circumstances surrounding it, that is, the manner in which she is transformed.

It is important to decide whether Eliza or Higgins is the main character, for the main plot will be constructed around the actions of this central character. If we try to put the subject of the play's action into the form of a dramatic question, we would ask, "Will Eliza become a lady?" The action is done either *by* or *to* Eliza, but in either case we may be certain that the passive *main* character does not occur in Shaw's work. We need not assume that he is the most interesting character in the play or that he is the one who occupies the author's greatest attention. It appears that Shaw was more interested in Eliza than in Higgins because he explains in detail what happens to her after the play is over. Nevertheless, Higgins must be the main character because he manipulates the action. In a comedy it is not necessary for the main character to undergo a change or show character development. Higgins remains the same from first to last; to use Shaw's term he is ''incorrigible.'' Eliza changes, but Higgins makes her change; she is his product. Thus, a more accurate way of stating the dramatic question would be: Will Higgins succeed in re-creating the common flower girl into a truly different person, inwardly as well as outwardly?

Once we see the dramatic problem of the play in this light, we can begin to trace the steps leading to the logical conclusion of *Pygmalion.* The first act is dramatically essential to the play not merely because it introduces the characters or serves as a prologue, but because it begins the action: Higgins makes such an impression on the flower girl that she is filled with a desire for her physical improvement, her external recreation. In Act II, the question is raised as to whether Higgins will succeed in his experiment.

As is usual in a play with a traditional five-act structure, the climax occurs in Act III and virtually resolves the question. Although the question is not definitely answered, certainly some strong indication is given the audience as to the direction which the following action will take. A shift in the direction of the action after the climax would surely confuse the spectators and might result in bringing the play to the level of romance. But *Pygmalion* is not romance, in spite of the subtitle, and thus Shaw makes his denouement consistent with his climax.

After the second act, the audience might expect the reception scene to contain the climax as it does in the movie and in *My Fair Lady,* but Shaw does not dramatize this scene. It is necessary to have a scene precede the ambassador's reception so as to show the developing process of Eliza's education, and Shaw is skillful enough to make the scene of Mrs. Higgins' at-home serve both as an expository scene of characterization and as climax. However, a few critics are determined to make the omitted garden party into the climax. Professor Bentley says:

> If again we call Act I the prologue, the play falls into two parts of two Acts apiece. Both parts are Pygmalion myths. In the first a duchess is made out of a flower girl. In the second a woman is made out of a duchess.

Since these two parts are the main, inner action the omission of the climax of the outer action—the ambassador's reception—will seem particularly discrete, economical, and dramatic.

But we need not be deceived by the subtlety and calmness of Shaw's climax. The dramatic question is answered at the home of Mrs. Higgins when Eliza encounters society and passes as acceptable to the Hills, and even to the much cleverer Mrs. Higgins. We now feel certain that, with more practice, Eliza will succeed in her official debut at the ambassador's party, although she probably would not be able to do so at the time of the climax. Nevertheless, what is important is the knowledge which one now has that Higgins is on the verge of succeeding with his experiment. Eliza's success will be Higgins' success. The question, ''Will Higgins be able to recreate the flower girl?'' is answered affirmatively.

But Higgins' success is not complete in Act III. In Act I, he had expressed a wish to Pickering to demonstrate what kind of a Pygmalion he could be in regard to Eliza if he had the chance. He wanted to see if he could create a new human being, not merely a duchess, out of flower girl. The climax, then, only indicates his accomplishment but does not actually show it. It remains for Act V to reveal to us the full extent of Higgins' achievement. Then we see that Higgins has succeeded so well—he has turned the frightened, easily-dominated Eliza into an independent woman—that he loses the prize possession itself. irony of such a success is evident. Thus, Pygmalion has created a masterpiece, a real person—and to Shaw a real person is one who is not dominated in spirit by the elements of his environment. Pygmalion loses his Galatea, for he has recreated her with the great humanizing qualities of character: independence of spirit and vitality of mind.

It is now possible to see why Shaw's ending is the only satisfying one, and why certain adapters such as Alan Lerner in *My Fair Lady* contradict the meaning of the play. Suppose Eliza's last line were changed from one of disdain (in answer to Higgins' confident order to her as his servant) to an acquiescent reply that indicates she will return to Higgins. If this were the case, then Higgins would not have really succeeded. He would have taken Eliza, the flower girl, the servant of society, and changed her physically but not spiritually. In the end, she will still be a servant girl at heart. Shaw's ending is not an arbitrary imposition of the author's temperament. Without the essential paradox involved in Higgins' accomplishment of recreation, the play becomes sentimental and one-dimensional.

The traditional structure serves Shaw well here. Professor Bentley is right in dividing the inner development of Eliza into two parts. But he does not go far enough, for the inner development is also dramatized; both inner development and plot structure are connected inseparably—that is, theme and action are virtually the same thing. *Pygmalion* is one of Shaw's best-constructed plays, and this is an important reason for its repeated success in production.

Source: Stanley J. Solomon, ''The Ending of *Pygmalion:* A Structural View'' in *Educational Theatre Journal,* Vol. 16, no. 1, March, 1964, pp. 59–63.

Myron Matlaw

In this essay, Matlaw examines Pygmalion's *ending and the ways that subsequent adaptations have strayed from Shaw's original vision. The critic ultimately affirms the play's original conclusion.*

Alan Jay Lerner, probably the most successful adapter of Shaw's *Pygmalion,* commented: ''Shaw explains how Eliza ends not with Higgins but with Freddy and—Shaw and Heaven forgive me!—I am not certain he is right.'' Many critics would agree with this sentiment. A recent analysis of the play goes so far as to dismiss the Epilogue as a bit of Shavian frivolity and to cite the ''happy ending'' Shaw himself wrote for Pascal's film as the proper denouement of a play which is persuasively categorized by one critic as a play which follows ''the classic pattern of satirical comedy'' [Milton Crane in *PMLA,* vol. 66, 1956].

Such an ending has been popular also with audiences and actors ever since the play first appeared in 1913. Shaw chided both Mrs. Patrick Campbell and Beerbohm Tree for their romantic interpretations in the first productions: ''I say, Tree, must you be so treacly?'' he asked during the rehearsals. Tree's stage business before the curtain fell left no doubts in the minds of audiences that Higgins's marriage to Eliza was imminent. Justifying it, Tree wrote Shaw: ''My ending makes money; You ought to be grateful.'' Shaw replied: ''Your ending is damnable: You ought to be shot.'' And he continued fulminating against romantic portrayals of an ending which caters to what, in the Epilogue written for *Pygmalion* later, he called ''imaginations. . . so enfeebled by their lazy dependence on the ready-mades and reach-medowns of the ragshop in which Romance keeps its stock of 'happy endings' to misfit all stories.''

> WHILE ONE OF THE MOST PENETRATING AND SUGGESTIVE OF THE ANALYSES OF SHAW'S WORK ACCEPTS THE ORIGINAL ENDING OF *PYGMALION,* IT SEEMS TO DO SO FOR THE WRONG REASONS.''

Nonetheless, the recurrent arousing of inappropriate audience expectations and the apparent inability of the play to arouse the appropriate expectations (or those which Shaw considered appropriate) raise a question about *Pygmalion*'s success on the playwright's terms. Perhaps even more important, they call for a re-examination of these terms; for I think that the ending is significant and dramatically inevitable, and that it is the ending Shaw himself rewrote for the film (thereby confusing the matter further)—rather than his Epilogue—which is frivolous. . . .

While one of the most penetrating and suggestive of the analyses of Shaw's work accepts the original ending of *Pygmalion,* it seems to do so for the wrong reasons. I cannot agree with the assertion in that analysis that ''the 'education of Eliza' in Acts I to III is a caricature of the true process.'' No educative process is in fact represented in the play (although Shaw inserted ''a sample'' for film production at a later date—a hint which was deftly developed in *My Fair Lady*). But more important, the conclusion that ''Eliza turns the tables on Higgins, for she, finally, is the vital one, and he is the prisoner of 'system,' particularly of his profession,'' seems to me to miss the point (Eriz Bertley in his *Bernard Shaw,* [New York], 1957).

Rather the reverse is true. The magnificent comic subplot underlines the point, for Doolittle was once, like Higgins, outside of class or ''system'' and had vitality. Both Doolittle and Eliza are brought to join the middle class. What is sharply contrasted, however, is the consequence of the transformation: for Doolittle it is a descent while for Eliza it is an ascent—the transformation makes the previously articulate (vital) father comically impotent while it gives the previously inarticulate (''crooning like a bilious pigeon'') daughter human life. In sum, Higgins, the life-giver, will continue his study of phonetics while Eliza will settle for the life her father describes so picturesquely in the last act when all the cards are put on the table. Higgins, that is, will continue to teach proper, *civilized* articulation, a superman attempting to transform subhumans into humans; while Eliza will lead an admirable if circumscribed middle-class existence, having been given humanity—life—by Higgins.

Her ability to undergo successfully such a transformation evidences her superior qualities and often makes her appear as the hero of the play. She is only a Shavian hero *manque,* however, and she is not the wife for Higgins. She can not even understand him, their values and interests being so different. Higgins genuinely admires Eliza, although he is first shocked and then amused by her values: in a most effective and inevitable denouement, the curtain falls as ''he roars with laughter'' —at the thought of her marrying Freddy. Admirable as she now is—especially when compared with what she was when he met her—she is not, and never can be, his equal. She is now part and parcel of the system of ''middle class morality'' which the early Doolittle and Higgins find ludicrous. Higgins and Eliza, then, still do not speak the same language, although this is true now only in the figurative sense. This does not, however, preclude the existence of an affinity between them, perhaps one comparable to the one existing between Caesar and Cleopatra. Nevertheless, marrying Eliza would be preposterous for Higgins, a superman with the vitality of a soul and a ''Miltonic mind'' (as he himself labels it) who lives on an entirely different plane, a plane where sex and marriage, indeed, are unknown.

What causes audiences to wish for it (as Eliza herself, for that matter, was wishing for it) is the Cinderella guise of the plot—which buttresses audiences' perennial desires, as Shaw rightly said in the Epilogue, for the marriage of the hero and the maiden—and the sentimental part of the myth which the title incidentally also calls to mind. The Cinderella guise, however, is accidental and irrelevant; it is purposely negated by the omission of scenes depicting the process of the transformation and by the omission of the grand ball scene, the highpoint of any Cinderella story. The title specifically and intentionally focuses attention away from the heroine and on Higgins, and on Higgins's life-giving qualities in particular.

It is very appropriate, therefore, that the most recent popular production is called *My Fair Lady,*

focusing attention, as the musical itself does, on the Cinderella theme. At the same time, with all the brilliance of this version, even with the dialogue culled from the original play, this one is a very different play throughout. All the noncomic lines. . . are omitted, for in *My Fair Lady* Higgins is the conventional romantic hero and not what he surely is in *Pygmalion:* the Shavian hero, standing alone, a superman embodying a life force divorced from human social and sensual drives, but representative of the vitality and creative evolution in which, in Shaw's philosophy, lies the ultimate hope of mankind.

Source: Myron Matlaw, ''The Denouement of *Pygmalion,*'' in *Modern Drama,* Vol. 1, no. 1, May, 1958, pp. 29, 33–34.

FURTHER READING

Bentley, Eric. *Bernard Shaw, 1856-1950,* amended edition, New Directions, 1957.

Though Bentley's book (originally published in 1947) is not adulatory, Shaw considered it ''the best book written about himself as a dramatist.'' Bentley states that his double intention in the book is ''to disentangle a credible man and artist from the mass of myth that surrounds him, and to discover the complex component parts of his 'simplicity.''' *Pygmalion* is discussed in detail, pages 119-126, and elsewhere in the book.

Crane, Milton. ''*Pygmalion:* Bernard Shaw's Dramatic Theory and Practice'' in *Publications of the Modern Language Association,* Vol. 66, no.6, December, 1951, pp. 879-85.

Crane begins with the question of whether Shaw was old-fashioned in his approach to drama or innovative. Wrapped up in this issue is the figure of Ibsen, who Shaw declared was revolutionary for giving his plays indeterminate endings and concluding with ''discussion,'' rather than the clear unraveling of a dramatic situation in the ''well-made play''—the popular form of the day. Crane demonstrates that Ibsen did not present a new innovation so much as modify earlier forms and claims that something similar holds true for Shaw as well. Although Shaw denied his audience a romantic ending in *Pygmalion,* Crane does not feel it is true of the playwright what many have said, ''that he is primarily a thinker, who chose for rhetorical reasons to cast his ideas in dramatic form.'' Rather than viewing his characters abstractly, as means to a rhetorical end, Shaw was passionately invested in their lives and destinies, which highlights a basic ''conventionality'' in his technique.

Dukore, Bernard F. ''The Director As Interpreter: Shaw's *Pygmalion* '' in *Shaw,* Vol. 3, 1983, pp. 129-47.

A three-part article analyzing, first, ''Shaw's concept of the question of directorial interpretation''; then his own directorial interpretation of *Pygmalion* (in the

London premiere and several subsequent productions); and finally, the revisions he made to *Pygmalion* as a result of the experience of directing the play. Dukore shows the careful separation Shaw maintained between "Playwright Shaw" and "Director Shaw": rather than explain to his actors the ideas in his play in a literary manner, Shaw was able to help them in very practical terms to develop their performances. Often these actors led him to new insights about his own characters. "While he recognized that there are a variety of appropriate ways to interpret any well-written role," however, Shaw also "rejected what he considered inappropriate interpretations."

Evans, T. F., editor. *Shaw: The Critical Heritage,* Routledge & Kegan Paul (London), 1976.
An extremely useful collection of 135 contemporary writings on Shaw's plays: reviews, essays, letters, and other sources. Arranged roughly in chronological order and grouped by play, the items "give a continuing picture of the changing and developing reaction to Shaw's dramatic work." *Pygmalion* is covered on pages 223-29.

Harvey, Robert C. "How Shavian is the *Pygmalion* We Teach?" in *English Journal,* Vol. 59, 1970, pp. 1234-38.
This article by a former high school English teacher begins with the observation that while Shaw lived, he absolutely refused to let his plays be published in school textbooks: "My plays were not designed as instruments of torture," he wittily commented. Harvey recognizes that despite the wishes of the playwright, there are definite values to students reading his work in a school setting. Too often, however, the work is taught to support grammar lessons, with the message that like Liza, students can succeed if they learn to speak "correctly." Harvey affirms that the real value of the piece for students is in trying to grasp its literary complexity. If anything, the play should show students "the social importance of all varieties of language . . . the equality of every dialect" rather than being used "to forge the very chains [Shaw] wrote the play to break."

Henderson, Archibald. *George Bernard Shaw: Man of the Century,* Appleton-Century-Crofts (New York), 1956.
A final, culminating book by Shaw's "official" biographer, incorporating much material from his previous works. Henderson studied Shaw first-hand and wrote on him for over fifty years.

Hill, Eldon C. *George Bernard Shaw,* Twayne (Boston), 1978.
A biography and critical study intended not for the Shaw specialist but for the general reader "who seeks an understanding of Shaw's life and work." *Pygmalion* is discussed in detail, pages 118-21.

Huggett, Richard. *The Truth about* Pygmalion, Heinemann (London), 1969.
Focusing predominantly on Mrs. Patrick Campbell, the actress who created Liza for the London premiere, this study is the result of three years of research into the play and its performances.

Kaufman, R. J., editor. *G. B. Shaw: A Collection of Critical Essays,* Prentice-Hall (Englewood Cliffs, NJ), 1965.

While none of the essays examines *Pygmalion* exclusively, the topics of these compiled studies overlap extensively with issues in that particular play. Notable contributions include a short, provocative piece by Bertolt Brecht, showing Shaw's influence on his work. Brecht states of Shaw's view towards society, "it should be clear by now that Shaw is a terrorist. The Shavian terror is an unusual one, and he employs an unusual weapon—that of humor." In his article "Born to Set It Right: The Roots of Shaw's Style," Richard M. Ohmann investigates the development of Shaw's position as a social outsider, "the critic of things as they are." Eric Bentley's "The Making of a Dramatist" examines the formative years 1892-1903 in Shaw's life.

MacCarthy, Desmond. *Shaw: The Plays,* Newton Abbott, 1951.
Originally published as a series of essays from 1907 to 1950, this book offers a unique chance to trace the development of a particular perspective on Shaw's long and prolific career. *Pygmalion* is discussed in detail, pages 108-13.

Miller, Jane M. "Some Versions of *Pygmalion*" in *Ovid Renewed: Ovidian Influences on Literature and Art from the Middle Ages to the Twentieth Century,* edited by Charles Martindale, Cambridge University Press, 1988.
A study of Ovid's version of the *Pygmalion* myth (including possible antecedents for it), and its influence on later works. Miller stresses the sexual implications of the Pygmalion-Galatea relationship in Ovid's story (which suggest possible consequences for Shaw's version). Miller states that the various versions of Pygmalion tend in general to be of two types: historical, which depict a social transformation and which usually contain "an element of social comment" (she places Shaw's *Pygmalion* in this category); and mystical, which explore "love as a divine experience." Miller suggests Shakespeare's *The Winter's Tale* as an early example of the "mystical" interpretation but comments that the form abounded in the nineteenth century in particular. Miller concludes that the "historicist" versions of Pygmalion, Shaw's included, "are interesting products of their time but lack the vitality of the Ovidian original."

Muggleston, Lynda. "Shaw, Subjective Inequality, and the Social Meanings of Language in *Pygmalion*" in *Review of English Studies: A Quarterly Journal of English Literature and the English Language,* Vol. 44, no. 175, August, 1993, pp. 373-85.
A detailed study of the social importance of *Pygmalion*'s exploration of accent and pronunciation as determiners "not only of social status but also of social acceptability." Although difficult only in places for readers not familiar with some linguistic vocabulary, the article's central argument is easily grasped: that Shaw rebelled against the idea that there was something inherently better about people of the upper classes and therefore demonstrated that social judgments of a person's merit depend on superficial, subjective qualities (like proper speech). *Pygmalion* is a "paradigm of social mobility," illustrating that social transformation is possible, and "a paean to

inherent equality,'' suggesting that a person's merit is distinct and separate from their level of social acceptability.

Quinn, Martin. "The Informing Presence of Charles Dickens in Bernard Shaw's *Pygmalion*" in the *Dickensian,* Vol. 80, no. 3, Autumn, 1984, pp. 144-50.

This article traces a number of connections between *Pygmalion* and various works of Dickens, who Quinn states "entered Shaw's life early and completely and was thereafter always at his fingertips when not on the tip of his tongue." Quinn shows that Dickens was specifically on Shaw's mind when writing *Pygmalion* in 1912, because he was completing at the same time an introduction to Dickens's novel *Hard Times.* The influence of Dickens was "pervasive" throughout Shaw's career, however. The value of Quinn's article is in documenting the exhaustive reading of "[a]n intellect as comprehensive as Shaw's," and inserting the name of Dickens, a novelist, among the list of dramatic artists considered to be Shaw's major influences: Shakespeare, Moliere, and Ibsen.

Shaw Bulletin, Shaw Review, Shaw: The Annual of Bernard Shaw Studies, the *Shavian.*

Publications of the Shaw Society of America (*The Shaw Bulletin,* 1952-1958; *Shaw Review,* 1951-1980; and the *Shaw* annual, 1981-present) and the Shaw Society, London (the *Shavian,* 1953-present). These journals have published extensively on all topics related to Shaw's work; check their title and subject indexes for further information.

Small, Barbara J. "Shaw on Standard Stage Speech" in *Shaw Review,* Vol. 22, 1979, pp. 106-13.

A short but enlightening study of Shaw's interest in diction and stage speech. Not entirely about *Pygmalion,* but its references to that play suggest the close relationship between Higgins and Shaw's own ideals of spoken speech. "Shaw was preoccupied with the dearth of good standard speech on the English stage," Small wrote. "Good diction was, for Shaw, associated with fine acting." Shaw did not blame individuals for their poor pronunciation; in his preface to *Pygmalion,* for example, he decries the problems stemming from English not being a language with phonetic spellings of words. These larger issues Shaw addressed through a phonetic system of his own devising, and other means, but regarding individual persons what Shaw hated most was pretension. "An honest slum dialect" was preferable to him "than the attempts of phonetically untaught persons to imitate the plutocracy."

Wagenknecht, Edward. *A Guide to Bernard Shaw,* Russell & Russell (New York), 1929.

A study written while Shaw was alive and at the peak of his career (he had won the Nobel Prize only a few years previously). Wagenknecht wrote that the purpose of his book is expository rather than critical: that is, "to gather together . . . all the information which, in my judgment, the student or general reader needs to have in mind in order to read Shaw's plays intelligently." As a study, it has largely been superseded by other later works, but it remains an important historical document.

SOURCES

Berst, Charles A. *Bernard Shaw and the Art of Drama,* University of Illinois Press (Urbana), 1973, pp. 197-218.

She Stoops to Conquer

OLIVER GOLDSMITH

1773

Most everyone has been the target of practical jokes, and most have been out on blind dates. Oliver Goldsmith bases his 1773 comedy *She Stoops to Conquer* on two such incidents, creating a complicated, convoluted plot based on miscommunication and mistaken identities. At the same time, Goldsmith explores a series of ethical and aesthetic issues.

Audiences responded favorably to *She Stoops to Conquer* when Goldsmith's play debuted in 1773 and have continued to do so ever since. Significantly, from its debut, it earned popular approval and remains today one of the few 18th century plays to be regularly performed for modern audiences. While the play proves funny and entertaining, it also marks an important step in the development of comic theory. Significantly, Goldsmith's play changed the face of comic theatre, eclipsing the popular sentimental comedy of the day, and inaugurated a new style of laughing comedy.

For those who believe the play's plot seems too far-fetched, Oscar James Campbell noted in an introduction to *Chief Plays of Goldsmith and Sheridan: The School for Scandal, She Stoops to Conquer, The Rivals* that the ''central idea of *She Stoops to Conquer* was suggested to Goldsmith by an incident of his boyhood. He had been told that the house of a Mr. Featherstone was an inn and directed there for entertainment. Goldsmith, always easily deceived by a practical joke, had gone to the squire's

house and treated him as a host. Out of this situation grew his characters and their games of cross-purposes.'' Other autobiographical elements in the play include resemblances between the young, vagabond Goldsmith who spent two years on a walking tour of Europe and the irresponsible, irrepressible Tony Lumpkin. Finally, Goldsmith, like his character Marlow, was at ease with serving women, but stiff in the company of proper ladies, in part because of insecurities about his physical appearance.

AUTHOR BIOGRAPHY

Born November 10, 1728, in Ballymahon, Ireland, Goldsmith was from a poor but not needy family, supported by his father's position as a minister. The family had expected that Goldsmith would attend university, but the marriage of an older sister required his tuition money as part of her sizable dowry. In 1745, Goldsmith entered Trinity College in Dublin under the sizar system, which allowed poor students to study in exchange for work. Perhaps because of his tenuous economic circumstances, Goldsmith did not distinguish himself academically. He failed to take his studies entirely seriously, violated college rules, and even took part in a riot in which several people died.

Completing his B.A. in 1749, Goldsmith attempted various careers, including the ministry and medicine. From 1753-56, he wandered across the British continent before arriving in London. There, Goldsmith embarked on a career writing reviews and essays for such periodicals as Ralph Griffith's *Monthly Review* and Tobias Smollett's *Critical Review,* as well as proofreading for the novelist and printer Samuel Richardson.

The first book to appear under Goldsmith's name proved a notable success. Entitled *The Citizen of the World; or, Letters from a Chinese Philosopher Residing in London to His Friends in the East,* it began as a series of essays in the *Publick Ledger.* Goldsmith, masquerading under the identity of an Asian visitor, satirized the faults and foibles of fashionable London society. The work brought Goldsmith to the attention of the city's literary elite, particularly members of The Club, which included writers like Samuel Johnson, James Boswell, Edmund Burke, and Thomas Percy, the painter Sir Joshua Reynolds, and the actor David Garrick. The

work also brought Goldsmith literary opportunities, but poor money management drove him to hack writing for survival, a pattern that unfortunately continued throughout his life.

In addition to periodical prose, Goldsmith wrote in various styles and genres. One of his most famous works, *The Deserted Village: A Poem,* laments the loss of Britain's rural lifestyle. Though politically a conservative Tory, Goldsmith condemned the enclosure of public land by wealthy landowners and the agricultural revolution, which drove small farmers off their land. Published in 1770, critics term the work a ''loco-descriptive'' poem, in which the narrator walks through and describes various natural and rustic settings, setting down in verse the thoughts these travels inspire.

Two of Goldsmith's other famous works stem from his aversion for Sentimentalism. According to Oscar James Campbell, Sentimentalism ''was founded on the belief that man is innately good and that he can be softened into virtue through tears which are made to flow from contemplation of undeserved suffering.'' In Goldsmith's 1766 novel *The Vicar of Wakefield,* the excessive sufferings of the deserving Vicar and his family call to mind the sufferings of Job, and critics today read the work as a parody of Sentimental fiction.

In his plays, Goldsmith challenged the Sentimental comedy, which had developed in response to the perceived immorality of Restoration theatre. Goldsmith articulated his position in an ''Essay on the Theatre; or, A Comparison between Laughing and Sentimental Comedy.'' The article differentiates between Sentimental comedy, called so only because it—like Dante's *Divine Comedy*—has a happy ending, and the more modern, humorous ''laughing'' comedy. In 1768, a Sentimental comedy by Hugh Kelly opened the same night as *The Good Natur'd Man: A Comedy,* Goldsmith's first play. These competing productions offered theatre audiences two completely different forms of comic entertainment. According to Campbell, Goldsmith's *She Stoops to Conquer* proved innovative and ''opened the door'' to a new kind of comedy.

In 1773, Goldsmith presented *She Stoops to Conquer.* Though generally well-received, not everyone applauded Goldsmith's comedy—advocates of Sentimental comedy like Horace Walpole attacked the play for lacking a moral lesson. Still, audiences in general approved and today it remains Goldsmith's most popular work.

PLOT SUMMARY

Prologue

Mr. Woodward, a contemporary comic actor, walks on stage weeping at the death of comedy. His last hope is that Goldsmith's play will make him laugh and revive the comic arts. (This prologue was written by the era's foremost actor and producer, David Garrick).

Act I, Scene i

Mr. Hardcastle has selected for his daughter's husband someone neither have met, the son of his old friend, Sir Charles Marlow. Kate fears she will not like him because her father described him as handsome but reserved.

Act I, Scene ii

At the Three Pigeons Tavern, Hardcastle's stepson, Tony Lumpkin, sings with his drinking buddies. The landlord interrupts, saying that two London gentlemen have lost their way. As a joke, Tony tells the men, Marlow and Hastings, that they remain far from their destination, Hardcastle's house. Then, Tony directs them to his stepfather's house, describing it as an inn, run by an eccentric innkeeper who fancies himself a gentleman.

Act II, Scene i

Hardcastle expects a visit from his prospective son-in-law, Marlow, and explains to the servants how they are to behave. Because the Hardcastles seldom see company, their servants are farmhands and become confused when Hardcastle explains their duties.

Marlow explains to Hastings that while he can be affable and boisterous with serving women and barmaids, he remains painfully shy among proper ladies.

Tricked by Tony, Marlow and Hastings mistake Hardcastle for a common innkeeper. Instead of treating him like a country gentleman, they behave rudely.

Hastings meets Miss Constance Neville, the niece of Mrs. Hardcastle, and is surprised to find her in an inn. She corrects his mistake, explaining that this is not the Buck's Head Inn but Hardcastle's house. Hastings urges her to elope with him. Constance hedges, reluctant to leave behind her inheritance of jewels, which Mrs. Hardcastle greedily guards. Hastings approves of her plan to get the

Oliver Goldsmith depicted at his desk

jewels but suggests they tell Marlow nothing. Hastings fears that if the reserved Marlow discovers that the mansion is not an inn, his embarrassment would drive him to leave, disrupting the lovers' plan.

When Marlow joins them, Hastings introduces Constance and Miss Kate Hardcastle, whom Marlow treats with extreme formality. Left alone together, Marlow's behavior becomes even more reserved, and at the end, Kate asks herself, "Was there ever such a sober, sentimental interview? I'm certain he scarce looked in my face the whole time." She finds Marlow attractive but wonders if anyone—perhaps she—can overcome his shyness?

When Mrs. Hardcastle joins Hasting's talk with Constance, her conversation reveals her pretensions and ignorance of fashionable London life. He pokes fun at Mrs. Hardcastle's incomplete knowledge of London's fashionable society, of which she so yearns to be a part.

Hastings and Tony converse. Hastings loves Constance and wants to marry her, while Tony detests the thought of marrying Constance but is being urged to by his mother (so that she can maintain control of Constance's jewelry). They develop a plan to help them both. Hastings asks Tony's assistance in eloping with Constance, and

Tony agrees, adding that he will also help her remove her inheritance of jewels.

Act III

Hardcastle, perplexed, wonders why his friend, Sir Marlow, recommended that Kate marry young Marlow, who seems rude and unmannered. When joined by Kate, they discuss Marlow's behavior and seem to be talking about two different people. In a sense, of course, they are. When with Hardcastle, whom he believes to be an eccentric innkeeper, Marlow behaves wildly and without manners. Knowing Kate to be a fine lady, however, Marlow remains shy and reserved. Father and daughter agree to reject a match with Marlow as unsuitable, but for different reasons—Hardcastle because of Marlow's apparent wildness, Kate because of his reserve.

Tony has Constance's jewels sent to Hastings but with no explanation about where they came from or what is to be done with them. Constance, unaware, asks Mrs. Hardcastle's permission to wear them. Constance believes that with the jewels in her possession, she can abscond with them when eloping. The jewels rightly belong to Constance, and Mrs. Hardcastle has difficulty finding a reason to refuse to give them to her. Tony suggests she say the jewels have been lost. Mrs. Hardcastle does so, but when she discovers the jewels have been lost, she tells Tony. He laughs, pretending to think her still playing a scene, though he knows the jewels are lost, because he took them.

When Kate discovers that Tony tricked the visitors into believing her father's house to be an inn, she urges all to maintain the deception. Consequently, Marlow mistakes Kate for a barmaid and flirts with her, behavior to which she responds. Hardcastle enters just in time to see Marlow seizing Kate's hand. Marlow rushes off, with Hardcastle even more convinced of Marlow's impropriety, while Kate insists she can prove the respectability of Marlow, to whom she has taken a fancy.

Act IV

Constance tells Hastings that they expect a visit from Marlow's father, Sir Marlow. Marlow wonders why Hastings has sent him a casket of jewels. Worried about their safety, Marlow returns them to the woman he believes to be the landlady but who is actually one of the Hardcastles' servants. The servant returns Constance's jewels to Mrs. Hardcastle, from whom they had been taken by Tony in the first place. When Hastings enters, Marlow reveals his infatuation with the barmaid (actually Kate). Hastings asks about the jewels, only to be told that Marlow has given them to the landlady (Mrs. Hardcastle). Hastings, who must continue the inn masquerade, cannot reveal the Hardcastles' identity. Consequently, Hastings decides he and Constance must elope without the jewels.

When Hardcastle tells Marlow that his servants have gotten drunk, he is astounded to learn they did so on Marlow's instructions! As Hardcastle storms out, outraged, Marlow realizes his mistake, confusing Hardcastle's house with an inn. Kate enters, confirming Marlow's suspicion. She conceals her identity, however, continuing to present herself as a barmaid. He tells her he would marry her, in spite of her lower class origins, if society—and his father—permitted, but he suspects that cannot be. She now understands his generous nature and sincerity.

With the jewels back in her possession, Mrs. Hardcastle urges Tony to marry Constance the following day, but unbeknownst to her, Tony already has arranged to provide horses enabling Constance and Hastings to elope. When Mrs. Hardcastle discovers their plan, she storms off, furious, ordering Constance to accompany her to her Aunt Pedigree's house, where she will be kept safe from Hastings and their unapproved marriage.

The act ends with Marlow angry with Hastings for concealing the true nature of the mansion, and Hasting incensed with Marlow for inadvertently returning Constance's jewels to Mrs. Hardcastle. Constance goes off to the supervision of Aunt Pedigree and all seems lost, until Tony insists he has a plan.

Act V, Scene i

Sir Marlow and Hardcastle enter, aware of Tony's joke and laughing about Marlow's mistaking Hardcastle's mansion for an inn.

When told of his son's love for Kate, Sir Marlow remains skeptical that his son could overcome his reserve with a proper lady. Kate, of course, fails to mention that when Marlow declared his love, her barmaid's disguise concealed her identity.

Act V, Scene ii

Instead of taking Mrs. Hardcastle and Constance to Aunt Pedigree's house, Tony leads them in a circle, until they find themselves tired, hungry, and—without realizing it—right back where they started. Mrs. Hardcastle becomes furious with Tony when she discovers his prank. Hastings, reunited with Constance, demands she leave the jewels behind and elope with him, but she refuses, urging "prudence." She hopes that, in time, she can marry with both Hardcastle's approval and her inheritance.

Act V, Scene iii

Kate, to convince Hardcastle and Sir Marlow that Marlow loves her, hides them where they can secretly observe the lovers' interview. Kate then confronts Marlow, who has come to say goodbye. Knowing that Marlow would become shy if he knew her true identity as a proper lady and Hardcastle's daughter, Kate continues her pretence of being a barmaid. Marlow passionately confesses his love, offering his heart despite the differences in their social classes. Finally, Hardcastle and Sir Marlow interrupt, revealing Kate's true identity.

Mrs. Hardcastle thinks that Constance and Hastings have eloped without the jewels, but they have not. They enter and beg Hardcastle's permission to marry. Hardcastle tells Tony that he has been of age—and therefore eligible to refuse Constance's hand in marriage—for three months. Mrs. Hardcastle has kept this secret from him in hopes of convincing them to marry so she could keep control of Constance's jewels. Tony refuses Constance, whom he does not love, enabling her to marry Hastings, whom she does love. The play ends with Mrs. Hardcastle's greedy plot foiled and both couples—Marlow and Kate and Hastings and Constance—ready to wed.

Epilogue

Spoken in Goldsmith's voice, the epilogue summarizes the action, hoping that the humorous tale of how Kate "stooped to conquer" justifies the author's abandonment of sentimental comedy.

CHARACTERS

Diggory

A talkative, likeable servant with poor table manners and a broad sense of humor. Mr. Hardcastle

Marlow and Kate

attempts to teach Diggory and other field servants to serve at a formal table, with comic results.

Diggory also delivers the letter which tells Tony that Hastings needs fresh horses in order to elope with Constance. Constance must read the letter aloud in front of her aunt. Realizing its contents, Constance pretends to read, instead fabricating a story about gambling. Tony's interest in gaming causes him to hand the letter to his mother, which spoils the secret elopement.

Miss Kate Hardcastle

The daughter of Mr. and Mrs. Hardcastle, Kate seeks in marriage a compatible and companionable husband, not money or status. In an effort to ascertain Marlow's true feelings, she pretends to be a barmaid to get him to announce that he loves her despite her low social position. In her intelligence and versatility, she resembles such Shakespearean heroines as Viola in *Twelfth Night* and Rosalind in *As You Like It*.

Mr. Hardcastle

Mr. Hardcastle loves the rustic life away from fashionable London, which he believes breeds "vani-

MEDIA ADAPTATIONS

- *She Stoops to Conquer* was adapted for film by Paul H. Cromelin in 1914.

- It was also adapted into a one-act play in Schulenburg, Texas, in 1965.

- Readings of Goldsmith's poems are included in a recording entitled *Johnson, Goldsmith, Cowper*, produced by Argo in 1972.

---

ty and affectation.'' He may be stuffy, long-winded, and old-fashioned, but he affectionately humors his wife, and loves his daughter, Kate. He wants the best for her, and in selecting a good husband for her, his objective is not money or status, but her happiness. A realist, Mr. Hardcastle sees the faults of Tony Lumpkin, Mrs. Hardcastle's son by her first marriage.

Mrs. Hardcastle

A vain and greedy widower, Mrs. Hardcastle remarried after the death of her first husband. Not evil as much as selfish and misguided, she lacks self-knowledge. While her husband enjoys rural pleasures, she yearns for a fashionable London social life and complains that they never entertain.

Her love for Tony Lumpkin, her son by her first husband, spoils him and makes it impossible for her to see his shortcomings clearly. While Mr. Hardcastle wants his daughter Kate to marry for compatibility and affection, however, Mrs. Hardcastle pushes Tony to marry Constance Neville because of her inheritance and social standing. Mrs. Hardcastle's greed and lack of perception prevent her from seeing that Tony does not love Constance.

Hastings

Marlow's friend, he loves Constance Neville, who returns his affection. He wants to marry her and

has the permission of her now dead father, though Mrs. Hardcastle, who covets Constance's jewels, opposes the match. Impetuous when it comes to marriage, Hastings urges Constance to abandon her inheritance and insists (impractically) that they can live on love.

While not evil, Hastings does not behave with complete honesty. On discovering the inn to be Hardcastle's house, he conceals this information from Marlow, fearing his friend will want to leave immediately and disrupt Hastings's marriage plans.

Like Tony, Hastings too can be a joker. For example, Mrs. Hardcastle tells Hastings, ''There's nothing in the world I love to talk of so much as London, and the fashions, though I was never there myself.'' Hastings makes amusement of her ignorance of the city and the pride that makes her pretend to more knowledge than she actually has. The scene's humor comes as their dialogue reveals to the audience her confusion between the fashionable and poor parts of London.

Landlord

The proprietor of the Three Pigeons alehouse, who informs Tony that Marlow and Hastings have arrived, searching for Tony's stepfather's house. The Landlord enables Tony to trick the travelers into thinking Mr. Hardcastle's house is an inn.

Squier Lumpkin

See Tony Lumpkin

Tony Lumpkin

Mrs. Hardcastle's son by her first marriage. Tony is a prankster and enjoys such practical jokes as burning the footman's shoes and disturbing his stepfather's wig. Tony sets the play's action in motion by lying to Marlow and Hastings, telling them that Mr. Hardcastle's house is an inn.

Ignorant and spoiled, though not unlikable, Tony is more concerned with having fun than advancing his education or social standing; Mr. Hardcastle says that the only schools Tony will ever attend are ''the alehouse and the stable.'' As he drinks with his buddies at the Three Pigeons alehouse, Tony sings a song that calls drink a better teacher than schoolmasters or preachers. Tony assures his friends that when he comes of age and inherits, he will spend his money with them drinking and gambling on horses. It is clear, however, that while Tony may come of age, he will never grow up.

Mrs. Hardcastle wants Tony to marry Constance Neville so that the family might benefit from the girl's inheritance; Tony cannot refuse until he legally comes of age. Despite his foolishness and immaturity, Tony does exhibit some character with his refusal to marry for money. Instead, he helps the lovers get the jewels and elope, though he serves his own interests as well as theirs in each case.

Maid

In Act III, the maid informs Kate about Tony's joke of telling Marlow the Hardcastle's house is an inn, and that Marlow believes Kate to be a barmaid.

Marlow

Marlow is Hastings friend and the son of Sir Charles Marlow, Mr. Hardcastle's old friend. Sir Charles has recommended his son as a suitable husband for Mr. Hardcastle's daughter, Kate. One peculiarity marks Marlow's behavior: while he can aggressively woo working-class women, he has no skill with proper ladies.

In a conversation with his daughter, Kate, Mr. Hardcastle describes Marlow as a scholar: young, handsome, brave, and generous. He is also, however, "one of the most bashful and reserved young fellows in the world." These qualities set Kate against him, because "a reserved lover . . . always makes a suspicious husband." Marlow's reported good looks, however, make the situation not impossible. In a soliloquy, Kate wonders: "Yet can't he be cured of his timidity by being taught to be proud of his wife?"

Sir Charles Marlow

Sir Charles Marlow has recommended his son, Marlow, as a suitable husband for his old friend Mr. Hardcastle's daughter Kate.

Constance Neville

Constance, Mrs. Hardcastle's niece, inherited jewels from her uncle, a director of the East India Company. Mrs. Hardcastle controls Constance's inheritance and she greedily hopes to keep these jewels in the family by marrying Constance to Tony, who has no romantic affection for Constance.

Constance loves and wants to marry Hastings, but is reluctant to elope and lose her jewels and Mr. Hardcastle's blessing. Not blindly materialistic, but practical, her attitude toward money and marriage resembles that of Jane Austen's heroines Elinor Dashwood in *Sense and Sensibility* and Jane Bennet in *Pride and Prejudice*.

Servants

Several servants fumble about awkwardly in the second act as Mr. Hardcastle attempts to train these farm workers in the niceties of London dinner service, with little success and a good deal of comedy.

THEMES

Appearances and Reality

Much of the comedy of Goldsmith's play depends on confusion between appearance and reality. After all, Marlow's misperception of Mr. Hardcastle's house as an inn drives the narrative action in the first place. Ironically, Goldsmith's comedy allows appearance to lead to the discovery of reality. Kate's deception leads her to discover Marlow's true nature. Falling in love when he thinks her a barmaid, he declares his decision to defy society and marry her in spite of the differences in their social class. Her falsehood allows him to relax with her and reveal his true self.

Truth and Falsehood

Thematically related to the theme of Appearance and Reality, Goldsmith uses falsehood to reveal the truth. Most obviously Tony's lie about Mr. Hardcastle's mansion being an inn produces the truth of the lovers' affections. Lying also leads to poetic justice. When Constance asks to wear her jewels, Mrs. Hardcastle lies and tells her they have been lost. Tony takes the jewels to give to Hastings, and when Mrs. Hardcastle goes to find them, they *have* been lost. Her lie has become true.

TOPICS FOR FURTHER STUDY

- Today, we take it for granted that people marry for love. This was not always the case, however. During the 18th century, for example, parents—usually fathers—selected their daughters' prospective husbands. A young women had the right to refuse their choice, and parents rarely forced her to marry a man she found entirely unappealing. Still, young women rarely had the right to select their own husbands.

- What is Goldsmith saying about this kind of arrangement? Does his play suggest that the right people end up married to their proper spouses? How would you feel about this kind of arrangement?

- Further research might be done into the 18th century's "marriage market," and the ways in which women reacted to it. The novels of Frances Burney or Jane Austen offer suitable comparisons. More generally, since much of *She Stoops to Conquer* revolves around parent-child relationships, you might investigate how parents really related to their children during this time.

- One thing that keeps Constance and Hastings apart is money. If she marries without Hardcastle's permission, she loses her inheritance of jewels. How important should money be in deciding whom and when to marry? Should couples be practical, or can people really live on love?

- You might research 18th century property law, under which all control of a woman's money passed to her husband after marriage. Until the Married Women's Property Act of 1867, the law also made it impossible for a women to own anything, even custody of their children. Nor could women vote, hold office, or attend universities. You might examine that status of women during the 18th century. In many ways, the status of working- and lower-class men was not much better. Your research might compare and contrast their various conditions.

- Even today, we still hear jokes about the city slicker and the country bumpkin. This common comic theme began as soon as society became urbanized, starting with classical writers like Juvenal satirizing the inhabitants of ancient Rome. Goldsmith's play depends on this kind of culture clash, between London residents like Marlow and Hastings, and country gentry like Mr. and Mrs. Hardcastle. How does this theme of culture clash function in the play? What might it signify about love, society, and lifestyles?

- Authors are not alone in exploring the tremendous changes which England experienced during the 18th century. Historians, social scientists, art historians, and anthropologists all work to uncover the complex web of related social changes. Select and research an aspect of this fascinating social upheaval. You might compare representations of English life in the paintings of Constable, Gainsborough, and Reynolds with the very different illustrations of Hogarth.

- Constance's inheritance comes from an uncle who worked for the East India Company. During the 18th century, people called someone who returned wealthy from colonies in the East or West Indies a "nabob." Nabobs figure prominently in 18th century literature. You might examine the historical background of these people, then read a play or novel in which they play significant parts.

- The comedy in *She Stoops to Conquer* results from a conflict between appearance and reality, between what things appear to be and what they are. We see this in Marlow's confusion of Hardcastle with an innkeeper and of Kate with a barmaid. In a sense, the action of the play revolves around Tony's lie, yet true love wins out in the end. What is Goldsmith saying about the role of honesty in society? How important and under what circumstances is it essential to be brutally honest? When do the ends justify the means? You might compare Goldsmith's play with a similar comedy by Oscar Wilde, *The Importance of Being Earnest,* which treats being earnest (i.e. honest), among other things.

Sex Roles

In many ways, Goldsmith's *She Stoops to Conquer* satirizes the ways the eighteenth-century society believed that proper men and women ought to behave. While the play shows the traditional pattern of male-female relations in Hastings's wooing of Constance, it also reverses the era's sexual etiquette by having Kate pursue Marlow.

Goldsmith's comedy raises serious issues, however. On the eighteenth century's "marriage market," many people married for money, land, or title. This practice often turned women into commodities, to be exchanged between fathers and prospective husbands more for economic than emotional reasons. In *She Stoops to Conquer,* the relationship between Mrs. Hardcastle and Constance depends entirely on her inheritance of colonial jewels, which provide Mrs. Hardcastle's sole reason for pressing Tony and Constance to wed. In this sense, Constance's jewels can be seen to symbolize the marketing of the female on the marriage market.

Though explored comically, the play also illustrates the tenuous status of contemporary working women and their constant danger of sexual harassment and the predatory nature of men. Goldsmith's comedy depends on our laughing because Marlow respects middle-and upper-class women but treats working class women as sexual objects. Historically, however, the situation for working women proved quite serious. During the eighteenth century, with more and more women entering domestic service, problems arose in which young female servants were vulnerable to unwelcome sexual advances from their employers and their families. Rape and sexual violence became common problems and figure prominently in eighteenth-century plays and novels. Novels by Austen, Burney, and Richardson treat the assault and seduction of young servants by their masters, in part to serve as a warning to those entering domestic service.

Culture Clash

As the play opens, Mr. Hardcastle associates his traditional attitudes with his life in the country. The comedy develops with the arrival of visitors from the city, Marlow and Hastings. Their lives of fashion represent innovation and change, though not necessarily for the better, as Mr. Hardcastle exclaims: "Is the whole age in a combination to drive sense and discretion out of doors?" The conflict between city and country values becomes clearer in light of countrified Tony's practical joke on supposedly sophisticated city residents like Marlow and Hastings. Mrs. Hardcastle also associates the urban with the fashionable and pretends to more urbanity than she actually possesses.

Obedience

The theme of obedience focuses primarily on the hierarchical relationship between parents and children, though Goldsmith's play suggests that obedience consists of more than blind servility. Children should obey their parents. Parents, however, should earn their respect and deserve to be obeyed by acting in their children's best interest. Kate obeys Mr. Hardcastle, but while they may not agree entirely on fashion and boyfriends, he acts as he does for what he believes to be her own good. Tony does not obey Mrs. Hardcastle and stymies her scheme to set him up with Constance. Greed, rather than paternal duty, motivates her actions, however, for she concerns herself primarily with maintaining possession of Constance's jewels, not with selecting a suitable mate for Tony. She does not deserve obedience, and no one condemns Tony for resisting her.

STYLE

Age of Sensibility

Many works written between 1750 and 1798 emphasized emotion and pathos, instead of drama and humor. The Sentimental comedy, called a comedy not because of its humor but because it had a happy ending, ruled the stage. *She Stoops to Conquer* reacts against this tradition, for Goldsmith's comedy actually evokes laughter. The prologue by Garrick and the epilogue by Goldsmith clearly situate the play as a challenge to sensibility, and positive audience response initiated a new age in stage comedy.

Comedy of Manners

While *She Stoops to Conquer* contains elements of farce, its comedy also stems from poking fun at the manners and conventions of aristocratic, sophisticated society.

Epilogue

In the concluding statement of *She Stoops to Conquer,* Goldsmith summarizes the plot and hopes that the comedy has conquered his audience as Kate has conquered Marlow's heart.

Farce

Many critics have described *She Stoops to Conquer,* a comedy characterized by broad humor and outlandish incidents, as a farce.

Foreshadowing

Goldsmith uses foreshadowing to create expectations and explain subsequent developments. For example, Mrs. Hardcastle in act one describes their house as "an old rumbling mansion, that looks for all the world like an inn." This helps the audience understand what gave Tony the idea for his practical joke and explains how the travelers' could mistake the Hardcastle's house for an inn.

Later, when Marlow indicates his anxiety speaking with ladies, but comfort flirting with wenches, this foreshadows his comical interludes with Kate. Kate's discussion with Mr. Hardcastle about desiring an outgoing husband leads the audience to anticipate her disappointment with the formal Marlow. Her statement that Marlow's shyness during their first meeting prevented him from even looking at her face makes us expect some comical treatment of identity and gives Kate's disguise as a barmaid credibility.

Irony

When Mrs. Hardcastle and Hastings discuss London's high society, she intends the conversation to show her sophistication and knowledge of city life. Instead, the conversation has exactly the opposite effect. Her confusion between fashionable and unfashionable neighborhoods shows her ignorance of high society, making her comments ironic.

Poetic Justice

Throughout the play, Mrs. Hardcastle tries maintain control over Constance's jewels. It is poetic justice that when Mrs. Hardcastle has hidden the jewels from Constance, claiming they've been stolen, they have in fact been stolen by Tony.

Prologue

David Garrick, the most famous actor and theatre producer of his time, wrote the introductory section of *She Stoops to Conquer.* Garrick claims that the "Comic muse, long sick, is now a-dying." He hopes that Goldsmith's play, with its humor, will challenge the traditional sentimental comedy and thus revive the muse.

HISTORICAL CONTEXT

The late 18th century marked a period of great transition for England. Between 1640 and 1688, the nation fought a civil war, executed its king, and restored its monarchy; it then established a government which balanced power between monarch and parliament. England had also fought a series of wars with the United Dutch Provinces and France, setting the stage for English dominance as a colonial power. The American Revolution loomed on the horizon, but most historians agree that the loss of the colonies had limited political or economic impact. England became an increasingly prosperous nation occupying a central position on the world stage.

The Shift to Industrialism

That said, not everything in this transition went smoothly. The agricultural revolution had begun in the 16th century with developments in farming and animal husbandry. By the 18th century, these improvements resulted in generally greater supplies of higher-quality, lower-priced food. Still, hunger persisted because bad harvests, war, and inflation caused food supplies and prices to vary from region to region. Further, the change from a system of many small farms to fewer large farms drove many farmers off their land and into the factories created by the industrial revolution. Goldsmith's poem *The Deserted Village* elegizes one such village that became vacant as England shifted from an economy largely rural and agricultural to one more urban, based on manufacturing and trade.

England's mercantile economy provided the impetus needed to drive the industrial revolution, just as surely as inventions like James Watt's steam engine drove the factories themselves. Still, new,

COMPARE & CONTRAST

- **1700s:** During the 18th century, entirely arranged marriages were rare, but a young women rarely had the right to select a husband entirely on her own. More customary was for the father to select the prospective husband, while the daughter had the right to accept or refuse him. In *She Stoops to Conquer,* Mr. Hardcastle has selected Marlow, the son of an old friend, but he assures Kate he would never control her choice.

  Today: The majority of people who marry make their own decisions and join together primarily for love.

- **1700s:** India was a British colony ruled largely by the East India Company, for whom Constance's uncle was a director.

  Today: India is one of the world's largest democracies.

- **1700s:** Mr. Hardcastle complains that life in the country has changed since he was a young man and offers no protection against the corruption of London life. Better roads and coaches carry mail and newspapers, connecting the city and country. London fashions and manners infiltrate even rural estates.

  Today: Many people live in suburbs which lie between urban and rural areas. Not only mass transit, but mass media and the Internet connect communities throughout the world.

- **1700s:** Mrs. Hardcastle's comment that ''since inoculation began, there is no such thing to be seen as a plain woman'' refers to the fact that, with advancing medical science and the advent of numerous vaccines against diseases, very few women were scarred by smallpox. A case of smallpox as a child left its mark on Goldsmith.

  Today: Children receive inoculations against a host of diseases, including measles and polio, which for earlier generations caused illness, disfigurement, and death.

---

largely unplanned cities sprung up around these factories. Rural migrants found they had left farm life behind for factory work that often offered lower wages and a diminished quality of life for themselves and their families.

England's Changing Economy

Changes in England's industrial, agricultural, and colonial economies translated into a demand for English goods and services. While some became impoverished, others flourished, as these changes stimulated the rise of the middle class. This led, among things, to the increasingly literate population which supported a new generation of writers like Goldsmith.

In general, these changes decreased the wealth among those landed and titled, and increased the wealth among those connected with commerce. As a result, children from old, titled, landed families married with those of untitled, cash-rich, but land-poor commercial families. It is this ''marriage market'' which provides the backdrop for Goldsmith's examination of the various motives for marriage in *She Stoops to Conquer.*

Sentimental Times and Goldsmith's Comedy

Finally, an explanation of the tone of Goldsmith's play, a comedy rooted in things quite serious. The 18th century's validation of empiricism offered a challenge to religious belief based solely on faith. Many people sought an accommodation between reason and faith. One such accommodation was Deism, which accepted as true certain observable ''facts''—for example, the world had been created, so there must be a creator—but resisted specifics about the nature of religious doctrine.

Such beliefs posed a problems, however: how can society develop a code for ethical conduct independent of the ten commandments? Sentimentalism, pioneered by Lord Kames, Francis Hutchinson, and Adam Smith, offered a psychological solution. They suggested that ethics arise from human sentiments, from sympathy and empathy.

Sentimental ethics work like this. A person contemplates an action—murder, for example—and wonders if it is wrong. To decide, one imagines the crime, first placing oneself in the victim's position, empathizing with the person's suffering. Then, one takes the objective position of an observer, attempting to feel sympathy for the person killed, for their family and loved ones. These two perspectives lead one to understand the emotions (the sentiments) involved and to condemn the action as evil.

Sentimentalism became a powerful force during the 18th century. It provided the philosophical underpinning for the American Revolution, which substituted the more Sentimental right to "Life, Liberty, and the Pursuit of Happiness" for John Locke's "Life, Liberty, and Property." It also motivated reform of the slave trade, prisons, and insane asylums. In the theatre, however, this philosophy led to the creation of the Sentimental Comedy, called so not because it provoked laughter, but because it ended happily. (For the same reason, Dante titled his poem *The Divine Comedy*). The Sentimental Comedy provided Goldsmith's target in *She Stoops to Conquer,* as he attempted—and succeeded—in writing a comedy that provokes not sympathetic tears but actual laughter.

CRITICAL OVERVIEW

In "An Essay on the Theatre; or, A Comparison Between Laughing and Sentimental Comedy," Goldsmith distinguishes between "hard" and "soft" comedy. Instead of the "Weeping Sentimental Comedy" which gratified audience sympathies at injustice suffered by innocent worthies, Goldsmith's 1773 essay advocated the "laughing comedy," which offered a "natural portrait of Human Folly and Frailty." *She Stoops to Conquer* opens with a prologue by actor and impresario David Garrick declaiming on the state of the theatre and sentimental comedy. Mr. Woodward, who speaks the monologue, weeps, saying, "Would you know the reason why I'm crying?/The Comic Muse, long sick, is now a-dying!" In *She Stoops to Conquer* and his earlier play *The Good-Natur'd Man,* Goldsmith sought to rescue that muse. His writing, according to Louis Kronenberger in an introduction to the 1964 Heritage Press edition of the play, led "an assault on the sentimental comedy that had held the boards for upwards of fifty years." No mere iconoclast, Goldsmith does more than critique the past. In fact, according to Oscar James Campbell in his introduction to *Chief Plays of Goldsmith and Sheridan: The School for Scandal, She Stoops to Conquer, The Rivals, She Stoops to Conquer* is "a virtual School for Comedy." Goldsmith's play incorporates and transforms elements of both the earlier Restoration Comedy of Manners and contemporary Sentimental Comedy and "opened the door" to a new kind of comedy.

Goldsmith's comedy has its roots in serious philosophical debate. In his 1651 *Leviathan,* Thomas Hobbes describes original human nature as a constant state of war, with minimal social cohesion and strong dominating weak. Hobbes's ideas influenced the Restoration comedy, an urban comedy of manners in which power and polish led to social manipulation and dominance. By the 1690s, Locke and others argued that people's innate moral sense made them naturally good and happy. This led to the "soft," "sentimental," or "reform" comedy, which lacked laughter and attempted to teach virtue by making audiences feel sympathy and empathy for the suffering of the innocent. These were comedies only in having a happy ending, for the same reason that Dante named his poem *The Divine Comedy.*

In *She Stoops to Conquer* Goldsmith tries to correct both the rakish mannerism of the Restoration comedy and the pathos of the Sentimental comedy. For example, while Restoration comedy privileged urban sophistication over rural simplicity, Goldsmith reverses the trend. "In Restoration comedies countrymen appeared as fools in London drawing rooms," noted Campbell. In *She Stoops to Conquer,* "Tony, on his own turf, easily hoodwinks the city dudes into mistaking an old house for an inn." For Goldsmith, country life seems not unfashionable exile but the repository of the traditional English virtues he portrayed in *The Deserted*

Village. In his portraits of Mr. Hardcastle and Kate, Goldsmith validates the familial warmth of country life. In the multiple marriages that mark its ending, the play shows the triumph of idealistic love instead of merely manners, all the while creating laughter and even "low" humor.

Goldsmith undermines Sentimentalism in ways which J. L. Styan, writing in an issue of *Costerus,* noted may be missed by contemporary audiences. For example, when Constance find Kate alone in the first act, she judges by her complexion that something emotional has happened. Constance asks, "has the last novel been too moving?" She wonders if Kate's sensibilities have been engaged by a Sentimental novel—of the kind Goldsmith satirizes in *The Vicar of Wakefield.* We quickly learn that Kate's emotional state has been heightened, not by a novel but by the imminent arrival of her suitor, an action that will initiate actual, not Sentimental comedy.

Goldsmith's play does more than simply respond to the past, however. By striking a balance between situation and characterization, *She Stoops to Conquer* proved innovative. What makes the play work for Styan are its "madcap situations" which resembles a farce in seeming "exaggerated, impossible, absurd, and ridiculous." According to Louis Kronenberger, the "farce idea that galvanizes it [is] the idea of having two young men directed to a private house—the very house they have been invited to visit—under the impression that it is an inn." The subtitle of the play, "The Mistakes of a Night," suggests the plot's farcical beginnings, though the play's success as a comedy, for Kronenberger, comes from the ways Goldsmith "ingeniously keeps exploring and extracting . . . the possibilities in his hoax."

Still, most critics see the play not as pure farce but as something more, largely due to its strong characterization. Styan observed that the "important farcical ingredient in Goldsmith's comedy depends upon the invention of a situation absurd enough to admit an exaggeration of character." True, "Marlow's being altogether at his ease with wenches and hopelessly shy with young ladies scores best as an amusing plot device." Further, "The spirit of this comedy is made to turn on . . . a marriage of convenience . . . inverted so that the lady takes the initiative, Miss Hardcastle becomes Kate, and the genteel heroine a barmaid who sets

about seducing the genteel hero." But it is the character of Kate, not merely her predicament, that makes the comedy work. According to Campbell, "Miss Hardcastle is the first heroine for many decades who has no taste for sentimental aphorism and tender hearts." This becomes clear in her response to Marlow's formal wooing during their initial meeting. She desires authentic emotional involvement, not sentimental claptrap and goes about getting it with her scheme to impersonate a barmaid.

In this, Goldsmith demands versatility of his characters, forcing them to present themselves in more than one way, as Styan noted. For example, compare the stiff, sentimental wooing scene in which Marlow first encounters Kate with later scenes between the more libertine Marlow and the "low" barmaid Kate, which provides comical counterpoint. For Campbell, characters like Mrs. Hardcastle and Tony Lumpkin, with his "pot house tastes and prankster ways . . . is a booby who lays booby traps for others," make the play "not farce, but comedy of continuous incident."

Two other elements of technical stagecraft enhance Goldsmith's comedy. One is his use of asides, in which a character makes a comment meant to be heard by the audience but not by other characters on stage. During Marlow's initial meeting with Kate, for example, Styan believes the characters' asides invite the audience into their thought processes and offer perspective on their actions. "The fact that the discussion here purports to be about hypocrisy makes the asides to pertinent that the farce shifts into a realm of social satire." Goldsmith also creates comic tension by the ways he orchestrates the stage action. The scene in which Marlow agrees to accept Kate despite their class differences resembles those in the typical sentimental comedy. But, according to Mark Anthony Houlahan in the *International Dictionary of Theatre-1: Plays,* Goldsmith "invigorates the cliches of sentiment by placing . . . [the characters] in an absurdly contrived and complex setting" in which the lovers—with Kate in disguise—can be observed by Mr Hardcastle and Sir Charles Marlow.

CRITICISM

Arnold Schmidt

A member of the English department at California State University, Stanislaus, Schmidt focuses

WHAT DO I READ NEXT?

- Students who enjoy reading Shakespeare might want to consider two of his plays which treat themes similar to those in Goldsmith's play, in particular love and the problems faced by young lovers whose marriage has been forbidden by parents. Critics see resemblances between Goldsmith's Kate and Rosalind, the heroine of Shakespeare's 1599 comedy *As You Like It.* Both plays feature smart and spirited women and both create comedy from forbidden loves, disguises, and mistaken identities.

- Those preferring tragedy might prefer Shakespeare's 1595 *Romeo and Juliet,* in which parental interference with the lover's plans for marriage leads to suicide and death. Leonard Bernstein and Stephen Sondheim successfully adapted *Romeo and Juliet* for the musical theatre in *West Side Story.*

- Like Goldsmith's play, Frances Burney's 1778 epistolary novel *Evelina, or a Young Lady's Entrance into the World* also portrays the eighteenth century's Britain's marriage market. It recounts the heroine's introduction into London society and explores the ways love and marriage influence female identity.

- In Mary Wollstonecraft's *Maria, or, The Wrongs of Woman,* late eighteenth-century England's marriage market leads a naive, sincere young women to destruction. Until the Married Women's Property Act of 1867, women who married lost control over their property under a legal convention known as "coverture." In this short, fragmentary, gothic novel, Maria's cruel husband has her imprisoned in a madhouse for her refusal to give him her money which she has saved for her daughter. Wollstonecraft's novel, written just 15 years after Goldsmith's play, offers a suitable contrast to *She Stoops to Conquer* for students interested in feminism and human rights.

- While any of Jane Austen's novels would serve as fine foils to Goldsmith's play, two in particular might be best to read next: *Emma* (1815) and *Sense and Sensibility* (1811). Both deal with the problems of love and marriage faced by young ladies in the eighteenth century. Structurally akin to *She Stoops to Conquer,* Austen's novels also develop themes in part by juxtaposing pairs of characters. In tone, Austen's irony might be contrasted with Goldsmith's comedy.

- Recalling the struggles of lovers Constance and Hastings, Wilkie Collins's 1868 novel *The Moonstone* also revolves around a young lady whose marriage stalls due to an Indian jewel. Different in style from Goldsmith's play, many critics see *The Moonstone* as one of the first detective novels, with an ending guaranteed to surprise.

- Oscar Wilde's funny, accessible 1895 comedy *The Importance of Being Earnest, A Trivial Comedy for Serious People* closely resembles *She Stoops to Conquer* in situation, theme, and tone. Both plays feature two citified male friends who woo two countrified female friends and both rely on disguise and double identities. Love triumphs at the end of both plays, which end in marriages all around.

---

his essay on how the advances of Goldsmith's era affected and enriched his comedy.

Not accidentally, ages of great social change frequently leave behind great comedy. Oliver Goldsmith's *She Stoops to Conquer* provokes laughter—often at situations that are quite serious. Parent-child relationships and marriage stand at the center of Goldsmith's play, as the characters attempt to strike some balance between authority and freedom, obedience and independence. While Goldsmith treats these themes lightheartedly, the play's humor conceals a somber undercurrent. By the time Goldsmith's play debuted in the late 18th century, Eng-

---

land had undergone great political, economic, and social transformations. These changes created what came to be know as the "marriage market," which provides the backdrop for *She Stoops to Conquer.* Simply put, the comedy asks how, at a time when many people married for money rather than love, can marriage join people who are both economically and emotionally compatible?

During the 17th century, England's Civil War moved the nation from a government by strong monarchy to one which balanced power between king and parliament. A series of wars with the United Dutch Provinces and France positioned England's ascent as a colonial power. The agricultural and industrial revolution had brought progress. By the mid-18th century, England had become an increasingly prosperous nation occupying a central position on the world stage.

These changes did not occur without costs, however. The agricultural revolution resulted in generally greater supplies of higher quality, lower priced food but drove many farmers off their land and into the factories created by the industrial revolution. England's mercantile economy provided the impetus needed to drive industrialization, but rural migrants often found that urban life and factory work compared unfavorably with agricultural work in the country. While some became impoverished, others prospered and rose to join England's growing middle class.

In general, these changes decreased the wealth among old, rural, titled families, and increased that of the newly rich commercial urbanites. As a result, children from old families, who were titled, married with those of untitled, cash-rich but land-poor commercial families. Such marriages created unions with money, land, and title. In *She Stoops to Conquer,* Goldsmith examines this "marriage market," seeking some balance between love and money.

The play's opening scene introduces the conflict between old and new, between country and city. Mr. and Mrs. Hardcastle discuss people who take trips to London, as they do not. Mr. Hardcastle remembers the days when rural life kept away the follies of town but no longer, for today, follies "travel faster than a stagecoach." Significantly, Tony's practical jokes reflects the long-standing comic jousting between the country bumpkin and the city slicker that goes back at least to the playwright Juvenal's satires of the late Roman empire. Mr. Hardcastle identifies himself as a barrier against the changing times, saying, "I love everything

that's old: old friends, old times, old manners, old books, old wine," and even his "old wife." As the times change, human relationships like marriage change with them, though not necessarily for the better. While traditional, Mr. Hardcastle seeks for his daughter a marriage with both financial and emotional security; Mrs. Hardcastle's mercenary attitudes resemble those of fashionable London society's marriage market. This conflict between husband and wife represents a conflict between traditional and colonial value systems.

Different styles of parenting have produced different kinds of children. By spoiling Tony, Mrs. Hardcastle prevented him from growing up. Tony is disobedient. On his way out to the Three Pigeons alehouse, he refuses Mrs. Hardcastle's request that he stay home "for one night at least." More legitimately, he also refuses to obey her command that he marry Constance. Mrs. Hardcastle conceals from Tony the fact that he's come of age. She uses deceit to manipulate him into a loveless marriage to Constance which permits Mrs. Hardcastle to keep controls of the Constance's jewels. While Mr. Hardcastle wants the best for his daughter in marriage, Mrs. Hardcastle concerns herself not with Tony's happiness but with the money and status the jewels might bring.

Mr. Hardcastle, on the other hand, seems honest, if stuffy, and his daughter Kate behaves honestly toward him (she may not tell him everything, but at least she never lies to him). Where Tony is obstinate, Kate is accommodating. While Kate wants to dress fashionably, Mr. Hardcastle wants her attire to be simple. They compromise: she dresses as she pleases during the day, when she receives visitors, and as he likes in the evening.

The play's action advances when Mr. Hardcastle announces, "I expect the young gentleman I have chosen to be your husband from town this very day." Kate's father assures her that he would never control her choice, but she responds anxiously, worried at the formality of their meeting will prevent her from feeling "friendship or esteem." During the 18th century, entirely arranged marriages were unusual, though a young women rarely had the right to select a husband entirely on her own. More customarily, a women's parents—primarily her father— selected a prospective husband, whom the daughter had the right to accept or reject. The young man Hardcastle has in mind, Marlow, is the son of an old friend, Sir Charles Marlow, but Hardcastle assures Kate he would never control her choice.

This exchange establishes the parameters of a successful parent-child relationship. The good father, Mr. Hardcastle offers guidance without being tyrannical, while Kate, the good daughter, seems willing to be compliant—but not at the price of marrying without emotional attachment. Here, we realize another difference between Mr. and Mrs. Hardcastle. While he selects an appropriate husband for his daughter, according to what he believes will make her happy, his wife has selected a zero (her own son) for Constance's fiance, a decision dictated not by concern for her own good, but by a selfish desire for gain.

She Stoops to Conquer portrays three strategies for parent-child relationships. In Tony's attitude toward his mother, Mrs. Hardcastle, we see resistance and deception. Likewise, deception characterizes her treatment of both Tony and Constance. Finally, the play offers the preferred option of compromise, as exemplified by Mr. Hardcastle's attitude toward his daughter Kate. This seems the best way for families to cope with decisions: insight and empathy on the part of the parents, intelligence and compromise on that of the child.

The play also offers three types of marriage. One possibility: a loveless, parentally-enforced marriage, as that arranged by Mrs. Hardcastle between Tony and Constance. Another option: marriage for love, but against parental wishes, as seen in Hastings's plans for eloping with Constance. Finally, the best solution, compromise between parent and child, as in Kate's marriage with Marlow—a marriage based on affection but also sanctioned by paternal authority.

The compromise solutions in *She Stoops to Conquer* reflect the 18th century's general validation of reasonable compromise and balance of power. During the 17th century, traditional writers like Robert Filmer argued for the divine right of kings based on the *Great Chain of Being*. According to nature, God ruled over man, kings over peasants, men over women, and fathers over families. Natural hierarchies justified both monarchy and patriarchy. In *She Stoops to Conquer*, the viewer sees a model of private sphere compromise between Kate and Mr. Hardcastle in regard to her clothing (and more importantly, her marriage). This attitude echoes the public sphere power-sharing arranged between king and parliament after the Restoration of 1660 and Glorious Revolution of 1688. Goldsmith's play balances tradition and structure with freedom and innovation.

Goldsmith's attitude toward marriage reflects other aspects of his social moment, however. While Marlow and Kate's wedding unites two old money families, Mrs. Hardcastle's efforts to wed Tony and Constance are an attempt to link traditional and colonial wealth. In effect, Mrs. Hardcastle attempts to colonize Tony and Constance in marriage, simultaneously extracting his Submission (playing the good son) and her jewels. The play's action makes this impossible but does not reject colonial wealth. It merely aligns colonial wealth in a marriage for love rather than in a forced, arranged marriage. Constance marries Hastings instead of Tony. Marriage itself still serves the same economic function of combining landed and colonial wealth.

In *She Stoops to Conquer*, comedy is serious business with serious social and monetary consequences. While raising legitimate issues about the responsibilities between parents and children, it also calls to mind the cultural and historical moment which produced it.

Source: Arnold Schmidt, in an essay for *Drama for Students*, Gale 1997

London Magazine

In this unsigned review which first appeared in the March, 1773, edition of London Magazine, *an overview of Goldsmith's* She Stoops to Conquer *is given.*

On Monday the 15th of this month [i.e. March] was first performed at this theatre a new comedy, called *She Stoops to Conquer, or The Mistakes of a Night*, written by Dr. Goldsmith. . . .

Mr. Hardcastle is a plain honest country gentleman. His wife is well-meaning, but foolish and positive, and so indulgent to her son, Squire Lumpkin, that she has given him no education for fear of hurting his health. This Squire is quite a spoiled child, regardless of his mother, fond of low company, and full of mischievous humour. Miss Hardcastle is a lively and amiable young lady, whom her father is desirous of marrying to young Marlow the son of Sir Charles. This Marlow is a fashionable young fellow, who has constantly lived in the pleasures of the town; and by being accustomed to the company of courtesans only, is in great dread of modest women, and behaves in their presence with a very awkward bashfulness. Miss Neville is a niece of Mrs. Hardcastle's, has a good fortune, and lives in the family. It is the purpose of the relations to have this young lady married to Squire Lumpkin; but this couple have not the least regard for each other. On the contrary, the Squire is enamoured with a vulgar country-beauty; and Miss Neville has a strong *penchant* for Mr. Hastings, the friend of Yound Marlow. These two gentlemen had never been at Hardcastle's, but the former is expected every moment from London; and Hastings, by an agreement with Marlow, was to accompany him thither as his friend, but in fact to have an opportunity of seeing and conversing with his mistress, Miss Neville.

Thus the whole story is situated at the beginning of the play; near which time the young Squire is discovered in an ale-house, revelling with his pot companions. At this time the landlord enters to inform him, that two gentlemen were at the door enquiring their way to Mr. Hardcastle's. He, on seeing them, guessed Marlow to be one of his coarse jokes upon the travellers, mischievously informs them that as it was late, and they cannot be accommodated that night at the ale-house, if they will walk on for about a mile, they will come to a very good inn, which they might know by seeing a pair of stag's horns over the gate. This, in truth, was Hardcastle's; but the Squire wanted fun, and he got it; for when the gentlemen arrived there, thinking themselves in an inn, they used very great freedom, to the utter astonishment of Hardcastle; for he accidentally heard Marlow named, and knew him; but he resolved to hold his tongue.

Soon after their arrival here, Hastings meets with Miss Neville, who undeceives him with respect to their mistake; but he begs her to conceal it yet from Marlow, whose natural diffidence would force him to quit the family immediately, which he had so freely, though unwittingly used. Miss Neville informs her cousin Miss Hardcastle of the whole; and this lady (being obliged to dress herself very plainly every evening to please a whim of her father's) agrees to pass herself upon Marlow as the bar-maid of the inn, in order to carry on the plot. From these different dispositions arise all the Mistakes of the Night.

After many laughable scenes which arise from the mutual misunderstanding of the several parties, Hardcastle at length flies into a violent passion, and accidentally mentions some circumstances to Marlow which alarm him. Marlow, in short, discovers his error, and consequently undergoes much confusion and agitation; but the arrival of his father adjusts

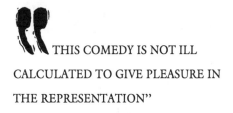

THIS COMEDY IS NOT ILL CALCULATED TO GIVE PLEASURE IN THE REPRESENTATION"

every difference, and he receives with joy the hand of Miss Hardcastle, who, in her character of barmaid, had greatly charmed him, and who, in consequence, might be said to have Stooped to Conquer.

While these things are transacting, the counterplot goes on successfully. Hastings gains over the Squire to his interest, and this hopeful son contrives to steal Miss Neville's jewels out of his mother's bureau, and gives them to Hastings, who was preparing to run away with his mistress. But the jewels being very valuable, he is unwilling to carry them with him on so hasty a journey, and gives them to Marlow to keep for him: Marlow, from the same laudable motives of security, consigns them to the keeping of Mrs. Hardcastle, whom he at this time supposed to be the landlady of the inn. Thus the old lady recovers the jewels; by which, and by means of a letter from Hastings to the Squire, which she read, she discovers the plot laid by the lovers for an elopement.

This plot known, Mrs. Hardcastle is greatly alarmed, as it threatened the destruction of her favourite scheme of marriage between her son and Miss Neville. She therefore determines to carry her that very night to her aunt's, about forty miles off. She soon hurries the young lady into the coach, and sets off under the guidance of the Squire on the horseback. Before their departure, however, the Squire whispers to Hastings not to despair yet, for he was still his friend, and would meet him behind the garden at a certain time which he named. Having set off, he leads his mother through danks, bogs, and quagmires, in a dirty condition, round through lanes and by-roads, till he landed her just at the back of her own garden, and then told her she was at least 40 miles from home, and upon a heath. Here, after a variety of roguish tricks with which he alarmed her, Hardcastle advances, and, after some misunderstanding, the parties recognize each other. In the mean time Hastings fled to his mistress, who was left in the coach; but they agree, instead of running away, to return to the family, and throw themselves upon the generosity of the Hardcastles. Mrs. Hardcastle will by no means consent to their union, insisting that Miss Neville cannot be married till her son is of age, who by articles was either to accept or refuse her hand—articles upon which her fortune depended. Hardcastle, however, obviates this, by informing the Squire that he has been already of age three months, and that he may do what he pleases. Lumpkin willingly refuses her, and her hand is consequently given to Hastings: with which the play concludes.

This comedy is not ill calculated to give pleasure in the representation; but when we regard it with a critical eye, we find it to abound with numerous inaccuracies. The fable (a fault too peculiar to the hasty productions of the modern Comic Muse) is twisted into incidents not naturally arising from the subject, in order *to make things meet;* and consistency is repeatedly violated for the sake of humour. But perhaps we ought to sign a general pardon to the author, for taking the field against that monster called Sentimental Comedy, to oppose which his comedy was avowedly written. Indeed, the attempt was bold, considering the strength of the enemy; and we are glad to observe that our author still keeps the field with flying colours.—But, (metaphor apart) it appears that the Doctor was too ardent. Well considering that the public were long accustomed to cry, he resolved to make them laugh at any rate. In aiming at this point, he seems to have stepped too far; and in lieu of comedy he has sometimes presented us with farce.

These redundancies are certainly the chief blots in his play. A stricter consistency in the fable, and a better attention to the unity of time in particular, would have exalted the comedy to a good and just reputation.

Source: Review of *She Stoops to Conquer* (1773) in *Goldsmith: The Critical Heritage,* edited by G. S. Rousseau, Routledge & Kegan Paul, 1974, pp. 119–22.

Louis Kronenberger

In this introduction to Goldsmith's play, Kronenberger proposes that She Stoops to Conquer *is a prime example of the theatre era from which it emerged, as well as evidence of the playwright's disdain for Sentimental comedy.*

Kronenberger served as a drama critic for Time *magazine from 1938 to 1961, and was regarded as an expert on eighteenth-century English literature and history.*

Oliver Goldsmith stands quite high in English literature, and a little apart, by reason of his three-pronged claims to recognition. There is his extremely famous poem, *The Deserted Village;* his extremely famous novel, *The Vicar of Wakefield;* his extremely famous play, *She Stoops to Conquer.* To have achieved three unquestioned classics that jointly run to about the length of an average-sized book is a notable example of how to travel down the ages with the lightest of luggage.

But though all three remain unquestioned classics, they no longer—if we are to be honest—enjoy a quite equal esteem or popularity. *The Deserted Village* has come to be a bit of a deserted poem. Certain of its lines and couplets have passed into the language, their authorship rather obscured; but the poem itself seems to be gradually passing out of circulation. Even as a high-school standby I suspect it is being replaced by something less pastoral and more vibrant. *The Vicar of Wakefield* has fared better, as it deserves to have done. For it has much of Goldsmith's kindliness and charm; and in any at all exhaustive journey through the English novel, one that stops at picturesque towns as well as populous cities, it must always have a place; it must, indeed—like *Cranford,* like *Our Village*—survive as the kind of minor work whose value rests on its being minor. Its voice may not carry far, or instantly rivet attention, but it is a genuinely individual one.

But of Goldsmith's three classics, it seems pretty certain that *She Stoops to Conquer* is much the best entrenched. It has so unequivocally survived as to seem, again and again, worth reviving; only a short time ago the Phoenix Theatre revived it in New York. So long as actors eye juicy character parts, they must glance at Tony Lumpkin; so long as producers eye time-tried comic plots, they must give thought to Goldsmith's; and in *any* journey through the English comic theatre, even one confined to Principal Points of Interest, it must surely have a place. Between 1728 and the 1870's, which is to say between *The Beggar's Opera* and Gilbert and Sullivan, *The School for Scandal* and *The Rivals* are *its* only rivals; and *The Rivals,* to my mind, is its inferior. *She Stoops to Conquer* is an extraordinary work on a very odd basis: that, without there being anything the least bit extraordinary about it, it stands alone of its kind among the comic classics of the English stage. Surely there should be at least a dozen *She Stoops to Conquer*s, a dozen farce comedies written between the age of Anne and the age of Victoria that, without ever seeming brilliant, are almost consistently lively; that, without ever turning bawdy, are not simpering or prim; that, with no great claim to wit, have a robust sense of fun; that, without being satirical, can spoof certain human weaknesses; and that, without being sentimental, remain friendly and good-natured.

Yet, unless they are moldering in unopened books on dust-covered shelves, far from there being a dozen such plays, where unmistakably is there another? What others manage (which is the crucial point) to sustain their good qualities throughout an entire evening? What others don't creep through a first act or crumble during the last, or don't plague us with a deadly subplot, or weary us with dialect jokes, or pelt us with petrified epigrams, or try our patience with spoonfuls of morality? *The Rivals,* for example, besides belonging to a different category or—what with mixing the satirical, the farcical, and the romantic—belonging to no category at all, makes us put up with Faulkland and Julia, who are decidedly bores. Goldsmith's lovers keep us far from breathless, but, by virtue of the uses Goldsmith puts them to, they are seldom boring.

Hence, instead of being recurrent in the English classic theatre, *She Stoops to Conquer* verges on the anomalous—a full evening's worth of good clean fun. It chiefly owes its vivacity, of course, to the farce idea that galvanizes it, the idea of having two young men directed to a private house—the very house they have been invited to visit—under the impression that it is an inn. The original title and surviving subtitle of the play, ''The Mistakes of a Night,'' suggests the quick, cumulative nature of the plotting, and the frank nature of the farcicality. Goldsmith sticks to the possibilities in his hoax, which means that he ingeniously keeps exploring and extracting them. (pp. v–viii)

[The central incident] had particular stage value by virtue of its comic reversal of values. To mistake a private house for an inn, as against mistaking one private house for another, starts off with confusion on one side that can quickly spread to the other, and that creates not just personal misunderstandings but social ''situations'' and *gaffes.* . . . The plot thickens, of course, and the fun

> *SHE STOOPS TO CONQUER HAS SO UNEQUIVOCALLY SURVIVED AS TO SEEM, AGAIN AND AGAIN, WORTH REVIVING''*

fattens by having the ''landlord'' stand aghast at the behavior of his guests; and the practical joke is kept going by the lubricating propinquity of the practical joker. Tony Lumpkin always stands ready to deceive or abet deception; no farce ever had more of a misleading man, whether at one moment by pretending to be in love with Miss Neville, or at another by driving Miss Neville and his mother over hill and dale in virtually their own backyard.

Tony, in the end, is much less a great character creation than a fat character part with pothouse tastes and prankster ways. But what is so lumpish in Tony is the more misleading thing about him: it conceals, it half denies, what is so sharp-witted. His mind must not be inferred from his manners. He is a booby who lays booby traps for others; he is the card-table simpleton who walks off with the winnings. The scene where he pretends to think his mother is shamming about the stolen jewels reveals how little of a fool he is and how greatly (in the theatre, above all) he can contribute to the fun.

Goldsmith does very well by Tony, and by us, in giving him Mrs. Hardcastle for a doting mother; theirs is perhaps the most enjoyable relationship in the play. The two pairs of lovers are to be praised, I think, not so much for qualities of character as for so lightly and briskly advancing the plot. Even Marlow's being altogether at his ease with wenches and hopelessly shy with young ladies scores best as an amusing plot device. Plot, as it must be in farce, is the real motive power of the play. But it proves the saving grace of the play as well, in that the plot, really, always calls the tune, always sets the level, refusing to halt for any detailed picture of manners or for more than a surface coat of romance.

Nothing is better known than that in *She Stoops to Conquer*—as earlier in *The Good-Natur'd Man* —Goldsmith was waging an assault on the sentimental comedy that had held the boards for upwards of fifty years. And the comedy of *She Stoops to Conquer* quite escapes being sentimental. But this, it seems to me, is chiefly through favoring plot situations over personal ones; which means, in the end, through scamping flesh and blood no less than sighs and tears. And if *She Stoops to Conquer* also escapes seeming genteel, it is chiefly from a certain air of the bucolic and rowdy—a sort of taproom indecorum that conceals the total absence of boudoir indecency. Where, at the beginning of the eighteenth century, George Farquhar had let the hero of *The Constant Couple* mistake a private house for a bordello, Goldsmith scarcely suggests that *his* private house has bedrooms. But Farquhar's racier amusement lasts for only a scene of two (which is all the situation proves worth) and his play, as a whole, is decidedly mixed and uneven; whereas Goldsmith's situation does last out a whole play; and his effect, if on occasion tame, is never jumbled.

What in the long run has so much helped *She Stoops to Conquer* must at the outset have seemed destined to harm it—its old-fashioned countryfied look, its genial humorist's good nature, its lack of something very new that must come to seem dated, of something very chic that in time must seem tacky. *She Stoops to Conquer* has its incidental merits: its best dialogue is thoroughly bright, it makes observations not just sound but astute, it contains social details that are revealing and vivid. But such things are just frequent enough to remind us that Goldsmith was a real writer, a man of real parts and cultivation. At the same time they are unobtrusive enough not to halt the flow of the fun— that immemorial fun born of human beings at cross-purposes and of situations gone askew and awry. (pp. viii–xi)

Source: Louis Kronenberger, introduction to *She Stoops to Conquer: or The Mistakes of a Night,* by Oliver Goldsmith, Heritage Press, 1964, pp. v-xi.

FURTHER READING

Bevis, Richard. "Oliver Goldsmith" in *Dictionary of Literary Biography,* Volume 89: *Restoration and Eighteenth-Century Dramatists, Third Series,* edited by Paula R. Backscheider, Gale, 1989. pp 150-69.

Presents extensive information about Goldsmith's life and how it relates to his writings. Traces Goldsmith's career from student to journalist to novelist, playwright, and poet, with discussion of all the major and much minor work.

Kroenberger, Louis. Introduction to *She Stoops to Conquer; or, The Mistakes of a Night,* by Oliver Goldsmith, Heritage, 1964, pp.v-xi.

Kroenberger discusses reasons for the continued popularity of Goldsmith's *She Stoops to Conquer,* which he attributes particularly to its farcical elements.

Styan, J. L. "Goldsmith's Comic Skills" in *Costerus,* Vol. 9, 1973, pp. 195-217.

Styan situates Goldsmith's *She Stoops to Conquer* within the context of restoration and sentimental comedy, and analyzes the elements that contributes to the play's dramatic and comedic success. These elements include Goldsmith's manipulation of farce, absurdity, and exaggeration, and the creation of characters who must themselves act different parts (for example, Kate acts first as a dutiful daughter, then as a barmaid). Finally, Styan considers Goldsmith's development as a playwright, comparing the successful *She Stoops to Conquer* with the earlier, less successful *The Good-Natur'd Man.*

A Streetcar Named Desire

TENNESSEE WILLIAMS

1947

A Streetcar Named Desire is the story of an emotionally-charged confrontation between characters embodying the traditional values of the American South and the aggressive, rapidly-changing world of modern America. The play, begun in 1945, went through several changes before reaching its final form. Although the scenario initially concerned an Italian family, to which was later added an Irish brother-in-law, Tennessee Williams changed the characters to two Southern American belles and a Polish American man in order to emphasize the clash between cultures and classes in this story of alcoholism, madness and sexual violence.

A Streetcar Named Desire was staged in the United States in 1947 in Boston and New York. A film version appeared in 1951, directed by Elia Kazan. The play, first published in book form in 1947 (New York: New Directions), was issued again with an introduction by the author in 1951. In 1953 an edition for actors was brought out by the Dramatists' Play Service. In England, editions appeared in 1949 (London: John Lehman) and 1956 (Secker and Warburg). Penguin Books now incorporates *Streetcar* with two of Williams' other plays, *Sweet Bird of Youth* and *The Glass Menagerie,* in a volume of its Twentieth Century Classics Series.

AUTHOR BIOGRAPHY

Tennessee Williams was born Thomas Lanier Williams on March 26, 1914, in Columbus, Mississippi, the son of Cornelius Coffin Williams and Edwina Dakin. The nickname Tennessee was not acquired until he was grown and attending college. Williams had an elder sister, Rose, who was later committed to a mental institution, and a younger brother, Walter Dakin. Because their father often worked away from home, Williams and his siblings were particularly close to their mother, a Southern belle and daughter of an Episcopal minister who enjoyed her status as a pillar of town society.

In 1918 the Williams family moved to St Louis. As Cornelius began to drink heavily and became increasingly moody, Edwina voiced her resentment at losing both her place in society and her close ties with her parents. In response to this unhappiness, and to the emotional pain of being bullied by children in the neighborhood, Williams began to read books and write his own stories; years later, in the foreword to *Sweet Bird of Youth* he commented that writing was "an escape from a world of reality in which I felt acutely uncomfortable. It immediately became my place of retreat, my cave, my refuge."

Beginning in 1929 Williams studied at the University of Missouri at Columbia, at Washington University in St Louis, and at the University of Iowa, meanwhile making a name for himself as a writer. Although this period was a creative one, and one in which his personal life settled down (he seems to have come to terms with his homosexuality at this point), there were also difficult times to endure. In response to his sister Rose's extreme mental instability, Edwina Williams consented to having a pre-frontal lobotomy performed on Rose, from which the young woman emerged severely changed.

Williams' emergence as a major new force in American theater occurred with the debut performance of *The Glass Menagerie* in 1944. He soon moved to New Orleans, the city which later figured strongly in *A Streetcar Named Desire,* and spent time in Europe and in Florida, where he bought a house. *Cat on a Hot Tin Roof* was the playwright's next major commercial success in 1955 but by this time Williams' physical health was deteriorating and he was relying increasingly on alcohol and drugs. Numerous other plays followed, some of

them successful, but his personal life remained in turmoil. In fits of paranoia, he quarreled with his agent, Audrey Wood, and his lover Frank Merlo. In 1966 his brother Dakin was contacted when Williams' health was particularly poor, and during the time he spent with Dakin he converted to Roman Catholicism. In the following years several unsuccessful plays were written and performed, and several of his earlier, acclaimed plays were revived. In 1983, after a spell of depression, Williams traveled to Sicily, remaining only a few days before returning to New York, where he died during the night of February 24 in the Elysee Hotel after choking on a barbiturate.

PLOT SUMMARY

Scenes 1 and 2

The play opens in a shabby district of New Orleans where Stanley Kowalski lives with his wife Stella. After they leave for the bowling alley, where Stanley is to play with his friend Mitch, a well-dressed woman arrives carrying a suitcase. This is Blanche DuBois, Stella's sister. Hardly believing that this is Stella's home, Blanche ungraciously accepts the invitation of the landlady, Eunice, to wait inside. She appears nervous and highly strung and searches out a supply of alcohol, supposedly to calm her nerves. When Stella returns they greet each other fondly, but there is a hint of unease between them.

On his return home, Stanley meets Blanche and they talk amicably, but as the conversation develops and as details of Blanche's past come out—particularly her marriage to a husband who is now dead, and the loss of Belle Reve, the family's property—we see Stanley beginning to distrust her. Blanche makes herself very much at home, taking long and frequent baths and drinking Stanley's alcohol, even whilst making disparaging comments about Stanley and Stella's standard of living.

Scene 3

The tension in the house continues in the next scene when the sisters return after an evening out to the house where Stanley is holding a poker party. Resenting the interest that Mitch, one of his friends, shows in Blanche, the now drunken Stanley shows his jealousy of Blanche and becomes violent with

Stella, who we now know is pregnant. After retreating briefly upstairs to the Hubbells' apartment, Stella returns to Stanley and they go off to bed together.

Scene 4

Despite this brutality and Blanche's attempts to persuade her to leave him, Stella insists that she loves Stanley and will not leave him. Overhearing Blanche's hostile comments about him, Stanley determines to follow his suspicions about her and to find out more about her recent past. He discovers that she left Laurel, her home town, because of rumors about her promiscuity and her relationship with a young student.

Scene 5

When Stanley hints to Blanche about what he knows, she is clearly terrified that it will all come out and tries to present a glossed-over version to Stella, focusing on her fear of growing old alone and hinting at a possible future with Mitch. After Stella's departure, Blanche flirts with a young man who arrives to collect newspaper subscriptions.

Scene 6

Blanche and Mitch's date in the next scene is not a success, but when they return home they speak more openly and Blanche tells Mitch of her dead husband who, we gather, was homosexual, and shot himself when she discovered him in bed with another man. Mitch comforts her and they discuss marriage.

Scenes 7 and 8

Shortly afterwards there is a birthday dinner for Blanche, but Mitch, having been told by Stanley about Blanche's past, does not show up. The meal is awkwardly silent and, to make it worse, Stanley presents Blanche with a bus ticket back home as a supposed birthday gift. Stella complains at his cruelty, but then goes into labor. Stanley takes her to the hospital.

Scene 9

Mitch then visits Blanche, who is alone in the apartment. In a drunken state he tells her that he knows about her past and, when she tries to explain, dismisses her explanation as lies. He tries to force her to have sex but she resists and threatens to call

Tennessee Williams

for help. Left alone again, she drinks more alcohol and loses herself in delusions of a rich millionaire who will look after her.

Scene 10

Stanley returns from the hospital to find Blanche dressed up in a ball gown and tiara, trying to pack her suitcase. He mocks her, tells her what he thinks of her, and allows his anger to be transformed into sexual violence as he carries her off to bed to rape her.

Scene 11

A scene change denotes the passing of time at this point and we next see Stella, returned from the hospital, unwilling to believe her sister's story and in agreement with Stanley that Blanche should be certified as insane. Blanche packs her things, believing that she is to leave with a rich admirer. While she is taking another bath and Stanley and his friends are again playing poker, a doctor arrives with a nurse from a mental hospital. Realizing what is about to happen, Blanche tries to escape, but is calmed by the gentle doctor. She leaves on his arm, stating that she has always placed her trust in the kindness of strangers. Stanley's friends are horrified and Stella is almost hysterical with tears, but

Marlon Brando as Stanley (on stairs at left) in a Broadway production

Stanley remains calm and soothes his wife into acquiescence. Life, it is suggested, will continue.

CHARACTERS

Doctor

The Doctor's role is to escort Blanche to the mental hospital. He is calm, professional, and treats Blanche respectfully in order for her to trust him.

Blanche du Bois

Blanche DuBois is a complex individual who provokes strong reactions from the other characters. We know that she has been a schoolteacher in Mississippi but was asked to leave her job because of an involvement with a student, that she was once a Southern belle from a wealthy family, and that she has a failed marriage and dubious past from which she has fled. Her complexity comes not from her history or background, but from the varied and often inconsistent facades she presents. At once strong in her desires and determined in her claims on the men who are around her, and yet weak and forever looking for someone to take care of her, she gives

off a series of conflicting signals. She is neurotic, psychologically deluded about her beauty and attractiveness, and perhaps also an alcoholic. Her sexual desires come through clearly from behind her talk with Mitch about keeping her reputation: when we see her flirting with the young man who calls at the door, we realize just how split her desires are from her surface talk and behavior. This point is made visually in the opening scene where the dainty and beautifully dressed woman who appears leads us to expect quite a different character to emerge than the brittle woman running from her past who begins to display her neuroses and obsessions during the course of the following acts.

Underneath Blanche's quite calculating exterior, there is always a hint of hysteria. In her stories about Belle Reve or her tales of previous lovers, there is something edgy in her conversation, a threat of something that might erupt if she is not handled carefully. This disjunction between emotional surface and depth is brought out throughout the play in the way that Blanche cannot face up to her past, but only reveals glimpses of it through her neurotic behavior and occasional comments. For example, she is forever taking baths as if to clean her conscience, but continues to talk about her past actions in terms which suggest that she has no conception of

MEDIA ADAPTATIONS

- In addition to its successful run on Broadway, *A Streetcar Named Desire* was made into a film by Warner Bros. and was released in 1951. Many of its original cast were retained, including Marlon Brando as Stanley, but Jessica Tandy, who played Blanche, was replaced with Vivien Leigh. The film, directed by Elia Kazan, received numerous Academy Award nominations and carried off four Awards, including Best Actress for Leigh and Best Supporting Actress for Kim Hunter (Stella).

- A made-for-television version appeared in 1984 with Ann-Margret as Blanche. Although this production reinstated some of the material which the censors had objected to in the 1950s, critics found it lacking in the spark and chemistry of the earlier version.

- An unrated television version of 1995 recreated the 1992 stage version which stared Jessica Lange and Alec Baldwin. Again, it is truer to the dialogue and actions of the original stage production than the censored 1951 film.

- Two sound recordings are available: HarperCollins's 1991 version stars Rosemary Harris and James Farentino in a 1973 recording of a production at the Repertory Theater of Lincoln Center. Caedmon's 1985 publication is from the same production.

- The play was adapted by the Dance Theatre of Harlem featuring Virginia Johnson as Blanche.

---

their moral implications. Admitting, for example, that it is her affairs which have led to her losing her job and being ruined financially, she can only ask Stella, in a roundabout fashion, "Haven't you ever ridden on that streetcar [named Desire]? . . . It brought me here." In similarly oblique terms, she describes a passionate affair as "someone you go out with—once—twice—three times when the devil is in you." Her flirtation with Stanley and the man at the door also suggest that she does not have the self-awareness to realize that what she is doing here is no different from the things she has done in the past which she claims to regret so much.

Not only does Blanche lack self-awareness, she is also utterly self-centered. As a house-guest in a small apartment, her behavior is intensely irritating. (If David Mamet's play *Oleanna* could be described as a play about a man who needs an answering machine, *A Streetcar Named Desire* is a play about a man who needs a guest room.) Not only must Blanche's presence disrupt Stanley and Stella's sexual intimacy, but it also spoils the routine of their everyday life, particularly because she is al-

ways in the bath when anyone else needs to use the bathroom. The fact that she freely (and dishonestly) drinks Stanley's whisky and that she sends the pregnant Stella off to run errands for her further emphasizes a selfish nature.

Yet, despite her contradictions, dishonesty, inconsistency, and selfishness, Blanche comes across as a sympathetic, if not entirely likeable, character. Williams himself commented that ". . . when I think about her, Blanche seems like the youth of our hearts which has to be put away for worldly considerations: poetry, music, the early soft feelings that we can't afford to live with under a naked light bulb which is now." Even though her faults are plain to see, Blanche still commands pity. Williams thought that this pity was an important element of the play. In a letter to Elia Kazan, the first director of *Streetcar,* he answered a question which Kazan had put to him, saying, "I remember you asked me what should an audience feel for Blanche. Certainly pity. It is a tragedy with the classic aim of producing a catharsis of pity and terror and in order to do that, Blanche must finally have the understanding and compassion of the audience. This without creating a black-dyed villain in Stanley. It is a thing (Misunderstanding with a capital M) not a person (Stanley) that destroys her in the end. In the end you should feel 'If only they had known about each other.' Perhaps part of the reason for this pity is that Blanche's tragedy does not come about only because of her actions, but because of the flaws of society itself. As the old gentility of the South is threatened by modernization and industrialization, and as women's roles become uncertain as they are caught between old ideals of beauty and gentility and the modern toleration of sexual license, Blanche appears to be stranded at a crossroads, with each choice of path risking society's disapproval and her ultimate destruction.

Pablo Gonzales

Pablo Gonzales is the other player at poker along with Stanley, Mitch, and Steve. He is coarse and loud, a strong, physical character who is, according to the stage directions, ''at the peak of [his] physical manhood.'' He also speaks Spanish.

Eunice and Steve Hubbell

Eunice and Steve Hubbell, the landlords who live upstairs from Stanley and Stella, are a vision of what Stanley and Stella could become. Eunice is overweight and run down from too many pregnancies while Steve is not particularly understanding or supportive of his wife. Domestic violence appears to be routine in their marriage. Despite their failings, however, Steve and Eunice are not unlikeable characters. They are hospitable and neighborly and take Stella in when she seeks refuge from Stanley. Their audible presence upstairs gives a sense of the cramped living conditions in which the play's actions occur.

Stanley Kowalski

Much of Stanley's character is seen through his relationship with Blanche. Stanley does not seem to have a life outside of the immediate action of the play, but when he is onstage he has a commanding presence, a quality underlined by Blanche's obvious sexual attraction to him. She even jokingly tells Stella that she has been flirting with Stanley to get him to see her side of the story about the loss of Belle Reve. While this may be her motivation, it's obvious that Blanche is genuinely attracted to Stanley and that flirting does not take too much effort on her part.

Blanche's response to Stanley's strong presence suggests that he is some kind of an animal. In earlier versions of the play, Stanley had a gentler, ineffectual side, but in the final writing of *Streetcar* Williams made him Blanche's complete opposite—angry, animalistic, and reliant on his basest instincts. These qualities are seen most clearly in Blanche's rather patronizing, but highly revealing comment to Stanley that ''You're simple, straightforward and honest, a little bit on the primitive side I should think. To interest you a woman would have to . . .'' The sentence is finished off for her by Stanley, but what we suspect she would have said is what she later says to Stella: that the only way to live with a man like Stanley is to go to bed with him. For Blanche, Stanley's sexual appeal and his primitive nature are closely bound up together. It is from the charge of such opposing feelings as attraction and disgust, expressed in this case through Blanche's eyes, that the play gains much of its energy.

Although Stanley responds in kind to Blanche's flirtations, telling her that ''If I didn't know that you was my wife's sister I'd get ideas about you,'' we know that actually he despises her and is enjoying the power that comes from being aware of the feelings she has for him. Stanley's actions are what would now be described as ''macho.'' But not only is he violent in his masculinity, he also appears to lack any sense of moral order: his rape of Blanche does not strike him as betraying any moral code, it is simply the outcome of their strained relationship and what he deems to be her inappropriate behavior in the immediate and more distant past.

This action is consistent with his character in the rest of the play and in the events which are meant to have taken place before the play begins. Stanley has power despite his lower social class, but, as he is well aware, it lies in his physical actions. Talking of his wooing of Stella and the difference in their social backgrounds, he comments, ''I pulled you down off them columns and you loved it.'' The social significance of his physical action, like his later rape of Blanche, suggests that the sources of power have changed in American culture and that Stanley is willing to grasp at whatever power he can find in order to assert his place in the family and society around him.

Where Stanley does have an identity independent from that created by the events of the play, he could be said to represent the new social order of modern America as a contrast to the decayed gentility of Blanche's Southern manners. This is also seen in the fact that Williams makes him an immigrant who is proud to be part of the new society of a multi-cultural America. As such an immigrant, he is not concerned about traditions or old hierarchies of land ownership or the power and wealth brought by family positions in society (he appeals instead to the local law of the Napoleonic code to prove that he has been swindled by Blanche's loss of Belle Reve). Stanley's determination to belong to American society and to claim his place there is emphasized by his impassioned outburst in response to being called a ''Polack.'' As he forcefully explains, ''I am not a Polack. People from Poland are Poles, not Polacks. But what I am is one hundred percent American . . . so don't ever call me a Polack.''

Stella Kowalski

Stella appears to be a simple character, but is actually more intriguing than her role as sister and wife to the play's two main protagonists would suggest. She acts as a foil to both characters, allowing their selfishness and emotional failings to be emphasized. She also acts as a measuring stick against which the audience can gauge society's reaction to the events portrayed on stage.

In relation to Stanley, Stella is sensitive and loving, practical and sometimes independent. She clearly loves Stanley, despite his many failings and his violence towards her, and she is willing to accept his temper as part of the passion they feel for each other: ''But there are things that happen between a man and a woman in the dark—that sort of make everything else seem—unimportant.'' She is carrying Stanley's baby, and indeed Stanley's rape of Blanche takes place while she is in the hospital giving birth. In her blinkered loyalty to Stanley at the end of the play and in her willingness to be reassured that what they have done for Blanche is right, her practical nature asserts itself: this is a marriage which she can convince herself she wants to save and will save for the benefit of herself and her child. Whether she is right or wrong to do this is not relevant: what is important to understanding the play is the knowledge that her action is not so unusual. Like many other people in society, Stella continues to function in her daily life despite considerable upheaval. Blanche draws attention to this stoical aspect of Stella's character when she comments, ''I never had your beautiful self-control.''

Stella's decision symbolizes a greater choice facing American society. She rejects Blanche's strategy of living in a glamorous past and chooses instead the rational, practical, sometimes flawed world which her marriage to Stanley represents.

Mexican woman

The Mexican woman appears briefly, speaks only Spanish, and is described as ''An old Mexican crone.''

Mitch

See Harold Mitchell

Harold Mitchell

Mitch is ''207 pounds, six feet one and one-half inches'' and lives with his sick mother. He is a foil to Stanley: he speaks in a more refined way, he is gentle and restrained while Stanley is rude and sexually forward. Blanche is aware of his kindness and even comments on it, saying, ''I thanked God for you, because you seemed to be gentle.'' Mitch is concerned with proper behavior: in contrast to Stanley, who walks around in his T-shirt and speaks frankly (even proudly) of his sweaty body, Mitch refuses to take his jacket off because he fears he might be perspiring too much.

Mitch's attempted rape of Blanche therefore comes as a shock. The action suggests how male views of female behavior were so idealized that if a man discovered any deviation from accepted norms of virginity and chastity, his reaction would be extreme. Mitch's actions reveal him as a deluded and rather pathetic man who has not fully grasped how relationships work and who has closed his eyes to the fact that men and women can deceive one another.

It is, of course, Mitch's assault on Blanche which leaves her in such a genuinely forlorn state that she becomes vulnerable to Stanley's cruelty and unwanted sexual advances in the later scene. Although Mitch may be upstaged by his more powerful friend, his actions bring about the destructive ending of the play.

Negro woman

The Negro woman is a neighbor whose presence at the opening of the play reminds the audience of the cosmopolitan society in New Orleans. She is vulgar in her conversation, fun-loving and good-humored.

Nurse

The Nurse who accompanies the Doctor is cold and professional, severely dressed, and speaks in a voice which is "bold and toneless as a fire-bell."

Young collector

The Young Collector calls to collect newspaper subscriptions. He is polite, reserved, and surprised by Blanche's unexpected sexual advances.

THEMES

A Streetcar Named Desire opens with the arrival of Blanche DuBois, a Southern belle who has lost her inheritance, at the New Orleans home of her sister Stella and Stella's husband Stanley. A conflict arises between Stanley and Blanche, and after several secrets about her past have been revealed, Stanley rapes Blanche while his wife is in the hospital giving birth. Stella, refusing to believe Blanche's accusations, gives consent for the increasingly hysterical Blanche to be placed in a mental hospital.

Class Conflict

A major theme explored symbolically in *Streetcar* is the decline of the aristocratic family traditionally associated with the American South. These families had lost their historical importance as the agricultural base of the Southern states were unable to compete with the new industrialization. A labor shortage of agricultural workers developed in the South during the First World War because so many of the area's men had to be employed either in the military or in defense-based industries. Many landowners, faced with large areas of land and no one to work on it, moved to urban areas. With the increasing industrialization which followed in the 1920s through the 1940s, the structure of the work force changed further: more women, immigrants, and black laborers entered the workforce and a growing urban middle class was created. Women gained the right to vote in 1920 and the old Southern tradition of an agrarian family aristocracy ruled by men began to come to an end.

In the context of this economic and cultural environment, Blanche represents the female aristocratic tradition of the Old South. Belle Reve, her family home, is typical of the plantations that were being sold off as the aristocracy bowed out to the new urbanization. Blanche's ultimate fate can be interpreted as the destruction of the Old South by the new, industrial America, represented by an immigrant to the U.S., Stanley Kowalski. Referring to his courtship of Stella, Stanley revealingly observes that, "When we first met, me and you, you thought I was common. How right you was, baby. I was common as dirt. You showed me the snapshot of the place with the columns [Belle Reve]. I pulled you down off them columns and how you loved it." By the end of the play, Stanley's aggression has triumphed over Blanche's inherited family superiority. As she departs for the mental hospital, her old-fashioned manners are still apparent when she says to the men, "Please don't get up." Their politeness in rising is a small gesture, however, considering their role in Blanche's destruction and in the fall of the Old South itself.

Sex Roles

Some of Blanche's difficulties can be traced to the narrow roles open to females during this period. Although she is an educated woman who has worked as a teacher, Blanche is nonetheless constrained by the expectations of Southern society. She knows that she needs men to lean on and to protect her, and she continues to depend on them throughout the play, right up to her conversation with the doctor from the mental hospital, where she remarks, "Whoever you are, I have always depended on the kindness of strangers." She has clearly known sexual freedom in the past, but understands that sexual freedom does not fit the pattern of chaste behavior to which a Southern woman would be expected to conform. Her fear of rejection is realized when Mitch learns of her love affairs back home. By rejecting Blanche and claiming that she is not the ideal woman he naively thought she was, Mitch draws attention to the discrepancy between how women really behaved and what type of behavior was publicly expected of them by society at large.

Violence and Cruelty

Violence in this play is fraught with sexual passion. Trying to convince Blanche of her love for Stanley despite his occasional brutality, Stella explains, "But there are things that happen between a man and a woman in the dark—that sort of make everything else seem—unimportant." Eunice and Steve Hubbell's relationship also has this element of violence, and there is the unnerving suggestion that violence is more common and more willingly accepted by the female partner in a marriage than one would like to believe.

Blanche translates Stella's comment into the context of sexual passion, claiming that, '' What you are talking about is brutal desire—just—Desire!—the name of that rattle-trap street-car that bangs through the Quarter, up one old narrow street and down another.'' Stella asks, ''Haven't you ever ridden on that street-car?'' and Blanche responds, ''It brought me here.—Where I'm not wanted and where I'm ashamed to be.'' It appears that the connection in Blanche's past between violence and desire in some way contributes to the events within the time scale of the play. This is not to excuse Stanley's later act of violence or to suggest that Blanche brings it on herself—rather, Williams is demonstrating how a cycle of violence, combined with passion and desire, is hard to break.

Madness

Considering how Tennessee Williams' sister Rose was the recipient of a lobotomy, the theme of madness running through *Streetcar* in the form of Blanche's neurosis and self-delusion may reveal some of the playwright's fears about the instability of his own mental life. His lingering regrets and guilt about Rose's treatment may also be seen in Stella's anguished cry as Blanche is taken away: ''What have I done to my sister? Oh, God, what have I done to my sister?''

STYLE

Scene Structure

The most striking feature of *Streetcar's* dramatic structure is its division into scenes rather than acts. Each of the eleven scenes that make up the play ends in a dramatic climax, and the tension of each individual scene builds up to the tension of the final climax. This structure allows the audience to focus on the emotions and actions of Blanche—the only character to appear in every scene. The audience is sympathetic to Blanche because they see more of her inner thoughts and motivations than the other characters on stage. Note, for example, how only the audience is aware of how much alcohol she is drinking. The scene organization adds to the audience's sense of tragedy—Blanche's destruction

TOPICS FOR FURTHER STUDY

- Investigate the emergence of industrialization and the decline of the old Southern aristocracy in the USA and analyze what bearing this has on *A Streetcar Named Desire*.

- With whom does the audience's sympathy lie in *A Streetcar Named Desire*?: Blanche? Stanley? Both? Neither?

- Discuss the importance of New Orleans—its geography, its transport system, its laws, its music and culture—as a setting for *A Streetcar Named Desire*.

- Examine the scene structure of *A Streetcar Named Desire*, paying particular attention to the beginnings and endings of scenes and the dramatic climaxes that they create.

is inevitable, signaling the inexorable passage of the drama and of her movement towards a final breakdown.

That Williams chose to organize his play this way may reveal his interest in film and the possibilities inherent in that medium for combining several visually dramatic incidents into a coherent experience. He also wrote a number of one-act plays during his career.

Motifs

In order to connect the separate incidents of Blanche's story, Williams provided dramatic motifs and details of setting which are repeated at significant moments during the play and which signal changes in mood and tone and highlight the reemergence of crucial themes.

As the title of the play suggests, the motif of the streetcar is a crucial one, pointing to the growth of the suburbs and the urbanization of the play as well as the unrelenting and unforgiving continuation of life itself. To arrive at Stella's apartment in New Orleans, Blanche must transfer from a streetcar called Desire to one called Cemeteries in order to get to the slum known as Elysian Fields. These were actual New Orleans names but their careful combination introduces the themes of death and desire that resonate through the play. Williams wrote that the streetcars' ''indiscourageable progress up and down Royal Street struck me as having some symbolic bearing of a broad nature on the life in the Vieux Carre,—and everywhere else, for that matter.'' An element of the play which is always heard rather than seen, the streetcar nonetheless adds much to the mood of the play and is a continual but subtle reminder of the play's setting.

Music

Music plays a similarly important part in the stage craft of the play. Two kinds of music dominate: the first type is what Williams called ''blue piano''—the blues music first associated with Southern Blacks. Later to develop into the music of New Orleans' bars and night clubs, it suggests unrestrained physical pleasure, animal strength and vitality and appears at significant emotional moments in the play—for example, when Blanche tells of the loss of Belle Reve and when she hears about Stella's pregnancy. It is also heard during moments of leisure, when people are drinking and having fun. But, in a darker mood, it appears at the moment of the rape in scene ten, signifying animal desires, and again at the very end of the play when Stanley is consoling Stella and enabling her to forget about Blanche.

In contrast to the recurring blue piano, which highlights the animal emotions of some characters, the polka known as the Varsouviana, heard only by Blanche, signals crucial moments in the development of the plot. Once the audience discovers that this music reminds Blanche of the scene on the ballroom floor when she renounced her husband, one anticipates imminent disaster whenever the music appears and reappears—particularly in the last scene of the play. It also accompanies moments of cruelty, like Stanley's gift to Blanche of a bus-ticket back home.

Both kinds of music underline the nature of the situation which is being played out on stage and stress the location of the play's actions both in the past lives of its characters and in the cultural context of New Orleans.

The dramatic organization of the play into scenes which build, through recurring themes and motifs, on the ongoing tension of the play suggest the accuracy of Arthur Miller's description of Williams' ''rhapsodic insistence that form serve his utterance rather than dominating and cramping it.''

HISTORICAL CONTEXT

Many of the major themes of *A Streetcar Named Desire* are embodied in the history and culture of New Orleans. The lively setting of the French Quarter, with its streetcars, bars, entertainment, and jazz and blues music, provides a rich background for the emotional events of the play; the setting also draws symbolic attention to changes which were taking place in American society, especially in the South during the post-World war II years.

Napoleonic Code

When Stanley feels he is being swindled by Blanche's loss of Belle Reve, he appeals to the Napoleonic Code, a set of laws devised by the French and implemented when they ruled the region known now as Louisiana. The state of Louisiana continued to operate under some of the precepts of the Napoleonic Code, such as the Code's emphasis on inheritance law: any property belonging to a spouse prior to marriage becomes the property of both spouses once they are married. Stanley, therefore, is legally correct to claim that, by depriving Stella of her share of the family inheritance, Blanche has also deprived him.

The South

On a more general level, the play represents the decline of the aristocratic families traditionally associated with the South. These once-influential families had lost their historical importance when the South's agricultural base was unable to compete with the new industrialization. The region's agrarian economy, which had been in decline since the Confederate defeat in the Civil War, suffered further setbacks after the First World War. A labor shortage hindered Southern agriculture when large numbers of male laborers were absorbed by the military or defense-based industries. Many landowners, faced with large areas of land and no one to work on it, moved to urban areas. With the increasing industrialization that followed during the 1920s

COMPARE & CONTRAST

- **1947:** Hungary becomes a Soviet satellite after Hungarian Communists, backed by the Red Army, seize power while Prime Minister Ferenc Nagy is on holiday. Anti-Communist sentiment builds in the U.S. The Truman Doctrine announces plans to aid Greece and Turkey and proposes economic aid to countries threatened by Communist takeover. The CIA is authorized by Congress to counter Moscow's attempts to establish governments through local Communist parties in Western Europe.

   Today: Communism has all but broken down since the collapse of the Berlin Wall. Revolutions in Czechoslovakia, Poland, and East Germany, as well as the break-up of the Soviet Union have eliminated many of the barriers between East and West. Eastern European countries are now undergoing a slow and difficult transformation to a market economy.

- **1947:** New technology: the first commercial microwave oven is introduced by the Raytheon Co. of Waltham, Massachusetts. Tubeless automobile tires, which seal themselves when punctured, are introduced by B.F. Goodrich. Howard Hughes' new seaplane, the Spruce Goose, the largest plane ever built, takes off for a one-mile flight across Long Beach Harbor before it is retired for good.

   Today: Most American homes have a microwave, as well as toasters, coffee makers, freezers, and numerous other examples of electrical gadgetry. Cars are commonplace but their emissions, along with those from airplanes and heavy industry, contribute to the global problem of pollution.

- **1947:** New consumable goods appear as America begins to recover from the effects of the Second World War. Frozen orange juice concentrate sales in the U.S. reach seven million cans. Reddi-Whip introduces whipped cream in aerosol cans. Sugar rationing ends on June 11. Monosodium glutamate (MSG) is marketed for the first time, and butylated hydroxyanisole (BHA) is introduced commercially to retard spoilage in foods.

   Today: Annual sales of convenience food reach new heights every year. Processed and "fast" food is readily available to Americans; consumers who maintain unhealthy diets and sedentary lifestyles significantly increase their risk of contracting heart disease and cancer. Additives are common in food and new developments, such as genetically engineered foods, continue to make headlines.

---

through the 1940s, the structure of the work force evolved more radically yet, incorporating large numbers of women, immigrants, and blacks. Women gained the right to vote in 1920 and the old Southern tradition of an agrarian family aristocracy ruled by men started to come to an end.

Women's Roles

Some of Blanche's difficulties can be traced to the narrow roles open to females during this period Although she is an educated woman who has worked as a teacher, Blanche is nonetheless constrained by the expectations of Southern society. She knows that she needs men to lean on and to protect her. She has clearly known sexual freedom in the past, but understands that sexual freedom does not fit the pattern of chaste behavior to which a Southern woman would be expected to conform. Her fear of rejection is realized when Mitch learns of her love affairs back home. By rejecting Blanche and claiming that she is not the ideal woman he naively thought she was, Mitch draws attention to the discrepancy between how women really behaved and what type of behavior was publicly expected of them by society at large.

Writing of the play's setting, Williams noted that "I write out of love of the South ... (which) once had a way of life that I am just old enough to remember—a culture that had grace, elegance, an inbred culture, not a society based on money." Through the destruction of Blanche and her struggles with the contradictory demands of society, Williams expressed a lament for the destruction of the old South, making clear his understanding that such change was inevitable.

CRITICAL OVERVIEW

A Streetcar Named Desire premiered in Boston and Philadelphia, then in New York on December 4, 1947, to almost unanimously laudatory reviews. The New Yorker described Streetcar as "deeply disturbing—a brilliant, implacable play about the disintegration of a woman, or, if you like, of a society."

Streetcar was highly praised by its first director, Elia Kazan, who, from his knowledge of Williams' character, was one of the first to point out psychological similarities between Williams and Blanche. Kazan noted that "I keep linking Blanche and Tennessee ... Blanche is attracted by the man who is going to destroy her. ... I also noticed that at the end of the play—all was an author's essential statement—Stella, having witnessed her sister's being destroyed by her husband, then taken away to an institution with her mind split, felt grief and remorse but not an enduring alienation from her husband. ... The implication at the end of the play is that Stella will very soon return to Stanley's arms—and to his bed. That night, in fact. Indifference? Callousness? No. Fidelity to life. Williams' goal. We go on with life, he was saying, the best we can. People get hurt, but you can't get through life without hurting people."

Other critics were not always so appreciative or understanding. The distinguished American critic Mary McCarthy summarized Blanche with considerably less sympathy, remarking that in her character Williams had "caught a flickering glimpse of the faded essence of the sister-in-law: thin, vapid, neurasthenic, romancing, genteel, pathetic ... a refined pushover and perennial and frigid spinster." McCarthy criticized Williams' for crafting Blanche's character with the trappings of "inconceivable" tragedy and melodrama, commenting that the playwright's work "reeks of literary ambition as the

apartment reeks of cheap perfume: it is impossible to witness one of Mr. Williams' plays without being aware of the pervading smell of careerism."

Audiences clearly disagreed: Streetcar ran for eight hundred and fifty performances on Broadway. It also won the Pulitzer Prize, the Drama Critics' Circle Award and the Donaldson Award.

The 1951 film adaptation won the New York Critics' Film Award and several Academy Awards.

CRITICISM

Joanne Woolway

Woolway is an author, editor, and educator affiliated with Oriel College, Oxford, England. Her essay examines Williams's themes of sex and violence, as well as the way in which the two are linked.

Violence in A Streetcar Named Desire is fraught with sexual passion. Trying to convince Blanche of her love for Stanley despite his occasional brutality, Stella explains, "But there are things that happen between a man and a woman in the dark—that sort of make everything else seem—unimportant." Eunice and Steve Hubbell's relationship also has this element of violence, and there is an unnerving suggestion that violence is more common and more willingly accepted by the female partner in a marriage than one would like to believe.

Blanche translates Stella's comment into the context of sexual passion, claiming that, "What you are talking about is brutal desire—just—Desire!— the name of that rattle-trap street-car that bangs through the Quarter, up one old narrow street and down another." Stella asks, "Haven't you ever ridden on that street-car?" and Blanche responds, "It brought me here.—Where I'm not wanted and where I'm ashamed to be." It appears that the connection in Blanche's past between violence and desire in some way contributes to the events within the time scale of the play. This is not to excuse Stanley's later act of violence or to suggest that Blanche brings it on herself—rather, Williams is demonstrating how a cycle of violence, combined with passion and desire, is hard to break.

The attraction between Blanche and Stanley gains an interesting perspective when compared to a work of classical literature by the Latin poet Ovid. In *Metamorphoses,* Philomela is raped by her broth-

WHAT DO I READ NEXT?

- Stanley Clisby Arthur's *Old New Orleans* (Gretna, La.: Pelican, 1990) provides an insightful picture into the setting of Williams' play and a view of the American South in the first half of the twentieth century.

- Williams' earlier play, *The Glass Menagerie* (1944), also portrays a Southern belle, Amanda Wingfield, who represents the playwright's ambiguous feelings about his mother's pretensions, possessiveness, and insensitivity. She also shares some similarities with Blanche Du Bois.

- The memoir of Williams' mother, *Remember Me to Tom* (New York: G.P. Putnam's Sons, 1964),

provides insight into the relationship between mother and son. This account was ghost-written by Lucy Freeman.

- Margaret Mitchell's 1936 bestseller, *Gone With the Wind*, is set in the antebellum era in the American South on through the aftermath of the Civil War. Depicting the porticoed mansions of Southern planters, the suffering of black slaves, and the unspoiled glamour of Southern belles, this novel (and the more famous film, which, like *Streetcar*, starred Vivien Leigh) was one of the last popular works to idealize the South.

---

er-in-law Tereus while visiting her sister Procne. He cuts out her tongue so that she cannot tell what he has done. Philomela, however, embroiders a story picture to convey to her sister the recent events and Procne, in revenge, kills their son and serves him up in a pie which she encourages Tereus to eat.

Similarly, in *A Streetcar Named Desire,* Stanley assaults his sister-in-law while his wife is away (in this case giving birth to their baby). But there are two substantial differences in the events which build up to the story's climax.

First, in Ovid's story there is no suggestion that Philomela associates sex with violence. There is no history of her previous lovers or any attraction between her and Tereus. In Williams's play, however, the issue of rape is confused because of Blanche's previous attraction for Stanley as well as her promiscuous past.

In a rape trial today, evidence of a woman's past sexual behavior would be discounted. If force was used by a man during sex, he has committed rape regardless of how the woman behaved in previous encounters. Williams was aware that many Americans did not always sympathize with the victim—it was all too easy to condemn women for their "loose" behavior and claim that female vic-

tims of rape brought sexual violence upon themselves. An indication of the chauvinism that still thrived during the 1940s can be found in the reviews by certain critics who covered the premiere of *Streetcar;* they interpreted Blanche's fate as the punishment for a fallen woman.

The issue is further complicated by Blanche's complex psyche. When talking about the combination of passion and violence in love, she appears strangely fascinated and not entirely repulsed by the thought. Speaking elliptically of the sexual arousal which violence can bring, Blanche comments, "Of course there is such a thing as the hostility of—perhaps in some perverse kind of way he—No! To think of it makes me. . . ." Violence is a phenomenon Blanche knows to be bound up with sex, even if she chooses to appear to Mitch as sexually naive.

A second important difference from Ovid's story is that Blanche's sister does not believe her story and, consequently, gives her no support. Whereas Procne concocts revenge on her unfaithful and violent husband, Stella is actually part of Blanche's downfall, supporting Stanley's cruel act of placing her in a mental institution. Not only is Stanley powerful, he is not checked in any way by the family structure that should provide some protec-

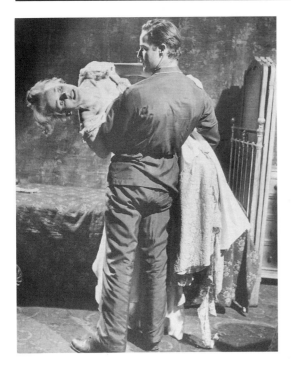

Marlon Brando and Jessica Tandy in the Broadway production

tion and support for Blanche. In this case, blood is most definitely not thicker than water.

Given that these two changes in focus appear to be deliberate, *Streetcar* paints a grim picture for women. Females in the play accept and perhaps even welcome sexual violence as part of life, and their family structures offer little protection from the predators.

Of course, there is more to it than that. It could be argued that *Streetcar* is only superficially about the roles and positions of women in society. Elia Kazan, *Streetcar*'s first director, commented on the issues which hover beneath the play's surface: "I keep linking Blanche and Tennessee . . . Blanche is attracted by the man who is going to destroy her. I understand the play by this formula of ambivalence. Only then, it seemed to me, would I think of it as Tennessee meant it to be understood: with fidelity to life as he—not us groundlings, that he—had experienced it. The reference to the kind of life Tennessee was leading at the time was clear. Williams was aware of the dangers he was inviting when he cruised; he knew that sooner or later he'd be beaten up. And he was. Still, I felt even this promise of violence exhilarated him."

While Blanche is often compared to Williams himself, Stanley-according to Williams's biographers-is based heavily on the playwright's brutal father, who taunted Williams about his effeminacy when he was a boy. In this light, the central issue in *Streetcar* is not necessarily violence towards women, but Williams's personal experience of brutality and the self-destructive enjoyment of fear which came out in the homosexual promiscuity he practiced as an adult.

Streetcar can be seen as an attempt to work through the purgatory of this fear and self-destruction. In addition to Ovid's *Metamorphoses, Streetcar* has referenced other classical models of literature. It is from Virgil's *Aeneid* that Williams took the name of the slum in New Orleans, "Elysian Fields": in Virgil's poem this is the place where the dead were made to drink water from the river Lethe to forget all traces of their mortal past. Both Blanche's drinking and her endless hot baths suggest that she is attempting to wash away her past and emerge through a sort of watery purgatory. She is not successful and the playgoer is left with little hope for Blanche's future. Through Blanche's bleakness and hopelessness, Williams expressed his own struggles with depression, moments of mental illness, and the alcohol and drugs that finally cost him his life.

Williams also offered a clue to the desolation and loneliness he felt in his often anonymous homosexual life in the play's epigram: "And so it was I entered the broken world / To trace the visionary company of love, its voice / An instant in the wind [I know not whither hurled] / But not for long to hold each desperate choice." The lines are from "The Broken Tower," by the poet Hart Crane who lived from 1899 to 1932. Like Williams he was homosexual and much of his poetry conveys a sense of isolation and failure. This is one of the last poems Crane wrote before committing suicide by jumping off the ship he was traveling on. He, presumably, was buried at sea, just as Blanche wished to be. The epigram is appropriate for a tragic play that tells the story of a woman's destruction at the hands of a cruel society.

Source: Joanne Woolway, in an essay for *Drama for Students,* Gale 1997

John J. Mood

A contributor to numerous journals, Mood served as an English professor at Ball State University. In this excerpt, he examines the symbolic nature of Blanche DuBois's entrance dialogue in A Streetcar Named Desire.

One of the most provocative entrance speeches in drama is the well-known enigmatic statement by Blanche DuBois, the second of Williams' numerous compelling women, in *A Streetcar Named Desire:*

> BLANCHE [*with faintly hysterical humor*]: They told me to take a streetcar named Desire, and then transfer to one called Cemeteries and ride six blocks and then get off at—Elysian Fields!

These words have often been noted and discussed for both their realistic and symbolic significance. They have never been examined, however, as a clue to the structural development and design of the play itself and of the course of the life and fate of Blanche as portrayed in the drama.

The statement can be seen as having two parts, the first of which (''take a street-car named Desire, and then transfer to one called Cemeteries'') deals with the events of Blanche's life before the play opens, and the second of which (''ride six blocks and then get off at—Elysian Fields'') deals with the play itself.

During the course of the play, the audience learns the story of Blanche's life prior to the time of the drama. What is vividly unfolded to us is that Blanche had taken the streetcar named Desire, and had transferred to the one called Cemeteries. We learn of Blanche's youthful loving desire for Allan Grey, her young husband. It was indeed a loving desire, and Blanche was one who could love greatly:

> When I was sixteen, I made the discovery— love. All at once and much, much too completely. It was like you suddenly turned a blinding light on something that had always been half in shadow, that's how it struck the world for me (*A Streetcar Named Desire,* New American Library, 1963).

This was loving desire, the same loving desire that Stella has for Stanley—not that ''brutal desire'' of which Blanche speaks. This is the loving sensual desire which leads not to death but to life and wisdom. It is that loving desire, that Eros, which, as Blanche sees, lights up the world.

But her discovery of her young husband's homosexuality and her shocked brutal words to him [''I saw! I know! You disgust me. . . .''] which result in his suicide—this traumatic event twists Blanche's loving desire into hate and self-loathing.

> " BLANCHE DIMLY REALIZES THAT SHE IS DEAD, THAT SHE IS STILL ON THE STREETCAR CALLED CEMETERIES, THAT SHE HAS MISSED THE STOP AT ELYSIAN FIELDS"

And disgust and self-hate result in her life of destructive lust for young men. Thus her loving desire becomes brutal desire, unloving desire. It becomes that sheer lust which is a kind of real death. Blanche, in short, has transferred to the streetcar named Cemeteries. She is psychically dead, and cannot stand the light [''The dark is comforting to me.''].

At that point in Blanche's life, the play begins. And ''Cemeteries'' takes on a subtly different meaning. Death can bring heaven or hell. Blanche can ''ride six blocks and then get off at—Elysian Fields!'' She can continue her course on the streetcar called Cemeteries toward the final death—or obtain heavenly bliss. And the latter will take *six blocks.* Another play by Williams, *Camino Real,* has no act divisions, only sixteen scenes (just as *Streetcar* has no acts, only eleven scenes. Blanche and Mitch have a moment of tenderness at the end of their first date. In response to this kindness, Blanche confesses to Mitch (and to the audience) the ugly story of how she destroyed her young husband. It is a remarkable moment of striking honesty. This moment of honesty elicits further kindness and even the beginning of love from Mitch: ''You need somebody. And I need somebody, too. Could it be—you and me, Blanche?'' And Blanche, ''*in long, grateful sobs*'' replies: ''Sometimes—there's God—so quickly!''

Thus, at the end of the sixth scene, the sixth block on her ride of death, Blanche indeed is on the threshold of finding ''God,'' ''Elysian Fields,'' loving desire. At that point, she has life within her grasp. It is the turning point of the play. But the opportunity passes. The very next scene quickly demonstrates that Blanche has resumed her illusions and games with Mitch, and thus her chance for life is lost. The final scenes portray this with an appalling inexorability. Had the incipient honesty

"TENNESSEE WILLIAMS HAS BROUGHT US A SUPERB DRAMA, *A STREETCAR NAMED DESIRE*"

and loving desire between Blanche and Mitch been nurtured with further openness and vulnerability, Stanley would never have raped her.

Near the end of the play, this fate is made explicit, The Mexican Woman appears, chanting her wares: "Flores? Flores para los muertes?" (Flowers? Flowers for the dead?) Blanche dimly realizes that she is dead, that she is still on the streetcar called Cemeteries, that she has missed the stop at Elysian Fields, that she is doomed to sterile dead lust, when, in a kind of real recognition, she observes in response to the old woman: "Death—. . . . The opposite is desire." She has dimly realized that desire *is* the opposite of death, that the desire which is the opposite of death is open, honest, forgiving, loving desire, the kind Stanley and Stella have for each other.

The most that Blanche can expect now is "Kindness." All that remains for her is her final tragic collapse.

Source: John J. Mood, "The Structure of *A Streetcar Named Desire*" in *Ball State University Forum,* Vol. 14, no. 3, Summer, 1973, pp. 9–10.

Brooks Atkinson

First published on December 4, 1947, this laudatory review by Atkinson appraises the play's debut and labels Williams's work as a "superb drama."

Tennessee Williams has brought us a superb drama, *A Streetcar Named Desire,* which was acted at the Ethel Barrymore last evening. And Jessica Tandy gives a superb performance as rueful heroine whose misery Mr. Williams is tenderly recording. This must be one of the most perfect marriages of acting and playwriting. For the acting and playwriting are perfectly blended in a limpid performance, and it is impossible to tell where Miss Tandy begins to give form and warmth to the mood Mr. Williams has created.

Like *The Glass Menagerie,* the new play is a quietly woven study of intangibles. But to this observer it shows deeper insight and represents a great step forward toward clarity. And it reveals Mr. Williams as a genuinely poetic playwright whose knowledge of people is honest and thorough and whose sympathy is profoundly human.

A Streetcar Named Desire is history of a gently reared Mississippi young woman who invents an artificial world to mask the hideousness of the world she has to inhabit. She comes to live with her sister, who is married to a rough-and-ready mechanic and inhabits two dreary rooms in a squalid neighborhood. Blanche—for that is her name—has delusions of grandeur, talks like an intellectual snob, buoys herself up with gaudy dreams, spends most of her time primping, covers things that are dingy with things that are bright and flees reality.

To her brother-in-law she is an unforgivable liar. But it is soon apparent to the theatregoer that in Mr. Williams' eyes she is one of the dispossessed whose experience has unfitted her for reality; and although his attitude toward her is merciful, he does not spare her or the playgoer. For the events of *Streetcar* lead to a painful conclusion which he does not try to avoid. Although Blanche cannot face the truth, Mr. Williams does in the most imaginative and perceptive play be has written.

Since he is no literal dramatist and writes in none of the conventional forms, he presents the theatre with many problems. Under Elia Kazan's sensitive but concrete direction, the theatre has solved them admirably. Jo Mielziner has provided a beautifully lighted single setting that lightly sketches the house and the neighborhood. In this shadowy environment the performance is a work of great beauty.

Miss Tandy has a remarkably long part to play. She is hardly ever off the stage, and when she is on stage she is almost constantly talking — chattering, dreaming aloud, wondering, building enchantments out of words. Miss Tandy is a trim, agile actress with a lovely voice and quick intelligence. Her performance is almost incredibly true. For it does seem almost incredible that she could understand such an elusive part so thoroughly and that she can convey it with so many shades and impulses that are accurate, revealing and true.

The rest of the acting is also of very high quality indeed. Marlon Brando as the quick-tempered, scornful, violent mechanic; Karl Malden as a stupid but wondering suitor; Kim Hunter as the patient though troubled sister—all act not only with color and style but with insight.

By the usual Broadway standards, *A Streetcar Named Desire* is too long; not all those Words are essential. But Mr. Williams is entitled to his own independence. For he has not forgotten that human beings are the basic subject of art. Out of poetic imagination and ordinary compassion he has spun a poignant and luminous story.

Source: Brooks Atkinson, in a review of *A Streetcar Named Desire* (1947) in *On Stage: Selected Theater Reviews from the New York Times, 1920–1970,* edited by Bernard Beckerman and Howard Siegman, Arno Press, 1973, pp. 286–87.

FURTHER READING

Arthur, Stanley Clisby. *Old New Orleans.* Gretna, La.: Pelican, 1990.
A historical exploration of New Orleans that provides background to *Streetcar's* setting.

Bloom, Harold, ed. *Tennessee Williams.* New York: Chelsea House, 1987.
A collection of critical essays contextualizing Williams' work with that of other modern writers, drawing out psychological similarities between Williams, Hart Crane, and Arthur Rimbaud.

Falki, Signi. *Tennessee Williams.* New York: Twayne, 1961.
An intelligent discussion of Williams' life and works in which the plays are organized into thematic groups and attention is drawn to recurring character types.

Hayman, Ronald. *Tennessee Williams: Everyone Else is an Audience.* New York: Yale University Press, 1993.
A biography which includes many quotations from Williams and opinions from his friends.

McCann, John S. *The Critical Reputation of Tennessee Williams.* Boston: G.K.Hall, 1983.
Charts Williams' reception among the important critics and writers of this century

Spoto, Donald. *The Kindness of Strangers: The Life of Tennessee Williams.* Boston: Little, Brown, 1985.
A literary biography beginning with Williams' parents and moving through the playwright's life, his theatrical encounters, life in the homosexual and drug culture of Florida, and his death. With bibliographical sources for further study.

Stanton, Stephen, ed. *Tennessee Williams: A Collection of Critical Essays.* Englewood Cliffs, NJ: Prentice-Hall, 1977.
A varied discussion of the major themes in Williams' work.

Tharpe, Jac, ed. *Tennessee Williams: A Tribute.* Jackson, Miss.: University Press of Mississippi, 1977.
Includes essays by people who knew and worked with Williams and provides an interesting critical perspective on his work.

2 9 7

You Can't Take It with You

GEORGE S. KAUFMAN AND
MOSS HART

1936

You Can't Take It with You opened in New York in December of 1936 to instant critical and popular acclaim. This depiction of a delightfully eccentric family, the third collaboration by playwrights George S. Kaufman and Moss Hart, proved to be their most successful and and longest-running work. Awarded the Pulitzer Prize in 1936, the comedy went on to run 837 performances on Broadway. Kaufman and Hart sold the film rights to Columbia Pictures for a record-setting amount, and the 1938 film won an Academy Award for best picture. Perenially appealing to audiences, *You Can't Take It with You* has become an American classic, regularly produced by high schools, colleges, and community theaters around the country. Successful Broadway revivals in 1965 and 1983 also attest to the play's timeless appeal.

You Can't Take It with You relates the humorous encounter between a conservative family and the crazy household of Grandpa Martin Vanderhof. Grandpa's family of idiosyncratic individualists amuse with their energetic physical antics and inspire with their wholehearted pursuit of happiness. Kaufman and Hart fill the stage with chaotic activity from beginning to end. Critics have admired the witty one-liners, the visual theatricalism, and the balanced construction of the play's three acts. Although *You Can't Take It with You* is undeniably escapist theater which prompts immediate enjoyment rather than complex analysis, it has clearly influenced American comedy. The formula origi-

nated by Kaufman and Hart—a loveable family getting into scrapes and overcoming obstacles—has been adopted as a format by most of today's television situation comedies.

AUTHOR BIOGRAPHY

George S. Kaufman and Moss Hart are remembered as masters of comedic playwriting. Each made important contributions to the American theater on his own, but they are best known for the successful and influential comedies they wrote together in the 1930s.

George S. Kaufman was born in Pittsburgh, Pennsylvania, on November 16, 1889, the descendent of early German Jewish immigrants. After graduating from high school in 1907, he briefly attended law school. Disenchanted with legal studies, he dropped out and proceeded to take on a series of odd jobs, ranging from salesman to stenographer. At the age of twenty he left Pittsburgh for New York City and began writing for the *New York Evening Mail.* After a stint as a columnist for the *Washington Times*—which ended when his editor objected to the young columnist's harsh satire—Kaufman returned to New York and soon became a theater news reporter for the *New York Times.* Later he was promoted to drama editor, a post he never gave up, even when he attained success as a playwright.

Although he rarely smiled and sometimes appeared almost gloomy, he was famous for his devastating sense of humor, particularly his one-liners. His peers considered him to be, as his friend Alexander Woollcott described him in Brooks Atkinson's *Broadway,* "the first wit of his time." Kaufman began applying this wit to playwriting in 1917. He would eventually become known as the "Great Collaborator," after a long career during which he collaborated on more than 40 plays. A gifted writer of dialogue, Kaufman had little interest in forming plots and left this up to his many writing partners.

Kaufman's first big hit—*Dulcy,* written with Marc Connelly—was produced in 1921. Both Connelly and Kaufman were part of the influential and now famous intellectual group called the Algonquin Round Table. These literary friends, who lunched and exchanged witticisms weekly at the Algonquin Hotel, included Tallulah Bankhead, Dorothy Parker, and Robert Benchley as well as several Kaufman collaborators such as Woollcott, Edna Ferber, and

Ring Lardner. But it was not until he was 40, that Kaufman teamed up with the partner with whom he would find his greatest success, Moss Hart.

Moss Hart, born October 24, 1904, was brought up in relative poverty by his English-born Jewish immigrant parents in the Bronx, New York. Inspired by an aunt who loved the theater, Hart was stagestruck at a young age. While still a teenager, he worked as an office boy for a theater manager; this manager produced Hart's first dramatic effort, *The Beloved Bandit,* in 1923. The show opened in Chicago and immediately flopped—one critic wrote a review in the form of an obituary for the play—and Hart's boss fired him after losing $45,000 on the production. Hart, still only nineteen, went on to take a job directing social activities at resorts in the Catskills. He gained somewhat of a reputation for the amateur theatricals he organized, but the six plays he wrote during this time were all rejected by producers.

Finally, in 1929, producer Sam H. Harris agreed to stage Hart's comedy *Once in A Lifetime* on the condition that the young writer revise the play with the well-known Kaufman. The twenty-six-year-old Hart idolized Kaufman and was thrilled at the prospect of working with him. This initial collaboration proved difficult, but when *Once in a Lifetime* opened in September, 1930, it was an unqualified success. This play, a satire of the movie industry, introduced the elements that would reappear in future Kaufman and Hart productions: numerous characters, chaotic activity, and witty dialogue. In the next ten years Kaufman and Hart would collaborate on seven more plays. Their third effort, *You Can't Take It with You,* (1936) was their most successful and longest-running work, claiming among its honors a Pulitzer Prize. (Kaufman's second; in 1931 his *Of Thee I Sing,* written with Morrie Ryskind, had been the first musical to win the Pulitzer Prize for drama). Some critics consider the duo's next play, *The Man Who Came to Dinner* (1939)—another story about a house filled with charming eccentrics—to be their best work.

Kaufman and Hart ceased collaborating in 1940 but both men continued to find success in the theatrical world. Kaufman collaborated on numerous popular plays throughout the 1940s and 50s, though most critics find that these works do not match the quality of his earlier efforts. He died on June 2, 1961. Hart went on to write six more plays on his own, as well as four screenplays, including those for *Gentleman's Agreement* (1947) and *A Star*

George Kaufman (at typewriter) and Moss Hart in 1937.

Is Born (1954). He won a Tony Award—formally known as an Antionette (or ''Tony'') Perry Award—in 1957 for directing the original production of Alan Jay Lerner's *My Fair Lady*. Not long before he died, on December 20, 1961, Hart completed an autobiography, *Act One,* which was praised by critics for its candor and insight.

PLOT SUMMARY

Act I, Scene i

You Can't Take It with You takes place in the living room of Grandpa Martin Vanderhof's home in New York City. The action begins on a Wednesday evening in 1936. The curtain rises on an eclectically decorated room containing a solarium full of snakes, a xylophone, and a printing press in addition to more common furniture items like chairs and tables.

The first scene of the play introduces the members of the eccentric Vanderhof-Sycamore household as they come in and out of the living room. Grandpa's middle-aged daughter Penny Sycamore sits at a rickety card table industriously typing a play. She is joined by her twenty-nine-year-old

daughter, Essie Carmichael, who makes and sells candy but really wants to be a dancer. Essie wears ballet slippers and dances rather than walks from place to place. Next, Rheba, the family maid, comes in and listens to Penny explain that her play's heroine has entered a monastery, and Penny can't think of a way to get her out. Then, Penny's husband Paul Sycamore emerges from the basement where he's been making fireworks. He is soon followed by his assistant Mr. De Pinna, a sort of permanent house guest who came eight years ago to deliver ice and has never left. Essie's husband, Ed Carmichael, comes in and goes to the xylophone and begins playing a tune. Essie is immediately up on her toes dancing to it. When the song is finished Ed goes to work at his printing press while Rheba's boyfriend Donald enters, bringing flies to feed the snakes.

At this point, Grandpa, the family patriarch who gave up business thirty-five years ago and now does whatever he likes, enters the bustling living room. He has just returned from watching the Columbia commencement exercises, one of the many activities—such as stamp collecting and going to the zoo—which he pursues just because he enjoys them. Not long after Grandpa arrives, Penny's younger daughter, Alice, enters. Alice is the one ''normal'' member of the family who has a secretarial job on Wall Street. After a few cheerful exchanges with her various relatives, she quiets down the group in order to tell them that her boss's son, Tony Kirby, will be calling for her later in the evening. She asks them all to behave as normally as possible because she likes this young man. She then goes upstairs to change.

When the doorbell rings, however, it turns out to be, not Alice's young man, but rather an Internal Revenue Agent named Henderson who has come to inform Grandpa that he owes twenty-two years' worth of unpaid income tax. But Henderson is scared off by a firecracker explosion before he can even get Grandpa to admit that the government does anything worth paying taxes to support. Finally, Tony arrives and gets a brief glimpse of Alice's family. As Alice whisks Tony back out the door, Essie's dance instructor, a loud Russian named Mr. Kolenkhov arrives. Kolenkhov and the rest of the family then sit down to dinner and Grandpa says grace, asking God to let them all continue living life just as they like.

Act I, Scene ii

Scene ii takes place later that same night. Alice and Tony have returned to the house after their date. They begin a conversation confessing how much they love each other. Alice admits she loves Tony but does not think they can ever marry because his traditional family could never accept her unconventional relatives. Tony does not think this is necessarily the case and convinces Alice that all that matters at the moment is their love for one another. The two become engaged and Tony departs.

At different points during this conversation Alice and Tony are interrupted by various family members who demonstrate the very eccentric behavior Alice thinks the Kirbys will be unable to accept. Penny comes through in her bathrobe looking for her play, "Sex Goes on Holiday." Essie and Ed return from the movies arguing about Ginger Rogers's dancing skill and casually mentioning that Grandpa thinks they should go ahead and have a baby. Donald passes by in his nightshirt carrying his accordion, and Paul emerges from the basement where he has continued making fireworks.

Act II

Act II opens a week later. Penny is talking to a drunken actress, Gay Wellington, who soon passes out on the couch. Tony Kirby and his parents are coming for dinner the next night, and Alice is getting things ready, consulting a list of things that need to be changed and put away. The rest of the family engage in their various amusements. Penny decides to complete a painting of Mr. De Pinna as a discus thrower which she began years ago, so he puts on a Roman costume and poses for her. Kolenkhov arrives to give Essie a dancing lesson, and she energetically pirouettes and leaps through the room while Grandpa throws darts.

At this moment, the Kirbys, in full evening dress, arrive. Tony has brought them a night early by mistake. The Kirbys are as shocked by the chaotic scene as the Sycamores are surprised to see the unexpected guests, but everyone tries to make the best of the situation. Penny gives hurried instructions about dinner to Rheba and they send Donald running to the market while everyone tries to sit down and have a conversation. But everything goes laughably awry as the drunken actress arises from the sofa, Kolenkhov seizes upon Mr. Kirby in an attempt to wrestle, and Penny starts a word association game which embarrasses the guests. Just when the Kirbys decide they can't stay for dinner after all and are about to leave, three F.B.I. agents show up and block the door. They have come to arrest Ed for the seemingly subversive circulars he has been printing. They search the house, and when they find the "munitions" (Paul's fireworks) in the basement they arrest everyone in the house, including the astonished Kirbys. And to top it all off, Mr. De Pinna has left his lit pipe downstairs with the fireworks, resulting in a large explosion at the close of the act.

Act III

Act III opens the next day as Rheba is setting the dinner table and Donald is reading to her a newspaper report of last night's arrests stating that all thirteen people were given suspended sentences for manufacturing fireworks without a permit.

Alice has broken off her engagement and is packed and ready to leave town. No one has called her a cab as she requested, and while she waits for one, Tony arrives to try and talk her out of leaving. At this point, Kolenkhov shows up with his friend, a former Grand Duchess named Olga who is now a waitress. He has brought Olga to make blintzes for the family and takes her into the kitchen to cook. Then, Mr. Kirby appears at the door looking for Tony. Alice is still trying to leave, but Grandpa stops her from going and gets everyone to stay and talk.

A scene from the 1983 National Theatre production in London

In the course of the ensuing conversation, everything gets resolved. It comes out that Tony purposely brought his parents to dinner on the wrong night because he wanted them to see Alice's family as they really were. Tony has decided to leave his job at Kirby & Co. and instead do something he really likes. Grandpa helps persuade Mr. Kirby that he should let his son pursue his dreams, since there is more to life than accumulating money. After all, ''you can't take with you'' when you die. To cap off the happy moment, a letter arrives from the I.R.S. saying that Grandpa's tax problems are resolved. The play concludes with everyone happily sitting down to a bountiful meal of Olga's blintzes.

CHARACTERS

Ed Carmichael

Essie's husband Ed, as the stage directions inform, is a ''nonedescript young man'' in his thirties. He is a musician and composer who likes to play the xylophone as well as ply his trade as an amateur printer. As a hobby, he uses his hand-press to print sayings which he comes across in the writings of the revolutionary Russian Communist Leon Trotsky, such as ''God Is the State; the State is

God.'' Proud of his work, he encloses these printed bills in the boxes with Essie's candy. Although Ed prints his slogans just for the fun of it, their political messages attract the attention of the F.B.I., who believe Ed is an insurrectionist attempting to undermine the United States government.

Essie Carmichael

Mrs. Sycamore's eldest daughter, Essie Carmichael, is a 29-year-old aspiring ballerina. She dances her way through the play, improvising steps to her husband Ed's xylophone music and eagerly following the instructions of her dance instructor, Mr. Kolenkhov. She makes candy, naming her newest confections ''Love Dreams,'' but she never takes off her ballet slippers even when she dons her candy-making apron. Like the other Sycamores, Essie is both happily absorbed in tasks which amuse her and wholly undisturbed by the eccentricities of her family.

Mr. De Pinna

Described in the stage directions as a ''bald-headed little man with a serious manner,'' the middle-aged Mr. De Pinna arrived at the Vanderhof residence eight years ago to deliver ice and ended up moving in. Although a minor character, he shows how open and accepting the Vanderhof-Sycamore family can be: everyone is obviously welcome in this house. Mr. De Pinna has clearly taken to this family's way of life. He helps Paul make firecrackers, poses in Roman costume for Penny's painting of a discus thrower, and remains undisturbed by the chaotic household.

Donald

Rheba's boyfriend, who, like her, is described in the stage directions in racist terms such as ''a colored man of no uncertain hue.'' Cheerful and at ease in the household, he is a minor comic character who willingly runs errands and occasionally offers amusing comments.

F.B.I. agents

The three F.B.I. agents (G-men)who come to investigate the seemingly political papers Ed Sycamore has been enclosing in candy boxes.

Grand Duchess Olga Katrina
See Olga

Henderson

Henderson is the Internal Revenue Department agent who comes to collect twenty-two years' back income tax from Grandpa Vanderhof.

Wilbur C. Henderson
See Henderson

Anthony Kirby, Jr.
See Tony Kirby

Anthony Kirby, Sr.
See Mr. Kirby

Miriam Kirby
See Mrs. Kirby

Mr. Kirby

Tony's father, the middle-aged Mr. Kirby, is a successful Wall Street businessman. He is a traditional authority figure who represents the conventional worldview the Vanderhof-Sycamores reject. Conservative and repressed, he has perpetual indi-

MEDIA ADAPTATIONS

- Frank Capra produced and directed an Academy Award-winning film version of *You Can't Take It with You.* The film stars James Stewart and Jean Arthur, Columbia, 1938; available from Columbia Tristar Home Video. The film adaption does alter the plot in some ways. Excerpts from Robert Riskin's screenplay were published in *Foremost Films of 1938,* edited by Frank Vreeland, New York: Pitman, 1939. Copies of the unpublished screenplay are available at the Margaret Herrick Library of the Academy of Motion Picture Arts and Sciences and the University of California, Los Angeles Theatre Arts Library.

- CBS produced a television adaption of the play featuring Jean Stapleton and Art Carney which aired May 16, 1979.

- A 1984 taped performance of the play featuring Colleen Dewhurst and Jason Robards is available from Columbia Tristar Home Video, Vestron Video, and Live Entertainment.

- The Moss Hart Papers at the Wisconsin Center for Theater Research include the script for an October, 1950, Pulitzer Prize Playhouse television adaption of the play, as well as an undated radio adaption by Tony Webster.

gestion and tells his wife he thinks ''lust is not a human emotion.'' He is initially shocked by Alice's family and says Grandpa Vanderhof's idea of doing only what makes you happy is a ''a very dangerous philosophy . . . it's un-American.''

Mrs. Kirby

Tony's mother, the middle-aged Mrs. Kirby, is the conservative female equivelent of her businessman husband. She, too, is shocked by the unconventional Vanderhof-Sycamores. She is affronted when Penny says spiritualism is ''a fake'' and seems to reveal she is dissatisfied with her marriage when in the word game she associates "honeymoon" with "dull" and almost admits that Mr. Kirby talks about Wall Street even during sex.

Tony Kirby

Tony Kirby is a Vice President of Kirby & Co., his father's business. The stage directions tell us he is a "very nice young man" who has recently attended Yale and Cambridge. He has fallen in love with Alice Sycamore and wants to marry her. Now that he's done with college he believes, as he tells Grandpa Vanderhof, that now "the fun's over, and—I'm facing the world," but his contact with Alice's family teaches him that if he makes the right choices his fun may just be starting. He purposely brings his parents to the Vanderhof-Sycamore house on the wrong night because, as he says to his father, "I wanted you to see a real family—as they really *were*. A family that loved and understood each other." Determined to do something that he wants to do, Tony rejects his father's business and embraces the Vanderhof's philosophy of seeking happiness over wealth.

Boris Kolenkhov (ko-len-kawv)

Essie's dance instructor Boris Kolenkhov is introduced in the stage directions as an "enormous, hairy, loud" Russian. A stereotypically- depicted comic character, he contributes to the chaotic activity in the Vanderhof-Sycamore home, encouraging Essie to dance and wrestling with the unsuspecting Mr. Kirby. He has a habit of conveniently arriving just in time for meals.

Olga

The Grand Duchess Olga is a Russian friend of Kolehnkov's who has fallen on hard times following the Communist Revolution in Russia. She is now a waitress and has a talent for making blintzes. She prepares the bountiful meal of blintzes which everyone sits down to at the conclusion of the play.

Rheba

Rheba is the Sycamore family's efficient, practical, and adaptable "colored maid." The stage directions introduce her in stereotypically racist terms—"a very black girl somewhere in her thirties"—common during the years preceding the Civil Rights movement. During the course of the play's action, however, Rheba emerges as a distinct individual, speaking her mind and holding her own within the eccentric household.

Alice Sycamore

Alice Sycamore is Penny's attractive younger daughter. The twenty-two-year-old Alice has, according to the stage directions, "escaped the tinge of mild insanity" that pervades her relatives, but her "devotion and love for them are plainly apparent." The only member of the family with a regular job, she is a secretary at a Wall Street firm and has fallen in love with the boss's son, Anthony Kirby, Jr. Although she loves Tony, she fears his conservative parents will never accept her family's eccentricities. Since Alice is a "normal" and likeable character, the audience is likely to sympathise with her and share her point-of-view.

Paul Sycamore

Penny's husband Paul Sycamore is in his mid-fifties. Quiet, charming, and mild-mannered, he never loses his composure, even when the fire crackers he makes in the basement with Mr. De Pinna unexpectedly explode. Like his wife and father-in-law, Paul possesses what the stage directions call "a kind of youthful air." A complete contrast to a disgruntled businessman such as Mr. Kirby, Paul contentedly pursues his chosen activities, such as making new "skyrockets" and building things with an Erector Set.

Penny Sycamore

See Penelope Vanderhof Sycamore

Grandpa Vanderhof

See Martin Vanderhof

Martin Vanderhof

Grandpa Vanderhof, as Kaufman and Hart describe him in the stage directions, is a 75-year-old "wiry little man whom the years have treated kindly." One day thirty-five years ago he gave up his business career, since, as he explains to Mr. Kolenkhov, it struck him that he "wasn't having any fun." So he "just relaxed" and has "been a happy man ever since." He now has "time enough for everything" and, as he tells Mr. Kirby, he no longer has "six hours of things I *have* to do every day before I get *one* hour to do what I like in." Grandpa collects stamps, throws darts, attends the commencement speeches at Columbia University, and encourages his family to follow his example and do only what makes them happy. He hasn't payed income tax in twenty-two years because he doesn't think the government does anything useful with the money. He provides the philosophical center of the play, explaining the folly of seeking material wealth at the expense of personal fulfillment, and asking only, as he says while saying grace before dinner, that their family be allowed ''to go along and be happy in [their] own sort of way.''

Penelope Vanderhof Sycamore

Grandpa Vanderhof's daughter, Penny Sycamore, is the first character on stage in *You Can't Take It with You.* Kaufman and Hart describe her in the stage directions as an endearing ''round little woman'' in her fifties, who loves nothing more than writing plays. As eccentric as the other members of her family, Penny was an enthusiastic painter but gave up this hobby for writing when a typewriter was delivered to the house by mistake eight years earlier. Charmingly blunt, she causes some embarrassment during the Kirbys' visit, first by calling Mrs. Kirby's beloved spirtualism ''a fake,'' and then by proposing a word association game and asking what everyone associates with the words ''sex,'' ''bathroom,'' and ''lust.'' Penny's enjoyment of life and direct speech are in marked contrast to Mrs. Kirby's seeming discontent and reserved acceptance of social conventions.

Gay Wellington

Gay Wellington, described in the stage directions as ''an actress, nymphomaniac, and a terrible souse,'' comes to the Sycamore house to discuss a script with Penny but then passes out on the couch. She occasionally awakens, usually just in time to contribute to the chaos that erupts following the Kirbys' unexpected visit.

THEMES

You Can't Take It with You contrasts the eccentric family of Grandpa Martin Vanderhof with the conservative Kirby family. Vanderhof's granddaughter Alice becomes engaged to her boss's son Tony Kirby. Although a dinner party meant to bring the two families together ends with an explosion and a night in jail, by the play's end both Tony and his father have come to appreciate Grandpa's carefree philosophy. All obstacles to the young couple's happiness are eliminated.

American Dream

The two families in *You Can't Take It with You* each represent different definitions (perceptions) of the American Dream. Mr. Kirby has attained financial success and a position of social and economic power. The play, however, asks its viewers to evaluate whether Americans should aspire to be like Mr. Kirby. His achievement is contrasted with Grandpa Vanderhofs' version of the American Dream, earning just enough money so that one can survive and do exactly what one wishes. Mr. Kirby may initially think Grandpa's ideas are ''un-American,'' but the Vanderhofs' infectious happiness and love for one another encourages the audience to revise their definition of the American Dream to include attainment of both material success and personal fulfillment.

Success and Failure

Throughout the play, the Vanderhof-Sycamore way of life calls into question conventional definitions of success and failure. Although Essie and Penny might be called ''failures'' because they lack talent in dancing and painting/playwriting respectively, the play depicts them as successful because each clearly finds joy in what she does. Tony Kirby initially thinks that in order to be ''successful'' he must forget about the dreams he had in college and accept his position as a vice president at Kirby & Co. But his contact with Alice's family convinces him that it is a mistake to give up one's dreams, as his father did when he was a young man. In the world of the play, failure to follow one's dreams and desires is the only genuine failure. The audience is encouraged to re-define ''success'' in terms of happiness rather than in terms of just money and status.

Individualism

The positive portrayal of eccentric and singular behavior in *You Can't Take It with You* also reflects the American belief in individualism. Many works in American literature celebrate individuals who rebel against the restraining conventions of society at large. All the Vanderhof-Sycamores could be classified as ''rugged individualists'' who follow the dictates of their own hearts and disregard those in the majority who disapprove.

Difference

The Vanderhof-Sycamores not only stand apart as ''different'' from the conventional world around them, but they also are willing to accept others who are different. Their openness is reflected—through humorous exaggeration—in the way that they allow anyone to move into their house or sit down at

TOPICS FOR FURTHER STUDY

- Look up a classic discussion of comedy—such as Aristotle's *Poetics,* Charles Baudelaire's *On the Essence of Laughter,* Sigmund Freud's *Jokes and the Comic,* or Northrop Frye's *The Mythos of Spring: Comedy*—and evaluate the form and content of *You Can't Take It with You* according to your chosen theorist's definition of comedy.

- Read either Ralph Waldo Emerson's essay "Self-Reliance" (1841) or the chapter "Economy" from Henry David Thoreau's *Walden* (1854). Consider how the ideas in your chosen text are reflected in *You Can't Take It with You.*

- Compare and contrast Frank Capra's film adaption of *You Can't Take It with You* with Kaufman and

Hart's original play. What alterations did Capra make which reflect his definition of family and community? How do the depictions of the business world in the play and film differ? Do the two versions emphasize the same political, economic, and social philosophies?

- Research the living and working conditions of minority groups—such as African Americans and Eastern European immigrants—in mid-1930s New York. What would life have been like for a real African American domestic worker or a Russian escaping persecution? Find authentic accounts to compare with the joking stereotypes presented in Kaufman and Hart's play.

their dinner table. And although the play's ethnic characters are depicted in a stereotypical manner which might offend late-twentieth-century sensibilities, the acceptance of African-American and Russian characters as part of the family was seen as quite liberal and open to the value systems of most 1930s audiences. The play's happy ending also reveals that differences may only be superficial, since Mr. Kirby, who once had dreams of being a trapeze-artist, may be more like Grandpa than anyone suspected.

Culture Clash

Much of the humor in *You Can't Take It with You* derives from the clash between the lifestyles of the two families. The Kirbys might be seen to reflect mainstream upper-middle-class American culture, while the Vanderhof-Sycamores resist the conventions of that same culture, making up their own rules. While themes of culture clash can often be used to show how divergent groups can come to understand each other, this is a secondary concern in Kaufman and Hart's play. The primary purpose of introducing a straight-laced family such as the Kirbys into the wacky world of the Vanderhof-Sycamores is to watch the sparks fly. The first act

clearly establishes the goofy nature of the family and raises audience expectation as interaction with citizens of the "real world" approaches. Laughs are generated from both the eccentric behavior of Grandpa Vanderhof and his family and the shocked reactions the Kirbys have to this oddball group.

STYLE

You Can't Take It with You has three well-balanced acts. Act I introduces the members of the eccentric Vanderhof-Sycamore family and sets up the play's central conflict: Alice Sycamore becomes engaged to her boss's son, Tony Kirby, but she does not think his family can accept hers. Act II depicts the laughably disastrous encounter between the two families when the Kirbys arrive for a dinner party on the wrong night. Act III then resolves all the problems that confront the family and the young couple.

Farce

You Can't Take It with You employs many elements of farce, which is defined most simply as broad comedy mixed with a healthy dose of improbability. Farce typically takes highly exaggerated characters and places them in unlikely situations. Key elements include witty wordplay and physical humor for broad comic effect to provoke simple, hearty laughter from the audience. Clearly, the dancing, xylophone-playing, firecracker-making members of the Vanderhof-Sycamore household are exaggerated, make witty verbal jokes, and engage in physical horseplay.

Romantic Comedy

The basic plot of *You Can't Take It with You* is that of a romantic comedy, a story of a love affair in which the couple must overcome obstacles—usually with comic results—before they can marry. Like many young lovers in Shakespearean comedy, Kaufman and Hart's Alice and Tony face difficulties on the path to their eventual happy ending. While straight-up romantic comedy is often derided by critics for being too cute or overly sentimental, Kaufman and Hart balance this element of their play with frequent interuptions from the loony family members.

Satire

Satire typically attacks political or social philosophies, showing them to be false or misguided through mockery and ridicule. Although *You Can't Take It with You* is not a harsh satire, it does gently ridicule the American tax system, welfare, and market capitalism through its ludicrous presentation of Henderson the I.R.S. agent, Donald and Ed's comments about "relief," and Grandpa's anti-materialist views. It also pokes fun at the typical perception of the Amercian Dream—one that encourages individuals to exert themselves in the pursuit of money and status without any regard for happiness and leisure activity.

HISTORICAL CONTEXT

In the mid-1930s when Kaufman and Hart wrote *You Can't Take It with You,* Americans were suffering through one of the worst economic periods in the history of the United States, an era known as the Great Depression. Many Americans lost their life savings, homes, and jobs in the stock market crash of 1929 and the numerous bank failures which followed. Unemployment rose to record heights for the time, reaching over 20% in 1935. Hopes raised by an apparent upturn in the economy in 1936 were dashed when the recovery collapsed in 1937.

After his election in 1932, President Franklin Delano Roosevelt instituted his "New Deal" legislation, a series of liberal reforms which put in place welfare, social security, and unemployment benefits. These relief efforts dramatically changed Americans' relationship with their government, which now provided many with a living either in the form of a job in a federal program or through welfare benefits. The nature of the presidency changed at this time as well; the executive branch gained powers no president since Roosevelt has seriously attempted to invoke.

Although the New Deal eased the effects of the Depression, the 1930s were an exceptionally tough time for the majority of Americans. The enormous hardships endured by ordinary people led many to question free market capitalism. Left wing ideas, such as socialism, gained in popularity during this decade, and labor unrest led to strikes across the country.

Not surprisingly, these political and economic factors influenced American popular culture. The art and literature of the 1930s gave rise to both works intended to argue political ideas and works intended to provide escape from the rigors of daily life. Newspapers contained more editorial columns than ever before and politically oriented magazines such as the *Nation* and the *New Republic* flourished; yet papers also included more comic strips and serialized stories than they had previously, and pulp detective and mystery fiction—prime escapist fare—flourished. Radio offered frequent news reports but also gave listeners lighthearted comedy programs such as *Amos 'n' Andy* and *Fibber McGee and Molly.* In the theater, propaganda plays such as Clifford Odets's *Waiting for Lefty* (1935) were balanced by farces such as Kaufman and Hart's plays.

Movies, too, touched on the harshness of the times with films like *I Am a Fugitive from a Chain Gang* (1936). More frequently, however, films offered optimistic escapism. Hollywood produced excellent slapstick and screwball comedies starring actors like Katherine Hepburn, Spencer Tracy, and Cary Grant, as well as classic animated features such as Walt Disney's *The Three Little Pigs* (1933)

COMPARE & CONTRAST

- **1930s:** During the Great Depression unemployment reaches a high of 20% in 1935. In 1938, unemployment is at 19.1%, which means 10.39 million Americans are unemployed.

  Today: In the mid-1990s unemployment runs as low as 5%. With 66% of Americans in the labor force, a larger proportion of Americans are working than ever before. Yet the disparity between the wealthiest 10% and the poorest 10% of the population is greater in the United States than in any other industrialized country except Russia.

- **1930s:** Starting in 1932, Franklin Delano Roosevelt's New Deal legislation combats the economic hardships of the Great Depression, introducing social security, acts creating jobs in the public sector, welfare, and unemployment benefits.

  Today: Social Security funding is endangered and economists warn that the system could collapse in the near future. Congress passes a Welfare Reform Act in 1996 limiting lifetime benefits to five years and requiring all welfare recipients to participate either in job training or employment programs.

- **1930s:** Beginning in 1938, Joseph Stalin, the communist dictator of the Soviet Union, kills 8 to 10 million people in an attempt to eliminate all his political enemies in an event later called the "great purge." In this same year, fascist general Francisco Franco starts a revolt in Spain which leads to a three-year civil war.

  Today: In Europe, genocidal slaughter takes place in Bosnia-Herzegovina during a civil war in the 1990s; thousands of people are killed in the name of "ethnic cleansing." In Africa, during the civil war in Rwanda, mass killings also take place in 1995 as two ethnic tribes attempt to eliminate one another.

- **1930s:** In 1930, life expectancy for American men was 58.1 years; American women were expected to live 61.6 years. By 1940, life expectancies for American men and women had risen to 60.8 years and 65.2 years respectively.

  Today: In 1990, the average life expectancy for men in the United States was 71.6 years, for women it was 79.2 years.

- **1930s:** In 1933, Frances Perkins becomes the first woman cabinet member when she accepts the post of Secretary of Labor.

  Today: Madeline Albright becomes the United States's first female Secretary of State in 1997.

- **1930s:** According to census records, the population of the United States rose from 123,202,624 in 1930 to 132,164,569 in 1940, an increase of approximately 7%.

  Today: In 1980, the U.S. population was 226,504,825. It grew to 248,709,873 by 1990, an increase of approximately 9%.

---

and *Snow White and the Seven Dwarves* (1937). Also enormously popular were upbeat films featuring the child actress Shirley Temple, including *Little Miss Marker* (1934) and *Heidi*. With little money to spend on entertainment, Americans also embraced a series of amusing "fads," often activities which were inexpensive (dance marathons, chain letters) or could be done at home (jig-saw puzzles, bridge).

The decade of the Great Depression is thoroughly documented both by still photography and motion pictures. Late-twentieth century society is familiar with images—for example the Dust Bowl, bread lines, and sit-down strikes—captured by 1930s photojournalists such as Margaret Bourke-White and Walker Evans. Magazines such as *Life* and *Fortune* published these photos and gave Americans a new perspective on themselves and their nation.

During this time of struggle and societal stagnation, ironically, a few women found their opportunities in the public sector expanding. The rapid growth of New Deal offices in Washington D.C. led to unconventional appointments and brought women into such government positions as the cabinet, treasury, and higher courts. Occasionally, as would be the case during World War II, women stepped into men's traditional role of family breadwinner—especially given that many men refused to work in clerical and secretarial positions that were typically identified with women. And despite open discrimination against married women (because many people believed wives shouldn't be allowed to work if their husbands already had jobs) the number of women in the labor force increased throughout the decade. Although the basic cultural assumptions about "women's place" in the home remained largely unchallenged in the 1930s, some women were drawn into newly active roles in government and the workplace.

Unfortunately, many ethnic minorities in America did not find even slightly increased in opportunities in the 1930s. At the start of the decade, three-fourths of all African Americans in the United States lived in rural areas. Existence for farm workers had already been harsh in the agriculturally depressed 1920s; conditions deteriorated during the depression of the 1930s. In urban communities as well, unemployment, worsened by discrimination, made life severely difficult for black workers. African-American leaders protested that New Deal programs did not offer equal relief or eliminate discrimination against black citizens. Although a legally supported system of segregation stayed in place in the Southern states and racist bias was in evidence throughout the country, some reform did begin in 1935 when President Roosevelt banned discrimination in the federal relief programs and African Americans made some gains in attaining their deserved rights and recognition during the second half of the decade.

The 1930s were a time dominated by economic and political concerns. Americans faced difficulties at home and saw unrest abroad, as civil war waged in Spain (1934-1936), Joseph Stalin exercised totalitarian power in Russia, and Hitler installed a fascist dictatorship in Nazi Germany. At the end of the decade the United States faced the frightening prospect of going to war as diplomacy throughout Europe and Asia failed and political tensions rose.

CRITICAL OVERVIEW

On its opening night in December of 1936, *You Can't Take It with You* became an instant commercial hit. Since then, the play's popularity has never waned; it has been successfully staged by theaters of all sizes for over six decades. Yet even while praising the skill with which Kaufman and Hart constructed their clever comedy, critics have generally categorized the play as an escapist farce, enjoyable yet lacking any significant content. When the play won the Pulitzer Prize in 1936, some questioned the choice, saying judges played it safe, choosing a popular work rather than a more controversial drama with greater depth and artistic merit.

In his *New York Times* review, Brooks Atkinson described *You Can't Take It with You,* as "a spontaneous piece of hilarity" composed with "a dash of affection to season the humor" by two writers with "a knack for extravagances of word and episode and an eye for hilarious incongruities." Most other reviews of the first production were equally positive, though some expressed surprise that the play was less satirical than Kaufman's earlier works. But perhaps because its humor was gentle and its message palatable, *You Can't Take It with You* appealed to audiences all across the country and touring companies shared the success of the Broadway production. The strong ticket sales were all the more remarkable considering the tough economic conditions of the Great Depression—and speak volumes of the play's appeal as escapist fare.

Over the years, critics' comments regarding *You Can't Take It with You* have been remarkably consistent. Frank Hurburt O'Hara, in his 1939 collection of essays *Today in American Drama,* praised Kaufman and Hart for creating a play that despite being "hilariously preposterous" still manages to be "more persuasive to audiences than most farces." Almost thirty years later, Richard Mason, in a 1967 *Theater Annual* article, would still admire the imagination and warmth in this play where "neither satire not any weighty preoccupation with issues is allowed to get in the way of the comedy ... any metaphorical values possessed by the play are quite overshadowed by its farce exuberance."

Pleasantly escapist, *You Can't Take It with You* is, as Ethan Mordden wrote in his 1981 book *The American Theater,* "one hit whose popularity is easy to understand." First opening in a decade when, as Mordden puts it, many "plays dealt with disoriented characters— alienated either by epic environmental pressures they don't understand or because they understand and dislike their environment," *You Can't Take It with You* offered audiences an amusing reversal: "the screwballs have their world in order; it's everyone else who's disoriented." And most critics would, along with Mordden, attribute the play's enduring appeal to the fact that although "very much of its time" Kaufman and Hart's comedy is "not dependent on timely allusions;" we can still easily understand Grandpa's message to "do what you want before it's too late."

In the 1990s, more criticism has been written on Frank Capra's 1938 film version of *You Can't Take It with You* than on Kaufman and Hart's original play. This reflects the burgeoning of popular culture and film studies, fields more interested in the 1930s Hollywood screwball comedies than the Broadway stage of the same era. But the lack of recent criticism may also indicate that many late-twentieth century scholars agree with Mason's judgement of all Kaufman and Hart's comedies: they "are there to be thoroughly enjoyed on the stage, but it is fatal to think about them."

CRITICISM

Erika Kreger

In this essay Kreger places Kaufman and Hart's play within the context of the Great Depression, noting that the work served as a welcome escape from the trials of 1930s America.

In the 1930s, Americans needed to laugh. The United States was suffering through the harsh economic times of the Great Depression and people went to theaters and movie houses to forget their troubles. So it is not surprising that in 1936 George S. Kaufman and Moss Hart's *You Can't Take It with You* was a commercial success. This screwball farce filled the stage with eccentric characters who did silly things and made witty remarks while fireworks literally went off in the background. Both frantic and funny, the play gave audiences just the sort of escapist entertainment they wanted.

You Can't Take It with You not only pleased Depression-era theater-goers, it went on in the decades which followed to become a classic American comedy, continually produced by theater companies of all kinds. Why has this play enjoyed lasting popularity when many other clever farces from the same era have been forgotten? Perhaps this

well-constructed work endures both because it skillfully employs classic comedic techniques and because it celebrates individualism, reiterating ideas Americans have embraced since the country's inception. Without exaggerating the philosophical importance of Kaufman and Hart's loveable bunch of screwballs, it is safe to say that *You Can't Take It with You* repackages, in the congenial form of Grandpa Vanderhof's worldview, the individualistic and anti-materialist ideals of American thinkers such as Ralph Waldo Emerson and Henry David Thoreau. As the idiosyncratic Vanderhof-Sycamores amuse, they also encourage the viewer to resist conformity, question the dominant culture's social and economic values, and seek personal fulfillment. The play fulfills its obligations as a farce, delivering verbal and physical comedy aplenty, but it also offers, with an appropriately light-touch, a message Americans want to hear.

But, as many critics have pointed out, any message *You Can't Take It with You* delivers is secondary to its main purpose: producing laughs. From the moment the curtain goes up, Kaufman and Hart keep audiences amused with sight gags and witty lines. Act I introduces the wacky Vanderhof-Sycamore family. They all follow their dreams, making the best of what life and chance have presented them: Penny writes plays because a typewriter was once delivered to the house by mistake, Essie dances and makes candy, Ed plays the xylophone and prints circulars on a hand-press, Paul make fireworks with the assistance of Mr. De Pinna, and Grandpa collects stamps and attends commencement exercises. None of them seems of mind that young Alice actually has a job as a secretary on Wall Street. In fact, no one seems to mind much of anything at all. No explosion is so loud and no behavior so strange as to disturb this family's balance.

Kaufman and Hart begin their play in a liberated realm—Grandpa Vanderhof's living room. This is a reversal of the traditional comic model literary critic Northrop Frye once proclaimed, where, as in many Shakespearean romantic comedies, the protagonists must escape a world of hypocrisy and habit and create their own new society of truth and freedom. In *You Can't Take It with You,* there is no need for Alice and Tony to run away and make a new community, for they start out in a fully formed alternative society. The "real world" remains safely off stage, and the Vanderhof-Sycamore world order—no jobs, no taxes, no formalities—holds sway. The humor and fun, of course, comes from watching the conservative Kirby family at first

WHAT DO I READ NEXT?

- *Harvey,* Mary Coyle Chase's 1944 comedy. This play, like *You Can't Take It with You,* won a Pulitzer Prize, and tells the story of another classic American eccentric, a charming man who keeps company with a huge, imaginary rabbit named Harvey.

- *Act One,* Moss Hart's well-received 1959 autobiography. This work offers insight into both the Broadway theater at mid-century and the Hart-Kaufman collaboration.

- *The Man Who Came to Dinner,* Kaufman and Hart's 1939 play. This fourth Kaufman-Hart collaboration, like *You Can't Take It with You,* depicts a crazy family and a rambunctious social occasion. Some critics consider this to be Kaufman and Hart's best work.

- *Ah Wilderness!,* (1933) by Eugene O'Neill. This nostalgic play, the only comedy O'Neill ever wrote, looks at family life in 1906 Connecticut.

- Dorothy Parker's essays, book reviews, and drama reviews from the 1930s can be found in *The Portable Dorothy Parker* as well as other anthologies of her work. Parker's famous satirical wit reflects the tone of the Algonquin Round Table, an intellectual group which influenced Kaufman.

- *The Importance of Being Earnest: A Trivial Comedy for Serious People,* (1895) a play by Oscar Wilde. This well-constructed comedy filled with famous witty lines is about the complicated courtship and betrothals of two upper-class English young men.

---

clash with and later attempt to adapt to this unorthodox world. The overall structure of the play, however, is quite traditional; three balanced acts, in turn, set-up, complicate, and resolve the humorous situation.

After Act I has introduced the unconventional cast of characters and made clear the problem of the play, that Alice and Tony want to marry but fear that their families are incompatible (a lighter version of Shakespeare's *Romeo and Juliet*), Act II generates hilarious complications by bringing Tony and his parents to dinner at the Vanderhof-Sycamore house on the wrong night. (This formula of a likeable but unusual family placed in ludicrous circumstances is a familiar one. Many critics credit Kaufman and Hart with originating this scenerio so often adopted by television situation comedies such as *The Addams Family* and *The Simpsons*.) This second act illustrates the broad comic techniques of farce, which place exaggerated characters in awkward physical positions and silly costumes. Kaufman and Hart start off with Essie, in her tutu, leaping through the living room, the balding Mr. De Pinna dressed like a Roman discus thrower, and Penny in the caricatured costume of "the artist." All funny sights even before the Kirbys show up in full evening dress (formal gown and tuxedo) to provide contrast. And the physical comedy continues throughout the scene, with Mr. Kolenkhov accosting the uptight Mr. Kirby in an attempt to wrestle, Donald running in and out to the store, and finally the chaotic arrival of the F.B.I., which is capped by a fireworks explosion and pandemonium. When reading a comedy (as opposed to actually seeing it produced), it is easy to overlook the importance of the visual and physical elements which are a crucial part of the humor. Kaufman and Hart certainly intended *You Can't Take It with You* to entertain both eye and ear; Kaufman in particular was well-known for adroitly choreographing the on-stage mayhem in productions he directed.

The play is filled not only with clever sight gags but also with great one-liners. Audiences never fail to laugh when Penny muses about her play's plot ("you know, with forty monks and one girl, something ought to happen") or when Grandpa sums up his sense of the government's value ("well, I might pay about seventy-five dollars, but that's all it's worth"). The caricatured Russian Kolenkhov energetically delivers some of the silliest lines in the play ("Life is chasing around inside of me, like a squirrel") and performers love the part. As the actor Gregory Peck said in *A Celebration of Moss Hart* about playing Kolenkhov, "it had that marvelous line—'Confidentially she stinks'—in it. I had the privilege of saying that, I think, four times at every performance, and for the first time in my life hearing an audience just tear the joint up. That was the surest-fire laugh line that any actor ever had." Hart and Kaufman's verbal wit shows up throughout the play, but perhaps a particularly good example of their ability to get big laughs from short lines is Penny's word game, where Mrs. Kirby's associations of bathroom—Mr. Kirby, honeymoon—dull, sex—Wall Street, are revealingly suggestive.

You Can't Take It with You might stand as a model for aspiring comedic playwrights, illustrating balanced structure as well as a skillful blend of physical and verbal humor. But its enduring appeal more likely can be credited to the other lesson it has to offer, that of Grandpa Vanderhof's life philosophy. Living out Grandpa's notions, the Vanderhof-Sycamores illustrate Ralph Waldo Emerson's idea, famously expressed in his 1841 essay "Self-Reliance," that to be an individual one must be a "nonconformist" and reject the "joint-stock company" of society which asks citizens to sacrifice their "liberty and culture." As Alice says about her family, "they do rather strange things" but "they're fun, and . . . there's a certain nobility about them." American audiences raised on individualistic beliefs are inclined to agree that there is something noble about folks who "just don't care about things that other people give their whole lives to." Society demands conformity, but in the world of Kaufman and Hart's play, those who follow society's dictates get little satisfaction from life, while those who make up their own rules find contentment. Echoing Emerson, *You Can't Take It with You* emphasizes the pleasure of following one's bliss. In this comedic world, nonconformists have fun. It really is a play about "play," in the sense of games and entertainment.

Grandpa laments the fact that most people have forgotten about having fun: they work because they are supposed to but no longer know what they are working for. He asks, "why should we live with such hurry and waste of life?" Grandpa himself used to "get down to the office at nine o'clock sharp, no matter how [he] felt" and "lay awake nights" worrying about contracts. He had been "right in the thick of it—fighting and scratching, and clawing"; the working world was a "regular jungle." Then one day he realized he "wasn't having any fun" so he "just relaxed" and has "been a happy man ever since." Grandpa's experience and realizations echo the well-known statements of Emerson's contemporary Henry David Thoreau, who in his 1854 book *Walden,* declared that "the mass of men lead lives of quiet desperation." Thoreau argued that people "labor under a mistake." Even when they try to have fun, an "unconscious despair is concealed even under what are called . . . games and amusements . . . there is no play in them, for this comes after work."

As theorist Stanley Cavell suggested in his discussion of 1930s film comedies, *Pursuits of Happiness: The Hollywood Comedy of Remarriage,* characters with individualistic and anti-materialist ideals like the Vanderhof-Sycamores underscore the difference between those who know what has true value in life and those who have forgotten what really counts. In Cavell's words "happiness is not to be won just by opposing those in power but only, beyond that, by educating them, or their successors." We see this in *You Can't Take It with You* where the happy ending depends upon Mr. Kirby and Tony learning to share Grandpa's ideals. In "screwball comedies" like this, as Cavell argued, fulfillment "requires not the fuller satisfaction of our needs as they stand but the examination and transformation of those needs." Grandpa wants Tony to make such a reassessment so that he will not "wake up twenty years from now with nothing in his life but stocks and bonds." Grandpa's advice to the Kirbys is very much in the tradition of Thoreau—who wrote that he went to live at Walden Pond so that he would not "discover that I had not lived." "You've got all the money you need," Vanderhof tells Mr. Kirby, "you can't take it with you." So now is the time to consider what will bring happiness. As Grandpa goes on to say, "how many of us would be willing to settle when we're young for what we eventually get? All those plans we make . . . what happens to them? It's only a handful of the lucky ones that can look back and say they even come close."

Certainly the Vanderhof-Sycamores are just such a "handful of lucky ones." They all seem to have followed the approach to life put forth in

Walden, which encourages its readers to ''simplify, simplify,'' to get back to the basics, and to relax like Thoreau for whom ''time is but a stream I go a-fishing in.'' Although the disasters of Act II cause some doubts about this philosophy at the opening of Act III—when Paul wonders if he's been wrong to have ''just been going along, enjoying myself, when maybe I should have been thinking more about Alice'' and Alice herself wishes her family ''behaved the way *other* people's families do''—the play's happy resolution affirms that Grandpa's way really is best.

Given the economic hardships of the 1930s, we can see why audiences of the time would want to believe Grandpa when he says ''life is simple and kind of beautiful if you let it come to you.'' Of course Kaufman and Hart, through occasional satiric moments, point out the impracticality of their philosophy with quips like Kolenkhov's reminder that ''you cannot relax with Stalin in Russia. The czar relaxed and what happened to him?'' Reminders of Depression-era reality aren't totally absent either, although they are always played for laughs. Donald's remark that going to pick up his relief check ''breaks up his week,'' the peculiar dinner menus, Kolenkhov's just-in-time-for-a-meal arrivals, and the F.B.I.'s investigation of Ed's seemingly subversive circulars bring to mind welfare, hunger, and bureaucratic paranoia respectively. But *You Can't Take It with You* does not aim for political satire but rather hopes to generate mirth, to, at least temporarily, help the audience forget the trials of the real world. The satire here is gentle and the hint of ''bad times'' only emphasizes the light-hearted good times we see depicted on the stage.

Comedy traditionally affirms the possibility of change and growth. There is always a new and better day to come. As Thoreau wrote, ''it is never too late to give up our prejudices. No way of thinking or doing, however ancient, can be trusted without proof.'' So even the older Mr. Kirby can learn to change his mind and see the world through Grandpa's eyes. When considered in the context of traditional American individualism, as expressed in the writings of Emerson and Thoreau, the Vanderhof-Sycamore philosophy which Mr. Kirby initially thinks is ''dangerous'' and ''un-American'' seems just the opposite: distinctly American. *You Can't Take It with You* deserves recognition not only as an excellent farce but as a classic celebration of American individualism. As Moss Hart said, ''I do not look down my nose at comedies; they are an ancient and honorable form of making certain truths palat-

''IN A WORLD IN WHICH THE SANITY USUALLY ASSOCIATED WITH SUNSHINE IS SADLY OVERVALUED, *YOU CAN'T TAKE IT WITH YOU* IS SOMETHING TO BE PRIZED''

able with laughter, and an age can be understood as well by its comedies as by its tragic dramas.''

Source: Erika Kreger, in an essay for *Drama for Students,* Gale, 1997.

John Mason Brown

In this review that first appeared in the New York Evening Post, *December 15 & 19, 1936, Brown praises the lighthearted nature of* You Can't Take It with You.

Brown was an influential and popular American drama critic who wrote extensively on British and American drama.

In a world in which the sanity usually associated with sunshine is sadly overvalued, *You Can't Take It With You* is something to be prized. It is moonstruck, almost from beginning to end. It is blessed with all the happiest lunacies Moss Hart and George S. Kaufman have been able to contribute to it. The Sycamore family is the most gloriously mad group of contented eccentrics the modern theatre has yet had the good fortune to shadow. Its various members comprise a whole nest of Mad Hatters. They are daffy mortals, as lovable as they are laughable. Their whims are endless. So, too, for that matter, is the fun they provide, except when Cupid is foolish enough to force his way into the family circle.

The Sycamores, bless them, live uptown in New York. They are, however, not nearly so far removed from Wall Street as they are from the rent-day worries to which most of us are heir. Grandfather Vanderhof . . . has for some years now refused, on very sensible grounds, to pay his income tax. More than that, though he still has some money, he has long ago retired from business in order to seek happiness in attending commencements, visiting zoos, and collecting snakes and stamps. All the members of his demented household have hobbies of their own and practice the gospel of relaxation which he preaches. His daughter, Mrs. Sycamore. . . , has abandoned painting, to which she temporarily returns, for playwriting because eight years ago a typewriter was delivered by mistake to the Sycamore bedlam. (pp. 177–78)

The quiet lunacy of the family is established by . . . Grandfather Vanderhof, [who] is as lovably gentle as he is unworldly. . . . Old though he is, he is happy because he has been able to remain a child of impulse in a sternly coercive world. He is more than strange. His strangeness is the measure of his wisdom and the point of his philosophy. His is a serenity and a goodness which make it possible for him, when saying ''grace,'' to speak directly to his Creator with a reverent simplicity such as has not been equaled hereabouts since *The Green Pastures* and such as should be the property of all bishops and archbishops in a Panglossian universe. (p. 179)

[Mrs. Sycamore's] head may be light, but her heart is filled with the same kindness which floods Grandfather Vanderhof's. She, too, sets about the business of being flighty and foolish with a blessed unconsciousness of how laughable she succeeds in being. So, also, does . . . her amiable husband. And so, for that matter, do the rest of the agreeably demented Sycamores.

It is only when workaday reason invades the Sycamore home; when dull normalcy makes its appearance; when an orthodox Cupid bursts into this inspired bedlam, that *You Can't Take It With You* suffers. The Sycamores . . . are too fortunate in their nonsense ever to be disturbed by something as illogical as ordinary common sense. (pp. 179–80)

Source: John Mason Brown, ''The Sensible Insanities of *You Can't Take It with You*'' (1936) in his *Two on the Aisle: Ten Years of the American Theatre in Performance*, W. W. Norton & Co., 1938, pp. 177–80.

Brooks Atkinson

In a review that first appeared in the New York Times *on December 15, 1936, noted critic Atkinson related the simple pleasures of Hart and Kaufman's play, particularly its eagerness to please an audience.*

Moss Hart and George S. Kaufman have written their most thoroughly ingratiating comedy, *You Can't Take It With You,* which was put on at the Booth last evening. It is a study in vertigo about a lovable family of hobby-horse riders, funny without being shrill, sensible without being earnest. In

Once in a Lifetime, Mr. Hart and Mr. Kaufman mowed the audience down under a machine-gun barrage of low comedy satire, which was the neatest trick of the season. But you will find their current lark a much more spontaneous piece of hilarity; it is written with a dash of affection to season the humor and played with gayety and simple good spirit. To this column, which has a fondness for amiability in the theatre, *You Can't Take It With You* is the best comedy these authors have written.

To people from the punctilious world outside, the Vanderhof and Sycamore tribes appear to be lunatics. For thirty-five years, grandfather has done nothing but hunt snakes, practice dart throwing, attend commencement exercises and avoid income tax payments. His son-in-law makes fireworks for a hobby in the cellar; various members of the family write plays, study dancing, play the xylophone and operate amateur printing presses. Being mutually loyal they live together in a state of pleasant comity in spite of their separate hobbies. If Alice Sycamore had not fallen in love with the son of a Wall Street banker there would be no reason for this comedy. The contrast between his austerely correct world and their rhymeless existence in a cluttered room supplies the heartburn and the humor. By the time of the final curtain even the banker is convinced that there is something to be said for riding hobbies and living according to impulse in the bosom of a friendly family.

Not that *You Can't Take It With You* is a moral harangue. For Mr. Hart and Mr. Kaufman are fantastic humorists with a knack for extravagances of word and episode and an eye for hilarious incongruities. Nothing this scrawny season has turned up is quite so madcap as a view of the entire Sycamore tribe working at their separate hobbies simultaneously. When Mr. Kirby of Wall Street and the Racquet Club walks into their living-room asylum his orderly head reels with anguish. The amenities look like bedlam to him. What distinguishes *You Can't Take It With You* among the Hart-Kaufman enterprises is the buoyancy of the humor. They do not bear down on it with wisecracks. Although they plan it like good comedy craftsmen, they do not exploit it like gag-men.

And they have assembled a cast of actors who are agreeable folks to sit before during a gusty evening. As grandfather, Henry Travers, the salty and reflective one, is full of improvised enjoyment. Josephine Hull totters and wheedles through the part of a demented homebody. As a ferocious-minded Moscovite, George Tobias roars through the room. Under Mr. Kaufman's direction, which can be admirably relaxed as well as guffawingly taut, every one gives a jovial performance—Paula Trueman, Frank Wilcox, George Heller, Mitzi Hajos, Margot Stevenson, Oscar Polk. Well, just read the cast. The setting is by Donald Oenslager, as usual.

When a problem of conduct raises its head for a fleeting instant in the Sycamore family, grandfather solves it with a casual nod of philosophy, ''So long as she's having fun.'' Mr. Hart and Mr. Kaufman have been more rigidly brilliant in the past, but they have never scooped up an evening of such tickling fun.

Source: Brooks Atkinson, review of *You Can't Take It with You* (1936) in *On Stage: Selected Theater Reviews from the New York Times, 1920–1970,* edited by Bernard Beckerman and Howard Siegman, Arno Press, 1973, pp. 182–83.

FURTHER READING

Atkinson, Brooks. ''The Giddy Twenties'' in his *Broadway,* MacMillan (New York), 1970, pp. 227-37.
    In this chapter from his book-length history of Broadway, Atkinson describes New York theater at the time George S. Kaufman came on the scene, discusses the influence of the Algonquin Round Table, and touches on the beginnings of Kaufman's collaborations with Moss Hart.

Cavell, Stanley. *Pursuits of Happiness: The Hollywood Comedy of Remarriage,* Harvard University Press, 1981, pp. 1-42.
    Cavell's introduction provides a useful interpretation of the film version of *You Can't Take It with You,* and his discussion of screwball comedies in the body of the book illustrates strategies for analyzing farce in both film and theater.

Frye, Northrop. ''The Mythos of Spring: Comedy,'' in his *The Anatomy of Criticism,* Princeton University Press, 1957, pp. 163-186.
    Frye's classic analysis of comedy does not deal with Kaufman and Hart specifically but offers a useful overview of the development of comic form from the Greeks through Shakespeare to the Victorian era.

Goldstein, Malcolm. *George S. Kaufman: His Life, His Theater,* Oxford University Press (New York), 1979.
    In this detailed and readable biography, Goldstein examines both Kaufman's life and work. Chapter 15, ''The Birth of a Classic,'' explains the development of *You Can't Take It with You* offers a reading of the play, and considers its influence on both collaborators.

Gould, Jean. ''Some Clever Collaborators'' in *Modern American Playwrights,* Dodd, Mead & Co. (New York), 1966, pp. 154-167.

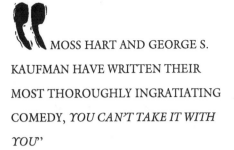

MOSS HART AND GEORGE S. KAUFMAN HAVE WRITTEN THEIR MOST THOROUGHLY INGRATIATING COMEDY, *YOU CAN'T TAKE IT WITH YOU*''

Gould provides concise biographical sketches of Kaufman and Hart, then moves on to a discussion of their most successful plays, devoting several paragraphs to *You Can't Take It with You* .

Hart, Moss. ''No Time for Comedy . . . or Satire: My Most interesting Work'' in *Theatre Arts,* Vol. 38, no. 5, May, 1954, pp. 32-33.
    An article written by Hart that discusses a number of his better-known works and presents his philosophy toward drama.

Mason, Richard. ''The Comic Theatre of Moss Hart: Persistence of a Formula'' in *Theatre Annual,* Volume 23, 1967, pp. 60-87.
    Mason discusses all of Moss Hart's comedies, examining closely the structure of each and arguing Hart contributed important comic elements to the farce form.

Mordden, Ethan. *The American Theater,* Oxford University Press, 1981.
    Mordden's book provides an excellent overview of the history of American theater. He charts the development of comedy as well as serious drama and offers an insightful discussion of Kaufman and Hart.

O'Hara, Frank Hurburt. ''Farce with a Purpose'' in *Today in American Drama,* Greenwood Press (New York), 1969, pp. 190-234.
    O'Hara includes a brief, complimentary discussion of Kaufman and Hart in this chapter dealing with 1930s farcical comedies.

Pollack, Rhoda-Gale. *George S. Kaufman,* Twayne (Boston), 1988.
    Pollack devotes a chapter of her brief biography to ''The Years with Moss Hart.'' She discusses the critical response to *You Can't Take It with You* and its impact on Kaufman's life rather than attempting any analysis or interpretation of the play itself.

SOURCES

Atkinson, Brooks. Review of *You Can't Take It with You* in the *New York Times,* December 15, 1936.

A Celebration of Moss Hart, University of Southern California, April 12, 1970, p. 16.

Thoreau, Henry David. *Walden,* Bantam, 1989, p. 111, 172-73, 178.

Glossary of Literary Terms

A

Abstract Used as a noun, the term refers to a short summary or outline of a longer work. As an adjective applied to writing or literary works, abstract refers to words or phrases that name things not knowable through the five senses.

Absurd, Theater of the See *Theater of the Absurd*

Absurdism See *Theater of the Absurd*

Act A major section of a play. Acts are divided into varying numbers of shorter scenes. From ancient times to the nineteenth century plays were generally constructed of five acts, but modern works typically consist of one, two, or three acts.

Acto A one-act Chicano theater piece developed out of collective improvisation.

Aestheticism A literary and artistic movement of the nineteenth century. Followers of the movement believed that art should not be mixed with social, political, or moral teaching. The statement ''art for art's sake'' is a good summary of aestheticism. The movement had its roots in France, but it gained widespread importance in England in the last half of the nineteenth century, where it helped change the Victorian practice of including moral lessons in literature.

Age of Johnson The period in English literature between 1750 and 1798, named after the most prominent literary figure of the age, Samuel John-

son. Works written during this time are noted for their emphasis on ''sensibility,'' or emotional quality. These works formed a transition between the rational works of the Age of Reason, or Neoclassical period, and the emphasis on individual feelings and responses of the Romantic period.

Age of Reason See *Neoclassicism*

Age of Sensibility See *Age of Johnson*

Alexandrine Meter See *Meter*

Allegory A narrative technique in which characters representing things or abstract ideas are used to convey a message or teach a lesson. Allegory is typically used to teach moral, ethical, or religious lessons but is sometimes used for satiric or political purposes.

Allusion A reference to a familiar literary or historical person or event, used to make an idea more easily understood.

Amerind Literature: The writing and oral traditions of Native Americans. Native American literature was originally passed on by word of mouth, so it consisted largely of stories and events that were easily memorized. Amerind prose is often rhythmic like poetry because it was recited to the beat of a ceremonial drum.

Analogy A comparison of two things made to explain something unfamiliar through its similarities to something familiar, or to prove one point based on the acceptedness of another. Similes and metaphors are types of analogies.

Angry Young Men A group of British writers of the 1950s whose work expressed bitterness and disillusionment with society. Common to their work is an anti-hero who rebels against a corrupt social order and strives for personal integrity.

Antagonist The major character in a narrative or drama who works against the hero or protagonist.

Anthropomorphism The presentation of animals or objects in human shape or with human characteristics. The term is derived from the Greek word for "human form."

Anti-hero A central character in a work of literature who lacks traditional heroic qualities such as courage, physical prowess, and fortitude. Anti-heros typically distrust conventional values and are unable to commit themselves to any ideals. They generally feel helpless in a world over which they have no control. Anti-heroes usually accept, and often celebrate, their positions as social outcasts.

Antimasque See *Masque*

Antithesis The antithesis of something is its direct opposite. In literature, the use of antithesis as a figure of speech results in two statements that show a contrast through the balancing of two opposite ideas. Technically, it is the second portion of the statement that is defined as the "antithesis"; the first portion is the "thesis."

Apocrypha Writings tentatively attributed to an author but not proven or universally accepted to be their works. The term was originally applied to certain books of the Bible that were not considered inspired and so were not included in the "sacred canon."

Apollonian and Dionysian The two impulses believed to guide authors of dramatic tragedy. The Apollonian impulse is named after Apollo, the Greek god of light and beauty and the symbol of intellectual order. The Dionysian impulse is named after Dionysus, the Greek god of wine and the symbol of the unrestrained forces of nature. The Apollonian impulse is to create a rational, harmonious world, while the Dionysian is to express the irrational forces of personality.

Apostrophe A statement, question, or request addressed to an inanimate object or concept or to a nonexistent or absent person.

Archetype The word archetype is commonly used to describe an original pattern or model from which all other things of the same kind are made. This term was introduced to literary criticism from the psychology of Carl Jung. It expresses Jung's theory that behind every person's "unconscious," or repressed memories of the past, lies the "collective unconscious" of the human race: memories of the countless typical experiences of our ancestors. These memories are said to prompt illogical associations that trigger powerful emotions in the reader. Often, the emotional process is primitive, even primordial. Archetypes are the literary images that grow out of the "collective unconscious." They appear in literature as incidents and plots that repeat basic patterns of life. They may also appear as stereotyped characters.

Argument The argument of a work is the author's subject matter or principal idea.

Aristotelian Criticism Specifically, the method of evaluating and analyzing tragedy formulated by the Greek philosopher Aristotle in his *Poetics*. More generally, the term indicates any form of criticism that follows Aristotle's views. Aristotelian criticism focuses on the form and logical structure of a work, apart from its historical or social context, in contrast to "Platonic Criticism," which stresses the usefulness of art.

Art for Art's Sake See *Aestheticism*

Aside A comment made by a stage performer that is intended to be heard by the audience but supposedly not by other characters.

Audience The people for whom a piece of literature is written. Authors usually write with a certain audience in mind, for example, children, members of a religious or ethnic group, or colleagues in a professional field. The term "audience" also applies to the people who gather to see or hear any performance, including plays, poetry readings, speeches, and concerts.

Avant-garde A French term meaning "vanguard." It is used in literary criticism to describe new writing that rejects traditional approaches to literature in favor of innovations in style or content.

B

Ballad A short poem that tells a simple story and has a repeated refrain. Ballads were originally intended to be sung. Early ballads, known as folk ballads, were passed down through generations, so their authors are often unknown. Later ballads composed by known authors are called literary ballads.

Baroque A term used in literary criticism to describe literature that is complex or ornate in style or diction. Baroque works typically express tension, anxiety, and violent emotion. The term ''Baroque Age'' designates a period in Western European literature beginning in the late sixteenth century and ending about one hundred years later. Works of this period often mirror the qualities of works more generally associated with the label ''baroque'' and sometimes feature elaborate conceits.

Baroque Age See *Baroque*

Baroque Period See *Baroque*

Beat Generation See *Beat Movement*

Beat Movement A period featuring a group of American poets and novelists of the 1950s and 1960s—including Jack Kerouac, Allen Ginsberg, Gregory Corso, William S. Burroughs, and Lawrence Ferlinghetti—who rejected established social and literary values. Using such techniques as stream of consciousness writing and jazz-influenced free verse and focusing on unusual or abnormal states of mind—generated by religious ecstasy or the use of drugs—the Beat writers aimed to create works that were unconventional in both form and subject matter.

Black Aesthetic Movement A period of artistic and literary development among African Americans in the 1960s and early 1970s. This was the first major African-American artistic movement since the Harlem Renaissance and was closely paralleled by the civil rights and black power movements. The black aesthetic writers attempted to produce works of art that would be meaningful to the black masses. Key figures in black aesthetics included one of its founders, poet and playwright Amiri Baraka, formerly known as LeRoi Jones; poet and essayist Haki R. Madhubuti, formerly Don L. Lee; poet and playwright Sonia Sanchez; and dramatist Ed Bullins.

Black Arts Movement See *Black Aesthetic Movement*

Black Comedy See *Black Humor*

Black Humor Writing that places grotesque elements side by side with humorous ones in an attempt to shock the reader, forcing him or her to laugh at the horrifying reality of a disordered world.

Blank Verse Loosely, any unrhymed poetry, but more generally, unrhymed iambic pentameter verse (composed of lines of five two-syllable feet with the first syllable accented, the second unaccented). Blank verse has been used by poets since the Renaissance for its flexibility and its graceful, dignified tone.

Bloomsbury Group A group of English writers, artists, and intellectuals who held informal artistic and philosophical discussions in Bloomsbury, a district of London, from around 1907 to the early 1930s. The Bloomsbury Group held no uniform philosophical beliefs but did commonly express an aversion to moral prudery and a desire for greater social tolerance.

Bon Mot A French term meaning ''good word.'' A *bon mot* is a witty remark or clever observation.

Breath Verse See *Projective Verse*

Burlesque Any literary work that uses exaggeration to make its subject appear ridiculous, either by treating a trivial subject with profound seriousness or by treating a dignified subject frivolously. The word ''burlesque'' may also be used as an adjective, as in ''burlesque show,'' to mean ''striptease act.''

C

Cadence The natural rhythm of language caused by the alternation of accented and unaccented syllables. Much modern poetry—notably free verse—deliberately manipulates cadence to create complex rhythmic effects.

Caesura A pause in a line of poetry, usually occurring near the middle. It typically corresponds to a break in the natural rhythm or sense of the line but is sometimes shifted to create special meanings or rhythmic effects.

Canzone A short Italian or Provencal lyric poem, commonly about love and often set to music. The *canzone* has no set form but typically contains five or six stanzas made up of seven to twenty lines of eleven syllables each. A shorter, five- to ten-line ''envoy,'' or concluding stanza, completes the poem.

Carpe Diem A Latin term meaning ''seize the day.'' This is a traditional theme of poetry, especially lyrics. A *carpe diem* poem advises the reader or the person it addresses to live for today and enjoy the pleasures of the moment.

Catharsis The release or purging of unwanted emotions— specifically fear and pity—brought about by exposure to art. The term was first used by the Greek philosopher Aristotle in his *Poetics* to refer to the desired effect of tragedy on spectators.

Celtic Renaissance A period of Irish literary and cultural history at the end of the nineteenth century. Followers of the movement aimed to create a romantic vision of Celtic myth and legend. The most significant works of the Celtic Renaissance typically present a dreamy, unreal world, usually in reaction against the reality of contemporary problems.

Celtic Twilight See *Celtic Renaissance*

Character Broadly speaking, a person in a literary work. The actions of characters are what constitute the plot of a story, novel, or poem. There are numerous types of characters, ranging from simple, stereotypical figures to intricate, multifaceted ones. In the techniques of anthropomorphism and personification, animals—and even places or things—can assume aspects of character. "Characterization" is the process by which an author creates vivid, believable characters in a work of art. This may be done in a variety of ways, including (1) direct description of the character by the narrator; (2) the direct presentation of the speech, thoughts, or actions of the character; and (3) the responses of other characters to the character. The term "character" also refers to a form originated by the ancient Greek writer Theophrastus that later became popular in the seventeenth and eighteenth centuries. It is a short essay or sketch of a person who prominently displays a specific attribute or quality, such as miserliness or ambition.

Characterization See *Character*

Chorus In ancient Greek drama, a group of actors who commented on and interpreted the unfolding action on the stage. Initially the chorus was a major component of the presentation, but over time it became less significant, with its numbers reduced and its role eventually limited to commentary between acts. By the sixteenth century the chorus—if employed at all— was typically a single person who provided a prologue and an epilogue and occasionally appeared between acts to introduce or underscore an important event.

Chronicle A record of events presented in chronological order. Although the scope and level of detail provided varies greatly among the chronicles surviving from ancient times, some, such as the *Anglo-Saxon Chronicle,* feature vivid descriptions and a lively recounting of events. During the Elizabethan Age, many dramas— appropriately called "chronicle plays"—were based on material from chronicles.

Classical In its strictest definition in literary criticism, classicism refers to works of ancient Greek or Roman literature. The term may also be used to describe a literary work of recognized importance (a "classic") from any time period or literature that exhibits the traits of classicism.

Classicism A term used in literary criticism to describe critical doctrines that have their roots in ancient Greek and Roman literature, philosophy, and art. Works associated with classicism typically exhibit restraint on the part of the author, unity of design and purpose, clarity, simplicity, logical organization, and respect for tradition.

Climax The turning point in a narrative, the moment when the conflict is at its most intense. Typically, the structure of stories, novels, and plays is one of rising action, in which tension builds to the climax, followed by falling action, in which tension lessens as the story moves to its conclusion.

Colloquialism A word, phrase, or form of pronunciation that is acceptable in casual conversation but not in formal, written communication. It is considered more acceptable than slang.

Comedy One of two major types of drama, the other being tragedy. Its aim is to amuse, and it typically ends happily. Comedy assumes many forms, such as farce and burlesque, and uses a variety of techniques, from parody to satire. In a restricted sense the term comedy refers only to dramatic presentations, but in general usage it is commonly applied to nondramatic works as well.

Comedy of Manners A play about the manners and conventions of an aristocratic, highly sophisticated society. The characters are usually types rather than individualized personalities, and plot is less important than atmosphere. Such plays were an important aspect of late seventeenth-century English comedy. The comedy of manners was revived in the eighteenth century by Oliver Goldsmith and Richard Brinsley Sheridan, enjoyed a second revival in the late nineteenth century, and has endured into the twentieth century.

Comic Relief The use of humor to lighten the mood of a serious or tragic story, especially in plays. The technique is very common in Elizabethan works, and can be an integral part of the plot or simply a brief event designed to break the tension of the scene.

Commedia dell'arte An Italian term meaning "the comedy of guilds" or "the comedy of professional actors." This form of dramatic comedy was popular in Italy during the sixteenth century. Actors were assigned stock roles (such as Pulcinella, the stupid servant, or Pantalone, the old merchant) and given a basic plot to follow, but all dialogue was improvised. The roles were rigidly typed and the plots were formulaic, usually revolving around young lovers who thwarted their elders and attained wealth and happiness. A rigid convention of the *commedia dell'arte* is the periodic intrusion of Harlequin, who interrupts the play with low buffoonery.

Complaint A lyric poem, popular in the Renaissance, in which the speaker expresses sorrow about his or her condition. Typically, the speaker's sadness is caused by an unresponsive lover, but some complaints cite other sources of unhappiness, such as poverty or fate.

Conceit A clever and fanciful metaphor, usually expressed through elaborate and extended comparison, that presents a striking parallel between two seemingly dissimilar things—for example, elaborately comparing a beautiful woman to an object like a garden or the sun. The conceit was a popular device throughout the Elizabethan Age and Baroque Age and was the principal technique of the seventeenth-century English metaphysical poets. This usage of the word conceit is unrelated to the best-known definition of conceit as an arrogant attitude or behavior.

Concrete Concrete is the opposite of abstract, and refers to a thing that actually exists or a description that allows the reader to experience an object or concept with the senses.

Concrete Poetry Poetry in which visual elements play a large part in the poetic effect. Punctuation marks, letters, or words are arranged on a page to form a visual design: a cross, for example, or a bumblebee.

Confessional Poetry A form of poetry in which the poet reveals very personal, intimate, sometimes shocking information about himself or herself.

Conflict The conflict in a work of fiction is the issue to be resolved in the story. It usually occurs between two characters, the protagonist and the antagonist, or between the protagonist and society or the protagonist and himself or herself.

Connotation The impression that a word gives beyond its defined meaning. Connotations may be universally understood or may be significant only to a certain group.

Consonance Consonance occurs in poetry when words appearing at the ends of two or more verses have similar final consonant sounds but have final vowel sounds that differ, as with "stuff" and "off."

Convention Any widely accepted literary device, style, or form.

Corrido A Mexican ballad.

Couplet Two lines of poetry with the same rhyme and meter, often expressing a complete and self-contained thought.

Criticism The systematic study and evaluation of literary works, usually based on a specific method or set of principles. An important part of literary studies since ancient times, the practice of criticism has given rise to numerous theories, methods, and "schools," sometimes producing conflicting, even contradictory, interpretations of literature in general as well as of individual works. Even such basic issues as what constitutes a poem or a novel have been the subject of much criticism over the centuries.

D

Dactyl See *Foot*

Dadaism A protest movement in art and literature founded by Tristan Tzara in 1916. Followers of the movement expressed their outrage at the destruction brought about by World War I by revolting against numerous forms of social convention. The Dadaists presented works marked by calculated madness and flamboyant nonsense. They stressed total freedom of expression, commonly through primitive displays of emotion and illogical, often senseless, poetry. The movement ended shortly after the war, when it was replaced by surrealism.

Decadent See *Decadents*

Decadents The followers of a nineteenth-century literary movement that had its beginnings in French aestheticism. Decadent literature displays a fascination with perverse and morbid states; a search for novelty and sensation—the "new thrill"; a preoccupation with mysticism; and a belief in the senselessness of human existence. The movement is closely associated with the doctrine Art for Art's Sake. The term "decadence" is sometimes used to denote a decline in the quality of art or literature following a period of greatness.

Deconstruction A method of literary criticism developed by Jacques Derrida and characterized by multiple conflicting interpretations of a given work. Deconstructionists consider the impact of the language of a work and suggest that the true meaning of the work is not necessarily the meaning that the author intended.

Deduction The process of reaching a conclusion through reasoning from general premises to a specific premise.

Denotation The definition of a word, apart from the impressions or feelings it creates in the reader.

Denouement A French word meaning "the unknotting." In literary criticism, it denotes the resolution of conflict in fiction or drama. The *denouement* follows the climax and provides an outcome to the primary plot situation as well as an explanation of secondary plot complications. The *denouement* often involves a character's recognition of his or her state of mind or moral condition.

Description Descriptive writing is intended to allow a reader to picture the scene or setting in which the action of a story takes place. The form this description takes often evokes an intended emotional response—a dark, spooky graveyard will evoke fear, and a peaceful, sunny meadow will evoke calmness.

Detective Story A narrative about the solution of a mystery or the identification of a criminal. The conventions of the detective story include the detective's scrupulous use of logic in solving the mystery; incompetent or ineffectual police; a suspect who appears guilty at first but is later proved innocent; and the detective's friend or confidant—often the narrator—whose slowness in interpreting clues emphasizes by contrast the detective's brilliance.

Deus ex machina A Latin term meaning "god out of a machine." In Greek drama, a god was often lowered onto the stage by a mechanism of some kind to rescue the hero or untangle the plot. By extension, the term refers to any artificial device or coincidence used to bring about a convenient and simple solution to a plot. This is a common device in melodramas and includes such fortunate circumstances as the sudden receipt of a legacy to save the family farm or a last-minute stay of execution. The *deus ex machina* invariably rewards the virtuous and punishes evildoers.

Dialogue In its widest sense, dialogue is simply conversation between people in a literary work; in its most restricted sense, it refers specifically to the speech of characters in a drama. As a specific literary genre, a "dialogue" is a composition in which characters debate an issue or idea.

Diction The selection and arrangement of words in a literary work. Either or both may vary depending on the desired effect. There are four general types of diction: "formal," used in scholarly or lofty writing; "informal," used in relaxed but educated conversation; "colloquial," used in everyday speech; and "slang," containing newly coined words and other terms not accepted in formal usage.

Didactic A term used to describe works of literature that aim to teach some moral, religious, political, or practical lesson. Although didactic elements are often found in artistically pleasing works, the term "didactic" usually refers to literature in which the message is more important than the form. The term may also be used to criticize a work that the critic finds "overly didactic," that is, heavy-handed in its delivery of a lesson.

Dimeter See *Meter*

Dionysian See *Apollonian and Dionysian*

Discordia concours A Latin phrase meaning "discord in harmony." The term was coined by the eighteenth-century English writer Samuel Johnson to describe "a combination of dissimilar images or discovery of occult resemblances in things apparently unlike." Johnson created the expression by reversing a phrase by the Latin poet Horace.

Dissonance A combination of harsh or jarring sounds, especially in poetry. Although such combinations may be accidental, poets sometimes intentionally make them to achieve particular effects. Dissonance is also sometimes used to refer to close but not identical rhymes. When this is the case, the word functions as a synonym for consonance.

Doppelganger A literary technique by which a character is duplicated (usually in the form of an alter ego, though sometimes as a ghostly counterpart) or divided into two distinct, usually opposite personalities. The use of this character device is widespread in nineteenth- and twentieth- century literature, and indicates a growing awareness among authors that the "self" is really a composite of many "selves."

Double Entendre A corruption of a French phrase meaning "double meaning." The term is used to indicate a word or phrase that is deliberately ambiguous, especially when one of the meanings is risque or improper.

Double, The See *Doppelganger*

Draft Any preliminary version of a written work. An author may write dozens of drafts which are revised to form the final work, or he or she may write only one, with few or no revisions.

Drama In its widest sense, a drama is any work designed to be presented by actors on a stage. Similarly, "drama" denotes a broad literary genre that includes a variety of forms, from pageant and spectacle to tragedy and comedy, as well as countless types and subtypes. More commonly in modern usage, however, a drama is a work that treats serious subjects and themes but does not aim at the grandeur of tragedy. This use of the term originated with the eighteenth-century French writer Denis Diderot, who used the word *drame* to designate his plays about middle- class life; thus "drama" typically features characters of a less exalted stature than those of tragedy.

Dramatic Irony Occurs when the audience of a play or the reader of a work of literature knows something that a character in the work itself does not know. The irony is in the contrast between the intended meaning of the statements or actions of a character and the additional information understood by the audience.

Dramatic Monologue See *Monologue*

Dramatic Poetry Any lyric work that employs elements of drama such as dialogue, conflict, or characterization, but excluding works that are intended for stage presentation.

Dramatis Personae The characters in a work of literature, particularly a drama.

Dream Allegory See *Dream Vision*

Dream Vision A literary convention, chiefly of the Middle Ages. In a dream vision a story is presented as a literal dream of the narrator. This device was commonly used to teach moral and religious lessons.

Dystopia An imaginary place in a work of fiction where the characters lead dehumanized, fearful lives.

E

Eclogue In classical literature, a poem featuring rural themes and structured as a dialogue among shepherds. Eclogues often took specific poetic forms, such as elegies or love poems. Some were written as the soliloquy of a shepherd. In later centuries, "eclogue" came to refer to any poem that was in the pastoral tradition or that had a dialogue or monologue structure.

Edwardian Describes cultural conventions identified with the period of the reign of Edward VII of England (1901-1910). Writers of the Edwardian Age typically displayed a strong reaction against the propriety and conservatism of the Victorian Age. Their work often exhibits distrust of authority in religion, politics, and art and expresses strong doubts about the soundness of conventional values.

Edwardian Age See *Edwardian*

Electra Complex A daughter's amorous obsession with her father.

Elegy A lyric poem that laments the death of a person or the eventual death of all people. In a conventional elegy, set in a classical world, the poet and subject are spoken of as shepherds. In modern criticism, the word elegy is often used to refer to a poem that is melancholy or mournfully contemplative.

Elizabethan Age A period of great economic growth, religious controversy, and nationalism closely associated with the reign of Elizabeth I of England (1558-1603). The Elizabethan Age is considered a part of the general renaissance—that is, the flowering of arts and literature—that took place in Europe during the fourteenth through sixteenth centuries. The era is considered the golden age of English literature. The most important dramas in English and a great deal of lyric poetry were produced during this period, and modern English criticism began around this time.

Elizabethan Drama English comic and tragic plays produced during the Renaissance, or more narrowly, those plays written during the last years of and few years after Queen Elizabeth's reign. William Shakespeare is considered an Elizabethan dramatist in the broader sense, although most of his work was produced during the reign of James I.

Empathy A sense of shared experience, including emotional and physical feelings, with someone or something other than oneself. Empathy is often used to describe the response of a reader to a literary character.

English Sonnet See *Sonnet*

Enjambment The running over of the sense and structure of a line of verse or a couplet into the following verse or couplet.

Enlightenment, The An eighteenth-century philosophical movement. It began in France but had a wide impact throughout Europe and America. Thinkers of the Enlightenment valued reason and believed that both the individual and society could achieve a state of perfection. Corresponding to this essentially humanist vision was a resistance to religious authority.

Epic A long narrative poem about the adventures of a hero of great historic or legendary importance. The setting is vast and the action is often given cosmic significance through the intervention of supernatural forces such as gods, angels, or demons. Epics are typically written in a classical style of grand simplicity with elaborate metaphors and allusions that enhance the symbolic importance of a hero's adventures.

Epic Simile See *Homeric Simile*

Epic Theater A theory of theatrical presentation developed by twentieth-century German playwright Bertolt Brecht. Brecht created a type of drama that the audience could view with complete detachment. He used what he termed ''alienation effects'' to create an emotional distance between the audience and the action on stage. Among these effects are: short, self-contained scenes that keep the play from building to a cathartic climax; songs that comment on the action; and techniques of acting that prevent the actor from developing an emotional identity with his role.

Epigram A saying that makes the speaker's point quickly and concisely.

Epilogue A concluding statement or section of a literary work. In dramas, particularly those of the seventeenth and eighteenth centuries, the epilogue is a closing speech, often in verse, delivered by an actor at the end of a play and spoken directly to the audience.

Epiphany A sudden revelation of truth inspired by a seemingly trivial incident.

Episode An incident that forms part of a story and is significantly related to it. Episodes may be either self-contained narratives or events that depend on a larger context for their sense and importance.

Episodic Plot See *Plot*

Epitaph An inscription on a tomb or tombstone, or a verse written on the occasion of a person's death. Epitaphs may be serious or humorous.

Epithalamion A song or poem written to honor and commemorate a marriage ceremony.

Epithalamium See *Epithalamion*

Epithet A word or phrase, often disparaging or abusive, that expresses a character trait of someone or something.

Exempla See *Exemplum*

Exemplum A tale with a moral message. This form of literary sermonizing flourished during the Middle Ages, when *exempla* appeared in collections known as ''example-books.''

Existentialism A predominantly twentieth-century philosophy concerned with the nature and perception of human existence. There are two major strains of existentialist thought: atheistic and Christian. Followers of atheistic existentialism believe that the individual is alone in a godless universe and that the basic human condition is one of suffering and loneliness. Nevertheless, because there are no fixed values, individuals can create their own characters—indeed, they can shape themselves—through the exercise of free will. The atheistic strain culminates in and is popularly associated with the works of Jean-Paul Sartre. The Christian existentialists, on the other hand, believe that only in God may people find freedom from life's anguish. The two strains hold certain beliefs in common: that existence cannot be fully understood or described through empirical effort; that anguish is a universal element of life; that individuals must bear responsibility for their actions; and that there is no common standard of behavior or perception for religious and ethical matters.

Expatriates See *Expatriatism*

Expatriatism The practice of leaving one's country to live for an extended period in another country.

Exposition Writing intended to explain the nature of an idea, thing, or theme. Expository writing is often combined with description, narration, or argument. In dramatic writing, the exposition is the introductory material which presents the characters, setting, and tone of the play.

Expressionism An indistinct literary term, originally used to describe an early twentieth-century school of German painting. The term applies to almost any mode of unconventional, highly subjective writing that distorts reality in some way.

Extended Monologue See *Monologue*

F

Fable A prose or verse narrative intended to convey a moral. Animals or inanimate objects with human characteristics often serve as characters in fables.

Fairy Tales Short narratives featuring mythical beings such as fairies, elves, and sprites. These tales originally belonged to the folklore of a particular nation or region, such as those collected in Germany by Jacob and Wilhelm Grimm.

Falling Action See *Denouement*

Fantasy A literary form related to mythology and folklore. Fantasy literature is typically set in non-existent realms and features supernatural beings.

Farce A type of comedy characterized by broad humor, outlandish incidents, and often vulgar subject matter.

Feet See *Foot*

Feminine Rhyme See *Rhyme*

Femme fatale A French phrase with the literal translation "fatal woman." A *femme fatale* is a sensuous, alluring woman who often leads men into danger or trouble.

Fiction Any story that is the product of imagination rather than a documentation of fact. characters and events in such narratives may be based in real life but their ultimate form and configuration is a creation of the author.

Figurative Language A technique in writing in which the author temporarily interrupts the order, construction, or meaning of the writing for a particular effect. This interruption takes the form of one or more figures of speech such as hyperbole, irony, or simile. Figurative language is the opposite of literal language, in which every word is truthful, accurate, and free of exaggeration or embellishment.

Figures of Speech Writing that differs from customary conventions for construction, meaning, order, or significance for the purpose of a special meaning or effect. There are two major types of figures of speech: rhetorical figures, which do not make changes in the meaning of the words, and tropes, which do.

Fin de siecle A French term meaning "end of the century." The term is used to denote the last decade of the nineteenth century, a transition period when writers and other artists abandoned old conventions and looked for new techniques and objectives.

First Person See *Point of View*

Flashback A device used in literature to present action that occurred before the beginning of the story. Flashbacks are often introduced as the dreams or recollections of one or more characters.

Foil A character in a work of literature whose physical or psychological qualities contrast strongly with, and therefore highlight, the corresponding qualities of another character.

Folk Ballad See *Ballad*

Folklore Traditions and myths preserved in a culture or group of people. Typically, these are passed on by word of mouth in various forms—such as legends, songs, and proverbs— or preserved in customs and ceremonies. This term was first used by W. J. Thoms in 1846.

Folktale A story originating in oral tradition. Folktales fall into a variety of categories, including legends, ghost stories, fairy tales, fables, and anecdotes based on historical figures and events.

Foot The smallest unit of rhythm in a line of poetry. In English-language poetry, a foot is typically one accented syllable combined with one or two unaccented syllables.

Foreshadowing A device used in literature to create expectation or to set up an explanation of later developments.

Form The pattern or construction of a work which identifies its genre and distinguishes it from other genres.

Formalism In literary criticism, the belief that literature should follow prescribed rules of construction, such as those that govern the sonnet form.

Fourteener Meter See *Meter*

Free Verse Poetry that lacks regular metrical and rhyme patterns but that tries to capture the cadences of everyday speech. The form allows a poet to exploit a variety of rhythmical effects within a single poem.

Futurism A flamboyant literary and artistic movement that developed in France, Italy, and Russia from 1908 through the 1920s. Futurist theater and poetry abandoned traditional literary forms. In their place, followers of the movement attempted to achieve total freedom of expression through bizarre imagery and deformed or newly invented words. The Futurists were self-consciously modern artists who attempted to incorporate the appearances and sounds of modern life into their work.

G

Genre A category of literary work. In critical theory, genre may refer to both the content of a given work—tragedy, comedy, pastoral—and to its form, such as poetry, novel, or drama.

Genteel Tradition A term coined by critic George Santayana to describe the literary practice of certain late nineteenth- century American writers, especially New Englanders. Followers of the Genteel Tradition emphasized conventionality in social, religious, moral, and literary standards.

Gilded Age A period in American history during the 1870s characterized by political corruption and materialism. A number of important novels of social and political criticism were written during this time.

Gothic See *Gothicism*

Gothicism In literary criticism, works characterized by a taste for the medieval or morbidly attractive. A gothic novel prominently features elements of horror, the supernatural, gloom, and violence: clanking chains, terror, charnel houses, ghosts, medieval castles, and mysteriously slamming doors. The term "gothic novel" is also applied to novels that lack elements of the traditional Gothic setting but that create a similar atmosphere of terror or dread.

Gothic Novel See *Gothicism*

Great Chain of Being The belief that all things and creatures in nature are organized in a hierarchy from inanimate objects at the bottom to God at the top. This system of belief was popular in the seventeenth and eighteenth centuries.

Grotesque In literary criticism, the subject matter of a work or a style of expression characterized by exaggeration, deformity, freakishness, and disorder. The grotesque often includes an element of comic absurdity.

H

Haiku The shortest form of Japanese poetry, constructed in three lines of five, seven, and five syllables respectively. The message of a *haiku* poem usually centers on some aspect of spirituality and provokes an emotional response in the reader.

Half Rhyme See *Consonance*

Hamartia In tragedy, the event or act that leads to the hero's or heroine's downfall. This term is often incorrectly used as a synonym for tragic flaw.

Harlem Renaissance The Harlem Renaissance of the 1920s is generally considered the first significant movement of black writers and artists in the United States. During this period, new and established black writers published more fiction and poetry than ever before, the first influential black literary journals were established, and black authors and artists received their first widespread recognition and serious critical appraisal. Among the major writers associated with this period are Claude McKay, Jean Toomer, Countee Cullen, Langston Hughes, Arna Bontemps, Nella Larsen, and Zora Neale Hurston.

Harlequin A stock character of the *commedia dell'arte* who occasionally interrupted the action with silly antics.

Hellenism Imitation of ancient Greek thought or styles. Also, an approach to life that focuses on the growth and development of the intellect. "Hellenism" is sometimes used to refer to the belief that reason can be applied to examine all human experience.

Heptameter See *Meter*

Hero/Heroine The principal sympathetic character (male or female) in a literary work. Heroes and heroines typically exhibit admirable traits: idealism, courage, and integrity, for example.

Heroic Couplet A rhyming couplet written in iambic pentameter (a verse with five iambic feet).

Heroic Line The meter and length of a line of verse in epic or heroic poetry. This varies by language and time period.

Heroine See *Hero/Heroine*

Hexameter See *Meter*

Historical Criticism The study of a work based on its impact on the world of the time period in which it was written.

Hokku See *Haiku*

Holocaust See *Holocaust Literature*

Holocaust Literature Literature influenced by or written about the Holocaust of World War II. Such literature includes true stories of survival in concentration camps, escape, and life after the war, as well as fictional works and poetry.

Homeric Simile An elaborate, detailed comparison written as a simile many lines in length.

Horatian Satire See *Satire*

Humanism A philosophy that places faith in the dignity of humankind and rejects the medieval perception of the individual as a weak, fallen creature. "Humanists" typically believe in the perfectibility of human nature and view reason and education as the means to that end.

Humors Mentions of the humors refer to the ancient Greek theory that a person's health and personality were determined by the balance of four basic fluids in the body: blood, phlegm, yellow bile, and black bile. A dominance of any fluid would cause extremes in behavior. An excess of blood created a sanguine person who was joyful, aggressive, and passionate; a phlegmatic person was shy, fearful, and sluggish; too much yellow bile led to a choleric temperament characterized by impatience, anger, bitterness, and stubbornness; and excessive black bile created melancholy, a state of laziness, gluttony, and lack of motivation.

Humours See *Humors*

Hyperbole In literary criticism, deliberate exaggeration used to achieve an effect.

I

Iamb See *Foot*

Idiom A word construction or verbal expression closely associated with a given language.

Image A concrete representation of an object or sensory experience. Typically, such a representation helps evoke the feelings associated with the object or experience itself. Images are either "literal" or "figurative." Literal images are especially concrete and involve little or no extension of the obvious meaning of the words used to express them. Figurative images do not follow the literal meaning of the words exactly. Images in literature are usually visual, but the term "image" can also refer to the representation of any sensory experience.

Imagery The array of images in a literary work. Also, figurative language.

Imagism An English and American poetry movement that flourished between 1908 and 1917. The Imagists used precise, clearly presented images in their works. They also used common, everyday speech and aimed for conciseness, concrete imagery, and the creation of new rhythms.

In medias res A Latin term meaning "in the middle of things." It refers to the technique of beginning a story at its midpoint and then using various flashback devices to reveal previous action.

Induction The process of reaching a conclusion by reasoning from specific premises to form a general premise. Also, an introductory portion of a work of literature, especially a play.

Intentional Fallacy The belief that judgments of a literary work based solely on an author's stated or implied intentions are false and misleading. Critics who believe in the concept of the intentional fallacy typically argue that the work itself is sufficient matter for interpretation, even though they may concede that an author's statement of purpose can be useful.

Interior Monologue A narrative technique in which characters' thoughts are revealed in a way that appears to be uncontrolled by the author. The interior monologue typically aims to reveal the inner self of a character. It portrays emotional experiences as they occur at both a conscious and unconscious level. images are often used to represent sensations or emotions.

Internal Rhyme Rhyme that occurs within a single line of verse.

Irish Literary Renaissance A late nineteenth- and early twentieth-century movement in Irish literature. Members of the movement aimed to reduce the influence of British culture in Ireland and create an Irish national literature.

Irony In literary criticism, the effect of language in which the intended meaning is the opposite of what is stated.

Italian Sonnet See *Sonnet*

J

Jacobean Age The period of the reign of James I of England (1603-1625). The early literature of this period reflected the worldview of the Elizabethan

Age, but a darker, more cynical attitude steadily grew in the art and literature of the Jacobean Age. This was an important time for English drama and poetry.

Jargon Language that is used or understood only by a select group of people. Jargon may refer to terminology used in a certain profession, such as computer jargon, or it may refer to any nonsensical language that is not understood by most people.

Juvenalian Satire See *Satire*

K

Knickerbocker Group A somewhat indistinct group of New York writers of the first half of the nineteenth century. Members of the group were linked only by location and a common theme: New York life.

L

Lais See *Lay*

Lay A song or simple narrative poem. The form originated in medieval France. Early French *lais* were often based on the Celtic legends and other tales sung by Breton minstrels—thus the name of the "Breton lay." In fourteenth-century England, the term "lay" was used to describe short narratives written in imitation of the Breton lays.

Leitmotiv See *Motif*

Literal Language An author uses literal language when he or she writes without exaggerating or embellishing the subject matter and without any tools of figurative language.

Literary Ballad See *Ballad*

Literature Literature is broadly defined as any written or spoken material, but the term most often refers to creative works.

Lost Generation A term first used by Gertrude Stein to describe the post-World War I generation of American writers: men and women haunted by a sense of betrayal and emptiness brought about by the destructiveness of the war.

Lyric Poetry A poem expressing the subjective feelings and personal emotions of the poet. Such poetry is melodic, since it was originally accompanied by a lyre in recitals. Most Western poetry in the twentieth century may be classified as lyrical.

M

Mannerism Exaggerated, artificial adherence to a literary manner or style. Also, a popular style of the visual arts of late sixteenth-century Europe that was marked by elongation of the human form and by intentional spatial distortion. Literary works that are self-consciously high-toned and artistic are often said to be "mannered."

Masculine Rhyme See *Rhyme*

Masque A lavish and elaborate form of entertainment, often performed in royal courts, that emphasizes song, dance, and costumery. The Renaissance form of the masque grew out of the spectacles of masked figures common in medieval England and Europe. The masque reached its peak of popularity and development in seventeenth-century England, during the reigns of James I and, especially, of Charles I. Ben Jonson, the most significant masque writer, also created the "antimasque," which incorporates elements of humor and the grotesque into the traditional masque and achieved greater dramatic quality.

Measure The foot, verse, or time sequence used in a literary work, especially a poem. Measure is often used somewhat incorrectly as a synonym for meter.

Melodrama A play in which the typical plot is a conflict between characters who personify extreme good and evil. Melodramas usually end happily and emphasize sensationalism. Other literary forms that use the same techniques are often labeled "melodramatic." The term was formerly used to describe a combination of drama and music; as such, it was synonymous with "opera."

Metaphor A figure of speech that expresses an idea through the image of another object. Metaphors suggest the essence of the first object by identifying it with certain qualities of the second object.

Metaphysical Conceit See *Conceit*

Metaphysical Poetry The body of poetry produced by a group of seventeenth-century English writers called the "Metaphysical Poets." The group includes John Donne and Andrew Marvell. The Metaphysical Poets made use of everyday speech, intellectual analysis, and unique imagery. They aimed to portray the ordinary conflicts and contradictions of life. Their poems often took the form of an argument, and many of them emphasize physical and religious love as well as the fleeting nature of life. Elaborate conceits are typical in metaphysical poetry.

Metaphysical Poets See *Metaphysical Poetry*

Meter In literary criticism, the repetition of sound patterns that creates a rhythm in poetry. The patterns are based on the number of syllables and the presence and absence of accents. The unit of rhythm in a line is called a foot. Types of meter are classified according to the number of feet in a line. These are the standard English lines: Monometer, one foot; Dimeter, two feet; Trimeter, three feet; Tetrameter, four feet; Pentameter, five feet; Hexameter, six feet (also called the Alexandrine); Heptameter, seven feet (also called the "Fourteener" when the feet are iambic).

Mise en scene The costumes, scenery, and other properties of a drama.

Modernism Modern literary practices. Also, the principles of a literary school that lasted from roughly the beginning of the twentieth century until the end of World War II. Modernism is defined by its rejection of the literary conventions of the nineteenth century and by its opposition to conventional morality, taste, traditions, and economic values.

Monologue A composition, written or oral, by a single individual. More specifically, a speech given by a single individual in a drama or other public entertainment. It has no set length, although it is usually several or more lines long.

Monometer See *Meter*

Mood The prevailing emotions of a work or of the author in his or her creation of the work. The mood of a work is not always what might be expected based on its subject matter.

Motif A theme, character type, image, metaphor, or other verbal element that recurs throughout a single work of literature or occurs in a number of different works over a period of time.

Motiv See *Motif*

Muckrakers An early twentieth-century group of American writers. Typically, their works exposed the wrongdoings of big business and government in the United States.

Muses Nine Greek mythological goddesses, the daughters of Zeus and Mnemosyne (Memory). Each muse patronized a specific area of the liberal arts and sciences. Calliope presided over epic poetry, Clio over history, Erato over love poetry, Euterpe over music or lyric poetry, Melpomene over tragedy, Polyhymnia over hymns to the gods, Terpsichore over dance, Thalia over comedy, and Urania over astronomy. Poets and writers traditionally made appeals to the Muses for inspiration in their work.

Mystery See *Suspense*

Myth An anonymous tale emerging from the traditional beliefs of a culture or social unit. Myths use supernatural explanations for natural phenomena. They may also explain cosmic issues like creation and death. Collections of myths, known as mythologies, are common to all cultures and nations, but the best-known myths belong to the Norse, Roman, and Greek mythologies.

N

Narration The telling of a series of events, real or invented. A narration may be either a simple narrative, in which the events are recounted chronologically, or a narrative with a plot, in which the account is given in a style reflecting the author's artistic concept of the story. Narration is sometimes used as a synonym for "storyline."

Narrative A verse or prose accounting of an event or sequence of events, real or invented. The term is also used as an adjective in the sense "method of narration." For example, in literary criticism, the expression "narrative technique" usually refers to the way the author structures and presents his or her story.

Narrative Poetry A nondramatic poem in which the author tells a story. Such poems may be of any length or level of complexity.

Narrator The teller of a story. The narrator may be the author or a character in the story through whom the author speaks.

Naturalism A literary movement of the late nineteenth and early twentieth centuries. The movement's major theorist, French novelist Emile Zola, envisioned a type of fiction that would examine human life with the objectivity of scientific inquiry. The Naturalists typically viewed human beings as either the products of "biological determinism," ruled by hereditary instincts and engaged in an endless struggle for survival, or as the products of "socioeconomic determinism," ruled by social and economic forces beyond their control. In their works, the Naturalists generally ignored the highest levels of society and focused on degradation: poverty, alcoholism, prostitution, insanity, and disease.

Negritude A literary movement based on the concept of a shared cultural bond on the part of black Africans, wherever they may be in the world. It traces its origins to the former French colonies of Africa and the Caribbean. Negritude poets, novelists, and essayists generally stress four points in their writings: One, black alienation from traditional African culture can lead to feelings of inferiority. Two, European colonialism and Western education should be resisted. Three, black Africans should seek to affirm and define their own identity. Four, African culture can and should be reclaimed. Many Negritude writers also claim that blacks can make unique contributions to the world, based on a heightened appreciation of nature, rhythm, and human emotions—aspects of life they say are not so highly valued in the materialistic and rationalistic West.

Negro Renaissance See *Harlem Renaissance*

Neoclassical Period See *Neoclassicism*

Neoclassicism In literary criticism, this term refers to the revival of the attitudes and styles of expression of classical literature. It is generally used to describe a period in European history beginning in the late seventeenth century and lasting until about 1800. In its purest form, Neoclassicism marked a return to order, proportion, restraint, logic, accuracy, and decorum. In England, where Neoclassicism perhaps was most popular, it reflected the influence of seventeenth- century French writers, especially dramatists. Neoclassical writers typically reacted against the intensity and enthusiasm of the Renaissance period. They wrote works that appealed to the intellect, using elevated language and classical literary forms such as satire and the ode. Neoclassical works were often governed by the classical goal of instruction.

Neoclassicists See *Neoclassicism*

New Criticism A movement in literary criticism, dating from the late 1920s, that stressed close textual analysis in the interpretation of works of literature. The New Critics saw little merit in historical and biographical analysis. Rather, they aimed to examine the text alone, free from the question of how external events—biographical or otherwise—may have helped shape it.

New Negro Movement See *Harlem Renaissance*

Noble Savage The idea that primitive man is noble and good but becomes evil and corrupted as he becomes civilized. The concept of the noble savage originated in the Renaissance period but is more closely identified with such later writers as Jean-Jacques Rousseau and Aphra Behn.

O

Objective Correlative An outward set of objects, a situation, or a chain of events corresponding to an inward experience and evoking this experience in the reader. The term frequently appears in modern criticism in discussions of authors' intended effects on the emotional responses of readers.

Objectivity A quality in writing characterized by the absence of the author's opinion or feeling about the subject matter. Objectivity is an important factor in criticism.

Occasional Verse poetry written on the occasion of a significant historical or personal event. *Vers de societe* is sometimes called occasional verse although it is of a less serious nature.

Octave A poem or stanza composed of eight lines. The term octave most often represents the first eight lines of a Petrarchan sonnet.

Ode Name given to an extended lyric poem characterized by exalted emotion and dignified style. An ode usually concerns a single, serious theme. Most odes, but not all, are addressed to an object or individual. Odes are distinguished from other lyric poetic forms by their complex rhythmic and stanzaic patterns.

Oedipus Complex A son's amorous obsession with his mother. The phrase is derived from the story of the ancient Theban hero Oedipus, who unknowingly killed his father and married his mother.

Omniscience See *Point of View*

Onomatopoeia The use of words whose sounds express or suggest their meaning. In its simplest sense, onomatopoeia may be represented by words that mimic the sounds they denote such as ''hiss'' or ''meow.'' At a more subtle level, the pattern and rhythm of sounds and rhymes of a line or poem may be onomatopoeic.

Opera A type of stage performance, usually a drama, in which the dialogue is sung.

Operetta A usually romantic comic opera.

Oral Tradition See *Oral Transmission*

Oral Transmission A process by which songs, ballads, folklore, and other material are transmitted by word of mouth. The tradition of oral transmission predates the written record systems of literate society. Oral transmission preserves material sometimes over generations, although often with variations. Memory plays a large part in the recitation and preservation of orally transmitted material.

Oration Formal speaking intended to motivate the listeners to some action or feeling. Such public speaking was much more common before the development of timely printed communication such as newspapers.

Ottava Rima An eight-line stanza of poetry composed in iambic pentameter (a five-foot line in which each foot consists of an unaccented syllable followed by an accented syllable), following the abababcc rhyme scheme.

Oxymoron A phrase combining two contradictory terms. Oxymorons may be intentional or unintentional.

P

Pantheism The idea that all things are both a manifestation or revelation of God and a part of God at the same time. Pantheism was a common attitude in the early societies of Egypt, India, and Greece—the term derives from the Greek *pan* meaning "all" and *theos* meaning "deity." It later became a significant part of the Christian faith.

Parable A story intended to teach a moral lesson or answer an ethical question.

Paradox A statement that appears illogical or contradictory at first, but may actually point to an underlying truth.

Parallelism A method of comparison of two ideas in which each is developed in the same grammatical structure.

Parnassianism A mid nineteenth-century movement in French literature. Followers of the movement stressed adherence to well-defined artistic forms as a reaction against the often chaotic expression of the artist's ego that dominated the work of the Romantics. The Parnassians also rejected the moral, ethical, and social themes exhibited in the works of French Romantics such as Victor Hugo. The aesthetic doctrines of the Parnassians strongly influenced the later symbolist and decadent movements.

Parody In literary criticism, this term refers to an imitation of a serious literary work or the signature style of a particular author in a ridiculous manner.

A typical parody adopts the style of the original and applies it to an inappropriate subject for humorous effect. Parody is a form of satire and could be considered the literary equivalent of a caricature or cartoon.

Pastoral A term derived from the Latin word "pastor," meaning shepherd. A pastoral is a literary composition on a rural theme. The conventions of the pastoral were originated by the third-century Greek poet Theocritus, who wrote about the experiences, love affairs, and pastimes of Sicilian shepherds. In a pastoral, characters and language of a courtly nature are often placed in a simple setting. The term pastoral is also used to classify dramas, elegies, and lyrics that exhibit the use of country settings and shepherd characters.

Pastorela The Spanish name for the shepherds play, a folk drama reenacted during the Christmas season.

Pathetic Fallacy A term coined by English critic John Ruskin to identify writing that falsely endows nonhuman things with human intentions and feelings, such as "angry clouds" and "sad trees."

Pelado Literally the "skinned one" or shirtless one, he was the stock underdog, sharp-witted picaresque character of Mexican vaudeville and tent shows.

Pen Name See *Pseudonym*

Pentameter See *Meter*

Persona A Latin term meaning "mask." *Personae* are the characters in a fictional work of literature. The *persona* generally functions as a mask through which the author tells a story in a voice other than his or her own. A *persona* is usually either a character in a story who acts as a narrator or an "implied author," a voice created by the author to act as the narrator for himself or herself.

Personae See *Persona*

Personal Point of View See *Point of View*

Personification A figure of speech that gives human qualities to abstract ideas, animals, and inanimate objects.

Petrarchan Sonnet See *Sonnet*

Phenomenology A method of literary criticism based on the belief that things have no existence outside of human consciousness or awareness. Proponents of this theory believe that art is a process that takes place in the mind of the observer as he or she contemplates an object rather than a quality of the object itself.

Picaresque Novel Episodic fiction depicting the adventures of a roguish central character (''picaro'' is Spanish for ''rogue''). The picaresque hero is commonly a low-born but clever individual who wanders into and out of various affairs of love, danger, and farcical intrigue. These involvements may take place at all social levels and typically present a humorous and wide-ranging satire of a given society.

Plagiarism Claiming another person's written material as one's own. Plagiarism can take the form of direct, word-for- word copying or the theft of the substance or idea of the work.

Platonic Criticism A form of criticism that stresses an artistic work's usefulness as an agent of social engineering rather than any quality or value of the work itself.

Platonism The embracing of the doctrines of the philosopher Plato, popular among the poets of the Renaissance and the Romantic period. Platonism is more flexible than Aristotelian Criticism and places more emphasis on the supernatural and unknown aspects of life.

Play See *Drama*

Plot In literary criticism, this term refers to the pattern of events in a narrative or drama. In its simplest sense, the plot guides the author in composing the work and helps the reader follow the work. Typically, plots exhibit causality and unity and have a beginning, a middle, and an end. Sometimes, however, a plot may consist of a series of disconnected events, in which case it is known as an ''episodic plot.''

Poem In its broadest sense, a composition utilizing rhyme, meter, concrete detail, and expressive language to create a literary experience with emotional and aesthetic appeal.

Poet An author who writes poetry or verse. The term is also used to refer to an artist or writer who has an exceptional gift for expression, imagination, and energy in the making of art in any form.

Poetic Fallacy See *Pathetic Fallacy*

Poetic Justice An outcome in a literary work, not necessarily a poem, in which the good are rewarded and the evil are punished, especially in ways that particularly fit their virtues or crimes.

Poetic License Distortions of fact and literary convention made by a writer—not always a poet—for the sake of the effect gained. Poetic license is closely related to the concept of ''artistic freedom.''

Poetics This term has two closely related meanings. It denotes (1) an aesthetic theory in literary criticism about the essence of poetry or (2) rules prescribing the proper methods, content, style, or diction of poetry. The term poetics may also refer to theories about literature in general, not just poetry.

Poetry In its broadest sense, writing that aims to present ideas and evoke an emotional experience in the reader through the use of meter, imagery, connotative and concrete words, and a carefully constructed structure based on rhythmic patterns. Poetry typically relies on words and expressions that have several layers of meaning. It also makes use of the effects of regular rhythm on the ear and may make a strong appeal to the senses through the use of imagery.

Point of View The narrative perspective from which a literary work is presented to the reader. There are four traditional points of view. The ''third person omniscient'' gives the reader a ''godlike'' perspective, unrestricted by time or place, from which to see actions and look into the minds of characters. This allows the author to comment openly on characters and events in the work. The ''third person'' point of view presents the events of the story from outside of any single character's perception, much like the omniscient point of view, but the reader must understand the action as it takes place and without any special insight into characters' minds or motivations. The ''first person'' or ''personal'' point of view relates events as they are perceived by a single character. The main character ''tells'' the story and may offer opinions about the action and characters which differ from those of the author. Much less common than omniscient, third person, and first person is the ''second person'' point of view, wherein the author tells the story as if it is happening to the reader.

Polemic A work in which the author takes a stand on a controversial subject, such as abortion or religion. Such works are often extremely argumentative or provocative.

Pornography Writing intended to provoke feelings of lust in the reader. Such works are often condemned by critics and teachers, but those which can be shown to have literary value are viewed less harshly.

Post-Aesthetic Movement An artistic response made by African Americans to the black aesthetic movement of the 1960s and early '70s. Writers since that time have adopted a somewhat different tone in their work, with less emphasis placed on the disparity between black and white in the United States. In the words of post-aesthetic authors such as Toni Morrison, John Edgar Wideman, and Kristin Hunter, African Americans are portrayed as looking inward for answers to their own questions, rather than always looking to the outside world.

Postmodernism Writing from the 1960s forward characterized by experimentation and continuing to apply some of the fundamentals of modernism, which included existentialism and alienation. Postmodernists have gone a step further in the rejection of tradition begun with the modernists by also rejecting traditional forms, preferring the anti-novel over the novel and the anti-hero over the hero.

Pre-Raphaelites A circle of writers and artists in mid nineteenth-century England. Valuing the pre-Renaissance artistic qualities of religious symbolism, lavish pictorialism, and natural sensuousness, the Pre-Raphaelites cultivated a sense of mystery and melancholy that influenced later writers associated with the Symbolist and Decadent movements.

Primitivism The belief that primitive peoples were nobler and less flawed than civilized peoples because they had not been subjected to the tainting influence of society.

Projective Verse A form of free verse in which the poet's breathing pattern determines the lines of the poem. Poets who advocate projective verse are against all formal structures in writing, including meter and form.

Prologue An introductory section of a literary work. It often contains information establishing the situation of the characters or presents information about the setting, time period, or action. In drama, the prologue is spoken by a chorus or by one of the principal characters.

Prose A literary medium that attempts to mirror the language of everyday speech. It is distinguished from poetry by its use of unmetered, unrhymed language consisting of logically related sentences. Prose is usually grouped into paragraphs that form a cohesive whole such as an essay or a novel.

Prosopopoeia See *Personification*

Protagonist The central character of a story who serves as a focus for its themes and incidents and as the principal rationale for its development. The protagonist is sometimes referred to in discussions of modern literature as the hero or anti-hero.

Protest Fiction Protest fiction has as its primary purpose the protesting of some social injustice, such as racism or discrimination.

Proverb A brief, sage saying that expresses a truth about life in a striking manner.

Pseudonym A name assumed by a writer, most often intended to prevent his or her identification as the author of a work. Two or more authors may work together under one pseudonym, or an author may use a different name for each genre he or she publishes in. Some publishing companies maintain ''house pseudonyms,'' under which any number of authors may write installations in a series. Some authors also choose a pseudonym over their real names the way an actor may use a stage name.

Pun A play on words that have similar sounds but different meanings.

Pure Poetry poetry written without instructional intent or moral purpose that aims only to please a reader by its imagery or musical flow. The term pure poetry is used as the antonym of the term ''didacticism.''

Q

Quatrain A four-line stanza of a poem or an entire poem consisting of four lines.

R

Raisonneur A character in a drama who functions as a spokesperson for the dramatist's views. The *raisonneur* typically observes the play without becoming central to its action.

Realism A nineteenth-century European literary movement that sought to portray familiar characters, situations, and settings in a realistic manner. This was done primarily by using an objective narrative point of view and through the buildup of accurate detail. The standard for success of any realistic work depends on how faithfully it transfers common experience into fictional forms. The realistic method may be altered or extended, as in stream of consciousness writing, to record highly subjective experience.

Refrain A phrase repeated at intervals throughout a poem. A refrain may appear at the end of each stanza or at less regular intervals. It may be altered slightly at each appearance.

Renaissance The period in European history that marked the end of the Middle Ages. It began in Italy in the late fourteenth century. In broad terms, it is usually seen as spanning the fourteenth, fifteenth, and sixteenth centuries, although it did not reach Great Britain, for example, until the 1480s or so. The Renaissance saw an awakening in almost every sphere of human activity, especially science, philosophy, and the arts. The period is best defined by the emergence of a general philosophy that emphasized the importance of the intellect, the individual, and world affairs. It contrasts strongly with the medieval worldview, characterized by the dominant concerns of faith, the social collective, and spiritual salvation.

Repartee Conversation featuring snappy retorts and witticisms.

Resolution The portion of a story following the climax, in which the conflict is resolved.

Restoration See *Restoration Age*

Restoration Age A period in English literature beginning with the crowning of Charles II in 1660 and running to about 1700. The era, which was characterized by a reaction against Puritanism, was the first great age of the comedy of manners. The finest literature of the era is typically witty and urbane, and often lewd.

Revenge Tragedy A dramatic form popular during the Elizabethan Age, in which the protagonist, directed by the ghost of his murdered father or son, inflicts retaliation upon a powerful villain. Notable features of the revenge tragedy include violence, bizarre criminal acts, intrigue, insanity, a hesitant protagonist, and the use of soliloquy.

Revista The Spanish term for a vaudeville musical revue.

Rhetoric In literary criticism, this term denotes the art of ethical persuasion. In its strictest sense, rhetoric adheres to various principles developed since classical times for arranging facts and ideas in a clear, persuasive, appealing manner. The term is also used to refer to effective prose in general and theories of or methods for composing effective prose.

Rhetorical Question A question intended to provoke thought, but not an expressed answer, in the reader. It is most commonly used in oratory and other persuasive genres.

Rhyme When used as a noun in literary criticism, this term generally refers to a poem in which words sound identical or very similar and appear in parallel positions in two or more lines. Rhymes are classified into different types according to where they fall in a line or stanza or according to the degree of similarity they exhibit in their spellings and sounds. Some major types of rhyme are ''masculine'' rhyme, ''feminine'' rhyme, and ''triple'' rhyme. In a masculine rhyme, the rhyming sound falls in a single accented syllable, as with ''heat'' and ''eat.'' Feminine rhyme is a rhyme of two syllables, one stressed and one unstressed, as with ''merry'' and ''tarry.'' Triple rhyme matches the sound of the accented syllable and the two unaccented syllables that follow: ''narrative'' and ''declarative.''

Rhyme Royal A stanza of seven lines composed in iambic pentameter and rhymed *ababbcc*. The name is said to be a tribute to King James I of Scotland, who made much use of the form in his poetry.

Rhyme Scheme See *Rhyme*

Rhythm A regular pattern of sound, time intervals, or events occurring in writing, most often and most discernably in poetry. Regular, reliable rhythm is known to be soothing to humans, while interrupted, unpredictable, or rapidly changing rhythm is disturbing. These effects are known to authors, who use them to produce a desired reaction in the reader.

Rising Action The part of a drama where the plot becomes increasingly complicated. Rising action leads up to the climax, or turning point, of a drama.

Rococo A style of European architecture that flourished in the eighteenth century, especially in France. The most notable features of *rococo* are its extensive use of ornamentation and its themes of lightness, gaiety, and intimacy. In literary criticism, the term is often used disparagingly to refer to a decadent or over-ornamental style.

Roman a clef A French phrase meaning ''novel with a key.'' It refers to a narrative in which real persons are portrayed under fictitious names.

Romance A broad term, usually denoting a narrative with exotic, exaggerated, often idealized characters, scenes, and themes.

Romantic Age See *Romanticism*

Romanticism This term has two widely accepted meanings. In historical criticism, it refers to a

European intellectual and artistic movement of the late eighteenth and early nineteenth centuries that sought greater freedom of personal expression than that allowed by the strict rules of literary form and logic of the eighteenth-century neoclassicists. The Romantics preferred emotional and imaginative expression to rational analysis. They considered the individual to be at the center of all experience and so placed him or her at the center of their art. The Romantics believed that the creative imagination reveals nobler truths—unique feelings and attitudes—than those that could be discovered by logic or by scientific examination. Both the natural world and the state of childhood were important sources for revelations of ''eternal truths.'' ''Romanticism'' is also used as a general term to refer to a type of sensibility found in all periods of literary history and usually considered to be in opposition to the principles of classicism. In this sense, Romanticism signifies any work or philosophy in which the exotic or dreamlike figure strongly, or that is devoted to individualistic expression, self-analysis, or a pursuit of a higher realm of knowledge than can be discovered by human reason.

Romantics See *Romanticism*

Russian Symbolism A Russian poetic movement, derived from French symbolism, that flourished between 1894 and 1910. While some Russian Symbolists continued in the French tradition, stressing aestheticism and the importance of suggestion above didactic intent, others saw their craft as a form of mystical worship, and themselves as mediators between the supernatural and the mundane.

S

Satire A work that uses ridicule, humor, and wit to criticize and provoke change in human nature and institutions. There are two major types of satire: ''formal'' or ''direct'' satire speaks directly to the reader or to a character in the work; ''indirect'' satire relies upon the ridiculous behavior of its characters to make its point. Formal satire is further divided into two manners: the ''Horatian,'' which ridicules gently, and the ''Juvenalian,'' which derides its subjects harshly and bitterly.

Scansion The analysis or ''scanning'' of a poem to determine its meter and often its rhyme scheme. The most common system of scansion uses accents (slanted lines drawn above syllables) to show stressed syllables, breves (curved lines drawn above sylla-

bles) to show unstressed syllables, and vertical lines to separate each foot.

Scene A subdivision of an act of a drama, consisting of continuous action taking place at a single time and in a single location. The beginnings and endings of scenes may be indicated by clearing the stage of actors and props or by the entrances and exits of important characters.

Science Fiction A type of narrative about or based upon real or imagined scientific theories and technology. Science fiction is often peopled with alien creatures and set on other planets or in different dimensions.

Second Person See *Point of View*

Semiotics The study of how literary forms and conventions affect the meaning of language.

Sestet Any six-line poem or stanza.

Setting The time, place, and culture in which the action of a narrative takes place. The elements of setting may include geographic location, characters' physical and mental environments, prevailing cultural attitudes, or the historical time in which the action takes place.

Shakespearean Sonnet See *Sonnet*

Signifying Monkey A popular trickster figure in black folklore, with hundreds of tales about this character documented since the 19th century.

Simile A comparison, usually using ''like'' or ''as'', of two essentially dissimilar things, as in ''coffee as cold as ice'' or ''He sounded like a broken record.''

Slang A type of informal verbal communication that is generally unacceptable for formal writing. Slang words and phrases are often colorful exaggerations used to emphasize the speaker's point; they may also be shortened versions of an often-used word or phrase.

Slant Rhyme See *Consonance*

Slave Narrative Autobiographical accounts of American slave life as told by escaped slaves. These works first appeared during the abolition movement of the 1830s through the 1850s.

Social Realism See *Socialist Realism*

Socialist Realism The Socialist Realism school of literary theory was proposed by Maxim Gorky and established as a dogma by the first Soviet Congress of Writers. It demanded adherence to a communist worldview in works of literature. Its doctrines required an objective viewpoint comprehensible to the working classes and themes of social struggle featuring strong proletarian heroes.

Soliloquy A monologue in a drama used to give the audience information and to develop the speaker's character. It is typically a projection of the speaker's innermost thoughts. Usually delivered while the speaker is alone on stage, a soliloquy is intended to present an illusion of unspoken reflection.

Sonnet A fourteen-line poem, usually composed in iambic pentameter, employing one of several rhyme schemes. There are three major types of sonnets, upon which all other variations of the form are based: the "Petrarchan" or "Italian" sonnet, the "Shakespearean" or "English" sonnet, and the "Spenserian" sonnet. A Petrarchan sonnet consists of an octave rhymed *abbaabba* and a "sestet" rhymed either *cdecde, cdccdc,* or *cdedce.* The octave poses a question or problem, relates a narrative, or puts forth a proposition; the sestet presents a solution to the problem, comments upon the narrative, or applies the proposition put forth in the octave. The Shakespearean sonnet is divided into three quatrains and a couplet rhymed *abab cdcd efef gg.* The couplet provides an epigrammatic comment on the narrative or problem put forth in the quatrains. The Spenserian sonnet uses three quatrains and a couplet like the Shakespearean, but links their three rhyme schemes in this way: *abab bcbc cdcd ee.* The Spenserian sonnet develops its theme in two parts like the Petrarchan, its final six lines resolving a problem, analyzing a narrative, or applying a proposition put forth in its first eight lines.

Spenserian Sonnet See *Sonnet*

Spenserian Stanza A nine-line stanza having eight verses in iambic pentameter, its ninth verse in iambic hexameter, and the rhyme scheme ababbcbcc.

Spondee In poetry meter, a foot consisting of two long or stressed syllables occurring together. This form is quite rare in English verse, and is usually composed of two monosyllabic words.

Sprung Rhythm Versification using a specific number of accented syllables per line but disregarding the number of unaccented syllables that fall in each line, producing an irregular rhythm in the poem.

Stanza A subdivision of a poem consisting of lines grouped together, often in recurring patterns of rhyme, line length, and meter. Stanzas may also serve as units of thought in a poem much like paragraphs in prose.

Stereotype A stereotype was originally the name for a duplication made during the printing process; this led to its modern definition as a person or thing that is (or is assumed to be) the same as all others of its type.

Stream of Consciousness A narrative technique for rendering the inward experience of a character. This technique is designed to give the impression of an ever-changing series of thoughts, emotions, images, and memories in the spontaneous and seemingly illogical order that they occur in life.

Structuralism A twentieth-century movement in literary criticism that examines how literary texts arrive at their meanings, rather than the meanings themselves. There are two major types of structuralist analysis: one examines the way patterns of linguistic structures unify a specific text and emphasize certain elements of that text, and the other interprets the way literary forms and conventions affect the meaning of language itself.

Structure The form taken by a piece of literature. The structure may be made obvious for ease of understanding, as in nonfiction works, or may be obscured for artistic purposes, as in some poetry or seemingly "unstructured" prose.

Sturm und Drang A German term meaning "storm and stress." It refers to a German literary movement of the 1770s and 1780s that reacted against the order and rationalism of the enlightenment, focusing instead on the intense experience of extraordinary individuals.

Style A writer's distinctive manner of arranging words to suit his or her ideas and purpose in writing. The unique imprint of the author's personality upon his or her writing, style is the product of an author's way of arranging ideas and his or her use of diction, different sentence structures, rhythm, figures of speech, rhetorical principles, and other elements of composition.

Subject The person, event, or theme at the center of a work of literature. A work may have one or more subjects of each type, with shorter works tending to have fewer and longer works tending to have more.

Subjectivity Writing that expresses the author's personal feelings about his subject, and which may or may not include factual information about the subject.

Subplot A secondary story in a narrative. A subplot may serve as a motivating or complicating force for the main plot of the work, or it may provide emphasis for, or relief from, the main plot.

Surrealism A term introduced to criticism by Guillaume Apollinaire and later adopted by Andre Breton. It refers to a French literary and artistic movement founded in the 1920s. The Surrealists sought to express unconscious thoughts and feelings in their works. The best-known technique used for achieving this aim was automatic writing—transcriptions of spontaneous outpourings from the unconscious. The Surrealists proposed to unify the contrary levels of conscious and unconscious, dream and reality, objectivity and subjectivity into a new level of "super-realism."

Suspense A literary device in which the author maintains the audience's attention through the build-up of events, the outcome of which will soon be revealed.

Syllogism A method of presenting a logical argument. In its most basic form, the syllogism consists of a major premise, a minor premise, and a conclusion.

Symbol Something that suggests or stands for something else without losing its original identity. In literature, symbols combine their literal meaning with the suggestion of an abstract concept. Literary symbols are of two types: those that carry complex associations of meaning no matter what their contexts, and those that derive their suggestive meaning from their functions in specific literary works.

Symbolism This term has two widely accepted meanings. In historical criticism, it denotes an early modernist literary movement initiated in France during the nineteenth century that reacted against the prevailing standards of realism. Writers in this movement aimed to evoke, indirectly and symbolically, an order of being beyond the material world of the five senses. Poetic expression of personal emotion figured strongly in the movement, typically by means of a private set of symbols uniquely identifiable with the individual poet. The principal aim of the Symbolists was to express in words the highly complex feelings that grew out of everyday contact with the world. In a broader sense, the term "symbolism" refers to the use of one object to represent another.

Symbolist See *Symbolism*

Symbolist Movement See *Symbolism*

Sympathetic Fallacy See *Affective Fallacy*

T

Tale A story told by a narrator with a simple plot and little character development. Tales are usually relatively short and often carry a simple message.

Tall Tale A humorous tale told in a straightforward, credible tone but relating absolutely impossible events or feats of the characters. Such tales were commonly told of frontier adventures during the settlement of the west in the United States.

Tanka A form of Japanese poetry similar to *haiku*. A *tanka* is five lines long, with the lines containing five, seven, five, seven, and seven syllables respectively.

Teatro Grottesco See *Theater of the Grotesque*

Terza Rima A three-line stanza form in poetry in which the rhymes are made on the last word of each line in the following manner: the first and third lines of the first stanza, then the second line of the first stanza and the first and third lines of the second stanza, and so on with the middle line of any stanza rhyming with the first and third lines of the following stanza.

Tetrameter See *Meter*

Textual Criticism A branch of literary criticism that seeks to establish the authoritative text of a literary work. Textual critics typically compare all known manuscripts or printings of a single work in order to assess the meanings of differences and revisions. This procedure allows them to arrive at a definitive version that (supposedly) corresponds to the author's original intention.

Theater of Cruelty Term used to denote a group of theatrical techniques designed to eliminate the psychological and emotional distance between actors and audience. This concept, introduced in the 1930s in France, was intended to inspire a more intense theatrical experience than conventional theater allowed. The "cruelty" of this dramatic theory signified not sadism but heightened actor/audience involvement in the dramatic event.

Theater of the Absurd A post-World War II dramatic trend characterized by radical theatrical innovations. In works influenced by the Theater of the absurd, nontraditional, sometimes grotesque characterizations, plots, and stage sets reveal a meaningless universe in which human values are irrelevant. Existentialist themes of estrangement, absurdity, and futility link many of the works of this movement.

Theater of the Grotesque An Italian theatrical movement characterized by plays written around the ironic and macabre aspects of daily life in the World War I era.

Theme The main point of a work of literature. The term is used interchangeably with thesis.

Thesis A thesis is both an essay and the point argued in the essay. Thesis novels and thesis plays share the quality of containing a thesis which is supported through the action of the story.

Thesis Play See *Thesis*

Three Unities See *Unities*

Tone The author's attitude toward his or her audience may be deduced from the tone of the work. A formal tone may create distance or convey politeness, while an informal tone may encourage a friendly, intimate, or intrusive feeling in the reader. The author's attitude toward his or her subject matter may also be deduced from the tone of the words he or she uses in discussing it.

Tragedy A drama in prose or poetry about a noble, courageous hero of excellent character who, because of some tragic character flaw or *hamartia*, brings ruin upon him- or herself. Tragedy treats its subjects in a dignified and serious manner, using poetic language to help evoke pity and fear and bring about catharsis, a purging of these emotions. The tragic form was practiced extensively by the ancient Greeks. In the Middle Ages, when classical works were virtually unknown, tragedy came to denote any works about the fall of persons from exalted to low conditions due to any reason: fate, vice, weakness, etc. According to the classical definition of tragedy, such works present the "pathetic"—that which evokes pity—rather than the tragic. The classical form of tragedy was revived in the sixteenth century; it flourished especially on the Elizabethan stage. In modern times, dramatists have attempted to adapt the form to the needs of modern society by drawing their heroes from the ranks of ordinary men and women and defining the nobility of these heroes in terms of spirit rather than exalted social standing.

Tragedy of Blood See *Revenge Tragedy*

Tragic Flaw In a tragedy, the quality within the hero or heroine which leads to his or her downfall.

Transcendentalism An American philosophical and religious movement, based in New England from around 1835 until the Civil War. Transcendentalism was a form of American romanticism that had its roots abroad in the works of Thomas Carlyle, Samuel Coleridge, and Johann Wolfgang von Goethe. The Transcendentalists stressed the importance of intuition and subjective experience in communication with God. They rejected religious dogma and texts in favor of mysticism and scientific naturalism. They pursued truths that lie beyond the "colorless" realms perceived by reason and the senses and were active social reformers in public education, women's rights, and the abolition of slavery.

Trickster A character or figure common in Native American and African literature who uses his ingenuity to defeat enemies and escape difficult situations. Tricksters are most often animals, such as the spider, hare, or coyote, although they may take the form of humans as well.

Trimeter See *Meter*

Triple Rhyme See *Rhyme*

Trochee See *Foot*

U

Understatement See *Irony*

Unities Strict rules of dramatic structure, formulated by Italian and French critics of the Renaissance and based loosely on the principles of drama discussed by Aristotle in his *Poetics*. Foremost among these rules were the three unities of action, time, and place that compelled a dramatist to: (1) construct a single plot with a beginning, middle, and end that details the causal relationships of action and character; (2) restrict the action to the events of a single day; and (3) limit the scene to a single place or city. The unities were observed faithfully by continental European writers until the Romantic Age, but they were never regularly observed in English drama. Modern dramatists are typically more concerned with a unity of impression or emotional effect than with any of the classical unities.

Urban Realism A branch of realist writing that attempts to accurately reflect the often harsh facts of modern urban existence.

Utopia A fictional perfect place, such as "paradise" or "heaven."

Utopian See *Utopia*

Utopianism See *Utopia*

V

Verisimilitude Literally, the appearance of truth. In literary criticism, the term refers to aspects of a work of literature that seem true to the reader.

Vers de societe See *Occasional Verse*

Vers libre See *Free Verse*

Verse A line of metered language, a line of a poem, or any work written in verse.

Versification The writing of verse. Versification may also refer to the meter, rhyme, and other mechanical components of a poem.

Victorian Refers broadly to the reign of Queen Victoria of England (1837-1901) and to anything with qualities typical of that era. For example, the qualities of smug narrowmindedness, bourgeois materialism, faith in social progress, and priggish morality are often considered Victorian. This stereotype is contradicted by such dramatic intellectual developments as the theories of Charles Darwin, Karl Marx, and Sigmund Freud (which stirred strong debates in England) and the critical attitudes of serious Victorian writers like Charles Dickens and George Eliot. In literature, the Victorian Period was the great age of the English novel, and the latter part of the era saw the rise of movements such as decadence and symbolism.

Victorian Age See *Victorian*

Victorian Period See *Victorian*

W

Weltanschauung A German term referring to a person's worldview or philosophy.

Weltschmerz A German term meaning "world pain." It describes a sense of anguish about the nature of existence, usually associated with a melancholy, pessimistic attitude.

Z

Zarzuela A type of Spanish operetta.

Zeitgeist A German term meaning "spirit of the time." It refers to the moral and intellectual trends of a given era.

Cumulative Author/Title Index

Nationality/Ethnicity Index

Subject/Theme Index

Doctor Faustus: 83, 88, 90
Oedipus Rex: 202, 208, 210, 213-214
Feminism
  A Doll's House: 106, 114-119
Film
  Cyrano de Bergerac: 41-42
  The Glass Menagerie: 125-126
  The King and I: 140, 151
  Pygmalion: 241, 250-251
  You Can't Take It with You: 301, 307-308, 315
Foreshadowing
  Oedipus Rex: 211
Forgiveness
  Doctor Faustus: 81-82, 90
Freedom
  Cyrano de Bergerac: 50

G

Ghost
  Doctor Faustus: 88, 91, 93
God
  Antigone: 2-3, 8, 10
  Cyrano de Bergerac: 52
  Doctor Faustus: 81-83, 87, 89-90
  Medea: 187-189
God and Religion
  Antigone: 8
Good and Evil
  Doctor Faustus: 86
Great Depression
  You Can't Take It with You: 307-309
Greed
  The Little Foxes: 160, 165-167, 172-173
Greed
  She Stoops to Conquer: 265, 269
Grief and Sorrow
  Antigone: 3-5
  Medea: 182-183, 188, 190
Grotesque
  Cyrano de Bergerac: 54
Growth and Development
  A Doll's House: 112
Guilt
  Medea: 192-193

H

Happiness and Gaiety
  The Cherry Orchard: 22-23
  Death of a Salesman: 61, 67
  Doctor Faustus: 86, 89, 91, 93
  The King and I: 142, 148, 151
  You Can't Take It with You: 298, 301-302, 306-307, 313

Hatred
  Cyrano de Bergerac: 45, 48-50
  The Little Foxes: 162, 165-167
  Medea: 182, 186
Heaven
  Doctor Faustus: 93
Hell
  Doctor Faustus: 81, 83, 88-90, 97, 105
Heroism
  Antigone: 8, 12-13
  The Cherry Orchard: 29, 32
  Cyrano de Bergerac: 41-42, 50-51, 54-55
  Death of a Salesman: 71
  Doctor Faustus: 90, 92-96
  Oedipus Rex: 213
  She Stoops to Conquer: 273
History
  Antigone: 9-10
  Death of a Salesman: 70
  Doctor Faustus: 79, 88, 90, 93, 96
  The Glass Menagerie: 130, 132, 139
  The King and I: 158
  Oedipus Rex: 202, 212, 215
  Pygmalion: 247
  You Can't Take It with You: 307, 315
Honor
  A Doll's House: 112
Honor
  Antigone: 2, 7
  Cyrano de Bergerac: 45, 55, 57-58
  Our Town: 231
  She Stoops to Conquer: 271
Hope
  The Cherry Orchard: 22-23, 28, 32
  Pygmalion: 248
  She Stoops to Conquer: 263, 265, 270
  You Can't Take It with You: 306-307
Human Condition
  Doctor Faustus: 88
Humanism
  Doctor Faustus: 91-92, 96
Humor
  Antigone: 11
  The Cherry Orchard: 22, 29-33, 36-37, 40-43
  Cyrano de Bergerac: 51-52
  Doctor Faustus: 86, 89, 93, 105
  The Glass Menagerie: 131
  The King and I: 150
  Oedipus Rex: 213
  Pygmalion: 246-248
  She Stoops to Conquer: 261, 263-265, 270, 272-275

You Can't Take It with You: 298, 305-312

I

Identity
  Pygmalion: 245
Identity and Search for Self
  A Doll's House: 112
Ignorance
  Doctor Faustus: 88
  Oedipus Rex: 204, 208, 210-211
  She Stoops to Conquer: 263, 270
Imagery and Symbolism
  Oedipus Rex: 211
  A Streetcar Named Desire: 288, 290
Individual vs. Self
  Death of a Salesman: 68
Individual vs. Society
  Death of a Salesman: 68
Individualism
  Doctor Faustus: 86
  You Can't Take It with You: 305
Irony
  Cyrano de Bergerac: 57-58
  Medea: 201

K

Killers and Killing
  Antigone: 1, 3, 9
  The Little Foxes: 170, 172
  Medea: 180, 182, 185-186, 192-193
  Oedipus Rex: 204, 208, 214
  Pygmalion: 248
Knowledge
  Death of a Salesman: 63-64, 70
  Doctor Faustus: 81, 87-89, 96-97
  The King and I: 142, 147-148
  Oedipus Rex: 210-211, 215, 217, 221
Knowledge and Ignorance
  Doctor Faustus: 87
  The King and I: 147
  Oedipus Rex: 208

L

Landscape
  Our Town: 222, 224-225, 230
Language and Meaning
  Pygmalion: 245
Law and Order
  Antigone: 1-4, 8, 10, 12, 18